PHYSIOLOGICAL
PSYCHOLOGY

PHYSIOLOGICAL PSYCHOLOGY

PETER M. MILNER

McGILL UNIVERSITY

HOLT, RINEHART AND WINSTON, INC.

NEW YORK   CHICAGO   SAN FRANCISCO   ATLANTA   DALLAS
MONTREAL   TORONTO   LONDON   SYDNEY

In addition to sources noted in the figure legends, we are indebted to the following sources for permission to print or adapt illustrations:

Figure 2.7: Copyright © 1964 by the American Association for the Advancement of Science.

Figure 3.5: Copyright *The CIBA Collection of Medical Illustrations* by Frank H. Netter, M.D.

Figure 3.7: Copyright *The CIBA Collection of Medical Illustrations* by Frank H. Netter, M.D.

Figure 7.3: Copyright © 1950 by The Macmillan Company.

Figure 9.13: From *Annals of the New York Academy of Sciences,* 1964. Reprinted by permission.

Figure 11.17: Copyright © 1966 by the American Association for the Advancement of Science.

Figure 12.5: From G. L. Rasmussen & W. F. Windle (Eds.), *Neural mechanisms of the auditory and vestibular systems,* 1960. Courtesy of Charles C Thomas, Publisher, Springfield, Illinois.

Figure 12.8: Adapted from *Speech and hearing* by Harvey Fletcher. Copyright 1929 by D. Van Nostrand Company, by permission of Van Nostrand Reinhold Company.

Figure 12.15: From G. L. Rasmussen & W. F. Windle (Eds.), *Neural mechanisms of the auditory and vestibular systems,* 1960. Courtesy of Charles C Thomas, Publisher, Springfield, Illinois.

Figure 12.22: From G. L. Rasmussen & W. F. Windle (Eds.), *Neural mechanisms of the auditory and vestibular systems,* 1960. Courtesy of Charles C Thomas, Publisher, Springfield, Illinois.

Figure 14.10: From M. Jouvet. The states of sleep. *Scientific American,* February 1967, 63. Copyright © 1967 by Scientific American, Inc. All rights reserved.

Figure 16.6: From J. L. Falk in *Nebraska Symposium on Motivation 1961.* Copyright © 1961 by the University of Nebraska Press and reprinted by permission of the publisher.

PREFACE

Twenty or thirty years ago physiological psychology was hardly recognized as a branch of experimental psychology; in some schools, indeed, any attempt to introduce physiological explanations was considered the worst type of heresy. Now, however, the picture is completely different. The logic of probing the nervous system for clues to behavior is almost universally accepted, and there is even some danger that the power of the approach may be overestimated by those outside the field. The last two decades have seen great advances in neurophysiology, neurochemistry, and in other biological sciences; the influence of these developments on psychology is such that no one seriously interested in any branch of the subject can afford to remain ignorant of them.

In a field where experiments are being performed and published at the rate of well over a thousand a year, and where many of the experiments are of questionable value, even the expert has difficulty in maintaining a clear and balanced view of more than one or two special areas. Students just entering the field have no hope of being able to do so, and the responsibility for guiding them toward the more significant contributions, and for training them to judge the merits of an experiment for themselves, rests heavily on their teachers. Work that supports current theories or prejudices is usually less closely scrutinized than experiments giving rise to surprising or revolutionary results. While in most cases this is reasonable, the tendency can be very troublesome if the theory happens to be wrong—as is illustrated by several examples in this book. I hope that the critical approach that I have adopted toward many of the investigations described will encourage readers to think for themselves and to question the criticisms as well as the experiments. In fact it is quite likely that by the time this text appears in print I shall myself have been forced to revise some of the views I have expressed.

Because this book is intended primarily for psychologists, some of whom may have had little contact with biological sciences, I have included elementary background material in physiology and anatomy. The book should be intelligible to readers without formal training in these disciplines, but a familiarity with the basic issues and methods of experimental psychology is assumed. The notes upon which the book is based have been used in my undergraduate courses for a number of years, and the final standings of the students have borne little relation to their previous exposure to "hard" biology.

Again, because this is a psychology text, the material has been organized around such problems as perception, motivation, and learning—cutting across anatomical and physiological classifications. I have in most cases related the experiments to some model or unifying theme, a procedure that emphasizes inconsistencies among experiments when they occur; this will perhaps encourage readers to seek better synthesizing principles or better experiments.

The relevance of physiological psychology for normal and abnormal human behavior is more apparent to the student if human observations are presented along with the data from animal experiments; I have done this whenever the opportunity arose. Interspecies comparisons, including those in which man is one of the species, usually indicate that corresponding parts of the nervous system determine similar types of behavior. However, this rule has some exceptions that should warn us never to take anything for granted.

During the writing of this book it has been my good fortune to be a member of the department assembled at McGill University by Professor D. O. Hebb a little over twenty years ago and to have enjoyed the stimulation of an active group of colleagues and students pursuing many lines of research in physiological psychology. I have learned something from all of them, and the contributions of many of them are recognized in the pages that follow.

Professor Hebb, more than anyone else, is responsible for this book having been written. He planted the idea and nurtured it by frequent and repeated encouragement, for which I am now very grateful. My wife Brenda has contributed a great deal to the book, especially to the sections dealing with human brain lesions, and her comments have done much to improve the writing.

Professor Paul Rozin's critical reading of an early draft of the manuscript and his very many helpful suggestions resulted in a greatly improved final version. I would also like to express my thanks to Professors Robert Malmo, Ronald Melzack, Joseph Mendelson, Gordon Mogenson, Aryeh Routtenberg, Case and Doreen Vanderwolf, and Dr. Imre Szabo—all of whom read parts of the manuscript, intercepted a number of errors, and suggested useful additions to it.

I must also acknowledge the debt I owe to many, many former students who struggled to learn physiological psychology from the early stencilled versions of this book, and who told me (either directly or by their puzzlement) where improvements were needed. Some former students have discovered deficiencies in the text in a harder way still—by using the notes to teach others—and a series of letters from one of them, Professor Graham Goddard, has been especially useful in writing the final version.

Finally, I should like to thank Susan Cook and Lynn Kernaghan, whose enthusiastic and accurate help eased many of the demanding jobs involved in the preparation of a work of this size.

P. M. M.

Montreal, Quebec
February 1970

CONTENTS

PHYSIOLOGICAL PSYCHOLOGY

CHAPTER 1

INTRODUCTION

It is customary to introduce psychology text-books by setting forth the author's idea of what psychology should be about; as often as not a homily on the philosophy of science is thrown in for good measure. I feel compelled to maintain this tradition, but, as there is nothing very original about my ideas on psychology and as I am quite unschooled in the philosophy of science, I shall be brief.

Like most other psychologists, especially those with physiological leanings, I aim to advance understanding of the behavior of living things, to answer the question "What makes this organism behave the way it does?" The method that I have adopted (and that is visible from time to time in this book) is to treat the question as if it had been asked about some man-made object like a radio or a motor car. I am interested in organisms as pieces of machinery, and I would like to know much the same things about them that I once wanted to know about the gadgets that I saw around me: first, *what* happens when the controls or inputs are manipulated and, a little later, *how* it happens.

It is the hope (and usually the belief) of physiological psychologists that behavior is not the product of an irreducible something called "consciousness," in the sense that the behavior of masses toward one another is a product of the (so far) irreducible force of gravity. If that hope remains unfulfilled, our understanding of behavior will forever be restricted to sets of probability formulas describing behavior that may occur in given sets of circumstances. This approach was once advocated by many so-called behaviorists and is not essentially different from the empirical search for "mental laws" carried out by earlier schools of psychology. From this point of view, psychology involves only the prediction of behavior according to scientific laws applied to a sealed "black box" (which earlier generations of psychologists would have called the "mind").

An inquiring schoolboy would probably feel cheated and dissatisfied, however, if the answer to his question about how cars work were that they obey empirical Laws of the Automobile from which, given wind velocity, road gradient and surface, pressure on the gas pedal, and other pertinent variables, the approximate speed and other behavior of the vehicle can be calculated. Our frustrated schoolboy could conclude only that motorcars have a nature unto themselves, with certain regularities of behavior that can be measured and classified but cannot usefully be made the object of further inquiry.

Of course, we know that such is not the case. Motorcars can also be explained in terms of smaller units like engines, gearboxes, steering apparatuses, and so on. Similarly, the behavior of electronic circuits can be reduced to the functioning of semiconductors, coils, magnetic circuits, electrons, and so on. Eventually, even in these examples, we arrive at a point beyond which further reduction is impossible at present, as when we are faced with the question "What is energy?" But there is a great deal of interesting territory between studying the object of inquiry as a total working unit and coming down to these ultimate questions. I believe that the same is true of the study of living organisms and that overall behavior results entirely from the functioning and interaction of more elementary components.

The easiest way to find out how the familiar machines around us work is to ask the men who make them (though, as an inveterate dismantler of clocks in my early youth, I think that it is not the most entertaining method). Failing that, one might ask someone who has already heard the answers. These methods cannot be applied to animate objects, however. After we have discovered *what* they can do by observing them (in their environment and, when necessary, in

1

the laboratory) we are on our own in answering the next question: how?

The nearest approach to this position in the world of inanimate objects is that in which a designer finds himself when he is asked to make something to fulfill a specified requirement never before presented. He is told what the machine must do and left to figure out how it can be constructed. In the case of the animal, we observe what it already does but still must figure out what sort of mechanism can behave that way. The psychologist does have one advantage. The working model is there before him, and, in theory at least, he can study the individual parts to see how they are assembled. Such investigations are the principal occupation of the physiological psychologist.

One thing that a designer of even the most complex self-organizing control machinery does not have to worry about, fortunately, is providing his invention with immediate awareness of its input, of the sort that animals (myself anyway) seem to enjoy. He can make a machine that will sort objects according to the wavelengths of light that they reflect, but he cannot point to one of its relays or transistors and say that when current flows through it the machine is experiencing the sensation of yellow. It would also be possible to build a machine that would scream and dance around when certain stimuli were presented and even one that would remember the experience as one to be avoided in future, but the inventor would not claim that he had built in the capacity to experience what we call "pain."

We should not dismiss this apparent difference between ourselves and machines (including the neural models constructed by theoretical psychologists) as imaginary. The basic mind-body problem will not be settled even when we have a good explanation of how neural circuits control behavior, or at least so it appears to me in my metaphysical innocence. On the other hand, I expect that the problem will eventually be solved. At the end of the last century philosophers, and even some scientists, thought that all the natural laws had been discovered. Since Bohr and Einstein there is less excuse for assuming that every phenomenon is

necessarily covered by our present collection of physical "laws." Perhaps as computers become more and more lifelike the differences between "them" and "us" will be easier to formulate.

Ideally, in a textbook on physiological psychology it should be possible to recount how research has uncovered the brain mechanisms involved in behavior, but unfortunately that is not yet the case. Nevertheless the data at present available are of great value in shaping psychological theory in many fields and in providing rational bases for classifying behavior. For example, that destruction of one part of the brain seriously interferes with the learning of nonsense syllables without having any measurable effect upon the learning of tactual or visual nonsense forms indicates that different neural circuits are involved in the two types of learning. This finding has implications for theories about intelligence. That patients with damage to another part of the brain cannot learn new material but can still remember what they learned before their injuries must have a profound influence on learning theories. The elicitation, by chemical injection or electrical stimulation, of stereotyped behavior patterns (some of them, like nest building in certain male animals, normally foreign to the subject) also has implications for theories of motivation and instinct.

These and other similar findings have considerably influenced the present trend away from such simple models of behavior as Hull's mathematical equations, in favor of models resembling complex computer programs. These models almost never aspire to cover all behavior but include only the data from perception experiments, for example, or those on problem solving. As this type of model has important commercial applications in the drive toward complete replacement of men by machines, there is no doubt that the trend will continue. The engineer will be close on the heels of the psychologist who discovers anything about the way the brain works—and may even be one jump ahead.

There are six parts in this book. The first consists of background information from other disciplines. One of the penalties imposed by an interdisciplinary subject like physiological psychology is that the student must be familiar with at least some aspects of the adjoining disciplines. The three chapters of the first section are thus devoted to the properties of neurons, the gross anatomy of the nervous system of higher vertebrates, and an introduction to some of the more important techniques used in research on physiological psychology.

The second part deals with the motor system. The approach is based on the assumption that overt behavior is the raison d'être of the nervous system and that all aspects of the system are aimed at increasing the efficiency and precision of motor activity. We therefore start at the root of the matter: the motor system.

The third part deals with sensory and perceptual mechanisms, from receptors to the cortex of the brain. Because of their greater accessibility and relative simplicity, the peripheral parts of both the sensory and motor systems are better understood than are the central parts. Circuits identified in the periphery may offer clues to what is taking place in the impenetrable tangle of the central nervous system, which is another reason for introducing the motor and sensory systems at an early point in the book. The third part of the book also contains chapters on the structure and certain functions (like language) of the cortex that transcend its role in perceptual analysis and learning.

The fourth section, a rather short one, covers sleep, arousal, and attention, topics that do not fall under either "sensory systems" or "motivation," though they are clearly related to both.

The fifth part of the book penetrates to the core of the problem of behavior, the topic of motivation. Special mechanisms have evolved to help animals to survive and to reproduce in suboptimal or unfriendly environments. They include neural mechanisms for temperature regulation, specific hungers, sexual and parental behavior, and various behaviors for avoiding injury. In most animals the instinctive response systems are refined and augmented by learning. In addition to the types of motivation already mentioned, this section also describes experiments on *self-stimulation* and explains their implications for a number of neural theories and models of motivation.

The final section reports the progress that has been made toward understanding the neural bases of learning and memory. Experimental attempts to localize learning mechanisms in nervous systems of varying degrees of complexity are described, and the section concludes with a discussion of some current theories about what happens at the subneural level (that is, at synapses or in the macromolecules of a neuron) when learning takes place.

Physiological psychology is at present in a very tantalizing phase, as readers of this book will discover. Empirical findings are multiplying at such a rate that they threaten to swamp us, but they still serve mainly to impress us with how much more we still need to know. We have enough information to tempt us into guessing how the brain may work, but we do not have enough information to inspire a great amount of confidence in most of these guesses.

PART ONE

FOUNDATIONS

In Chapter 1 we noted that the task of discovering how the brain works bears some resemblance to that of the designer commissioned to produce a machine for a specified new job. Many of the things that animals and people do are known; psychologists must think of ways that nervous systems might be put together to generate such behavior.

The design engineer would not progress far if he had to start from scratch, knowing nothing about the properties of materials and having to invent and build all the components that he wished to incorporate as he went along. A case in point is Babbage, who invented the principle of the general-purpose digital computer in the early nineteenth century. He spent years and several fortunes trying to construct the machine, using the technology of the time, but never completed it. He could not have been expected also to invent the modern components necessary to make his idea practicable.

The physiological psychologist must also rely heavily upon developments in other branches of science to provide him with the information about components of the nervous system that he needs to explain behavior. Whether he is trying to assemble a hypothetical brain that will produce lifelike behavior or to take a real brain apart, his task is hopeless without an idea of what elementary parts like nerve cells are capable of.

We know a great deal more about the functioning of neurons now than we did twenty years ago, thanks to the efforts of a few brilliant neurophysiologists, but much remains to be discovered, especially about changes that take place during development and learning. Some of the neural properties that psychologists must know are introduced in Chapter 2.

The neuroanatomist also has provided much helpful information to physiological psychologists. It is true that we cannot tell very much about how the brain works from visual inspection, especially of cut and stained sections of it, but if we are to work with the brain we must learn our way around in it.

We soon discover that the brains of animals have certain features in common. Many of the distinctive structures in the brains of such lower vertebrates as fish are recognizable in the brains of mammals, and the brain of one mammalian species is quite similar to those of others. This similarity is very important; if we had to study the correlation between form and function separately for every species we would never come to the end of it, and the task would seem almost pointless. That the brains of monkeys and apes are so similar to those of men is especially useful because, although the human brain interests us most, the amount of experimentation that we can do on it is very limited. Implicit in comparative studies is the assumption (not always completely justified) that homologous structures have the same functions at different stages of evolution.

The main purpose of Chapter 3 is to provide the student with a vocabulary of anatomical terms and a gross map of the mammalian nervous system so that he can follow the procedures of the many experiments in physiological psychology that involve specific brain structures. Detailed interconnections within structures are not included, although they should be interesting to psychologists theoretically because of the light they may throw upon how structures perform their functions. It would be confusing, however, to introduce these data until the functions themselves have been described, and in any case it cannot be claimed that great progress has so far been made in interpreting the fine detail of neural connections.

The final chapter of this part presents some of the more common techniques used to study brain functioning. There are surprisingly few techniques either for measuring physiological variables or for introducing them into psychological experiments. The three most important are, first, preventing part of the brain from functioning either by destroying it or, temporarily, by local application of drugs or cold; second, exciting parts of the brain with electrical current or local application of certain drugs; and, third, recording electrical fluctuations (and sometimes chemical or thermal changes) at various points in the brain. Electrical recording techniques are available for measuring the discharges of individual neurons, the total activity of a few hundred neurons, and gross voltage changes from variations in the polarization voltage of very many neurons in large volumes in neural tissue.

Use of one or more of these techniques in conjunction with one or more of the large array of tests devised by experimental psychologists accounts for much of our present information about the relations of the nervous system to behavior. There are many experiments that we would like to carry out for the valuable information they would almost certainly provide but that demand techniques that have not yet been adequately developed. Advances are being made all the time, however, and in recent years some experiments formerly considered impossible—recording the discharges of single neurons in conscious, behaving animals, for example—can now be performed under certain circumstances. Unfortunately, knowledge of the activity of one or two out of many billions of neurons has limited value, and no one has yet succeeded in investigating the interactions among neurons in complex pathways.

The limitations as well as the possibilities of presently available methods must be recognized if we are to design practicable and useful experiments. They are discussed in Chapter 4.

CHAPTER 2

NEURONS

The "textbook neuron" of 1940, and even later, was a very simple object—misleadingly simple—and the psychological theorist who attempted to use it to explain behavior usually found himself in trouble. We now know, thanks largely to such developments as the electron microscope and microelectrode recording, that neurons are extremely complex and vary widely one from another. We still do not know all there is to know about neurons, but at least today most psychologists are aware of this limitation.

The ultimate aim of neuropsychology is to explain how neurons, acting in concert, can bring about the behavior we see in the total organism; it is obviously of the utmost importance, therefore, that we first find out what individual neurons can and cannot do. This effort involves us in the study of pure physiology; there is no easy road to "interdisciplinary" subjects. An effective physiological psychologist has to be well informed on certain aspects of physiology, as well as to have a sound background in psychology.

Until the middle of the nineteenth century it was commonly believed that the nervous system was a continuous network of pipes, similar to the vascular system, through which fluid or electricity could flow. The work of the anatomists His, Kölliker, Ramón y Cajal, and others led Waldeyer (1891) to propose the "neurone doctrine." Waldeyer argued that the nervous system is made up of many individual cells called "neurones" (now usually spelled "neurons") and that nervous energy is conducted from one to another. Even as recently as 1935 there were still a few scientists who

were not convinced that neurons are really distinct from one another, but with the advent of the electron microscope it became possible to demonstrate the gaps between individual cells (see Figure 2.3).

Early studies of the physiology of neurons were conducted largely with excised pieces of peripheral nerve, which function normally for some time if kept in a suitable environment, so that many of the properties that were discovered and attributed to neurons in general really applied only to particular bits of single, rather unrepresentative neurons. Furthermore, because electrical excitability was a conspicuous feature of such preparations and the passage of nerve impulses was usually detected by electrical means, an exaggerated idea of the importance of the nerve's electrical properties was fostered. For many years the most widely accepted theory of neural transmission was that the electrical current set up by an impulse in one neuron was responsible for firing other neurons with which the first made contact.

This theory, though incorrect, served to stimulate a great deal of useful research on such simple neural circuits as the junctions between nerve and muscle and the connections in the spinal cord responsible for reflex responses. But eventually evidence against the electrical theory of neural transmission became too strong to be ignored, and in the last ten or fifteen years a more complex and realistic model of the neuron has evolved.

STRUCTURE

Before we can talk about the neuron in more particular terms we must first know what it looks like and what its various parts are called. Neurons occur in an almost infinite variety of forms, and there are exceptions to almost any generalization about them. The diagram in Figure 2.1 and the description here are of a "standard," or idealized, neuron; most real neurons differ from this example in one way or another.

Protruding from the cell body, or *soma*, are a number of irregular tapering processes known

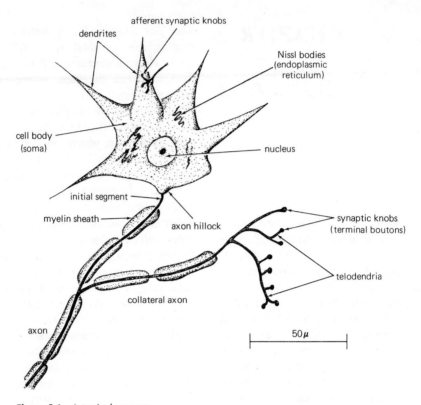

Figure 2.1   A typical neuron.

as *dendrites* (from *dendron,* "tree") and a single filamentous process called the *axon.* In mammals the cell body may be anywhere from a few micra (1 micron = 1/1,000 mm) to more than 100 micra (100 μ) in diameter; dendrites may be up to several millimeters long. The axon may be up to a meter or more in length (though a few centimeters is more common) and from a fraction of a micron to about 20 μ in diameter. A few of the neurons of some invertebrates are very large. The axons of the giant neurons of the squid, for example, are about 1 mm in diameter.

There is no sharp demarcation between the dendrites and the cell bodies of neurons of the type shown in the figure. The surfaces of both are studded with the synaptic knobs of afferent neurons (a few are shown in Figure 2.1), so that together they constitute the receiving area of the neuron. Although the cell bodies of most neurons combine the function of signal reception with the usual *trophic* functions of cells

(that is, the absorption and use of chemical nutrients), in some neurons these functions are performed in separate regions. In such neurons the cell body has nothing to do with the reception or transmission of impulses. Bodian (1962) has therefore made the sensible suggestion that the nutritive and information-processing functions be differentiated in labeling the parts of the neuron. He suggests the names *dendritic zone* for the receptive surface, wherever it may be located, and *perikaryon* for the nucleated cytoplasmic mass that is responsible for growth and nourishment. The dendritic zone may, and usually does, include the membrane of the perikaryon, as well as the dendrites, but in such cells as the unipolar cells of the dorsal-root ganglion (see section on classification of neurons later in this chapter) the dendritic zone may be several feet from the perikaryon, which is then simply an appendage of the axon.

Bodian defined the axon as the specialized part of the cell that conducts impulses without decrement away from the dendritic zone and toward the *synaptic knobs* (or *terminal boutons*) that form the junctions with the next elements in the neural circuit. It usually emerges from the cell body at a clearly demarcated elevation of the membrane called the *axon hillock*. The axon receives no synaptic connections (though this rule also has exceptions), and its entire length, with the exception of a short *initial segment* (see Figure 2.1), is sheathed by a number of *satellite cells*. In peripheral nerves (those outside the brain and spinal cord) the satellite cells are called *neurilemma* (or Schwann cells); in the central nervous system they are called *oligodendroglia*. Several small axons may share a satellite cell, as in Figure 2.2a, or a single axon may be swaddled in layer upon layer of the fatty membrane of its "personal" satellite cells (Figure 2.2b). The latter kind of axon is known as a *myelinated* axon. An axon usually divides into several branches soon after it leaves the dendritic zone, and each branch finally breaks up into a profusion of terminal fibrils, or *telodendria*, which wind among the dendrites and cell bodies of other neurons, often making repeated synaptic contact with them.

The inside of the neuron is filled with a fluid (*cytoplasm*) in which are suspended the nucleus and a number of granule-like structures that will absorb basic dyes (Nissl stains). These structures have various names: *Nissl bodies, Golgi apparatus, neurofibrils, tigroid bodies,* and so on, depending on their appearance. Under the electron microscope they are revealed as complex folded membranes, the larger ones forming what is called an *endoplasmic reticulum* similar to that found in secretory cells in other parts of the body. These membranes are rich in *ribonucleic acid* (RNA), a substance that regulates the manufacture of proteins and other requirements of the cell (see Chapter 21). It is therefore assumed that the larger cell inclusions participate in synthesis of substances used in maintaining the cell and transmitter substances that are released onto other cells to excite or inhibit them. There are some smaller inclusion bodies called *mitochondria*, whose function is to oxidize sugars and fats to produce an energy-rich substance, *adenosine triphosphate* (ATP). Mitochondria congregate in regions of high metabolic activity in the cell, for example, in the synaptic knobs.

Figure 2.3 shows an electron micrograph of three synaptic knobs lying against a dendrite of another cell. The diameter of the knobs is about 1 μ, and the gap between each knob and the juxtaposed dendritic membrane (the *synaptic cleft*) is about 0.02 μ wide. The membrane

Figure 2.2 Cross sections of (a) a group of unmyelinated axons sharing a single neurilemmal cell and (b) a single axon sheathed in many layers of neurilemmal membrane, that is, a myelinated axon. (After Gardner, 1968.)

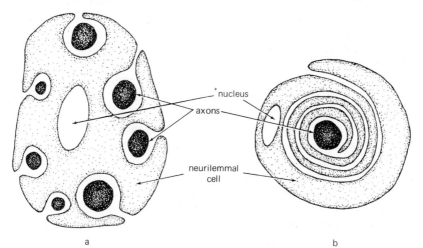

a   b

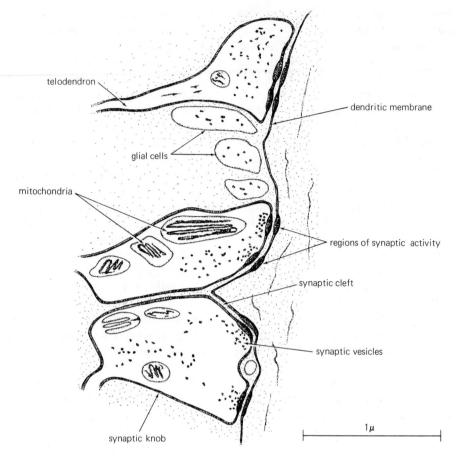

telodendron

dendritic membrane

glial cells

mitochondria

regions of synaptic activity

synaptic cleft

synaptic vesicles

synaptic knob

1 μ

Figure 2.3 Electron micrograph of three synaptic knobs lying against the membrane of a dendrite. (After Palay, 1958.)

itself is about 0.005 μ thick, and it consists of a sandwich of *lipoid* material (fat) between two layers of protein, but these are too thin to be seen in the figure. The dark parts of the membrane along the synaptic cleft are believed to be regions of synaptic activity.

The large objects in the cytoplasm of the lowest knob are mitochondria. The smaller granules are *synaptic vesicles*, believed to contain the transmitter substance ejected into the synaptic cleft by the knob when it is fired by an arriving impulse. The synaptic vesicles are about 0.03 μ in diameter. The part of the dendritic membrane shown in the drawing is typical of the whole surface of the dendritic zone, which may be encrusted with a total of up to several thousand such afferent connections.

Only a very small part of the cell membrane is free from contact with either synaptic knobs or glial cells. Glial cells are present in great numbers throughout the central nervous system; their main role seems to be to hold the neurons together and to synthesize and store material for use by the neurons. It is reported that the neurons' only access to the nutrients carried by the blood is through glial cells, which can thus act as a useful filter. The satellite cells around axons are a form of glia.

Electron microscopy and some recent neurophysiological experiments have cast doubt on the classical idea that synaptic knobs end only on the cell bodies and dendrites of other cells. In some instances they appear to end on other synaptic knobs. It is also now considered likely that neurons sometimes influence one another directly through their dendrites. These deviations from unidirectional conduction through the nervous system may be of importance for mechanisms of behavior.

CLASSIFICATION OF NEURONS

Neurons are classified according to the number of processes issuing from the perikaryon. In *unipolar cells* only the axon is connected to the cell body and the latter has no dendrites (Figure 2.4a). In *bipolar cells* there is one afferent process in addition to the axon (Figure 2.4b). The afferent process usually also conforms to Bodian's definition of an axon, but, as axons are conventionally defined as conducting *away* from the cell body, some people have preferred to call it a "dendrite," even though, except at the tip, it has none of the functional properties of a dendrite. The most common type of neuron in the vertebrate nervous system is the *multipolar cell*, in which the axon and many dendrites all sprout from the perikaryon, as shown in Figure 2.1.

Neurons may also be classified according to whether they have long axons (*Golgi type I*) or short axons (*Golgi type II*). Short axons, for the purpose of this classification, are those whose branches remain in the immediate vicinity of the cell body (perhaps within a radius of 1-2 mm).

Neurons also differ in the rates at which impulses are conducted along their axons.

Gasser classified nerve fibers in three main types, A, B, and C; A and B fibers are myelinated (as in Figure 2.2b). The difference between types A and B has no psychological importance; type-B neurons are found only in the *preganglionic* part of the *autonomic nervous system* (see Chapter 3). Type-A fibers vary in diameter from 1 to 20 μ, and the velocity at which impulses are transmitted along them in meters per second is about six times their diameter in micra. The C fibers are much smaller, from 0.3 to 1.3 μ in diameter, and the velocity of impulse transmission is rather less than twice the diameter.

Gasser subdivided the A fibers on the basis of conduction speed: The fastest were called "A-alpha," those of intermediate velocity "A-beta," and the slowest "A-gamma." As the speed of conduction is directly proportional to the diameter, these designations are sometimes applied to the three diameter ranges of myelinated fibers. Alternatively, Lloyd has suggested a classification based directly on fiber diameter. Group I is made up of myelinated fibers 12–21 μ in diameter, Group II of those 6–12 μ in diameter, and Group III of those 1–6 μ in diameter. He classifies Gasser's C fibers as Group IV.

STAINING NEURONS

Neurons can be seen clearly under the ordinary light microscope only after they have been dyed in some way. The best technique for making

Figure 2.4 A unipolar neuron (a) and a bipolar neuron (b).

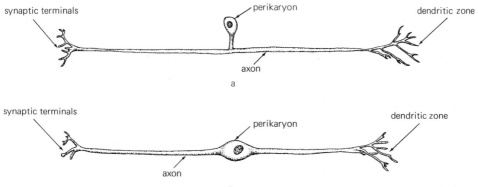

a whole single neuron visible is the *Golgi stain* (or some modification of it), in which the slice of neural tissue is impregnated with a silver salt. By a process similar to that used in developing photographic film, metallic silver is deposited in just a few of the neurons. Those neurons that are affected are silvered completely, and, as the neighboring, unstained cells remain quite transparent, thick slices of tissue can be used without obscuring the view of the stained neurons. Sometimes very long stretches of axon, or dendrite, can be followed in one slide. Unfortunately there is no way of predicting ahead of time which neurons will be stained. Figure 5.10 shows Golgi staining.

A somewhat different method of silver staining, developed by Ramón y Cajal, is used to stain all the neurons in a section. It affects cell bodies, dendrites, and unmyelinated axons; staining these axons is very useful in tracing nerve tracts (bundles) in the central nervous system. As all cells are stained by this method, only thin sections (up to about 50 μ thick) can be used, which sometimes complicates the problem of following tangled tracts. A more recent advance in the silver-staining technique (Nauta, 1957) overcomes this disadvantage. It enables the histologist to stain the axons of only those neurons that have recently been killed and are undergoing degeneration. By destroying a particular group of neurons and later using the Nauta stain on a series of sections through the brain, the experimenter can find out where the axons of the killed cells go.

Nissl stains, as mentioned earlier, have an affinity for the RNA-rich membranes and inclusion bodies of the cell; they do not stain axons. They are useful for locating and identifying cell groups in the brain called *nuclei*. (Not to be confused with the nuclei *within* cells.) Brain nuclei can be differentiated from one another by the sizes and shapes of the cell bodies that they contain, as well as by their location with respect to other nuclei, and a stain that emphasizes the perikaryon is ideal for giving this information.

None of the stains so far mentioned is very suitable for staining myelinated axons. For them the histologist uses some version of the *Weigert technique*, in which the fatty membrane is stained by *hematoxylin*. This chemical does not stain neurons, only satellite cells, but the cell groups can be seen as clear areas in the sections. It is possible to stain the same section for both fibers and cell bodies (Figure 2.5), using Luxol fast-blue for myelin and neutral red for cell (Klüver & Barrera, 1953).

Another method, analogous to the Nauta stain, is also available for myelinated fibers; it is the *Marchi method*, in which osmium is used to stain the myelin residue left by the degenerating axons of injured cells. It is thus possible to follow the tracts from experimentally cut fibers as black spots through a series of sections. Osmium salts are also used to prepare sections for inspection under the electron microscope.

Most stains cannot be used on living tissues because several stages of the staining procedure are lethal, but nerve fibers in the skin or cornea of the eye, for example, absorb methylene blue to a greater extent than do the surrounding tissues and can thus be rendered visible in the living animal. Unstained neurons, living or dead, may be observed with a special apparatus, the *phase-contrast microscope*, which makes use of differences in the refractive indexes of transparent objects in the visual field to render them visible.

Pomerat used phase-contrast microphotography to make some excellent time-lapse (speeded motion) movies of living neurons and glial cells. They show the cells in vigorous motion, especially during growth, and it is also possible to see the movements of granules along internal tracts within each cell body and axon. (The film *Dynamic Aspects of the Neuron in Tissue Culture* is available from the Tissue Culture Association, 99N El Molino Avenue, Pasadena, California 91101.) Some still photographs from the film are reproduced in Pomerat, Hendelman Raiborn & Massey (1967).

PHYSIOLOGY OF NEURONS

For the purpose of discussing its physiological mechanisms it is possible to regard the neuron as a slightly porous bag full of fluid (Figure 2.6). The bag is the membrane, the fluid is the

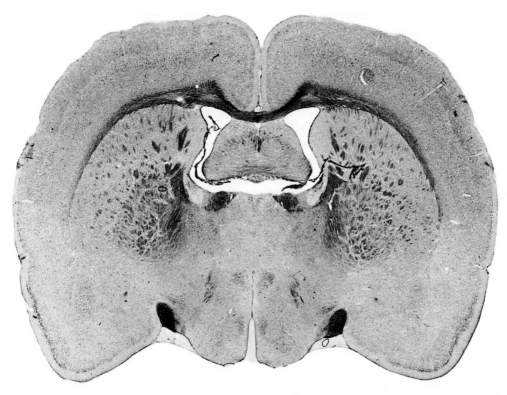

Figure 2.5 A section of rat brain at the level of the hippocampal commissure, stained by the method of Klüver and Barrera for both cell bodies and fiber tracts. (From Pellegrino & Cushman, *A stereotaxic atlas of the rat brain.* New York: Appleton-Century-Crofts, 1967.)

cytoplasm, and the whole thing is surrounded by a pool of *extracellular fluid*.

Many of the interesting properties of neurons depend upon the difference in constitution between the extracellular and intracellular fluids. The differences arise partly from the inability of some large molecules to pass through the semipermeable membrane and partly from the action of energy-consuming (chemical) processes in the membrane that transport ions in a preferred direction through the membrane. These ion-transport reactions are usually called *ion pumps*.

When an electrolyte dissolves in water it dissociates into positively charged (for example, Na^+) and negatively charged (for example, Cl^-) ions. These ions are in constant random motion as a result of thermal agitation, and two principles operate to maintain a homogeneous distribution of ions throughout the solution. The first is that like charges repel one another

and that opposite charges attract, so that if a number of similarly charged ions should arrive simultaneously in one spot they would be rapidly dispersed by mutual repulsion. They would also attract ions with the opposite charge

Figure 2.6 Constituents of neuronal cytoplasm and extracellular fluid.

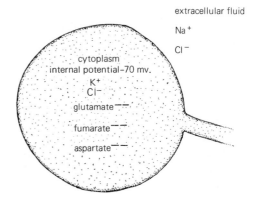

extracellular fluid

Na^+

Cl^-

cytoplasm
internal potential-70 mv.

K^+
Cl^-
glutamate$^-$$^-$
fumarate$^-$$^-$
aspartate$^-$$^-$

into the region. The establishment of all but very weak and transient gradients of electrical potential (that is, voltage differences) in the solution would thus be prevented.

The other principle tends to prevent inequalities of concentration of any substance in the solution. Regardless of the charge, if there are more particles of a constituent in one part of the vessel than elsewhere, purely random movements will ensure that more of them move out of that region than move in. Suppose that an inhomogeneity exists, and imagine an open window between the regions of high and low concentration. All particles of the substance are equally mobile, so that the window will naturally be traversed by more particles from the concentrated side than from the dilute side. There will be a net flow of particles down the concentration gradient from the concentrated to the dilute region until the difference is eliminated.

In solutions of several different elements this principle applies to each component separately; it is not possible, for example, to maintain a high concentration of sodium in one part of a vessel and a high concentration of potassium in another, for the particles of each substance flow down their own concentration gradient to ensure homogeneous distribution.

This equilibrium can, however, be artificially upset in a number of ways. If an electrical charge is applied between conducting plates in a solution, the positively charged ions (*cations*) will move to the negative plate (*cathode*), and the negatively charged ions (*anions*) will seek the positive plate (*anode*). A process that is almost the converse of this one occurs in the neuron. The active pumping of ions through the membrane against their concentration gradients causes a separation of electrical charges, and voltage appears between the inside and the outside of the membrane.

According to the findings of Hodgkin (1951) and others, the constituents of the cytoplasm and extracellular fluid that are most responsible for the electrical properties of the neuron are sodium chloride (NaCl), potassium chloride (KCl), and the salts of some amino acids that are found inside the cell. The cell membrane

is relatively permeable to chloride ions (Cl^-), but the large amino-acid radicles (for example, *glutamate*$^{--}$, *fumarate*$^{--}$, and *aspartate*$^{--}$, see Figure 2.6) cannot penetrate the membrane, thus providing a steady negative bias to the inside of the neuron. Sodium ions (Na^+) and potassium ions (K^+) also do not pass through the membrane very freely, but when a sodium ion does collide with the inside of the membrane it is likely to enter into some sort of chemical reaction that carries it to the outside, whereas a potassium ion striking the outside of the membrane is liable to be drawn inside through a similar mechanism.

These metabolic processes establish voltage and concentration gradients across the cell membrane. According to Eccles (1957), the concentration of sodium inside a *motoneuron* (a large neuron in the spinal cord) of the cat is roughly one-tenth that in the surrounding fluid. Each sodium ion extruded from the cell takes with it a single unit of positive charge. Some idea of the cumulative effect of this drain can be obtained from one simple calculation: If only sodium ions were involved and no other ions were allowed to move through the membrane, a potential difference on the order of 5,000 volts would appear between the inside and the outside of the neuron when nine-tenths of the sodium had been driven out. Of course such an enormous voltage would destroy the membrane, and it is fortunate that ordinarily two other ionic migrations take place that almost completely neutralize it. The first is the influx of positively charged potassium ions because of the potassium pump. The other is the efflux of negatively charged chloride ions until an equilibrium is reached between the conflicting requirements of minimizing both the electrical and concentration gradients.

If, in the same example, the concentration of chloride were the same inside and outside the membrane, those chloride ions nearest the membrane would be repelled by the internal negative charge and attracted by the positive charge outside. The chances that they would be pulled out of the cell would be high. On the other hand, any chloride ions on the outside would be discouraged from entering by the repulsion of the internal charge and the attraction of the external positive voltage. This drift out of the cell would continue, reducing the negative charge of the cell but never completely neutralizing it. If it were ever neutralized there would be nothing to counteract the large difference in concentration built up between the inside and the outside. With more chloride ions on the outside of the cell than on the inside and no potential difference to maintain it, chloride ions would be forced to enter the cell along the concentration gradient. Somewhere between the two extremes of zero concentration gradient and zero potential gradient an equilibrium condition is established. For most

neurons this equilibrium occurs when the internal voltage is about −70 to −80 millivolts (mv), the unneutralized remainder of the thousands of volts that would otherwise have accumulated.

This equilibrium is that of the resting neuron, one that is not being bombarded by afferent impulses. An impulse arriving at a synapse along the axon of an afferent neuron releases a chemical transmitter substance onto the postsynaptic membrane of the neuron (Figure 2.7a), causing it to become more permeable at that point. Eccles (1964) has hypothesized a mechanism, illustrated schematically in Figure 2.7b, by which molecules of the transmitter

Figure 2.7   A model of synaptic transmission. (a) Release of transmitter substance from a synaptic vesicle through the presynaptic membrane. Molecules of transmitter substance open pores in the postsynaptic membrane when they impinge upon it. (b) The postsynaptic membrane enlarged. Molecules of transmitter substance occupy receptor sites on the membrane and move the adjacent barriers at the openings of pores through the membrane. (After Eccles, 1964.)

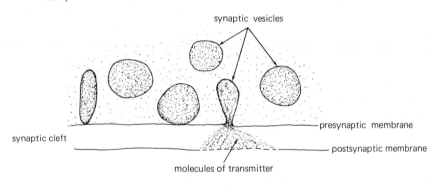

substance become attached to *receptor sites* and cause pores in the membrane to open. If the synapse is a normal excitatory one, the membrane develops holes big enough to let both sodium and potassium ions through. The potassium is under no great pressure to move in either direction; there is not very much of it on the outside, and the excess internal concentration is largely held there by the negative charge. It is a different matter with the sodium. There is a lot of sodium outside the membrane, and it is attracted into the cell by the internal negative charge; it therefore pours in through the holes. In the cat motoneuron as many as 10^7 sodium ions might enter during the fraction of a millisecond that the membrane is rendered permeable. (The transmitter substance in this case is probably *acetylcholine*, which is destroyed by the enzymes *cholinesterase* and *acetylcholinesterase* as soon as it is released.) At an average motoneuron synapse in the cat the influx of positively charged ions is sufficient to reduce the internal voltage by about half a millivolt. The resulting charge is called an *excitatory postsynaptic potential* (EPSP). After the acetylcholine has been eliminated, the membrane immediately recovers its impermeability to sodium, and the normal voltage is restored in a matter of three or four milliseconds, probably through migrations of potassium and chloride ions. The insurgent sodium is eliminated more slowly by the action of the sodium pump.

If a number of synapses are active simultaneously or within a few milliseconds of one another, their effects sum, and a larger change in cell potential results. If this change exceeds a critical value of 10–20 mv (that is, if the internal voltage of the cell changes from, say, −70 to −55 mv) something dramatic—and not completely understood—happens to the axon at the point where it joins the dendritic zone: It becomes highly permeable to sodium ions. Through this region the flow of ions is great enough to wipe out completely the internal negative charge. In fact, under the influence of the large concentration gradient, the sodium keeps flowing even after the membrane potential has been reduced to zero, causing the charge

on the inside of the cell to become positive (Figure 2.8).

We have discussed "large numbers" of ions, but it must be recognized that this term is relative. The amount of sodium that finally enters the cell, even during a complete discharge, is hardly enough to produce a detectable change in the internal concentration. The same reasoning used to illustrate the change in voltage that would occur if only sodium ions were removed from the neuron shows that, if they all returned without any further compensating readjustment among the other ions, the internal voltage of the cell would rise to several thousand volts.

When the initial segment of the axon becomes permeable, the charge of the cell body is neutralized almost instantly, but it takes longer for the ions carrying the charge to penetrate the long, thin axon. The farther reaches of the axon membrane resemble the initial segment, however, in that they become permeable to sodium ions if the potential difference falls below the critical value at any point. A relatively small number of ions moving down the thin core thus suffice to open the door to much greater numbers by providing the necessary depolarization and triggering the increase of membrane permeability. The process spreads along the axon in a way analogous to the spread of a flame along a match or a piece of string. The heat from the burning part of the match heats the neighboring length until it reaches the critical combustion temperature. When that part burns in its turn, its heat sets fire to the next length, and so on. In the axon the "hole" of permeability moves along, fed by the very current that flows through it.

This process is modified somewhat in the myelinated axon. The myelin coating is not continuous but has gaps, called *nodes of Ranvier*, between the satellite cells (see Figure 2.1). Ions can flow into the axon only at these points and at the initial segment. Because of the greater separation between the internal and external charges in the myelinated regions, the electrical capacity of the axon is much reduced, and fewer ions are therefore needed to produce the change of voltage necessary to trigger

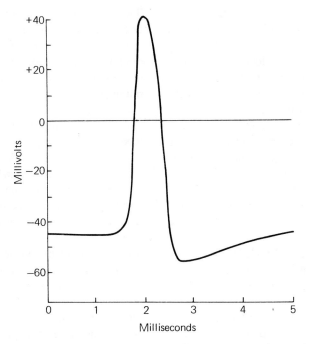

Figure 2.8 Action potential measured inside a squid giant axon showing "overshoot" into the positive region because of the influx of sodium ions through the axon membrane under the pressure of the concentration gradient. (After Hodgkin & Huxley, 1939.)

membrane permeability (just as fewer molecules are needed to produce a given pressure change in a vessel of small capacity than in a large one). The section of axon between the nodes rapidly discharges to the critical voltage, and a new "hole" appears at the next node. The impulse thus "leaps" from node to node, giving rise to what is called "saltatory conduction." The rate of impulse transmission is thus faster in myelinated than in unmyelinated axons.

We have referred to "holes" in the membrane that let sodium ions through to the inside of the cell, but the process is clearly not that simple. If it were, the neuron would discharge once and never recover. It appears that only a limited amount of sodium is allowed through the membrane at each impulse, as if a turnstile could make only a certain number of revolutions in one direction before it had to be unwound to be used again. During the "unwinding" phase, the membrane transports cations (mainly potassium) to the outside of the cell and so restores the internal potential. At this

moment the membrane is quite insensitive to further stimulation of any sort, the neuron is *refractory*; only when the internal voltage has returned to normal or at least to more than the triggering potential can the membrane discharge again.

If a large number of impulses are transmitted in a short time, there will be an accumulation of sodium ions inside the cell and a loss of potassium from it. The fatigue, or adaptation, which eventually cuts down the firing rate, may be due in part to this redistribution of ions. Equilibrium is then restored over the next few minutes or hours by the sodium and potassium pumps.

Neurophysiologists still do not agree on whether reduced potential across the membrane of the dendritic zone makes it permeable, or whether that part of the cell responds only to chemical stimuli. At one time it was assumed that impulses are propagated along dendrites in the same nondecremental manner as along axons, but later observations have cast doubt on this assumption. It is now commonly believed that dendrites are capable of electrotonic conduction only (that is, they conduct as if they were passive tubes of electrolyte, with no contribution from the membrane). During a discharge of the cell body, a wave of depolarization would thus spread decrementally up the dendrites, arriving, very much attenuated, at the ends of the branches. Depolarization through synaptic action near the tips of the dendrites would be similarly attenuated by the time it reached the cell body.

Some data do not fit this hypothesis, however. Hild and Tasaki (1962) have shown that nondecremental conduction occurs along the dendrites of some cells cultured in vitro. They extracted small quantities of cat and rat brain and allowed the neurons to grow in a culture medium on slides. Then, under the phase-contrast microscope, they placed a stimulating microelectrode against the tip of a dendrite and a recording microelectrode against the wall of the same dendrite near the cell body. Clear indications that electrical impulses travel without decrement down the dendrites after each stimulation were obtained. This finding seems to establish that the dendrites of some neurons can behave as axons do under some circumstances, but it should be remembered that the cells cultured in vitro had no synaptic connections, which may influence the behavior of the dendritic membrane under normal conditions.

INHIBITION

In addition to the excitatory synapses already described, which allow ingress to sodium ions and consequent depolarization of the cell, there are other inhibitory synapses that when activated (fired) lead to an *increase* in the internal charge (*hyperpolarization*). Eccles (1964) has provided substantial evidence that at these synapses the transmitter substance opens up small holes in the postsynaptic membrane that are permeable only to potassium and chloride. (Sodium ions are smaller than potassium ions, but in solution each always carries around a "cage" or crystal of water molecules, which prevents it from passing through small holes.)

The potassium is thus able to move out of the cell without the entrance of any sodium.

It may seem strange that potassium should migrate to the outside against the attraction of the internal charge, but thanks to the potassium pump there is actually more potassium inside the cell than can be held there by the charge alone. If only inhibitory synapses are active, therefore, the internal voltage will become slightly more negative than it was before. This reaction is known as an *inhibitory postsynaptic potential* (IPSP). It must be remembered, however, that inhibition manifests itself only when the neuron would otherwise be fired, that is, when it is undergoing depolarization. Under these conditions there is less internal attraction for the potassium than at the equilibrium potential, and it is even more likely to flow out through the inhibitory synapses. The more sodium that enters (through excitatory synapses), the more potassium ions will leave, forming a short circuit for the current. This short circuit prevents the internal potential from becoming sufficiently positive to reach the critical value at which an impulse is triggered at the axon junction. If more excitatory synapses become active, the effect of the inhibitory synapses may be overcome, but it will take longer for the critical voltage to be reached, and, if the cell is firing repetitively, the frequency of discharge will be reduced by inhibition.

Generation of inhibitory postsynaptic potentials is not the only means by which transmission is blocked at a synapse, however. It has been known for some time that there are some spinal inhibitory pathways that are not depressed by strychnine, a substance that normally interferes with the action of the transmitter substance at inhibitory synapses. Frank and Fuortes (1957) recorded from the insides of neurons undergoing strychnine-resistant inhibition and found that excitatory postsynaptic potentials were reduced although the inhibitory input produced no sign of hyperpolarization. They inferred that the inhibitory influence was acting not upon the cell but upon the excitatory afferents to it, and they called the effect *presynaptic inhibition*.

Eccles has studied this effect further by placing microelectrodes in the afferent terminals themselves. He has found that during presynaptic inhibition the terminals undergo long-lasting partial depolarization. This reduced membrane potential attenuates any arriving excitatory impulses, and less transmitter substance is released (Eccles, Eccles, & Magni, 1960, 1961). Angel, Magni, and Strata (1965) have studied presynaptic inhibition in the visual pathway of cats.

A possible site for presynaptic inhibition is the *axoaxonal synapse* (a synapse on a synaptic knob) described by Estable (1961). E. G. Gray (1962) and Szentágothai (1964a) have also observed such structures in electron micrographs.

FUNCTIONAL CHARACTERISTICS OF NEURONS

The hypothetical neurons that have been described in this chapter may sound formidably complex, but the real ones are even more so. One very important property that has not been mentioned so far is the ability of at least some neurons in the central nervous system to fire spontaneously (without synaptic input). Perhaps most neurons would do so if they were not under almost continuous inhibitory influence. Some neurons change their sensitivity, or their spontaneous rate of firing, in accordance with the presence of hormones and other constituents of the blood. These neurons may more properly be considered receptors (neurons with specialized dendritic zones), which will receive fuller consideration in Chapter 8.

Most neurons fire repeatedly if input to the cell is maintained, the frequency of firing being roughly proportional to the intensity of the afferent bombardment. The reason is not clear, but it seems that, once the axon has been triggered and has admitted a burst of sodium ions, potassium ions are ejected in such quantity as to override the slower influx of ions at synapses and to drive the internal potential to something approaching its resting value. Then, when the initial segment of the axon becomes impermeable again, the cell potential falls once more because of the leaks at the synapses, and the cell is refired. Some cells fire repeatedly after a single afferent impulse. In such instances, assuming that other afferent pathways are not disturbing our measurements, we think that either a long-lasting transmitter substance has been deposited on the cell membrane or the membrane is very slow to recover from the effect of the transmitter substance.

Unfortunately, with present-day techniques it is not possible to study a single neuron of the central nervous system in isolation. We cannot therefore determine whether its more complex behavior is caused by intrinsic properties or by interaction with other neurons and glial cells. Although this state of affairs is not very satisfactory, it is not strictly speaking a problem for the physiological psychologist. In general, he uses neural phenomena, but not the explanations for these phenomena, in his theorizing. It is true that the more he knows about the explanations, the more successful he may be in closing gaps in the physiological data, but, if one *theory* of neural functioning should prove wrong and be replaced by a better one, serious changes in psychological theory do not usually follow. The discovery of new neural *phenomena*, on the other hand, may entail profound changes in the thinking of physiological psychologists, opening up new possibilities for model building. The most important discovery that we can look forward to is one that would provide the basis for an explanation of learning, the storage of information. Several mechanisms have been suggested as possible candidates, but none is completely satisfactory. Discussion of this problem will be postponed to Part Six, after presentation of necessary information on the requirements for such a process.

Summary

Neurons occur in an almost infinite variety of shapes and in a wide range of sizes, but they all possess the following parts: a dendritic zone, which receives input connections from many sources and sums excitatory and inhibitory effects; an axon, which generates impulses whenever the summed input exceeds a critical value and conducts them without decrement away from the dendritic zone; and a perikaryon (usually, but not always, within the dendritic zone), which contains the nucleus of the cell and carries out the main nutritive and metabolic processes.

Neurons always occur in conjunction with satellite cells, glial cells called "neurilemma" or "oligodendroglia." In some cases these cells coat axons with a fatty membrane known as "myelin."

Neurons are rich in endoplasmic reticulum, membranes that play a part in the synthesis of proteins. Some of the proteins produced by neurons are capable of irritating the membranes of other neurons, and they therefore act as transmitter substances when released at axon terminals.

Neurons are usually classified according to the number of processes issuing from the cell body. In unipolar cells the single fiber sprouting from the cell divides into two, one end going to the dendritic zone and the other to the axon terminals. Bipolar cells have one process leading to the dendritic zone and one to the synaptic knobs. Multipolar neurons, by far the most common, have numbers of dendritic processes and one axon issuing from each cell body.

The velocity of impulse transmission depends upon the diameter of the axon and whether or not it is myelinated. Impulses travel more quickly along thick or myelinated axons than along thin or unmyelinated ones.

Microscopic observation of neurons usually involves staining them with silver, which darkens unmyelinated parts of neurons, or with Nissl stains, which color the RNA-rich membranes in the cell bodies. Other stains have also been developed to show myelinated fibers and degenerating fibers, the latter being useful for tracing the connections from an area that has been experimentally destroyed.

The neuron membrane actively pumps sodium ions from the cell, leaving the large negatively charged amino-acid radicles behind to give the inside of the cell a net negative voltage of about 70 mv.

When the postsynaptic membrane is made porous by the release of transmitter substance onto it, sodium ions leak back into the cell at a high rate and partly neutralize the negative charge. If the membrane potential is driven below a critical value, an impulse, whose size does not depend on the triggering voltage, is generated in the initial part of the axon and transmitted to the axon terminals, where it causes the release of transmitter substance onto the next neuron of the pathway.

At some synapses release of the transmitter substance opens only smaller pores, allowing potassium ions to escape from the cell but not the ingress of sodium. This loss of potassium neutralizes the effect of sodium entering through excitatory synapses and inhibits the firing of the neuron.

Inhibition is also produced by partial depolarization of synaptic knobs, which renders them less effective when excitatory impulses reach them. This mechanism is called "presynaptic inhibition."

Many neurons apparently fire "spontaneously," but it is rarely possible to be sure that no chemical transmitter substance is acting upon them. Neurons do not fire each time they receive an impulse, but the firing rate (until adaptation or fatigue sets in) is roughly proportional to the rate of excitatory afferent bombardment. Because neurons in the central nervous system are interconnected in complex networks, it is never possible to know exactly what synaptic influences are acting upon the individual cells whose activity is being measured; definite interpretation of the results is thus rarely possible.

This problem is a headache for neurophysiologists, but psychologists are more interested in what neurons do than in how they do it.

CHAPTER 3

GROSS NEURO-ANATOMY

In his student days, Lashley, the pioneer of physiological psychology, was given sections of a frog brain to study under the microscope and is said to have had the idea that to understand the animal's behavior one needed simply to trace the neural pathways to see how the frog was "wired up." It is doubtful that Lashley was the first to conclude this, and it is quite certain that he was not the last; many beginners in this field think that, as neuroanatomical knowledge becomes more complete and detailed, it will answer all our psychophysiological questions.

The shortcomings of this idea are soon revealed, however. Even supposing that it would be possible to trace all the neural connections accurately, which seems doubtful except perhaps in the very simplest organisms, there are other factors to be taken into account. For example, all connections are not equally effective; some synapses may suppress activity, and others may excite; some cells may respond to synaptic input only if other conditions, like temperature or composition of the blood, are also favorable; time relationships between neural activities may be important; and the type of transmitter substance may influence such factors as duration and intensity of activity. Microscopic examination of stained dead tissue can tell us little or nothing about these things.

But, although neuroanatomy may not answer all our questions, it is nevertheless an indispensible tool. First and most important, it has provided a convenient map on which the readily distinguishable parts of the nervous system are displayed and named. Without such a map it would be impossible for one investigator to communicate with another; imagine trying to describe a dance to someone who could not distinguish an arm from a leg.

Furthermore, although function in the more psychologically interesting parts of the brain does not always bear a clear and simple relation to structure, relations do exist, and a major preoccupation of physiological psychologists is to extend and clarify them. Some rational ordering of the nervous system is essential if this work is to proceed in an efficient way.

The primary purpose of this chapter is to supply a rough chart so that we can begin to find our way around in the nervous system. The emphasis is on the relative locations of the various structures, and only the most elementary facts about the pathways among them are introduced at this point. More detail about functional connections and the fine structure of such individual parts as the retina, the cerebral cortex, and so on, will be introduced later in the book as the need arises.

COMMON ANATOMICAL TERMS

Animals have three principle axes: nose to tail, back to belly, and side to side (because of bilateral symmetry, it is rarely necessary to differentiate between the right and left sides; it is more useful to view this axis as starting in the middle and extending to each side). The Latinate equivalents of these directions are conventionally employed in anatomy: *rostral* to *caudal, dorsal* to *ventral,* and *medial* to *lateral* (Figure 3.1). *Ipsilateral* means on the same side; *contralateral* means on the opposite side.

In the curious posture of man both his nose and his belly point in the same forward direction; for primates, the terms "anterior" and "posterior" are therefore sometimes used instead of "rostral" and "caudal" to describe the front-back direction in the head and to describe the ventral-dorsal direction in the spinal cord. Furthermore, the dorsal and ventral parts of the head, which are usually carried at the top and bottom by both man and beast, are sometimes labeled "superior" and "inferior" (or "basal") respectively. These directions are shown in

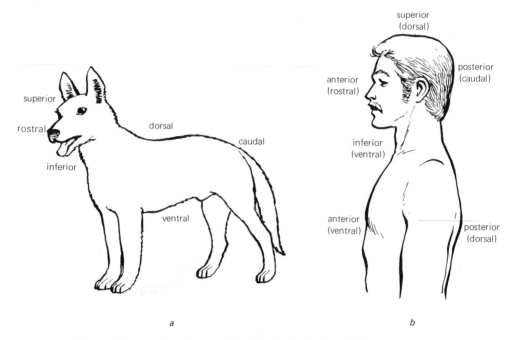

Figure 3.1   Some directional relationships in the bodies of (a) common vertebrates and (b) primates.

Figure 3.1. Whenever possible the terms "rostral," "caudal," "dorsal," and "ventral," will be used for both animal and man in this book; they are strictly applicable to the latter only if he is imagined to have his head thrust back at an angle of about 90 degrees to its usual position.

Two other useful pairs of terms are: *distal-proximal* and *afferent-efferent*. The distal part of a nerve fiber or limb, for instance, is the end farther from the brain or the center of the body; the proximal part is, of course, the other end. An afferent process is one that is approaching the center, an efferent process one that runs in the opposite direction. These terms can be used only for parts that are polarized in some way, nerve cells or blood vessels, for example, which normally carry impulses or fluids in only one direction.

The brain has approximately the consistency of a raw egg. In order to examine its structure we must first harden it with a fixing agent like alcohol or formalin. It may then be dissected layer by layer or sliced very thin, mounted on slides and stained for microscopic inspection. Brain sections are most commonly cut perpen-

dicular to the rostral-caudal axis (ie parallel to the vertical plane through both ears); they are called *coronal*, or *frontal*, sections. Sections perpendicular to the lateral axis (vertical slices from front to back of the head) are called *sagittal*, or *longitudinal*, sections; the medial sagittal section divides the brain into its two hemispheres. *Horizontal* sections are perpendicular to the dorsal-ventral axis. There are, of course, an infinite number of possible planes of section; special angles are sometimes used to show the features of particular structures.

For descriptive convenience the nervous system is divided into two parts: a *peripheral nervous system* and a *central nervous system* (CNS). The former, with minor exceptions, lies outside the bony protection of the skull and vertebral column. It is further divided into *somatic* and *autonomic* components. The somatic part consists of nerves to skeletal (striped) muscles and from many receptors. The autonomic, or visceral, part consists of the motor nerves to the heart, to smooth muscles (of blood vessels, digestive and reproductive organs, and so on), and to glands. It also contains the nerves of receptors from visceral structures. The autonomic motor system is subdivided once more into the *sympathetic* and *parasympathetic* nervous systems (Figure 3.12). In general, the sympathetic system mobilizes the body during stress, and the parasympathetic system runs the internal economy under normal conditions.

All parts of the nervous system are composed of neurons and various kinds of supporting tissue, which were described in Chapter 2. The cell bodies usually appear in clusters or groups, called *nuclei* in the central nervous system, and *ganglia* in the peripheral nervous system. The axons of the cells in peripheral ganglia form bundles called *nerves*, which run to and from muscles, receptors, glands, and so on. Axons also form bundles within the central nervous system, there called *tracts* or *fasciculi*. By an extension of the nomenclature of the peripheral system, neurons forming long tracts in the central nervous system are sometimes called *ganglion cells* to differentiate them from neurons with short axons or others not associated with tracts. Short-axon neurons connecting the other cells within a nucleus are called *internuncials*.

Tracts consist mainly of myelinated axons and, when exposed, have a characteristic white sheen, from which they take the name "white matter." Concentrations of cell bodies or unmyelinated axons look dark by comparison and are known as "gray matter." This gray-white distinction is lost when tissue is stained, but, as mentioned in Chapter 2, Nissl stains make gray matter visible, and Weigert stains darken white matter (Figure 3.2). A rough idea of the course of a tract can be obtained in this way, but individual fibers (axons) often leave and join the tract at many points along the route, so that it is never certain whether or not any of the axons starting at one end cover the full distance. This difficulty can be overcome by the special staining techniques that allow us to follow degenerating axons.

Of late these purely anatomical techniques of tracing pathways have been augmented by such physiological methods as stimulating some point in the living animal and plotting the points at which nerve impulses can then be picked up. Even so, it seems likely that we still do not have a complete, or even entirely accurate, picture of the connections of the central nervous system. This lack need not worry the psychologist unduly, however. It is easy to exaggerate the significance of the presence or absence of a direct pathway between two structures, for the fact is that, even when no link is apparent, indirect connections involving only a few synapses can almost always be discovered.

DEVELOPMENT OF THE VERTEBRATE NERVOUS SYSTEM

The gross anatomical features of the nervous system are strikingly similar throughout the mammalian series. The information derived from experiments on the nervous system of one animal would otherwise be of doubtful significance in understanding the behavior of other species. There is much experimental evidence that homologous structures usually have similar functions, though there are exceptions, and the principle should not be applied automatically.

Structural resemblances among brains are also convenient for the student of anatomy. He has to memorize the names and locations of the parts of the brain of only one animal, and he can then apply his knowledge to many other species with little modification. Most neuroanatomy textbooks are intended for medical students and are therefore devoted principally to the human brain. It is convenient for us to adopt the same basic model.

The brain of the mammal, and especially that of the human, is a highly evolved structure; at first sight it appears to be only a disorganized collection of tracts and nuclei. A closer examination does little to dispel this impression. Order begins to emerge only as we trace the development of the system *ontogenetically*, *phylogenetically*, or both. We owe a great deal to Herrick's (1948) work on the neuroanatomy of the lower vertebrates for our present somewhat clearer conception of the organization of the mammalian nervous system.

In early embryos, and in primitive *chordates*, the nervous system consists of a nerve net in the form of a tube closed at both ends. Sensory

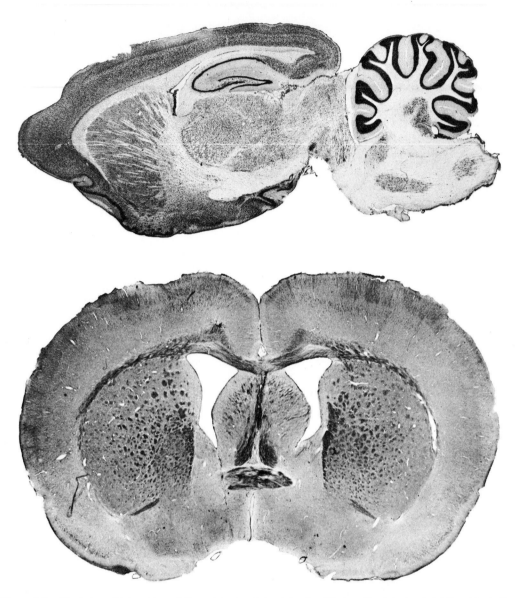

Figure 3.2 (*Top*) A sagittal section of the rat brain, stained by the Nissl method (using toluidine blue). The section was taken about 2.5 mm lateral to the midline. The cerebral cortex, corpus callosum, caudate-putamen (shot through with bundles of internal capsule fibers), hippocampus, thalamus, and cerebellum are prominent. (*Bottom*) Coronal section of rat brain stained by the Weigert method. The section is at the level of the anterior commissure, which can be seen crossing the midline below the columns of the fornix. On either side of the lateral ventricles may be seen the caudate-putamen (shot through with bundles of internal capsule fibers).

nerves enter the dorsal side of the tube and motor nerves leave the ventral side (Figure 3.3a), with a diffuse intermediate nerve net connecting them. Functionally, the development of the brain seems generally to pursue the following sequence. At first the neural tube consists of a string of largely autonomous seg-ments, with only diffuse connections from one to another. Mutations leading to the concentration of chemical and other sensitivity around the mouths of animals (to provide more efficient selection of food), and others that changed the nervous system to enable the animal to use that increased sensitivity to control its movements, have been perpetuated because of the advantages they confer in the competition for survival. We thus find the evolution of a large *olfactory* nucleus and some concentration of motor control at the head of the neural tube.

Other receptor systems in the head also become specialized and feed their information into the developing region of behavioral control, where it can be used most effectively. For increased diversity and complexity of sensory input greater processing capacity is required, and at some stage part of the originally olfactory forebrain is invaded by other sense modalities and converted into circuits necessary for a higher level of behavioral control. The forebrain grows to accommodate the extra load, and the increased number of neurons ensure more refined sensory analysis and more flexible motor

Figure 3.3 Evolution of the mammalian brain. (a) Section of the simple neural tube, showing sensory and motor nerves. (b) Enlargement of the anterior end of the neural tube to form the three divisions of the brain. (c) Further expansion and lateral growth of the forebrain. (d) Division of the forebrain into diencephalon (thalamus and hypothalamus), striatum (basal ganglia), and cortex (cerebral hemisphere). The figure shows the relative positions of these structures. (After Gardner, 1968.)

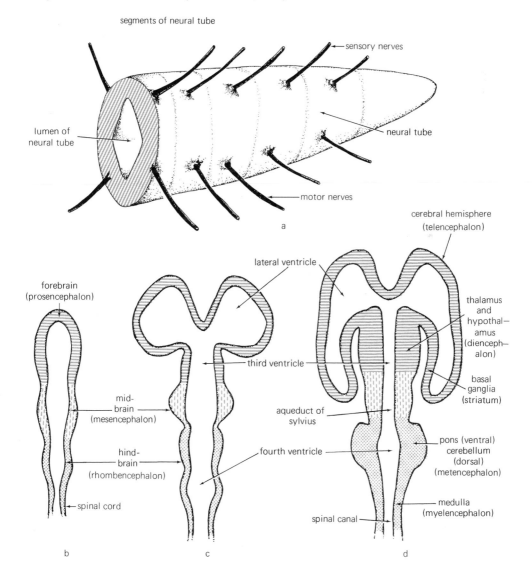

control. At first this greater control is exerted mainly through the older pathways between the lower motor centers and the segmental motor pools, but eventually additional direct connections evolve between the higher center and the segmental levels.

This process is repeated with yet another invasion of the most anterior region of the brain and the establishment of an even higher level of sensory and motor processing. It is possible that the brains of primates are still evolving to accommodate an even higher level of sensorimotor integration.

The structural changes that accompany these developments are the ones that make the pattern of the mammalian brain so difficult to unravel. They are illustrated in Figure 3.3. At an early embryonic stage, the mammalian neural tube looks something like that shown in the horizontal section of Figure 3.5b. The posterior segments eventually become the spinal cord, and the three bulges evolving from anterior segments of the tube develop into the *hindbrain* (*rhombencephalon*), the *midbrain* (*mesencephalon*), and the *forebrain* (*prosencephalon*), and lose their segmental character. In the course of further growth (Figure 3.3c, d) the hindbrain becomes differentiated into the *medulla oblongata* (*myelencephalon*) and the *metencephalon*, which comprises the *pons* and *cerebellum*. The midbrain has developed no major subdivisions; its main distinguishing nuclei are the *inferior* and *superior colliculi*. The core of neural tissue at this level is called the *tegmentum*.

The forebrain undergoes the most dramatic growth. It first divides into the *diencephalon* (composed of the *thalamus* and *hypothalamus*) and the *telencephalon*. The parts of the brain below the level of the telencephalon, that is, from the medulla to the diencephalon inclusive, are often called the *brainstem*. With the concentration of function at the anterior end of the neural tube, the extra neurons form bulges and eventually the end balloons out as shown in Figure 3.3c, d. The ever-lengthening walls of the telencephalon are pressed back against the part of the brainstem behind them by the resistance of the skull, so that eventually a sort of

sandwich is produced. As the higher levels of behavioral control establish their communications with the lower levels, long axons push their way through the folds and knit the whole mass together. The outer layer is then the cerebral cortex, and the fold sandwiched between it and the thalamus consists mainly of the *striatum* and the *archipallium* (or primitive cortex). The part of the cortex lying between the archipallium and the most recently evolved part of the outer layer (*neocortex*) is sometimes called *transitional cortex*. Only the *spinal cord* and the *lower brainstem* retain their tubular form, and even there the original organization is greatly modified by the presence of the long ascending and descending pathways required to maintain rapid communication with the higher levels.

The *lumen* (channel) at the anterior end of the neural tube is contorted by these maneuvers into the left and right *lateral ventricles* (see Figure 3.7). In the diencephalon the channel is flattened in the vertical plane to form the *third ventricle*, and farther back, in the rhombencephalon, it is flattened in the horizontal plane to form the *fourth ventricle*. Between these two, as it passes through the midbrain, it narrows to become the *aqueduct of Sylvius*. Posterior to the fourth ventricle it becomes the even narrower spinal canal.

The consequence of all this growth is a hierarchical control of behavior in which the final common motor paths (that is, the motoneurons) are under the influence, first, of direct sensory input from muscles, second, of other *intrasegmental reflex circuits* (control by input from nearby skin receptors), third, of *intersegmental reflex circuits* (control by more remote sensory input), fourth, of reflex centers in the lowest part of the brain, fifth, of more complex motor centers in the *striatum*, and sixth, of the *motor cortex*. Each of these control levels is influenced by sensory information of corresponding degrees of abstraction, as well as by activity descending from the motor centers situated above it in the hierarchy. As the newer mechanisms develop, they do not replace the older ones but instead bind them into a more complex integration.

GENERAL ANATOMY OF THE HUMAN BRAIN

Bearing in mind the rough design outlined for vertebrates, we may now turn to a more detailed study of our specific example, the human brain. After the brain has been removed from the skull, almost the whole of its visible surface consists of cerebral cortex, the area of which is still further increased by the formation of *convolutions*, or *gyri* (Figure 3.4). The brains of the higher mammals, including that of man, are beginning to produce yet another major fold, this time from the rear, where the *temporal lobe* extends forward to cover part of the cortex called the *insula* or the *island of Reil* (Figure 3.5). The cerebellum, which has many thin convolutions, or *folia*, may be seen below the posterior cortex in Figure 3.4. The dorsal and lateral cortical surface is arbitrarily divided into four lobes, which take their names from the overlying bones of the skull: the *frontal, parietal, occipital,* and *temporal* lobes.

In the ventral view (Figure 3.6) it is possible to see a few subcortical structures. Starting at the posterior end, we see that the spinal cord merges into the medulla, which then disappears

into a sort of tunnel formed by the pons (bridge) and the cerebellum. Rostral to the pons we see the *mamillary bodies,* part of the hypothalamus. The rest of the hypothalamus is obscured first by the *pituitary gland,* an organ that regulates *endocrine gland* secretion, and then by the *optic chiasm,* in which the optic nerves from the eyes meet and partly cross (*decussate*). More rostral still, we see the *olfactory bulbs.* The *olfactory nerves,* which connect the receptors in the nose to the bulbs, are very fine and delicate and are always broken in the process of removing the brain from the skull.

In order to see the structures shown schematically in Figure 3.3d, we have to cut the brain open. Figure 3.7b shows a section in the plane indicated in Figure 3.7a. The section passes through the lumen of the neural tube in several places: at the fourth ventricle in the hindbrain, the third ventricle at the diencephalic level, the dorsal part of the lateral ventricles where they spread out from the third ventricle, and in the temporal lobe where the lateral ventricles curl round into the *inferior horns.*

The lower part of the section shows the

Figure 3.4 Lateral surface of the human brain, showing the positions of the main gyri.

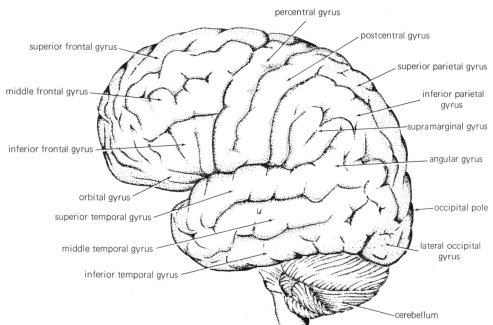

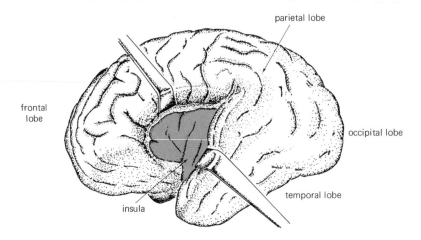

Figure 3.5 Lateral surface of the human brain; the temporal lobe is displaced by hooks to reveal the insula (island of Reil). (After Netter, 1957.)

Figure 3.6 Ventral surface of the human brain, showing locations of the 12 cranial nerves.

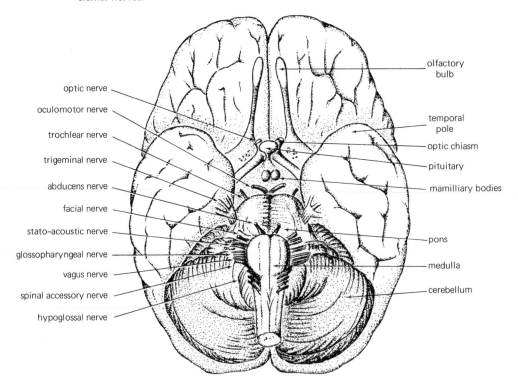

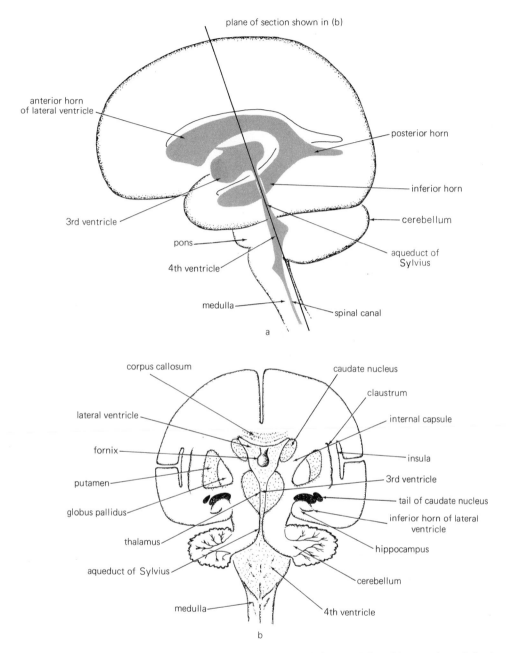

plane of section shown in (b)

anterior horn
of lateral ventricle

posterior horn

inferior horn

cerebellum

3rd ventricle

aqueduct of
Sylvius

pons

4th ventricle

medulla

spinal canal

a

corpus callosum   caudate nucleus

claustrum

lateral ventricle

internal capsule

fornix

insula

putamen

3rd ventricle

tail of caudate nucleus

globus pallidus

inferior horn of lateral
ventricle

thalamus

hippocampus

aqueduct of Sylvius

cerebellum

medulla

4th ventricle

b

Figure 3.7 (a) A view of the human brain showing location of the ventricles. (b) A section of the human brain along the plane indicated in (a), showing ventricles and internal structures.

pons and the midbrain. More rostral, on either side of the third ventricle, lies the *thalamus.* It is a paired collection of nuclei; the two main parts of the body are joined together by an isthmus of tissue called the *massa intermedia,* which bridges the third ventricle as may be

seen in Figure 3.10. The thalamus is shown in more detail in Figure 3.8.

Surrounding the thalamus is a group of nuclei called the *basal ganglia* (some neuroanatomists include the thalamus among the basal ganglia, but the label is more useful if that

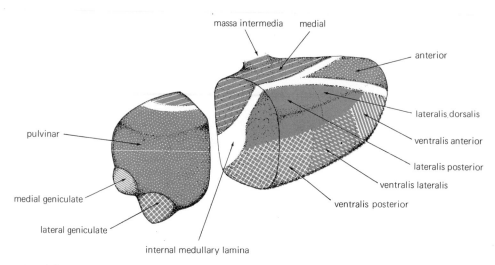

Figure 3.8 Schematic view of the right thalamus, which is sectioned to show the internal arrangement of constituent nuclei. The subdivisions of the main nuclear groups (medial, anterior, lateral, and ventral) will be referred to in later chapters. (After Netter, 1957.)

structure is excluded). These nuclei are fragments of the original striatum, which was forced back over the thalamus during the growth of the forebrain. They are shown more completely in Figure 3.9. The dorsal fragment is the *caudate nucleus*, so called because of its long tail, which extends back and around into the temporal lobe. Lateral to the thalamus is the *lenticular* (lens-shaped) *nucleus*. It is separated from the caudate nucleus by the *internal capsule*, a massive bundle of fibers from the overlying cortex. The medial part of the lenticular nucleus is paler than the rest and is therefore named *globus pallidus*. The lateral

Figure 3.9 A lateral view of the left basal ganglia. The claustrum is not shown as it would obscure the view of the lenticular nucleus.

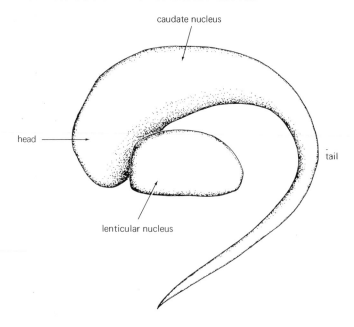

part is called the *putamen*. Another fragment of the striatum has been split off the lateral border by the fibers of the *external capsule* and is called the *claustrum*. That nucleus lies just beneath the surface of the insula, the region of the cortex buried by the temporal lobe.

The next oldest part of the forebrain, which in lower mammals like the rat occupies the space just beneath the neocortex in the posterior half of the brain, is the *archipallium*, consisting mostly of the *hippocampus*. In primates, the continuing growth of the neocortex has crumpled most of this structure into the medial part of the temporal lobe, where it lies just below and lateral to the inferior horn of the lateral ventricle. It has been curled into a shape that an imaginative neuroanatomist considered to resemble a seahorse, or hippocampus. A long fiber tract, the *fornix* (arch) joins the hippocampus to the hypothalamic region. From the hippocampus it passes around the thalamus into the third ventricle, then descends around the front of the thalamus and turns back into the

hypothalamus. The section shown in Figure 3.7b cuts the fornix as it passes through the third ventricle. The hippocampus and some associated structures were at one time believed to be involved in olfaction and were given the name of *rhinencephalon*, or "smell brain."

The area between nuclei in the brain is occupied by tracts connecting the different nuclei to one another and to the neocortex (which occupies the outer boundary of the section) and linking the different areas of the cortex. One conspicuous tract, or *commissure*, made up of fibers joining the cortices of the two hemispheres is the *corpus callosum*.

Figure 3.10 shows the medial surface of the brain after a midline sagittal section. We see the location of the medulla and fourth ventricle at the caudal end of the brainstem. The spinal canal expands laterally to form this ventricle and then narrows again to the aqueduct of Sylvius in the mesencephalon. The aqueduct is surrounded by a mass of cells called the *central gray*. Dorsal to the aqueduct are the *inferior* and

Figure 3.10   Midline sagittal section of the human brain.

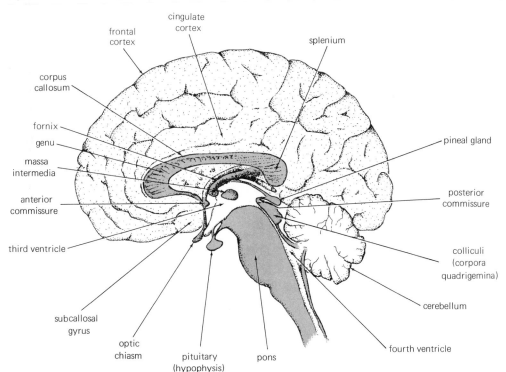

superior colliculi (*corpora quadrigemina*). The inferior colliculi are relay nuclei for the auditory system, and the superior colliculi are, among other things, reflex centers for the visual system.

The main sensory and motor tracts pass through the ventral and lateral regions of the medulla and mesencephalon, and the nuclei of many cranial nerves are also to be found there. A relatively undifferentiated mass of cells called the *reticular formation* occupies much of the space between the tracts and nuclei. It corresponds to the "intermediate net" of the primitive neural tube. The mesencephalic part of the reticular formation is sometimes called the *tegmentum*. The part in the medulla is called the bulbar reticular formation.

Rostrally, the aqueduct opens into the third ventricle, the lateral walls of which are made up of the thalamus and the hypothalamus. The two sides of the thalamus are joined at one point by the massa intermedia, which is cut by our section. The sensory tracts from the spinal cord (*medial lemnisci*), which lie medially in the hind- and midbrain, pass laterally into the thalamus at this level. The descending motor tracts (*cerebral penduncles*) pass around the thalamus in the internal capsule and become the *pyramidal tract* in the midbrain. None of these tracts is visible in the midline-sagittal section except where they decussate in the medulla. They are shown schematically in Figures 10.1 and 6.1b.

At the base of the brain, below the hypothalamus, the section cuts the pituitary gland, or *hypophysis*. The posterior part of this structure is an outgrowth of neural tissue, but the anterior part has negligible neural connections with the brain and is apparently under the influence of secretions from the hypothalamus, which are carried to it in the bloodstream by a *portal vein* system (see Chapter 16). Another neurosecretory structure, the *pineal gland*, is located medially below the *splenium* of the corpus callosum. This body is perhaps best known as the unpaired midline structure that Descartes considered the most likely seat of the soul.

The only other parts of the brain cut by our section are the commissures, tracts joining one hemisphere to the other. The *posterior commissure*, at the posterior extremity of the thalamus, contains fibers linking the two halves of the diencephalon and the mesencephalon. The *anterior commissure*, at the other end of the thalamus, contains fibers from a number of rhinencephalic structures, including the olfactory bulbs and parts of the medial temporal lobe. Rhinencephalic fibers also cross in a part of the fornix where its two branches merge in the dorsal part of the third ventricle.

The remaining commissures are the optic chiasm, where half the optic nerve crosses over, and the corpus callosum, which, as has been mentioned, is the major link between the sides of the cortex. The space, shaped like an inverted comma, between the descending columns of the fornix and the *genu* of the corpus callosum has a thin membrane called the *septum pellucidum*, which separates the two lateral ventricles at this point. In lower animals cells associated with the fornix columns, and other rhinencephalic tracts, form nuclei in the vicinity of the septum. They constitute the *septal area*.

It is very difficult to picture the brain in three dimensions from a few two-dimensional cross sections. The illustrations in Netter (1957) or a good neuroanatomy textbook will undoubtedly be helpful, but there is no substitute for dissection of an actual brain, or at least of a model, for clarifying the true spatial relations among the parts.

SPINAL CORD

The spinal cord still retains some of the features of the primitive neural tube. It is organized segmentally, with sensory nerves feeding into the dorsal side of each of the 31 segments and motor nerves issuing from the ventral side of each. Between the two sides is a core of gray matter, roughly H-shaped in cross section (Figure 3.11). Surrounding this core are the ascending and descending neural pathways that distinguish the higher animal. Adjacent to the core are the shortest and oldest links, the inter-

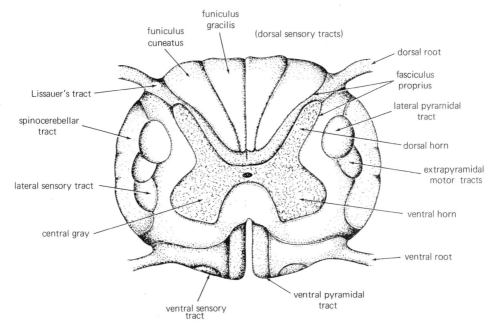

funiculus
gracilis

funiculus
cuneatus

(dorsal sensory tracts)

dorsal root

fasciculus
proprius

Lissauer's tract

lateral pyramidal
tract

spinocerebellar
tract

dorsal horn

extrapyramidal
motor tracts

lateral sensory tract

ventral horn

central gray

ventral root

ventral pyramidal
tract

ventral sensory
tract

Figure 3.11 Cross section of the spinal cord in the cervical region. Motor tracts are labeled on the right and sensory tracts on the left.

segmental pathways of the *fasciculus proprius*. These connections do not extend beyond the length of the cord, and many of them span only a few segments.

The long, ascending sensory pathways are distributed in the outer parts of the cord. In the dorsal sector they consist of the *funiculi gracilis* and *cuneatus*; the *spinocerebellar tracts* run up the lateral borders, and just medial to their ventral parts are the *lateral spinothalamic tracts*. The *ventral spinothalamic tracts* occupy part of the ventral sector of the cord.

There are two main motor pathways. The first is the *lateral corticospinal* (or lateral pyramidal) *tract*, located dorsal to the lateral spinothalamic tract and consisting of crossed fibers of the pyramidal tract on their way to join the direct sensory inflow to the spinal motor mechanisms. The other motor pathways are in the ventral sector of the cord and include the uncrossed part of the pyramidal tract and a group of pathways (extrapyramidal tracts) from subcortical motor centers of the brain. These tracts deliver input directly to the motor nuclei of the cord.

The *ventral horns* of the H-shaped central gray core contain the motor pools, including the cell bodies and dendrites of the motoneurons whose axons emerge from the ventral roots and go to the skeletal musculature. The autonomic motor pools, which feed to the smooth muscles, glands, and heart, are located between the ventral and dorsal horns in the lateral part of the gray matter (*lateral horn*).

THE PERIPHERAL NERVOUS SYSTEM

The peripheral nervous system originates in 31 pairs of spinal nerves, which emerge between the spinal vertebrae, and 12 pairs of cranial nerves, which leave the brainstem directly. There are somatic and autonomic components of both cranial and spinal nerves, and, with a few exceptions (mostly cranial nerves), peripheral nerves combine sensory and motor functions. At the point where spinal nerves meet the cord, however, each branches into a dorsal root that is for all practical purposes only sensory and a ventral root that is only motor. This functional difference between the dorsal and ventral roots was discovered in 1811 by Bell and independently (and much more conclusively) by Magendie in 1822. It has proved of immense value in experimental work on spinal reflexes.

The cell bodies of all spinal, and most cranial, sensory fibers lie outside the central nervous system. Those of spinal nerves lie in the dorsal roots, where they produce swellings called *dorsal-root ganglia*. There are no synapses in these ganglia; primary sensory neurons (connected directly to receptors) are unipolar, and the axons pass uninterruptedly through the ganglia. The cell bodies of skeletal (somatic) motoneurons lie within the central nervous system in the ventral horns of the cord and in the motor nuclei of the brainstem. The axons go directly to the skeletal muscles with no further synapses. When an axon reaches its muscle it branches and innervates a large number of muscle fibers (usually between 100 and 1,000 in man). The muscle fibers innervated from a single motoneuron axon are called a *motor unit* because they inevitably fire simultaneously.

Spinal Nerves

On leaving the vertebral column, each spinal nerve sends a branch to innervate the muscles and skin of the back. From the regions of the spine related to the arms and legs the rest of each nerve joins other spinal nerves to form *plexuses*, from which emerge the peripheral nerves to the limbs. The need for intercommunications throughout the body parallels that for supplies carried by the blood, and, in fact, many peripheral nerves run alongside blood vessels and have similar fields of distribution. The vascular and nervous systems also minimize the ill effects of accidental damage in similar ways. Because of the mixing of fibers from different spinal nerves in the plexuses and the overlapping distributions of the endings from different nerves, the destruction of any one nerve produces a less specific and less severe disturbance than would otherwise occur. The nerve fibers remain distinct, of course, but the cross connections in the plexuses permit

axons from several spinal nerves to contribute to one peripheral nerve and vice versa.

The autonomic motoneurons of the central nervous system, located in the lateral horns of the cord and in some of the motor nuclei of the brainstem, are not (with one ambiguous exception) directly connected to the innervated organs. Their axons constitute only the first stage of the peripheral autonomic system; each synapses with a second neuron in a peripheral ganglion. The neuron in the central nervous system is therefore called a *preganglionic neuron*, and the neuron that innervates the organ is called a *postganglionic neuron*.

The organs innervated by the autonomic system are shown in Figure 3.12. *Smooth muscles* control the lens and iris of the eye; they also regulate peripheral blood flow by constricting or dilating small vessels. They are present in hair follicles to raise the hairs. (We humans do not have much hair left, but the muscles are still there and produce "goose pimples" when they contract.) Smooth muscles are responsible for the *peristaltic* movements of the digestive tract and are also present in the *trachea* and lungs. They control *anal* and *urethral sphincters* and the *urogenital system* in general. Although the autonomic motor system is sometimes considered to be outside voluntary control, parts of it can be controlled to some degree, and most autonomic responses can be brought under voluntary control by rewarding required responses (see Chapter 20).

The heart is a special sort of muscle, which combines some of the features of smooth and striated muscles. It also comes under autonomic control, as do the various glands of the body.

As mentioned earlier, the autonomic system may be divided into two parts, a sympathetic division, which is fed by spinal nerves from the *thoracic* and upper *lumbar* regions of the spinal cord (it is sometimes called the *thoracolumbar system*—see Figure 3.12), and a parasympathetic division, which is fed by cranial nerves and spinal nerves originating in the *sacral* segments of the cord (hence the *craniosacral system*). The sympathetic system is largely *adrenergic* [*adrenaline (epinephrine)* is the transmitter substance]

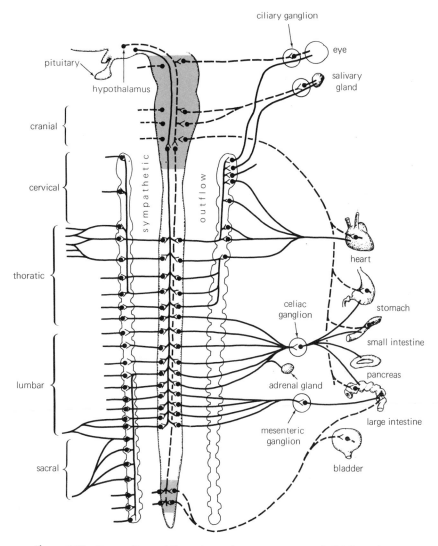

Figure 3.12 Connections of the autonomic nervous system. Solid lines show the sympathetic system and broken lines the parasympathetic system. The sympathetic outflow to the skin and blood vessels is shown at left. (After Gardner, 1968.)

at the junction between the postganglionic cell and the innervated organ, whereas the parasympathetic system is mainly *cholinergic* (*acetylcholine* is the transmitter substance) at the final junction.

The sympathetic system is the more diffuse; many of its postganglionic neurons lie in ganglia that form two chains (the *sympathetic trunks*) running close to the spinal vertebrae down the entire length of the column. They send fibers to join each of the spinal nerves

close to the points at which they emerge from the vertebral column (Figure 3.13). These links are called *gray rami communicantes* (from *ramus*, "branch"). They are gray because the postganglionic axons lack myelin. In the thoracic and upper lumbar regions the sympathetic ganglia receive input from a preganglionic branch of each spinal nerve. These fibers are called *white rami communicantes*, as they are myelinated.

Not all the preganglionic fibers pass through

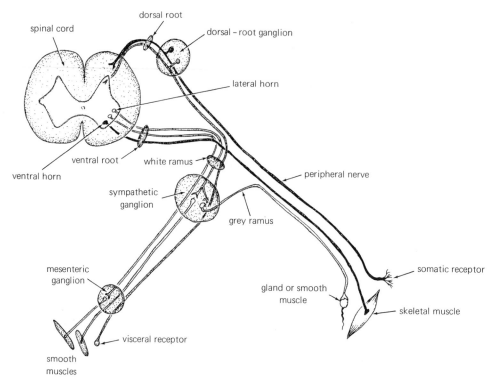

Figure 3.13 Sensory and motor connections to a segment of the spinal cord. Some motor fibers return to the peripheral nerve through the gray ramus communicans after synapsing in the sympathetic ganglion, the remainder go through autonomic nerves to internal organs.

the white rami synapse in the ganglia of the sympathetic trunk. Some continue straight through to form plexuses and later synapse in the *celiac ganglion* (*solar plexus*) or in one of the *mesenteric ganglia* (of which only one is shown in Figure 3.12). One preganglionic nerve, the *lesser splanchnic nerve,* continues without synapse to the medulla, or internal core, of the *adrenal gland.* It is the ambiguous case already mentioned; there is some justification for considering the adrenal medulla to be composed of postganglionic cells, which, instead of delivering epinephrine through axons to other organs, pour the transmitter substance straight into the bloodstream whenever they are stimulated.

In general, the postganglionic fibers that return to the spinal nerves through the gray rami innervate the blood vessels, sweat glands, and hair follicles of the skin. The other fibers innervate the organs and blood vessels of the head, heart, lungs, and gastrointestinal and

urogenital systems. Because of the extensive interconnections in the sympathetic trunk and the release by the adrenal medulla of the sympathetic transmitter agent epinephrine into the blood, which distributes it to all the other organs, the sympathetic system tends to be widespread in its action, though this tendency has been overstated by textbook writers.

The parasympathetic, or craniosacral, division of the autonomic system has a much more discrete organization than does the sympathetic division. Each preganglionic nerve goes to a ganglion that is close to, or connected with, the organ innervated; the postganglionic fiber is thus typically very short. In this way the autonomic component of the *third cranial nerve,* for example, goes only to the *ciliary ganglion* and is involved only in focusing the lens and regulating the iris of the eye. Such specific termination means that the eye can be adjusted without at the same time producing salivation, pilo-erection, or more catastrophic effects still.

The *tenth cranial nerve* (the *vagus*) has a more global influence. It wanders about the body cavity innervating the smooth muscles of the lungs, the heart, and most of the abdominal viscera. The parasympathetic outflow from the sacral part of the cord is directed primarily to the sphincters, bladder, colon, and genital organs.

Autonomic nerves carry sensory fibers from receptors in the viscera, but, apart from their origin and their peripheral course, visceral afferents are indistinguishable from somatic afferents. Their cell bodies lie in the dorsal-root ganglia or in the equivalent ganglia in the head, and they have no extra synapses outside the central nervous system as do the autonomic motor nerves.

Cranial Nerves

The spinal nerves leave the cord at each segment in a relatively stereotyped and regular pattern, but the cranial nerves present a more complex picture. One of them, the optic nerve, is not really a peripheral nerve at all but a tract of the central nervous system that has strayed out of the skull. The others have evolved from the nerves that originally belonged to the anterior segments of the primitive neural tube, when these segments were fused to form the brain.

The principle functions of the specific cranial nerves are listed here. Their points of emergence on the ventral side of the brainstem are shown in Figure 3.6, and the more important ones are discussed in greater detail later in the book when we deal with the special senses. Further information about the location of cranial-nerve nuclei and the peripheral courses of the nerves can be found in any standard textbook of neuroanatomy.

1. *Olfactory nerve* (sensory). A short nerve connecting the *olfactory epithelium* (lining) of the nose to the olfactory bulb.

2. *Optic nerve* (sensory). A tract from the ganglion cells of the light-sensitive retina in the eye. The tract also contains some efferent fibers believed to control the sensitivity of the retina.

3. *Oculomotor nerve* (motor). Innervates the *extrinsic* (turning) and *intrinsic* (focusing and pupil-control) muscles of the eye.

4. *Trochlear nerve* (motor). Innervates one extrinsic eye muscle (the *superior oblique*).

5. *Trigeminal nerve* (mixed). Motor fibers to the muscles of mastication. It also carries *proprioceptive* (position sense) afferents from the same muscles and afferents of touch, pain, and so forth from the face, scalp, cornea, jaws, teeth, anterior two-thirds of the tongue, and *dura mater* (the outer membrane of the brain).

6. *Abducens nerve* (motor). Innervates one extrinsic eye muscle (the *lateral rectus*).

7. *Facial nerve* (mixed). Innervates facial and scalp muscles (except those served by the trigeminal nerve) and *lachrymal* and *salivary* (*sublingual* and *submaxillary*) glands. It conveys taste from the anterior two-thirds of the tongue.

8. *Auditory* or *Stato-acoustic nerve* (sensory). Innervates the organs of balance and hearing. It also has efferent fibers, believed to influence the sensitivity of receptors.

9. *Glossopharyngeal nerve* (mixed). Motor nerve to the vocal organs and one (*parotid*) salivary gland. It conveys taste from the posterior third of the tongue and sensation from the back of the mouth.

10. *Vagus nerve* (mixed). Motor fibers to tongue, vocal organs, and thoracic and abdominal viscera; sensory fibers from the back of the external ear (*pinna*), vocal organs, and thoracic and abdominal viscera.

11. *Spinal-accessory nerve* (motor). Innervates the vocal organs and back muscles.

12. *Hypoglossal nerve* (motor). Innervates tongue muscles.

As may be inferred from their functions, the third, seventh, ninth, and tenth cranial nerves contain some autonomic fibers of the parasympathetic division.

Summary

The purpose of this chapter has been to provide an approximate map of the vertebrate nervous system, showing the shape of the various grossly distinguishable parts and where they lie in relation to one another. More detailed information about the connections and fine structure of the parts will be presented in later chapters as necessary.

The nervous system is too soft to be handled and investigated in its natural state; it must first be hardened by a fixing agent. It may then be dissected. The myelinated tracts and layers may be distinguished by their shiny white appearance, the cell masses by their gray color. For more detailed study serial sections are stained either for cell bodies or for myelin, and the form of the brain is reconstructed from these sections.

The present complex structure of the mammalian brain can best be understood by examining how it developed from the simple neural tube of the primitive chordate. Concentration of neural functioning at the anterior end of the tube obviously had survival value, and animals evolved in that direction. This end expanded into two large bulbs, which then folded back on themselves to provide the basic pattern of the mammalian brain.

The posterior end of the tube has evolved into the segmented spinal cord. The cord merges at its rostral end into the posterior part of the brain, the medulla oblongata, which, together with the pons and cerebellum, constitutes the hindbrain. The midbrain has no major subdivisions; it includes the colliculi and midbrain tegmentum. The forebrain has shown the most spectacular development. The hypothalamus and thalamus form the diencephalic part, and the remaining structures constitute the telencephalon. The older part of the telencephalon is the striatum, including the caudate, globus pallidus, putamen, and claustrum nuclei. Next we find the archipallium (represented by the hippocampus), and the whole is surrounded by the cerebral cortex made up mainly of neocortex and transitional cortex.

The lumen of the neural tube expands at the head end to form ventricles. In the medullary region it flattens in the horizontal plane to form the fourth ventricle; in the diencephalon it is flattened medially to form the third ventricle, and in the telencephalon it forms two lateral bubbles, which eventually attain labyrinthine horn shapes called the "lateral ventricles."

The dorsal and lateral views of the human brain show only convoluted cortex. The area is rather arbitrarily divided into four parts, frontal, parietal, temporal, and occipital lobes, according to the overlying bones. Another area, which is hidden by the temporal lobe, is called the insula. On the ventral surface of the brain it is possible to see part of the brainstem: the medulla, the pons and cerebellum, and the posterior part of the hypothalamus. Covering the rest of the hypothalamus are the pituitary and the optic chiasm. Farther forward are the olfactory bulbs.

An approximately frontal section along the track of the ventricular system reveals most of the other structures of the brain. The thalamus lies next to the third ventricle, the basal ganglia around it. The hippocampus lies inside the temporal lobe, and the cerebral cortex encloses everything. The large tracts, like the corpus callosum joining the two hemispheres and the internal and external capsules containing fibers from the cortex to subcortical structures and the spinal cord, are also conspicuous.

The spinal cord consists of 31 segments, each with a pair of motor nerves issuing ventrally and a pair of sensory nerves entering dorsally. The spinal neurons (gray matter) are concentrated around the spinal canal in the center of the cord and, are surrounded by ascending and descending tracts. The motor paths descend mainly in the lateral and ventral sectors close to the gray core; the sensory tracts ascend in the most superficial position. Two large sensory tracts, the gracile and cuneate funiculi, run in the dorsal sector, spinocerebellar tracts run in the lateral sector, and other tracts run in the lateral and ventral sectors.

The peripheral nervous system may be divided into somatic and autonomic components. The somatic component has no synapses and consists of motor nerves feeding to striped muscles and sensory nerves from receptors.

The autonomic system is a motor system for smooth muscles and glands. One synapse is interposed between each spinal (preganglionic) neuron and postganglionic neuron to the innervated organ. Although visceral sensory fibers run in the same nerves as autonomic motor fibers, they do not otherwise differ from somatic sensory fibers; they are therefore not usually considered part of the autonomic system.

There are two parts to the autonomic system, the sympathetic and the parasympathetic. Both cooperate to maintain the normal functioning of such vegetative systems as digestion, blood circulation, temperature regulation, and so on, but the sympathetic system is especially involved during stress, and it has a more widespread influence than does the parasympathetic system.

Preganglionic sympathetic fibers leave the spinal nerves in the thoracic and lumbar regions soon after the nerves emerge from the cord and pass through short nerves called "white rami" to two chains of ganglia running parallel to the cord. After synapsing in the ganglia, some of the postganglionic fibers return to the peripheral nerve through other short nerves called "gray rami," but others form separate nerves to the internal organs. Some preganglionic fibers continue through the ganglia of the sympathetic chains without synapsing; they synapse later in other ganglia distributed throughout the body cavity.

The parasympathetic system is fed by preganglionic input from cranial nerves and some nerves in the sacral region of the cord. The peripheral ganglia in this system are usually small and very close to the innervated organs, so that the postganglionic nerves are short.

Apart from the peripheral nerves that leave the cord, there are 12 pairs of nerves that leave the brain directly; they are known as "cranial nerves." Many of them carry sensory input from the skin, or motor output to the muscles, of the head and face; they also include sensory nerves for smell, taste, vision, hearing and balance.

CHAPTER 4

RESEARCH TECHNIQUES IN PHYSIO- LOGICAL PSYCHOLOGY

Progress in any field of science is dictated jointly by the ideas that people have and by the methods available for testing those ideas. The relationship is not quite as simple as it may seem, however, for new techniques often give rise to new problems, instead of helping to solve old ones. Many techniques become available, not because of recognized needs, but because of developments in other branches of science, and their application may result in discoveries of phenomena not previously imagined.

For a long time ideas in psychology ran far ahead of the means for testing them, especially in physiological psychology. For centuries the only information about the functioning of the nervous system came from the accidents of disease and injury. Battle wounds have provided much information about the way the brain works from the time of the ancient Greeks to the present day. For example, the relationship between peripheral nerves and movement and sensation was already known to philosophers in the third century B.C. from studies of injured people.

The only other significant source of infor-

mation in the search for mind-brain relationships was the study of neuroanatomy. The gross features of the brain were also known to the early Greeks, but little further progress was made until a good microscope had been developed and until the discovery, toward the end of the nineteenth century, of techniques for sectioning and staining neural tissue.

The late nineteenth century also saw the introduction of two very important techniques for experimental study of the nervous system in animals: lesions (destruction or removal) and stimulation of parts of the brain. (It is true that Flourens and Rolando had pioneered these methods early in the century, but, as in most pioneering work, the results were far from conclusive.)

LESIONS

Ablation

At first, ablations were confined to the outside, or cortex, of the brain, which was the most accessible part. In the early experiments of Ferrier (1876), S. Brown and Schäfer (1888), Pavlov, and others, parts of the brain were cut or spooned out. These techniques frequently caused irritation and *epileptogenic* (convulsive seizure producing) scarring in the neighboring tissues, which were damaged but not completely eliminated (Pavlov, 1927, p. 321). Lashley (1929) used hot-wire *thermocautery* (burning) for most of his cortical destructions in rats, but this method is also likely to produce scarring, and, besides, the depth of the lesion is difficult to control.

The use of suction to remove cortical tissue, developed by Penfield around 1930 for operations on the brains of human patients, has the advantage of removing all remnants of tissue not adequately vascularized and thus of reducing the number of insufficiently nourished cells left at the border of the wound. It also keeps the operative field reasonably free from blood, so that the extent of the lesion can be more accurately judged. This method is used almost exclusively today for ablation of any neural tissue accessible to a pipette. The pipette, usually of glass or metal, is connected to a vacuum pump through a bottle; the bottle acts as a trap for the tissue that is sucked up by the pipette and prevents it from passing through the pump (Figure 4.1).

Some investigators, those who wish to make an experimental study of impairments produced by long-standing epileptic attacks for example, are interested in deliberately producing irritative lesions. One fairly reliable method is to implant a small silver cup, or disk, containing aluminum-hydroxide or alumina cream (Barrera, Kopeloff & Kopeloff, 1944). In many animal species, chronic seizures will begin a few weeks or months after implantation. The method seems to work best, however, with dogs and primates; it is difficult, if not impossible, to produce chronic seizures in rats by this method.

Ablation of neural structures buried beneath the cortex presents different problems. The first and most important is that of locating the particular structure; the second is to make the lesion without damage to the surrounding (especially the overlying) structures. It cannot be claimed that the perfect solution to either of these problems has been found, but the *stereotaxic instrument*, which was invented by Horsley and Clarke (1908), is a practical tool that has been of great value in making subcortical lesions and in performing many other experiments on the deep parts of the brain. A

modern stereotaxic instrument is shown in Figure 4.2. It consists essentially of a frame that holds the subject's head firmly in a standard position. Bars or plugs, which fit into the *external auditory meatus* (ear canal), determine the position of the skull in two planes; the position in the third plane is controlled by pins or clamps holding either the upper teeth or the rims of the eye sockets. The rest of the instrument consists of three sets of guide rails that allow an electrode carrier to be moved through measured distances in the three principal axes: anterior-posterior, lateral, and vertical. The electrode carrier can usually be tilted to allow the electrode to be inserted into the brain at angles other than the vertical if that is more convenient. In this way, an electrode or other slender implement can be directed to any preselected point within the cranial cavity, the two horizontal coordinates being set first and then the needle lowered to the desired point.

In order to use this instrument effectively, it is necessary to know the coordinates of the subcortical structures to be investigated; *brain atlases* have therefore been prepared for the animals most commonly used in physiological and psychological experiments. A section from de Groot's atlas of the rat brain is shown in Figure 4.3. Unfortunately, there is some individual variation in the shape of the skull in most species, which limits the accuracy of stereotaxic placements based only on atlas coordinates.

Figure 4.1 Apparatus for ablating brain tissue by suction.

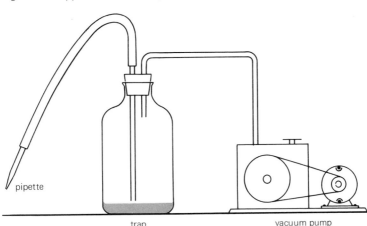

pipette

trap

vacuum pump

Figure 4.2 A stereotaxic instrument for use on small animals. (Courtesy of David Kopf Instruments.)

Greater accuracy can be obtained if corrections are made for departures from the standard ratios of length to width of the skull. In the rat it is common to measure distances from the *skull sutures* (the joints between cranial bones), rather than from the coordinates given in relation to ear bars and teeth clamps, as the sutures tend to be more closely related to the position of the brain.

Subcortical lesions are almost always made electrically, either by a radio-frequency (RF) current, which destroys tissue by heat, or by a direct current (DC), which destroys tissue by a combination of heat and *electrolysis*. In the latter process oxidization at the anode is probably the major cause of damage. It is difficult to make large electrolytic lesions; RF is therefore usually used in larger animals like the cat and monkey. Electrolytic lesions have been

Figure 4.3 Section from the de Groot atlas of the rat brain. (After De Groot, 1959.)

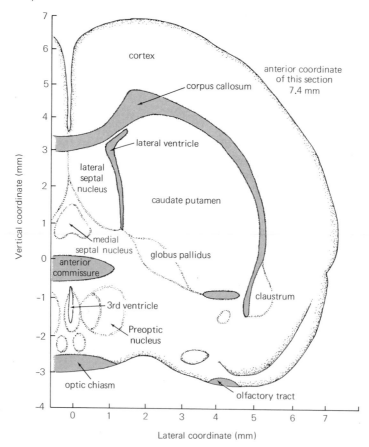

used extensively in rat experiments, mainly because the apparatus is simple but also because it provides more control over the size of small lesions. The method has, however, been criticized (Reynolds, 1965a) as more likely than other methods to produce irritative lesions, especially if, as is usual, steel electrodes are used. The metal salts produced by oxidization of the electrode material poison cells bordering the lesion and cause them to behave in abnormal ways, making it impossible to tell whether a change in the animal's behavior results from loss of tissue or from the irritation and abnormality of the surviving cells. This objection can be overcome to a great extent by the use of electrodes made of noble metals (metals that have no chemical reaction to oxygen); platinum tips are often employed. Reynolds claimed that irritative tissue damage then results from the pressure of electrolytically released oxygen, but such damage is not very likely; considerable quantities of hydrogen are released at a steel cathode, but no significant lesion is produced there. Furthermore, the brain is sufficiently flexible to stand considerable mechanical distortion without permanent ill effects.

Another, and more precise, method of producing a lesion is with intense *ultrasonic* vibrations (Krieckhaus, 1964). By this means it is possible to make a subcortical lesion without disturbing the overlying tissue at all, and the lesions are very clean because there is no interference with the blood supply. A transducer to convert electrical oscillations into sound waves is curved so that the waves it generates focus a few centimeters away from its surface. It is positioned so that the focal point is the structure to be destroyed. When the intensity of the sound is properly adjusted, the cells at the focus are torn apart by the vibrations without any harm to tissues where the waves are less concentrated.

The technique, when properly applied, is more accurate than are others because the apparatus can be used at low intensity as a sort of *sonar*, locating subcortical reference points like the ventricles by measuring sound reflections. That the brain is not distorted by the introduction of a foreign body like an electrode is also important in increasing the accuracy of

this method. Unfortunately the apparatus is expensive and requires expert handling to realize its full potential.

Some investigators (for example, Settlage & Bogumill, 1955) have used *gamma radiation* from radioactive isotopes to produce brain lesions. This method has a number of theoretical advantages: The size of the lesion can be adjusted by the length of exposure, and therefore accurately replicated, and radiation does not interfere with large blood vessels passing through the area. Unfortunately the radiation apparently produces peculiar effects at a distance from the intended locus of the lesion (Harlow, 1958), and the method has never become popular.

Reversible Lesions

In some experiments it is desirable to produce a temporary lesion (to find out, for example, whether an animal with a lesion is unable to learn a particular response or merely unable to perform that response). One way to do so is to cool the part of the brain in question to below about 25° C., as many neurons cease to conduct at that temperature (Dondey, Albe-Fessard & Le Beau, 1962). When the area is allowed to return to normal body temperature, the neurons fire normally again. If the temperature is reduced below freezing at any time, however, the affected cells are destroyed by ice crystals, and a permanent lesion is produced.

This technique has been used to make subcortical lesions in human patients for therapeutic purposes. The area of suspected disturbance is first cooled to a moderate degree to see whether or not a permanent lesion would have the desired effect. If cooling causes improvement, it is intensified until freezing takes place. If the first cooling does not produce improvement, the area is allowed to warm up, and another region is cooled; the process is repeated until a suitable locus for the permanent lesion is found.

Small areas of the brain can be cooled or heated to a moderate degree by inserting U tubes or concentric tubes, thermally insulated except at the tip, and circulating cool or warm fluid through them (Figure 4.4). Insulating such

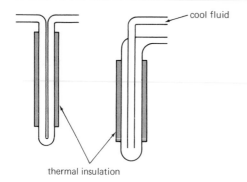

thermal insulation

Figure 4.4 Cooling probes for cooling subcortical areas: (a) U tube and (b) concentric tubes. If liquid refrigerant gas is pumped down the inner tube of the concentric probe and allowed to vaporize at the tip, no thermal insulation is required.

probes is difficult if they are not to become too big; for more intense cooling, a refrigeration technique is therefore used. A liquefied gas like butane or propane is pumped down the inner tube of a concentric probe, allowed to vaporize near the tip, and exhausted through the outer tube. The heat required to evaporate the gas is absorbed from the tissue around the end of the probe, which is thus rapidly cooled.

A rather specialized type of temporary lesion can be produced by putting a small amount of 10-20 percent potassium chloride (KCl) solution on the cortex or in some subcortical structure. (Not all subcortical structures can be treated in this way, however.) Waves of depression, or neural inactivity, spread slowly from this region until the whole subcortical structure (or cortical hemisphere) is engulfed. When the KCl solution is removed, the structure slowly recovers, supposedly with no permanent ill effects. To prepare the animal for the administration of cortical *spreading depression*, a hole is made in the skull; care is taken not to damage the dura mater (the outer protective membrane). Then a plastic tube is implanted and held in place by screws and fast-setting *acrylic-resin cement* (see discussion of implanted electrodes later in this chapter). The outer end of the tube is closed with a plug, except during the introduction of solutions.

In order to depress the activity of the cortex of one hemisphere, the cap of the tube over that hemisphere is removed, and a little KCl solution is squirted in from a syringe. To allow the cortex to recover, the cap is again removed and the solution rinsed out with physiological saline solution. The KCl in the tissue soon diffuses out, or is carried away by the blood. Recovery is not immediate; it may be several hours before the animal behaves normally again.

STIMULATION

Electrophysiology is as old as the knowledge of electrical currents. It was Galvani's chance observation of the twitching of a frog's leg hanging on a metal hook that led him to the discovery that electricity could be generated by the contact of two dissimilar metals, and for some time the nerve-muscle preparation was the only "voltmeter" available.

In the early days of neurophysiology much work was done on the characteristics of the current that would excite nerves, and it was soon discovered that the rate of change in the current was important. A direct current (DC) produced practically no effect except when it was turned on and off. The standard stimulator for many years was therefore an *induction coil*, with a vibrating interrupter to convert direct current from a battery into pulses, which were picked up in a secondary coil whose distance from the primary coil could be changed in order to adjust the strength of the applied stimulation. This primitive device was not abandoned until well into the electronic age, and no doubt there are still a number to be found in physiology laboratories. It is not very satisfactory because the mechanical vibrator produces erratic output pulses, and it is impossible to vary most of the parameters of stimulation. The modern stimulator is an electronic circuit consisting of an oscillator, which controls the repetition rate of the pulses, and other circuits to determine the shape (usually rectangular), duration, and amplitude of each pulse. Optimum parameters for most brain structures are sharply rising pulses of 50-300 per second, 0.1-1.0 msec long.

For experiments in which the old induction coil is adequate, a much better alternative has existed for many years in most laboratories: the alternating current (AC) supplied by the power companies. This current reverses its polarity 120 times per second (100 per second in most of Europe) and is highly effective for stimulating nerves, as anyone who has inadvertently come into contact with a power line will testify. Many physiological psychologists use small step-down transformers as convenient and simple sources of stimulation for experiments in which the wave form and frequency need not be adjusted. A variable potentiometer ("volume control") may be used to adjust the stimulating voltage.

Probably the earliest attempts to stimulate the brain electrically were made by Rolando (1809). He observed movements of the body of an animal in response to a battery voltage administered to the cerebellum but nothing from stimulating the cortex. He concluded that the cortex was electrically unexcitable. This view persisted (presumably nobody was skeptical enough to check it) until Fritsch and Hitzig (1870) mapped the motor cortex of the dog by eliciting body movements through electrical stimulation. Apart from more mapping work on the motor areas of other animals, little further work was done for another half-century. Then neurosurgeons, working with conscious human patients, found that they could elicit sensations from parts of the cortex by electrical stimulation and were able to plot the sensory areas. Soon afterward the stereotaxic instrument made it possible to stimulate subcortical structures and pathways in anesthetized animals. This technique, in conjunction with the recording of evoked potentials, provided a valuable adjunct to anatomical studies of neural pathways.

It is not, of course, possible to study the behavior of an animal clamped into a stereotaxic instrument. Even with local anesthesia to prevent pain from the instrument and surgical procedures, few animals would be cooperative enough to tolerate such restriction without some disturbance of behavior. W. R. Hess (1957) overcame this difficulty by screwing a platform to the skull as a support for electrodes implanted in the brain through holes in the skull

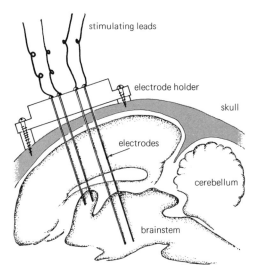

Figure 4.5 Hess's electrode holder screwed to the skull to allow stimulation of the brain of an unanesthetized animal. (After R. Hess, Koella, & Akert, 1953.)

(Figure 4.5). The operations were performed while the animals were under anesthesia, and behavioral testing was conducted later when they had recovered. Hess did not attempt to implant the electrodes into precise loci at the time of operation; the exact positions of the electrodes were determined later by *postmortem* examination of the brain. (Such examination is, of course, a standard check on the accuracy even when the electrodes are aimed stereotaxically). By implanting electrodes in a large number of cats, Hess was able to obtain information about the effects of stimulating most of the subcortical structures that interested him.

Hess also used the different characteristics of neurons to achieve differential excitation of overlapping pathways or systems. When neurons are exposed to a depolarizing electric current from a stimulating electrode, they immediately set up compensatory processes to maintain their polarization. If the applied current is increased slowly enough, the cell can adjust its repolarization rate so that the membrane potential never falls to the critical firing value—one reason why a direct current, or a slowly alternating one, is relatively ineffective as a stimulus. In general, small, slow-firing cells are more sluggish in their compensatory reactions than are larger cells with higher rates of firing and conduction (see Chapter 2). It is therefore possible to fire the small cells preferentially, despite their basically higher thresholds, by using pulses of slowly rising wave form, as shown in Figure 4.6. Hess was mainly interested in the autonomic systems in the diencephalon, which probably involved small cells; he therefore used slowly rising pulses almost exclusively in his behavioral work. Some of his results are discussed in later chapters.

The technique of stimulating predetermined points in the brains of freely moving animals is now very advanced. In general, some form of electrode holder is screwed to the skull of the animal; electrodes are then implanted with the aid of a stereotaxic instrument and cemented to the holder with a fast-setting acrylic resin. When the animal is to be stimulated, electrical connections to the electrodes are made through one of the many varieties of miniature plugs commercially available.

In work with a small animal like the rat, an electrode or other device may be held in place by screwing three or four jeweler's screws a short distance into the skull and pouring acrylic plastic around them and the implanted electrode, thus embedding the whole in a firmly attached "skullcap." For a larger animal this method of fixing may not be strong enough to withstand the animal's attempts to remove the foreign object. Then it is usual to make slots or "keyholes" in the skull with a dental burr and to screw bolts firmly to the skull as shown in Figure 4.7. The bolts can then be used to support electrodes or more complex structures.

Delgado (1963) has attached transistorized stimulators to the heads of monkeys, timing them to go on and off automatically by means

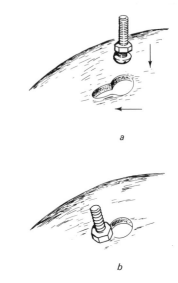

Figure 4.7 Insertion of bolts into keyhole slots in the skull: (a) keyhole and bolt before insertion, (b) after insertion.

of a built-in miniature wristwatch movement. Robinson, Warner, and Rosvold (1965) have devised a miniature receiver capable of applying stimulation to one of a number of remotely switchable electrodes with any parameters that can be obtained from a standard stimulator. Receivers are screwed to four bolts attached to the head and powered by small batteries that are continuously recharged in the light by "sun batteries" placed on top of the stimulator. The animals can thus be stimulated at various points as the experimenter desires over a period of several years, without ever having to be caught or handled after the initial implantation of the apparatus.

Stimulating electrodes are of two basic types, *monopolar* and *bipolar*. Current must flow in a closed circuit, of course, and monopolar electrodes must therefore be used with a return connection from the animal to the stimulator. A so-called *indifferent electrode* is used for this purpose; it may consist of a wire attached to one of the screws in the skull or embedded in the skin at any point on the body. If the animal is made to stand on a metal floor the current from the electrode may be made to return through its feet, though this technique provides a pathway of too variable a resistance for most

Figure 4.6 "Damped" wave form used for preferentially stimulating small hypothalamic neurons. (W. R. Hess, 1932.)

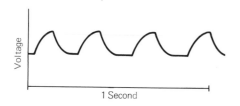

1 Second

purposes. The essential feature of the indifferent electrode is that it is of sufficient area so that the current density (microamperes per square centimeter) is not great enough to stimulate any nerve endings or neural tissue that may lie close to it. An area 10-20 times that of the exposed monopolar electrode tip should be enough to prevent stimulation of tissue at the indifferent contact.

The current density is naturally at a maximum where the area through which the current is passing is smallest, that is, at the tip of the stimulating electrode. At threshold value, therefore, only the neurons in the immediate vicinity of the tip will be excited. With an increase in total current, the critical current density will be reached farther from the tip, but, as the current is spreading more or less radially in all directions around the tip, the density falls off proportionally to the square of the distance. It is thus necessary to increase the current by about four times to double the diameter of the stimulated region. There are, however, eight times as many cells in a sphere of twice the diameter; moreover, the cells near the electrode will receive suprathreshold stimulation when the current is increased, so that the total firing will increase faster than the increase in current.

The negative pole (or cathode) of the electrode is usually considered more effective than the positive pole (or anode) in firing neurons, but this is not always so. The exceptions are probably caused by the fact that, in structures where the neurons are all oriented in a particular direction, it is possible to induce a negative current to flow into the sensitive axon hillock by applying a positive voltage near a remote part of the dendritic zone. Strong negative current through the dendrites is not an effective stimulus because the dendrites are not very sensitive to electrical stimulation.

Bipolar electrodes consist of two leads placed close together. Usually they are both insulated from the brain except at the tips, and the tips are within a millimeter or two of each other. The path of the current through the tissue is thus very short, and the current density may be high enough to fire neurons along its entire length. Another form of bipolar electrode is the concentric electrode, consisting of one central insulated wire inside a surrounding tube.

Monopolar electrodes take up less space than do bipolar ones and also have the advantage of requiring fewer connections when multiple stimulations (or recordings of brain potentials) are to be carried out. The bipolar electrode is used when it is important that the stimulation (or potential measurement) be confined to a small area of the brain. This precaution is most necessary during recording studies because a monopolar electrode is influenced by changes in bioelectric potential that take place anywhere between its location and the location of the indifferent electrode, which may be a considerable distance away.

Most electrodes for stimulation are made of stainless steel. Although in theory the metal is eroded by the stimulating current, depositing toxic ions in the surrounding tissues, it has been found that with the very small currents used animals can be stimulated intermittently over a period of years with no apparent damage to the brain. Alternative electrode materials are silver (more toxic than stainless steel), gold, tungsten, and platinum.

A minor bonus of using stainless steel or other ferrous alloy is that the iron deposited in the tissues surrounding the tip can be stained, which facilitates location of the stimulation points in sections of the brain after the experiment. Just before the animal is killed, a small anodal current is passed for a few seconds through the electrode. The brain is then perfused, or soaked, with a solution of potassium ferrocyanide, which reacts with the deposited iron salt to form ferric ferrocyanide, or Prussian blue.

In addition to electrical stimulation, the technique of chemical stimulation has now come into common use. A *cannula*, or a guide through which a cannula can be introduced, is implanted. It can be combined with an electrode for electrical stimulation or recording. In one arrangement (Shinshu Nakajima, 1964) a length of stainless-steel tubing is implanted so that it ends just above the part of the structure to be stimulated; it is cemented to the skull in the same way that electrodes are. A cannula consisting of another length of hypodermic tubing that fits snugly inside the implanted guide is prepared with a "stop," so that it can penetrate the guide and protrude a fraction of a millimeter into the brain at the bottom. A polyethylene tube fits over the stop, and when the cannula is in place the tubing slides over the end of the guide as shown in Figure 4.8. This tube prevents the cannula from being pulled out and also seals the top of the guide so that injected fluid does not escape up the space between the cannula and the guide. The other end of the polyethylene tube is attached to a microsyringe containing the solution to be injected; the tube may be quite long, allowing the animal considerable freedom of movement. To avoid damage to the tissues near the tip of

Figure 4.8 Cannula-and-guide assembly for injecting chemicals into the brain. The cannula guide is cemented to the skull; the cannula and the polyethylene tubing that connects it to the syringe are removed when not in use, and a cap is placed over the end of the cannula guide.

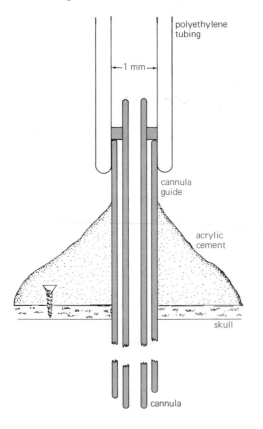

the cannula, only a few microliters of fluid are injected at a time, and the injection must be performed slowly over a period of minutes.

Sometimes the active substance is applied in solid form, either pressed into the end of a cannula or fused to the tip of a needle that is either permanently implanted or introduced through a guide in the same way as the cannula.

RECORDING FROM THE BRAIN

Electric Potentials

The same electrodes used for stimulating can be used to pick up bioelectric potentials from the brain. For most purposes stainless steel or some similar material is satisfactory, but in experiments in which steady or very slowly changing potentials are to be recorded, as well as in others in which it is necessary to reduce signals unrelated to the experiments (*artifacts*) to the absolute minimum, a *non polarizable electrode* is used. Normally, when a current passes between two electrodes immersed in an electrolyte, one or both surfaces undergo chemical change, and, as they are then different from each other, a difference in potential appears between them. This principle is that of the common rechargeable battery and is known as "polarization"; it is a nuisance when it happens to recording electrodes because the polarization voltage is confounded with the voltage that is being picked up from the brain.

Nonpolarizable electrodes are really electrodes that have already been polarized as far as possible, so that current flow does not produce any further change in the chemical composition of the electrode surfaces. Current is carried through an electrolyte, such as the fluid in the brain, by ions (charged atoms or parts of molecules). When these ions give up their charges to the metal electrode, they are deposited there as neutral atoms (for example, hydrogen, sodium, or chlorine) or as free radicles (for example, sulphate or carbonate). Most of these deposited substances are highly reactive; sodium and the other alkali metals, for example, capture a hydroxide (OH) radicle from the water and release hydrogen at the electrode.

This reaction does little harm unless the gas bubbles grow so big that they insulate the metal from the tissue. The release of chlorine, on the other hand, results in formation of the chloride or some other oxidization product of the electrode material. The two electrodes will then be composed of different materials, giving rise to an electrochemical potential that may mask or interfere with the voltage measurement.

In order to overcome this difficulty it is necessary to coat both electrodes with chloride before the measurements are carried out. Silver electrodes can be coated with silver chloride by making them anodes in cells with a chloride electrolyte like KCl solution. Mercury electrodes covered by a layer of *calomel* (Hg_2Cl_2) are sometimes used. On such a coated electrode more chlorine atoms merely add to the chloride already there; they do not change the composition of the surface. On the other hand, when an alkali-metal atom (sodium, for example) is released at the electrode, it captures one of the chlorine atoms to form soluble sodium chloride, thus slightly reducing the thickness of the silver or mercury chloride layer, but again there is no change in the composition of the surface unless enough current passes to remove a substantial part of the chloride.

Calomel is toxic and must not come in contact with neural tissue; a saline-soaked wick or a tube filled with *agar gel* is therefore interposed between the electrode and the tissue. Caspers (1961) has used permanently implanted electrodes of both the calomel and silver-chloride types in rats. Rowland (1961) has developed even smaller nonpolarizing electrodes, four or five of which can be implanted in the brain of a rat for recording changes in DC potential during learning and other forms of behavior.

All the electrodes described so far are suitable for measuring gross changes in potential within a region of neural tissue, but they are too large to detect the firing of individual neurons. To record such sharply localized discharges, it is necessary to have an electrode tip not much bigger than the area invaded by the action current from the neuron. If the electrode is too big, much of its surface is outside the field of the discharge current and acts merely as a short circuit for the current picked up by the fraction of the tip that is in the field. The smaller the electrode tip, the more nearly its potential approaches that of the discharging membrane. Extracellular *microelectrodes* are usually no larger than a few microns in diameter at the tip. To record the voltage inside a neuron, the electrode must be able to penetrate the cell with minimum damage, and such intracellular microelectrodes have tips less than 1 μ in diameter.

There are two basic types of microelectrode: glass pipettes filled with a conducting electrolyte like KCl solution and metal microelectrodes coated with insulation except at the tips. Glass microelectrodes are made by heating small-diameter glass tubing until it is soft and drawing it out to the required size. Machines are available for doing it semiautomatically. These electrodes are easy to make, but filling them can be rather tedious, as all bubbles must be carefully eliminated. They have the further disadvantage that the concentrated electrolyte with which they must be filled to achieve a low enough resistance may diffuse into the region under investigation and change conditions there. (Sometimes, however, this characteristic can be turned to advantage.) These electrodes are also delicate and liable to become plugged up.

Some metal electrodes are made by enclosing a ductile metal like platinum or silver in a glass tube and pulling the whole thing in a flame. The glass coating serves to support and to insulate the metal. Stainless steel and tungsten wires can be dissolved away electrolytically until the tip has a fine point, but they must then be insulated. This is usually done by submerging the electrode in synthetic varnish and lifting it out gently, tip first.

Recently a technique has been developed to measure the total amount of neural activity in a small region of the brain with an electrode intermediate in size between the microelectrode and the gross electrode (10-200 μ diameter). Any neuron near the tip produces a small voltage pulse on the electrode each time it fires, and if many neurons are firing in the vicinity the recorded effect is rather like that of random-noise voltage. This "noise" voltage can be amplified and fed to a meter, which provides a measure of the average level of neural firing in the region.

As we saw earlier, in Chapter 2, the potential difference across the membrane of a neuron is usually less then 0.1 volt, which (except in the electric organs of some fish) is the largest voltage encountered in bioelectrical measurements. The voltages picked up outside the skull in *electroencephalography* (EEG) are a thousand times smaller, and sometimes it is necessary to detect potential changes as small as 1 μv. These voltages require a great deal of amplification before they can drive such recording instruments as the *cathode-ray tube* or the electromagnetic pen.

When the junction between electrode and tissue has a very high electrical resistance, as is the case with most microelectrodes, the amplifier must pass negligible current, or most of the voltage will be lost in the resistance instead of appearing at the amplifier-input terminals. A current amplifier is therefore used at the input stage of the equipment, to provide a replica of the input voltage at adequate current, while absorbing negligible current from the electrode.

If only the rapid fluctuations of voltage are of interest, an amplifier basically similar to the audio stages of a radio is suitable. When the investigator is dealing with such minute input potentials, however, it is very likely that voltages picked up from power lines (60-Hz "hum") and other sources of interference may be many times greater than the voltage under study. Fortunately these voltages usually appear simultaneously on both leads from the subject and can thus be eliminated by the use of a *differential amplifier*, which amplifies only the voltage difference between the two input leads and rejects any voltage common to both (B. H. C. Matthews, 1934). A grounded cage, or shielded room, around the subject eliminates interference from nearby radio and television transmitters, electric motors, and other radiating equipment.

If the DC component of the signal is important or if changes occurring over periods of more than a few seconds are to be faithfully recorded, special amplifiers must be used. High-gain amplifiers have multiple stages, each feeding the next through a network (such as a capacitor and resistor or a transformer) that will not pass DC or very low frequencies. It is possible to design a coupling network that will allow direct currents and very low-frequency currents to pass, but the supply voltage to the first amplifier stage forms part of the input to the second stage. Any fluctuation of the supply voltage will therefore be amplified 10,000 times or more by the subsequent amplifier stages, and inevitably produce inaccuracies in the measurement of small DC bioelectrical potentials.

A better technique, therefore, is to "chop" the DC input voltage into pulses with a mechanical or electronic switch and then to feed the resulting pulses into a normal amplifier (or one tuned to the chopping frequency). The output of the amplifier is finally restored to the original DC form. By this technique, DC potentials of 1 μv or less can be measured with a drift in the zero input reference level of no more than a few microvolts per week.

There are several ways of dealing with the amplified bioelectric potentials, depending on the sort of analysis required. DC or slowly fluctuating voltages may be read directly on a voltmeter scale or fed to a paper-chart recorder (a meter with a pen attached to the pointer, so that it can trace a line on a strip of paper moved past it at a constant rate by a clockmotor). The signals may also be fed into a digital voltmeter, whose output is periodically punched onto computer tape for subsequent analysis; or fed directly into a computer.

More rapidly changing voltages (up to about 100 per second) such as those picked up through gross electrodes from the brain, can be recorded on paper by a high-speed electromechanical oscillograph, as in the conventional EEG machine; the tracing is then analyzed by eye (see Figures 14.2, 14.9, and so on). This method is satisfactory for clinical purposes but not for most research purposes; for the latter more precisely quantified measures are usually required. One way to analyze the signal is to perform some sort of frequency analysis. The voltage may be recorded on magnetic tape and analyzed by playing it at various speeds through a tuned filter. The filter allows only a narrow band of frequencies to pass to the recording or integrating apparatus, and this frequency will be related to the original signal frequency by the ratio of playback and recording speeds of the tape. (For example, if the filter is tuned to 10 Hz and the tape is played at the same speed as was used for recording, the 10-Hz component of the signal will be monitored. If the tape is run at five times the recording speed, the 2-Hz component of the signal will be passed by the filter because it will be played back at 10 Hz.)

Alternatively, many filters, each tuned to a different frequency band, may be put in the output of the amplifier and the frequency or *spectral analysis* performed on the incoming signal. If a high-speed digital computer is available, the same analysis can be obtained by converting the EEG signal into digital form (*analogue-to-digital converters* are made to do this job) and feeding it into a computer that has been programmed to perform the required frequency analysis.

Bioelectric potentials may have to be recorded on magnetic tape for various reasons in addition to that mentioned. Standard tape recorders are very inefficient at the low frequencies encountered in physiological measurement, but this weakness can be overcome by a frequency-modulation (FM) technique. The frequency of an audio oscillator is controlled by the EEG signal voltage, so that for every voltage there is a corresponding oscillator frequency (1,000 Hz might correspond to zero volts, 1,500 Hz to $+1$ volt, 500 Hz to -1 volt, and so on). The FM signal is recorded on the tape and played back into a circuit that reconverts each frequency to its equivalent voltage. In this way even DC voltages may be recorded on tape.

When brain potentials are being picked up from several different points simultaneously, it is sometimes useful to determine the extent to which they are related. *Cross correlation* is the method used. Analogue computers have been developed to perform this operation; alterna-

tively, the voltages can be converted into digital form and the correlations worked out on a suitably programmed digital computer.

Some voltages from the nervous system are time-locked, which means they bear a constant time relationship to an external event, such as an electrical stimulus, a click, or a flash, that is under the experimenter's control. A single recording of such an evoked response may be uninterpretable because of the high level of spontaneous background activity, which is essentially unrelated to the signal, but if the stimulus is repeated, the time-locked response may be detected by recording (or photographing) a number of responses on top of one another (Figure 4.9). The random variations blur the image, but the blurred line has a mean path corresponding to any response that is present in all the tracings.

A similar effect can be obtained by adding sequential tracings to one another electrically in a memory device known as a *computer of average transients* (CAT). The signal is divided into many small time elements, starting with the event that triggers the evoked response. The average value of the voltage during each of these short intervals is stored in a separate memory bin. This process is repeated after each of a number (as many as several hundred) of presentations of the stimulus; the average voltage during each of the small intervals is added to the sum from that interval already in the memory bin from previous presentations. If the voltages picked up are unrelated to the stimulus, there will be about as many negative as positive values in each interval, and the sum will never depart far from zero. On the other hand, if the stimulus produces an evoked potential, this voltage will be present during some of the time intervals every time the stimulus is presented, and the voltage will accumulate in the corresponding memory bins. A sequential readout of the memory will then give a plot of the evoked potential clear of random noise.

The CAT has proved useful in many experiments, for example, the extracranial recording (through scalp electrodes) of *evoked potentials* in human subjects. The evoked potential from a single stimulus is masked by the EEG voltage

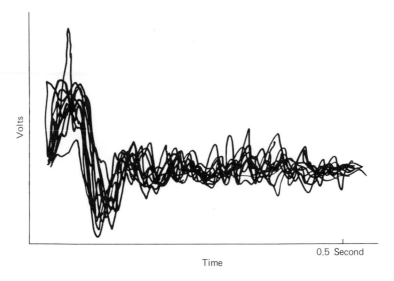

Figure 4.9 Superposition of ten oscilloscope records of evoked potentials in order to reduce errors of interpretation caused by random variations in the signal. Each sweep of the time base is triggered by the stimulus that evokes the brain potential; that is, the records are *time-locked* to the signals.

picked up at the same time, but the average EEG tends toward zero over many trials because it is not timelocked to the stimulus, whereas the average evoked potential, which is time-locked to the stimulus, remains constant.

When it is necessary to record electrical events too rapid for mechanical recording instruments, the cathode-ray oscilloscope is used.

It is a very useful tool in which a beam of electrons, focused on a fluorescent screen, takes the place of the pen in a mechanical oscilloscope. The electron beam can be deflected by electrical or magnetic fields and, having almost no weight, responds for all practical purposes instantaneously.

The oscilloscope shown in Figure 4.10 is one

Figure 4.10 A cathode-ray tube.

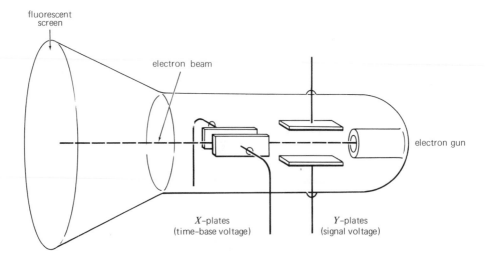

in which the beam is deflected by electrostatic force. If a voltage is applied between the Y-plates, the negatively charged electrons of the beam are attracted by the positive plate and repelled by the negative plate, resulting in a vertical deflection of the spot on the screen. Similarly, the beam can be deflected horizontally by a voltage applied to the X-plates.

The instrument may be used in conjunction with light-sensitive film, just as a mechanical pen is used with a moving strip of paper. The beam is deflected in the vertical plane by the amplified output from the brain, and the film is drawn horizontally past the screen. The spot then traces a graph of the change of signal voltage over time.

For short periods of time, a similar effect can be obtained by driving the electron beam from left to right at a constant velocity (with what is known as a *time-base* voltage on the X-plates), at the same time as it is being moved up and down by the signal. The spot is returned to the left of the screen at very high speed so that the fly-back is not visible.

If the phenomenon observed is repetitive or can be triggered by a stimulus, the time-base voltage can be synchronized with each occurrence of the event; if the events occur at more than about 10 per second, a steady picture appears due to the persistence of vision. Unique or infrequent events may be recorded photographically, or a cathode ray tube with a long-persistence or storage screen can be employed. The phosphor in such screens continues to glow for some time after it has been excited by the electron beam making the screens unsuitable for use with rapidly changing signals.

Recording Temperature

Techniques have been evolved for measuring temperature changes in the nervous system. At first the method was used to measure blood flow, as reduced blood flow usually results in a fall in temperature. More recently, temperature changes have been found correlated with behavior and with sensory input. Temperature measurements are relatively easy to make with *thermistors*, beads of semiconducting material whose electrical resistance varies greatly with temperature. The beads can be attached to the tips of hypodermic needles and implanted in the brain stereotaxically. The leads pass through the needle, and connection is made to them, as to electrodes, through a plug attached to the skull. Temperature measurements are made by connecting the thermistor in a resistance-measuring circuit, which usually plots the resistance changes (with conversion to temperature) on a paper chart.

Chemical Analysis

The chemical processes of the brain are attracting a great deal of interest at the moment. It is possible to take samples of the fluid at a given point in the brain by slowly forcing a normal saline solution down one tube and collecting it, along with the exudate from the brain, through an adjacent or concentric tube. Fluid is often collected from the cortex of anesthetized animals by removing part of the skull, piercing the dura mater, and placing a metal ring around the wound. The fluid that collects in the ring is withdrawn from time to time and analyzed. Physical and physical-chemistry methods are now available to measure extremely small quantities of organic substances in the samples.

Unfortunately, some of the most interesting chemicals are very short-lived in a free state in the brain. As soon as they are liberated they are broken down by *enzymatic action*. A drastic method of ascertaining the normal distribution of these substances is to freeze a small animal instantly by dropping it into liquid air or nitrogen, which stops all enzymatic reactions. The brain is then removed, ground up, treated with solvents to extract the required chemicals before the temperature becomes high enough for the reactions to start again.

Radioactive tracers also have their use in physiological psychology. A substance incorporating radioactive atoms, such as carbon 14, can be fed or injected into an animal and later traced to see whether or not it has been incorporated into neural tissue and, if so, where. The location can be determined by the technique of *autoradiography*, in which slices of the tissue are placed against (or coated with) a photographic emulsion and left in the dark for a long time until the radioactivity has produced an image on film. When the film is developed, it shows a silhouette of the structures that have taken up the tracer element. Alternatively, samples of the tissue may be tested with a Geiger counter to measure the absorption of tracer element in particular structures.

Summary

Present-day knowledge about the functioning of the nervous system has been acquired with the aid of three main techniques: lesions, stimulation, and recording. Cortical ablations can be done under direct visual control; the most common method is to remove tissue by suction, as it is less likely to cause irritative scarring. An epileptic lesion can be obtained, if required, by implanting alumina cream.

Subcortical lesions are usually produced by electrolysis or radio-frequency cautery. An electrode is introduced into the area to be destroyed by means of a stereotaxic instrument, which holds the head of the subject in a standard position and allows a probe to be moved into any predetermined position in the brain. The coordinates of the structure to be located are usually read from atlases that have been prepared for most animals used in brain experiments.

Less frequently used methods of producing lesions involve ultrasonic sound waves, radioactive isotopes, and freezing. Cooling probes can produce reversible lesions if the temperature is not allowed to fall below the freezing point. A reversible lesion that spreads over the cortex of one hemisphere can be produced by applying a small quantity of KCl solution to that hemisphere.

Stimulation of brain tissue may be achieved electrically or chemically. In the former case an electrode is placed at the point to be stimulated, either by visual guidance or by means of a stereotaxic instrument, and a small current (usually a fraction of a milliampere) is passed through the tissue. Most modern stimulators deliver rectangular pulses of current whose amplitude, duration, and repetition rate can be independently adjusted over a wide range. The most effective parameters for stimulation vary somewhat from structure to structure, but a sharply rising pulse lasting 0.1–1.0 msec, at a repetition rate of 50–300 per second, is close to the optimum for most.

In an investigation of the effects of stimulation upon behavior, electrodes must be implanted for a long period of time. Usually a support is screwed to the skull, and the electrodes are cemented to it. During testing a lead from the stimulator is plugged into each electrode.

Chemicals for stimulating the brain are applied through a hollow needle, or cannula, which may be implanted in the same way that an electrode is. Solutions are injected through a flexible polyethylene tube attached to the cannula during testing; solid chemicals are pushed into the end of a small needle, which slides down the inside of the implanted tube.

Bioelectric potentials can be recorded from the same type of electrodes as are used for stimulation, unless very slow potentials must be picked up, in which case nonpolarizing electrodes must be used. They are usually made of chlorided silver or mercury. If the firing of single neurons is to be detected, very small electrodes, whose tips measure about 1 μ in diameter must be used. They may be of metal coated with insulation, or they may be glass pipettes filled with conducting solution. Spike discharges from a number of adjacent neurons may be picked up simultaneously with intermediate-size electrodes (with diameter between 10 and 200 μ).

In order to amplify small bioelectric potentials without interference, differential amplifiers are used. They amplify only the differences between the two input leads and reject any voltages that appear between both leads and ground. To amplify small DC potentials, the signals are chopped into pulses, amplified in a tuned amplifier, and restored to DC form.

Amplified signals are usually fed into a recording or analyzing device. Simple electromechanical pen recorders are capable of recording up to about 100 events per second and are used mainly for recording brain potentials in the range of a fraction of a hertz to about 60 Hz. Impulses from single neural elements, which last about a millisecond each, are observed with the aid of a cathode-ray oscilloscope and (if necessary) photographed.

Various computer techniques are used to analyze neural potentials. Filters may be used to indicate what frequencies are present, or correlations among the voltages at various points in the brain may be calculated.

If an event is evoked by a stimulus or is under the experimenter's control, it is possible to use an averaging technique to improve the signal-to-noise ratio of a response. A simple method is to photograph a number of traces of the event on top of one another, so that any recurring deflection can be distinguished from the random fluctuations. Another method is to present the stimulus repeatedly and to use a computer of average transients (CAT) to calculate the average voltage during each of many consecutive time intervals after the stimulus. Any genuine evoked response will appear every time and be added; random events will tend to cancel one another out in repeated presentations and will disappear.

In addition to electrical recordings, temperature recordings have sometimes been found useful. They can readily be taken with the aid of thermistor elements implanted in the brain. Standard resistance-measuring equipment can then be used to determine the temperature.

Chemical samples can also be recovered from the brain, through cannulas similar to those used to inject chemicals. In order to prevent the destruction of short-lived substances, it is necessary to freeze the brain instantly by dropping the animal into liquid air or nitrogen. The brain is then ground up and the substances extracted before the temperature rises to the point at which enzyme reactions can take place.

PART TWO

MOTOR MECHANISMS

A characteristic of almost all animals is that they can move. As Sperry (1952) has pointed out, control of movement is by far the most important function of the nervous system; sensory systems, central integrating and storage mechanisms, and the motor system proper are all employed in energizing and guiding movements. As long as the motor system continues to function, an animal has some hope of survival, even though sensory input is restricted. If the motor system fails, the animal is doomed, no matter how effective its sensory apparatus may be. Very simple organisms have no nervous systems; the sensory input impinges directly upon motile cells, the precursors of muscle cells. The history of animal development is essentially that of improvement in environmental control of the motor cells.

In most vertebrates the skeletal muscles are controlled by input from receptors in the muscles themselves, from receptors in the skin and neighboring joints, from higher levels of reflex control (organs of balance, for example), and from sensory circuits of great complexity that involve learned components and may integrate the inputs from several sense modalities.

It seems logical, therefore, to start our study of the nervous system with the part that constitutes the raison d'être for the rest; there is also a more practical reason for doing so. Simple reflexes have been very thoroughly investigated for many years, and a number of fundamental principles applicable to that level of neural functioning have been established; in all probability they are also applicable to the more complex mechanisms we shall encounter later. Furthermore, we cannot go very far in the study of the motor system without some mention of sensory input; we are thus forced to adopt a more holistic approach than would be necessary if we started with sensory processes. By the time we are ready to study the sensory systems we shall have some idea of the basic functions they have evolved to serve.

CHAPTER 5

THE SPINAL MOTOR SYSTEM

The organs through which the motor system produces its effects upon the environment of the animal (internal or external) are called *effectors.* They include glands, smooth muscles, and *striated* (or *skeletal*) *muscles.* Smooth muscles and glands are innervated by the autonomic part of the motor system; the former are responsible for digestive movements, control of blood flow, erection of hairs, focusing of the eyes, and operation of internal sphincters and genital organs. Glands regulate the body chemistry; and the sweat glands help to regulate its temperature. In some animals there are cells in which granules of pigment can be moved, producing changes in skin color.

The secretory cells of the glands function in much the same way as do nerve cells. They manufacture substances under the direction of RNA in the endoplasmic reticulum (see Chapter 2), and, when stimulated by excitatory substances released by nerve endings or carried in the blood, they expel the secretion into the bloodstream or into ducts for delivery to the stomach, mouth, eyes, and so on.

Smooth muscles and striated muscles are basically similar, the main difference being that smooth muscles contract more slowly than do skeletal muscles. A muscle consists of a large number of individual cells called *muscle fibers,* which resemble nerve cells in some respects.

The fiber has a chemically sensitive region called the *end plate,* where the motor axon terminates and which corresponds to the subsynaptic membrane of the neuron. When the motoneuron axon fires, it releases acetylcholine in the underlying end-plate region (Figure 5.1), depolarizing the muscle fiber and generating an electrical impulse that is propagated in both directions toward the ends of the fiber.

Immediately after the impulse has passed, the muscle undergoes a brief contraction. The term "contraction" is applied to muscles in a special sense and does not necessarily mean that they shorten. If the ends of a muscle are fixed, contraction will register as a stronger pull on the supports, which is called *isometric contraction.* The more usual case, in which the muscle exerts a constant pull and grows shorter, is called *isotonic contraction.*

A. F. Huxley and Niedergerke (1954) and H. E. Huxley and Hanson (1954) arrived independently at the same hypothesis about the basic mechanism of muscle contraction. Subsequent research supports their hypothesis and has extended it so that it now seems likely that all cellular movement (including the streaming of cytoplasm inside stationary cells) is triggered by the proposed mechanism.

Each muscle fiber is made up of millions of longitudinally aligned filaments, thick ones composed of molecules of the protein *myosin* and thin ones composed of the protein *actin.* The actin filaments are attached to transverse membranes called *Z lines* (Figure 5.2); and the actin filaments from two adjacent Z lines mesh with myosin filaments, which occupy the spaces between the lines. When an electrical impulse passes down the muscle fiber it causes an activating substance (thought to be calcium) to be released through the deactivation of a calcium "sink," which normally holds the calcium bound to it (Gergely, 1959, 1964; Podolsky & Costantin, 1964). This process allows the myosin to break down adenosine triphosphate, or ATP (see Chapter 2), and use the energy so released to haul in the actin filaments from both sides by means of ratchet-shaped bridges pointing in opposite directions at the two ends of the myosin filaments (Figure 5.2). For more

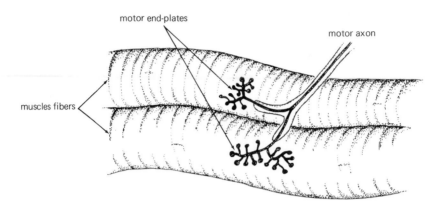

Figure 5.1 Terminals of a motoneuron axon at the end plates of two striated-muscle fibers.

detailed information about this mechanism of muscle contraction the reader should consult H. E. Huxley (1965, p. 18).

A striated muscle consists of many thousands of muscle fibers bound together in a sheath and attached to a bone, eyeball, or other organ by tendons. Muscles can only pull; they cannot push, and therefore each joint is provided with two groups of muscles, one to hold the joint extended (*extensors*) and the other to flex it (*flexors*). Usually a number of muscles, called

synergistic muscles, combine to pull on a joint. Muscles whose action is in opposition (extensors and flexors) are called *antagonistic* muscles.

A section of a typical striated muscle is shown in Figure 5.3. As may be seen, it is well supplied with sensory endings, as well as with motor nerves. As mentioned in Chapter 3, one motoneuron innervates a large number of muscle fibers, and the total group is called a "motor unit." A moderate-sized muscle contains several hundred motor units.

Figure 5.2 (a) The arrangement of actin and myosin filaments that gives rise to the striations of skeletal muscle. (b) An enlarged myosin filament, with bridges, or hooks, to draw actin filaments toward the center during muscle contraction. (After H. E. Huxley, 1965.)

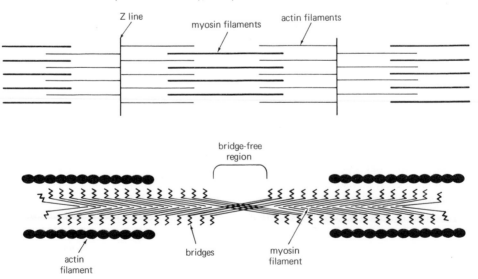

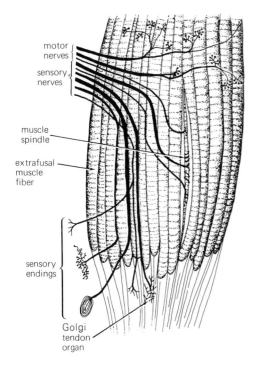

motor
nerves

sensory
nerves

muscle
spindle

extrafusal
muscle
fiber

sensory
endings

Golgi
tendon
organ

Figure 5.3 Denny-Brown's diagram of the motor and sensory nerve supplies to a striated muscle. (After figure in Creed, Denny-Brown, Eccles, Liddell & Sherington, 1932.)

The motoneurons innervating one muscle do not form a compact mass but are scattered throughout several segments of the spinal cord and are called the *motor* (or *motoneuron*) *pool* for that muscle.

Muscle Spindles

The skeletal effector system is a little more complex than this picture indicates. About 30 per cent of the motor nerve is made up of axons much smaller than the rest (3–8 μ in diameter, compared to 12–14 μ), and it has been found that they end not on ordinary muscle fibers but on very weak fibers called *intrafusal muscle fibers*, which lie inside small structures called *muscle spindles* (Figures 5.3 and 5.4). Because the velocity of the impulses in these small-diameter axons falls into Gasser's gamma category (see Chapter 2), the neurons are often called "gamma motoneurons," but the name is

not a very satisfactory designation of muscle-spindle efferents, especially as it now turns out that some muscle spindles are innervated by larger motor fibers with impulse velocities in the alpha range (60–120 m per second). In this chapter, motoneurons ending in muscle spindles will be called *intrafusal motoneurons*. When necessary to avoid ambiguity, those ending on ordinary muscle fibers will be called *extrafusal motoneurons*.

The anatomy of the muscle spindle is shown in Figure 5.4. The intrafusal muscle fibers, of which there may be 2–10 per spindle, occupy the end, or *polar*, regions. They are attached in the middle to an elastic nonmuscular zone called the *nuclear bag*, which contains several receptors, the most important being the *annulospiral*, or *primary receptor* of the nuclear bag. Located in the *myotube region*, an elastic part of the structure situated between the two contractile ends of the spindle, this receptor is very sensitive to stretch. It stretches and fires when the intrafusal motor system is fired, provided that the points of attachment at the ends of the spindles do not move.

This effect was observed by Leksell (1945), who found that by judicious compression of the motor nerve he could block impulses in the large axons without disturbing conduction through the smaller, slower-conducting axons. He expected the slow impulses to produce a contraction of the muscle, but his instruments were not sensitive enough to detect any change in tension, although the gamma impulses could be picked up in the nerve entering the muscle. Leksell did find, however, that when he moved his recording electrode to the dorsal root he could pick up strong bursts of sensory impulses returning to the cord during stimulation of the motor nerve, and he rightly assumed that these impulses were generated by the stretch receptors in the muscle spindles, indicating that the motor impulses were firing the intrafusal muscle fibers.

Muscle spindles are scattered through all skeletal muscles. The ends are usually attached to the sheaths of extrafusal fibers, so that their lengths vary in accordance with those of the

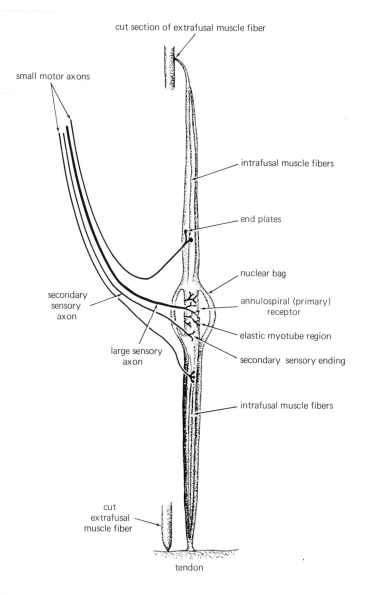

cut section of extrafusal muscle fiber

small motor axons

intrafusal muscle fibers

end plates

nuclear bag

secondary
sensory
axon

annulospiral (primary)
receptor

elastic myotube region

large sensory
axon

secondary sensory ending

intrafusal muscle fibers

cut
extrafusal
muscle fiber

tendon

Figure 5.4 A muscle spindle isolated from the surrounding extrafusal muscle fibers. (After Barker, 1948.)

muscles. When the muscle as a whole contracts isotonically, the muscle spindle is shortened, and the tension on the annulospiral ending is reduced. On the other hand, when the muscle relaxes (it gets longer), its spindles will be stretched and the annulospiral receptors may fire (see Figure 5.5). The primary receptor may thus be stretched in three different ways: by contraction of *intra*fusal fibers, by reduction in the firing of *extra*fusal fibers (so that they re-

lax), and by application of an external force that lengthens the whole muscle.

It has been found that the afferent axon from the primary ending of the nuclear bag (annulospiral receptor) returns to the segment of the cord that contains the motor pool for its muscle and sends a branch directly to extrafusal motoneurons in that pool. We thus have a direct feedback loop from the muscle to its own motoneurons, as shown in Figure 5.6. The link

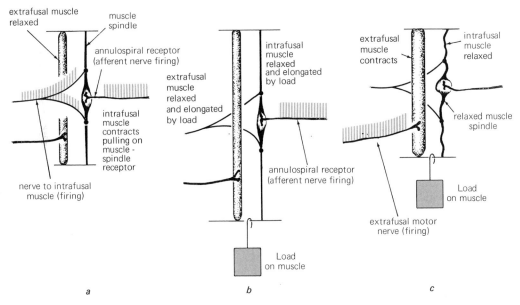

Figure 5.5 Three conditions of a muscle spindle. (a) No weight is suspended from the muscle. Initially there is no firing in the motor nerve to the extrafusal muscle but firing has just started in the small nerve to the intrafusal muscle, causing it to contract. It is important to remember that the *intrafusal* muscles are much too weak to produce any external movement, even when the muscle is unloaded, so that their contraction has no effect other than to stretch the nuclear bag and hence to generate impulses in the annulospiral receptor. These impulses return to the spinal cord via the sensory nerve. (b) There is no motor input to either the extrafusal or the intrafusal muscle but a force is applied to the muscle as a whole, causing it to elongate. As the muscle spindle elongates along with the rest of the muscle, the annulospiral receptor is stretched and generates impulses as before. (c) The load remains on the muscle but firing of the nerve to the extrafusal muscle causes the muscle to contract and counteract the effect of the load. The tension is thus removed from the muscle spindle; if there is no activity in small motor nerve fibers to the intrafusal muscle, the nuclear bag is relaxed and no annulospiral receptor impulses are generated.

between the muscle spindle and its extrafusal muscle is mechanical; the path from the spindle back to the muscle is neural.

What is the effect of this feedback? It has already been pointed out that, if the muscle increases in length (which can happen either because an extra load is applied or because its motoneurons fired less frequently), the stretch receptors of its muscle spindles will probably be fired. This activity in turn bombards the motoneurons and causes them to fire more vigorously, thus counteracting the tendency of the muscle to lengthen further. Conversely, if the load is removed from a muscle so that it shortens, the spindle also shortens and delivers fewer impulses to the motoneuron pool, reducing the firing frequency of motoneurons and allowing the muscle to return to approximately its former position. Feedback is thus a very

powerful device for maintaining the muscle at a fixed length and the limb in a fixed position. The rigidity of *decerebrated* animals (animals that have lost cerebral control of spinal mechanisms because of a complete section of the brainstem at the level of the colliculi) is partly caused by the fact that, when an attempt is made to flex the limb, the receptors of the extensor-muscle spindles immediately fire and increase the tone of the extensor muscles to counteract the flexing force.

Nevertheless it is obvious that under normal circumstances we can adjust the position of our limbs without evoking appreciable resistance. With such powerful control of muscle length, how do we make the muscle adopt a new length? To answer this question we must remember the other way in which primary receptors can be influenced: through the intrafusal

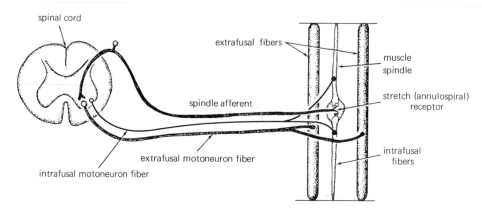

spinal cord

extrafusal fibers

muscle spindle

spindle afferent

stretch (annulospiral) receptor

extrafusal motoneuron fiber

intrafusal fibers

intrafusal motoneuron fiber

Figure 5.6 Connections of stretch reflex arc. If the stretch receptor is stimulated, the afferent signal fires motoneurons that cause the extrafusal muscles to contract and to reduce the stretch on the spindle receptor.

motor system. If there is an increase in the rate of delivery of impulses to the intrafusal muscle fibers (where the impulses come from will be explained later), the stretch receptors will fire, although the limb has not moved. In order to relieve the stretch, the muscle has to shorten, and the increased bombardment of the extrafusal motoneurons by the feedback from the spindles ensures that this shortening takes place. If the input to the intrafusal fibers is unchanged the limb resists attempts to move it, but with changed input to the intrafusal system the same feedback mechanism will force the limb to adopt a new position, which will then be held as long as the input to the intrafusal system remains at the new level.

If we use the familiar feedback analogy of the thermostatically controlled furnace, we can view the input to the intrafusal motor system as corresponding to the variable setting of the thermostat, the annulospiral receptor to the temperature-sensing device, and its connections with the motor pool to the control connections from the sensor to the furnace. The point at which the temperature-sensing device turns the furnace on can be adjusted, but, once set, the temperature is maintained at that point. A closer, though perhaps less familiar, analogy is the power steering of a car, in which a weak force (the driver) adjusts the position at which a more powerful hydraulic system holds the wheels of the car. Usually the system is designed so that the driver also applies some force

directly to the wheels, as well as to the hydraulic amplifier valve; a similar dual control seems to operate in the muscle servosystem also. There are direct connections from the input to the extrafusal motoneurons, as well as to the intrafusal control motoneurons.

Tendon Reflexes

The muscle-spindle feedback loop can be seen in action in the familiar "knee jerk" or tendon reflex. When the limb is hanging in a relaxed position and a tendon to an extensor muscle is tapped smartly, the muscle is stretched and a volley of impulses elicited from its spindle receptors. They travel to the cord, fire the motoneurons in the extensor motor pool, and produce a sudden contraction of the muscle a fraction of a second later.

The Intrafusal System in Reflex Movements

Reflexes are relatively stereotyped movements or postural adjustments in response to particular stimuli. It might be argued that the tendon reflex should not be classified with other reflexes, for it is only the accidental outcome of maltreating a mechanism that is in continuous operation during every movement that the muscle makes. There is ample evidence that many movements operate through the mediation of the intrafusal system. Granit (1955a) cites experiments that he conducted with

Eldred and Merton demonstrating that the Magnus-Kleyn postural reflexes operate in this way. When an animal's head is thrust back, there is a tendency for its forelegs to extend and its hindlegs to flex (as in a cat about to jump up onto a table). When its head is thrust down, there is a tendency for the reverse to happen; the forelegs flex and the hind legs extend (as when a cat sniffs a mouse hole). Rotating the head from side to side produces extension of the limbs on the side toward which the head is turned and flexion of the limbs on the other side. If the animal is standing, the body is thus partly rotated in the same direction as the head. These Magnus-Kleyn reflexes appear very clearly in the decerebrate animal, where they are not disturbed by central influences. They have been found to be initiated by receptors in the joints of the neck.

Eldred, Granit, and Merton (1953) prepared a decerebrate cat (allowing spinal and hindbrain mechanisms to be studied free from other brain influences) so that they could record the impulses from the stretch (annulospiral) receptor in a spindle of the *soleus muscle*, an extensor in the calf of the hind leg. They also recorded the muscle tension, which is a good measure of the firing rate in the extrafusal fibers of the motor nerve. The experimental arrangement is shown diagrammatically in Figure 5.7. To confirm that the recording electrode was on a fiber from the muscle-spindle receptor, the Achilles tendon was tapped to elicit a tendon reflex. That the receptor was of the correct type was demonstrated by the cessation of firing in the afferent axon during the resulting muscle contraction, as shown in Figure 5.8a. If the electrode had been on a fiber from a *Golgi tendon organ* (see discussion in the next section of this chapter) the firing would have increased

Figure 5.7 The experimental preparation used by Eldred, Granit, and Merton (1953). The oscilloscope records impulses picked up from a single afferent axon from the muscle spindle; the strain gauge records the contraction of the extrafusal muscle (and thus, indirectly, the activity of the extrafusal motoneuron).

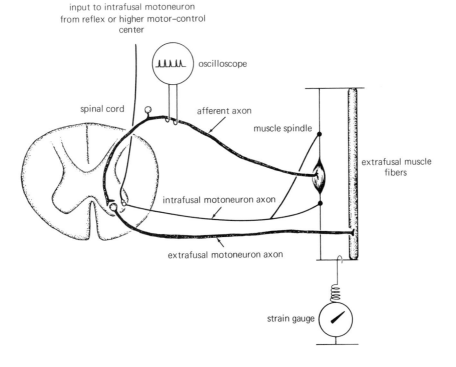

during the muscle contraction. With constant input to the intrafusal muscle, contraction of the extrafusal muscle shortens muscle spindles and their receptors, but stretches tendons.

The head of the cat was held up, causing the hind-limb extensors to relax. The low firing rate of the stretch receptor (Figure 5.8b) indicated that the intrafusal muscle was also relaxed. Then the head was suddenly pushed down, and immediately there was a strong contraction of the extensor muscle, and at the same time the firing rate in the spindle afferent greatly increased. The muscle spindle must have shortened even more than did the rest of the muscle, to put the nuclear bag into tension, and this finding is a strong indication that the input from the neck-joint receptors first fires the intrafusal system, which then excites the extrafusal system through spindle-receptor feedback.

This point can be demonstrated more conclusively by cutting the dorsal roots to prevent signals from the muscle-spindle receptors from getting back to the motoneurons. Now, when the head is thrust down, the response from the stretch receptor is more vigorous than before, but there is no contraction of the muscle (Figure 5.8c). As the extrafusal system is not directly affected by the cutting of the dorsal roots, we would expect a response from the muscle if the impulses from the neck-joint receptors went directly to the extrafusal motoneurons. In the absence of an appreciable response we must assume that the input goes mainly to intrafusal motoneurons and influences the extrafusal cells through feedback.

Similar results were obtained from the same preparation when other postural reflexes were elicited. Further experiments have shown that the *withdrawal reflex* (the retraction of a limb from a noxious stimulus), the scratch reflex (the dislodging of irritating objects from the skin), and in fact all the reflexes tested are mediated in the same way, the input being mainly to the intrafusal system. The same results were obtained for a number of motor effects engendered by brain stimulation, though Granit reported that stimulation of the motor cortex,

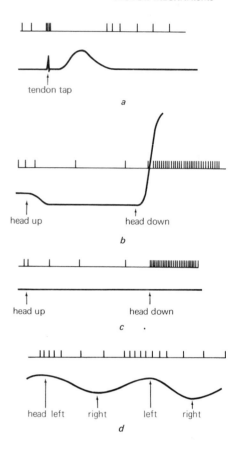

Figure 5.8 Recordings from the preparation shown in Figure 5.7. The upper line in each is the record of action potentials in the afferent axon from the spindle; the lower line is the record of extrafusal muscle tension. (a) The tendon reflex test to confirm that the electrode is on a spindle afferent. The tendon is tapped smartly to produce a sudden stretch of the muscle. This produces a brief burst of activity in the annulospiral receptors, but as the stretch is over before the reflex contraction of the muscle ensues all tension is removed from the spindles during the contraction and activity in the afferents from the spindles ceases. If the fiber had been from a Golgi tendon organ, its activity would have increased during the contraction as well as during the tap. (b) Extension of the hind limb when the head is thrust down. Despite shortening of the muscle, the spindle receptor is more active, indicating increased tension within the muscle spindle. This could only come about by contraction of the intrafusal muscles. (c) The same manoeuver after the dorsal root has been cut between the recording point and the spinal cord. The reflex movement is absent, but the muscle spindle still shows increased tension when the head is pushed down. The reflex input from the neck is therefore firing the intrafusal, but not the extrafusal, motoneurons. (d) Reflex limb extension to head turning is also mediated via the intrafusal motor system. (After Eldred, Granit, and Merton, 1953.)

besides firing intrafusal fibers, also fired extra-fusal fibers directly.

Behavioral Relevance of the Muscle-Spindle Feedback

The muscle-spindle servomechanism has a great advantage over a system in which the muscles must be controlled by firing from the output of a motor-system path directly onto the motoneurons. In a primitive system such as the latter, the position of the limb can be maintained against variable loads only by a corresponding variable input from the motor-system afferents. For example, without feedback, if somebody jostled you and caused more of your weight to be thrown onto one leg, that leg would require more input to its extensors to prevent it from buckling. If this adjustment had to be dealt with at the level of the brainstem, you might have fallen by the time the problem had been analyzed and the requisite compensation dispatched. With the servomechanism, each value of the output from the higher-level control corresponds not to a certain muscle contraction but to a particular position of the muscle, independent of load, and this relationship greatly simplifies the problem of making accurate movements.

The mechanism constitutes a very elementary example of how the problem of *motor equivalence* may be solved by neural systems, a problem raised insistently by Lashley (Lashley & McCarthy, 1926, Lashley, 1930a). The point is that we never perform an act like opening a door in exactly the same way twice. There are always minor or major variations in the movements made, depending on which hand happens to be nearer the knob, whether or not we are carrying anything, and so on.

The muscle-feedback mechanism cannot by itself solve the problem at the levels of complexity described in the above examples, but the principle involved in the solution may well be the same at all levels. Input instructions determine the result independently of conditions at the specific muscles involved. The servomechanism allows this achievement without requiring storage of an impossibly large number of alternative sets of instructions at the higher levels. We shall return to this point later.

Golgi Tendon Organs

There are dangers in having too effective a mechanism controlling muscle position because most muscles are strong enough to do considerable damage to tendons, and even to bones, if they are fired at maximum power. Fortunately in muscle tendons there are a number of Golgi tendon organs, receptors with relatively high firing thresholds. They deliver inhibitory volleys to the motor pool for the muscle when for any reason the tension in the tendon becomes dangerously high. In the decerebrate animal, if the experimenter exerts a strong force against the rigid muscle, resistance will suddenly evaporate, and the limb will move to a new position, at which rigidity returns. This effect is known as the *clasp-knife effect* for obvious reasons. The sudden loss of tone results from the firing of the high-threshold tendon organs, which inhibit both extra- and intrafusal motoneurons for the limb and put the stretch reflex out of action momentarily, before the force on the leg damages the tendons.

Reciprocal Innervation

There are other situations in which the normally useful muscle-spindle reflex would prove an embarrassment. Consider the flexing of an arm. Contraction of the flexor muscles will inevitably stretch the extensors, and for smooth movement the latter should relax freely. We have seen, however, that the stretch reflex would immediately be thrown into action to resist this relaxation, and the antagonist muscles would then fight in earnest. In order to avoid this undesirable state of affairs, there are neural connections among antagonist muscle pools to inhibit one as the other produces contraction. This system is known as *reciprocal innervation*. The actual connections involve, at least to some extent, the stretch receptors, as shown in Figure 5.9. When the stretch receptor for the extensor is pulled, it fires an inhibitory volley to the motoneurons of the antagonist flexors, as well

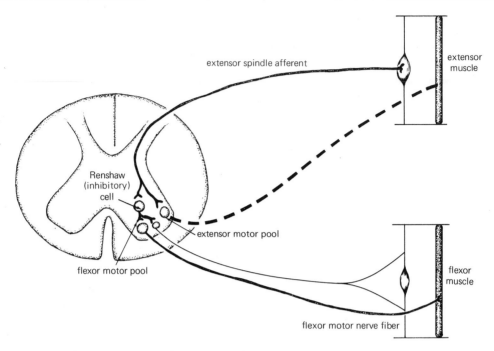

Figure 5.9 Reciprocal innervation of antagonist muscles. Extensor stretch-receptor activity inhibits the flexor motor pool, and vice versa, though the symmetrical connections from the flexor stretch receptor to the extensor motor pool are not shown in the diagram to prevent undue confusion.

as the excitatory volley to its own muscle pool. This inhibitory volley forestalls any effort by the antagonist stretch receptors to hold the muscle rigid. As the inhibition is applied to intrafusal, as well as to extrafusal motoneurons, the flexor spindles will be relaxed and will not feed back much input to the extrafusal neurons in any case.

It is usually assumed that a single neuron cannot have both excitatory and inhibitory endings in different axon branches (except, possibly, in the case of presynaptic inhibition), as such endings would involve the manufacture of two different transmitter substances and the delivery of each to the appropriate synaptic knobs. A possible alternative assumption would be that there are different types of subsynaptic membranes at excitatory and inhibitory points, but the more common assumption is that an inhibitory neuron lies between the afferent and the motoneuron that it inhibits. It is known that the motor pools in the cord have many inhibitory neurons distributed among the motoneu-

rons, and it appears likely that inhibitory reflex connections go to these cells instead of directly to the motoneurons. That is certainly what happens in the case of the most direct of all inhibitory feedback systems, that involving recurrent connections from the motoneuron to the inhibitory neurons in its own pool, which we shall now discuss.

RECURRENT COLLATERAL INHIBITION

Each motoneuron axon branches before it leaves the spinal cord, and one of the branches returns to the region of the cell body (a *recurrent collateral*) and terminates on inhibitory cells called *Renshaw cells*. The Renshaw cells, in turn, end on motoneurons, especially on the one whose recurrent collateral fires them, and its neighbors. There is thus a very short negative-feedback loop that prevents a motoneuron from being fired repeatedly in rapid succession. There are several interesting consequences of this action, but before we discuss them it is necessary to digress briefly on the subject of field effects in neural interaction.

FIELDS OF NEURONS

The diagrams that physiologists and physiological psychologists draw often show neurons with only one or two afferent synapses from specific points ending on their bodies. Simplifications of this sort are essential for clarity, but they misrepresent the facts. Figure 5.10 shows two motoneurons and their dendrites in the spinal cord of a puppy. The dendrites of one cell spread through a large part of the ventral quadrant of the cord, and some even cross to the other side of the midline. They probably spread an equal distance along the axis of the cord also. As a single motor pool contains several hundred cells of this sort and the motor pools for several muscles overlap one another, the resulting tangle of dendrites may be imagined.

The afferent axons also branch repeatedly, each terminating in hundreds or thousands of synapses. A motoneuron receives at least several thousand synaptic contacts, those on the cell body producing a large post-synaptic potential when they fire and those on dendrites producing changes in potential proportional to distance from the cell body. The odds are high that the firing of a single axon entering a motor pool influences to some degree every neuron in the pool.

We could, in theory, work out to what extent

each motoneuron would be depolarized when a particular excitatory axon fired by counting the endings of the axon on each cell, measuring the distance of each along a dendrite, allowing for reduced potentials with distance from the cell body, and so on. But this effort would be about as useful as trying to specify the velocity of individual air molecules in a tornado or individual electrons in a vacuum tube. Taking the measurements is impracticable in the first place, and such information, even if obtained, would be less valuable than a plot of the average effect at various points from some center of disturbance. Such a plot of the average effect of synaptic activity in a motoneuron pool or other collection of cells is called a *field*, analogous to a magnetic, electrical, or gravitational field. The overall field includes both excitation and inhibition; when net excitation momentarily exceeds a certain threshold, neurons will fire.

The input from muscle-spindle afferents to the motoneuron pool probably produces a relatively homogeneous field, one that excites all the motoneurons of the pool about equally. If Renshaw cells were to have smaller fields concentrated in the vicinity of the motoneurons whose recurrent collaterals fire them, it would explain how the motor units of a muscle share the load and why they do not all fire together during normal movement.

To begin with, let us imagine what would happen in a motor pool if no inhibitory feedback were operating and, second, all the motoneurons had approximately the same thresholds and equally strong connections from the spindle afferents. At modest levels of input from stretch receptors none of the neurons would receive enough input to fire, and the muscle would remain relaxed. As stretch increased, a point would be reached at which input to all the motoneurons would pass the threshold; the whole pool would then discharge, causing a violent twitch of the muscle. After the neurons had recovered from refractoriness and the muscle had relaxed again, the spindle receptors would produce suprathreshold input again, and the twitch would be repeated. It would be quite impossible to obtain smooth, graded responses from such a system.

Figure 5.10 A section of the spinal cord of a puppy stained by the Golgi technique to show two motoneurons in the ventral horn. (After Ramón y Cajal, 1952, Figure 130.)

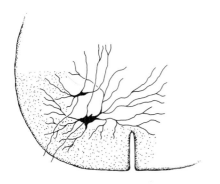

Of course it might be that the second condition would not hold and that some of the motoneurons might have lower thresholds than others, but then the more sensitive ones would fire whenever the muscle was used at all, and the units with the highest thresholds would hardly ever fire. We know that the actual operation is quite different; the units are "rotated" so that each carries the load part of the time. This hypothetical explanation will therefore not serve.

Let us reconsider the effects of local inhibitory fields, centered on recently fired motoneurons and tapering off around them (Figure 5.11). It is clear that, as soon as a motoneuron has fired, all the other neurons within the resulting inhibitory field will have raised thresholds and that the next neuron to fire will be in a remote part of the pool. The firing of that neuron produces another area of raised threshold around itself and so on. The inhibitory effect dies away in 50–100 msec, but during that time the neurons in the middle of the field will not be able to fire, and those on the fringe will need greater input to fire them.

The effect is shown diagrammatically in Figure 5.12. A linear array of motoneurons is shown along the horizontal axis, and the momentary thresholds of each are plotted vertically just after one of them has fired (Figure 5.12a). Any cells that have thresholds below the average input will fire within a short time unless they are prevented by further inhibition; a moment later the picture is therefore as seen in Figure 5.12b. Later, when the peaks of inhibition have died down a little, another motoneuron will fire in the trough between them (Figure 5.12c). In this way the firing will be distributed among the neurons of the pool.

If the intensity of the input is increased, as in Figure 5.12d, two things will happen: Cells closer to the inhibitory fringe will fire, and they will fire earlier during the decay of inhibition. More motoneurons will thus be fired, and they will be fired more frequently, resulting in a nicely graded increase of muscle tone with increased input. In the absence of inhibitory feedback, increasing input would merely increase the rate at which jerky, full-strength

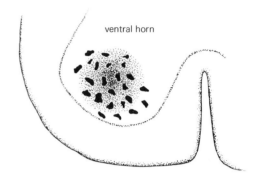

Figure 5.11 A pool of motoneurons in the spinal cord. The depth of shading around the neuron that has just fired indicates the strength of the inhibitory field set up by recurrent-collateral inhibition.

muscle twitches would succeed one another. Recurrent negative feedback seems to be one of the devices the nervous system employs to convert all-or-none into graded effects.

This mechanism has been described in some detail, not because psychologists have a profound interest in the activity of the motor pools, but because it illustrates circuits that may be important at all levels of the nervous system. In fact, it offers another simple example of motor equivalence. A certain input is delivered to the motor pool, and the local feedback *at the level of the pool itself* determines which of the large number of motor units that might possibly fire will in fact do so. Suppose that we must fire about 50 motor units in a particular muscle as part of a movement; it would be an advantage to fire the more rested units, but if the choice had to be made at the higher motor centers they would become hopelessly cluttered with information on which motor units had fired at what times. Fortunately, the choice does not have to be made at that level; the rested units are selected automatically at the level of the motor pools.

Human subjects have, nevertheless, found it possible to acquire voluntary control over individual motor units in some of the small muscles of the hand when the muscle concerned is thoroughly relaxed, though increased tension always recruits unselected units rather than firing the selected units more rapidly (Basmajian, 1963). Basmajian's experiment indicated that some central (possibly motor cortex) neu-

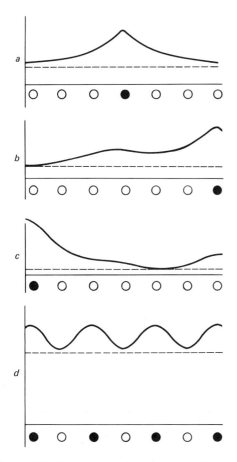

Figure 5.12 The pattern of motoneuron firing according to the hypothesis presented in the text. The abscissas indicate distance along a section through a motor pool, and the circular shapes below represent some of the motoneurons. The solid neurons are those that have just been fired. The ordinates represent the momentary intensities of inhibition along the section (or the intensity of input required to fire the neuron at each point). The average intensity of the excitatory input delivered to all the neurons is indicated by the broken horizontal lines. (a) The middle neuron has just fired. (b) Shortly afterward the neuron at the right end fires, and the one at the extreme left is about to fire. (c) The fifth neuron from the left has the lowest threshold and is about to fire. (d) As excitatory input increases the neurons fire more frequently despite higher levels of inhibition, so that several can fire simultaneously.

rons of the motor system are not homogeneously connected to the motoneurons of a muscle pool as postulated for spindle afferents; they must have at least slightly stronger connections to certain motoneurons than to others. At low firing rates (lower than about 10 per second,

at which frequency the recurrent inhibition from one impulse has dissipated before the next impulse is generated) only the motoneuron receiving the strongest input fires. As input becomes stronger, however, the first neuron is still partly inhibited when the next impulse arrives, and another motoneuron therefore fires instead.

The limited degree of voluntary control over motoneurons revealed by this experiment would be of no value as a means of spreading the load among motor units even if we could train ourselves to use it, because it can be maintained only under conditions of extremely weak contraction, when such sharing is not necessary.

Recurrent-collateral inhibition is another possible analogue of the motor-equivalence phenomenon, in which any one of a number of movements may be used to achieve a certain end like the opening of a door. At one level of nervous-system function, activity merely indicates that the door should be opened with no commitment to method. At lower levels decisions are made on which of the many tactics used in the past is most applicable to the present stimulus situation (pushing a swinging door or turning a knob, using a key, and so on). At still lower levels these instructions are interpreted in terms of proprioceptive (body position) and other sensory input, to determine what movement should be made next (raising the arm, turning the shoulder to the door, and the like), and then, lower still, we find the mechanisms we have been discussing in this chapter. They determine which motor units shall be used at any instant to perform the movements dictated from above.

ELECTROPHYSIOLOGY OF THE SPINAL CORD

In the course of describing the lower levels of motor organization it has already been necessary to mention a few experiments in which the electrical activity of nerves was measured. Further electrophysiological measurements related to spinal reflex activity will be described here, with more attention to the techniques involved.

Spinal reflexes are of varying degrees of

complexity, as we have seen. One rough way to classify them is into *segmental* and *interseg-mental reflexes*. In a segmental reflex the affer-ent nerve arrives at the same segment of the cord from which the motor nerve originates; in an intersegmental reflex several segments of the cord are involved. We can use the conven-ient segregation of the spinal nerves into sen-sory and motor roots to study some of the electrical concomitants of segmental reflexes.

In the simplest experimental arrangement, the influence of peripheral events is eliminated by cutting both dorsal and ventral roots. An electrode (which may consist of a pair of wires insulated from each other but bare at the tips, where they are separated by a distance of 1 mm or less) is placed against each nerve stump. The one on the dorsal stump is used for stimulation, and the one on the ventral stump is connected to an amplifier and oscilloscope for recording the electrical activity in the motor nerve.

In such experiments it is customary to stim-ulate with short pulses of current, the duration being in the order of a millisecond and the intensity anywhere from a few hundredths of a milliampere to several milliamperes, depend-ing upon what percentage of the axons in the nerve are to be fired. Stronger currents fire axons with higher thresholds (usually those with smaller diameters) and, by increased spread, those farther away from the tip of the electrode. The pulses are usually presented at regular intervals, perhaps once every few sec-onds, to allow the nervous system to recover from the previous shock before the next is applied. The voltage picked up by the electrode in the ventral root may vary from a few micro-volts to several millivolts, and it is displayed on a cathode-ray oscilloscope (with a camera for permanent recording), as described in Chapter 4.

The output of the ventral root after a mod-erately strong shock to the dorsal root is shown in Figure 5.13. After about 1 msec there is a large, brief spike, or sharp wave, followed by a series of waves of lower amplitudes, lasting 10–20 msec. The spike indicates a synchronous volley of impulses in many of the motoneuron axons; the waves represent less synchronous,

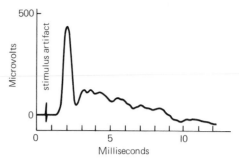

Figure 5.13   The response evoked in a cut ventral root by stimulation of the cut dorsal root.

delayed firing of other motoneurons. As the strength of the shock increases, the initial spike soon reaches maximum amplitude. The later waves do not reach their maximum value until a shock of about twice that current is applied.

It has been found that the time an impulse requires to traverse a synaptic junction is around 0.8 msec; allowing for conduction time through the nerve stumps and the fine terminals of the afferent nerve, the initial spike must therefore reflect direct firing of motoneurons by the incoming sensory fibers. For that reason the connection involved is called the *two-neuron arc*. The later waves could conceivably be caused by other two-neuron arcs whose axons make long detours in the cord, but in fact they are not. The delay in their firing has been shown to be caused by the interposition of more syn-apses in the path. Each synapse contributes a delay of about 0.8 msec, to which is added conduction time through the axon of the inter-neuron. The passage of impulses through different numbers of interneurons before they arrive in the motor pool is responsible for the long duration and lack of synchrony of the later waves. These connections are called *polysyn-aptic*, or *multisynaptic, arcs*.

If the dorsal root is left intact and the stimu-lating electrode is applied to a peripheral nerve from a muscle, a pronounced initial spike and only a small amount of delayed activity are recorded from the ventral root. If, on the other hand, stimulation is applied to a *cutaneous nerve* (from the skin), there is no initial spike from the ventral root but only the asynchronous polysynaptic waves. Further analysis confirms the suspicion that the two-neuron arc is exclusively part of the muscle-spindle feedback circuit (Figure 5.6) described earlier. As we have seen, this mechanism must react as quickly as possible for efficient operation.

During these experiments the ventral root must always be cut to prevent the pickup of *antidromic impulses* (impulses traveling backward along an axon toward the cell body) engendered by the electrical stimulation of peripheral nerves that contain both sensory and motor fibers. It is also necessary to cut the peripheral nerve involved in the experiment before it connects with any muscle, so that the stimulation does not produce twitching and thus fire muscle and joint receptors to confound the afferent signal. In some experiments the muscle is paralyzed by *curare* or some other drug that blocks neuromuscular transmission, as an alternative to cutting the nerve.

The application of a single pulse that simultaneously fires large numbers of axons in a sensory nerve is not a *physiological stimulus*; it is not likely to occur during the normal functioning of the nervous system. The receptors feeding into a spinal segment are never fired simultaneously, and, when some are fired, they usually emit trains of impulses in sequence rather than a single isolated impulse like that produced by a shock to the nerve. Variations in the type of signal delivered through the stimulating electrodes allow us to study slightly more realistic conditions.

If the stimulation of the dorsal root is reduced until single pulses just fail to produce a response in the ventral root and if two identical pulses of that strength are then applied in rapid succession, the second will often cause firing in the ventral root. The shorter the interval between the two stimulations, the bigger the motoneuron response will be (except that when stimulations are less than a millisecond or so apart there is a reduction in firing of the afferent nerve because of refractoriness). When the impulses are spaced more than about 10 msec apart, the facilitating effect of the first volley upon the second is reduced to negligible proportions. This phenomenon is called *temporal summation*, and it occurs because the partial depolarization of many motoneurons

caused by the first volley, though not strong enough to trigger an axonal impulse, persists for a few milliseconds and is able to summate with the depolarization produced by the next input volley and thus to fire the neuron.

Spatial summation, in which a neuron is fired by the combined actions of several groups of simultaneously discharging synaptic inputs, can be demonstrated by splitting the sensory root into two parts and applying to each a small stimulus that either just fails to produce a response in the ventral root or produces only a very small one. Then, when both branches of the nerve are stimulated simultaneously the ventral-root response is much larger than the sum of the separate responses. Many motoneurons have synaptic connections from axons in both branches of the nerve. When either branch is stimulated alone, not enough synaptic knobs are active on any one neuron to depolarize it to the point of triggering an impulse, but, when both branches are stimulated together, many neurons receive input from both and are depolarized beyond the critical point.

It is possible to confirm that many motoneurons receive synapses from both branches of the divided root by stimulating them with maximal shocks. Under these conditions, many neurons fired by one branch will also be fired by the other; when both branches are stimulated simultaneously, the output of the ventral root will be much *less*, instead of more, than the sum of the separate responses, quite the opposite from when threshold shocks are employed. This phenomenon is known as *occlusion*, and it is sometimes used in electrophysiological studies of the central nervous system to determine whether or not two pathways involve a common set of neurons at any point. If they do, maximal stimulation of both pathways simultaneously evokes an output voltage smaller than the sum of the outputs when the two pathways are stimulated one at a time with shocks of the same intensity.

Afterdischarge

When stimulation of the dorsal root is strong enough to excite polysynaptic arcs, its effect on subsequent input naturally lasts longer. Usually the effect of persisting interneuronal activity is to facilitate subsequent input.

If a nerve that gives rise to polysynaptic activity is fired repetitively (by trains of pulses at a high repetition rate), interneuronal activity builds up and maintains itself for several seconds after the stimulation has been turned off. This effect is known as *afterdischarge*. Two theories have been put forward to explain this. One is that long-lasting depolarizing substances accumulate at the interneuronal synapses and continue to produce neural firing for some time, until they diffuse away or are destroyed. The other, suggested by Lorente de Nó (1935a, b), is that impulses circulate in closed loops of neurons (Figure 5.14). Neither of these theories is entirely satisfactory; it is difficult to see why the duration of the afterdischarge should depend upon the duration and intensity of the input if it is caused by reverberation in closed loops. One might predict that, after a burst of forced firing, enough neural fatigue would develop to curtail reverberations rather than to encourage them.

On the other hand, Burns (1958) has shown that an afterdischarge can be stopped dead by a single large shock to the spinal cord, though the same shock applied during the stimulus that produces the afterdischarge has no such effect. It is difficult to see how the shock could influence either the accumulation of a transmitter substance or any other chemical process related to afterdischarge. The effect of the shock can best be explained by assuming that it fires the whole population of cells in that part of the cord, leaving them all refractory for an instant, during which time the reverberation has nowhere to go and is quenched.

Perhaps the answer to the dilemma is that both hypotheses are partly right. The stimulation may produce a chemical or other effect that makes the neurons more sensitive to normal input so that they can participate in reverberatory firing. In support of this interpretation, neural transmission has been found to become more efficient for a short time as a result of being driven for a few seconds at a high rate by electrical stimulation. The phenomenon is called *post-tetanic potentiation*.

Post-tetanic Potentiation

If the nerve from a muscle is stimulated at an intensity that generates small monosynaptic spikes from the ventral root (Figure 5.15), and if the nerve is then subjected to a burst of stimulation for several seconds at as high a frequency as possible without refractory blocking (about 500 pulses per second), the size of the ventral-root response to a single stimulus exactly like those applied before this *tetanizing* burst is much increased for several minutes. It has been shown in further experiments that this potentiation results from increased effectiveness of the synapses traversed by the tetanic volleys; the motoneurons do not become more sensitive to input arriving at other synapses.

The probable explanation for post-tetanic potentiation is that the synaptic knobs release more transmitter substance at each impulse after they have been used at a high rate for some time and then rested for a moment. Possibly neurons have some mechanism that adjusts the availability of transmitter substance to the rate of use. During the tetanic burst this mechanism goes into high gear to keep up with the increased drain, and it continues to run at the higher rate for a short time afterward, thus providing the synaptic knobs with an over-

Figure 5.14   Closed loops of neurons, in which it would be possible for activity to reverberate.

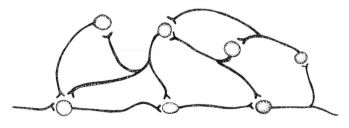

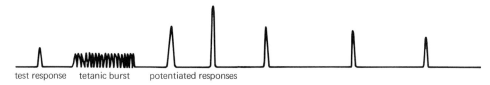

test response   tetanic burst   potentiated responses

Figure 5.15 Ventral-root responses to a standard sensory impulse before (test response) and after (potentiated responses) tetanic firing of the sensory nerve. The potentiation lasts about 1 minute.

abundance of transmitter substance. That it takes several seconds for potentiation to reach a maximum after the end of the tetany lends credence to this theory.

It has alternatively been suggested that the axon becomes hyperpolarized during the tetany and that it is the increased amplitude of the electrical impulse that causes more transmitter substance to be released.

If post-tetanic potentiation takes place in the interneurons involved in reverberatory activity during an afterdischarge, it could account for the fact that a single shock does not suffice to start the afterdischarge. A burst of stimulation is necessary to arouse post-tetanic potentiation.

REFLEX ACTIVITY

Although the principle of the reflex is important to psychologists, specific examples are usually less so. However, several common examples are mentioned here for purposes of illustration, including certain autonomic reflexes that are useful as measures of arousal or emotional states. Spinal or bulbar (medullary) reflexes are seen most clearly in decerebrate animals, for in normal animals they are often masked or modified by "voluntary" responses.

"Magnet" Reflex

If the plantar surface of an animal's foot is touched, the limb will extend to increase the pressure of contact. The function of the reflex in the normal animal is presumably to brace the limb as it makes contact with the ground, so that it can bear the weight of the animal. It works in the opposite direction to that of the previously mentioned withdrawal reflex, which is dominant when the stimulus to the foot is noxious, causing flexion and withdrawal from the source of trouble.

Crossed-Extension Reflex

When the foot is pricked or burned, its limb is withdrawn, and the contralateral limb is at the same time extended. This reflex thus functions to provide support by the uninjured limb when a greater part of the body's weight is shifted onto it. The reflex may also play a part in coordinating limb movements in walking. Its pathway is through connections from the flexor afferent fibers on one side of the body to the extensor motor pools on the other side.

Scratch Reflex

Even a spinal preparation (an animal with the upper part of the spinal cord completely sectioned) will move its most convenient foot to a region of its trunk that is being irritated and will then scratch back and forth with it. This reflex not only involves elaborate tonic adjustments to reach the required posture, but also demonstrates generation of cyclic activity from a steady input, a process that occurs at all levels of the nervous system. We can only speculate about the mechanism that performs the conversion, but oscillation is a well-known consequence of feedback, and there are, as we have seen, several such circuits in the motor system.

An electric bell converts continuous voltage from a battery into the back-and-forth motion of its hammer through a form of feedback. The position of the hammer controls the current flowing through an electromagnet, which in turn determines the position of the hammer. When the hammer has been attracted to the magnet it opens a switch in the electromagnetic circuit. A spring then pulls the hammer away from the magnet, and the switch closes again. The magnet attracts the hammer once more, and once more the switch opens; the cycle is repeated as long as the voltage is maintained.

It is quite likely that a similar mechanism provides the basis for the scratch reflex, and other similar reciprocating movements of an animal. Signals from receptors in the joint, generated when the limb is flexed, fire extensor muscles and inhibit flexors; then, when the limb has extended, the joint receptors stop firing, and the flexors fire again (Figure 5.16). This explanation cannot be the whole story, however, for Sherrington (1906) (who discovered many of these spinal reflexes) found that the scratch reflex persists even when the limb is restrained to prevent proprioceptive feedback. We must therefore assume that other internal connections bypass the peripheral feedback, as shown in Figure 5.17.

In the hypothetical circuit shown in the diagram, input is fed to both antagonist pools, but, owing to slight asymmetry, one fires a little sooner and more strongly than does the other. Subsequently the reciprocal inhibitory connections will prevent the second from firing at all. It is assumed, however, that the transmission in the first path adapts, or becomes fatigued, quite rapidly, thus reducing the inhibition to the unfired pool and allowing it to start firing. The reciprocal inhibition then cuts off the first activity completely, and the second path fires at full strength for a time, giving the first pool time to recover. When the second path is fatigued the transmission switches back to the first path and so on.

Among the movements and activities involving reciprocal feedback connections similar to those for scratching are tail wagging, burrowing, walking, swimming, flying, chewing, breathing, and many others. The feedback pathways for these reflexes probably have several alternative branches also; that is, there is usually a proprioceptive branch of the feedback and other internal pathways that can perform the same functions should the proprioceptive branch fail for any reason.

Breathing

Breathing (the Hering-Breuer reflex) has been investigated in some detail, and the existence of dual control of feedback has been well estab-

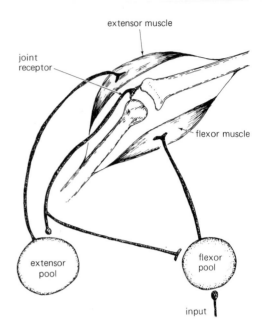

Figure 5.16 A neuromechanical circuit to produce reciprocating movement of a joint. Input fires the flexor muscle until output at the joint receptor is great enough to inhibit the flexor pool and excite the extensor pool. The joint is then extended until the stretch receptor in the joint stops firing, when flexion begins again.

Figure 5.17 A neural circuit producing reciprocating motor behavior. The first pool to fire inhibits the other through connections that adapt (decay in transmission efficiency) fairly quickly. When the inhibition is weakened to the extent that the second pool can start to fire, its fresh inhibitory connections will immediately stop the firing of the first pool. Each pool will thus fire for a short time in turn and will then give way to the other.

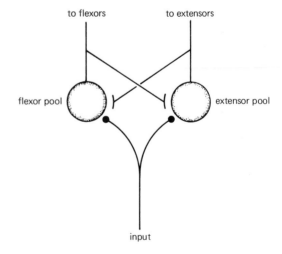

lished in this case (Salmoiraghi & Burns, 1960). The important neurons for this reflex are not in the spinal cord but scattered throughout the reticular formation in the medulla (or bulb) below the floor of the fourth ventricle in the brain. There are two types of cells, those that fire as the animal inhales and those that fire as it exhales. In normal respiration exhaling is a passive process. It is therefore not likely that the participating neurons are part of any "expiration center," if there is such a thing; they are more likely to be responsible for inhibiting inspiratory neurons during the expiratory part of the cycle.

As the lungs expand, stretch receptors are fired and send impulses through the vagus to inhibit the inspiratory neurons, causing the lungs to collapse. At this point the inhibition of the inspiratory neurons ceases, allowing them to fire again. They fire spontaneously at a rate that depends upon the concentration of carbon dioxide in the blood flowing through the capillaries in the medulla. As the concentration increases (up to a point) the neurons fire more vigorously.

If the vagus nerves, which carry the afferents from the stretch receptors in the lungs, are cut, breathing does not stop, but it becomes slower and deeper. Neurons in the respiratory center continue to fire in rhythmic bursts, even if the efferent path to the lungs is cut and the animal is maintained on artificial respiration at a rate different from that of activity in the respiratory center. This independence rules out the possibility that afferents other than those passing through the vagus control the breathing rate after the vagus has been cut.

When the neurons in the center are firing in bursts, free from afferent control, they presumably do so because of reciprocal connections within the center similar to those described for the scratch reflex (Figure 5.17). The afferents through the vagus (which may in any case play only a minor role) can thus be dispensed with (Burns & Salmoiraghi, 1960).

Breathing reflexes combine elements of the autonomic and somatic systems; the sensory input comes from the viscera, and the motor outflow is to the skeletal muscles. There are many other such mixed reflexes, including swallowing, weeping, focusing the eyes, and some components of sexual activity. Some of these reflexes also involve complex sequences and combinations of actions, some of them skeletal and some visceral in origin. In swallowing, for example, the closure of the windpipe has to be very delicately timed in relation to the other movements, and the sequence is apparently under complete control of the central mechanism and not dependent upon proprioceptive feedback at all (see Chapter 6).

Defecation and Micturition

The reflexes of elimination can be elicited in more or less complete form in the spinal animal. That is, they are organized in the spinal cord and not in the brain. They involve adoption of particular postures, contraction of the bladder or abdominal wall, and opening of the appropriate sphincters. Spinal dogs and cats even give a terminal scratch on the ground as part of the pattern.

In the spinal animal the stimulus for micturition is increased pressure in the bladder, which fires pressure-sensitive receptors that in turn fire autonomic motoneurons to contract smooth muscles in the bladder wall, increasing the internal pressure still further. At the same time impulses pass up the spinal pathways to produce the appropriate postural adjustments, and the sphincters are opened. When the bladder is full, a slight stimulus like scratching the skin of the pelvic region is likely to trigger the reflex because of the slight increase in tone it induces in the muscles of the bladder. Human patients with spinal-cord transection are thus able to acquire a useful degree of voluntary control over the reflex.

In the intact animal control of the reflex normally comes from higher centers which receive information from the pressure receptors of the bladder. The central control can facilitate or inhibit the reflex pathways for a wide range of pressures, according to circumstances.

Sexual Reflexes

Many components of sexual behavior are also organized in reflexes at the spinal level. Stimulation of the skin of the thighs or genital region of a spinal male dog will result in erection of the penis and ejaculation of semen. Further examples are given in Chapter 17.

It is clear that most of the activities that we consider to be motivated by primary drives— eating, breathing, copulating, and so on—have components that occur automatically through spinal and bulbar reflex mechanisms. Normally the reflexes can be brought in and out of action by higher-level control. If the higher control is eliminated the reflexes become continuously accessible.

Other Autonomic Reflexes

As we saw in our discussion of the anatomy of the autonomic system, its activity is relatively diffuse, especially that of the sympathetic division. Not only are many responses emitted together, but they are produced by a wide variety of stimuli, somatic as well as visceral. Nevertheless, a number of surprisingly specific reflexes are also to be found.

One that is purely autonomic is the control of heart rate by blood pressure. The receptors are pressure-sensitive cells in the *carotid sinus* (an enlarged region of the main artery to the head). They send afferents through the vagus to a cardiovascular center in the medulla, from where the impulses travel back to the heart, causing it to slow down as the pressure rises. Emotional factors may, however, override or disturb this reflex regulation of blood pressure.

The electrical resistance of the skin, especially that on the palm and other hairless surfaces, varies with the activity of the sweat glands and can be used as a convenient measure of sympathetic activity. Any pleasant, unpleasant, or novel stimulus is reflected in a reduction of resistance known as the *psychogalvanic reflex* (PGR), or *galvanic skin reflex* (GSR). It can readily be conditioned to neutral stimuli, though both conditioned and unconditioned

responses have a tendency to be attenuated by habituation with repeated elicitation. Other motor effects more specific to particular emotional states are blushing, weeping, pilo-erection, salivation (or the inhibition of salivation), and so on. Why one type of emotional arousal should elicit one sort of autonomic activity and another a different sort is puzzling, but apparently a considerable degree of innate organization of the motor system underlies the experiences of embarrassment, grief, joy, fear, and so on.

Spinal Shock

If the spinal cord is cut, all reflexes from the parts of the cord below the cut are profoundly depressed for a time. In lower vertebrates like the fish and the frog, the reflexes return in a few minutes; in man they may not return for several weeks. The reason for the depression is that impulses from the brain are necessary to maintain the excitability of motoneurons and interneurons. Hongo, Kubata, and Shimazu (1963) have shown that during sleep or low arousal the activity of the intrafusal motor system, upon which all reflexes depend, is reduced. These facilitating impulses are eliminated by cutting the cord. It is not clear why recovery occurs, but it probably results from what is known as *denervation hypersensitivity*. Cells that have not fired for some time become hypersensitive and require less input to fire; they can thus work with a lower level of background facilitation.

The complete loss of all reflexes, even the two-neuron stretch reflex, during spinal shock is most striking. Sherrington found that even strong electrical stimulation of a big cutaneous nerve, which would normally produce a most violent withdrawal reflex, had no effect during spinal shock.

It is clear that a stimulus delivered to a perfectly intact reflex connection is not normally adequate to produce a response by itself; it is absolutely dependent upon input from a second source, located in the brain, to start the movement. Here we have what may be regarded as a prototype of motivational activity. In more complex behavior—for example, eating—it is not enough that tasty food be placed before the animal; the animal must also be hungry before it will eat. We may draw a parallel between the facilitating effect of hunger upon the pathways involved in eating and the effects of downstream facilitation necessary to allow spinal-reflex pathways to function.

Summary

The ultimate object of all nervous activity is to produce behavior, which it can do only through the motor systems. Sensory systems have evolved to allow better control of the motor system; they would be useless to an animal lacking a motor system.

Spinal motor mechanisms are more accessible than are most of the central parts of the motor system and have been studied in more detail. For this reason and because they often illustrate principles assumed to operate at higher levels, our study of physiological psychology has begun with them.

The organs that act as intermediaries between the nervous system and the environment are called "effectors." Skeletal muscles are most important for dealing with the external environment; smooth muscles and glands influence primarily the internal environment.

A muscle fiber contracts when it receives an impulse from a motoneuron at its end plate. Contraction results from the interaction of millions of filaments of the two proteins actin and myosin. Each motoneuron innervates a large number of muscle fibers (a motor unit). A moderate-sized muscle contains several hundred motor units. Several muscles usually act on a joint; those producing extension of a limb are called "extensors"; those whose contraction bends the limb are called "flexors." Muscles that have similar effects are called "synergists," and those with opposing effects are called "antagonists."

In addition to the large motoneurons that fire the large extrafusal muscle fibers, there are small motoneurons in each motor pool (about 30 per cent of each nerve) that innervate very small fibers inside structures called "muscle spindles." The sole purpose of these small fibers is to pull a stretch (annulospiral) receptor located in the middle of the spindle.

This link between the motor and sensory systems is part of a feedback circuit that tends to make the position of a muscle dependent on the input flowing from motor centers to the motor pools, and not on the load. Reflex input to a motor pool synapses almost exclusively with the small motoneurons, firing them and causing the intrafusal fibers to contract. This action pulls the stretch receptor, causing it to fire. Its output returns to the spinal cord and fires the large motoneurons.

When the muscle has contracted sufficiently, the muscle spindles (which are embedded in the muscle) become shorter, and the stretch receptors fire less vigorously. Their firing rate cannot, of course, fall below that necessary to hold the muscle in its new position. If the load on the muscle is heavy, more input to the extrafusal fibers is necessary before the muscle spindles are shortened enough; the extra input is derived from the increased firing of the stretch receptors and not from increased input from the reflex mechanism. Many experiments have shown that reflex responses usually operate through the muscle-spindle feedback path.

Sensory feedback, indicating the effects the motor system is having, provides a powerful mechanism for decentralizing decisions on details of behavior; possibly similar feedback (involving much more complex sensory input) at the central levels of motor integration may explain "motor equivalence," Lashley's term for the ability to use any of many alternative responses to achieve a specific goal.

Reciprocal inhibition of muscles by their antagonists is necessary to avoid conflict resulting from the operation of stretch receptors in the passive member of an antagonistic pair of muscles. When flexors are being fired by afferent impulses from their own muscle spindles, the same input pathway inhibits the extensor motoneurons.

Motor units share the load among themselves under all but very light load conditions. This sharing is probably produced by a short negative-feedback path by which a firing motoneuron inhibits itself and the surrounding neurons for a short time. A collateral of the main axon runs back to the vicinity of the cell body and fires Renshaw (inhibitory) cells there. During the time that the motoneuron is prevented from firing again, some other motoneuron must fire if the muscle contraction is to be maintained. And, of course, if the contraction is not immediately maintained, more input to the motor pool is generated by the muscle spindles (which begin to stretch), and more motoneurons are fired.

The electrical activity of the motor root has been measured during stimulation of the sensory root in preparations in which both the dorsal and ventral roots of the spinal nerve have been cut. When single pulses of current are administered to the sensory root, a complex wave form emerges from the motor root. The largest component occurs within 1 msec and is attributed to the two-neuron arc between the muscle-spindle afferents and the motoneurons. Following that peak is a slowly declining series of asynchronous wavelets that continues for 10–20 msec.

Temporal and spatial summation can be demonstrated with this preparation. If two subthreshold input pulses are presented in close succession, temporal summation fires some motoneurons, producing a wave from the ventral root. Spatial summation may be demonstrated by dividing the dorsal root into two branches and simultaneously presenting sub-threshold pulses to both. Motoneurons that receive synapses from axons in both branches then receive inputs above threshold and fire.

Prolonged stimulation of the sensory root evokes an afterdischarge lasting several seconds. In theory this afterdischarge could be caused by reverberation through closed neuronal loops in the cord or by accumulation of some excitatory substance. Experimental evidence can be cited to eliminate each of these possibilities, but it is still possible that both could act together to produce the afterdischarge. A long-lasting aftereffect of intense activity has also been discovered; it is called "post-tetanic potentiation." The size of a response in the ventral root to a stimulus in the dorsal root is magnified for several minutes following stimulation of the dorsal root at a high rate (500 pulses per second) for a period of about a minute. It is believed that this tetany mobilizes extra supplies of transmitter substance at the synaptic terminals and that the extra supply remains for several minutes after the need ceases.

The spinal cord has circuits capable of generating various relatively stereotyped responses (reflexes) in response to particular stimuli. Although the responses are usually simple, the connections that produce them are considerably less so. Reflex responses that involve phasic (cyclical) movements are of particular interest because they obviously cannot be produced by simple connections from a receptor to a motor pool; there must be some intermediate circuit with oscillatory properties. Such circuits could, in theory, employ proprioceptive feedback from the oscillating limb to switch the input from one set of muscles to the antagonists and back at appropriate moments (like the valves in a steam engine or the contact of an electric bell), but in almost all cases that have been investigated it has been found that oscillations can still be elicited in the absence of proprioceptive feedback. A circuit has been suggested as a possible candidate for producing reciprocating motor activities. The neurons involved in the two antagonistic movements receive excitatory input at the same time, but they inhibit each other through paths that adapt (and recover) very quickly. When one group is firing the other is quiescent, at least for a time. Eventually, however, the inhibitory path weakens, and the second group breaks through, immediately inhibiting the first group and monopolizing the firing until its inhibiting power in turn becomes weak. Then the first group takes over again and so on.

Experiments on the phasic motor activity of breathing indicate that cells whose activity cycles are consistent with this theory are present in the medulla. It is probable that in normal breathing only one group of cells—those that fire when the animal inhales—is actually connected to muscles. The second group, which fires during exhalation, merely serves to inhibit inhalation periodically.

All spinal reflexes cease for a time when connections to the brain are severed. This phenomenon is called "spinal shock"; it is quite brief in fish and amphibians, but it may last for several weeks in man. It appears that central facilitation of motor pools is essential for normal motor activity of any sort; not enough excitation is provided by the sensory input alone. The mechanism of recovery from spinal shock is still not understood, but the tendency of neurons to become more sensitive when they receive less than normal input (denervation hypersensitivity) may account for it.

CHAPTER 6

CENTRAL MOTOR MECHANISMS

The motor outflow from the brain to the spinal cord and motor nuclei of the cranial nerves is divided by anatomists into two parts, the *pyramidal system* and the *extrapyramidal system*. The pyramidal pathway takes its name from the symmetrical wedge-shaped bulges it forms on the ventral surface of the medulla, just caudal to the pons. At one time it was believed that all the fibers passing along this route to the spinal cord originated in the motor cortex, a strip of cortex lying on the rostral border of the *Rolandic* (or *central*) *fissure* (Figure 6.1a). It has since been found, however, that, in humans, only about 40 per cent of the axons passing through the medullary pyramids come from cells of the motor cortex, about 20 per cent come from cells of the *somatosensory area* in the *post central gyrus* (Figure 3.4) and the rest come from cells in other parts of the brain.

THE PYRAMIDAL SYSTEM

Not all the efferents from the motor cortex pass through the pyramidal tract; many are apparently extrapyramidal. It is therefore almost impossible to investigate the pyramidal system through physiological experiments on the motor cortex, and most of the data reported here apply to mixed pyramidal and extrapyramidal effects. Altogether there are about a million fibers in each of the bilateral pyramidal tracts in man. Most are very thin and poorly myelinated, but about 3 per cent are large and heavily myelinated. The large fibers are believed to be the axons of giant motor-cortical neurons called *Betz cells*.

Anatomy

The motor cortex is *topographically* organized, as shown in Figures 6.1a, b. These diagrams are based on data gathered from stimulating the motor cortex during brain operations on unanesthetized man, but similar maps have been produced for many other mammals. (Animals below the mammalian level have only rudimentary neocortex and do not have pyramidal motor systems.) The toes and feet are represented at the dorsal end of the motor strip, near and within the longitudinal fissure (Figure 6.1b), the arm and hand account for a large part of the lateral surface, and the relevant areas for the face and tongue are located toward the fissure of Sylvius at the ventral end of the strip.

The axons of many neurons in the motor cortex contribute to the internal capsules, which descend between the thalamus and the basal ganglia (Figure 3.7b) and become the *cerebral peduncles* (Figure 6.1b). The pyramidal fibers become more scattered as they pass through the pons, but they bunch together again when they leave it and become the medullary pyramids. The left and right tracts decussate at the caudal end of the medulla. In man about 80 per cent of the fibers cross over, though great individual differences are reported, including cases in which there is no crossing whatever at this level. The crossed pathway descends in the lateral corticospinal tract of the cord; the uncrossed part descends mainly in the ventral corticospinal tract, though some of its fibers join the crossed fibers from the other pyramidal tract in the ipsilateral corticospinal tract. The lateral corticospinal fibers end on interneurons near the dorsal horn. The ventral fibers apparently end more directly in the motor pools, some on interneurons, some (especially those for the distal muscles) directly on motoneurons. Some of the descending fibers, presumably uncrossed, terminate in ipsilateral motor pools, according to Lawrence and Kuypers (1965).

Penfield (1950) has described a second motor

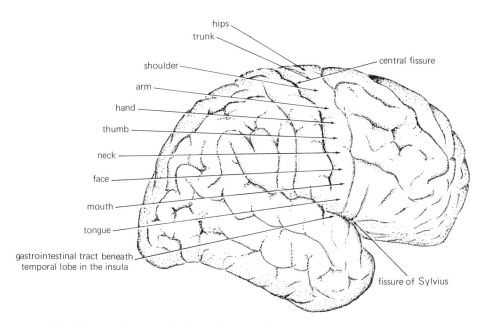

Figure 6.1a Topographical organization of motor cortex.

area in the human cortex, running along the border of the Sylvian fissure. There stimulation produces both ipsilateral (on the same side as the stimulation) and contralateral (on the opposite side) movements of arms and legs, and occasionally the patient reports a strong desire to move a particular limb or inability to move some part. Penfield has also found what he calls the "supplementary motor area" on the medial surface of the longitudinal sulcus, just anterior to the foot area of the precentral motor cortex. Stimulation in this area produces a response in which the contralateral arm is slowly raised, and the head and eyes turn as if looking at the upraised hand.

According to Chang, Ruch, and A. A. Ward (1947), it is possible to cause contraction and relaxation of single muscles in monkeys by finding the appropriate points on the motor cortex and stimulating them with threshold voltage. According to J. W. Ward (1938), however, coordinated movements, rather than individual muscles, are represented cortically in cats. These different results may arise from differences in experimental animals, technique, type of anesthesia, or parameters of stimulation (see Mihailović & Delgado, 1956). Certainly, at average levels of motor-cortex stimulation

in higher mammals, patterns of movement are more commonly produced than are muscle twitches, and, as we shall see, small lesions in the motor cortex do not always paralyze particular muscles but may prevent certain movements. The controversy probably arises from too naïve a view of the function of the motor cortex, however. Some cortical neurons are now known to synapse on motoneurons for particular muscles (see the discussion of Evarts' experiments later in this chapter) but by far the majority feed into subcortical motor nuclei belonging to the extra-pyramidal system. During stimulation with gross electrodes both types of neuron must be fired.

Even before the discovery of the excitable motor cortex in dogs by Fritsch and Hitzig (1870), Jackson (1870) made the astute observation that some epileptic fits start with jerks of single parts of the body, like a finger or the mouth; he predicted that a part of the cortex would be found to control such movements. If a grand mal seizure develops, the movements spread first to adjacent muscles and then progressively through the whole body. Jackson suggested that the first movements are caused by spontaneous electrical discharge of the neurons in part of the motor cortex (caused by

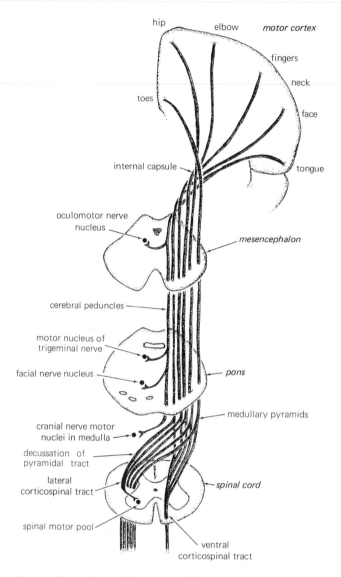

Figure 6.1b Pathway of the pyramidal tract.

irritation from a scar or other disease state), which then spreads progressively through the rest of the motor area.

This suggestion has proved correct, and it is useful in localizing the focus of epileptic attacks originating in the motor cortex. It also furnished information on the organization of the human motor cortex in the days before stimulation of the exposed brain during operations became common. From the way in which the movements spread to affect more and more

of the body it was possible to say which parts of the body are represented by adjacent or overlapping parts of the motor cortex. Nowadays seizures caused by an epileptic focus in the motor cortex are called "jacksonian fits."

Lesions of the Pyramidal Tract

Lesions of the pyramidal tract produce a wide variety of effects, depending upon the species, the extent of the lesion, and the time elapsed after the lesion. In general, the lower the species on the phylogenetic scale, the smaller is the effect of a lesion. In rats and cats there is temporary loss of tone (*flaccid paralysis*) in the affected limbs, but after a few days it is difficult to detect any differences in motor behavior. Monkeys can stand and grasp cage wires after four or five days and can pick up food from the floor after two weeks, but they never recover the ability to move digits independently of one another (Lawrence & Kuypers, 1965). In man lesions produce severe flaccid paralysis for one or two weeks. Then the proximal muscles begin to recover, so that the shoulder or hip joint can be moved. Later more distal muscles improve, but the fingers rarely if ever recover their previous dexterity.

Lesions in the medullary pyramids produce the symptoms mentioned with few complications, but, because the motor cortex contains extrapyramidal neurons besides those that send axons to the pyramidal tract, cortical lesions usually engender "release" phenomena as well. Some of the inhibitory regulation of the motor system is lost, and as the recovery of function proceeds it is accompanied by an abnormal increase in muscle tone and heightened susceptibility to reflex activity. Sometimes a tendon reflex will become so sensitive that one jerk will trigger a second and so on, producing a train of jerks known as *clonus*. The syndrome of rigidity and clonus is called *spasticity*.

A cortical lesion can cause a loss of some movements, although the muscles that participate in them may still be functional and able to participate in other movements. For example, a patient may be able to open and close his fist yet unable to move his fingers separately. It sometimes happens that vigorous movement on the unaffected side will induce weaker movement of the same sort (called *associated movement*) on the paralyzed side. Such movement may be controlled through the uncrossed pathways from the uninjured cortex which are no longer subject to suppression and interference from the previously more powerful crossed connections.

Although the motor cortex is topographically related to the body, the arrangement is by no means a simple one in which all the cells in one part of the cortex are connected to a particular limb or muscle. Glees and Cole (1950) showed, using monkeys, that if the area that moves the thumb upon stimulation is ablated, degenerating fibers can be found in the lateral corticospinal tract as far caudal as the lumbar region, well beyond the point at which all nerves to the thumb have left the cord. In other words there are many neurons that have nothing to do with the thumb occupying the same part of the motor cortex as do those that move the thumb.

Glees and Cole also followed the course of recovery of thumb movements after flaccid paralysis caused by a lesion. They had the monkeys open a small drawer (as in a matchbox) to obtain food. The drawer could be pulled open only by grasping a small projection between the finger and thumb, and it was held closed by a weight-and-pulley arrangement that could be adjusted to the point at which the subject could no longer exert enough pull to open the box. Figure 6.2 shows how grasping strength improved during the first 10 days after the operation in a monkey with a typical lesion of the thumb area of the motor cortex.

After complete recovery the brain was reexposed, and it was then found that stimulating the borders of the lesion now produced thumb movements whereas this had not happened during the first operation. When these areas

Figure 6.2   Recovery of strength in a monkey's thumb after ablation of the thumb area of the motor cortex. (After Glees & Cole, 1950.)

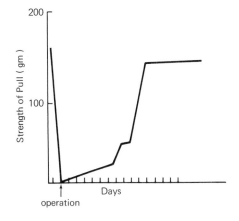

were also ablated, flaccid paralysis returned, and again partial recovery occurred with time. Glees and Cole suggested that such recovery results from regression to less differentiated functioning of the motor cortex. They argued that some of the diffuse connections they had demonstrated anatomically in the experiment described earlier can partly take over the function of the destroyed cells. Although this suggestion is a likely one, it does not explain why recovery takes so long. Nor does it explain how the animal recovers from a large lesion of the motor cortex. Some sprouting and growth of new connections may also be required.

Recording Experiments

Penfield and Jasper (1954) have found, during brain operations on unanesthetized man, that changes in the pattern of electrical activity are recorded from the motor cortex when patients make voluntary movements. The wave form of the resting activity is slower and larger than that during movement. This change is analogous to the so-called arousal, or activation, pattern of other parts of the cortex recorded when the subject is paying attention to a stimulus or working on a problem (see Chapter 14). The change in potential apparently accompanies increased differentiation of neural firing.

The results of an experiment by Jasper, Ricci, and Doane (1960) lent further support to this belief. Microelectrodes were used to record the activity of single neurons in the cortices of monkeys during avoidance conditioning. It was found that, after conditioning had been established, some of the neurons in the motor cortex fired more rapidly during application of the conditioned stimulus (CS), whereas others were inhibited. It should be noted that the changes began several seconds before any overt movements were made, as if the activity constituted the preparation, or intention, to move, rather than an immediate trigger for movement (Figure 6.3).

Evarts (1966) has also measured the time relationships of the firing of motor-cortex neurons during an instrumental response. He confined his measurements to pyramidal-tract

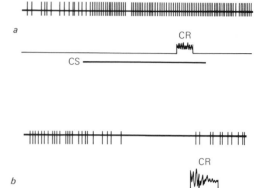

Figure 6.3 Unit activity of motor-cortex cells during avoidance conditioning. The upper line shows cell discharges, the middle line motor responses and the lower line the conditioned stimulus (a flashing light). (a) A cortical cell whose firing rate increases during the CS. (b) A cortical cell that is inhibited during the CS. (After Jasper, Ricci & Doane, 1958.)

neurons, which were identified by their antidromic responses to stimulation of the medullary pyramids. His experiment also differed from that of Jasper and his colleagues in that he measured reaction time and the reinforcement was fruit juice rather than shock. Monkeys were trained to release a telegraph key as quickly as they could after a light was turned on. Responses within 350 msec were rewarded.

Some large pyramidal-tract neurons fired about 120 msec after the light came on, resulting in muscle activity 50–100 msec later. A quite close temporal relationship was observed between the firing of most pyramidal-tract neurons and the opening of the key. Evarts pointed out a paradoxical feature of his data: There were no latencies of less than 100 msec between the appearance of the light and the first spike from pyramidal-tract neurons, although latencies as short as 30 msec are common when the response of pyramidal-tract neurons to flash is measured in anesthetized monkeys.

In a later experiment, using the same technique for isolating pyramidal-tract neurons, Evarts (1968) showed that most of them fired at a rate related to the force to be exerted by their associated muscle. Monkeys were trained to move a lever back and forth rhythmically between two stops. The interval between stop contacts had to be within the range 400–700 msec for the monkey to be rewarded with a few drops of fruit juice. The lever could be loaded with different weights, so that the monkey had to exert force during either wrist flexion or extension (Figure 6.4).

The activity of the pyramidal-tract neurons most closely associated with wrist movements

was not a pure function of the force to be exerted against the lever; the rate of change in the force also had an effect. During steady application of force, the neurons fired more rapidly, the stronger the force, but when the force was changing, the relationship became more complex. There was a sudden extra burst of firing just before an increase in motion of the wrist and a brief reduction just before any decrease in motion.

Figure 6.4 The apparatus used by Evarts. In order to obtain fruit juice, the monkey must move the vertical rod back and forth at a certain rate. The force to be exerted is determined by the weight-and-pulley arrangement. The direction of the force depends upon which pulley is used. (From Evarts, 1968.)

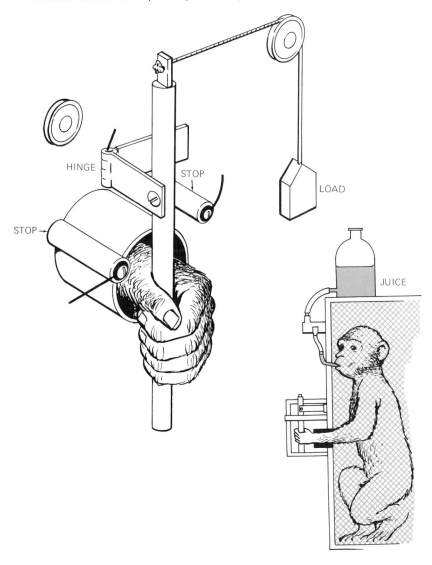

This finding is consistent with the idea that the fast-conducting pyramidal-tract neurons provide direct early input to initiate muscle contraction or relaxation and that a slower system, working through the muscle-spindle feedback mechanism, is partly responsible for firing motoneurons, as soon as the load levels off.

As Evarts has pointed out, however, there are many possible explanations of the data. One serious problem is that it is never possible to say exactly which muscle the specific neuron under investigation is most directly connected with.

THE EXTRAPYRAMIDAL SYSTEM

Anatomy

The division of the motor system into pyramidal and extrapyramidal systems is confusing and unfortunate. It was probably engendered by a historical accident arising from the early assumption that the pyramidal system was *the* motor system. Other parts of the brain subsequently found to have motor functions were therefore lumped together as extrapyramidal. It is difficult to define a clear functional distinction between the two systems, and, except for the short part of the pathway through the medulla, the pyramidal and extrapyramidal systems are not anatomically separate either.

The main structures in the extrapyramidal motor system are shown in Figure 6.5. They include the *cingulate* and motor cortices, the basal ganglia (globus pallidus, putamen, caudate nucleus, and claustrum), parts of the thalamus (*nucleus ventralis anterior* and the *intralaminar nuclei*), the *subthalamic nuclei*, the cerebellum, *red nuclei*, the *substantia nigra*, and various components of the reticular formation. Even the cortical area just posterior to the motor cortex (which is primarily concerned with sensory input from the body) is involved in motor functioning. Lende (1963) has demonstrated complete overlap of motor and somatosensory cortex in the most primitive mammals, and even in primates, as mentioned earlier, many

motor-system neurons are to be found scattered among sensory cells. From the point of view of the psychology student, entirely too much is known about the anatomical connections between these nuclei and structures, but the elaborate diagrams still have not been translated into satisfactory models to explain the parts these elements play in controlling movements.

Simplifying the findings of Nauta (1964) and Nauta & Mehler (1966), we can state generally that the caudate and putamen receive connections from all parts of the cortex and feed their output to the globus pallidus. This structure feeds into the subthalamic and other brainstem nuclei in which there are apparently innate connections capable of producing basic motor patterns used by the animal, but it also has strong connections with the nuclei of the thalamus (*ventralis lateralis* and ventralis anterior) that project to the motor cortex and the premotor area just anterior to it. There the impulses are presumably mixed with sensory input from the dentate nucleus of the cerebellum.

In higher mammals there is also an interesting closed loop from the globus pallidus to the *centre median,* one of the nonspecific "arousal-system" nuclei of the thalamus (Figure 10.2), and from there to the putamen and back to the globus pallidus. It seems that the caudate-putamen complex, which was at the highest motor level in animals with no motor cortex, has tapped the large fund of sensory information available in the mammalian cortex and also feeds some of its output through the globus pallidus and thalamus to the motor cortex, from where it may be delivered quickly and directly to the spinal motor centers. In primates the extrapyramidal motor system may provide a very important component of the input to the pyramidal system, though the major efferent path originates in the lower brainstem and descends into the extrapyramidal tract of the cord (Figure 6.5). The striatum (the complex of caudate, putamen, and globus pallidus) may thus still be the primary initiator of motor activity, even in mammals. The cortical connections do not dominate the system, but perhaps they add to its flexibility and learning capacity.

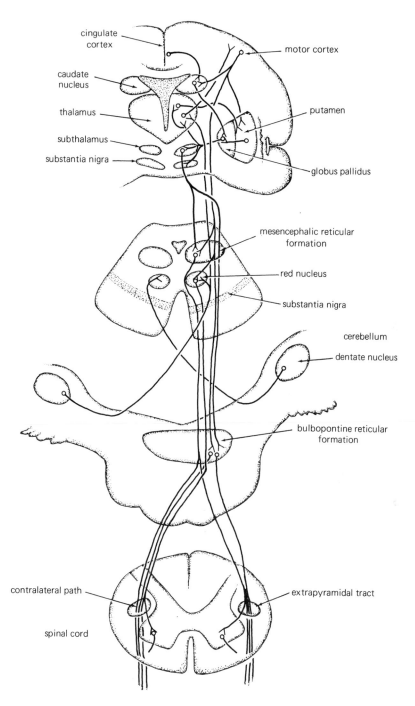

Figure 6.5 The extrapyramidal system. The sections are not all to the same scale.

Stimulation Experiments

Several experiments have shown that electrical stimulation of many parts of the extrapyramidal system at voltages too low to produce movement can modify the excitability of the motor system globally. Two methods of measuring the excitability of the motor system have been employed. One is to elicit tendon reflexes (knee jerks, for example) at regular intervals and to record their amplitudes with and without the extrapyramidal stimulation; the other is to stimulate the motor cortex with pulses every few seconds to evoke movements and, as before, to measure the effect of additional extrapyramidal stimulation on the amplitude of the movements.

Stimulation of the cingulate cortex, parts of the motor cortex, the caudate nucleus, the cerebellum, or the bulbar part of the reticular system reduces or eliminates the movements ordinarily elicited by either of these two techniques in the lightly anesthetized animal. They are therefore called the "inhibitory," or "suppressor," parts of the extrapyramidal system. Stimulation of the *vestibular nucleus*, the hypothalamus, the mesencephalic part of the reticular system, or part of the cerebellum increases the amplitude of movement in the same preparation.

Stimulation of the subthalamic nuclei, also in the lightly anesthetized animal, causes walking movements (Waller, 1940). These movements can be suppressed by concurrent stimulation in the medial thalamus (R. G. Grossman, 1958). Stimulation of the caudate nucleus at higher voltages produces such phasic movements as pawing. It can also cause turning of the head and trunk away from the stimulated side. Stimulation of the cerebellum in unanesthetized cats can produce various movements, usually in three phases: an immediate effect, a rebound at cessation of the stimulation, and a sequence of slow movements in various parts of the body over a period of two or three minutes (S. L. Clark, 1939). One report of cerebellar stimulation in man described similar results. At one point on the cerebellar cortex, stimulation yielded simultaneous flexion of both knees; afterward the knees flexed again twice without the application of further stimulation.

All sorts of postural movements, like rolling over, body flexions, and so on, have been reported as resulting from stimulation of different points in the reticular formation in unanesthetized animals (Sprague & Chambers, 1954). The results indicated that light anesthesia had changed the effect of the stimulation from the normal complex mixture of specific movements and changes of muscle tone to a simpler inhibition or facilitation of all movements. Probably there are specific and nonspecific systems throughout most of the motor system, and anesthesia has a greater effect on the specific parts than on the parts controlling general excitability level. Or the anesthetic may have a greater effect on excitatory than on inhibitory circuits.

Stimulation of inhibitory points in the anesthetized animal produces a generalized loss of tone, as we have seen, but there are a few points at which stimulation stops movements in unanesthetized animals without any loss of tone. Hunter and Jasper (1949) found that they could stop walking or running (even to the extent of causing a cat chasing a mouse to "freeze") by stimulating the intralaminar nuclei of the thalamus (nuclei embedded in the internal medullary laminae—see Figure 3.8) with a low voltage. There is a close similarity between this *arrest reaction*, produced by stimulation, and the freezing of an animal in response to surprising or frightening stimuli, which leads us to suppose that the electrical stimulation is tapping an innate protective mechanism.

Guiot, Hertzog, Rondot, and Molina (1961) produced arrest of speech in human patients by exploratory stimulation of the thalamus during surgical treatment of Parkinson's disease. Sometimes the rate of speaking increased steadily during the stimulation, then finally stopped. As far as could be ascertained, this effect was obtained from the reticular nucleus of the thalamus, a net-like structure that encloses most of the thalamus and forms a part of the same nonspecific system as the intralaminar nuclei.

Lesion Experiments

Lesions of the extrapyramidal system produce various effects, some of which are very puzzling. In the inhibitory parts of the system, they are likely to intensify the spasticity produced by cortical lesions (that is, the limbs become stiffer and more difficult to control). Decerebrate rigidity following section of the brainstem at the level of the colliculi is an extreme example of the loss of central inhibitory control. The stretch-reflex mechanism is highly facilitated by excitatory brainstem nuclei, like the vestibular nuclei, which are below the lesion, and receives no counteracting inhibition.

Lesions of the vestibular nuclei reduce the tonic stiffness of the spastic, but the affected limbs still respond excessively to stimulation of reflexes. Such responsiveness can be reduced by lesions of the mesencephalic reticular formation. Lesions of the cerebellum produce *ataxia* (failure of coordination), disequilibrium, and tremor (the so-called *intentional tremor*, which becomes worse during voluntary movement).

Another condition that has been attributed to dysfunction of the extrapyramidal system is *Parkinson's disease*, which is characterized by postural rigidity and tremors (about five per second) that become worse when the patient is *not* making voluntary movements. This disease results from lesions in the globus pallidus or substantia nigra, and the symptoms can often be relieved, surprisingly, by making further lesions, either in the globus pallidus or in the nearby internal capsule, though surgical treatment is less often necessary since the discovery of satisfactory drug therapy.

Involuntary movements, such as *chorea* (jerks and tics), *athetosis* (writhing), and *hemiballismus* (flailing of arms and legs) have been attributed to extrapyramidal lesions. Degeneration of many parts of the system have been found to be associated with these motor abnormalities.

Lesions of the postcentral gyrus (somatosensory cortex) produce temporary loss of strength, as well as clumsiness. Monkeys with such lesions maintain bizarre postures for long periods, provided they cannot see the affected limbs (Cole & Glees, 1954). This effect is quite different from that of interrupting the sensory input at the spinal level. Lashley (1917a) mentioned a patient with a lesion of the proprioceptive path in the cord, who was not able to maintain a posture for more than a few seconds when blindfolded yet was under the impression that he was holding it for much longer.

IMPLICATIONS FOR BEHAVIOR

So far we have discussed mainly the physiology and neurology of the central motor system, and it is rather discouraging to find that it has so little relevance to the major psychological problems in this area.

In J. B. Watson's time (the early 1920s) there was some interest in the motor system among behaviorists because of the motor theory of thought. But their conception of the motor system was based on a much-simplified picture of the pyramidal system. Responses were believed to be organized in the motor cortex and controlled by conditioned-reflex connections to that area from the sensory areas of the cortex. Later behaviorists, perhaps recognizing the disparities between their theories and actual physiological mechanisms, tended to denigrate physiological explanations, even though, as Hebb (1951) pointed out, they continued to use out-of-date physiological ideas.

In any case the subtler problems of motor behavior have never been taken seriously by the neo-Pavlovian school. Hull and his followers have been satisfied to call a complex sequence of movements a response (R) and to leave it at that, just as they have been content to call a complex and varying sensory flux a stimulus (S). Physiological psychologists cannot afford to leave such gaps in their understanding as those obscuring the relations between the outside world and the processes underlying behavior. If we are to understand learning and motivation, it is essential to know how the final output of the system is regulated and what kind of signals the system is designed to accept. These problems, then, are those that the motor system poses for the psychologist.

Lashley, as usual, was a pioneer in this field.

Some of his earliest psychological research was devoted to testing the Pavlovian theory that, during conditioning, connections are established between the motor and sensory areas of the cortex through the intervening association cortex (Lashley & Franz, 1917). Having found no disturbance of learned responses consequent to cuts and other lesions around and through the motor cortex in rats, he was forced to abandon the theory in its original form. The "engram" (or neural substrate) of learning was not to be found in the cortex according to Lashley.

Later, in a more theoretical vein, Lashley (1951) made one of the few suggestions ever offered on how a response might be built up from its individual movements. He first rejected the idea that each movement produces a feedback signal that elicits the next movement as a conditioned reflex (a process now sometimes called *Markov chaining*, in which each movement depends only upon the immediately antecedent condition of the organism). One argument against this idea is that in some responses (playing a fast passage of music, for example) there is not enough time for feedback from one movement to reach the brain before the next movement occurs. Another serious difficulty is that in many responses the same movement is made more than once and is followed in each case by a different movement; the problem of how two different movements can become conditioned to an identical feedback signal then arises. Of course, there are several ways to avoid this difficulty, but the original simple theory does not survive the necessary additions and changes.

Lashley suggested that each response involved two distinct processes, one consisting of neural activity continuing for the duration of the response and facilitating all its component movements, the other being a series of neural activities organized by internal connections to regulate the timing and sequence of the individual movements. One neural activity preselects and facilitates the different movements that are going to be employed in the response; the other "scans" these preselected movements and triggers them at the right times.

It is difficult to think of an alternative to the broad outline of this theory. Many examples can be cited—from such innate patterns as swallowing to the highest forms of learned response like uttering grammatical sentences—to fit the general scheme. Certainly we have the impression from introspection that some process of "mental" organization occurs before the movements of a response begin, and the preparations are by no means confined to the first movement of the contemplated response. (To type the word "contemplated," we do not have the pure idea of pressing the "c" key and then waiting to see what movement will next appear, as the Markov-chaining theory would predict. Somewhere in the nervous system there is an activity corresponding to the whole word and beyond that, in all probability, a still higher order of activity corresponding to the meaning that is to be conveyed by the sentence in which the word is to appear.)

It is quite another matter, however, to provide adequate experimental evidence, as opposed to anecdotes, to support or illuminate this theory of motor function. No systematic research program has yet been devoted to the problem, and most of the experiments related to it have been conducted with different problems in mind.

In a series of experiments, mostly performed with salamanders, P. Weiss (1926, 1952) uncovered some interesting facts about the way walking movements develop. The central nervous systems of amphibia are able to regenerate themselves throughout the life of the animal (as those of warm-blooded animals are not), so that if an extra muscle or limb is grafted onto the body of such an animal it will eventually be innervated by the nerves present in the region. This phenomenon makes possible a number of interesting experiments.

The normal sequence of leg-muscle contractions in walking can be simplified as shown in Figure 6.6. Let us say that the flexor and *adductor* (muscle drawing the limb to the body) are contracted initially. Then, while the flexor is still contracted, the adductor relaxes, and the *abductor* (antagonist of the adductor) contracts to bring the limb forward. Next, the flexor

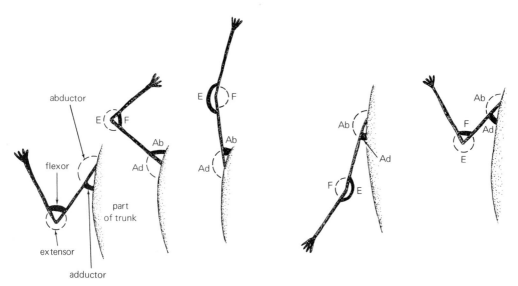

Figure 6.6 The sequence of muscle contractions during forward locomotion of an amphibian. Contracting muscles are shown by solid lines, relaxed muscles are dotted. (After Weiss, 1952).

relaxes, and the extensor contracts, bringing the limb to its extreme forward position. The weight of the body is then transferred to the foot, and, with the limb still extended, the adductor brings it back to the side in a wide sweeping movement that propels the body forward. Finally, the foot lifts, and the joint flexes to complete the cycle. The cycle, which continues indefinitely, can be summarized as flexor-abductor-extensor-adductor, or FBED. The movements of each leg are coordinated with those of the others, so that, when the left leg is at the F stage of the cycle, the right leg is at the E stage.

Weiss wanted to know, first, whether the sequence of movements was learned through strengthening or selection of the connections that were reinforced by successful locomotion. He grafted an extra right leg onto the body of the salamander just behind the normal left leg. Because the grafted leg was the mirror image of the normal leg, it had to point backward in its new position, as shown in Figure 6.7. When the appropriate nerves had established connections to the new limb, he found that the two adjacent limbs always performed identical movements, although the movements of the supernumerary limb then impeded locomotion. The animal never learned to reorganize

the sequence of movements in the extra limb; it therefore seems reasonable to conclude that the connections are innately determined in some way.

Another similar experiment yielded even more striking proof that, in the salamander, walking movements are not learned. When the budding forelegs of the developing animal were removed and grafted onto the opposite sides of the body, both forelegs opposed the activities of the hind legs in locomotion, and the animal

Figure 6.7 Supernumerary right forelimb grafted behind normal left forelimb of salamander. (After Weiss, 1952.)

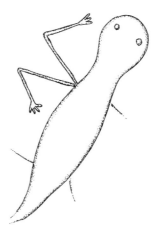

never succeeded in walking properly. If the connections had been selected on the basis of their value to the animal as it began to move about, we would expect a different sequence of movements to be adopted by the reversed legs to allow them to cooperate with the hind legs.

As Weiss pointed out, however, his experiments also cast doubt on any theory of rigid innate determination of nervous connections in the spinal cord. If the central connections of the motoneurons that grew to the grafted limbs had been determined once and for all by the genes in the egg, the limbs would have made random movements or movements corresponding to those of the trunk muscles that the neurons were originally to innervate. Instead each muscle behaved in all its movements as it would in its normal location. Weiss called this phenomenon the *myotypical response*. Although he was reluctant to explain it in terms of connections, the most likely explanation seems to be that suggested by Sperry (1951): When a motoneuron grows toward a muscle and makes functional contact with it, some substance is transferred from the muscle to the neuron so that the dendritic zone of the latter can attract certain interneurons in the cord and repel the rest. All motoneurons to extensor muscles from a part of the cord in the region controlling the forelegs will thus attract the same central connections and become part of the same motor pool. (Being part of the same pool does not imply spatial contiguity: it means merely that all the neurons have similar connections.)

These experiments do not tell us much about the central organization that generates the sequence FBED when the animal walks, but they do at least tell us that such an organization exists and that very likely chemical mechanisms operate during growth to ensure that its output is applied to the correct motoneurons.

In mammals, although the peripheral nervous system is capable of regeneration—so that nerves can be transferred to different muscles and can establish connections with them—the muscles thus innervated do not continue to act typically (as they would in the myotypical response); instead they behave as would the muscles to which the nerves were originally connected. The central nervous connections of the mammalian spinal cord are thus presumably not plastic and, once formed, they cannot be modified. Sperry has performed numerous grafting experiments on rats, cats, monkeys, and other animals and has found that, if the nerves to the ankle muscles of a rat, for example, are crossed, the unfortunate animal will continue to lift its foot when it should lower it and vice versa for the rest of its days.

Anokhin (1947) performed similar nerve-crossing operations in cats and found considerable recovery of normal functioning. If the upper part of the spinal cord was cut, however, any reflexes involving crossed nerves were reversed, showing that the motor-pool connections had not changed. Monkeys also eventually learn to modify their movements to compensate for crossed nerves, but, when a reflexive movement is evoked or the monkey is surprised into making a sudden movement, behavior is still the reverse of that intended. Similarly, people with damaged peripheral nerves that have grown, either naturally or with surgical help, into muscles different from those that they originally innervated can learn to avoid making inappropriate movements most of the time, but the learning is at the conscious level and is likely to break down under stress.

In amphibia the central nervous systems thus remain plastic throughout life and will reorganize themselves according to innate patterns. In higher mammals, on the other hand, a certain amount of plasticity is present only at the higher levels of the nervous system, in the form of learning. Intermediate animals cannot relearn, nor will their nervous systems undergo the required changes to correct for peripheral disturbances at maturity. Sperry has suggested that during embryonic development warm-blooded animals are similar to amphibians and that the specificity of the initial neural connections depends upon a chemical factor. The connections of a spinal motoneuron presumably depend upon some substance that it absorbs from the muscle it innervates. Once made, however, these connections are fixed for life. As we shall see later, a similar phenomenon has been observed in the sensory systems.

One bit of information from the Weiss studies has contributed directly to our understanding of the mechanism responsible for the firing sequence FBED, but we are not at all certain that it is applicable to animals higher in the phylogenetic scale than the salamander. In one experiment Weiss showed that the sequence of movement was not changed by radical destruction of the sensory nerves to the limbs. This finding implies that the timing of movements does not depend upon feedback from the movements themselves and that, though feedback may play a part in the intact animal, there is nevertheless a neuronal system capable of producing the required sequence without outside support.

This system is reminiscent of the mechanism already described for the control of breathing (see Chapter 5). In the latter a *pneumotaxic* (autonomous respiratory) *center* apparently provides the intermittent excitation required by the inspiratory neurons, even after the feedback from the peripheral stretch receptors has been cut off. The mechanism postulated to account for this process was a recurring adaptation and recovery of reciprocal inhibitory connections, leading to periodic transfer of activity from one group of neurons to another and back again. More complex inhibitory connections could possibly be postulated to explain the switching of activity through a series of motor pools to provide walking or, for example, swallowing movements.

Doty and Bosma (1956) have performed several experiments on the swallowing reflex that have contributed in important ways to our knowledge of the motor system. If a sensory nerve (*superior laryngeal nerve*) from the tongue of a dog is stimulated, reflexive swallowing occurs. A steady input of 30 impulses per second to the nerve will produce repeated swallowing at a rate of about 20 swallows per minute, which is close to the maximum possible rate. Higher or lower frequencies of stimulation have less effect, and above about 100 per second swallowing ceases entirely. If, however, the input is broken up into irregular bursts, the maximum swallowing rate can be obtained with 20–30 impulses per second, whatever their temporal pattern within wide limits. To quote from Doty's summary (1951, p. 157): "Exploratory analysis using continuous stimulation by variously grouped pulses showed the optimal response to be surprisingly independent of temporal patterning; as though each pulse were counted by the CNS irrespective of when (within hundreds of milliseconds) it was delivered." In this instance the motor-control mechanism integrates sensory input from the lingual nerve, which acts as the primary activator or drive of the controlling circuit, whereas in the breathing "center" the concentration of carbon dioxide in the blood provides the drive stimulus. Obviously, it would be equally possible for similar response-generating mechanisms to be activated instead by central, nonsensory signals, as in voluntary control of swallowing or walking.

The swallowing reflex is interesting from other points of view. It involves a complex sequence of movements in which at least 10 muscles of the tongue and pharyngeal region work together with perfect timing to transfer the contents of the mouth to the esophagus, without losing any of them into the respiratory system. Doty and Bosma studied this reflex, recording the electrical activity of many mouth and throat muscles during swallowing. In this way they were able to examine the timing of one muscle's firing relative to that of the others. This timing proved to be extremely stable under a wide variety of such conditions as anesthesia and different eliciting stimuli (electrical stimulation of the laryngeal nerve, squirting water into the mouth, swabbing the back of the tongue, and so on). Even when some muscles were cut out, prevented from moving, or desensitized with a local anesthetic, the remaining muscles continued to fire in the normal order. The only differences noted appeared under general anesthesia; then the reflex was more difficult to elicit, and during the response each muscle contracted for a shorter time and more weakly than usual. The duration of the whole swallow was shortened, but the order and relative timing of the muscles remained the same. This finding suggests that for swallowing too there is a center that is self-sufficient once it has been raised above its excitation threshold by a certain intensity of input. Whether or not the various muscles that the center controls fire has no influence on the progress of the firing within the center.

It should be clearly understood that the term "center" in this context is used simply for convenience; it does not imply a specialized concentration of neurons at one spot in the nervous system. In general, the neurons for a particular function are spread through a number of nuclei or (as are many brainstem "centers") scattered throughout the reticular formation.

Stimulation of the upper part of the brainstem, the diencephalon and septal area, has been most fruitful in evoking complex patterns of movement. This work was started by W. R. Hess (1957), who received the Nobel prize for his contributions. Hess placed electrodes in the thalamic and hypothalamic regions of cats and studied the animals' reactions to stimulation for several days after they had recovered from the operation. Some of the points stimulated gave rise to states of general excitement, others to quieting. The excitement was accompanied by dilation of the pupils, increased blood pressure, increased depth and frequency of respiration, (or panting), and increased muscle tone. Opposite effects were obtained from stimulation at some other points: The cat sometimes collapsed in a heap on the ground with complete loss of muscle tone; its blood pressure fell, as did its heart rate; and the rate and depth of respiration were reduced. Sometimes there was no loss of tone, but the cat would find a suitable place to sleep and after the usual preliminaries would settle itself in the characteristic posture and go to sleep.

Stimulation of some parts of the hypothalamus gave rise to salivation, sometimes accompanied by panting, in which case the cat would usually adopt the sitting, open-mouthed posture of the overheated animal. Stimulation of other points produced salivation accompanied either by chewing and licking or sometimes by aggressive behavior. Sneezing, retching, and vomiting were also obtained by stimulating various points in the septal area and hypothalamus. These responses represent, of course, very complex sequences of muscle action, but of the same general type as in the swallowing reflex. Defecation and micturition also occurred in complete form (including the preliminary search for a suitable place and the terminal scratching on the ground) after stimulation of the septal area or anterior hypothalamus.

Behavioral effects related to feeding were also obtained by stimulation in these regions. The cat would sniff along the ground or in the air and could be made to gulp food even though it had been sated before stimulation. If there was no food around, the cat would gnaw at and swallow inedible objects. As mentioned earlier, stimulation of the subthalamus leads to restless walking, and rhythmic leg movements can be obtained from this region even in the anesthetized animal.

In a somewhat similar series of experiments performed more recently upon chickens Holst and Saint Paul (1963) obtained similar results. A chicken with electrodes in the brainstem can be stimulated not only to make a number of isolated movements and sounds but also to perform complete characteristic actions. Eating may be elicited in sated hens, as in other animals, or hens can be made to spit out the contents of their mouths with gestures of disgust. Other points of stimulation cause them to sit or incubate eggs. A hen or cock may also attack the nearest object. Different types of attack are obtained, depending upon the point of stimulation: either the pecking and feather pulling that establishes rank in the farmyard or the spur fighting with which the cock drives away predators or rivals (or provides illegal entertainment). Interesting stereotyped patterns of behavior have also been demonstrated during brainstem stimulation in monkeys by Delgado (1965).

These experiments raise the problem of the relationship between response and motivation, or drive. Some of the stimulations, as we have noted, cause straightforward movements, which do not vary appreciably from one stimulation to the next, nor do they depend upon the environment to any significant extent. On the other hand, responses like pecking at food or an enemy are goal-directed and are obviously modified by the presence and position of a suitable goal. In such cases and especially if the response contains learned elements, the stimulation is usually considered to be arousing a drive, rather than to be evoking a response.

Careful analysis of the examples, however, seems to show that there is no clear-cut criterion to differentiate responses to stimulation of the motor system and those to stimulation of the drive mechanism. Even the simplest responses like walking and breathing are influenced to some extent by feedback from proprioceptors in the joints and muscles. Greater participation of feedback, including signals from distance receptors like those in the eye, makes it easier for us to view a particular response as motivated, but in principle the internal mechanisms need not differ much from those involved in the simpler responses.

More will be said about the physiology of drives in a later chapter, but for the present it is worth noting that in some instances there is a strong functional resemblance between a drive state, which predisposes an animal to a certain course of action, and the first component of Lashley's hypothetical response mechanism, which "sets" the movements that will be released in sequence by the lower-order scanning system.

It is true that often a drive represents an even higher level of the motor hierarchy than Lashley attributed to his "priming" mechanism, but there are examples, perhaps intermediate between the more commonly recognized drives and simple motor responses (breathing and excretory responses, for example), in which it seems redundant to postulate a separate level of motor control between the drive state and the sequence of actions that it sets in motion. In these instances drive state and overall facilitation of the response are the same thing neurally.

One further aspect of the response attracted Lashley's attention and should be mentioned here, although little related experimental work can be reported: timing. Timing is important in initiating the whole response and also in determining the rate at which the component movements occur once the response has started.

In describing the experiment of Jasper, Ricci, and Doane (1960) earlier in this chapter, we noted that changes in the activity of the motor cortex were not correlated exactly with the movements but started several seconds before any activity could be detected in the muscles. This finding seems to be further evidence that there is a preliminary setting of the motor system before a response and that it is independent of the mechanism that actually initiates the response. Some other mechanism, closely related to the scanning system, is responsible for translating this setting into overt action. If this all-important trigger impulse is not forthcoming, the response never begins. Something of the same sort can be inferred from watching the intentional movements, or vicarious trial-and-error behavior, of an animal about to jump or to do something that it is not very sure about.

In voluntary responses (perhaps "optional responses" would be a better term), triggering must be controlled by a complex network of excitation and inhibition. It is very difficult to design experiments that throw unambiguous light on this process, but it seems likely that rapid (usually one-trial) learning not to make a response that has been punished by shock (passive avoidance) involves learned inhibition rather than loss of the response tendency. The preparation for the response occurs as before in the nervous system, but the triggering spark is never allowed to reach the motor system, and the response tendency eventually dies away.

A recent discovery that may eventually lead to better understanding of the mechanism of response initiation has been made by Walter, Cooper, Aldridge, McCallum, and Winter (1964). They discovered that a stimulus, to which a response must be made after a short interval, generates a sustained negative potential which can be recorded through the scalp with suitable nonpolarizing electrodes and DC amplifiers. This potential lasts until the response has been made (or the intention to make it abandoned).

This slow potential shift was labeled *contingent negative variation* by its discoverers, presumably because its appearance is contingent upon the association of a response with the stimulus that elicits the potential. In the original experiments, a click was followed at intervals of several seconds by a series of flashes. Normal evoked potentials with no negative shift were produced by both the click and the flashes. When the subject was asked to press a button to stop the flashes, however, the interval between the two evoked potentials was filled by a large negative shift of the recorded base line, as shown in Figure 6.8.

If on any occasion the subject decided not to respond, the negative voltage did not appear. The second stimulus was not actually necessary; if the subject had been told to press the button after the lapse of an estimated interval (for example, 2 seconds), the negative shift would have appeared during the delay period.

These findings have been replicated, with close attention to possible artifacts, by Low, Borda, Frost, and Kellaway (1966). The effect has also been demonstrated in monkeys; recordings were taken directly from the cortex during operant-conditioning performance (Low, Borda & Kellaway, 1966). Other workers have shown that increased effort to make the response or to detect the second stimulus, as well as increased motivation to make the response, all result in increases in the negative potential (Irwin, Knott, McAdam & Rebert, 1966; Rebert, McAdam, Knott & Irwin, 1967). It has been suggested that the wave may represent the activity of an inhibitory system that is blocking motor activity until such time as the signal to respond is received (Donald, 1968).

As we shall see when we study various possible mechanisms involved in learned behavior (Chapter 18), the most probable model is one based on the idea that the animal can try out various alternative response possibilities "in its mind" before selecting the one that seems most appropriate. Such a model requires that the animal be equipped with a mechanism for preventing the response tendency that is active in the brain from reaching the musculature prematurely. This system would correspond to the response trigger that we have already postulated on other grounds.

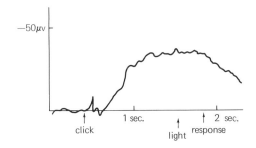

Figure 6.8 A slowly changing negative potential recorded from the vertex of the skull during the interval between a warning signal (click) and a response released by a light signal.

There is much evidence that a frightened animal takes longer than usual to respond and may completely fail to do so. This behavior is aggravated by lesions in the medial thalamus (Vanderwolf, 1962). Strangely enough, stimulation of the same general region also arrests or slows down a response.

The opposite effect can be obtained by administering excitatory drugs like *amphetamine*. Animals then seem to have trouble withholding responses they would normally make under the circumstances, even though such responses have been punished, extinguished, or "fatigued" previously. Similar behavior also occurs after an animal has sustained lesions in the hippocampus or other parts of the *limbic system* (a group of mostly rhinencephalic structures involved in motivation) or in the frontal lobes (see Chapter 19). A confusing variety of treatments seem to interfere with the timing of response initiation in the mammal, which may be an indication of how many systems participate in this most important function.

AUTONOMIC RESPONSES AND ACTIVATION

Most actions of the motor system constitute "public" behavior, but there are some inconspicuous or internal effects that are revealed only through the use of special equipment. One such response, mentioned in Chapter 5, is the galvanic skin response (GSR), or psychogalvanic reflex (PGR). This response is a combination of two closely associated effects of exciting autonomic efferents to the skin. The more important effect of the two is a change in the electrical resistance of the skin owing to the secretion of sweat; the other is generation of a small voltage by activated glands and smooth muscles. The usual technique for detecting these changes is to measure the resistance between two electrodes on the palm or fingers with a DC bridge. Any emotional disturbance shows as a drop in the resistance, which has a latency of a little under 1 second. The resistance usually returns to basal level, or nearly so, within a few seconds. There are also long-term changes in the basal resistance level (BRL), reflecting the subject's general level of activity, temperature, and state of mind (R. Kaplan, 1963).

The GSR is one of the measures taken by the so-called lie detector. Other measures that also indicate emotional disturbance are those of heart rate and, to some extent, respiration pattern. The simplest method of recording heart rate is to hold the subject's pulse, a method used in the eighteenth-century to detect criminals. A more convenient and sophisticated technique is to amplify the action potentials of the heart and to apply them to a *polygraph recorder* or a counter of some sort. The heart rate usually increases when the subject is disturbed, but in some cases increased anxiety causes it to fall. Respiration is, of course, under greater voluntary control than is the heart or the GSR response, but in strong emotion we lose this control, and various respiratory reflexes take over. Involuntary gasps, screams, sobbing, and laughter are obvious enough without special measuring equipment, but subtler changes in the regular pattern show up

when breathing is mechanically recorded. Another autonomic effect manifest in extreme cases is the *arteriole reaction*, which causes blushing, or flushing, or the opposite under conditions of emotional disequilibrium. A more sensitive measure is also available in the form of a *plethysmograph*, which measures the blood flow, usually through a finger or earlobe.

One of the most important measures of relatively hidden motor activity is the *electromyograph*, which measures the electrical activity of muscles. This device enables an experimenter to quantify the tonus in a muscle that is not moving a limb; the muscles most often chosen are those of the head involved in expression and posture, rather than those involved in gross bodily movement. Malmo and his colleagues have used this technique extensively to demonstrate that mental stress may show itself as tension in certain muscles (which may subsequently ache) (Malmo & Shagass, 1949) and to measure degree of concentration on a task (A. K. Bartoshuk, 1955a, b). From recording electrodes placed on a muscle not engaged in performing the experimental task (usually something rather short like mirror drawing or tracking) they found that the passive muscle's tension rises continuously during the performance and falls precipitately at the end. The activity of such muscles seems to have some relation to the background facilitating bombardment of motoneurons by downstream impulses from the brainstem, but the relation is not simple. It appears that "drive," or activation, is correlated not with the amplitude of the electromyogram but with its rate of increase, or "gradient," during the task (Malmo, 1965).

Summary

The central motor system has been divided rather artificially into pyramidal and extrapyramidal systems. The pyramidal system is simple, recently evolved, and in most species, not very important. It consists of a relatively small number of neurons (about 2 million in man and fewer in other animals) in the motor cortex, adjacent somatosensory cortex, and, to a lesser extent, the rest of the cortex, which send their axons directly to motoneurons or interneurons in spinal motor pools. These axons constitute the pyramidal tract.

The motor cortex is a strip lying immediately anterior to the central fissure, and the body musculature is represented topographically along this strip, with the hind feet at the dorsomedial extremity and the head at the lateral end. The pyramidal tract decussates in the medulla, so that the muscles of the left side of the body are represented in the right hemisphere of the brain and vice versa. These relationships have been mapped through experiments in which movements of various muscles have been elicited by electrical stimulation of points in the motor cortex.

Lesions confined as closely as possible to the pyramidal tract produce transient flaccid paralysis, but lower mammals recover almost completely and quite quickly. Primates take longer to recover, and certain fine movements of the extremities never return to normal.

It has been found that, after recovery from a small cortical lesion, the cortex in the vicinity of the lesion has taken over some of the function of the missing area, but this finding cannot explain recovery after the whole of the pyramidal tract has been cut. Presumably the extrapyramidal system is capable of assuming control after a period of reorganization.

Recording the activity of single neurons of the pyramidal tract has shown that it is closely associated in time with muscle activity and that the neurons fire faster when more force is exerted. An activity proportional to the rate of change of force appears to be superimposed on this basic relationship. The extra activity during change may serve to initiate action quickly before slower tonic activity through muscle-spindle feedback becomes effective.

Other neurons in the motor cortex (probably not pyramidal-tract neurons) have been found to fire well in advance of any muscle response. They seem to be involved in setting up the next response before it is evoked ("thinking about" the next response).

The anatomy of the extrapyramidal system is quite complex. Several midbrain and subthalamic structures appear to contain innate circuits capable of producing certain relatively stereotyped responses when excited by downstream input. Some of the input to these structures comes from the globus pallidus, which also delivers impulses more directly to spinal motor centers and to the *centre median* nucleus of the thalamus. The globus pallidus receives input from the caudate-putamen complex, which, in turn, receives an important afferent component from all parts of the cortex (including the motor cortex). There is a feedback loop from the *centre median* to the globus pallidus through the caudate-putamen complex and another, longer path through the cortex and the caudate-putamen. The subthalamic nuclei also feed back to the motor cortex through the motor nuclei of the thalamus (ventralis lateralis and ventralis anterior). Cerebellar input reaches the system mainly through the ventralis lateralis. The final outflow of the extrapyramidal system descends in spinal tracts ventral to the lateral pyramidal path and lateral to the ventral pyramidal path.

The striatal motor centers constitute the highest motor level in submammalian species. In the mammal these structures have acquired connections with many parts of the cortex, and these connections no doubt give them access to much useful sensory information suitably processed by the cortex. It is unlikely, however, that the cortex has assumed the dominant position in the motor system.

Various effects of stimulation in the extrapyramidal system have been reported. In the lightly anesthetized animal low-level stimulation of parts of the cortex, caudate nucleus, parts of the cerebellum, or bulbar reticular system produces inhibition of the motor system. Stimulation of part of the hypothalamus or the mesencephalic reticular system has a facilitating effect.

Stimulation of subthalamic nuclei can produce walking movements; other specific movements are obtained from stimulation of the reticular formation and hypothalamic regions in intact animals. Thalamic stimulation can produce "freezing" behavior.

Extrapyramidal lesions produce a variety of motor disturbances. Destruction of inhibitory parts causes excessive muscle tone and hyperreflexia. Other lesions have been implicated in Parkinson's disease (stiffness and tremor when at rest), involuntary movements, and (from the cerebellum) ataxia and tremor that becomes more pronounced during voluntary movements.

Learning theorists have paid little attention to the motor system in recent years, but it is clear that any attempt to devise a physiological theory of behavior is doomed without some prior understanding of the way in which the sequences of movement that constitute responses are put together in the nervous system. Lashley has suggested a two-level process in which one activity sets up the response as a whole and another brings in the movements at the right times like the conductor of an orchestra.

Central "prewired" (innately connected) systems apparently produce sequences of neural firing that control many basic activities like walking, swallowing, breathing, and so on. These systems have been studied through grafting new limbs onto animals and showing that, when the limbs become innervated, the movements of the individual muscles are exactly the same as those of muscles in adjacent limbs. The activity of the muscles engaged in swallowing has been measured and found to follow a constant sequence independently of the intensity of stimulation or any surgical or anesthetic interference with the muscles.

There is no clear-cut demarcation between the motor system and the motivational system, as usually defined. Some structures clearly have motor functions; stimulation always produces the same movements. Other structures produce quite variable movements, which have only goals in common. For example, an animal may always eat when stimulated, but the actual movements that it makes depend upon the location of food and other environmental factors. In such an instance we are inclined to say that the stimulated structure is "motivational." Intermediate effects are more difficult to classify, suggesting that there is a continuum between structures that produce movement relatively uninfluenced by sensory input and those in which sensory input is dominant in determining the final sequence of movements.

Another problem relating to the motor system is the timing of responses. Although there is only slight evidence (from single-neuron recording experiments) that a timing mechanism exists, it seems probable that patterns of motor-system firing can occur without producing overt responses and may be held in readiness for at least a number of seconds. At the appropriate time the balance between inhibition and facilitation is tipped in favor of facilitation, and the response is emitted. Withholding a response is associated with a negative potential on the surface of the cortex, which may reflect inhibitory activity. Lesion experiments to be discussed later suggest that the hippocampus, frontal lobes, and perhaps other parts of the limbic system are mainly responsible for maintaining the inhibition of preset responses until they are required.

The autonomic motor system produces less conspicuous behavior than does the skeletal system, but instruments like the "lie detector," which monitors heart rate, respiration rate, and resistance on the palm of the hand, allow us to investigate its activity.

PART THREE

SENSORY
SYSTEMS

The study of sensory mechanisms involves us in some very difficult problems, verging on the metaphysical. What do we mean when we say that we feel a touch or see a light? In principle, at least, we can specify a sequence of neural activities connecting a pattern of receptor firing to the pattern of muscular contractions by which we indicate our appreciation of the stimulus, but where among all this firing are our sensations represented? The classical answer seems to be "in the sensory areas of the cortex." In many discussions of sensory discrimination, for example, it is implied, if not stated explicitly, that there are specific cells in the cortex whose firing represents or in some way causes specific sensations. The evidence that supposedly supports this view is that electrical stimulation of the sensory cortex during brain operations on conscious human beings occasions sensations that resemble, according to the patients, those produced by normal stimulation of receptors (Penfield & Rasmussen, 1950). Furthermore, destruction of the sensory cortex, in some cases at least, results in loss of sensation.

In our present ignorance about the relationship between neural activity and sensation, it might be prudent to sidestep this issue and to concern ourselves only with the mechanisms relating receptor activity to the responses that it can evoke. But then we run into another difficulty: Some stimuli produce no immediate response, and, still more troublesome, most stimuli can evoke any number of responses, depending upon the organism's instructions, previous experience, motivation, and so on.

From a more practical point of view we may regard the function of the sensory systems as to provide the motor and motivational systems with information about the relations between the organism and its environment. If a part of the animal is being damaged, information is needed to direct the withdrawal of that part; if food is available to the right, the information must be in a form that will guide the animal in that direction when other sensory information indicates that internal food supplies are running low. Information that food is in the mouth must elicit chewing, swallowing, and so on.

In the primitive animal, most sensory input is an immediate goad to action—approach or escape—and such immediate connections are still important in the modalities of pain, taste, smell, and so on in the most highly developed animals. During the course of evolution, however, sensory modalities have sprung up that do not in themselves have strong affective or motivational properties; they exist to improve performance dictated by motivations from other sources. Visual input, for example, allows an animal to distinguish objects of no immediate significance. Different values may become attached to these visual inputs, depending upon what "affective" input is presented at about the same time.

The distinction between affective and informative sensory input has been made on various occasions. Head (1920) called the primitive modalities capable of arousing emotions and drives *protopathic* and those capable of making fine discriminations *epicritic*. A somewhat similar dichotomy was presented by Hebb (1955), who called one type the "arousal function" and the other the "cue function," but he believed that all sensory input had components of both types. Hebb is quite right, of course, in pointing out that no sense modality falls completely into one or the other category. We receive information even from a painful stimulus, and abstract art suggests that meaningless visual stimulation can be attractive. This problem has also been reviewed by Pfaffmann (1960).

It seems that, with increasing complexity of the nervous system, there is a corresponding increase in the interaction among the modalities. The frog, for example, is almost entirely dependent for obtaining food upon reflex tongue flicks toward any object moving in its visual field. It will starve to death in the midst of a swarm of flies if none of them moves. It does not recognize them as food, or, if it does, it cannot make an appropriate response.

In higher animals, the motor system has access to sensory input from all modalities; different inputs from a single object appear to be pooled at some level, at which each has the power to elicit a common neural activity representing the object. The clear recognition of this mechanism must also be credited to Hebb (1949, 1966). In his treatment of perception he speculated that sensory input from a class of objects might establish a pattern of cortical firing (he called it a *cell assembly*) that would eventually become semi-independent of the input originally responsible for building it and would become capable of firing in response to other modes of input from the same or similar objects. In other words, a particular group of cortical neurons might at first be excited by visual stimuli from triangles, but many of the same group would later fire if triangular objects were touched, three dots were seen, and so on. This ability to establish neural representations of classes of objects and to arouse them from a wide variety of sensory inputs, constitutes true generalization, one of the most useful attributes of the perceptual system.

Generalization in this sense does not mean inability to distinguish between stimuli (as in the stimulus generalization described by Hull, 1943, for example); it means the ability to abstract some common feature from a number of discriminable stimuli and to respond only to it. For example, in the familiar two-point discrimination test, the subject is able to say whether he has been touched by one or by two sufficiently separated points at any place on the body. He has abstracted the quality of singularity or duality, independent of the particular touch receptors stimulated. The same neural activities can be elicited by seeing the symbols 1 or 2 or by hearing one or two clicks. There is no limit to the combinations of receptor activities that can elicit such concepts.

It is certain that the ability to operate with concepts rather than with raw sensory data confers a tremendous advantage upon the higher animal. It appears to demand at least multiple interconnections within and among sensory modalities and considerable plasticity (modifiability) among the connections. The only structure that has such characteristics in abundance is the cortex, and it is not surprising that this structure predominates in animals that are good at generalizing and forming concepts. Nor is it surprising that there are strong sensory connections to the cortex, especially from those modalities that are capable of providing the richest variety of discriminations.

Although in general this book is organized in terms of behavioral rather than of anatomical categories, it is clear that sooner or later in our study of sensory systems we shall have to know more about the properties of the cortex. To avoid scattering this information throughout the chapters and breaking the continuity of our discussion of the different modalities, this part of the book will begin with a chapter devoted to some of the general properties of the cortex and including some speculations on its part in concept formation.

Then we shall go to the other extreme of the sensory pathway and examine some of the general properties of receptors, after which chapters on the different modalities—olfactory, gustatory, somatosensory, visual, and auditory—will complete the section. In each case, we shall follow the sensory input as far as the cortex, but the reader will discover, unfortunately, that few experiments have thrown much light on the rather high-powered speculations on the cortical role in perception that scientists have indulged in.

CHAPTER 7

THE CORTEX

A very large proportion of the cells in the sensory systems of higher mammals lies in the cerebral cortex, and it is thus reasonable to suppose that this region is important for sensory analysis. As a preliminary to the study of these systems it is therefore necessary to learn something about the anatomy and physiology of the cortex and about the development of ideas relating the cortex to behavior.

The cortex of an organ or other object is its rind or bark, the outer covering. The cerebral cortex is the part of the brain that lies on or near the surface and encloses the rest. During the course of evolution the vertebrate nervous system has undergone great modification, but the anterior end, and in particular the cortex, has shown the most spectacular growth. The mammalian cortex can be divided into three main types: the most primitive, *archicortex* (which includes the hippocampus); the *paleocortex*, which evolved later, (of which the *pyriform lobe* is an example), and the neocortex, or *isocortex*, which developed most recently and constitutes the major part of the cortex of the mammal.

Although the frog has a single layer of cells, and reptiles and birds have multilayered structures that correspond to the neocortex of higher animals, the neocortex does not reach its full development in animals below the mammal. In man, by far the majority of all brain cells lie in the cortex. The increase in size of the cortex during evolution from one species to another within the class of mammals exceeds that of any other region of the nervous system. For such

reasons it has long been assumed that the cortex must be the "seat of intelligence," the structure in which the interactions and other computations necessary for reasoning and learning take place. This assumption has been largely borne out by lesion experiments in which changes in animal behavior have been studied after all or part of the cortex has been removed.

Some people have gone further and suggested that particular mental abilities depend upon the activity of specific areas of the cortex. An early, and extreme, version of this view was expressed by Gall at the end of the eighteenth century. Gall was an anatomist who thought he could discern a relationship between the mental characteristics of his acquaintances and the shapes of their skulls, and he attributed this relationship to differential growth of different cortical areas. Unfortunately for his theory, the skull varies a good deal in thickness, so that measurements of the outside are not an adequate indication of the development of the underlying cortex. Furthermore, Gall had no adequate way of measuring mental abilities, and many of his conclusions were based upon the skull measurements of single individuals whom he considered outstanding examples of particular propensities like "amativeness" or "secretiveness." Gall's colleague Spurzheim popularized these ideas under the name *phrenology* and certainly achieved much publicity, and even widespread acceptance, for them. At one time phrenology occupied a position in the scientific world similar to that occupied today by psychoanalysis, as Dallenbach (1955) has pointed out. It is a moot point whether such publicity helped or hindered the scientific study of cortical functioning in the long run.

Soon after Gall had made public his theory about the cortical localization of function, Rolando (1809) first used electrical stimulation of the brain in an attempt to find where movements originated (with little success, however), and Flourens (1823) performed early experiments on the effects on animal behavior of surgically extirpating parts of the brain. Flourens' results were opposed to the conclusions of the phrenologists, though it must be remembered that he was working with animals and the phrenologists with human beings. He found that partial destruction of the cortex had no effect upon behavior and that the whole cerebrum had to be removed in order to interfere with such "higher" mental processes as perception, and control of voluntary movements. Perhaps as a reaction to the spread of a commercialized and increasingly disreputable form of phrenology, the implications of this study were exaggerated in academic circles, and they continued to influence psychological theorizing long after more sensitive methods of measuring behavior had shown them to be incorrect.

In 1836 Dax noticed that speech was often disturbed in patients who had suffered strokes or other damage to the left side of the brain. Later Broca (1861), on the basis of postmortem examinations of the brains of patients who had been rendered speechless by strokes, claimed that speech was controlled by a relatively small area of the cortex in the third convolution of the frontal lobe of the left hemisphere. Then in 1870, nearly 70 years after Rolando's pioneer work, Fritsch and Hitzig succeeded in localizing the motor cortex in the dog by electrical stimulation.

Progress toward any accurate localization of other functions in the cortex was slow, mainly because, until well into this century, only the crudest measures of behavior were available for use with animals, or even with humans; it was, of course, impossible to make experimental brain lesions in man. Even when fairly sophisticated methods of testing animals became available and were applied, the results sometimes did nothing to further the advance of cortical localization. For example, Lashley (1929) in a famous series of experiments with rats showed that cortical lesions interfered with learning and retention of a maze-running habit to an extent that depended upon the size of the lesion (Law of Mass Action) but not upon the locus of the lesion (Law of Equipotentiality).

The Law of Equipotentiality, in particular, lent support to the antilocalization school, and proved surprisingly influential among psychologists and even (although based on rat experiments) among neurologists. It also became as-

sociated in some way with the Gestalt reaction against structuralism and the extreme conditioned reflex theory of behavior put forth by J. B. Watson (1926). As a result and perhaps also because of its outstanding originality, Lashley's research was accepted less critically than would otherwise have been the case.

The Law of Equipotentiality has been interpreted in various ways. The most extreme interpretation was that the whole cortex was equipotential for all its functions. Although a few people seem to have thought that this idea was implied by Lashley's work, it is doubtful that anyone with any knowledge of the field would have entertained the idea for a moment. That damage to the occipital lobe of the cortex can lead to blindness or partial blindness (see Chapter 11) but never to loss of movement and that lesions of the precentral gyrus can lead to difficulties with movement but not to blindness are evidence enough to refute it.

A less extreme interpretation and apparently the one intended by Lashley, was that the cortex as a whole is equipotential for certain functions like learning and problem solving. This interpretation is not so easy to refute, but, as we shall see, it has received little support from present-day research on more advanced mammals than the rat.

The weak form of the Law of Equipotentiality is that parts of the cortex are equipotential for particular functions (for example, that parts of the striate, or visual, cortex are equipotential for vision). There is every reason to believe, with reservations, that this interpretation is valid not only for many cortical areas but also for many subcortical structures. A remarkable feature of brain-lesion studies is how often no change in behavior can be detected until the whole of a particular area or structure has been eliminated. In these examples, however, the meaning of "equipotentiality" has subtly changed from Lashley's original. He meant that the same deficit was produced regardless of the lesion's location and not that a small part could do the work of the whole, as is clear from his Law of Mass Action, which states that the larger the lesion, the more severe the deficit. The Law of Mass Action and the Law of Equipotentiality, as conceived by Lashley, are not mutually independent, and, in fact, on close analysis each seems to imply the other. This relationship can lead to confusion because some people seem to use the two laws interchangeably.

Neither the methodological difficulties encountered by Lashley and others nor the antilocalization climate among psychologists and some neurologists deterred neuroanatomists from trying to determine the functions of different parts of the cortex by tracing their connections. Many schemes for differentiating one region from another according to structural details were proposed.

The very earliest method of "mapping" the cortex had been merely to extend the name of the overlying bone to the underlying region of the brain. The frontal lobe is beneath the frontal bone of the skull, the parietal lobe beneath the parietal bone, the occipital lobe beneath the occipital bone, and the temporal lobe beneath the temporal bone. After the advent of the microscope and staining methods that make the structure of neurons easily distinguishable, maps of the cortex based upon the occurrence and arrangement of neurons in the different regions could be drawn. A. W. Campbell (1905) drew up one such *cytoarchitectonic map*, dividing the cortex into about 20 regions; Brodmann (1909) produced a widely used map with about 50 numbered areas. Later others elaborated on these early attempts until by the time of the Vogts (Vogt & Vogt, 1919) and Economo and Koskinas (1925) divisions numbered 200 or more.

The differences between many adjacent regions in these later maps were so small as to be imperceptible to all but the anatomists who first detected them. This problem was pointed out by Lashley and Clark (1946), who found only a few regions of the cortex that they could recognize from anatomical sections alone if they did not know beforehand what part of the cortex the sections had come from.

In about 1930 another anatomical technique for dividing up the cortex was developed. It depends upon a phenomenon called *retrograde degeneration*. Some neurons apparently cannot

survive long if their axon terminals make no contact with efferent neurons. Probably an essential chemical passes from one cell to the other at the synapses. The relay cells of the thalamus, which transmit sensory and other input to the cortex, are of this type; after a cortical lesion there is secondary loss of cells through retrograde degeneration in the part of the thalamus that projects to that area.

The nuclei of the thalamus are relatively easy to distinguish from one another in microscopic sections; after a unilateral cortical lesion it is easy to tell which nuclei have suffered retrograde degeneration because the intact side can be compared with the partly degenerated side. By making a series of cortical lesions and studying the resulting thalamic degeneration, it is possible to construct a map of the areas that receive projections from each of the thalamic nuclei. The technique has the disadvantage that it is only practicable in work with animals, but the brains of higher subhuman primates are sufficiently similar to the human brain for homologous areas to be estimated with reasonable accuracy.

The retrograde-degeneration technique revealed that the occipital visual area receives projections from the *lateral geniculate nucleus*, the superior temporal auditory area from the *medial geniculate nucleus*, the postcentral gyrus (somatosensory area) from the *ventralis posterior nucleus*, the precentral gyrus (motor cortex) from the *ventralis lateralis nucleus*, the frontal cortex from the *medialis dorsalis nucleus*, the cingulate and *subicular cortex* from the *anterior thalamic nuclei*, and the posterior temporal cortex from the *pulvinar* (Figure 7.1).

Many of these are areas that receive sensory projections, and can be located by the technique of evoked potentials, which was introduced in the 1930s. A recording electrode is placed on the cortex of an anesthetized animal and stimuli applied to the sense organs (spots of light to the eye, clicks or tone pips to the ear, tactile stimuli to different parts of the body, and so on). If the electrode is on the appropriate sensory projection area it will pick up an evoked potential for each application of the stimulus, and in that way the areas devoted to the differ-

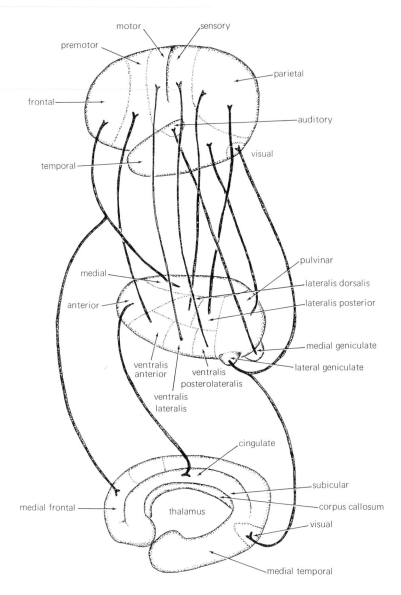

Figure 7.1 Connections between thalamus (center, not to scale) and the sensory cortex (lateral surface above, medial surface below).

ent modalities can be located. What is more, with patience it is possible to plot the field within a particular modality. Figure 7.2 shows the locations on the cortex of the peak potentials evoked by touching different parts of the body of a rat. Woolsey (1958) and his students have performed such measurements on many different species. It should be noted, however, that the evoked-potential method does not always produce the same map of sensory areas

as does the retrograde-degeneration method, though the overlap is considerable (Doty, 1958).

Yet another way to plot what appears to be the same sensory projection was used by Foerster (1936) and Penfield and Boldrey (1937) on unanesthetized human patients during brain operations. The sensory cortex was stimulated electrically, and the patient was asked to report what he noticed. Figure 7.3

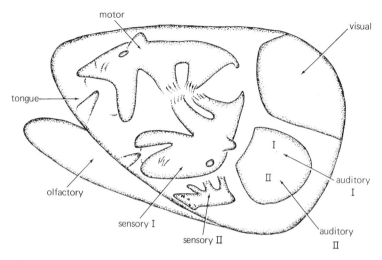

Figure 7.2   Sensory and motor areas of the rat cortex. (After Woolsey, 1958.)

shows the "sensory homunculus" projected on the cortex as revealed by this method.

Through evoked potentials it has been discovered that most of the sensory modalities are represented at least twice each in the cortex. The evoked potentials in the second area are somewhat smaller and usually of longer latency; they also show a greater tendency toward ipsilateral representation. There is also more overlap of modalities among the secondary areas. For example, in the cat the second somatosensory area coincides with an area where auditory evoked potentials can also be obtained (Figure 12.15).

Figure 7.3   A cross section of one hemisphere of the sensory cortex showing a "sensory homunculus" (After Penfield & Rasmussen, 1950.)

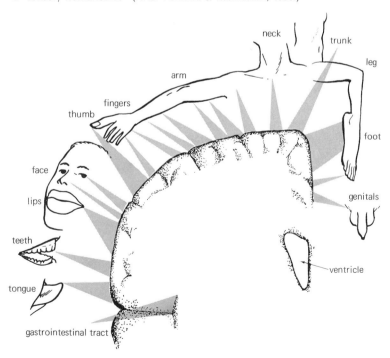

In the rat and other low-order mammals, the cortex is almost completely occupied by sensory and motor areas, but in animals higher on the phylogenetic scale much of the frontal, temporal, and parietal cortex does not respond directly to sensory input. These "silent" regions were originally considered to be association areas, in which signals arriving in the sensory areas could mingle and become associated with one another. They may very well have other functions, however. K. H. Pribram (1958) has suggested that cortical areas that receive signals directly from the environment be called *extrinsic cortex* and those that receive afferents from nonsensory thalamic nuclei be called *intrinsic cortex*. This suggestion may be logical, but, as is usual in such matters, it will probably be a long time before these terms replace the established designations "sensory" and "association."

We see that the history of cortical subdivision has proceeded along a sort of parabolic trajectory, starting with frontal, temporal, parietal, and occipital; reaching a very large number during the architectonic-mapping phase; and falling again to a few physiologically defined areas in more recent times. As far as the psychologist is concerned, the acid test of such subdivisions is whether or not they can be shown to mean anything behaviorally. Does a lesion of an anatomically or physiologically defined area produce a more isolated and clearcut behavioral disturbance than a lesion that ignores such boundaries? In sensory and motor areas it certainly does. There is a close correspondence between the sensory areas found by the evoked-potential technique and those revealed by Penfield's more behavioral stimulation method, and we saw in Chapter 6 that the motor cortex as mapped through stimulation corresponds to the region where lesions produce motor weakness. Later we shall examine the effects of lesions in different areas on subtler aspects of behavior like maze learning and problem solving and we shall discover that the original four subdivisions—frontal, parietal, temporal, and occipital—are still almost as useful as any that have subsequently been adopted.

FINE ANATOMY OF THE CORTEX

It is commonly stated that there are about 9 billion (9×10^9) neurons in the human cortex, but this figure may be too high because parts of some cells appear in more than one slice and may be counted twice. Sholl (1956) favored a figure between 5 and 7 billion. There are probably even more neurons in the cortices of such large mammals as the elephant and the whale, though the cortical cells in these animals are farther apart than in the cortex of man and the proportion of small to large neurons is smaller. In man there are many more small, short-axon interneurons than there are large, long-axon cells.

The thickness of the cortex does not vary much with species. It is approximately 2 mm thick in the rat, which has a smooth cortex, and varies from 1.5 mm at the convexities to about 3 mm at the bottom of the sulci of the primate cortex. The cortex is made up of several layers, as is clear from Nissl-stained sections (see Figures 2.5, 7.4). Neuroanatomy textbooks

Figure 7.4 A section of Nissl-stained cortex, showing layers.

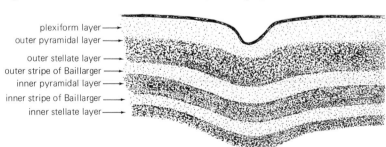

plexiform layer ⟶
outer pyramidal layer ⟶
outer stellate layer ⟶
outer stripe of Baillarger ⟶
inner pyramidal layer ⟶
inner stripe of Baillarger ⟶
inner stellate layer ⟶

state dogmatically that there are six basic layers, and in fact a common definition of isocortex (or neocortex) specifies that it must have six layers at some stage of development. Nevertheless, few inexperienced observers will spontaneously recognize six layers in sections of the cortex. During the nineteenth century, before the figure six had been decided upon, various eminent histologists estimated the number of layers as between five and eight, and there was no general agreement on where one layer stopped and the next began.

It was Brodmann who somehow managed to raise the idea of a six-layered structure almost to a law of nature, but the layering differences in different regions of the cortex are so great that his idea can be sustained only by subdividing layers in some places or making arbitrary distinctions where in fact there is a gradual and smooth transition. Sholl has raised doubts about the traditional view, and perhaps the time is ripe to break with it and to describe roughly what is actually seen in a typical section of the cortex.

Plexiform Layer

The outer layer is always very distinct; the few neurons present have horizontally directed (in the same plane as the layer itself) axons. Most of the layer consists of the tips of the apical dendrites of cells in lower layers and some thin axons from below that run parallel to the surface for a short distance (Figure 7.5). In the Nissl section this layer is almost transparent.

Outer Pyramidal Layer

Below the plexiform layer is a layer consisting mainly of small *pyramidal cells* (so called because of their shape). They send their axons down into the white matter below the cortex and their apical dendrites are in the outer layer. As we penetrate this layer more deeply the pyramidal cells become bigger, and *stellate cells* (*star cells, bushy cells, spider cells,* and so on, also named for their shapes) begin to appear. These cells have dendrites and axons that branch profusely in the vicinity of the cell

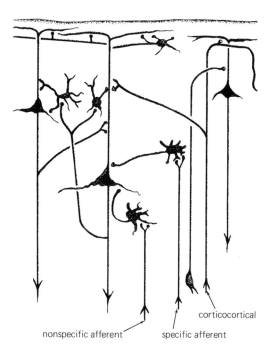

nonspecific afferent   specific afferent   corticocortical

Figure 7.5   Examples of neural connections in the cortex. (After Lorente de Nó, 1949.)

bodies; some of the axons ascend to the outer layer, where they run horizontally and form a dense plexus with the tips of the apical dendrites of the pyramidal cells.

Outer Stellate Layer

At a deeper level the number of pyramidal cells diminishes, and the cells are mainly stellate. It is at this level that the main afferents from the thalamus terminate, sending axonal branches horizontally to form a layer of white matter that is quite pronounced in the sensory areas of the cortex. In the visual cortex it is known as the *stripe of Gennari*; elsewhere it is called the *outer stripe of Baillarger*.

Inner Pyramidal Layer

Below this level the number of pyramidal cells begins to increase again. The apical dendrites of these cells do not all reach the surface layer, but some end in the upper pyramidal layers, and their axons also send branches toward the surface, which end in the upper layers, though the main shafts of the axons descend to the underlying white matter.

Inner Stellate Layer

The pyramidal cells become larger still at the bottom of the inner stellate layer and are again joined by stellate cells, including spindle-shaped *Martinotti cells*, which send their axons toward the surface.

Apart from the specific afferents from the thalamic relay nuclei, which, as we have seen, end mainly in the middle of the outer stellate layer, there are nonspecific afferents that end in all layers of the cortex, especially in the inner stellate layer, and association fibers from other parts of the cortex that also end in all layers, especially in the outer pyramidal layer.

This general description of structure applies to most parts of the cortex, but in some regions there may be many fewer stellate cells in the middle layers, the cells may be smaller, the pyramidal cells in one of the layers may be much larger than in other parts of the cortex, and so on.

The main direction of flow of fibers in the cortex is perpendicular to the surface, but some axon branches are distributed in random directions, usually in the vicinity of the cell bodies. The basal dendrites and the tips of the apical dendrites of the pyramidal cells, of course, run mainly parallel to the surface. According to Sholl, the average radius of the dendritic field of a neuron in the visual cortex of the cat is about 160μ, and the density of distribution falls off exponentially from the cell body outward. The field of apical dendrites in the plexiform layer of the cortex is even greater.

The axon of a stellate cell usually terminates within the dendritic field of the cell, but collateral branches of long-axon cells may travel a millimeter or so away from the cell. It is probable that a majority of these intracortical connections are inhibitory in nature; otherwise the tendency toward a buildup of epileptic activity around closed loops of neurons would be very great. The afferent axons branch within a terminal zone about 600μ in diameter; a

single afferent fiber thus may fall within the fields of more than 5,000 cortical neurons.

Most of the long axons of cortical cells travel perpendicularly downward and enter the white matter below. From there they either return to a different part of the cortex at any distance from the point of origin in either hemisphere, or they leave the cortex to end in the thalamus, basal ganglia, or almost any other part of the brain. Those entering the pyramidal tract—but no others—pass beyond the pontine region into the spinal cord. Many axons branch and no doubt end in several different places.

In summary, there are two main types of neurons in the cortex, those with intracortical connections and those with axons that leave the cortex, usually to return to it at another point. The axons of most of the latter neurons also have recurrent collaterals with intracortical connections.

CORTICAL CONDUCTION

It is clear from its structure that the cortex cannot efficiently transmit information laterally within its layers for any distance. Such horizontal pathways involve many short steps and are highly diffuse because of the multiple connections at each step. For long-range conduction the extracortical fibers running in the subcortical white matter are clearly much more suitable. These inferences from anatomy have been confirmed by numerous experiments.

Burns (1950, 1954) has studied the transmission characteristics of cortex isolated from the underlying white matter to avoid the complicating influences of the extracortical pathways. A slab of cat cortex was circumsected and undercut without disturbing its blood supply (which flows down from the pia mater, one of the outer membranes of the brain). Recording and stimulating electrodes were placed on the slab. Burns found that a small stimulus produced a wave of activity in which the surface of the cortex went negative. The wave traveled out from the stimulating electrode at about 2 m per second, decreasing in amplitude as it went, so that it never went farther than about 1 cm from its origin. It could be stopped by a shallow cut through the cortex, and it was therefore probably generated by the firing of fine axons (0.5-1 μ in diameter) in the plexiform layer. These axons could come from the horizontal cells in that layer, or they could be the horizontal terminal branches of axons from cells in lower layers. The negative wave was assumed to represent the depolarization of apical dendrites by the synaptic action of these axons.

With higher stimulation currents, the surface-negative wave was accompanied by a series of surface-positive waves, which traveled without decrement to the borders of the cortical slab. These waves lasted 0.5–5 seconds at a frequency of about 70 per second. The surface-positive wave was not interrupted by the cut through the upper layers of the cortex but was stopped by a cut that included the outer stellate layer. Burns concluded that the short-axon connections of the stellate cells in that layer and the collateral connections of pyramidal cells were responsible for conducting the impulses laterally through the cortex.

These experiments clearly demonstrated that there are multisynaptic pathways through the cortex, which are available under certain circumstances, but that they are ever used for long-distance communication through the cortex is doubtful. Apparently activity has to be quite intense before it is so transmitted, and once started it spreads in an uncontrolled manner like an epileptic seizure, to which it may well be related.

It was at one time believed, under the influence of Pavlov, that conditioned reflexes could be explained by transcortical-conduction effects. The center for the conditioned stimulus was thought to acquire connections through the cortex with the center for the conditioned response. Very few psychologists now accept this oversimplified view of learning. Lashley (1921, 1924) inaugurated the attack by showing that lesions and cuts distributed over many parts of the cortex had no effect upon learned responses, though they could hardly fail to interrupt connections between the sensory and motor areas involved in performance. Later

Sperry and Miner (1955) demonstrated that lateral pathways more than a few millimeters long were not important for the efficient functioning of the visual cortex. They trained cats to perform a very difficult visual discrimination and then diced the visual cortex with multiple slashes or pushed insulating strips of mica through it so that it was effectively reduced to a large number of small islands interconnected only through the subcortical white matter. When the cats recovered from the operations they were still able to perform almost as fine visual discriminations as before.

The experiments of Hubel and Wiesel (1962) and Mountcastle (1961a), in which microelectrode recordings were taken from cells at different depths in the sensory cortex, suggest that cells within a narrow vertical column respond to the same stimulus but that cells in adjacent columns may respond to a completely different stimulus, emphasizing the absence of lateral, as compared with vertical, excitatory interconnections. The possibility of extensive lateral inhibitory connections was not ruled out by this experiment, however.

Loucks (1961), Doty, Rutledge, and Larsen (1956), Rutledge and Doty (1962), and others have demonstrated that the connections from electrodes on the cortex to the rest of the brain are mainly through pathways leaving the cortex near the stimulation points. In these experiments animals were taught to respond to electrical stimulation of the cortex, and then the cortex beneath the electrode was either separated from the rest by a circular cut down to the white matter, or it was undercut so that, although the cortex remained intact, the region under the electrode was no longer joined to the white matter. The circumscribing lesion had no effect upon the response to stimulation, but in those animals in which the cortex had been undercut the response disappeared, though in most such cases it was subsequently possible to retrain the animal with a higher stimulation voltage.

Further information about the ways in which impulses are conducted from one part of the cortex to another can be inferred from some observations by Rusinov, which have been repeated and extended by Morrell (1961a). In the original experiments Rusinov found that, when part of the motor cortex was anodally polarized with a current of 2–10 μamp, the response that would ordinarily have been produced by an electrical stimulus at that motor point could be produced by any peripheral stimulus like a flash or click. The effect of the polarization was to produce what was called a *dominant focus of excitation*. For example, if the polarizing electrode were placed on the part of the motor cortex responsible for flexion of the left forelimb, that limb would flex to any flash, touch, sound, or the like presented to the animal during polarization. Furthermore, a sort of conditioning seemed to take place so that when such flexion was elicited repeatedly by flashes, for example, the limb movement continued to be produced by flashes for about 20 minutes after the polarizing current had been turned off. During this time the response did not occur to stimuli, like sounds, that had not been presented repeatedly during polarization.

This experiment is obviously of great interest to learning theorists, and it will be discussed from that perspective later; Morrell's modification of the procedure is of more immediate interest here. He recorded with a microelectrode from a single cell in the polarized zone and implanted a stimulating electrode in the cortex nearby. He was able, with this arrangement, to reproduce the effects reported by Rusinov. The stimulus could be set so that, in the absence of the anodal current, it had no effect upon the cell from which recordings were being taken but, when the current was flowing, it caused repetitive discharges of that cell. After the cell had been fired in this way repeatedly it could then be fired without the aid of anodal current for about 40 minutes. Circumsection of the region containing the observed cell, to separate it from any transcortical connection to the stimulating point, had little effect upon the response except to eliminate some of the later components of the discharge. Undercutting the region abolished the short latency part of response, leaving a long latency burst of firing.

Apparently over the rather short distances

used in this experiment there are two pathways between cortical cells, one through *U fibers* in the white matter (the descending and ascending axons of pyramidal cells), which provide a fast path, and one through the cortex either via very fine horizontally directed fibers in the outer layers or via polysynaptic pathways.

Another phenomenon involving lateral conduction through the cortex is spreading depression. Leão (1944) first drew attention to the fact that, during physiological experiments in which the cortex of an animal was exposed for some time or allowed to become dry or irritated in any way, there were periods when it went completely dead electrically. The wave of depression originated at some particular point and spread it at the remarkably low rate of 3–6 mm per minute until it had engulfed the whole cortex. The state of depression at any point lasted about five minutes.

Grafstein (1956) investigated the activity of individual cells during spreading depression and found that the cells on the border of the depressed region went through a phase of very intense activity before finally becoming quiescent. She also noticed that, when a direct current was passed through the cortex from a depressed region to a normal region, the velocity of the spread increased when the cathode was on the normal cortex and decreased when it was on the depressed cortex, which suggested that a cation was somehow involved in the spread. Her theory was that the increased activity of very many neurons released so much potassium that it depolarized neighboring cells and caused them to fire, thus releasing more potassium, and so on. After a period of wild activity during which they lost a significant fraction of their intracellular potassium and absorbed excessive quantities of sodium, the cells were refractory until the metabolic pumps had at least partially restored the normal resting state.

Spreading depression can be initiated by applying potassium chloride (KCl) solution to the dura, and in recent years a number of investigators, notably Bureš and Burešová (1960), have found this technique convenient for producing reversible dysfunction of the cortex during behavioral experiments. We shall discuss several examples in later chapters.

It is significant—or a very strange coincidence—that the rate calculated by Lashley (1941) for the spread of the scintillating *scotoma* (blind spot) that accompanied his own attacks of migraine (see Chapter 11) is almost exactly the same as that for spreading depression. It is possible that the bright flickering border of the "blind" region reflected intense activity of the cells at the leading edge of a wave of spreading depression sweeping across the visual cortex and that the scotoma itself was caused by the depression. It is not clear what starts the spreading depression in such cases, but it may be related to the disturbance of blood supply that usually accompanies migraine.

THEORIES OF CORTICAL FUNCTIONING

It seems that the only types of lateral conduction through the cortex are pathological and incapable of conveying significant information. Under normal conditions impulses leap from one point to another through U fibers of all lengths, so that cells in many parts of the cortex become involved in any activity that starts there. It is statistically certain that many of these long-axon, corticocortical connections form loops. A neuron at point A in the cortex, let us say, sends an axonal branch to point B, where it synapses with several thousand other cortical neurons. Some of the latter will be fired by the first neuron, and let us suppose that they send axons to points C, D, E, and so on, where each synapses with thousands of new cells. Sooner or later, some cells that send branches back into the region around A and synapse with the first cell are sure to be reached by the activity. Other neurons may go to points B, C, D, and so on and form loops within the larger loop. But for the presence of inhibitory neurons, one could imagine this process continuing until all the neurons in the cortex become involved, producing a form of epileptic seizure completely beyond the control of any input.

P. M. Milner (1957) has suggested that, once a small fraction of the cortical neurons have been recruited to snowballing activity of this sort, they drive up the level of inhibitory activity, which prevents further spread; a controlled burst of firing is thus confined to a limited group of neurons. A short time later the activity in the network dies down (because of either fatigue, adaptation of the synapses, or inhibition from cells beginning to escape from the inhibition set up by the group), and a similar burst of activity establishes itself in another group of cells. The process bears some resemblance to that described in Chapter 5 to account for the sharing of effort among motoneurons in a motor pool, except that in this case the participating neurons are able to fire one another. According to this view, there is an endless sequence of brief bursts of firing in one complex loop after another in the cortex, each involving thousands or perhaps tens of thousands of neurons. These networks would fire due to their interconnections whether or not there was any input to the cortex, but of course input, when present, would have an important effect upon the pattern of activity.

When Hebb's postulate (1949) that associations occur among neurons that fire together is applied to the neurons of these networks, we see that the more often the constituent neurons fire together, the more stable and more easily aroused as units the networks become. Networks that fire at random may be so variable that they never become stabilized, but those that are repeatedly fired by a particular sort of input could soon become well established. Such organized groups of neurons might well be the cortical representations of concepts mentioned in the introduction to Part Three. Hebb, in his brilliant pioneering work on the neurophysiology of percepts and concepts, called such a collection of jointly firing neurons a "cell assembly." The mechanism he suggested for the establishment of such assemblies was not completely satisfactory, however, and the account given here is an alternative designed to overcome some of the difficulties in the original.

Concepts would be of little use if it were not possible to form associations among them. One group of neurons must therefore be able to "learn" to arouse another group that is often forced by sensory input to fire just after the first group has fired. It is possible that the mechanism involved relies on the rebound properties of some neurons. If such a neuron is strongly inhibited it fires vigorously for a time when the inhibition is removed. Such cells are sometimes called "off" cells. Presumably, at the end of each burst of "concept" activity there is an "off" burst from cells that have been strongly inhibited by it. These cells will therefore be firing when the next organized group begins to fire, and eventually some of them will become incorporated into that group. They may then act as a nucleus from which the full activity of the second group can grow, thus increasing the probability that it will fire after the first group, even when the sensory input originally necessary to fire the second group is no longer present.

As mentioned in the introduction to Part Three, concepts can be aroused by input from several modalities and from many different patterns of input within a modality. The networks that have been postulated here are distributed throughout the cortex and are therefore accessible to many different inputs. Also, because they are widely distributed and each has a multiplicity of internal connections and loops, they cannot be eliminated by a small lesion anywhere in the cortex. Such a lesion would destroy perhaps 10–20 per cent of the connections within each network, but in a well-established assembly the remaining interconnections would be enough to carry on. As the networks representing other concepts would also have lost a similar proportion of their connections, including their inhibitory connections with other networks, the relative probabilities of each residue firing would not be greatly changed by such a lesion. A particular input would still fire the remaining cells of its concept network, and most of the output associations would be strong enough to work as before.

This possibility would explain the results of Lashley's experiments, mentioned earlier in the chapter. That the primate cortex does not exhibit complete equipotentiality could indicate that the neurons for some classes of concept, though still spread out, tend to be more highly concentrated in one or another part of the cortex.

If the activity corresponding to concepts is widely distributed throughout the cortex (and probably such other structures as the thalamus), direct experimental investigation will be extremely difficult if not impossible. Certainly only inferential evidence for the model presented here has emerged from the experiments to be described in the following chapters.

Summary

The cortex is the most recent large structure to have evolved in the nervous system. It reaches its full development only in the mammal and increases greatly in relative size as we ascend the mammalian series. Probably the most long-standing problem in physiological psychology is that of the relations between the cortex and behavior, particularly intelligent behavior.

Differences in the structure of different areas of cortex have been mapped, but apart from conspicuous features that distinguish sensory and motor cortex from the rest, no architectonic differences that clearly indicate function have been found. Other methods of subdividing the cortex—the locus of retrograde degeneration after a cortical lesion, evoked-potential mapping, and stimulation—have also proved useful mainly in outlining sensory and motor functions. Ablation experiments in animals and the study of people with accidental or therapeutic cortical lesions have told us more about the functions of association (or intrinsic) cortex.

The cortex is a layered structure, consisting of columns of cells oriented perpendicularly to the surface, except in the outermost layer, which consists largely of horizontally disposed dendritic branches. There are two basic cortical-cell types: those with long axons, mostly pyramidal in shape, and those with short axons.

A number of experiments support the view that the lateral interconnections among columns of cells within the cortex are not of great functional importance in normal intracortical conduction. The most important connections among different columns appear to be made through axons that leave the cortex and return again after traveling for distances ranging from a fraction of a millimeter to several centimeters through the underlying white matter. At least two forms of abnormal activity can spread for indefinite distances within the cortex, however; paroxysmal discharge and spreading depression.

Measurements of dendritic and axon-terminal fields suggest that there are innumerable possibilities for closed feedback paths involving cortical neurons. Even more such loops must be possible if thalamic and other neurons participate in the circuits. It seems clear that powerful inhibitory components must be present to prevent excessive buildup of activity in these pathways. The combination of closed feedback circuits and lateral inhibition could produce segregation of many small networks of widely distributed cortical neurons that fire together. It is proposed that each such network of cells could acquire connections with various sensory inputs that have a common property and that the network would then represent that common property or abstraction.

CHAPTER 8

RECEPTORS

In this chapter we shall deal briefly with several general properties of receptors, taking examples from various sensory modalities. We shall investigate the mechanisms through which stimuli influence rate of impulse generation, adaptation, and the relations between stimulus intensity and receptor output, that is, the coding of sensory information.

Receptors are the windows of the nervous system. In the jargon of data processing they constitute an "interface" between the environment and the nervous system. In primitive organisms a single cell is both receptor and effector. The membrane, or part of it, reacts to changes in the environment in such a way as to activate proteins similar to actin and myosin within the cell and thus to cause movement. In higher animals muscle cells still respond to local stimuli by contracting, but their sensitivity has become highly specialized, so that normally they respond only to chemical transmitters released by motoneurons at their end-plate regions. Muscle cells and the rest of the nervous system are shielded from the outside world and rely on a few specialized cells, the receptors, for information about it.

Receptors function in basically the same way as do neurons, and, in fact, some of them are the slightly modified dendritic zones of neurons. All other receptors have no axons and do not fire; rather they have direct influence on the dendritic zone of a sensory neuron. They differ from neurons in that they are located where they will be exposed to environmental stimulation and have evolved special sensitivities, to temperature changes, light, traces of airborne chemicals, or other stimuli.

It must be stressed, however (and this point will be raised many times in our discussion of the sensory processes), that, despite their specialization, receptors do not completely exclude all other types of input. The photoreceptors of the eye, for example, will respond to mechanical stimulation, and thermal receptors will respond to chemical stimulation (application of menthol, for example) or to pressure (Zotterman, 1959). Recordings from sensory nerves have revealed many similar examples.

The receptors that collect information about the world outside the organism are of greatest interest to most psychologists. But the brain also has to know what is going on in the rest of the body (as far as the nervous system is concerned, the body is the part of the environment that is of most immediate concern), and receptors can therefore be found in all parts of the body, even inside the brain itself.

TYPES OF RECEPTORS

Receptors are *transducers*; that is, they convert one form of energy into another, leaving the informational content relatively unchanged. They can be divided into two general catagories, according to whether they are normally excited by mechanical or by chemical stimuli. The former are called *mechanoreceptors*, the latter *chemoreceptors*. In Chapter 2 we noted that, in order to generate an impulse propagated along its axon, a cell must be depolarized to a critical potential. In neurons the flow of depolarizing current is induced by the action of minute quantities of chemical on the subsynaptic parts of the membranes. In chemoreceptors like olfactory receptors similar chemical depolarization takes place on the membranes, and propagated action potentials may then be generated in the axons of the receptor cells, exactly as in a neuron. The changed membrane potential of a receptor resulting from the depolarizing action of a stimulus is called the *generator potential*.

The taste buds of the tongue and the photoreceptors of the eye are examples of receptors that do not have axons and do not generate spike discharges. Such receptors are innervated by dendrites from the first neuron of the sensory path, and it is probable that depolarization of the receptors causes currents to flow through the closely apposed neuronal membranes (Figure 8.1). An alternative possibility is that, when such a receptor is depolarized, it releases a transmitter substance onto the dendrites of the innervating neuron.

Frequently, when the receptor cell has no electrically excitable zone and does not generate an impulse, the first sensory neuron that innervates it is spontaneously active, even in the absence of stimulation. The effect of stimulating the receptor is then to modulate the rate of spontaneous neuronal discharge by speeding up or slowing down the flow of depolarizing current into the dendrites of the neuron. There is thus no stimulus too small to fire the pathway, and the sensory neuron has no well-defined threshold. The detection of a stimulus then depends upon the ability of the central "decoding" nuclei to discriminate changes in frequency of the input.

Chemoreceptors subserve the senses of smell and taste, and many are present in the brain to monitor levels of carbon dioxide, glucose, hormones and other chemicals in the body fluids. It is not so obvious, perhaps, that the visual receptors are fundamentally chemoreceptors, but light breaks photopigments like visual purple (rhodopsin) down into their chemical components, and presumably one of these components acts upon the receptor membrane (or perhaps upon the membrane of the neuron that innervates the receptor) to increase its permeability to ions.

Temperature-sensitive receptors probably also rely upon a chemical phenomenon. The

Figure 8.1 The receptor cell does not itself generate an impulse, but the depolarizing current that flows into it when it is stimulated also flows through a closely apposed sensory-nerve terminal and depolarizes it sufficiently to generate impulses there.

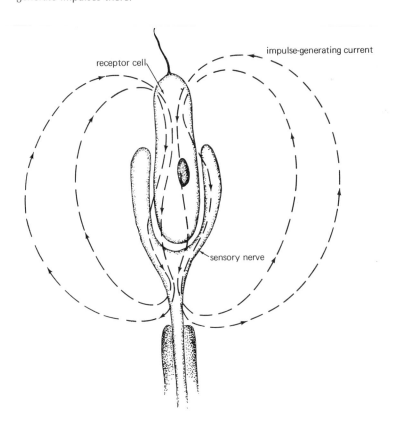

rates of many enzyme reactions are very sensitive to temperature; thus a depolarizing substance may be bound in an inactive form at one temperature and released at a slightly different temperature.

There are two schools of thought on the mechanism of depolarization in mechanoreceptors. One obvious possibility is that mechanical distortion opens pores in the membrane, allowing sodium ions to enter the cell (Figure 8.2). Another possibility is that movement releases a transmitter substance onto the membrane, which would make these cells basically chemoreceptors like the rest. Acetylcholine and other chemical agents have been shown to fire some mechanoreceptors, but the effect can be eliminated by cholinergic blocking agents like curare or *hexamethonium* without reducing the receptor's sensitivity to mechanical stimuli. This result tends to favor the hypothesis of

mechanical opening of pores, though it does not completely rule out the possibility that depolarization is mediated by some still-unknown transmitter substance. Mechanoreceptors are found in the ear and the vestibular apparatus (which signals the position and rate of movement of the head), the muscles (the annulospiral receptor of the muscle spindle that we have already studied is such a receptor), the joints, and throughout the skin and viscera.

Pain receptors may be fired by thermal, mechanical, or chemical means, as anyone who has suffered a sensitive tooth will know. It is most unlikely that there is only one type of pain receptor; in fact, there may not even be such a thing as a specialized pain receptor. It is very important to keep in mind that we are not directly aware of receptor activity; our sensations result from patterns of activity in the brain. We can be quite sure that there is no

Figure 8.2 Ion flow through pores opened in the membrane by mechanical distortion of a free nerve ending.

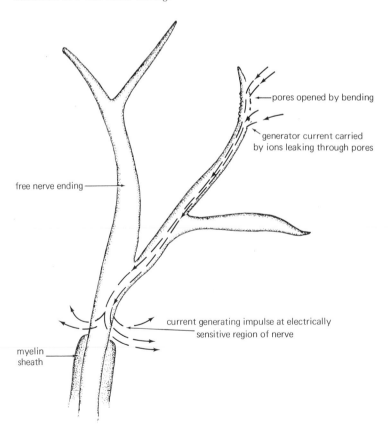

one-to-one correspondence between the activity of an individual receptor and the activity that it produces in the brain; the effect at the center will depend upon the overall pattern of receptor firing and probably upon other factors as well.

ADAPTATION IN RECEPTORS

The earliest work on the coding of sensory information was done by Adrian (1928) shortly after the development of electronic amplifiers, which made it possible to record the activity of single axons in peripheral nerves. He and his collaborators showed that the sensory message consists of trains of impulses whose amplitude is independent of the stimulus and that there is some correspondence between the frequency of firing and the strength of the applied stimulus. They also observed the decline in impulse frequency over time, which underlies the phenomenon of adaptation to a steadily applied stimulus. Touch receptors may stop firing completely within a second after application of steady pressure to the skin or the bending of a hair and may then give another short burst of activity when the stimulus is removed.

On the other hand, some receptors show only partial adaptation, which is clearly related to a need for information about the steady value of a stimulus, as in the stretch receptors of the carotid sinus, which are part of the system regulating blood pressure, or the position receptors of the joints. It can also be inferred that the transducers responsible for maintaining the body temperature at about 37° C. must be nonadapting, though the temperature receptors in the skin adapt quite rapidly over a considerable range of temperatures.

The mechanism of sensory adaptation is still largely unknown, though it is presumably related to the one that produces adaptation in neurons. One possibility is that the membrane potential of an excitable cell tends to be held constant by a chemical feedback system that accelerates the ion pump when the potential falls. A sustained generator potential will thus be reduced by an increased counterflow of ions. One would then expect the cell to overcom-

pensate and experience reduced sensitivity for a time after the removal of the stimulus, but although many receptors do, touch and pressure receptors do not. They respond briefly at the onset of a mechanical disturbance and again when it is removed. If we accept the hypothesis that the membrane of such a receptor becomes porous when it is distorted, we can explain the adaptation as a plastic flow of the membrane, which relieves the stress and allows the pores to close again. When the stimulus is removed the membrane must return to its old shape, which will briefly open the pores once more. This does not explain, however, why some mechanoreceptors fail to adapt.

J. A. B. Gray (1959) has suggested that sometimes the dynamic characteristics of the tissue around a receptor may result in application of a brief stimulation to the sensitive region during the onset and cessation of a steady stimulus. For example, a touch to the skin might set up a wave, and receptors would be stretched only as the wave passed through them.

Experiments by Katz (1950), Gray and Sato (1935), and Loewenstein (1959), to be described shortly, have shown that in at least some types of adapting receptors the decay of impulse frequency follows a time course similar to that of the generator potential. Shigehiro Nakajima (1964), however, demonstrated that the rapidly adapting stretch receptor of the crayfish quickly ceased to generate impulses, even though the generator potential was artificially held constant. He therefore concluded that in some instances adaptation is a function of spike generation.

INFORMATION CODING BY RECEPTORS

After Adrian's early experiments B. H. C. Matthews (1931, 1933) made a quantitative study of the relation between the stimulus and the frequency of generated impulses. The receptor he used was the muscle-spindle stretch receptor, to which measured stimuli can easily be applied and which adapts to only a limited extent. By hanging different weights on the muscle while recording impulses from a single

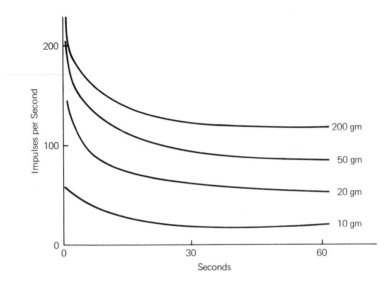

Figure 8.3 Frequency of impulses in the afferent nerve, plotted against the duration of different loads applied to a muscle-spindle receptor from the frog.

sensory fiber from a stretch receptor in it, Matthews obtained curves of impulse frequency plotted against load similar to that shown in Figure 8.3. If instead of plotting the load on the muscle against frequency of impulses, we plot the logarithm of the load, the curve is approximately a straight line over most of the working range of the receptor (Figure 8.4), which is often taken to mean that Fechner's *psychophysical relationship* [sensation $= a \cdot$ log

Figure 8.4 Frequency of impulses in an afferent nerve, plotted against the logarithm of the load on a muscle-spindle stretch receptor in the frog. The readings were taken 1 second after application of the load. (After B. H. C. Matthews, 1931.)

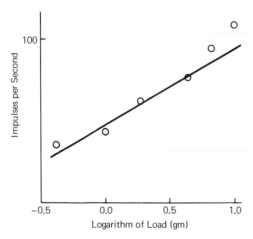

(stimulus intensity)] is a consequence of the characteristics of the receptor. The receptor generates an impulse frequency proportional to the logarithm of the stimulus (over the normal range of input). Thus the sensation, which is also proportional to the logarithm of the stimulus, must be directly proportional to the frequency generated by the receptor and transmitted along the sensory nerve.

Other measures of the relationship do not fit the logarithmic curve quite so closely. Hartline and Graham (1932) recorded the frequency of impulses from an *ommatidium* (light-sensitive element) of the horseshoe crab (*Limulus*) at different brightnesses. The frequency 3.5 seconds after the onset of light is plotted against the logarithm of the intensity of light in Figure 8.5. The relationship is distinctly nonlinear. If, however, the logarithm of the impulse frequency is plotted against that of the intensity, a straight line is obtained. This curve corresponds to the power law proposed by Stevens (1957, 1961): sensation $=$ (stimulus intensity)^b, or $S = I^b$. It so happens that the empirical constant b for the curve obtained by Hartline and Graham for the *Limulus* eye is approximately 0.3, which is close to the value 0.33 based on brightness judgments by human subjects that Stevens gave for the visual system, but this approximation is no doubt coincidental.

Probably no simple mathematical expression exactly describes the input-output characteristics of all receptors; the logarithmic relationship is adequate for most, but the power law may be more accurate for some. The apparent correspondence between the subjective intensity of a sensation and the frequency of impulses generated by receptors is very surprising in view of the many factors that influence the signal on its way to the brain.

It has already been pointed out that the generation of impulses by receptors is a two-stage affair; the physical stimulus produces a generator potential by depolarizing the cell, and the generator potential initiates spike activity in an axon, either its own or that of the first sensory neuron. It would be interesting to know more about how these two processes are related quantitatively. For example, does the nonlinearity of transduction arise in the first or the second stage? Experiments related to this problem have been performed by several investigators. Katz (1950) was able to measure the generator potential of a muscle stretch receptor in the frog by placing an electrode made of agar jelly on the afferent nerve very close to the receptor. The generator potential was conducted through the cytoplasm of the receptor axon, which was short enough not to impose too great a resistance in the recording circuit (see Figure 8.6). The electrode picked up both the generator potential and the impulses propagated along the axon when the muscle was stretched through a measured distance by an electromagnetic device. The results are shown in Figure 8.7; the generator potential appears as a shift in the base line of the trace, upon which the spike discharges are superimposed. Katz found a linear relationship between the generator potential and the spike frequency. The presence of the large spikes tended to make accurate measurement of the generator potential difficult, so they were eliminated through the application of *procaine*, a local anesthetic that has little effect on the depolarization process but suppresses the electrical excitability of the axon. Katz then found that the generator potential was roughly a logarithmic function of

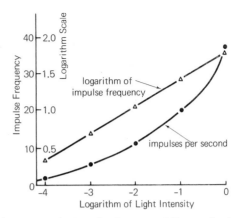

Figure 8.5 The impulse frequency 3.5 seconds after the onset of light (dots) and the logarithms of the same values (triangles) plotted against the logarithms of the light intensity in arbitrary units. (After Hartline & Graham, 1932.)

the stretch. The psychophysical function is thus introduced into the sensory system at its very first link.

More recently, J. A. B. Gray and Sato (1953) and Loewenstein (1959) have studied similar phenomena in the *Pacinian corpuscle* (Figure 8.8). This mechanoreceptor attains a length of up to 1 mm and is found in the skin, joints, and many other places. It is constructed rather like an onion, with many layers surrounding a central neural ending; it adapts very rapidly. In order to measure its excitability, the receptor was mounted so that it could be stimulated by a blunt probe driven by a loudspeaker unit, a method that allows both the intensity and the speed of application of the stimulus to be accurately controlled and measured. Gray and Sato found that, as in the stretch receptor, a generator potential could be recorded from the nerve whenever the corpuscle was touched by the probe. (Incidentally, in this instance the logarithmic law fitted the data better than did Stevens' power law.)

As can be seen in Figure 8.9a the generator potential reached a peak about 2 msec after the sudden application of a stimulus and had completely decayed about 10 msec later. It seems that in these receptors the ion permeability outlasts the movement by only 1-2 msec and that the resting potential is restored immediately. If the stimulus is applied more slowly,

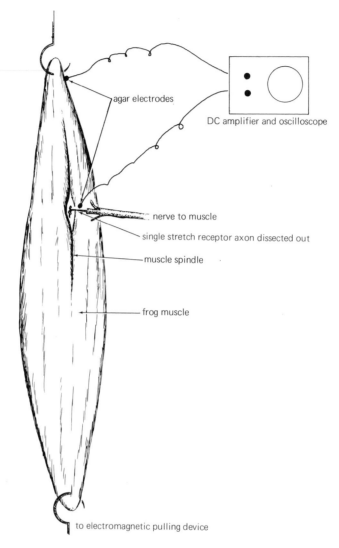

agar electrodes

DC amplifier and oscilloscope

nerve to muscle

single stretch receptor axon dissected out

muscle spindle

frog muscle

to electromagnetic pulling device

Figure 8.6 The preparation used by Katz: a frog muscle (greatly enlarged), showing one muscle spindle and the stretch-receptor axon dissected away from the main nerve to the muscle. One agar electrode is placed on the nerve very close to the receptor; the other electrode is placed on a tendon. The muscle can be stretched by means of an electromagnetic pulling device.

the restoration process cancels out some of the depolarization, and the peak generator potential is reduced (Figure 8.9b, c).

Loewenstein (1959) was able to show, in a series of ingenious experiments, that the capsule of the Pacinian corpuscle has nothing to do with the activity of the receptor except for modifying the effects of mechanical forces upon the sensitive inner core. All the layers of the capsule

could be dissected away without affecting the generator potential or the firing of the nerve to a mechanical stimulus. If the nerve was cut, however, and the ending within the capsule was allowed to degenerate, stimulating the capsule produced absolutely no electrical response.

By delicate manipulations Loewenstein managed to place two tiny stimulating probes at different points on the surface of a single

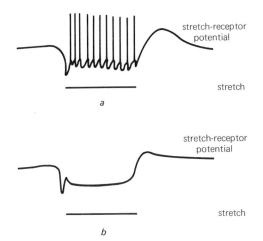

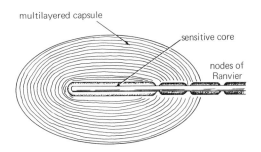

Figure 8.8 Cross section of a Pacinian corpuscle showing the core consisting of a sensory nerve-ending.

Figure 8.7 Potentials recorded from an axon close to the stretch receptor of a frog muscle during application of stretch. (a) Without procaine. (b) After application of 0.5 per cent procaine to block spike generation. (After Katz, 1950.)

nerve ending dissected from a Pacinian corpuscle (Figure 8.10a). Each of the probes, moved separately, produced a generator potential; when both were moved simultaneously the potentials summated as shown in Figure 8.10b. This finding supports the theory that at each point on the nerve ending distortion of the membrane will produce a momentary leakage current that contributes to the total generator potential.

Very rapidly adapting receptors like the Pacinian corpuscle cannot signal information about static stimuli (the position of a joint or tendon or the pressure on the skin, for example). They do not even provide accurate information about the intensity of a changing stimulus because the rate of change has such an important effect upon receptor output. Engineers frequently employ this type of information in feedback-control circuits to help maintain stability; perhaps rapidly adapting receptors in muscle spindles and joints also serve this purpose. Rapidly adapting receptors would also be useful in producing initial arousal to a change in stimulus without occupying transmission paths later, when the situation has been attended to and appraised.

Figure 8.9 Generator potentials from a Pacinian corpuscle during application of an electrically controlled tactile stimulus. (a) The stimulus onset as brief as possible. The stimulus stays on after application. (b) The stimulus onset occupying about 2.5 msec. (c) The stimulus onset occupying about 5.5 msec. (After J. A. B. Gray & Sato, 1953.)

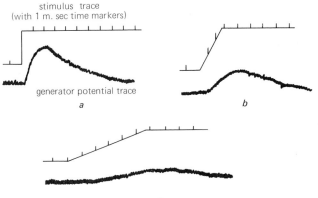

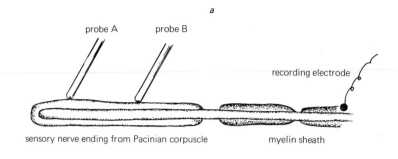

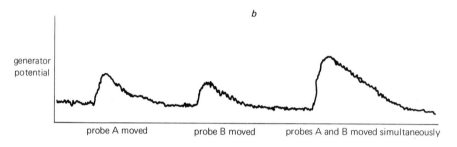

Figure 8.10 (a) Two mechanical probes positioned at different points along the sensory-nerve ending dissected from a Pacinian corpuscle. (b) Potentials recorded during movements of each probe separately and together, illustrating summation of generator potentials. (After Loewenstein, 1959.)

Nonadapting or more slowly adapting receptors provide information on the intensity of a steady stimulus, coded, as we have seen, as frequency of axonal discharge. In practice, many receptors fire together, and more information is contained in the pattern of their firing. This matter will be considered more fully in the next chapters.

Summary

Receptors respond to stimuli with changes in membrane potential. The structures and locations of most render them particularly responsive to single types of stimulation—light, temperature, or mechanical deformation, for example.

Those most sensitive to mechanical stimuli are called "mechanoreceptors"; those most sensitive to chemical input are called "chemoreceptors." Some receptors are the specialized endings of primary sensory neurons; many receptors, however, are not parts of neurons but are innervated by primary sensory neurons.

The change in receptor-membrane potential produced by a stimulus is called a "generator potential." When it reaches a critical value the axon of the sensory neuron fires; it has been found that the firing rate is proportional to the generator potential over wide limits. The generator potential is not, however, a linear function of stimulus intensity; in most instances it is approximately proportional to the logarithm of the intensity or is related to it by a power law.

Many receptors respond strongly to the onset of a stimulus but either completely cease to respond after a short time or continue at much reduced rates. This phenomenon is known as "adaptation." The mechanisms of adaptation are not understood, but it seems certain that more than one are involved. One of them may be a membrane reaction to counteract the depolarization produced by the stimulus; another may be a "healing" of breaches through which ions leak after mechanical deformation. It has also been shown that the generation of impulses by the axon slows with continued firing, even though the generator potential may remain constant.

The initial bursts of activity by receptors, before adaptation sets in, probably serve to start the response to a stimulus briskly or to attract attention to a new stimulus. Adaptation prevents constant stimuli from masking new input or distracting attention from more important stimuli.

CHAPTER 9

TASTE AND SMELL

The sense of taste depends upon chemical sensitivity to fluids and substances in aqueous solution. Smell, in air-breathing animals, depends upon chemical sensitivity to gaseous and airborne substances. In fish, however, both gustatory and olfactory receptors are stimulated by traces of chemicals in solution; the difference between taste and smell lies in the location and sensitivity of the receptors. Smell and taste, even in land animals, are closely associated functionally. What we commonly think of as the taste of a substance is the result of its action on both the gustatory and olfactory systems; if one or the other sense is eliminated, the subjective "taste" is profoundly altered.

These chemical senses evolved because of their value in feeding, finding mates, and avoiding poisons, predators, and unhealthy environments. Smell, which is more sensitive to volatile chemicals, provides advance information and is able to guide the animal toward or away from an odoriferous object. Taste is a contact sense and has strong reflex connections that promote consumption and digestion of food (through salivary and gastric secretions) or the forcible ejection of potentially harmful substances from the mouth.

TASTE

In some fish taste chemoreceptors are distributed over the whole body, so that taste is simply another cutaneous sense like those of tempera-

ture or pain. Some insects have taste receptors on their feet, as well as on their proboscises. Although most land-dwelling vertebrates have lost this sense from all the skin except that of the mouth and tongue, there is no good anatomical or physiological reason for considering taste to be different from the other relatively protopathic (motivating) cutaneous senses in these animals. Taste fibers join the same peripheral nerves from the tongue and gullet as do the fibers from pressure, temperature, and pain receptors, and some nerve endings in the tongue respond to both taste and temperature or both taste and touch.

Although we recognize four "primary" tastes: salt, sweet, bitter, and sour, this classification is convenient only for experimental purposes. It has never been shown that every taste can be synthesized through suitable mixtures of these four, a minimum requirement for acceptance of the assumption that they are primaries; nor does it seem likely that any attempt to do so would be conclusive. Taste comparisons are much more difficult to conduct than are color comparisons, for example. In the first place, it is difficult to eliminate confusing stimulation of the olfactory system, and, second, it is impossible to eliminate the aftereffects of one stimulation completely so that a second may be applied within a reasonable time. These aftereffects consist of selective adaptations, producing insensitivity to some tastes relative to others or aftertastes that supplement and modify subsequent stimulations. Furthermore, pure primary stimuli are difficult, perhaps impossible, to obtain.

As a corollary to the idea of primary tastes, early sense physiologists assumed that each had its own receptors and conduction system to the brain. Similar assumptions had been made about other modalities as well. We shall see that present-day physiological measurements do not support these assumptions.

One of the arguments for assuming that there are specific receptors for each primary taste was that different parts of the tongue have different relative sensitivities to different tastes. The back is sensitive to bitter, the tip to sweet, and the lateral surfaces to salt and sour, but, according to Patton (1960), the back is only about six times more sensitive to quinine than is the tip and four times more than are the sides. The relative differences in sensitivity to other tastes from one area to another are even smaller. The middle part of the dorsal surface of the tongue is quite insensitive to all tastes.

Many efforts have been made to find the physical and chemical correlates of tastes but with limited success. Salty tastes are elicited by cations like Na^+ and K^+ (or even by non-metallic cations like NH_4^+ but not by H^+). The taste of a salt also depends upon its anion to some extent; for example, sodium sulphate tastes salty but not quite the same as sodium chloride; apparently the sulphate anion modifies the taste.

The hydrogen ion is different from other cations, in that it elicits a sour taste. There is a tendency for weak acids like citric and acetic acids (lemon juice and vinegar), in which only a small proportion of the molecules dissociate into hydrogen ions and acid radicles, to taste more sour than a solution of the same pH (hydrogen-ion concentration) of a strong acid like HCl, in which most of the molecules are dissociated into ions, presumably because the buffering action of the initially undissociated molecules of the weaker acids replenishes the supply when hydrogen ions are absorbed by various reactions in the mouth.

There does not seem to be any single chemical structure that is essential for conferring the property of sweetness. It is puzzling that, although a wide range of substances taste sweet (many sugars, some amino acids, lead acetate, beryllium salts, very dilute salt solutions, glycols, and others), quite small differences in the structure of chemical isomers (compounds of the same atoms differently arranged) can change them from sweet to tasteless. It is believed that there must be different types of receptor sites on the membrane of each "sweet" receptor, to which molecules differing in structure can become attached, opening pores and causing the cell to be depolarized. Each site accepts only molecules of a specific shape, but one cell may accommodate a variety of different sites (Evans, 1963).

There seems to be a close association between sweet and bitter mechanisms. Most bitter substances are organic, but again some dilute salts taste bitter, and, after the tongue has become adapted to salt, even distilled water tastes bitter to some people (Bartoshuk, McBurney, & Pfaffmann, 1964). Slight changes in the structures of many sweet compounds can convert them into bitter ones, and many synthetic sweetening agents like saccharin have bitter aftertastes. Another indication of a relationship is that a substance, *gymnemic acid,* inhibits both sweet and bitter receptors, regardless of the different substances that elicit these tastes (R. M. Warren & Pfaffmann, 1959).

The classical bitter substances are *alkaloids,* plant bases like strychnine, nicotine, quinine, and caffeine. Many of these substances are toxic, which ensures the evolutionary selection of animals that can detect and reject them from their diets. It is interesting that many people with otherwise normal sensitivity to bitter substances are unable to taste the compound *phenylthiocarbamide* (PTC), further evidence that there are separate receptor sites for different substances on the same cell membranes. It may thus be futile to look for a common chemical property shared by compounds that taste the same. Each may have its own site and its individual way of stimulating the same receptors.

We may say, then, that the characteristics that give substances their tastes are only very roughly known. Acids are sour, salts are salty, and many organic compounds are either sweet or bitter, with a tendency for the lighter molecules to be sweet and the heavier ones to be bitter. There is no way, at present, to predict the taste of a substance from its chemical structure, nor are the actions of the substances on the receptor membranes understood.

Another peculiar feature of the sense of taste is its variability from species to species. Perhaps this variability should not surprise us, in view of the differences in diet of different animals and the importance of taste in determining what is eaten and what is rejected.

Kare and Ficken (1963) have conducted a number of comparative studies of taste preference and have found for example, that fowls are indifferent to many sugars (dextrose, maltose, sucrose) but have a strong aversion to xylose. Calves, on the other hand, like xylose second only to sucrose, though they are indifferent to maltose and lactose. Rats have a strong liking for most sugars, including xylose, but maltose is first choice; they avoid xylose in high concentrations. Dogs show still a different pattern, and cats are indifferent to all sugars, except possibly when starving.

Saccharin solution is strongly preferred to water by rats and pigs, calves are indifferent to it, chickens avoid it slightly, and dogs do not like it at all. There are marked individual differences even within species, however. Some rats show little preference for saccharin at concentrations enjoyed by most rats. Nachman (1959) has bred from rats that seem to avoid saccharin and has found that the behavior is inherited. Calves, chickens, and some other animals are astonishingly indifferent to hydrogen-ion concentration; they will ingest solutions so acid that humans would regard them as intolerably sour.

Although there has been no systematic attempt to correlate data on preference with electrophysiological data, differences among species are also found in the responses of tongue nerves to chemical stimulation of the receptors. NaCl is a more effective stimulus in rats than is KCl, but the reverse is true in cats and dogs. There is little neural response to sugar in cats but more in rats and guinea pigs. Many animals have water-sensitive taste receptors; such receptors have been found by electrophysiological recording in the frog, cat, dog, pig, pigeon, chicken, and monkey. No fibers responding to water have been found in the rat, sheep, goat, calf, or man (see Kitchell, 1963). It is difficult to make much sense of these differences, for all these animals require water and drink it from time to time. Some change in activity of nerves from the mouth must indicate the presence of water in such animals.

Great care must be taken not to confuse preference thresholds with taste thresholds. The fact that the preference thresholds of animals,

from bees and blowflies (Frisch, 1950; Dethier & Bodenstein, 1958) to rats, cats, and men (Richter, 1947; Kare & Ficken, 1963), vary with the needs of the animal has misled some investigators into believing that receptors change their sensitivity according to those needs. This view has repeatedly been shown to be false. Pfaffmann and Bare (1950) recorded from the afferent nerves of normal and salt-deficient rats (the rats had been *adrenalectomized*, that is, their adrenal glands had been removed, which caused them to excrete excessive sodium). There was absolutely no difference in the threshold concentration of salt solution that caused firing in the nerves of the two groups, though the salt-deficient rats showed a preference for a solution almost at the receptor threshold and the normal rats had a much higher average preference threshold. Nachman and Pfaffmann (1963) achieved the same results, using intact rats that had been deprived of sodium. Koh and Teitelbaum (1961) found that normal rats demonstrate detection thresholds much below the normal preference thresholds when they have been punished with shock for failing to discriminate between dilute salt solution and water.

Although preference and aversion thresholds are interesting in themselves, they should never be confused with or used to measure detection thresholds. Before pursuing our investigations into the activity of afferent neurons, we must digress to take a closer look at what is known of the anatomy of the taste pathway.

Anatomy of the Taste System

The receptors for taste occur in clusters called "taste buds." The buds are oval in shape and nearly 0.1 mm long. Each contains 10–15 cells, not all of which are active receptors at any given time. The receptors are slender cells with *microvilli* (hairs) protruding from a pore at the top of each bud, as shown in Figure 9.1. The cells remain functional for only a few days. *Epithelial* (skin) cells at the border of the bud are continually dividing and migrating to the center. On the way they become innervated by the sensory nerve to the bud, and Beidler (1963) believes that it is this connection that confers the special receptor properties upon the cells, causing the morphological and functional changes. After only three or four days of active life, the cells lose their neural connections and degenerate.

There are about 10,000 taste buds in the normal human adult and rather more in children. The chicken has only 24, but the catfish has 100,000 taste buds over its whole body. In terrestrial vertebrates the taste buds are located in various *papillae* (small elevations) on the tongue, palate, larynx, and pharynx. They are supplied by a network of nerve fibers, each of which branches and innervates several receptors. Other branches sometimes end freely in the surrounding epithelium.

Taste fibers from the anterior two-thirds of the tongue enter the *lingual nerve* along with those from pain, touch, and temperature receptors. They then pass into a branch of the *chorda tympani*, a nerve that traverses the middle ear to join the seventh cranial (facial) nerve (see Chapter 3). Primary afferent taste fibers terminate in the *nucleus of the solitary tract* (Figure 9.2; Makous, Nord, Oakley & Pfaffmann, 1963). The receptors in the posterior third of the tongue are connected to the same nucleus of the medulla through the glossopharyngeal nerve. Those in the larynx and pharynx communicate with the nucleus through the vagus nerve.

It is usually claimed that the second-order neurons, originating in the nucleus of the solitary tract (those receiving synapses from the primary sensory nerves), project to the contralateral *ventralis posterior medialis* (VPM) nucleus of the thalamus (Figure 9.3), their axons having crossed over to ascend in the medial lemniscus. This claim has been questioned by Frommer (1961), who found, recording from the thalamus with small electrodes, that the response was mainly ipsilateral. Emmers, Benjamin, and Blomquist (1962), using a similar technique, found a bilateral distribution of taste afferents in the ventroposterior part of the ventral nucleus in the rat. They also found predominantly ipsilateral taste projection to the homologous part of the thalamus in the squirrel

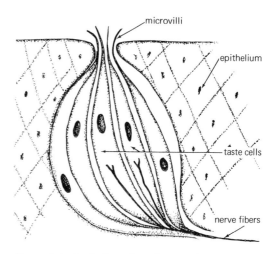

Figure 9.1 Vertical section of a taste bud.

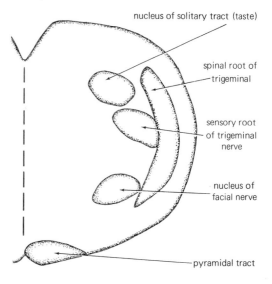

Figure 9.2 A cross section of the rat medulla, showing location of the solitary-tract nucleus, in which taste activity can be recorded.

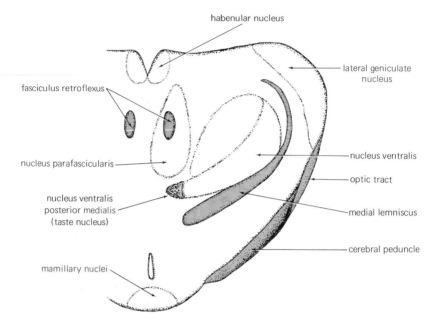

Figure 9.3 A cross section of the rat thalamus, showing the location of the relay nucleus for taste. (After Benjamin, 1963.)

monkey (Blomquist, Benjamin & Emmers, 1962).

The region of the thalamus to which taste afferents project is an architectonically distinct subnucleus (that is, the cells are recognizably different in shape) in the most medial part of the ventral nucleus (Figure 9.3). It is just below the *parafascicular nucleus* in the rat and just below the *centre median* in the monkey. Only impulses from taste stimulation are recorded there. Lesions in this subnucleus produce ele-

Figure 9.4 Area for taste on the ventrolateral cortex of the rat (According to Benjamin & Akert, 1959).

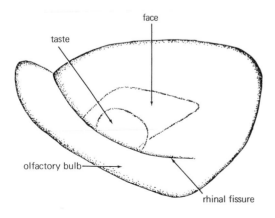

vations of the threshold for quinine avoidance (Ables & Benjamin, 1960) and impairment of preferences for sucrose and salt (Oakley & Pfaffmann, 1962) in the rat.

The cortical projection of the gustatory system is not known with the same degree of confidence as is the thalamic projection. Bagshaw and Pribram (1953) found that the avoidance threshold for quinine solutions was raised in monkeys through large lesions that included the anterior insula and the anterior parts of both the upper and lower banks of the Sylvian fissure. Benjamin and Pfaffmann (1955) ablated rat cortex in which they had evoked potentials with stimulation of the chorda tympani and the ninth cranial nerve (an area at the bottom of the sensory area for the face and just above the *rhinal fissure*; see Figure 9.4), and they too obtained an increase in the threshold for quinine avoidance. The impairment was considerably attenuated 140 days after the operation, however, and no deficit was obtained in rats that had been overtrained or totally untrained on the discrimination task before the operation (Benjamin, 1959).

Lesions in this cortical area of the rat produced retrograde degeneration of the subnucleus for taste in the medial part of the ventralis posterior thalamic nucleus, indicating it is the cortex to which that nucleus projects. (Benjamin & Akert, 1959). It is puzzling that a cortical lesion that produces degeneration in a thalamic nucleus should have less effect upon behavior than does a lesion in that nucleus alone, but it does. Apparently after retrograde degeneration small neurons remain in the thalamus to subserve taste discrimination.

In the squirrel monkey the situation is even more puzzling. Ablation of the cortex that receives projections from the chorda tympani and ninth cranial nerve had no significant effect upon taste discrimination, nor did it produce degeneration in the thalamic nucleus for taste (Benjamin, 1963). Benjamin was of the opinion that taste input was projected not to the cortex but to the claustrum, which is close enough to the insula in the monkey to be accidentally damaged by cortical ablations. In the rat the claustrum is not distinguishable from the deep cortex in the area where lesions produce deficits of taste discrimination (De Groot, 1959).

M. J. Cohen, Landgren, Ström, and Zotterman (1957) and Landgren (1957a, b) recorded from single cells in the part of the cat cortex that receives projections from the chorda tympani, the motor area for mastication close to the rhinal fissure and anterior to the *ectosylvian gyrus* (Figure 12.14). They found few pure taste cells there, though a number of cells that responded to mechanical or thermal stimulation of the tongue also responded to gustatory stimuli. Apparently it is an area of convergence for tongue afferents, and its significance as a taste area has not yet been conclusively determined.

Afferent Taste Mechanisms

K. Kimura and Beidler (1961) were able to record directly from single receptor cells in taste buds in the tongues of rats and hamsters. Typical responses to solutions placed on the tongue are shown in Figure 9.5. A steady depolarization of up to 10 mv occurred as long as the stimuli were present. In the taste

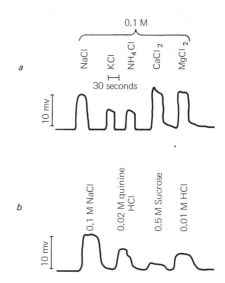

Figure 9.5 Recordings of DC potentials inside single taste cells. (a) A rat taste cell as various chloride solutions are applied to the tongue. Water rinses were applied for about 30 seconds between each chemical stimulation. (b) Responses of a hamster taste cell to salty, bitter, sweet, and sour stimuli. (After K. Kimura & Beidler, 1961.)

cell whose record is shown in Figure 9.5b salty, bitter, sweet, and sour stimuli depolarized receptors to different degrees. No highly specific receptor cells were found, though some depolarized cells were unaffected by some stimuli and only weakly depolarized by others.

One nerve fiber of the lingual nerve innervates several receptor cells, and it is not surprising that these fibers do not show taste specificity any more than the receptors do. If the functional properties of the receptor are determined by the nerve, as was suggested earlier, we may expect all the receptors innervated by a particular fiber to have roughly the same spectrum of taste sensitivity and this spectrum to be reflected in the activity of the nerve.

Pfaffmann (1955) has made many measurements of single-fiber activity in the chorda tympani of various animals during stimulation of the tongue with different sapid (that is, flavored) substances. Some of the results are illustrated in the histograms in Figure 9.6. It should be noted that only occasional fibers responded to single stimuli. Most of the fibers had a preferred substance, which produced a

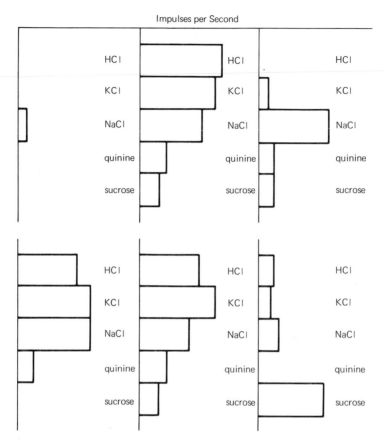

Figure 9.6 The activity of six different chorda-tympani fibers during separate stimulation of the tongue with five different substances in the rat. (After Pfaffmann, 1955.)

maximum firing rate, but they nevertheless fired, though less rapidly, to all, or almost all, of the other stimuli used.

Although not shown in Figure 9.6, fibers that respond to water have been found in many

Figure 9.7 The integrated response of the chorda tympani to NaCl solutions (of the molar concentrations shown) flowing over the tongue of a rat. Each concentration flowed for about 10 seconds and was followed by distilled water for about 20 seconds. (After Beidler, 1961.)

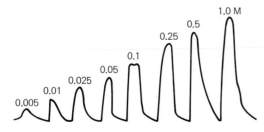

animals, especially birds; again this sensitivity is not unique, and the same fibers fire to other substances as well.

When a solution is placed on the tongue, the firing rate in the chorda tympani rises to a maximum within about 50 msec and then falls to a lower rate, which is maintained for several minutes if the solution remains on the tongue. The relationship between the concentration of a saline solution and the firing rate it produces is indicated in Figure 9.7. The relationship turns out to be roughly a power function (Beidler, 1961).

Responses to gustatory stimuli in single neurons of the nucleus of the solitary tract have been studied by Pfaffmann, Erickson, Frommer, and Halpern (1961) and by Makous, Nord, Oakley, and Pfaffmann (1963). The results are very similar to those obtained from the single fibers of the chorda tympani. Many neurons responded to cooling as well as to chemical stimulation and some to mechanical stimulation also, which may explain why thirsty rats will spend long periods "drinking" at a cool-air jet and will even learn to press a lever to gain access to it (Hendry & Rasche, 1961).

Benjamin (1963) has recorded from single taste neurons in the thalamus of the squirrel monkey. The responses were very meager (perhaps because the animals were under nembutal anesthesia), but they were otherwise quite similar to those of cells in the rat medulla, though somewhat more specific. Almost one-third of the units responded to just one of the standard stimuli (NaCl, HCl, quinine, and sucrose). Several cells gave "off" responses to acid. They responded to the water rinse after acid had been placed on the tongue but gave no immediate response to the acid itself. A number of cells responded to both NaCl and sucrose; several to NaCl, HCl, and quinine; but none to both quinine and sucrose. Some cells were sensitive to temperature changes, as well as to several of the taste stimuli.

Cohen, Landgren, Ström, and Zotterman (1957) and Landgren (1957a, b), as mentioned earlier, recorded from single cortical cells in the "taste" area of the cat. They found convergence of many modalities in these cells; the specificity of cortical taste cells in the cat was much less than that of taste cells in the monkey thalamus.

It is difficult to reconcile such lack of specificity, especially at the cortical level, with the view that our subjective experiences correspond to the activity of particular cortical cells, but whether or not we are justified in pushing the hypothetical cells responsible for the subjective appreciation of taste down into the thalamus or into some other subcortical structure is impossible to say. The lower levels of the taste system are certainly capable of sustaining learned responses to gustatory stimulation and must therefore have mechanisms for discriminating one taste from another. *Anencephalic* infants (infants born with no telencephalon) are capable of responding to sweet substances and rejecting bitter ones.

One way in which relatively unspecific taste receptors may produce sharply discriminable sensations (and reflex activities) is by means of a mechanism employing lateral inhibition. Pfaffmann (1955) argued that the diffuse patterns of afferent gustatory impulses must be decoded by a central mechanism, and P. M. Milner (1958) has provided a simplified model of how this decoding might be accomplished (Figure 9.8).

We first reduce the scope of the problem to two fibers, one of which responds strongly to salt and weakly to quinine, whereas the other gives a stronger response to quinine than to salt. The second-order cells then send collaterals to an inhibitory network, which feeds back to the input of the second-order cells. The thresholds of all the second-order neurons are thus raised to a value just below that of the largest input falling on any of them. If the inhibition increases further, it cuts off all activity in the second level cells and eliminates its own input. If the inhibition starts to fall, the second-order cells fire faster and restore it by increasing the input to the inhibitory network.

When quinine is presented, therefore, the afferent that is more sensitive to it will fire its second-order cell, but the other second-order cell will not receive enough input to overcome the inhibition. When salt is presented, the reverse occurs, and the other second-order cell will fire.

The circuit would cause cells at the higher levels of the pathway to respond more selectively to gustatory input than the receptors do. That thalamic cells are more selective lends some support to the model. It may, however, be less important than was once believed to separate the overlapping signals before they reach the brain. The brain may be quite capable of using the total pattern of input.

SMELL

The sensitivity of the olfactory system is much greater than that of the taste system. For some substances a few hundred molecules constitute an adequate olfactory stimulus, even in humans, who are often considered to have a somewhat degenerate olfactory system (De Vries &

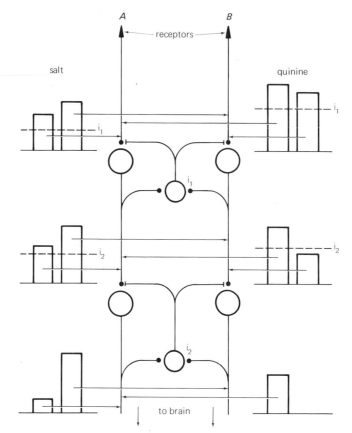

Figure 9.8 The hypothetical mechanism for "sharpening" taste discrimination during transmission through sensory relay nuclei. The presynaptic inhibition level (i) is determined by the total activity in the pathway and reduces the transmission from the weakly stimulated receptors relatively more than that from the more strongly excited ones. Receptor A is supposed to be more sensitive to quinine but less sensitive to salt than is receptor B. The histograms on the left therefore represent the average activity in the paths indicated by the arrows when salt is applied to the tongue, and the histograms on the right of the diagram represent the comparable activity when quinine is applied. (After P. M. Milner, 1958.)

Stuiver, 1961). This sensitivity enables animals to discriminate at a distance among a great variety of objects that emit traces of volatile substances. Sensitivity to specific chemicals is a fundamental property of living cells and it is not surprising that olfaction evolved long before vision or hearing as an important means of discriminating distant objects.

The olfactory nerve is the only sensory nerve that goes directly to the telencephalon without synapsing in the thalamus, a reminder that the forebrain, so important for all fine discriminations in the higher vertebrate, evolved from an olfactory ganglion. Without the sense of smell,

most animals would perish, unable to find either food or mates. The value placed upon herbs and perfumes by humans is some indication that this modality has not been completely superseded at the upper end of the phylogenetic ladder.

In spite of its antiquity and importance, however, the olfactory system is the least studied of the five classical senses. Moulten and Tucker (1964) commented that there are 40 theories of olfaction and very few established facts. This lag may be attributed to several causes: One is the great difficulty of providing standard stimuli. The nose is so sensitive that

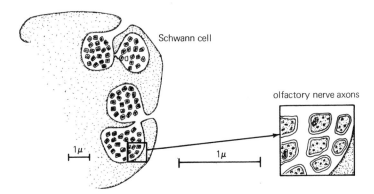

Figure 9.9 Cross section of a satellite cell (Schwann cell) in the olfactory nerve, showing arrangement of the axon bundles in each enclosing space. (After De Lorenzo, 1963.)

background contamination is difficult to eliminate, and it is almost impossible to construct instruments sensitive enough to measure the stimuli being presented. A second reason is that much of the olfactory system is inaccessible to study. The primary afferent nerves are very short, extremely fine (about 0.2μ in diameter, less than half the wavelength of blue light), and surrounded by bone along much of their path. A further peculiarity of the olfactory nerve, one

that makes it difficult to record from, is that bundles of the very thin axons share the same space in the enveloping satellite cells, as shown in Figure 9.9. Finally, once it leaves the olfactory bulbs the olfactory pathway is apparently very diffuse.

The receptors for smell lie in an area of olfactory epithelium that occupies the upper part of the nasal passage (Figure 9.10). In man the area of the olfactory epithelium is about 240

Figure 9.10 The lateral wall of the nasal cavity. In normal breathing air flows below the olfactory epithelium. Sniffing causes the air to swirl past the receptors. (After Adey, 1959.)

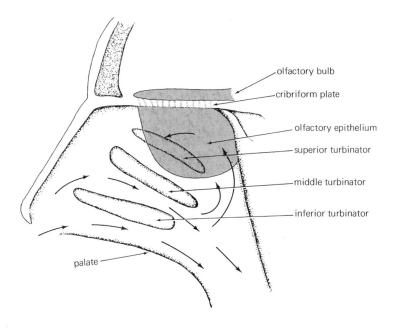

mm², and it contains about 30 million receptors per nostril. Each receptor has many fine hairs, or *cilia*, which increase the area of exposed membrane. It has been calculated that the total area is several times that of the outer body surface.

The sensitivity of the system can be varied in several ways, of which the most effective involves the pattern of respiration. Sniffing forces more air between the *superior turbinator* (see Figure 9.10) and the septum (membrane separating the nostrils) of the nose and thus increases the amount of odorant in contact with the receptors at a given time. In normal respiration, only about 5 per cent of the inhaled air passes over the olfactory epithelium, and more than half the odorant is adsorbed on the non-

olfactory epithelium before it reaches the olfactory surface (De Vries & Stuiver, 1961). Arrest of respiration or breathing through the mouth reduces the stimulation of receptors still further.

The rate of flow of inhaled air past the olfactory epithelium also depends upon the width of the aperture between the upper turbinator and the septum, and this aperture can be reduced by vasodilation which causes the tissue to swell. Autonomic activity can regulate the sensitivity of the olfactory system in much the same way that it regulates the light entering the eye by varying the pupil diameter. Tucker and Beidler (1956) have shown that the rabbit's olfactory-nerve response to an odor is increased by stimulation of the cervical sympathetic

Figure 9.11   Three receptors of the olfactory epithelium. (After De Lorenzo, 1963.)

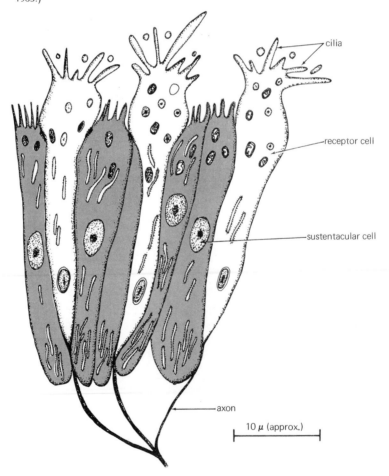

cilia

receptor cell

sustentacular cell

axon

10 μ (approx.)

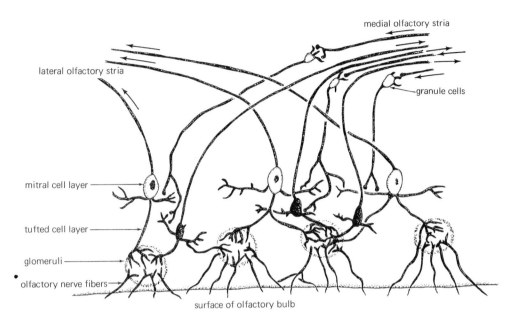

lateral olfactory stria

medial olfactory stria

granule cells

mitral cell layer

tufted cell layer

glomeruli

olfactory nerve fibers

surface of olfactory bulb

Figure 9.12   Olfactory-bulb connections.

nerve, but whether this increase results from vasoconstriction or from a more direct effect of the sympathetic system upon receptors is not known. In the tortoise, stimulation of the sympathetic system has the opposite effect. The apertures to the nasal cavity are reduced, and the response to olfactory stimulation falls to about a quarter its normal value (Tucker, 1963).

Olfactory Receptor Mechanisms

The olfactory receptor is a neuron with a long, slender cell body surrounded by *sustentacular cells* of the olfactory epithelium (Figure 9.11). A slight swelling of the cell occurs where its body projects above the epithelial surface, and from this swelling emerge a number of cilia about $0.1\ \mu$ in diameter and up to $100\ \mu$ long. These cilia are moistened by fluid from glands, and, along with microvilli of the sustentacular cells, form a "felty" layer on the surface, the olfactory mucosa. The axons of a number of receptors gather into bundles and become embedded in Schwann cells (Figure 9.9). These bundles then pass through small holes in the base of the skull (the *cribriform plate*) to the olfactory bulb (Figure 9.12).

The mechanism by which odorous substances excite the receptors is still not known with certainty, but it now seems to be generally accepted that it is similar to that by which chemicals excite taste receptors or, for that matter, that by which transmitter substances influence the dendritic zone of a neuron. It is supposed that there are receptor sites on the neuronal membrane of such a nature that only molecules with particular shapes can be adsorbed by them. When such a site is occupied, the membrane is rendered in some way permeable to ions and becomes depolarized (or possibly, on some occasions, hyperpolarized). The name given to this theory is the *steric theory of odor*.

Moncrieff (1954) found that chemicals with similar odors tended to be adsorbed onto various agents like activated charcoal, silica gel, fuller's earth, and so on to similar degrees, even though they were quite different chemically. He also found that odors were strongly adsorbed by the olfactory mucosa of a freshly slaughtered sheep (Moncrieff, 1955). Amoore (1964) summarized many years' experiments devoted to showing that molecules with similar shapes, which will fit into hypothetical receptor sites

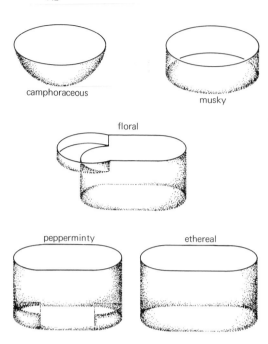

Figure 9.13 Five shapes of receptor sites on the membrane of an olfactory receptor. Molecules that fit into the sites will elicit responses. Molecules with a positive charge have a pungent odor whatever their shape, and those with a negative charge have a putrid odor. (After Amoore, 1964.)

of particular configurations, smell alike. He constructed models of seven receptor sites that he considered adequate to explain all odors (Figure 9.13).

Amoore (1952) predicted that the odor of cedar wood could be simulated by the simul-

Figure 9.14 Responses of single neural elements in the olfactory mucosa of the frog. (a) Responses of one neural element to puffs of butyric acid, valeric acid, cyclohexanol and n-butanol. (b) Responses of another unit to puffs of musk xylene, nitrobenzene, benzonitrite and pyridine. (After Gesteland, Lettvin, Pitts & Rojas, 1963.)

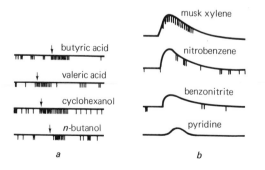

taneous stimulation of four different sites: those for camphoraceous, musky, floral, and minty odors, the reason being that the molecule of cedar-wood oil would fit into all these sites. Johnston (1963) was able to produce a good match for cedar wood by mixing the four suggested primaries in suitable proportions.

Ottoson (1958, 1959, 1963) has recorded slow potentials in response to odors in the olfactory mucosa of the frog and the rabbit. He calls these potentials *electro-olfactograms* (EOGs). They are presumed to be the combined generator potentials of large numbers of olfactory receptors. Several interesting facts have been demonstrated by this recording technique. It has been shown, for example, that the amplitude of the response is approximately a logarithmic function of the concentration of the stimulus, but the range is quite short, only 1–1.5 logarithmic units. That is, an odor saturates the olfactory receptors when it is 10–30 times the threshold concentration.

It is also possible to show that some odors produce much longer-lasting depolarization than others do, presumably because the active molecules remain adsorbed to the membrane longer. Adaptation curves for the depolarizing mechanism can also be plotted for various odors. The potential falls to about half the initial value in less than a second during sustained stimulation but then remains steady for a long time. The olfactory receptor cannot therefore be considered to adapt rapidly.

Despite the technical difficulties occasioned by the small size and close packing of the receptors, Gesteland, Lettvin, Pitts, and Rojas (1963) succeeded in recording from single olfactory receptors in the frog as various odors were presented. The results suggest that, as in taste, each olfactory receptor will respond to a rather wide range of substances (Figure 9.14). Each odor presented excited between a third and a half of the cells sampled, though the individual cells responded differently to different odors. If the olfactory system of the frog is typical, recognition of a particular smell requires comparison of firing rates in an appreciable fraction of the fibers of the olfactory nerve. Gesteland and his colleagues suggested that there must be several different receptor sites on the membrane of each receptor. The sensitivity of a receptor to a given substance would thus depend upon the number of receptor sites on its membrane to which that substance could be adsorbed.

Anatomy of the Olfactory System

After they pass through the cribriform plate the olfactory nerves terminate in *glomeruli* in the olfactory bulb (Figure 9.12). In the rabbit each glomerulus is the junction of about 26,000 afferent nerve fibers with the dendrites of about 24 *mitral cells* and 60 *tufted cells* (Allison & Warwick, 1949). The glomeruli lie near the surface of the bulb; the next deeper layer consists of the perikarya of the tufted cells and their accessory dendrites. The axons of these cells pass through the anterior commissure to the contralateral olfactory bulb, where they synapse with granule cells.

The next layer consists of the perikarya of mitral cells and their dendrites. The axons of the mitral cells make up the *lateral olfactory tract* (or *stria*), which is the main olfactory connection to the rest of the brain. Deeper still in the bulb there is a layer of granule cells. They receive impulses mainly from fibers entering the bulb through the anterior limb of the anterior commissure and send axons to the accessory dendrites of the tufted and mitral cells. This centrifugal path could provide regulatory feedback of the type found in other sensory modalities.

In man the lateral olfactory stria connects the olfactory bulb to the *periamygdaloid* (or *pyriform*) *cortex* in the region of the *uncus* (the medial part of the temporal pole, Figure 3.6), passing over the surface of the olfactory tubercle in the anterior hypothalamus. The path is shown for a rat in Figure 9.15. Fibers leave the tract along the way, so that only a fraction of them reach the uncus and amygdaloid region. It was once believed that the *medial olfactory stria*, which connects the two bulbs through the anterior commissure, also gave off fibers as it passed through the parolfactory area of the frontal lobe, but electrophysiological evidence does not support this belief. Short-latency re-sponses to electrical stimulation of the olfactory bulb are picked up in the olfactory tubercle, the amygdala, the full lengths of the claustrum and putamen, and the periamygdaloid cortex (Berry, Hagamen & Hinsey, 1952). According to K. H. Pribram and Kruger (1954), only the corticomedial part of the amygdaloid complex receives fibers directly from the olfactory bulb. Other parts of the so-called rhinencephalon ("nose brain"), like the septal area and the hippocampus, respond only after long latencies, suggesting that the connections to these regions from the olfactory system are indirect (Adey, 1959).

Central Olfactory Mechanisms

The electrical activity of the olfactory bulb has attracted much attention, but no very significant picture of it has emerged. Gross electrodes pick up waves of spontaneous activity registered there. For example, Adrian (1942) found that each breath of laboratory air produced waves having a frequency of 15-20 per sec. in the olfactory bulbs and periamygdaloid cortex of the hedgehog. In the intervals between inspirations electrical activity was irregular and of low voltage. Filtered air did not produce these waves. At the other extreme strong odors blocked the rhythmic activity generated by mild olfactory stimulation. Moulton and Tucker (1964) suggested that such suppression might be caused by centrifugal inhibition, perhaps orignating in the trigeminal nerve. Certainly some olfactory input reaches the brain through the trigeminal nerve; Allen (1941) showed that a dog could still discriminate some strong odors like camphor and creosote after its olfactory nerve had been cut.

The relationship, if any, between the pattern of gross electrical activity in the olfactory bulbs and the perception of odors is not at all clear. The potential is not always correlated with the level of activity of such neural elements as the mitral cells. Adrian (1951, 1953) recorded from single cells, or small groups of cells, in the mitral layer of the olfactory bulb of the rabbit and found that, although each cell had a lower threshold for one odor than for others, most would fire to any odor that was strong enough.

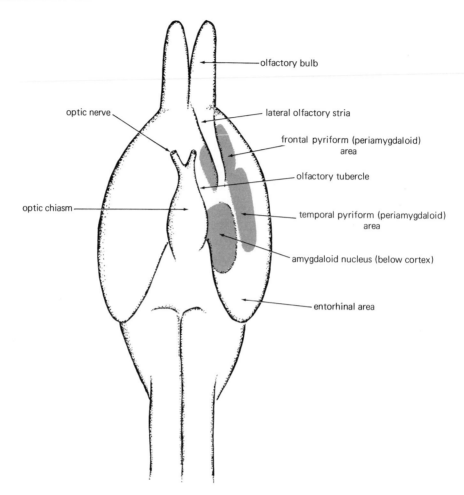

optic nerve

optic chiasm

olfactory bulb

lateral olfactory stria

frontal pyriform (periamygdaloid)
area

olfactory tubercle

temporal pyriform (periamygdaloid)
area

amygdaloid nucleus (below cortex)

entorhinal area

Figure 9.15 Ventral view of a rat brain. Shaded areas are primary olfactory projections. (After Adey, 1959.)

Walsh (1956) found three types of cells in the mitral layer of the olfactory bulb. Those most frequently encountered discharged continually at about 10 impulses per second, regardless of respiration or odor. A second type fired during the inhalation of air (even purified air), and the third type responded to one or more odors. One cell, for example, responded to butyl acetate but not to the isomer ethyl butyrate or to other esters (types of organic salts).

Mozell (1958) spaced four small electrodes along the total length of the olfactory bulb in the rabbit and recorded the integrated output of the cells in the vicinity of each electrode as different odors were presented. His results

parallel quite closely those obtained from the olfactory mucosa by Ottoson (1958). Some substances, like heptane, produced rather long responses; amyl acetate gave much shorter responses. Amyl acetate, however, produced responses in all parts of the bulb. Heptane and ether, on the other hand, tended to arouse larger responses in the posterior, than in the anterior end. There is considerable point-to-point projection from the olfactory mucosa to the olfactory bulb, so that if different substances, because of their different rates of diffusion, were to reach different parts of the mucosa, some parts of the bulb might give bigger responses to some odors than to others.

Mozell, like Ottoson, found that the maximum response was obtained with only 10–50 times the threshold concentration of an odorous substance. He suggested that this range might explain why, although smell is remarkable for the variety of stimuli that can be distinguished, intensity discrimination in this modality is poor. The amount of sniffing required to detect an odor does extend the range of information about its intensity, however.

Attempts have been made to identify the olfactory areas of the brain and to investigate the manner in which they function by testing animals with various lesions. The lesions are usually made in rhinencephalic structures to which olfactory projections have been found by both anatomical and physiological methods. Swann (1934) ablated the septal area, amygdaloid complex, fornix, the olfactory bulb, and anterior commissure in rats. The animals then had to choose between two alleys, both of which were blocked by scented wood shavings (the scent was creosote in one, anise in the other). The scent and the food were moved from side to side at random. The only lesions that had any effect upon this discrimination were complete section of the olfactory bulb and cutting the anterior limb of the anterior commissure. Allen (1941) has criticized this experiment on the grounds that creosote is an irritant that will stimulate trigeminal receptors; but the fact that section of the olfactory bulb produced an impairment in learning seems sufficient answer to this criticism.

Allen (1941) also found that lesions in most of the rhinencephalon had no effect upon olfactory discrimination. He trained dogs to make a conditioned leg flexion with the smell of clove vapor as CS and to inhibit the response to a different odor (asafetida); subsequent lesions in the periamygdaloid, amygdala, and hippocampal areas had no effect upon the conditioned response. The dogs were also still able to distinguish food from nonfood substances by smell. The lesions did abolish the ability to inhibit the positive response when the differential odor (asafetida) was presented. Nor could the dogs learn new discriminations between positive and negative odors. They tended to respond to everything after the lesions. In a later experiment Allen (1949) found that lesions in the frontal cortex had similar effects upon olfactory discrimination but did not prevent discrimination of visual or auditory conditioned stimuli.

Santibañez and Pinto Hamuy (1957) showed that large lesions in the temporal lobe of the monkey caused loss of olfactory discrimination (between orange and vanilla) but that the animals were able to relearn it. T. S. Brown, Rosvold, and Mishkin (1963) made smaller lesions to try to pinpoint the area in the temporal lobe necessary for successful olfactory discrimination but found that both superior and inferior temporal-lobe ablations produced similar effects. Neither lesion had any effect upon simultaneous discriminations (both odors present at the same time, as in Santibañez and Pinto Hamuy's experiment), but both lesions impaired the ability to make successive discriminations. The monkey had to respond to cherry presented alone, for example, but not to pine presented alone. The experimental animals all tended to respond to the negative odor more frequently than did the intact control animals. In visual discriminations, the control task, only the monkeys with inferior temporal lobectomies showed impairment.

These results do not lend themselves to simple interpretation. It appears that even lesions in the primary-projection cortex of the olfactory system do not produce complete anosmia (loss of the sense of smell), but they do interfere to some extent with the association of meanings, especially "negative" meanings, to olfactory stimuli. It is likely that the input to the olfactory tubercle is adequate to maintain most olfactory functions; this area is contiguous with the anterior hypothalamus and connected through the medial forebrain bundle to other hypothalamic and brainstem nuclei related to eating and sexual behavior. Stimulation in any of these areas in the rat produces sniffing and exploratory activity, which could be interpreted as searching for the origin of an interesting smell.

The peculiar long-term adaptation to some odors is an interesting phenomenon, presumably involving a process similar to learning, that has not been studied physiologically. Those who work with animals, for example, soon become quite insensitive to their smell. This insensitivity is not merely a failure to notice the odor; the detection threshold is very significantly increased. The same thing happens to the threshold for the perfume of a familiar soap or for the "taste" (mostly odor) of toothpaste. Frequently eaten foods lose some of their savor, and it may take many weeks of abstinence to effect complete recovery. In view of this phenomenon, the professional "nose," who blends teas, whiskeys, perfumes, and so on is a paradox. Apparently long training sharpens his olfactory sense so that he can discriminate minute differences in the stimulus.

It is possible that investigations of patients with brain damage would throw some light on the olfactory mechanisms, but little, if any,

work has been done so far. Epileptic patients with foci in the temporal lobe sometimes have olfactory *auras* (their seizures are heralded by hallucinations of smell). Penfield reported that conscious patients stimulated in the olfactory bulb or near the uncus during operations sometimes experience smells or stenches; the examples mentioned were the smell of burning rubber and of manure. Of stimulations near the uncus that of the amygdaloid nucleus was the most likely to produce olfactory experiences (Penfield & Jasper, 1954). These observations served to confirm what had been assumed from anatomical findings, that the amygdaloid region receives olfactory input, but they do not add appreciably to our knowledge of the physiological mechanisms of olfaction.

Summary

The chemical senses of taste and smell take advantage of the fundamental chemical selectivity of cells to provide a relatively elementary mechanism for distinguishing between various environmental stimuli.

It is assumed that receptor sites on the membranes of taste and olfactory receptors selectively adsorb molecules of certain shapes and electrical charges. When a receptor site is occupied, the cell membrane becomes permeable to ions and the cell is then depolarized; this generates afferent impulses in a sensory nerve.

Microelectrode recordings indicate that chemoreceptors are almost invariably sensitive to a number of different stimuli, as if each possessed different types of receptor sites in different proportions. Although two receptors may both respond to two substances, A and B, for example, one may be more sensitive to A and the other more to B.

The anatomical path of the taste system is hardly distinguishable from that for the cutaneous sense from the head. It eventually terminates in the lower end of the somatosensory cortex, near the area for the mouth, or possibly in the claustrum. The olfactory pathway is unique in that it goes straight to the forebrain, without synapsing in the thalamus. The main projection seems to be to the amygdaloid nucleus and the cortex overlying it.

Although the results from different experiments are not easy to compare, the indications are that thalamic cells show more taste specificity than do cells in earlier or later parts of the taste pathway. The cortical cells, in particular, show a great deal of convergence, not only of different tastes, but also of different modalities of tongue sensation. The electrophysiology of the olfactory system has been less thoroughly studied, but the mitral cells of the olfactory bulb seem to be more selective than the receptors are.

Cortical lesions have relatively slight effects on taste and smell discriminations, the implication being that the cortex is not required to decode the fairly simple input patterns and that there are direct subcortical paths to eating, sexual, and other mechanisms that depend upon gustatory and olfactory information.

CHAPTER 10

THE SOMATO-SENSORY SYSTEMS

Although there are many elaborate ways to classify sensory systems functionally, textbook writers usually group them according to the paths they take to the brain. Hence the vestibular apparatus, which provides information about the position and movements of the head, is part of the *kinesthetic system* (from *kineo*, "to move") and although it may also be classified as part of the visual system because one of its most important functions is to prevent loss of fixation during head and body movements, most textbooks nevertheless place it with the auditory system, no doubt because the sense organs for the two systems are close together and both are connected to the brain by the eighth cranial nerve (see Chapter 3).

Similarly, the skin senses (touch, pressure, pain, warmth, cold, itch, vibration, and so on) are often considered together with the *proprioceptive* systems (*proprio*, "of one's own"), which provide information about what goes on inside the body. This method is convenient because many of the receptors in the skin look, and probably function, like receptors in joints, muscles, and parts of the viscera and because the afferents from both systems travel to the brain through the same spinal and bulbar routes.

It was clear to early anatomists that sensory information is transmitted to the brain through nerves. Aristotle thought some emanation of the stimulating object traveled through the nerves; Descartes thought the stimulus released "vital spirits," which flowed through the nerves, but he did not attempt to explain the different effects produced by different modes of stimulation.

In 1826 Müller published his doctrine of the specific energies of nerves, which stated that the sensation aroused by a stimulus depended not upon the stimulus presented but upon the properties of the sensory nerves it excited. The optic nerve always signals sensations of light, even when stimulated mechanically (by a blow to the eye, for example); the auditory nerve always signals sound; and so on for the other senses. Müller recognized that the classical sense of touch includes a complex set of submodalities, but he did not go so far as to suggest that there are different nerve energies for temperature, pain, and the like, nor did he suggest that there are different nerve energies for different colors or tastes. According to Boring (1929), the extension of Müller's doctrine to the submodalities of skin sensation was proposed by Natanson (1844) and Volkmann (1844). Later Helmholtz (1862) went even further and suggested that each neuron of the auditory nerve gives rise to a sensation of sound at a particular pitch, opening the way for a mosaic theory of perception. It is clear that Müller and his followers all thought each sensation was produced by the firing of specific brain neurons that had "private lines" from the peripheral organs. Different combinations of these elementary sensations were supposed to generate more complex perceptions.

There are two major aspects of sensory specificity: the "local sign," which indicates the location of the stimulus in space or on the skin, and the modality or quality of the stimulus, whether it is a touch or an itch, a light or a sound, for example. The specific-energies theory stated that each point on the skin was equipped with a number of nerve endings sensitive to different types of stimulation. (Touch, pain, warmth, and cold were the modalities usually specified.)

Although it was not a necessary corollary of

the law of specific nerve energies that different sensory qualities implied different receptor structures, that assumption has also often been made. When histologists began to discover different forms of nerve endings in the skin and when at the same time the concentration of skin sensibility in spots responding to one or another modality was discovered (Blix, 1884), the obvious inference was drawn: that there must be some correspondence between the morphology of the endings and their specific sensitivities.

Soon afterward Frey (1895) attempted to deduce which types of endings were associated with each of the four main modalities of skin sensibility (touch, warmth, cold, and pain) from the relative concentration of endings in parts of skin that he thought to be differentially sensitive to these types of stimuli. Free nerve endings were thus classified as pain receptors because they are the only endings found in the cornea of the eye, which Frey believed to be sensitive only to pain.

The obvious test of Frey's classification is to mark sensitive spots on a piece of skin and then to examine it histologically to see whether or not there are endings of the specified type beneath the spots. This experiment was performed many times during the succeeding half-century, almost invariably with negative or ambiguous results (Weddell, 1941; 1961). Frey's classification has suffered further setbacks. For example, Lele and Weddell (1956) have confirmed, through very rigorous experiments, that stimulation of the cornea can cause sensations of touch, warmth, and cold, as well as of pain. (Frey did conduct an experiment to confirm the general opinion that the cornea was sensitive only to pain; he dipped a hair in hot or cold water, shook the water off, and poked the hair into the eye. Almost all the subjects said that they felt pain each time.)

The greatest blow to the theory, however, was the discovery that there are few specialized endings in hairy skin, unless the baskets of free nerve endings around the hair follicles can be regarded as such (Hagen, Knoche, Sinclair & Weddell, 1953). Hairy skin is, of course, sensitive to all modes of stimulation. Oppenheimer, Palmer, and Weddell (1958) have shown that some so-called "specialized endings" are really abnormalities associated with degenerating or regenerating nerve fibers and appear much less frequently in the skin of children. Bazett, McGlone, Williams, and Lufkin (1932), in attempting to identify temperature receptors, found at least seven clearly distinguishable types of nerve endings in the skin of the human male prepuce, but they were able to find only the usual four modes of sensibility—touch, warmth, cold, and pain—there.

One very constant type of ending is the Pacinian corpuscle (see Figure 8.8), and it is hard to believe that this structure does not modify the response of the ending in any way. Nevertheless, as we saw in Chapter 8, Loewenstein (1959) has shown that the sensitivity of the ending as a mechanoreceptor is virtually unaffected by the removal of the capsule. C. C. Hunt (1961) has found that Pacinian corpuscles are selectively excited by vibration; perhaps, as suggested by the experiments of Mendelson and Loewenstein (1964), the capsule reduces the sensitivity of the ending to other forms of stimulation.

A. G. Brown and Iggo (1963) have provided what they consider evidence in favor of the specificity of some endings. They crushed a cutaneous nerve (which caused both the ending and the distal part of the nerve to degenerate) in cats and then watched the course of regeneration. They found that the nerve tip was very insensitive to touch until the specialized structure had regenerated, but the correlation does not necessarily imply a causal relationship.

It would be strange if the elaborate structures around the ends of sensory nerves were there purely for the entertainment and edification of histologists. Perhaps they serve to protect the nerves against intense stimulation of the plantar surfaces, finger tips, and similar areas, which are subject to considerable wear and tear.

In any case, we must certainly accept the evidence that special endings are not necessary for the detection of different modalities of stimulation. Skin with only free nerve endings is no less capable of detecting various stimuli than is skin with encapsulated endings. Despite the absence of experimental support, Frey's scheme was nevertheless so "obvious" and simple that it flourished for more than 50 years, and even today many biologists accept it without question, not having heard that it is dead (or at least suffering from serious complications).

The function, if any, of the specialized nerve endings has no real bearing on the more important problem of the validity of the law of specific nerve energies. It would obviously be quite possible for certain endings, free or encapsulated, to be specifically sensitive to heat, cold, and so forth and for these nerves to deliver their signals to different parts of the brain in order to produce different sensations. This hypothesis is simple, attractive, sensible, and clearly able to survive a good deal of contradictory evidence if necessary.

Among psychologists there have always been opponents of Müller's doctrine, especially in relation to the sensation of pain (see Melzack & Wall, 1962, 1965). One school, for example, has maintained that there is no special modality for pain, that the sensation is caused by excessive or disorganized firing in other modalities (Nafe, 1934; Hebb, 1949). An even more extreme view is that there are no specific receptors or pathways at all. An alternative is that different qualities of sensation are caused by different firing patterns in afferent nerves (Sinclair, 1955), but before we pursue these matters further we must learn a little more about the sensory pathways than was shown in Chapter 3.

PATHWAYS OF THE SOMATOSENSORY SYSTEM

Peripheral nerves have been classified, as we saw in Chapter 2, into three main groups: A, B, and C (Gasser, 1935). The largest and most rapidly conducting sensory fibers are those that carry information from the muscle-spindle stretch receptors and Golgi tendon organs to the cord. In cutaneous nerves, unconnected to muscles, there are A fibers ranging in diameter from 3 to 17 μ and about four times as many C fibers, most of them less than 1.3 μ in diameter.

The sensory nerves from a given segment of the spinal cord innervate an area of skin called a *dermatome*. On the trunk these dermatomes are strips running around the body like belts. It should be noted that one dermatome is completely overlapped by the two adjacent ones, the upper half by the lower half of the one above and the lower half by the upper half of the one below. The whole body surface is thus adequately innervated by alternate dermatomes, providing insurance against damage and conferring increased sensitivity and acuity.

As mentioned earlier all the cell bodies of afferent nerves (except cranial nerves) lie in the dorsal-root ganglia just beside the spinal cord. There is some segregation of fibers according to size as they enter the cord: Most A fibers enter directly into the *dorsal columns*; the C fibers and the remaining A fibers enter *Lissauer's tract*, which is at the tip of the dorsal horn (Figure 3.11). This division is perpetuated throughout the somatosensory system but in a very complex way, with much interaction among the pathways.

The sensory system is analogous to the motor system in that there is a relatively direct and specific path to the cortex, phylogenetically recent, and a variety of older pathways, the least differentiated of which seems to correspond to the common afferent nerve net of primitive animals.

Like the motor system, the somatosensory system has been divided rather arbitrarily into two parts: the *lemniscal system* and the *extralemniscal system* (Figures 10.1, 10.2). A further resemblance to the pyramidal and extrapyramidal motor systems is that only in the medial lemniscus, the midbrain pathway from which the lemniscal system takes its name, are the two systems anatomically distinct.

The Lemniscal System

In general, the large, myelinated A fibers tend to feed into the lemniscal system and the small, unmyelinated C fibers into the extralemniscal system, but there is a great deal of interaction between the different pathways, which makes it impossible to sort out the central connections except by making assumptions about the information conveyed by the different sizes of peripheral fiber. At present we have only frag-

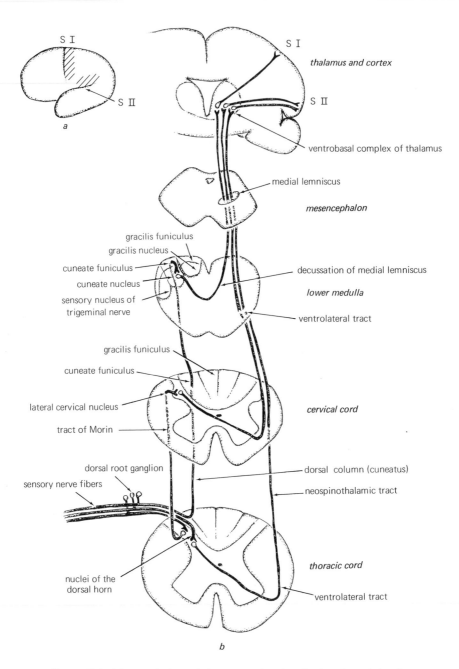

Figure 10.1 (a) Lateral view of the cortex showing the location of the first and second somatosensory areas (S I and S II). (b) Three main divisions of the lemniscal somatosensory system, including the dorsal columns, the tract of Morin, and the neospinothalamic tract. (The lower sections are shown on a larger scale than the upper sections.)

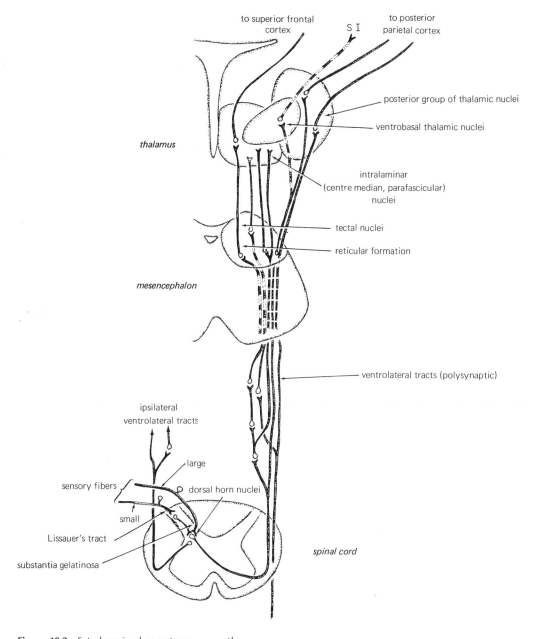

to superior frontal
cortex   S I   to posterior
                                       parietal cortex

posterior group of thalamic nuclei

ventrobasal thalamic nuclei

thalamus

intralaminar
(centre median, parafascicular)
nuclei

tectal nuclei

reticular formation

mesencephalon

ventrolateral tracts (polysynaptic)

ipsilateral
ventrolateral tracts

large

sensory fibers

dorsal horn nuclei

small

Lissauer's tract

spinal cord

substantia gelatinosa

Figure 10.2 Extralemniscal somatosensory pathways.

mentary data on which to base such assumptions.

Upon entering the cord, almost all the fibers bifurcate, sending one branch up the cord and the other down for a few segments. The larger A fibers from the skin and deep tissues ascend into the lower medulla via the dorsal columns (gracilis and cuneate funiculi), and end in the nuclei of the dorsal columns (gracilis and cuneatus nuclei).

The second-order neurons of the dorsal-column nuclei have axons that cross the midline and converge to form the medial lemnisci, flat bundles of fibers close to the midline on either side (Figure 10.1). As this tract ascends through the brainstem, the lower parts swing laterally at about the level of the pons until the flat bundles lie horizontally instead of vertically. They continue in this orientation through the mesencephalon and terminate in the posterior thalamus. The zone of lemniscal termination coincides closely, but not exactly, with the nucleus ventralis posterior (VP) of the thalamus; Rose and Mountcastle (1959) call it the *ventrobasal complex* (VB). The cells representing the contralateral hind limbs are in the lateral part of the nucleus; those representing the head are in the medial part.

From there the thalamic cells project to the first and second somatosensory areas of the cortex (S I and S II). It is believed that most of the afferents reaching the thalamus by the lemniscal route eventually project to S I because there we find the cortical cells with the most precise somatotopic localization and the shortest firing latencies. In primates S I lies in the postcentral gyrus (Figure 10.1a) parallel to the motor cortex and with a corresponding somatotopic arrangement, with the feet at the top of the gyrus within the longitudinal fissure and the head at the ventrolateral end of the gyrus. S II lies on the upper bank of the Sylvian fissure, with representation of the head adjacent to that of the head in S I and representation of the feet at the posterior end.

The second component of the lemniscal system is the *neospinothalamic pathway*. It originates in cells of the dorsal horn that receive collaterals from the cutaneous A fibers. The axons of these cells cross over and join the ventrolateral tracts on the contralateral sides of the cord. They leave these tracts at the upper end of the medulla and join the medial lemniscus, passing with it into the thalamus. There is some evidence suggesting that thalamic cells receiving neospinothalamic synapses project predominantly to the second somatosensory area, but, on the other hand, many thalamic neurons have branched axons that terminate in both sensory areas.

The third lemniscal pathway, the tract of Morin, is phylogenetically older than are the others and seems to be less important in monkeys and men than in lower animals. It also originates in dorsal-horn cells, possibly in-

cluding collaterals of axons in the spinocerebellar tracts, and ascends the cord just below the dorsal horn to the level of the *lateral cervical nucleus*, an island of gray matter lateral to the upper end of the dorsal horn and just below the medulla (Morin, 1955). The axons of the cells in the lateral cervical nucleus cross and join the medial lemniscus. As the neospinothalamic tract increases in size during phylogeny, the tract of Morin declines. It is believed that the thalamic terminations and, of course, the cortical projections of the two systems are similar.

The main input to the somatosensory systems from the head comes through the fifth cranial nerve, with primary-neuron perikarya in the Gasserian ganglion (seen in Figure 3.6 at the junction of the three divisions of the trigeminal nerve). The fibers bifurcate as they enter the brainstem; the descending branch enters the *spinal trigeminal nucleus*, and the ascending branch enters the *main sensory trigeminal nucleus*. The main sensory nucleus corresponds to the nuclei of the dorsal columns. Most of its efferents go to the most medial part of the medial lemniscus of the opposite side, though the face has much stronger ipsilateral representation in the lemniscal system than does the rest of the body. The fibers continue with the medial lemniscus to the medial part of the VP nucleus of the thalamus.

The spinal trigeminal nucleus corresponds to the dorsal-horn nuclei of the spinal nerves and contains cells whose axons also join the medial lemniscus, as well as many others that are extralemniscal.

The Extralemniscal System

The extralemniscal system corresponds to the undifferentiated afferent system of primitive chordates. Both small myelinated and small unmyelinated peripheral fibers feed into it. The small fibers enter the cord in Lissauer's tract at the tip of the dorsal horn, where they split into short ascending and descending branches. Collaterals from these branches pass medially into the *substantia gelatinosa*, a mass of small cells and dendrites occupying the tip of the dorsal horn just medial to Lissauer's tract (Figure 10.2). The cells of the substantia gelatinosa are very extensively interconnected, not only ipsilaterally, but also, through commissural fibers, with similar cells on the opposite side. According to Szentágothai (1964b), however, they have no other efferent paths. The only cells influenced by activity in the substantia gelatinosa are those lying in the adjacent part of the dorsal horn, whose dendrites lie within the structure. The bodies of these neurons, like others in the dorsal horn, receive synapses from collaterals of A fibers, so that they are influenced by both A and C afferents. Szentágothai has been able to trace the axons of these neurons into the dorsolateral (spinocerebellar) tracts only. Wall (1961) also traced their axons into these tracts, but he presented neurophysiological evidence for a wider distribution. Collaterals may pass into the tract of Morin or synapse with other dorsal-horn cells, which in turn send axons into the ventrolateral tracts.

Many second-order cells of the extralemniscal system have short axons and end in the cord a few segments above their points of origin. They form a pathway that may make many synapses before reaching the medulla (Bowsher, 1965; Noordenbos, 1959). The upper neurons of this system, together with long ascending fibers, end, for the most part, in the reticular formation of the medulla and pons. Some end in the lower layers of the superior and inferior colliculi (*tectal nuclei*).

The axons of some reticular neurons eventually reach the nonspecific nuclei of the thalamus, principally the *centre median* and the nucleus parafascicularis. From there they project to all parts of the cortex but, in primates, especially to the superior frontal gyrus and the parietal area just posterior to the first sensory area. Some fibers in the ventrolateral tracts (*paleo spinothalamic* fibers) bypass the reticular formation and feed straight into the nonspecific thalamic nuclei (the intralaminar nuclei, according to an anatomical study by Mehler, Feferman, and Nauta, 1960).

Some of the ventrolateral fibers that pass through the reticular formation end not in the nonspecific nuclei of the thalamus but in a group of cells lying lateral and dorsal to the specific ventrobasal nuclei. Bowsher (1965) called it the "VP shell"; it corresponds to what Rose and Woolsey (1958) called the "posterior group of thalamic nuclei" (PO). These nuclei also receive input from other modalities. They overlap to some extent with the auditory relay (medial geniculate) nucleus and receive input from the superior colliculus and the vestibular system. The cortical projection of the posterior group or VP shell is largely to S II.

The Spinocerebellar System

Apart from the cells on the border of the substantia gelatinosa already mentioned, many more medially placed dorsal-horn cells (for example, *Clarke's nucleus,* or *column*) receive collaterals from the large myelinated primary neurons and discharge their efferent axons into the spinocerebellar tracts on both sides of the midline.

These pathways end in the cerebellar cortex, to form a somatotopic map of the body as shown in Figure 10.3. Snider (1950) has shown that there are connections from these cerebellar areas to the somatosensory areas of the cerebral cortex, as well as in the opposite direction from the cerebral cortex to the cerebellum. That

Figure 10.3 Areas of the cerebellar cortex of the monkey that respond to tactual stimulation. The representation is ipsilateral in the anterior area and bilateral in the paramedian lobule on either side of the vermis. (After Snider, 1950.)

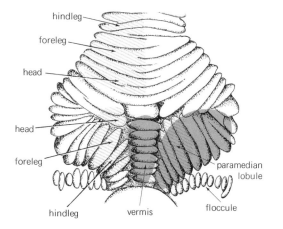

cerebellar lesions are reported to produce little, if any, sensory loss is regarded as evidence that these connections have no significance for perceptual mechanisms. They are usually assumed to subserve smooth motor functioning.

Descending cerebellar efferents in the spinal cord are capable of exciting or inhibiting dorsal-horn cells, presumably thus modifying the information sent up the cord, but again there is no evidence that the modification affects cells that are part of the somatosensory system.

The partial tracing of the sensory pathways, of which we have just given a very simplified account, has involved an immense amount of patient work by neuroanatomists and neurophysiologists. One of the most potent methods of analysis is to record from single cells, or axons, at different points in the system during various manipulations of the skin and joints of the animal. In the lemniscal system there are many cells with small fields and specific modalities; the extralemniscal system contains cells that are sensitive to a wide variety of stimulations over large parts of the body. The lemniscal system is largely, though not entirely, contralateral in its cortical projection; the extralemniscal system is responsive to both ipsilateral and contralateral stimulation. In general, because of the greater number of synapses and smaller fibers, the extralemniscal system responds with longer latencies than does the lemniscal system at the equivalent level. With these cues to assist in identification, it is possible, after recording from hundreds or even thousands of cells, to arrive at some statistical estimate of the extent to which each system projects to the various pathways and cortical areas. It must be emphasized, however, that this picture is only a statistical one. There is considerable individual variation in the anatomy of the spinal cord (as in the rest of the nervous system). Anatomists find different degrees of decussation in different specimens, for example, and different ratios of particular types of fiber in different tracts.

Although Figures 10.1 and 10.2 give a rough idea of the main afferent paths of the somatosensory system, they cannot be used with any confidence to predict the outcome of a lesion or other intervention, not only because of individual variation, but also because they are highly simplified. The extent of collateral branching in most of the tracts is only partly known, and that it occurs at all is not often mentioned in anatomy textbooks.

Centrifugal Pathways

The picture may seem quite complex enough as it stands, but there is yet a further complication; descending pathways carry feedback from higher to more peripheral levels.

This centrifugal system has been less thoroughly studied than have the ascending systems, but it seems certain that an important component originates in the sensorimotor cortex and in the second sensory area (Lundberg, Norrsell & Voorhoeve, 1963). Some fibers descend to the ventrobasal part of the thalamus (very generally, cortical areas receiving projections from certain thalamic nuclei send return connections to the same nuclei). Other fibers descend in the pyramidal tract and pass into the dorsal-column nuclei (Magni, Melzack, Moruzzi & Smith, 1959), where they both facilitate and inhibit the cells relaying sensory impulses (Towe & Jabbur, 1961; Jabbur & Towe, 1961).

Hagbarth and Kerr (1954) showed that stimulation of the sensorimotor cortex, the second sensory area, and sometimes the cingulate cortex, suppressed evoked responses in the ventrolateral pathways of the cord. Stimulation of the anterior vermis of the cerebellum and parts of the reticular formation had a similar effect.

A word of caution about the interpretation of recordings from gross electrodes must be interjected at this point. The recording of an evoked potential in a tract or at a point in a nucleus or on the cortex is frequently reduced in amplitude by a tonic (steady) bombardment of impulses from a nonspecific source (for example, stimulation of the reticular formation). At one time this effect was believed always to arise from inhibition, but single-cell microelectrode recordings do not support this uniform interpretation. Hagbarth and Fex (1959), for instance, used microelectrodes to show that responses from dorsal-horn cells are sometimes facilitated and sometimes inhibited by stimulation of central areas. The reason that a facilitatory bombardment can reduce an evoked potential may be that it keeps many dendrites and cell bodies partly depolarized, thus reducing the size of the slow postsynaptic evoked potential.

Recent work by Andersen, Eccles, and Sears (1964) has shown that stimulation of the sensorimotor cortex can influence the afferent terminals of peripheral nerves by presynaptic inhibition. These workers found a somatotopical organization in the pre- and postcentral gyri but not in S II; stimulation of the leg area of the primary sensorimotor cortex will thus inhibit afferents from the leg and so on.

THE PROBLEM OF "LOCAL SIGN"

Let us return now to the theoretical questions raised earlier in this chapter. It has been suggested that the centrifugal feedback just described serves the function of reducing the divergence of impulses in the sensory pathways. Such divergence would prevent accurate localization of a stimulus and perhaps cause mixing of sensory qualities. Most of the mechanisms for preventing diffusion that have been hypothesized have been based on W. H. Marshall and Talbot's original theory of visual acuity (1942). Ruch (1960) adapted this model to the touch modality as shown in Figure 10.4. At each synaptic level the afferents display *reciprocal overlap*, which means that they branch and end on several adjacent higher-order cells, each of which therefore has several afferent branches ending on it. At first sight this arrangement would seem merely to diffuse the fields of the afferent fibers; but it is further assumed that much convergence is required to fire the cells. Only a few of the higher-order cells, those receiving many converging branches from active afferents, will therefore be fired.

P. M. Milner (1958) modified Marshall and Talbot's scheme by suggesting that the "fringe" neurons are silenced by inhibitory feedback. When there is only a little input the threshold

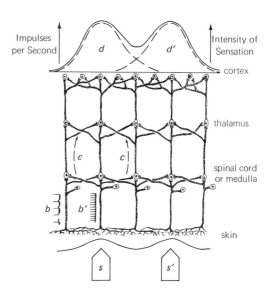

Figure 10.4 Ruch's illustration of the neural mechanism of two-point discrimination. The two stimulating points are indicated at s and s'; b is the firing rate of the receptor stimulated at the periphery of its field by s, b' the firing rate of another receptor stimulated at the center of its field. The arrows c show how the activity is concentrated on a few central neurons in the thalamus, resulting in as clear a discrimination between the activities d and d' generated at the cortex as at the skin, in spite of overlapping connections along the way. (From Ruch, 1960.)

of the higher-order cells is relatively low, and only a small amount of convergence will suffice to fire them; when input is great the threshold is automatically raised, and much more convergence of afferent impulses is required (see Figure 9.8).

Mountcastle and Powell (1959b) presented a similar model, backed by solid experimental evidence for the requisite inhibitory activity in the sensory pathways. Unfortunately, however, single-cell recordings have so far failed to reveal any cells in the cortex that respond to stimulation in an area of skin small enough to explain the accuracy with which we can localize stimuli. There are several plausible explanations that do not involve abandoning a "specific energy" theory of local sign; we shall return to them shortly, but it should be pointed out now that it may be a mistake to expect the local-sign information to be invested in single cells at the cortical level or at any other level.

The information on locus of stimulation is

certainly present in the cortex in the form of activity in many cells with overlapping peripheral fields. (The peripheral field, or just the field, of a higher-order sensory neuron is the area of skin where appropriate stimulation will excite the neuron.) The potency of this form of parallel-path information transmission can be judged from the following example. Suppose that we have three neurons, with peripheral fields *A*, *B*, and *C*, arranged as in Figure 10.5. We can now locate a stimulus in each of seven zones marked on the diagram. A stimulus in zone 1 fires only neuron *A*; one in zone 2 fires both *A* and *B*; one in zone 3 fires *B* alone, and so on. We can do even better if we assume that the firing of the afferents is more vigorous when the stimulus is near the center of the field, as indicated by the experiments of Mountcastle and Powell (1959b). Moderately strong firing in *A* and *B* and very weak firing in *C* would mean that the stimulus was near point *X*; stronger firing in *C* and weaker firing in *A* and *B* would mean that the stimulus was near point *Y*. If this amount of information can be derived from a simple analysis of the activity of three neurons with large fields, there is no doubt that the millions of neurons that fire in response to a single stimulus could convey far more information than we could possibly use.

Figure 10.5 The peripheral fields of three cortical neurons, showing how the firing pattern (not taking into account gradations in firing rate) can indicate in which of seven zones a stimulus has been applied.

What is not clear, however, is how this information is abstracted, or decoded. It would not be difficult to design a model of a neural circuit that could fire a single neuron for each pattern of cortical activity, but then we would be back to the problem of why no such neurons have ever been located. If we think in terms of action systems, rather than "sensation" cells, however, we discover that there is no need for such specificity. When we are stimulated at a particular point we can move our head and eyes to look at it or our limbs to touch it. For every stimulated point there is an activity of the motor system that can produce a related posture. A posture is produced not by firing a single motoneuron but by the interplay of many efferents, that is, by a pattern of output. An increase in the firing rate of one fiber relative to others will change, for example, the angle of a finger very slightly, just as a slight increase in the firing rate of one sensory cell relative to others will indicate that the stimulus has moved to a slightly different position on the skin. If we consider only the responses that a stimulus might evoke, we see that the nervous system could convert directly from a sensory pattern to a motor pattern. The highly specific sensory neuron implicit in the models of Müller and his followers, which would indicate the exact location and quality of a stimulus, is not a necessary intermediary. The pattern theory leaves many questions still unanswered, but it is worth consideration as an alternative to an approach that lacks experimental support.

Contact Sensitivity of the Skin

At the time when the models of Ruch and P. M. Milner were being formulated it was believed that the receptive fields, even at the level of the peripheral-nerve fibers, were too big to provide the tactual acuity demonstrated by psychophysical measurements. Careful study of the properties of peripheral-nerve fibers has shown this assumption to be false, however. Such studies have also shown that receptors are quite specific in their sensibilities, though not exactly in the ways that Frey predicted.

Most of the A fibers in a cutaneous nerve

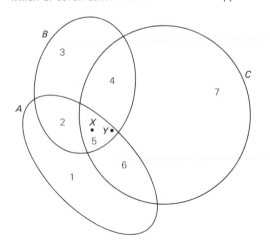

from hairy skin have endings around the hair follicles. As each nerve serves a number of hairs and as each hair receives endings from several nerve fibers, the receptive fields of these fibers are quite large. C. C. Hunt and McIntyre (1960b) determined that in the cat these fields ranged from 3 mm² to more than 800 mm², with the smallest fields near the distal parts of the limb and the largest on the trunk. The small fields tended to be associated with large-diameter fibers (in the 10–17 μ range) and the large fields with slenderer fibers (in the 2–4 μ range).

These fibers, which were also described by Maruhashi, Mizuguchi, and Tasaki (1952), vary widely in their sensitivity to stimulation of the hairs, adapt very quickly if hairs are held in a bent position, typically have no continuous background discharge, and are unaffected by moderate temperature changes.

The next most common fiber, according to C. C. Hunt and McIntyre (1960a), was one that responded to touch of the skin at one or more very small spots. They were probably the receptors that Tapper (1964) described as associated with small elevations of the skin. Fibers with up to five of these "punctate fields," arranged in a cluster a few millimeters in diameter, have been isolated, but most of them, about 10 per cent of all the A fibers in a nerve from the leg of a cat, respond to touch at just one point. The distribution of these sensitive spots is quite dense enough to account for tactual acuity without having recourse to the analysis of overlapping fields. Unfortunately, however, the place specificity of peripheral fibers seems to be lost at the first sensory relay.

Most of these touch fibers have a steady background discharge that is dependent upon temperature. In fact, the receptors act like temperature receptors, except that they are not as sensitive to temperature and are more sensitive to mechanical stimuli. Each has a range of temperature within which it fires. The temperature-sensitive band for a particular fiber may be below, above, or in the region of the normal body temperature. The receptors adapt slowly and incompletely to both touch and temperature change.

Hunt and McIntyre also described fibers that were fired only by fairly heavy pressure on some part of the skin and others that required noxious stimulation like a pinch or a pinprick to fire.

Most of the afferent fibers in a cutaneous nerve do not fire if the skin or hair is stimulated at a frequency of more than about 100 Hz, but C. C. Hunt (1961) has found some fibers that show very little response to vibrations below 85 Hz yet are extremely sensitive to vibrations in the range from 100–600 Hz. Many of the receptors feeding these fibers were found in the membrane close to the bone (periosteum). That they were indeed vibration-sensitive receptors was confirmed by stimulating them with a vibrating hair. After staining, they were found to be Pacinian corpuscles.

It has not proved possible up to now to record from C fibers with the usual microelectrode technique, but W. W. Douglas and Ritchie (1957) ingeniously demonstrated that these fibers carry many impulses generated by light touch. They exposed the central end of a cutaneous nerve in the cat and stimulated it electrically to send antidromic volleys toward the skin. These volleys were recorded in a nerve twig innervating a small patch of skin, and, because of their slow velocity, the impulses passing down the C fibers arrived at the recording point later than did those in A fibers and could thus be readily distinguished from them (Figure 10.6). Having noted the normal size of the C-fiber volley, they then gently stimulated the skin innervated by the twig with a piece of cotton gauze and saw that the volley was immediately very much attenuated. This result can mean only that *orthodromic* impulses generated by the brushing of the skin were colliding with the antidromic impulses and preventing them from reaching the recording electrodes. (When two impulses traveling in opposite directions in a nerve fiber collide, they eliminate each other because the short length of axon just behind each is absolutely refractory and cannot be refired in time to conduct the other impulse.)

Iggo (1960) has also shown that some C fibers respond to touch. He succeeded in dissecting single C fibers from a cutaneous nerve

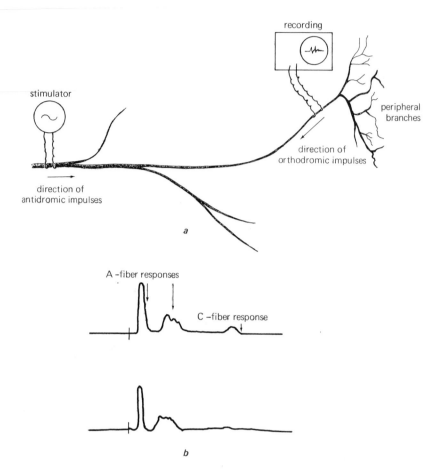

Figure 10.6 (a) The apparatus in W. W. Douglas and Ritchie's experiment. Activity induced in a small peripheral twig by a single impulse delivered to the more central part of a nerve is recorded on an oscilloscope. (b) The record in the absence of peripheral stimulation, showing the dispersion of impulses in A fibers and C fibers of various diameters because of the different velocity of impulses (upper trace), and the attenuation of the C-fiber response during stimulation of the skin (lower trace). (After W. W. Douglas & Ritchie, 1957.)

of cats and recording from them. He found that all had quite small receptive fields (4–25 mm²) and that their sensitivity varied over a wide range. Some fired at the slightest deflection of a hair (and, unlike myelinated hair fibers, adapted very slowly); others could be fired only by pricking or pinching with a force that would be painful in human subjects. Attempts to fire these fibers by injection of pain-producing substances were not successful, however. Most of the fibers exhibited several seconds of after-discharge when a stimulus had been removed. Some of the receptors were sensitive to both mechanical and thermal stimuli, and the sensi-

tivity of mechanoreceptors was changed by changes in temperature.

In summary, then, we see that tactual stimulation of the skin fires receptors with distinct characteristics and that these receptors deliver impulses to the cord through all types of afferent fibers.

We pass now to the second-order cells of the tactual system. Perl, Whitlock, and Gentry (1962) found that the cells of the dorsal-column nuclei in cats responded to three types of skin stimulation. About 40 per cent of those sampled in their microelectrode study responded only to hair flexion at rates of up to 30 per second.

At higher flexion rates, however, they gave only initial bursts, as when a hair is displaced and left in the displaced position.

The fields of these neurons, like those of the peripheral-nerve fibers innervating hair roots, vary in size according to the region of the body that they occupy. Fields near the extremities are small (the smallest found was about 10 mm^2); those on the body are large (up to about 2,000 mm^2). These dimensions are not markedly larger than are those of the fields of peripheral fibers. Stimulation of the skin outside the field reduces the response to a stimulus in the field, indicating some lateral inhibition in the nuclei of the dorsal columns.

About 25 per cent of the cells investigated responded to touch and were clearly fed by the temperature-sensitive touch receptors described by those working on peripheral nerves. The neurons had a background firing rate that depended upon the temperature of the skin in the receptive field. There is a striking difference between the characteristics of these second-order neurons and their peripheral fibers, however: The former have no punctate receptive fields. One cell in the dorsal-column nuclei with a field of only 200 mm^2 was found, but that was the smallest. Most of the touch-and-temperature-sensitive second-order neurons have receptive fields several thousand millimeters square, some as large as 30,000 mm^2.

Stimulation of the skin at the border of the field does not inhibit activity produced by stimulation within the field, as it does in cells that respond to hair movements; in fact, summation is the most common effect. It is clear, therefore, that there is a great deal of convergence of touch fibers on second-order cells in the dorsal-column nuclei, very little of it of an inhibitory nature. Why peripheral fibers that have such exquisitely distinct fields should merge their effects is not clear. We must assume that the brain cannot use sensory information in the mosaic form that Müller and many others thought it would require. Information about local sign is not necessarily lost by convergence, but it is probably being recoded into a form more suited to analysis by the brain.

Other neurons in the nuclei respond to vibra-tion of receptors at frequencies of up to 350 Hz. About 15 per cent of the cells in the sample of Perl and his colleagues were of this type. These cells presumably received afferents from the Pacinian corpuscles, some of which are apparently in the viscera, as several cells that discharged in response to every heartbeat were found. The cells responsive to hair stimulation tend to be located in a different part of the nuclei from that occupied by cells responding to touch and vibration.

Morin, Kitai, Portnoy, and Demirjian (1963) and Oswaldo-Cruz and Kidd (1964) have recorded from cells in the lateral cervical nucleus in the cat and have found that most of the cells respond to ipsilateral touch. There are some cells with small fields, but most have very large fields involving most of the body.

The characteristics of neurons at the next stage, the ventrobasal (VB) complex of the thalamus, have not been studied through such careful exploration of the adequate peripheral stimuli as was performed in the studies of neurons in peripheral-nerve and dorsal-column nuclei. The work of Poggio and Mountcastle (1963) indicates, however, that there is little change in either the fields or the type of stimulation required to fire thalamic third-order cells from those associated with second-order cells. There appears to be little additional convergence of modalities in this part of the thalamus. Much the same conclusions may be drawn about neurons in the primary somatosensory cortex (S I), according to Mountcastle and Powell (1959b), though it must be emphasized again that more careful investigation of the types of skin stimulation adequate to fire these neurons might change this conclusion.

An interesting finding by Powell and Mountcastle (1959), who were recording from single neurons of the postcentral gyrus in monkeys, was that, as the microelectrode was pushed through the layers of the cortex perpendicularly to the surface, many neurons with very similar characteristics were encountered. This finding reinforces the evidence mentioned in Chapter 8 and other data that we shall encounter later leading to the conclusion that cortical cells are organized in vertical columns, communicating much more with their neighbors above and below than with those beside them at the same level.

The type of information that is transmitted through the ventrolateral pathways is not as clear-cut as is that recorded in the dorsal pathways. According to Wall (1961) all types of receptor afferents converge on dorsal-horn cells. C. C. Hunt and Kuno (1959) also reported convergence on spinal interneurons in the cat of input from a number of receptive fields. Many cells responded to stimulation of either side of the body. Not all the neurons sampled by Hunt and Kuno gave evidence of convergent input, however; possibly those that do not are part of the neospinothalamic pathway, which joins the lemniscal system in the mesencephalon.

As has been mentioned, the majority of fibers in the ventrolateral tracts are relatively short and branch a great deal, so that there is ample opportunity for mixing afferents in this polysynaptic route even before it reaches the medulla. In the reticular formation there is further convergence, not only of afferents from different fields and modalities within the somatosensory system, but also of afferents from auditory, visual, and other modalities (Moruzzi, 1954).

Mountcastle (1961a) and his colleagues have demonstrated that in the *posterior group* (PO) of thalamic nuclei in the cat (part of Bowsher's VP shell) most of the cells have exceedingly large fields, some of them consisting of the total body surface (Figure 10.7). There appears to be an equally widespread convergence of inhibition on some of the cells. One PO cell with a fairly small excitatory field could be inhibited by stimulation anywhere else on the body. A more frequent finding was that a cell could be inhibited by simultaneous stimulation of the part of the body symmetrically opposite to the excitatory field.

This lack of modal specificity in the posterior group of thalamic nuclei is not absolute. Some cells show the typical hair-receptor response,

Figure 10.7 Receptive fields of eight representative neurons in the posterior group of thalamic nuclei of the cat. Responses ipsilateral to the recording electrode are shown on the right sides of the diagrams. (From Poggio & Mountcastle, 1960.)

receptive fields of units driven by mechanical stimuli

receptive fields of units driven by noxious stimuli

with rapid adaptation and an "off" response when the stimulus is removed; others behave as touch cells do, with a sustained burst during contact and prompt cessation of activity when the stimulus is removed. Of the cells in this nucleus sampled by Poggio and Mountcastle (1960) a large proportion required very strong, presumably painful, stimulation to fire. There was a steady recruitment of activity during continued stimulation (over a period of 5-10 seconds), followed by an afterdischarge lasting 15 seconds or more after stimulation was discontinued. Casey (1966), although not disputing that these cells may be involved in the perception of pain, has discovered that cells in the posterior group and in other extralemniscal thalamic nuclei that respond only to injurious stimulation when the animal is under light anesthesia respond also to touch when the animal is unanesthetized. They do, however, respond more vigorously to noxious stimuli than to innocuous stimuli.

Although Mountcastle seemed inclined to attribute pain conduction to the extralemniscal system, it is clear that the system also has various other functions, especially arousal. The extensive mixing of inputs of all types in the pathways makes the interpretation of experiments quite difficult.

Carreras and Andersson (1963) recorded from neurons in the second sensory area in the cat and found many cells there with fairly small contralateral fields, resembling those of cells in S I. In addition they found cells with large bilateral fields, some of which responded only to noxious stimulation.

KINESTHESIS

It may seem arbitrary to introduce the subject of kinesthesia at this point in a chapter on the somatosensory systems. Pain or temperature sense may seem to have more in common with what we have just been discussing. The reasons for adopting this order are that the lemniscal pathways for touch and kinesthesis are very similar and that they have usually been investigated together as a matter of experimental convenience.

Boyd and Roberts (1953) and Skogland

(1956) recorded activity in afferents from receptors in the knee joints of cats. They found that, as the joint is rotated steadily, a receptor will start to fire at a certain angle, will fire progressively more rapidly for the next 10-15°, and will then slow down and stop as the angle of peak stimulation for that particular receptor is passed. Different receptors fire at different angles, so that the whole movement is covered by a series of receptors, each monitoring part of the range. If the joint is left in a position at which a receptor is firing, the receptor will adapt slightly.during the first few seconds, after which the firing rate will be maintained indefinitely.

Mountcastle, Poggio, and Werner (1963) have made quantitative measurements of the relation between the firing rates of cells in the ventrobasal group of thalamic nuclei and the angles of the joints that drive the cells in monkeys. The characteristics of these cells are not quite the same as those of the afferent fibers in cats. Some neurons fire maximally when the limb is fully extended and others when it is completely flexed. The relationship between angle (θ) and firing frequency (F), for all the thalamic neurons sampled, is a power function: $F = a \times \theta^{0.7}$ where a is an empirical constant. The rate of adaptation is very slow after the first few seconds, as may be seen in Figure 10.8.

Figure 10.8 The firing rate of a neuron in the ventrobasal thalamic complex of the monkey produced by extension of the contralateral knee to the angles shown. Each curve represents the average of five trials, starting with the knee flexed. (After Mountcastle, Poggio & Werner, 1963.)

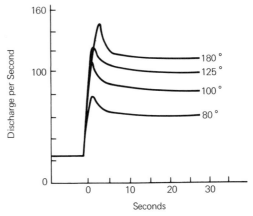

It is not clear whether the different ranges of angles to which thalamic and receptor cells respond in these experiments are caused by convergence and recoding at the thalamic level or simply by the difference in species of animal tested.

Cells with properties similar to those of VB cells are also found in the cortex (Mountcastle & Powell, 1959a) but have not yet been studied in such careful detail. In general, the neurons responding to movements of joints are in the anterior part of the postcentral gyrus near the motor area, and those responding to stimulation of the skin tend to be in the posterior part of the gyrus.

Some of the cortical cells responding to joint movement are inhibited by stimulation of the skin near the joint; frequently two neurons are spaced so closely that both can be picked up at the same time by the microelectrode, and one of them fires when the limb is flexed, the other when the limb is extended.

As in other cortical modalities, there is columnar organization, and vertical penetration reveals cells in all layers that respond to the same movement of a joint.

It must be emphasized again that no muscle afferents like those from muscle spindles are

Figure 10.9 Three recordings from a single fiber in the lingual nerve of a cat as the temperature of the tongue is reduced in steps of 2° C. The upper tracing in each case shows the temperature, the lower the discharges in the fiber. (After Hensel & Zotterman, 1951.)

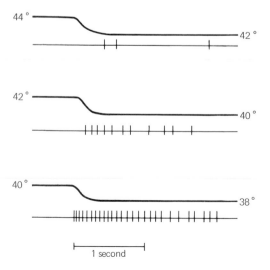

found in this part of the kinesthetic system. The input from muscle spindles bears no consistent relationship to the angle of the limb, for the receptors can be fired by the intrafusal muscles quite independently of the joint position. The information from these receptors would thus not be suitable for providing a *body image*. The spindle receptors indicate the disparity between the "required" and the actual muscle length, which might be interpreted centrally as the load, or effort, involved in maintaining a posture.

TEMPERATURE SENSE

Much early knowledge about the peripheral mechanism of thermal sensibility was derived from the tongue of the cat. Hensel and Zotterman (1951) recorded from the lingual nerve, or the chorda tympani (both nerves from the tongue) while changing the temperature of the tongue by placing a *thermode* (a copper block through which water at the required temperature was circulated) in contact with it. Figure 10.9 shows the effect of sudden cooling, in steps of 2° C., on the activity of one fiber. After a brief period of adaptation the discharge settles down to a steady rate. If the steady impulse frequencies are plotted against temperature, a curve like one of those in Figure 10.10 is obtained. When the peak activity occurs at a temperature below about 37° C. (body heat), the fiber is called a "cold" fiber; when the peak occurs at a higher temperature, the fiber is called a "warm" fiber, but the distinction is perhaps arbitrary. Peaks of activity may occur at any temperature between 20–45° C. for different fibers. Some have double peaks, one in the cold region and another (quite high) in the warm region, above the threshold for pain, which is about 48° C. (Dodt & Zotterman, 1952). It has been suggested that these receptors are responsible for the illusion of paradoxical cold, which some people experience when they touch very hot objects. It probably also explains why a grid made up of warm and cold bars feels more dangerously hot than does one that is uniformly warm (Geldard, 1953). Apparently a central integrating mechanism interprets the firing of both warm and cold fibers as indicating a higher temperature than the firing of warm fibers alone.

The temperature-sensitive fibers in the tongue nerves from which recordings have been made are very small myelinated fibers (A fibers of the smallest group). As we have seen, there are many fibers in cutaneous nerves that respond to both touch and temperature, most of them being in the same size group. Whether or not they participate in temperature perception is not known, but they do not seem to be as sensitive to temperature as those in the tongue investigated by Zotterman. Hensel, Iggo, and Witt (1960) have found C fibers in cutaneous nerves that are extremely sensitive to temperature changes and unresponsive to touch. Cooling the skin 0.3° C. may change the frequency of discharge by as much as 22 impulses per second; these fibers have temperature vs. impulse frequency characteristics very similar to those shown in Figure 10.10 for afferents from the tongue of the cat.

The central pathways of the temperature system are much less well understood than are those for touch and kinesthesis. Most, if not all, the spinal afferents are assumed to travel in the ventrolateral pathways because a cordotomy that severs these pathways and leaves the dorsal columns intact usually abolishes temperature sensation in the part of the body below the cut. *Syringomyelia*, a disease that causes local destruction of the core of the spinal cord, abolishes temperature sensation in the dermatomes served by the diseased segments, indicating that the afferents cross over close to their points of entry into the cord.

It seems likely that many of the temperature-sensitive afferents ascend in the neospinothalamic tract and reach the VB complex of the thalamus. Landgren (1960) has recorded from various cells in the lateral part of the nucleus ventralis posterior medialis (VPM) that are sensitive to cooling of the tongue. One cell in the same region responded to heating of the tongue. These cells were, as far as could be determined, pure temperature cells; many other cells were found that were sensitive to temperature changes, but they responded to other types of stimulation, usually touch or pressure, as well. Hécaen, Talairach, David, and Dell (1949)

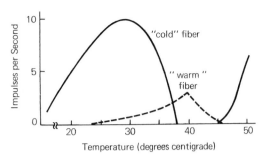

Figure 10.10 Steady firing rate of one sample "cold" fiber and one "warm" fiber in the lingual nerve of cat, as the temperature of the tongue is varied. (After Dodt & Zotterman, 1952.)

found that a lesion in the VP and *centre median* nuclei of the thalamus that eliminated chronic intractable pain also produced a loss of temperature sensations in man.

Landgren (1957b) has located neurons fired by temperature changes of the tongue in the lateral part of S I in the cat. Of 36 such cells 12 were responsive only to temperature changes, and the remaining 24 were also fired by touch or pressure. It therefore seems that a few specific temperature afferents remain relatively isolated from other modalities all the way to the cortex, though convergence with afferents from other modalities is more common.

That there must be some interaction between temperature-sensitive and other afferents seems clear from the subjective reports of patients with various disturbances of the sensory pathways or those of human subjects stimulated in unusual ways. In some pathological states light touching will engender pain described as burning, and, according to Melzack, Rose, and McGinty (1962), normal subjects report pricking and stabbing sensations when they are stimulated by a small, warm probe. In the latter experiment, increasing the area of the warm stimulus without changing its temperature led to subjects' recognition of the stimulus as warm.

PAIN

Of all the skin senses pain is the most conspicuous, the most intensively studied, the most important from a clinical point of view, and the least understood. One difficulty is that pain is not a single modality any more than "touch" is. Many unpleasant experiences are lumped together under the heading of pain, including aching, stinging, pricking, burning, smarting, soreness, and many others. The pain from a speck in the eye is quite different from a toothache or a sprained ankle. It is never certain in experiments on pain that all the subjects are describing the same experience or that they are using terms in the way intended by the experimenter.

All sensations are accessible only through introspective report, but the fact is particularly troublesome in the case of pain. We can confidently assume that a normal person exposed to electromagnetic radiation of a certain frequency and intensity, for example, will see light and that we can teach him to report it as such, but we have much less confidence that a stimulus painful to one person will also be painful to another or even to the same person at a different time. The point at which heat becomes painful or an electric shock becomes unbearable is a very personal matter and also varies with the subject's state of mind. Although some people suffer pain for no apparent reason, others with every reason to feel pain (wounded soldiers or injured athletes, for example) sometimes do not. The investigator also must face such vexing questions as whether an intolerable itch is painful or not. It is certainly unwelcome and highly motivating; in fact, it often seems preferable to feel sore than to itch.

When we turn to animal experiments we are even more in the dark. We can never be certain that animals feel pain at all, in the sense that we do. All that we can say is that their reflexive responses to noxious stimulation resemble ours and that they avoid the sort of stimuli that would cause us pain. Of course, animals and human beings also avoid situations and stimuli that are not in themselves injurious (smells, high places, darkness or light, and so on), but we do not automatically assume that these stimuli cause pain to animals. There is no watertight behavioral indicator of pain, and our best argument for supposing that animals experience noxious stimuli in the same way we do comes from faith in our evolutionary kinship with them.

Because of the poor correlation between painful stimuli and reported sensations, there has always been more reluctance to apply Müller's doctrine of specific energies to pain than to other modalities. A naïve person might well arrive at the conclusion that pain results from excessive stimulation of other modalities, and examples of this theory certainly antedate that of Müller. The idea was put forward again in more recent times by Nafe (1934), though already in 1931 Adrian, Cattell, and Hoagland had shown that very high rates of fiber activity could be induced by directing a pulsating jet of air onto the skin, without apparently aversive effects. Later Hebb (1949) suggested that pain was a disorganization of central activity that could result from unusual or excessive input. Others, for example Sinclair (1955) and Wall (1960), have rejected Müller's doctrine more completely and have suggested that all sensations, including pain, result from specific spatiotemporal patterns of input. (Müller's theory does, of course, offer a special example of a spatiotemporal pattern, but one gets the impression that the antispecificity faction has put its money on temporal coding and actually attributes little importance to spatial coding.)

Disregarding controversy over hypotheses, however, investigators have carried out various studies of pain receptors and pain pathways along the same lines as those devoted to other skin senses. Some of these studies have already been mentioned. C. C. Hunt and McIntyre (1960b) found that 2–3 per cent of the small A fibers in their sample could be fired only by injurious stimulation of the skin. Iggo (1959, 1960), also in cats, found that about 30 per cent of his sample of C fibers required noxious stimulation to fire. Furthermore, many of them responded when the skin temperature was raised above 48° C., which is near the pain threshold in human subjects. They could not, however, be fired by injections of substances that cause pain to people. The fields of these low-sensitivity receptors are quite small (about 10 mm^2 in the skin around the knees in cats) and exhibit unusual degrees of afterdischarge when the stimulus is removed.

It seems reasonable that, as only noxious stimulation can fire some fibers, those must be the ones responsible for painful sensations. But, before we congratulate ourselves on the simplicity of the peripheral mechanism, there are several other facts that must be taken into account. One is that, if the blood supply to a region is cut off for some time, there is a period when a slight stimulus will trigger a most unpleasant tingling, burning pain, which has a long afterdischarge. Yet it is difficult to believe that the thresholds of pain receptors are lowered by lack of oxygen.

Another problem is exemplified by the history of one of Weddell's patients (1961). Shortly after a nerve to one of the patient's fingers had been crushed the finger became *hyperalgesic* (extremely sensitive to pain) at the border of the denervated area near the skin with normal sensibility. Light stroking of the sensitive region produced almost unbearable pain. Histological examination revealed that this border zone was being invaded by sprouts branching from nerves in the normal area.

Many other examples of a similar nature, in which reduced innervation of the skin has resulted in increased susceptibility to pain, can be cited. Weddell (1941) and Weddell, Sinclair, and Feindel (1948) have suggested that a particularly unpleasant type of pain results when a pain receptor becomes isolated from other types of receptor. Anoxia (lack of oxygen) has this effect because the larger A fibers, with their higher metabolic rate, stop conducting sooner than do the C fibers when deprived of their blood supply. The reverse effect is obtained with local anesthetics, which apparently more readily block C fibers than A fibers and can produce an area of *analgesia* (insensitivity to pain) that remains sensitive to touch.

Zotterman (1939) appears to have been the first to suggest that there might be an inhibitory interaction between afferents, such that firing of A fibers would prevent the long-lasting afterdischarge of activated C fibers. Wortis, Stein, and Joliffe (1942) and Noordenbos (1959) have elaborated on this idea, but the most thoroughly

worked-out model of how the fast and slow afferents interact has been presented by Melzack and Wall (1965).

The basic mechanism of Melzack and Wall's model is shown in Figure 10.11. During innocuous stimulation of the skin, both A and C afferents are stimulated and produce a net excitatory effect in cells of the substantia gelatinosa. These cells depolarize the terminals of both A and C fibers on the transmission cells of the dorsal horn, producing presynaptic inhibition and preventing those cells from being fired too vigorously. If a noxious stimulus is presented, however, though few extra A fibers will be recruited, many extra C fibers will fire, thus increasing the inhibition of substantia-gelatinosa cells and reducing the inhibition of the input to the dorsal-horn cells, which will therefore fire at a much higher rate.

A central decoding system sensitive to the firing frequency of the transmission cells has been postulated. When this frequency is low, the activity is interpreted as representing various innocuous modes of stimulation, but a high frequency is interpreted as pain. An additional control of the "pain gate," through the centrifugal descending system, has been postulated by Melzack and Wall, but this control need not concern us here.

The model explains how pain can result from an increase in the activity of C fibers or from a decrease in the activity of A fibers, which has the effect of eliminating the inhibition of

Figure 10.11 Melzack and Wall's model of pain transmission in the spinal cord. A fibers excite (e) substantia-gelatinosa cells and C fibers inhibit them (*i*). The cells deliver presynaptic inhibition to the terminals of the A and C fibers on transmission cells in the dorsal horn. (After Melzack & Wall, 1965.)

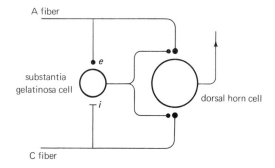

dorsal-horn cells by the substantia gelatinosa. It fits the anatomical and the clinical data well, but, of course, direct physiological verification is lacking, and the actual mechanism is probably a good deal more complex.

The spinal part of the pain pathway is assumed to coincide closely with that for temperature because lesions that cause loss of pain almost invariably cause loss of sensibility to temperature in the same parts of the body. Syringomyelia, for example, leads to bilateral loss of both pain and temperature sense in the affected segments, and cutting the ventrolateral tract causes loss of both types of sensation caudal to the lesion in the opposite side of the body. Sectioning the dorsal columns usually has no effect upon the perception of pain or temperature, though there have been occasional reports that pain is rendered more unpleasant after such operations.

The more central parts of the pathways for pain have been investigated in cats by Kerr, Haugen, and Melzack (1955). On the assumption that stimulation of tooth-pulp nerve is a reliable pain stimulus, they explored the brainstem with recording electrodes during such stimulation. They found evoked activity in five main areas: the medial lemniscus, the *trigemino-*

bulbothalamic tract (corresponding to the spino-bulbothalamic path from the spinal cord), the *central tegmental fasciculus*, the *central gray*, and the reticular formation (Figure 10.12). Pathways from these areas were followed into the ventralis posterior, *centre median*, parafascicular, and periventricular nuclei of the thalamus. The lemniscal path was the only one not affected by nitrous-oxide anesthesia, and it was therefore assumed to be unconnected with pain afferents (Haugen & Melzack, 1957).

Poggio and Mountcastle (1960) claimed that most thalamic cells that can be fired only by noxious stimulation of the body lie in the posterior group of thalamic nuclei (PO). These neurons register a slow buildup of activity during continued stimulation and afterdischarges that last a quarter of a minute or more. As mentioned previously, Casey (1966) found similar cells not only in PO but also in other projection nuclei of the extralemniscal system. He reported, however, that in the unanesthetized monkey these cells could also be fired by touch, though they fired more rapidly when noxious stimulation was applied.

Cells responding only to noxious stimuli have also been found in the cortex (Carreras & Andersson, 1963), mostly in the middle part

Figure 10.12 The brainstem of a cat, showing regions implicated in transmission of pain. (According to Kerr, Haugen, & Melzack, 1955.)

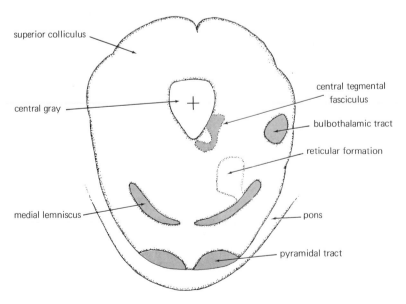

of the *anterior ectosylvian gyrus* in the cat (see Figure 12.14), corresponding roughly to the foreleg in S II, the second somatosensory projection area. All the neurons in the sample had large receptive fields, and half could be fired by noxious stimuli applied to any part of the body, including the cornea (the only place where a weak mechanical stimulus was sufficient to fire them). The experiments of Carreras and Andersson were carried out with the cats under light nembutal anesthesia, and it is possible that their *nociceptive* (pain-receptive) neurons would be less specific in the unanesthetized animal.

The very small proportion of cells in the thalamus and cortex that respond exclusively, or even almost exclusively, to noxious stimulation seems incommensurate with the massive effect of a painful stimulus upon behavior. Much of the motor response is no doubt evoked at the spinal-reflex level, but the explanation for the widespread central effects may be that pain is accompanied by strong arousal, a state not peculiar to pain; the cells involved can be fired by a great variety of stimuli. Perhaps the few nociceptive cells in the thalamus and cortex are responsible for the sensation of pain. We do not know how many cells are necessary to produce a sensation; we do not, indeed, have the slightest idea what a sensation is in neural terms. The behavioral effects of pain, on the other hand, are well known; as we noted earlier, however, they are not exclusive to painful stimuli. Fear and anxiety can be elicited by the weakest of stimuli. As we shall see later, the behavior associated with these emotions depends upon activity in a set of medial reticulo-limbic structures. As Melzack and Casey (1968) have pointed out, pain afferents have ample opportunity to activate this system. .

Frontal lobotomy (cutting the fibers connecting the frontal lobes to the rest of the brain) often provides some relief to patients with intractable pain. The usual comment of the patient is that the pain is as intense as ever but that it does not bother him as much as it did before the operation. Possibly this reaction is caused by interference with the arousal (or limbic system) aspects of the input, while the "sensory" components remain undisturbed.

In an effort to obtain some confirming behavioral evidence of the brainstem pathways described in the experiment of Kerr and his colleagues, Melzack, Stotler, and Livingston (1958) investigated the effects of lesions in four of these pathways in cats. The apparatus was a box with two compartments, the floor of each of which could be heated or had holes through which pins could be raised to present painful stimuli to the occupant. The cats were first tested to see whether or not they would escape these stimuli by moving into the adjacent compartment. Those that would not were eliminated from the experiment.

Then the cats were divided into four groups, each sustaining lesions in either the dorsal columns (control lesions), the spinothalamic tract, the rostral part of the central gray, or the central tegmental fasciculi.

The results were somewhat confusing, but on the whole they supported predictions based on the earlier recording study. The cats with dorsal-column lesions showed no deficit in escaping the noxious stimuli. The cats with spinothalamic lesions escaped in only about half the trials. Those with central-gray lesions started badly but improved from day to day until, on the fifth day, they escaped on about 70 per cent of the trials. The cats with the central-tegmental lesions behaved in a most unexpected way, however. They became hyperresponsive, escaping with an urgency not observed in any of the other animals. They also showed signs of spontaneous pain, rubbing and biting at their paws and crying. It was suggested that the central tegmental fasciculus might carry descending inhibitory impulses.

Stimulation Experiments

That ventrolateral cordotomy usually eliminates pain from parts of the body caudal to the lesion would lead us to assume that the dorsal columns (which are intact after this operation) do not carry pain impulses. Weddell (1961), however, reported that patients described electrical stimulation of the dorsal columns as unpleasant, like that of a bump or an electric shock. He was of the opinion that such sensations should not be interpreted as pain, but his view serves only to illustrate the inadequacy of our definitions of pain. It also suggests that Weddell had forgotten that there are collaterals from the dorsal columns to the dorsal horn and ventrolateral tracts at all levels. Strangely enough, similar electrical stimulation in the ventrolateral tracts had no effect, probably because the parameters of stimulation were more suited to firing large than small fibers. Patients of Spiegel and Wycis (1961) stimulated in the spinothalamic tract at the mesencephalic level experienced sensations of tingling, burning, pricking, and so on. The sensations were usually diffuse and referred to the opposite side of the body from the stimulated tracts. Pain was also elicited from patients by stimulation of the superior and inferior colliculi in the region where spinotectal fibers terminate. Cats also gave "pain suggestive" responses to stimulation in the superior and inferior colliculi.

M. E. Olds and Olds (1963) stimulated numerous structures in the rat brain, giving the animals the opportunity to turn the stimulation off by pressing a lever. "Pure" escape responses were obtained from areas in the mesencephalon corresponding to all those in which Kerr and his colleagues had recorded tooth-pulp responses, as well as in the lower layers of the superior colliculus (Figure 10.12). Whether such stimulation is painful or not, the rat agrees with man in not liking to have its lemniscal system stimulated electrically.

Delgado (1955) and Delgado, Rosvold, and Looney (1956) found that monkeys also responded with aversion to stimulation of the medial lemniscus and the VP nucleus of the thalamus. It is possible that there was current spread to the *centre median*. Hécaen, Talairach, David, and Dell (1949) elicited pain sensations from the *centre median* and nearby VPM of the thalamus with electrical stimulation in human patients undergoing surgical lesions for intractable pain.

Stimulation of the nucleus medialis dorsalis in patients did not produce experiences of pain or even of fear, nor did Delgado evoke aversive

responses from the same nucleus in monkeys, though the region is one in which neurons responding only to noxious stimuli have been reported. Olds and Olds did, however, report escape behavior in rats stimulated there.

Penfield and Boldrey (1937) reported a very few instances of pain resulting from cortical stimulation in conscious patients during brain surgery. The patients described most of these sensations as tingling, numbness, or "electricity." Hallucinations of movement were also experienced.

In view of the paucity of pain experiences from cortical stimulation, many neurologists have suggested that pain impulses "enter consciousness" in the thalamus. Massive lesions in the lateral thalamus, like those often produced by *thrombosis* of the *thalamogeniculate artery* (obstruction by a blood clot), can lead, after periods of analgesia, to one of the most unbearable forms of pathological pain. It has been claimed that this pain can be eliminated by extending the lesion into the *centre median* (Talairach, Hécaen, David, Monnier & Ajuriaguerra, 1949), but it would be unwise to conclude that this nucleus is therefore the center for pain. One neurosurgeon has cynically stated that as long as there is any brain left, it will develop the ability to respond to pain.

It should be clear by now that we can find many questions but can supply only a few answers about the mechanisms of pain. Many difficult problems have not even been mentioned here. Pain is probably the only sense modality accessible to study by experimental lesions and stimulation in human subjects, yet we still do not know to what extent it is a specific modality and in what ways it interacts with other sense modalities. We do not even know where the main sensory area for pain is located or if the concept of a sensory area for pain has any meaning.

We might guess that pain results from some pattern of activity in the reticular core of the nervous system (which extends along the spinal cord and up through the reticular formation of the brainstem, the more medial of the thalamic nuclei, and the limbic system) and that this pattern can be established in the normal animal only by stimulation of high-threshold receptors. Under abnormal or pathological conditions the pattern can appear spontaneously or with input from other receptors, especially when input to the system from large A fibers is reduced.

CORTICAL MECHANISMS OF SOMESTHESIS

Among the skin senses it is clear that the modalities of touch and body-position sense lie toward the epicritic or informative end of the continuum; pain, itch, tickle, and temperature sense are relatively protopathic, or affective, though we make considerable use of temperature to identify objects by "touch" and may even use pain for this purpose (with sharp objects, for example). Vibration produced by moving the fingers over a surface is important for the identification of textures.

When we try to identify an object by handling it we use information about the positions of our joints, skin contact, vibration, and to a lesser extent temperature and noxious stimulation. This multimodal activity ascending to the cortex is integrated not only across modalities but also along a temporal dimension, so that information derived from one scan is stored and added to that derived from subsequent scans until the object is recognized. Movement is very important for judging shape, as well as texture; it is certainly no accident that the sensory cortex is so closely linked to the motor cortex.

Kinesthetic information about the posture of the body at any instant is essential for determining what movements are necessary to reach for something or to adopt a new posture, so that again we see the value of the overlap of the sensory and motor cortices.

The somatosensory system rivals the visual and auditory systems in its integrating capacity, that is, its ability to combine information from different loci, different modalities, and different instants in time. It also has in common with the other relatively epicritic modalities a capacity for abstraction. A simple example is that mentioned in the introduction to Part Three:

the ability to tell that one has been touched by two points, wherever on the body they are. Presumably the innumerable combinations of pairs of stimuli that can excite the concept of duality must have some common property in order to permit such recognition.

One suggestion on how this property is detected is that of a scanning mechanism that converts spatial patterns of stimulation into temporal, or sequential, information. It is easy to eliminate some unwanted information, the locus of stimulation for example, from a temporal pattern. In the instance mentioned, a scanning process similar to that of attention may explore the area of interest and send impulses to a "counter" each time it meets a stimulus. This hypothetical mechanism certainly corresponds to our introspective notion of what happens when we are touched at several points and must count them one by one, but the process of distinguishing one from two seems more immediate.

An engineer faced with the problem of instantly counting small numbers of simultaneous, randomly located events might arrange for each event to generate a standard impulse, then add all the impulses and measure the size of the sum. In neural terms this model could perhaps be simulated by having all the inputs from touch receptors converge on cells with graded thresholds, some fired by touching any single point, others requiring convergent input from afferents fired when two points are simultaneously touched, and so on. It would not matter which two peripheral points were touched; convergence would ensure that the same set of central neurons was always fired. It would be necessary only to associate this set of neurons with a network whose activity had come to represent the concept "two," and all other examples of dual stimulation would immediately be recognized without further learning.

Duality is a relatively simple example of generalization. To recognize a letter traced on the hand, the perceptual mechanism would have to be equipped with detectors for lines and for the angles between them independent of locus, size, and so on. Such detectors must be complex, but they are by no means impossible to imagine, and, as we shall see when we deal with the visual system, cells with the required properties have been discovered there.

The simpler analyses are performed in transmission nuclei of sensory pathways, but vast numbers of neurons must be required to detect more complex properties, which suggests that this process takes place in the cortex. That the modalities in which the most complex analysis is required (somesthesis, vision, hearing) have larger cortical sensory areas than do the more protopathic senses lends further support to this idea. We might have expected experiments on sensory cortex to shed some light on these property-detecting mechanisms, but, although we now know a good deal about the relationship between the locus of a cortical lesion and the specific deficits that ensue, these data have not yet been very helpful to perceptual theorists in their efforts to find out how the cortex performs its functions.

Lesions that affect somatosensory discriminations are, as we might expect, concentrated in and around the somatosensory cortical areas. Rats with ablations of both S I and S II (as delineated by electrophysiological mapping) showed greater loss of preoperatively learned roughness discrimination than did rats with ablations of only one or the other of the sensory areas or of the frontal or occipital cortex (Zubek, 1951, 1952b). A cat with ablations of S I and S II was unable to relearn the roughness discrimination at all (Zubek, 1952a). The ability to discriminate a wedge from a cylinder by touch was unaffected by any cortical lesion (Zubek, 1952c), as was temperature discrimination (Downer & Zubek, 1954).

J. Marshall (1951) encountered a number of patients with small "cortical" lesions (mostly caused by missile wounds) who had lost sensibility to pain and temperature, but in view of the negative findings of Downer and Zubek and of many other investigators, including those working with well-defined cortical lesions in human subjects, it seems likely that subcortical structures had also been damaged in Marshall's patients.

Kruger and Porter (1958) showed that unilateral lesions of S I and S II in the monkey produced some impairment of tactual form discrimination with the contralateral paw; the deficits were more severe when the lesion was extended to include the precentral gyrus. Disturbance of motor functioning was probably not a contributory factor in aggravating such deficits, as monkeys showed no loss on a visual-discrimination problem in which the same response movements were used. This result indicates that the sensory projection to the supposedly motor area of the precentral gyrus is enough to provide residual tactual acuity when the classical sensory areas have been ablated.

Weight discrimination in animals was not impaired by bilateral lesions of either the precentral gyrus (motor) or the posterior parietal lobe and only transiently by lesions of the postcentral gyrus (S I), according to Ruch, Fulton, and German (1938). Large parietal-lobe lesions, including the postcentral gyrus, did, however, produce lasting impairments of weight discrimination. Blum (1951) also observed an impairment of weight discrimination in a monkey with extensive lesions of the parietal lobe invading the postcentral gyrus and part of the posterior temporal lobe but failed to find it in five other monkeys with similar lesions that had spared the postcentral gyrus.

In animals unilateral cortical lesions have only slight effects as a rule. For most areas, commissural paths through the corpus callosum ensure that both hemispheres are provided with all the incoming information, and either side can perform a satisfactory analysis. The somatosensory domain is different, however. Tactual input, except for that from the face, is almost all projected to the contralateral cortex, so that unilateral lesions do produce deficits. Ettlinger and Kalsbeck (1962) give monkeys a routine neurological examination and tested them for visual reaching toward a moving object and for tactual discrimination. The tests were administered before operation, after unilateral ablation of the posterior parietal lobe, and again after removal of the other parietal lobe. After the first operation all the deficits were contralateral to the lesion. They included reduced accuracy in picking up a sugar pellet from a moving belt and deficits in tactual discrimination. It is interesting that, although the monkeys had trouble reaching for food, once they had grasped it they conveyed it straight to the mouth without fumbling. After the second lesion there was practically no change, except that the deficits became bilateral. When bilateral removals were performed in one operation the animals appeared to be blind for a few days and were very clumsy for a time, but their behavior was otherwise similar to those who had undergone two-stage operations. (Transient blindness has been reported by all experimenters who have performed single-stage bilateral posterior-parietal lobectomies.) Lesions that affected the anterior part of the parietal lobe, including the postcentral gyrus, produced much the same deficits but in more severe forms.

These data suggest that the two hemispheres work almost independently of each other in the somatosensory modality, but that is far from the case, as may be inferred from the immediate transferability (with little loss) of tactual discriminations learned with one paw to the opposite paw. This interaction is probably mediated by the corpus callosum. According to Ebner and Myers (1962), section of the middle portion of the corpus callosum alone is sufficient to prevent transfer of a roughness discrimination from one paw to the contralateral one in monkeys. Although Sperry (1962) and his collaborators have reported cases in which section of all the forebrain commissures in monkeys did not completely prevent transfer of training between opposite paws, he has since come to consider it probable that the subjects outwitted the experimenters in these experiments by using nontactual information.

H. Teitelbaum, Sharpless, and Byck (1968), having shown that in the cat there are functional connections from S I in one hemisphere to S II in the opposite hemisphere but none to the contralateral S I, speculated that transfer of a tactual discrimination from one paw to the opposite one would be prevented by a lesion of S II ipsilateral to the trained paw. They confirmed this speculation experimentally.

Rather surprisingly, they discovered that the lesion also prevented transfer in the other direction. Apparently the transcallosal connections between the two second sensory areas are crucial for transfer of training. Connections between S I and the contralateral S II are not effective for this purpose.

A cat can learn a tactual discrimination after the contralateral S I has been ablated, but the training cannot be transferred to the other paw. Damage to S I does not prevent a discrimination from being transferred from the paw opposite the intact hemisphere to the paw opposite the damaged hemisphere.

Semmes and Mishkin (1965) have provided further evidence of interhemispheric interaction, showing that lesions of sensorimotor and posterior parietal cortex in monkeys disturb tactual discrimination by the ipsilateral, as well as by the contralateral, paw. The monkeys took longer to learn a roughness discrimination than did monkeys with all cortex except sensorimotor cortex removed unilaterally. There was no disturbance of tactual size judgments.

The question whether or not the posterior parietal lobe is a "tactual association area" is still controversial. Several animal experiments have suggested that this lobe is important for somesthetic learning. H. B. Pribram and Barry (1956) and M. Wilson (1957) compared monkeys with bilateral lesions of the posterior parietal lobes and others with lesions in the inferior temporal lobes (an association area that had previously been shown to be important for visual discrimination; see Chapter 11). The monkeys were required to discriminate stimuli either tactually (in the dark) or visually. Those with parietal-lobe lesions had no difficulty with the visual tasks but were impaired on the tactual problems; the opposite was true of the monkeys with the inferotemporal lesions.

This experimental design is known as *double dissociation* (Teuber, 1955). Two tasks are given to two groups of animals with different lesions. If one group exhibits a deficit only on one of the tasks and the other group only on the other, the experimenter has established beyond reasonable doubt that one part of the brain is more important than other parts for a particular function and that damage to that area does not produce global impairment on every task. In Wilson's experiment, the monkeys probably were still capable of associating meanings with stimuli that they could distinguish, but the ability to discriminate among tactual stimuli was impaired by the parietal-lobe lesions, and the ability to discriminate among visual stimuli was impaired by the inferotemporal lesions.

M. Wilson, Wilson, and Chiang (1963) have shown that monkeys with parietal-lobe lesions form tactual-learning sets even more slowly than do normal monkeys but acquire visual-learning sets without difficulty. "Learning set" is the name given by Harlow (1949) to the ability of some animals to learn a new discrimination in one or a few trials after experience with many similar problems. The animal is usually trained by presenting a few trials with one discrimination, and then, whether or not it has learned that discrimination, a new pair of discriminanda is introduced for the same limited number of trials and so on. Eventually, after hundreds of discriminations, the animal becomes able to learn each new one very quickly, often in a single trial. It is assumed that the improvement is partly a result of the animal's learning to pay attention to the essential features of the specific kind of problem. This ability seems particularly susceptible to disruption by cortical lesions. Monkeys have more difficulty acquiring tactual-learning sets than acquiring visual ones, possibly because they find tactual discriminations harder than visual ones in the first place.

Comparison of animal data with those derived from testing human patients with parietal lesions is complicated by the asymmetry of the human brain and by the difficulty of being precisely certain what lesion each patient has. Semmes, Weinstein, Ghent, and Teuber (1960) tested a group of war veterans with brain damage produced by missile wounds for *pressure sensitivity, two-point threshold, point localization*, and so on. They found some bilateral deficits after lesions of the left hemisphere but only contralateral deficits after lesions of the right hemisphere. This difference between the two groups was not statistically significant, how-

ever, and other workers have not been able to confirm it (see discussion later in this chapter). Semmes and her colleagues reported that patients who had suffered loss of sensory acuity in only one hand were usually impaired with both hands on more complex tactual tasks like discrimination learning. Weinstein (1962) demonstrated a loss of tactual size discrimination in patients with right-sided lesions, and this loss was more severe if the patient had also suffered sensory loss. This type of deficit was found less frequently in patients with left-sided lesions.

It is not very satisfactory to base conclusions about cortical localization on patients with gunshot wounds because it is impossible to know what subcortical structures have also been clipped by penetrating missiles and bone splinters. Furthermore, parts of the brain remote from the main track of the missile might well sustain permanent damage from the shock waves at impact.

Corkin (1964) tested patients who had undergone cortical removal for relief of epilepsy, using a battery of tests similar to that used by Semmes and her colleagues. She found no lasting sensory defect in any patient whose central Rolandic region (pre- and postcentral gyri) was undamaged. The deficits that she did find were mainly contralateral, but there were some bilateral effects, particularly on the test of point localization (in which the hand is touched twice at an interval of about a second and the subject must say whether or not the two contacts are at the same place). These deficits occurred equally often after right- and left-sided lesions.

The other sensory tests given by Corkin (of pressure threshold, as measured by a series of hairs of graded stiffness, and of two-point discrimination threshold, in which two points on the hand of varying distances apart are touched simultaneously) did not reveal any significant ipsilateral deficits (Corkin, Milner & Rasmussen, 1964).

In view of the controversy over the function of the posterior parietal lobe and over whether or not lesions there produce "pure" *astereognosis* (inability to recognize objects by touch), it is interesting that Corkin found impairment of tactual object recognition only in those patients who also had sensory deficits, that is, in those whose lesions invaded the Rolandic area.

Semmes (1965) agreed with Corkin that pure astereognosis does not exist, although her analysis of the findings in patients with missile wounds revealed some who lacked sensory deficits (in pressure threshold, point localization, and so on) yet still had difficulty recognizing shapes tactually. Semmes believed that such difficulty may have arisen from some general impairment of the ability to orient in space ("spatial ability") and not from a specific tactual-association deficit.

The "spatial" difficulty showed up more obviously in map-reading tests (Semmes, Weinstein, Ghent & Teuber, 1955), in which the subject was given a map indicating the path that he was to take among nine spots marked on the floor. He was not allowed to turn the map relative to his body as he proceeded along the path, so that most of the time the direction of the path on the map was not the same as that to be taken in the room.

The subjects were tested with both visual and tactual maps. As might be expected, the mode of the map's presentation was not very important; subjects with impaired spatial ability could not follow the tactual map any better than they could follow the visual one.

Those brain-injured subjects who showed impairment on the map-reading task also tended to have difficulty discriminating shapes tactually, which led Semmes (1965) to the conclusion previously mentioned: that both deficits in subjects with no sensory loss were caused by a deficit of spatial ability that was not specific to any modality and probably resulted from damage to the posterior parietal lobe.

Orbach (1959) found that blind monkeys, who also had lesions of the occipital and posterior parietal lobes, performed badly in a locomotor maze, though the same subjects were unimpaired on a stylus-maze test. B. Milner (1965) and Corkin (1965) tested human patients with various surgical lesions of the cortex on visually and tactually guided stylus mazes respectively and found that, although there was

a high correlation (0.77) between the scores on the two mazes, small parietal-lobe lesions, either in the Rolandic area or more to the posterior, had little effect upon performance. Lesions in the right frontal or right temporal lobes produced a more severe deficit. (Lashley's choice of the maze to test the theory of cortical localization of function was unfortunate; even in man maze performance appears to be affected by lesions in many parts of the cortex.)

As B. Milner (1965) has pointed out, the lack of correlation between performance on the stylus and locomotor mazes in the monkey or on the stylus maze and map-reading task in man may result from the greater need for good spatial orientation in the second tasks. In the stylus maze the maze and the subject remain in the same relative positions throughout, whereas in the locomotor maze the orientation of the subject to the maze is continually changing.

Hécaen, Penfield, Bertrand, and Malmo (1956) tested patients with surgical lesions and found, as did Corkin, that parietal-lobe lesions produced no increase in sensory thresholds unless there was also invasion of the Rolandic area. They also noted difficulties with such complex sensorimotor activities as dressing, constructing block designs, using scissors, and so on, which resulted from lesions in the right posterior parietotemporal area. (Lesions in the same area in the left, dominant hemisphere would produce severe language disturbance, and thus would never be made for the relief of epilepsy.)

Many patients tended to ignore the contralateral (left) side of their body, and of space in general. One patient, for example, would come to the table with his left hand in his pocket and would try to eat with only his right hand until reminded to use both.

The patients also had some trouble finding their way about, were unable to draw the simplest figures from memory, and were not much better at copying them. One, who worked in a clothing store, found it easier to dress the dummies than himself, because, as he said, they did not move their limbs about as he did. This story suggests that information on limb position is defective or cannot be used by these patients.

After strokes some patients have spontaneous movements of the contralateral limbs, and, particularly with right-sided lesions, they claim to be unaware of these difficulties or even deny strenuously that they occur. Critchley (1953) mentioned one of Lhermitte's patients, a distinguished scientist, who had had a stroke that left him paralyzed on the left side. He denied that anything was wrong with him, and he was seriously concerned about the sanity of his niece when she kept talking about his paralysis.

The phenomenon seems to be some form of hallucination of the body image. Some less seriously affected patients recognize what is happening to some extent and report that they feel phantom limbs that move, even though the real limbs do not. One patient, asked to stretch his arms out in front of him, admitted that only the right arm had been raised but said that he felt as if both were up. Such hallucinations raise some interesting questions about the structures necessary for perception of body position and how it is possible to have sensations of movement and position when the higher sensory and motor systems are damaged. Unfortunately, the damage from strokes is certainly not confined to the cortex, and it is idle to speculate about the mechanism when the extent of the lesion is unknown.

The asymmetry of the human brain shows itself in the syndromes that we have been discussing. Piercy, Hécaen, and Ajuriaguerra (1960), in an analysis of 3,000 patients, found that *constructional apraxias* (such as inability to copy designs with match sticks) were more than twice as frequent after right-sided brain injuries than after left-sided injuries. Nathanson, Bergman, and Gordon (1952) found that about 70 per cent of patients with unilateral paralysis who denied being ill had damage to the right hemisphere. Language difficulties are the most frequent result of left-sided lesions. We shall have more to say about them in Chapter 13.

Summary

The somatosensory systems include the skin senses of touch, pressure, pain, temperature, itch, vibration, and so on and the body senses of joint position, muscle tension, and visceral state. The afferents for these modalities follow similar routes to the brain through the spinal cord and the medulla.

Although there are receptors with many different types of encapsulated endings, especially on the hands and feet, little relationship has been found between shape and function. Pacinian corpuscles have, however, been identified as vibration receptors.

The early theory that each modality employed separate afferent fibers and that the location of a stimulus was indicated by a mosaic of pathways (Müller's doctrine) has not been supported by experimentation, but the modifications required to reconcile it to present data are not as great as some extremists have suggested.

Recordings from single sensory fibers show that some A fibers respond mainly when hairs are moved, others mainly when pressure or high-intensity stimulation is applied, and others mainly to vibration. Some are sensitive to touch at discrete points on the skin, and the same ones are also slightly sensitive to temperature. Other myelinated afferents are exclusively involved in joint position, muscle-spindle activity, or other kinesthetic functions.

The endings of C fibers range from high sensitivity to touch or temperature change to sensitivity only to intense or noxious stimulation. We thus see that there is not much more mixing of modalities in the sensory pathways than Müller postulated; within each modality, however, there is considerable interaction among neighboring afferents.

Somatosensory afferents take two main paths to the brain: the lemniscal, which passes through the medial lemniscus in the medulla, and the extralemniscal, which follows a more diffuse path through the reticular formation and tectal nuclei of the brainstem.

The most important lemniscal path ascends through the dorsal columns (gracilis and cuneate funiculi) of the spinal cord. Its fibers synapse in the gracilis or cuneate nuclei in the medulla, from where second-order fibers decussate to form the main body of the contralateral medial lemniscus. Other afferents synapse in the spinal cord near their points of entry and ascend in the neospinothalamic tract (part of the ventrolateral spinal pathway). The third lemniscal route is through the tract of Morin lying just ventral to the dorsal horn; its fibers synapse in the lateral cervical nucleus and cross over to join the medial lemniscus. The fibers of the medial lemniscus end in the ventrobasal complex of the thalamus and are relayed to the primary and secondary areas of the somatosensory cortex (S I and S II).

The extralemniscal pathway is very heterogeneous. The fibers ascend in the ventrolateral tracts of the cord, each with one or more synapses along the way. When they reach the medulla most of them synapse either in the reticular formation or in the tectal nuclei, and activity is relayed to the intralaminar (parafascicular and *centre median*) or to the posterior group of thalamic nuclei. Some of the ascending fibers do not synapse in the lower brainstem but go straight to the intralaminar thalamic nuclei. The extralemniscal outflow of the thalamus is distributed widely through the cortex.

Some somatosensory afferents go to the cerebellar cortex through the spinocerebellar tracts and are relayed from there to the cerebral cortex. There is also a complex network of descending fibers that have inhibitory effects upon incoming signals.

The lemniscal system is characterized by a primarily contralateral projection to the cortex, short latency, small peripheral fields, and little mixing of modalities. Unilateral input to the extralemniscal system projects to both hemispheres, has longer latency and larger peripheral fields in general than does the lemniscal system, and reveals more overlapping of modalities.

The activity of units in the somatosensory cortex is often very similar to that of single skin receptors, despite much overlapping of adjacent endings in relay nuclei. Lateral inhibition is usually invoked to explain the lack of "smearing." It has also been suggested that lateral inhibition may operate to narrow the fields of some cortical neurons further so that they fire only to very precisely specified stimuli. No such cells have been found, however, and it seems unlikely that they exist. The overall firing pattern in a group of cells is an extremely potent way of conveying information, making it unnecessary for specific cells to represent each discriminable input.

The firing rate of joint receptors and connected cortical cells is determined by the angle of the limb. Some cells fire at their maximum rates when the limb is fully extended and some when it is fully flexed.

Most of the research on temperature sense has been done on small A fibers from the tongue, though most temperature receptors in the skin conduct through C fibers. Apparently, however, the characteristics are similar in each case. Cold fibers have peak activity when the receptor is at a temperature below 37° C. (body temperature), the exact value depending upon the individual fiber. Another peak usually occurs in cold fibers at a high temperature, near the pain threshold. Warm fibers are those that reach peak activity when the receptor is above 37° C.

The temperature afferents from the body ascend in the ventrolateral pathway (possibly in the neospinothalamic tract) and reach the ventrobasal complex of the thalamus. Some S I cells are fired by cooling the tongue, but the cortex does not contribute significantly to temperature discrimination.

The modality of pain is very difficult to

study, partly because of a natural reluctance to use painful stimuli on animals or people and partly also because of the absence of a clear, objective definition of a painful stimulus. There is a widely held view that there are no specialized receptors for pain and that the central activity we recognize as pain is elicited by some characteristic of the firing pattern of receptors in other modalities. Against this view we may set the repeated observations that some peripheral fibers (both A and C) fire only when the skin is stimulated by a strong pinch, pinprick, or other noxious stimulus.

The pain mechanism does not involve simply these high-threshold receptors, however; other modalities interact more with pain than they do with one another. The ability to experience pain is so essential for survival that we seem to be very well supplied with potential pain receptors, most of which are inhibited by other input except under pathological conditions. Several investigators have suggested ways in which, under normal circumstances, large, fast-conducting touch fibers might inhibit the activity of low-threshold pain fibers.

Most pain afferents travel to the medulla through the ventrolateral spinal pathways and synapse in the reticular formation and the lower layers of the colliculi. Some cells fired maximally by noxious stimuli are found in the posterior group of thalamic nuclei and a few in the somatosensory cortex. Arousal and avoidance behavior involve reticulolimbic brain structures, to which most sensory inputs, including pain, project.

Although cutting the ventrolateral pathways of the cord usually prevents perception of pain from the part of the body below the cut, at least for a time, suggesting that pain signals do not ascend in dorsal pathways, electrical stimulation of the dorsal columns is nevertheless described as painful by subjects. Stimulation of the tectal region and some intralaminar thalamic nuclei is also painful, but cortical stimulation is not.

One probable function of the somatosensory cortex is to detect certain characteristics of tactual stimuli (length, relative angle, and so on). Other characteristics of these stimuli (temperature, hardness, texture, for example) are analyzed before the signals reach the cortex. All the analyzed information is then integrated, or synthesized, in association cortex, so that the neural representations of one or more concepts are aroused.

Simple tactual, shape, or temperature discrimination is not affected by ablations of S I and S II in the rat, but roughness discrimination is impaired. In the monkey, tactual discrimination is impaired contralateral to a lesion of the somatosensory cortex. Very large parietal-lobe lesions are required to produce impairment of weight discrimination.

The main effects of somatosensory lesions occur only on the contralateral side of the body, but the two hemispheres are connected through the corpus callosum, so that training with one limb can be transferred to the contralateral limb. After section of the corpus callosum, or ablation of S II on the untrained side of the cortex, no transfer takes place.

Some ipsilateral deficits of roughness discrimination have been reported after extensive lesions of the sensorimotor cortex. Bilateral posterior-parietal-lobe lesions produce selective impairment of tactual form discrimination, learning, and formation of learning sets.

Patients with cortical damage show no deficit of tactual discrimination unless they have also suffered loss of tactual acuity or sensitivity. After parietal-lobe lesions both people and monkeys have difficulty with spatial orientation but little difficulty with stylus mazes, where there is a constant relationship between the body and the maze.

Right posterior-parietal-lobe lesions also impair complex activities like dressing, copying block designs, using scissors, and so on and cause neglect of the left side of the body. Gross disturbances of the perception of limb movements and hallucinatory disturbances of body image may also occur.

CHAPTER 11

THE VISUAL SYSTEM

The visual systems of animals are sensitive to energy in the form of electromagnetic radiation at wavelengths between 0.7 and 0.4 μ. (The more common unit of length used in optics is the millimicron, or mμ, which is 10^{-9} meters. Many scientific journals have now adopted "nano" as the standard prefix meaning 10^{-9} for all physical measures, and wavelength measurements will therefore be given here in *nanometers*, or nm. Another unit of length, which was frequently used to measure light wavelengths at one time, is the *angstrom* (A), which is 10^{-10} meters. This unit is now used mainly in electron microscopy.)

Many nocturnal vertebrates are insensitive to the long-wavelength end of the spectrum (between 650 and 700 nm), and some insects are sensitive to wavelengths too short for human beings to see (ultraviolet light). The receptors of vertebrates are sensitive to ultraviolet light, but these short waves are filtered out on their way through the eye and do not normally reach the receptors. In animals with color vision the wavelength of the light determines what color is seen.

Many simple organisms like worms have light-sensitive receptors distributed over the body surface; in some single-celled organisms the whole membrane is sensitive to light. Such animals may be able to detect the intensity and rough direction of a light source, but they do not have vision in the sense of being able to recognize objects in the environment. In order to do that, it is necessary to have a mosaic of individual receptors, each responding to light only from a certain angle.

A simple optic system for achieving this result is shown in Figure 11.1a, which is a diagram of the eye of the nautilus, a mollusk related to the squid. The eye consists of a spherical cavity lined with light-sensitive cells. Light is admitted through a small hole at the top, and the light reaching each receptor comes from a rather narrow angle in line with the hole; the cavity thus acts as a pin-hole camera.

The compound eye of an arthropod works in a similar way. It consists of a bundle of thin translucent rods, called "ommatidia," each of which picks up light from a small angle and uses it to excite a receptor cell. The ommatidia point in slightly different directions, so that each receptor "sees" a different part of the surroundings. By relating the activity of the different receptors, the central nervous system is able to discriminate among different patterns of light falling on the eye.

The octopus and other higher cephalopods improve on the pin-hole camera of the nautilus by having a lens at the opening of the eye cavity. The lens has much the same effect as does the hole, but it allows more light to enter without increasing the angle seen by each receptor (Figure 11.1b). The lens, however, also introduces a complication: Only objects at a certain distance are brought into sharp focus on the receptor surface; to obtain sharp resolution of objects over a range of distances some adjustment is necessary. In the octopus and many fish the lens can be moved nearer or farther from the receptors by muscular action. Most higher vertebrates accommodate the eye to objects at different distances by changing the curvature of the lens.

THE STRUCTURE OF THE HUMAN EYE

The structure of the human eye is shown in Figure 11.2. The light first passes through the cornea, which is curved and acts as a lens to focus it roughly on the *retina* (the sensitive inner surface of the eyeball opposite the cornea). Behind the cornea is another lens, whose

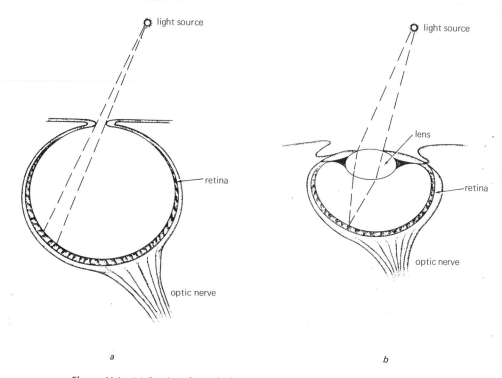

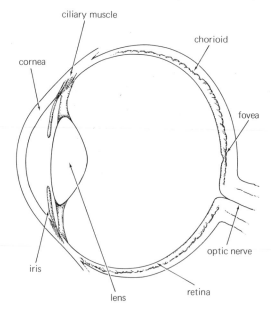

Figure 11.1 (a) Section through the "pin hole" eye of *Nautilus*. The amount of light entering the eye is limited by the diameter of the hole. If the hole is made bigger, the ability to resolve adjacent objects is reduced. (b) Section through the lens eye of the octopus. A larger aperture (which admits more light) is possible with no loss of resolving power, thanks to the focusing action of the lens.

shape can be changed to provide fine focusing adjustments. The natural shape of this lens tends to be spherical, but when the *ciliary muscles* that control it are relaxed it is partly flattened by the pressure of the fluid in the eyeball. Distant objects should be in focus on the retina under these conditions. Contraction of the ciliary muscles, which lie around the eyeball in the zone where the lens is attached, takes some of the tension off the lens, and it reverts to a more spherical shape. This process allows focusing of closer objects on the retina. With increasing age the lens loses some of its elasticity, so that it does not spring back as far when the ciliary muscles contract, and nearby objects can no longer be properly focused without the assistance of external lenses.

The mechanism of central nervous control of the ciliary muscles to produce reflexively the sharpest possible image of the object to which we happen to be attending, is clearly remarka-

Figure 11.2 A cross section through the human eye.

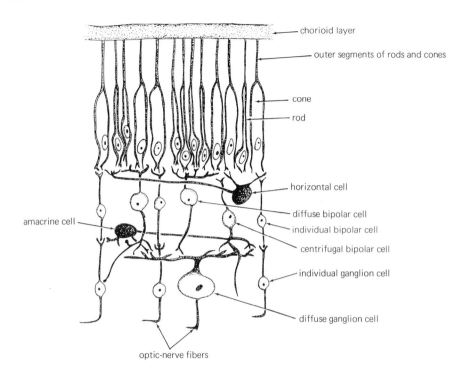

Figure 11.3 The connections of a few typical cells in the retina. Light must pass through the inner layers (at the bottom of the figure) before reaching the light-sensitive outer segments of the rods and cones. Neural activity travels in the opposite direction toward the optic-nerve fibers. (After Polyak, 1941; Everett, 1965.)

ble. Unfortunately, we know very little about it.

Between the cornea and the lens there is an aperture, the *pupil*, whose diameter is controlled by muscles that move an opaque membrane, the *iris*. The dilator muscles are innervated by the sympathetic nervous system; the sphincter muscles constrict the pupil and are innervated by the parasympathetic nervous system. The pupil dilates in the dark and constricts in bright light. When it is constricted, imperfections in the lens produce less distortion of the image, and the depth of focus (the range of distances at which objects are simultaneously in focus) is increased. The eye thus takes advantage of better light by improving its optics, and it can trade acuity for increased sensitivity in dim light. The pupil also constricts during sleep and other periods of increased parasympathetic activity.

The image of the outside environment is focused upon the retina, a screen of neural elements at the back of the eyeball. The retina extends approximately 100° around the visual axis of the eye. In most diurnal animals it is backed by a light-absorbing *chorioid layer*, which reduces the amount of reflected and scattered light, but in nocturnal animals any light penetrating the retina is reflected by a layer known as the *tapetum* so that nearly twice as much light passes through each receptor. A considerable increase in sensitivity is thus obtained but at the expense of "fogging" and loss of contrast in bright light.

The retina consists of three main neural layers (Figure 11.3), which are almost transparent. The receptors (thin rod- or cone-shaped structures) form the outer layer (lying next to the chorioid layer, with their light-sensitive outer segments pointing away from the lens). The next layer consists of *bipolar cells*, whose dendrites make contact with the receptor cells and whose axons synapse with the ganglion cells of the inner layer. The axons of the ganglion cells pass over the inner surface of the retina to converge at the *optic disk* (the blind spot), where they penetrate the other layers and emerge from the back of the eyeball as the optic nerve.

In addition to these three basic layers, there are two sets of cells with lateral connections. The first consists of *horizontal cells*, which lie just inside the receptor layer and link the dendrites of the bipolar cells over a considerable distance. The second set is made up of *amacrine cells*, which extend laterally in a layer between the ganglion cells and the bipolar cells. There are also *centrifugal bipolar cells*, which connect ganglion cells and possibly efferent optic-nerve fibers to the receptor layer.

The part of the retina that lies about the visual axis is called the *macula*, and its middle few degrees are very thin. The axons of the ganglion cells skirt the region to form a depression called the *foveal pit*, or *fovea*. There the receptors are almost all slender cones, about 1.5 μ in diameter; there are very few rods. The density of cones falls off rapidly with distance from the fovea, and the density of rods increases, reaching a maximum about 20° away and then declining steadily to the edge of the retina. There are about 125 million rods and about 6.5 million cones in the human retina.

In the foveal region there are almost as many ganglion cells as there are receptors, but there are only about 1 million ganglion cells altogether in each retina, which means that in the periphery there must be more than 100 receptors per ganglion cell. Even allowing for the fact that peripheral vision is poor, there must be a considerable amount of data compression in the retinal layers before the signals are passed on to the brain. (Strictly speaking, the retina is part of the brain that has strayed out of the skull, and the optic nerve is really a tract of the central nervous system.)

The firing of ganglion cells is influenced by brain activity via centrifugal fibers in the optic nerve. Granit (1955b) found that stimulation of the mesencephalic reticular formation produced both facilitation and inhibition of retinal cells, and Spinelli, Pribram, and Weingarten (1965) recorded efferent impulses in the optic nerve in response to auditory and tactual stimuli. Spinelli and Weingarten (1966) and Weingarten and Spinelli (1966) later measured efferent activity in single optic-nerve fibers to nonvisual stimuli and changes in the responses of single afferent fibers to light stimuli during nonvisual sensory stimulation.

VISUAL RECEPTORS

There are two main types of visual receptor in the vertebrate eye: rods and cones (Figure 11.4). The outer segments of both are similar in appearance and contain stacks of light-

Figure 11.4 Rods and cones from the retina of a monkey, with electron micrograph of part of the outer segment of a cone showing laminar structure. (After Dowling, 1965.)

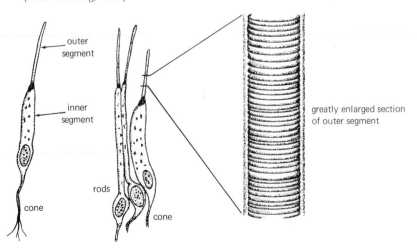

absorbing membranes reminiscent of the *lamellae* in *chloroplasts*, the sites of photosynthesis in plants. The inner segments of the rods are thin and cylindrical; those of the cones are fatter and bottleshaped, though they vary considerably and are almost as slender as rods in the densely packed foveal region. Under the electron microscope it is clear that the spacing between the light-absorbing disks in the outer segment of the rod is smaller than that between the disks of the cones (Dowling, 1965).

The rods contain a purple pigment called *rhodopsin*, which may be extracted so that its light absorption can be measured in vitro (outside the body). There are three absorption peaks, two in the ultraviolet part of the spectrum (radiation that does not reach the retina in the intact eye) and one at a wavelength of 500 nm (the part of the visible spectrum that looks green to us). When green is absorbed from white light, which is a mixture of all visible wavelengths, it leaves light that looks red and blue, accounting for the purple color of rhodopsin. The absorbed light provides the energy for a series of chemical reactions that convert the rhodopsin through a number of orange-colored intermediate substances into *retinene* (a yellow *carotenoid*) and a protein called *scotopsin*. With more light the retinene is further bleached to colorless vitamin A.

Rhodopsin is resynthesized continuously from scotopsin and vitamin A or retinene, but this process takes a long time; in bright light most of the opsin is in bleached form. In complete darkness the scotopsin is eventually all converted into rhodopsin.

Proteins similar to scotopsin combine with other carotenoids to produce light-sensitive substances that are found in cones and have absorption peaks for light of other wavelengths. For example, *iodopsin*, which is found in the cone receptors of chicken retinas, has an absorption peak at about 560 nm and is bleached by light to a different opsin. The opsins from cone pigments are usually called *photopsins*.

DUALITY OF THE HUMAN VISUAL SYSTEM

It is surprising, and indeed intriguing, to find the theme of duality running through the sensory systems of higher animals. The skin, as we have already seen, has a rapid, spatially localized system and a slower, more diffuse system; as we shall see later, the ear also has two sets of receptors with rather different properties. Many, though not all, vertebrate retinas also contain two distinct types of receptor, the rods and the cones, which have different functional properties and different distributions (and possibly different central connections, though the input is so compressed as it is funneled through the optic nerve that this point is difficult to determine).

It seems clear that cones are important for color vision. Nocturnal animals, which have poor color vision or none at all, have only rods in their retinas; animals with useful color vision have both rods and cones, and some have only cones. In man color sensitivity falls off outside the fovea, as cones become sparser (Boynton, Schafer & Neun, 1964). The rods, when adapted to the dark so that they contain maximum concentrations of rhodopsin, are considerably more sensitive to white light than are the cones; in dim light we depend upon rod vision. Under these conditions colors appear as different shades of gray. This type of vision is called *scotopic*, or dark vision. Daylight vision, in which the rods are ineffective because their rhodopsin is almost entirely bleached out, is called *photopic*.

When the threshold sensitivity of the dark-adapted eye is measured at different wavelengths, it is found to follow the scotopic curve shown in Figure 11.5, with peak sensitivity at a wavelength of 500 nm. Rhodopsin absorbs light most effectively at this wavelength, and, in fact, the threshold-sensitivity curve and the absorption curve are very similar when the transmission characteristics of the fluids in the eyeball are taken into account.

The sensitivity curve for the photopic process (cone vision) cannot be measured so easily because the transition to color vision is not distinct enough to serve as an indicator of when the cones begin to respond. One way of plotting the relative sensitivity of the cones at different wavelengths is to take the measurements in fairly bright light. The rods then have little effect upon central vision because their input to ganglion cells is inhibited by cone activity

(Gouras, 1965). The subject adjusts the brightness of light at each wavelength until it looks
as bright to him as does a standard patch of
white light. Another method is based on the
fact that there are few rods in the fovea; the
experimenter measures the threshold for very
small test spots viewed in central vision. At
threshold values, however, it is difficult for the
subject to achieve stable fixation, and if his gaze
wanders, rods are stimulated.

The cones adapt to darkness much more
quickly than do the rods because the enzymatic
recombination of vitamin A with the various
photopsins takes place more rapidly than does
the recombination of vitamin A with scotopsin.
(This statement is true of recombination in
vitro, as well as in the eye, and the fact has been
used as a chemical method of separating
scotopsin from iodopsin; see Wald, 1959). If
the course of dark adaptation is plotted by
exposing the eye to a bright light for a time
and then taking sample threshold measurements
after the subject has been in darkness for varying lengths of time, a curve like that in Figure
11.6 is obtained. After about five minutes the
cones have completely adapted to the dark and
are more sensitive than the still half-bleached
rods. Shortly thereafter, however, the rods
overtake the cones, and a new phase of adaptation starts, which continues 20–30 minutes
more. The exact shape of the recovery curve
depends upon the size and location of the test
patch of light (obviously, if it is a small patch
presented to foveal vision, the recovery of the
rods will have less effect) and upon the brightness and duration of the preadaptation light.
Measurements of the cone plateaus of the
dark-adaptation curve at various wavelengths
of test light provide another means of determining the spectral-sensitivity curve of cone
vision. An average spectral-sensitivity curve for
cone vision is shown along with the scotopic
curve in Figure 11.5; the peak sensitivity of
photopic vision falls at a longer wavelength
than does the peak for scotopic vision.

This difference between the two kinds of
vision generates relative changes in brightness
of different hues as the level of illumination
changes. Some fully dark-adapted cones are
more sensitive than rods at the long-wavelength

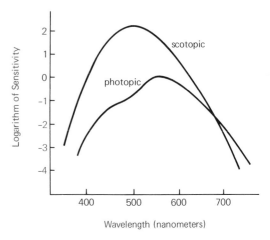

Wavelength (nanometers)

Figure 11.5 Scotopic- and photopic-sensitivity curves
of the human eye. (After Judd, 1951.)

(red) end of the spectrum; none are as sensitive
as rods in the middle (green region) of the
spectrum. Red flowers, appearing in daylight
as bright as the surrounding green foliage, turn
dark quickly in the dusk and may look quite
black while the greenery is still light gray. This
phenomenon is called the *Purkinje shift*; it is
less noticeable in foveal vision because of the
paucity of rods in that region. For the same
reason, after dark adaptation, very dim light is
seen best a few degrees away from central
vision. For the first 5–10 minutes after the
subject enters the dark, however, the fovea is
still the most sensitive region of the eye.

The functional differences between the two
systems are thus highly correlated with the
biochemical and morphological differences.
This relationship, when first proposed, was

Figure 11.6 A dark-adaptation curve for an average
human subject, showing rapid adaptation of cones,
followed by slower but more profound adaptation
of rods. (After Hecht, 1929.)

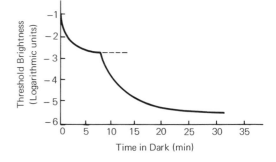

Time in Dark (min)

called the *duplicity*, or *duplexity*, *theory*, and the names are still sometimes applied to the rod-cone distinction, though the "theory" is no longer a theory in the sense that psychologists usually use the word.

FUNCTIONING OF VISUAL RECEPTORS

As we saw in the previous section, light falling on the outer segment of the receptor releases carotenoids and opsins. According to Wald (1959), retinene and vitamin A are bland, inert substances not very likely to have any effect upon neurons. He believed that the released opsin was the active substance that influenced the membrane potential of the receptor.

There is a steady electrical potential of about 50 mv across the chorioid membrane of the retina; the inner surface is positive. The voltage spreads to neighboring tissues, as if the eyeballs were small electric batteries; eye movements thus produce changes in current in these tissues. This effect has been used to detect and measure eye movements electrically. It can also produce misleading artifacts in EEG recordings taken from the front part of the head.

The retinal potential changes with illumination of the eye; the temporal course is as shown in the electroretinogram (ERG) in Figure 11.7. Part of the wave is almost certainly the summed generator potential of large numbers of receptors; other parts may reflect depolarization and hyperpolarization of different layers of cells. This wave occurs only in response to gross changes in illumination of a large part of the visual field in man.

Figure 11.7 Potential change across the retina of the eye during a brief flash of light (electroretinogram).

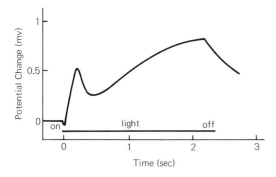

Little is known about the electrical events in the individual receptors of warm-blooded animals when light falls upon them, but Parry (1947) was able to record from the *occellar nerve* of the locust, which connects the simple eye (*occellus*) to the *circumesophageal ganglion* ("brain"). Rather surprisingly, he found that the membrane became hyperpolarized at the onset of light; that is, the inside of the nerve became more negative. When the light was turned off the potential overshot slightly into the hypopolarization range, but the cell still did not fire. Cells in the circumesophageal ganglion fired when the light went off, however. This "off" response is clearly related to the alerting effect of a shadow passing over the insect.

For many years this observation of the hyperpolarizing effect of a stimulus was considered unique, but recently Tomita (see MacNichol, 1966) succeeded in penetrating the visual receptor of a carp with a microelectrode and found that it too was hyperpolarized by light. It thus begins to appear possible that hyperpolarization is a common response in visual receptors. It is not universal, however: The eccentric cell (the excitable cell of the arthropod ommatidium) is depolarized by light and generates impulses that are propagated along the optic nerve (MacNichol, 1958).

As far as we know at present, the visual receptors of vertebrates do not generate action potentials. In fact, there is no evidence that any retinal cells except the ganglion cells do so. All the intrinsic neurons are very short (the whole retina is only a few hundred microns thick), so that *electrotonic* (electrical conduction through the cytoplasm) conduction of graded generator, or postsynaptic, potentials could possibly take the place of impulses and control the liberation of transmitter substances at the synaptic junctions.

NEURAL ACTIVITY IN THE RETINA

In the retinal layer adjacent to that in which individual receptor potentials were recorded from carp, Tomita recorded from cells that were also hyperpolarized by light but whose responses increased in amplitude as the area of the illuminating spot was increased. This finding indicates that the element summates the responses of numerous receptors. (The total area of the light spot would not be expected to alter the illumination, and thus the potential, of an individual receptor as long as that receptor was completely covered by the spot.) The summating elements are large and probably correspond to giant horizontal cells in the fish retina. Under the microscope it is clear that these cells synapse extensively with the receptors. Similar potentials were picked up from horizontal cells by MacNichol and Svaetichin (1958) and by Motokawa, Oikawa, and Tasaki (1957).

RETINAL MECHANISMS OF COLOR VISION

Both these groups of investigators found cells next to the receptor layer that behaved in a most interesting way as the wavelength of the stimulating light was changed (Figure 11.8). Some cells were hyperpolarized by the onset of light at all visible wavelengths, the spectral sensitivity characteristic being similar to that of the photopic sensitivity curve (Figure 11.8a). Others were hyperpolarized maximally by blue-green light, were relatively unaffected by yellow light, and were hypopolarized at longer wavelengths (Figure 11.8b). Still others (Figure 11.8c) were hypopolarized by violet light, hyperpolarized by green light, and hypopolarized again as the wavelength increased beyond about 600 nm.

These "color-sensitive" cells were at first thought to be *Müller's fibers* (a form of glial cell), but MacNichol (1966) has remarked that the histological evidence could just as readily point to their being bipolar cells. The main reason for rejecting the possibility initially was that these cells do not behave like typical neurons (they have no action potentials, for example), but once it was accepted that other retinal neurons behave equally atypically this objection lost much of its weight.

How the response to light was reversed as the wavelength changed still remains to be explained; in order to explore possible explanations, it is necessary to examine another of Tomita's experiments. Figure 11.9 shows the

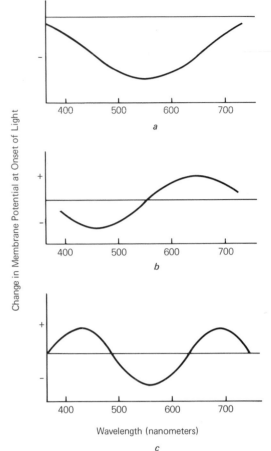

Figure 11.8 Changes in polarization of cell membranes in a fish retina at the onset of standard-intensity light at different wavelengths. (a) "Luminosity" detectors. (b) "Red-green" detectors. (c) "Red-green-red" detectors. Negative corresponds to membrane hyperpolarization. (Data from MacNichol & Svaetichin, 1958; and Motokawa, Oikawa & Tasaki, 1957.)

effect of different wavelengths of light on the membrane potentials of three cones in the retina of the carp. The first one had a maximum response to wavelengths in the red part of the spectrum (600 nm or more), the second had a peak response in the yellow region, and the third responded maximally to blue-green light.

These findings seem to provide a direct answer to the question of how we perceive color, which has vexed psychologists and physiologists since Newton first discovered the physical basis for color in the seventeenth century. Even before Tomita performed his experiments there

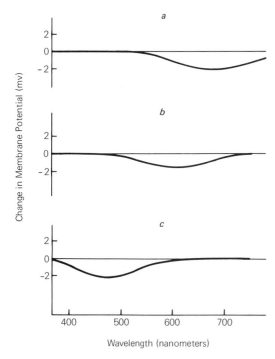

Figure 11.9 Responses of three different types of cone in the carp retina to the onset of light at different wavelengths. Negative potential corresponds to membrane hyperpolarization. (From data of Tomita cited by MacNichol, 1966.)

Figure 11.10 Absorption curves for the outer segments of three types of cones in the primate retina. (Data from Marks, Dobelle & MacNichol, 1964; Brown & Wald, 1964.)

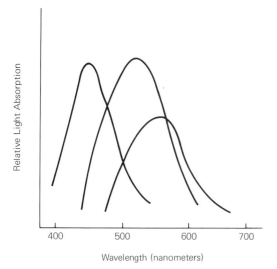

had been strong, though indirect, evidence of three different kinds of cones responding to different wavelengths of light; this evidence came from a series of measurements of light absorption in the outer segments of single cones in various vertebrate retinas, including those of man. Marks, Dobelle, and MacNichol (1964) and P. K. Brown and Wald (1964) had independently succeeded in constructing microspectrophotometers, which focus a beam of light on a spot only about 1 μ diameter and pass it through a single cone in a fragment of retina mounted on a slide. Light of varying wavelengths is passed through the cone, and the amount transmitted at each wavelength is compared with that from an identical beam passing through another part of the retina not occupied by receptors. The difference was assumed to be caused by the absorption of some light by the pigment of the cone.

Such experiments are very difficult to perform because the light must be kept extremely dim in order not to bleach the pigment excessively before the measurements are completed. All preliminary operations must take place in infrared light for the same reason. Once the tissue is cut off from its blood supply the resynthesis of retinal pigments ceases.

The results of the two experiments correspond fairly well with each other, though not too closely with Tomita's experiments on carp receptor potentials. In a population of cones it was found that the absorption peaks clustered in three groups, one in the region of 445–450 nm, another between 525 and 535 nm, and a third at 555 nm, according to Brown and Wald, or at 570 nm, according to Marks and his colleagues (Figure 11.10), corresponding to colors of violet, yellowish green, and either yellow or greenish yellow.

These colors are certainly not what we would consider subjectively to be "pure" colors. In fact, there are good reasons for thinking that there are four subjective "primaries"—blue, green, yellow, and red—and that they are arranged in mutually antagonistic pairs, blue-yellow and green-red. This view was first put forward by Hering (1878), who suggested that there were three types of receptor, each capable of producing two types of output, one during the breakdown of photochemicals and the other during their resynthesis. One receptor would thus signal either blue or yellow, another red or green, and the third black or white.

Clearly the biochemical and physiological bases of Hering's theory do not stand up in view of later findings, but its logic is sound, and Hurvich and Jameson (1957) have brought it up to date with much additional evidence. In order to quantify the relationship between the wavelength of a stimulus and the strength of the subjective experience of color that it elicits, they balanced one color, for example blue, against its opponent, yellow. A series of lights of different wavelengths were presented and a standard blue light mixed with each until the observer reported neither blue nor yellow in the color that he saw. The intensity of the yellow component of the test wavelength was then assumed to equal the amount of blue that had had to be added to cancel it.

When the wavelength of the test light passed the point at which no blue had to be mixed to cancel the yellow component (below the point in the spectrum at which pure green is seen), the process was reversed, and yellow was added until the blueness was canceled. A similar method was used to measure the intensities of the red and green components of light of different wavelengths. The resulting curves are shown in Figure 11.11. They bear a striking resemblance to the retinal potentials recorded by Svaetichin (Figure 11.8b).

It would appear that, at an early stage in their journey through the retina, the signals from the three different sorts of cone receptors are recoded by transmission cells to give the double *opponents* signal, with one color of each pair represented by hyperpolarization of the transmission cell and the other by hypopolarization.

It is relatively easy to determine the effects of light upon the activity of the retinal ganglion cells, for they generate impulses that are transmitted along the optic nerve. As we shall see, there are many types of ganglion cell, coded to deliver different aspects of the visual signal to the brain; those that seem related to color vision were first investigated by Granit (1943).

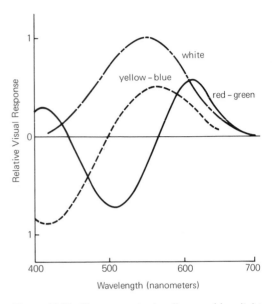

Figure 11.11 The amount of yellow or blue light (dotted line) required to neutralize the blue or yellow component of the sensation evoked by a test patch of spectral light, plotted against the wavelength of the test patch. The solid line is a plot of the amount of green or red light needed to neutralize the red or green component of the same test patch. The curves can be interpreted as showing the intensities of primary-color experiences evoked by spectral light at any wavelength. The achromatic brightness evoked by the light at different wavelengths is shown by the broken line. The curve indicates the amount of white light required to match the brightness of the spectral light, the subject ignoring color as far as possible. (After Hurvich & Jameson, 1957.)

He found that many ganglion cells responded over the whole visible spectrum with a peak sensitivity (in bright light) at about 560 nm; he called them *dominators*. He also found cells that responded to a narrower range of wavelengths, with peaks at different points (corresponding to various colors) for different cells. He called them *modulators*. Many dominators had subsidiary peaks corresponding to modulator peaks.

It is interesting that Granit used cats in his experiments because these animals are not noted for their ability to use color vision. A rather different picture has emerged from recent experiments on the spectral response of optic-nerve fibers. C. R. Michael (1966b) has clearly demonstrated opponent-process effects with blue and green light in optic-nerve fibers

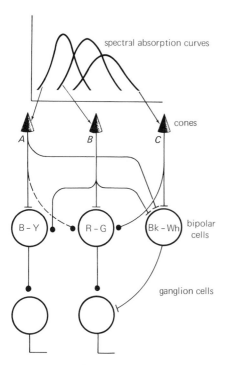

spectral absorption curves

cones

bipolar cells

ganglion cells

Figure 11.12 Hypothetical connections of a mechanism that will provide an opponent, four-primary output from a three-primary cone system. Flat endings represent hyperpolarizing connections; round endings represent hypopolarizing connections.

of the ground squirrel. He showed, for example, that some fibers are fired by a green or yellow light and inhibited by a blue light. Other fibers had the reverse characteristics.

A relatively simple model of how the conversion from the trichromatic response of the cones to the opponent-process signal in subsequent elements might occur is shown in Figure 11.12, adapted from P. M. Milner (1958). The cone with its peak in the short-wavelength region of the spectrum is labeled A, that with its peak in the green region B, and that with the peak in the yellow region C. Bipolar or other intermediate cells are shown for the three opponents processes described by Hering: blue-yellow (B-Y), green-red (G-R), and black-white (Bk-Wh). They are acted on by the cones in such a way that excitation of A hyperpolarizes the B-Y cell and hypopolarizes the R-G cell (which accounts for the red component of the sensation from very short-wave violet light). Excitation of B has the opposite effect upon

both intermediate cells: It hypopolarizes the B-Y cell and hyperpolarizes the R-G cell. Excitation of C hypopolarizes the R-G cell. All the cones have hyperpolarizing effects upon the B-W cell, which is the one that responds to the general level of illumination regardless of the color seen. The effect of light of various wavelengths would then be to produce membrane potentials in the three second-order cells similar to those found by Svaetichin and others.

It is clear that the bipolar cells help in some way to determine the firing pattern of the ganglion cells, but the actual mechanism is unknown, and it is probably far from simple. It is known, for example, that there is more total activity in the optic nerve when the eye is in darkness than when it is under steady illumination (Arduini & Pinneo, 1962), which strongly suggests that inhibition is an important feature of the visual input to ganglion cells. For the purpose of constructing the model it has merely been assumed that hyperpolarization and hypopolarization will have opposite effects upon any ganglion cell with which a bipolar cell synapses. Ganglion cells that synapse with the B-W bipolar cells will thus be equivalent to Granit's dominators, and those that also have connections with the B-Y and R-G bipolar cells will resemble the modulators, or, more exactly, the opponent ganglion cells of C. R. Michael.

RETINAL CODING OF INFORMATION ON FORM

Although the mechanism for transmission of color information along the optic nerve has been the subject of much research, the earliest work on the optic nerve was not concerned with color. Hartline (1938) recorded from single fibers in the optic nerve of the frog and discovered that some fibers responded to flashes of light with bursts of impulses, others stopped firing during flashes and produced bursts of impulses when the light went off, and still others produced bursts of impulses at both the on and the off. For obvious reasons he called them "on," "off," and "on-off" fibers. Granit (1947) placed microelectrodes on the surface of the retinas of frogs and other animals, and obtained the same effects; he attributed the "off" response to the release from inhibition of ganglion cells.

Kuffler (1953) investigated the ganglion-cell response to light in more detail. Instead of illuminating the whole retina, as earlier investigators had done, he used very small spots of light (about 100 μ in diameter), which could be moved to different parts of the retina in relation to the ganglion cell from which he was recording.

When he placed a single spot at the point where it produced a maximum effect (usually close to the electrode, unless the recording was from an axon), he found much the same effects that Hartline and Granit had found. The cell either fired vigorously when the light came on, or it was inhibited by the light and fired as it went off. If the spot was then moved 0.5 mm or more away from the center of the receptive field of the ganglion cell, the response was often the reverse: "on" cells become "off" cells and vice versa. When the light spot was in intermediate positions, the ganglion cell gave "on-off" responses (Figure 11.13 a, b, c).

With two light spots Kuffler was able to demonstrate the interaction between adjacent regions of the retina even more clearly. If he put one spot at the center of the field of an "on cell," eliciting a response as shown in Figure 11.13a and then put another spot of light on the retina about 0.5 mm away, the response of the cell was attenuated (Figure 11.13d). Receptors that influence ganglion cells by the most direct path, through bipolar cells, thus appear to have effects antagonistic to those that influence them through additional lateral connections.

This experiment was the first of a very fruitful series in which patterned stimuli were presented to the eye while the activity of single neurons of the visual system was observed, and it revealed a rather simple form of data processing, often called "lateral inhibition," within the retina. Which elements are responsible for the lateral spread is unknown, but it is most likely that they are the horizontal and the amacrine cells.

The consequences of lateral inhibition for perception have been studied in the eye of the

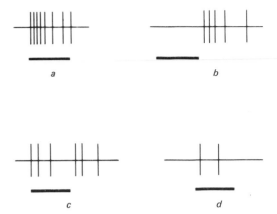

Figure 11.13 The firings of a retinal ganglion cell, resulting from a flash of light (indicated by the bar under each oscilloscope record): (a) a spot of light on the center of the field, (b) a spot of light near the periphery of the field (c) a spot of light in an intermediate position, and (d) two spots of light, one on the center and the other on the periphery of the field. (After Kuffler, 1953.)

horseshoe crab (*Limulus*), which has many large individual light-sensitive units (ommatidia), each with its own nerve fiber connecting it to the *cephalic ganglion* (brain) (Figure 11.14). As far as is known, the only interaction among the receptor elements occurs through the lateral branches of the optic-nerve fibers, which may be seen in the figure. The system is thus extremely simple and most suitable for investigating basic visual phenomena.

Hartline, Wagner, and Ratliffe (1956) demonstrated inhibitory interaction among ommatidia in *Limulus*, using an experimental arrangement similar to that of Kuffler. They

Figure 11.14 A section through part of the eye of *Limulus polyphemus*, showing ommatidia and optic-nerve fibers with interconnecting lateral branches. (After MacNichol, 1958.)

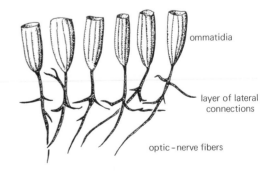

ommatidia

layer of lateral connections

optic-nerve fibers

shone a spot of light on one receptor and then showed that the frequency of impulses in the nerve fiber from that ommatidium was reduced by shining light on the surrounding receptors. Later Hartline and Ratliffe (1957) showed that the inhibitory effect was proportional to the firing rate of the neighboring nerve fibers,

Figure 11.15 (a) A sharp edge between light and dark regions. (b) Gradual transition between light and dark. Immediately below is a plot of brightness and below that a plot of the firing rate of an optic-nerve fiber of *Limulus polyphemus* as the corresponding ommatidium is moved from the dark to the light end of the "ramp." (Data from Ratliffe & Hartline, 1959.)

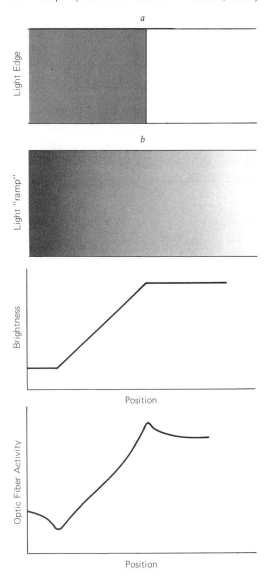

rather than to the intensity of the light on surrounding receptors. They did so by manipulating the inhibition on the neighboring elements so that their firing rates were reduced without any change in the light falling on them. When their firing rates were reduced in this manner, that of the receptor that they were inhibiting increased.

Ratliffe and Hartline (1959) went on to study the effects of lateral inhibition upon the response of the eye of *Limulus* to simple visual patterns like an edge between two areas of different brightness (Figure 11.15a) or a light "ramp," in which the intensity of the light varies linearly with distance from one edge (Figure 11.15b). It is not practicable to record from all the optic-nerve fibers, even in a simple eye like that of the horseshoe crab, but the total pattern can be reconstructed if the activity of only one fiber is sampled and the pattern moved so that the ommatidium innervated by it occupies each position on the pattern in turn. When the rest of the eye is masked, leaving only that ommatidium exposed, its response follows the intensity of the light closely, as one would expect, but if the rest of the eye is also exposed the responses are modified by lateral interactions.

When the test ommatidium is well inside the illuminated area of the first stimulus (Figure 11.15a), it is surrounded by other brightly illuminated receptors and is thus relatively strongly inhibited. When it is near the edge of the lighted area, its neighbors to the left are in the darker region and are firing at a lower rate, exposing the test element to less inhibition and allowing it to fire more rapidly. As soon as the edge of the illumination is moved past the test ommatidium, so that it receives light from the less bright side, its activity falls to a very low level because it is not only dimly illuminated, but it is also still being strongly inhibited by its neighbors to the right, which are still in the light. This source of inhibition declines as the edge is moved farther from the ommatidium and its immediate neighbors also become dimly illuminated.

From this experiment it is clear that cells near a visual edge fire more rapidly or more slowly than do those well inside the uniformly illuminated areas, producing an enhancement of contour that is probably useful in sharpening perception.

The ramp stimulus (Figure 11.15b), when seen by human subjects, generates an illusion originally described by Mach (*Mach bands*). A dark line is seen at the dark transition zone and a bright line at the lighter end of the stimulus figure. The activity of the *Limulus* ommatidium was found to be enhanced when it was just inside the bright plateau and depressed just inside the darker plateau, the principle being the same as that which caused the enhancement or firing near a contour. This effect, caused by lateral inhibition, can explain the illusion and was, in fact, suggested by Mach when he discovered the phenomenon. We do not know whether or not *Limulus* experiences the Mach-band illusion, but Ratliffe and Hartline's experiment (1959) suggests that it could.

Experiments on the electrical activity of the retina have revealed another feature of the visual mechanism: The major response to a change in illumination is quite brief. The "on" response of the frog's optic nerve consists of a burst lasting about 0.1 second, followed by a steady discharge at a much lower rate. In view of the constant slight movement of the eye (Ditchburn & Ginsborg, 1953), this transient response is probably at least as important as is the lateral inhibition mechanism just described for enhancing the retinal activity near the contours of a visual image. Each time the eye moves, receptors on the border are moved into a region of increased or decreased illumination and give either vigorous "on" or "off" responses.

Evidence for the importance of eye movements in maintaining a clear image of the environment comes from experiments with human subjects, in which an optical system holds the image steady on the retina. The simplest method for stabilizing an image on the retina is to "burn" an afterimage there with a bright flash, but the decay of this afterimage complicates the interpretation of the results. Riggs, Ratliffe, Cornsweet, and Cornsweet (1953)

attached a small mirror to the cornea and used it to reflect a vertical line onto a screen, the length of the path being adjusted so that as the eye moved the reflected image moved through the same angle and continued to fall upon the same part of the retina. They found that perception of the line soon faded. Using a somewhat different technique, in which the stimulating pattern was attached to a contact lens so that it moved with the eyeball, Ditchburn and Ginsborg (1952) and Ditchburn and Fender (1955) arrived at the same result. The manner in which the visual images fade is quite complex, and the related phenomena have proved useful in the study of perception (Pritchard, Heron & Hebb, 1960), but the main point, for our present purpose, is that the signal from the retina is drastically reduced if the receptors are prevented from frequently crossing the contours between light and dark.

Ditchburn, Fender, and Mayne (1959) went one stage further and added movements to the stabilized image, to determine which components of normal eye movement are instrumental in maintaining the image. There are three main types of movement: tremors, with a frequency of up to 150 per second, and amplitudes of 0.5 minute of arc (1 min arc = $\frac{1}{60}°$) or less; flicks, occurring every second or so, with amplitudes of up to 50-min arc; and slow drift, which takes place between flicks and has about the same amplitude. They found that tremors were not very successful in restoring the fading of stabilized images but that flicks were. We can therefore assume that the image on the retina must be moved to a different set of receptors every second or so, in order to provide the optimum signal to the rest of the visual system.

MORE COMPLEX INFORMATION PROCESSING IN THE RETINA

So far we have discussed very simple processing of information capable of being performed by a single-layered structure like the eye of *Limulus*; the multilayered vertebrate retina has been found capable of much more sophisticated computations. One of the first indications of just how complex the retinal output might be came from some experiments on the visual system of the frog by Maturana, Lettvin, McCulloch, and Pitts (1960). Many of their observations were based on fibers of the optic nerve, though some were made after further processing in the optic tectum.

One group of optic-nerve fibers responded to any sharp edge in a receptive field that ranged from 2-4° in diameter. These fibers were named *boundary detectors*. Their response seems to depend more upon the sharpness of the edge than upon the difference in brightness of the two sides. Another set of cells responds best to small dark spots moved across their receptive fields, which are 3-5° in extent. Edges or spots with diameters of more than a few degrees do not fire these fibers, which are usually referred to as *bug detectors*. Both types of fiber respond to targets as small as 3 min arc. A third group of optic-nerve fibers responds only to moving edges or to edges changing in brightness or contrast, over a field of 7-11°, and a fourth type responds to dimming of the light, corresponding to Hartline's "off" fibers.

In the optic tectum, which is the next stage of the amphibian visual system, there are *newness* cells, which adapt immediately to movement in a particular direction but still respond to movement through their fields in another direction. They take 20 seconds or so to recover from a single stimulus unless the light is momentarily extinguished. The fields of these neurons are very large. *Sameness* neurons have characteristics opposite to those of newness cells and have even larger fields, sometimes encompassing the whole visual field. These cells do not respond immediately to an object brought into the field, but once they "notice" it they respond to it as long as it stays in the field, with strong bursts taking place every time it starts to move or changes direction. The steady response can be erased by a short period of darkness or by leaving the object stationary for about two minutes.

Some of these cells behave even more peculiarly. If a target is brought into the field and moved back and forth, the cell responds to it with the usual bursts, especially when it changes direction. If a second target is then brought into the field and moved vigorously, the cell will begin to respond to its movements, and it is found that, when this second object is kept still, the cell is no longer responding to the changes of direction or movements of the first. After a time it will begin to respond to that target again, but when it does it will no longer respond to movements of the second. It is as if the cell can pay attention to only one target at a time. Maturana and his colleagues did not say whether or not the experimental preparation was capable of making eye movements, but presumably it was not. Many of these findings have been confirmed by Grüsser-Cornehls, Grüsser, and Bullock (1963).

More recently Maturana and Frenk (1963) have demonstrated specialized cells for detecting movement and horizontal edges in the retina of the pigeon. Movement-sensitive cells have also been demonstrated in the retina of the rabbit by Barlow and Hill (1963) and in the ground squirrel by C. R. Michael (1966a). Retinal ganglion cells that respond to movements of an object in a particular direction are common in the pigeon, the rabbit, and the ground squirrel, animals whose laterally placed eyes look at different parts of the environment, but they seem to be absent in the cat and higher animals with *binocular fields*. A simple model of the mechanism of sensitivity to directional movement is shown in Figure 11.16.

Spinelli (1966) has used a scanning technique to plot the visual fields of optic-nerve fibers in the cat. A white target of 0.2° was moved over a square field of 25° × 25° at a speed of one line in 3.5 seconds and 50 lines per scan. The output of the nerve fiber at each position of the target was stored in a computer, and, after 50 scans, all points where the total activity had exceeded a predetermined value were plotted by the computer, revealing fields like those shown in Figure 11.17. The fields of some of the fibers were circular, or annular, as found by Kuffler (1953), but many were much more complex, including some distinct edge and bar

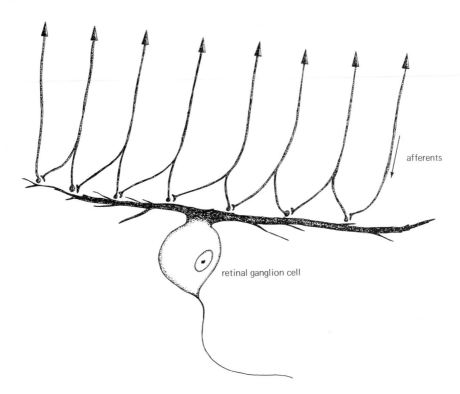

Figure 11.16 A possible mechanism for directional sensitivity of retinal ganglion cells. Each afferent to the ganglion cell has a branch that exerts presynaptic inhibition on the ending of its neighbor to the left. If a disturbance moves from left to right, each excitatory ending will have a chance to fire the ganglion cell before it is inhibited, but if the disturbance moves from right to left the inhibition is applied before the excitation arrives at each synapse, preventing any response from the ganglion cell.

detectors and others sensitive to sloping and curved lines in various orientations. Why these fields have never been detected by conventional plotting techniques is not clear, but they are highly reproducible by this method.

THE CENTRAL VISUAL SYSTEM

Pathways

The central pathways of the mammalian visual system are shown in Figure 11.18. The optic nerves enter the optic chiasm, which lies below the hypothalamus, and undergo some decussation. In lower animals the nerve from the right eye crosses completely to the left side and vice versa, but in animals with binocular vision some of the fibers do not cross. In primates only about half the optic nerve fibers, those from the nasal hemiretinas, cross. The fibers from each temporal hemiretina join those from the opposite nasal hemiretina and continue to the ipsilateral thalamus. This arrangement ensures that each half of the visual field will be projected to the contralateral side of the brain. Owing to the reversing effect of the lens, the right visual field is projected onto the nasal half of the retina of the right eye and the temporal half of the retina of the left eye. At the optic chiasm the axons from both these areas finish up on the left side of the brain. The axons of the ganglion cells then continue (now called "optic tracts," rather than "optic nerves") around the hypothalamus; in mammals most of them synapse in the lateral geniculate nuclei of the thalamus. The remaining fibers, of small diameter, continue to the mesencephalon and

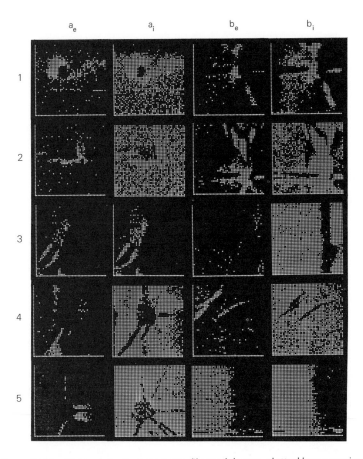

Figure 11.17 Fields of single optic-nerve fibers of the cat, plotted by a scanning and computer-averaging technique. The columns marked a_e and b_e show points on the field that each elicit more than three standard deviations above the mean activity of the fiber; the columns a_i and b_i show all points where the target elicits any impulses. The white areas in the figures with e subscripts thus represent excitatory fields; the dark areas with i subscripts represent inhibitory fields. (From Spinelli, 1966.)

terminate in the pretectal nuclei and the superior colliculi (or optic tectum). In lower vertebrates this area is the main terminus of the optic nerve, and it may be regarded in evolutionary terms as an older and more diffuse pathway corresponding to the extralemniscal spinotectal pathways of the somatosensory system.

Most of the neurons of the lateral geniculate nuclei project to the visual cortex (Brodmann's *area 17*) on the same side. In primates there are six layers in each lateral geniculate. The fibers from each eye go to alternate layers, so that there is not much interaction between them at that level. The main convergence between the afferents from corresponding fields in the two eyes occurs in the cortex.

The evidence from microelectrode studies in the lateral geniculate nuclei and visual cortex has so far indicated that the analysis of afferent information there is quite similar to that which takes place in the retina. It seems that, as binocular vision evolves and the fields of the two eyes overlap increasingly, much of the analysis that in more primitive animals is done in the retina is performed in the thalamus and cortex, where the input from equivalent points in both eyes converges (Baumgartner, Brown & Schulz, 1964).

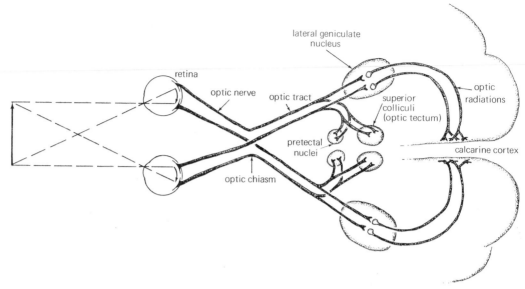

Figure 11.18 Pathways of the mammalian visual system.

Color Perception

Color cells with very similar opponent-color characteristics to those found by C. R. Michael in the retina of the ground squirrel (see "Retinal Mechanisms of Color Vision" earlier in this chapter), have been found by De Valois, Smith, Karoly, and Kitai (1958) and by Wiesel and Hubel (1966) in the lateral geniculate nuclei of the monkey. In the dorsal layers of the geniculate nuclei De Valois and his colleagues found cells that fired to the onset of one of a pair of opponent colors (for example, green) and to the turning off of the other (for example, red). De Valois, Jacobs, and Abramov (1964) reported that after the eye has been exposed to one wavelength, a small shift in wavelength in the direction of the opponent color will fire the geniculate cell corresponding to that produced by the opponent color. For example, the "red on, green off" cell will give an "off" response when the eye has been in red light and is then exposed to orange.

This observation is presumably related to the observed phenomenon of color contrast or complementary afterimages, exploited by Land (1959) in his demonstrations that it is possible to see full-color images even though the physical stimulus does not include all the wavelengths of the visible spectrum. We assume that the red and green systems are mutually inhibitory, so that adaptation to red will leave the green system in a hypersensitive or uninhibited state in which it can be fired by almost any color that contains less red than the adapting stimulus.

Wiesel and Hubel (1966) investigated both the spatial and color characteristics of lateral geniculate cells in the monkey and identified four different types of cells. Type I, the most common, had two concentric fields; the center of each gave an "on" or "off" response to one color, and the surround gave the opposite response to the opponent color (for example, red-on-center, green-off-surround). Type II had no such organization but gave "on" responses to one color and "off" responses to another color at all points in their receptive fields. Type III seemed to correspond to brightness cells; each had either an "on" or an "off" center and an opposite surround, but the characteristics did not change with wavelength. Type IV cells were found only in the two ventral layers of the nucleus. They gave short "on" responses at all wavelengths in the center of the field and a maintained suppression of activity as long as red light was present in the surround. During that time large spots of light of any wavelength between 400–580 nm had no effect on type IV cells. When red light was turned off there was no burst of activity; each cell merely resumed firing at its spontaneous rate. The only other cells found in the ventral two layers were of type III (insensitive to wavelength differences). Neither the efferent connections nor the functions of these layers is known at present.

Wiesel and Hubel presented a somewhat simplified explanation of the characteristics of the first three types of cell that took no account of the several levels of neural interaction between the geniculate cells and the retinal cones; they also called the cones with peak sensitivity in the yellow part of the spectrum "red" cones, which might mislead some readers. Basically, however, their explanation followed lines quite similar to the model in Figure 11.12.

Form Perception

The extraordinarily interesting results of Hubel and Wiesel's recordings of unit activity in the visual cortex of cats are widely known to students of perception. These investigators found that some neurons had fields elongated in one direction, not circular like those in the retina

and the lateral geniculate nuclei (Figure 11.19). These cells, which they called *simple cortical cells*, were assumed to be connected to a number of geniculate cells whose fields were arranged in a line. Most of the simple cortical cells had inner and outer fields that gave opposite types of response. That is, if the cell gave an "on" response to a spot of light in the center of the field, it would give an "off" response to the same stimulus displaced to the outer region of the field. Sometimes the field was asymmetrical, with an "on" region on one side and an "off" region on the other side.

Some other cortical neurons were not affected by small spots of light in the visual field but did respond to bars of light with roughly the dimensions of the simple fields (about $\frac{1}{8}$° wide and 1° long). The bar had also to be oriented in a particular direction to produce a response. The strange feature of these cells is that they respond to appropriately oriented shapes over quite a large part of the visual field; they seem to be line orientation detectors. Hubel and Wiesel thought that these cells, which they called *complex cells*, were fed by a number of simple cells, all of whose fields had the same orientation but were located in different regions of the cat's visual field. The

Figure 11.19 Arrangements of visual fields. (a, b) Fields of geniculate cells. (c, d, e, f) Various types of cortical-neuron field. Each type of cell has many orientations. (After Hubel & Wiesel, 1962.)

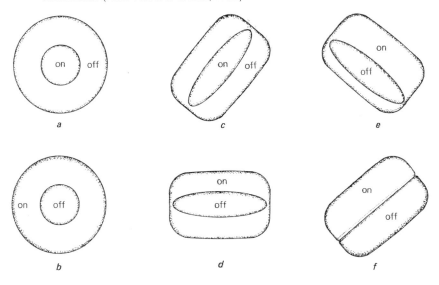

discovery that tilting the cat (and the stereo-taxic instrument) made a cortical cell fire to the stimulation of a different set of retinal cells means, however, that the connections are more complex than was thought, and involve other inputs. Cells responding to movement in only one direction were also found in the visual cortex, and this finding has been confirmed and investigated further by Baumgartner and his colleagues (1964).

Hubel and Wiesel, like Powell and Mount-castle (1959; see Chapter 10), found that the organization of the cortex is columnar. As a microelectrode was driven through the cortex, it encountered a number of active cells, and when penetration was perpendicular to the surface it was found that the visual fields of those cells were oriented in the same direction. Simple cells in the same column had overlap-ping fields. Adjacent columns of cells were usually responsive to lines of different orienta-tion.

Most of the cells explored in these experi-ments had fields in the middle 5° of the cat's visual field, corresponding to the *area centralis* of the retina. In accord with the accepted topo-graphical projection from retina to cortex, cells in the anterior parts of the visual cortex re-sponded to stimuli on the superior retina (low objects), and posterior cells responded to stim-uli on the inferior retina (high objects). The medial cortex responded to the far contralateral visual field, stimulation of which also fired cortical cells in the second visual area, lateral to the primary projection area.

Within the projection of the retinal area centralis four out of five cortical cells responded to light presented to either eye. Usually when a cell could be influenced by either eye its field had the same orientation in each, and there was summation if both eyes were stimulated simul-taneously. Some cells, in fact, *required* summa-tion from both eyes.

Somewhat similar binocular interactions were observed by Burns, Heron, and Grafstein (1960), who used diffuse illumination of the whole visual field. In general, they found sum-mation of the two eyes on visual cortical neu-rons, but in some neurons they found the op-posite effect. The cell responded less when both eyes were illuminated than when only one was illuminated.

In view of the findings of Maturana and his colleagues, Hubel and Wiesel, and others, the question arises whether the connections of cells that respond to specific properties of a stimulus (like movement or orientation) are innate or acquired through experience, as Hebb (1949) suggested. In order to answer this question, several experiments on very young kittens were designed to follow the development of respon-siveness of neurons in the visual cortex.

Hubel and Wiesel (1963) recorded from cells in the cortices of four kittens, all less than 20 days old. In one the eyes were still unopened, in another no pattern vision had been allowed, and in the other two one or both eyes had been open for a few days.

All the cells were very unresponsive, com-pared to those of adult cats; they were like those of adult cats under deep anesthesia. Stimuli had to be presented very infrequently to prevent fatigue, but, apart from that, the types of re-sponse were essentially the same as those of adults. Most cells responded maximally to lines with particular orientations and some to movement in particular directions.

Other kittens were reared for two to three months with one eye occluded (Wiesel & Hubel, 1963a, 1963b). When that eye was un-covered and the other eye covered, the young cats appeared quite blind. They showed no visual placing and walked off the edges of tables. Although a flash in the previously occluded eye produced an evoked potential in the visual cortex, it did so with a latency of 35–40 m sec (compared to 25–30 m sec for the normal eye), and the response lacked the negative component. Microelectrode recordings were taken from a total of 84 cells in these animals, and all but one were completely unaffected by any stimulus applied to the eye that had been occluded. Histological investigation revealed that the cells in the layers of the lateral genicu-late nuclei receiving connections from the affected eye were atrophied.

When both eyes had been occluded during rearing (Wiesel & Hubel, 1965), though the animals behaved as if blind, the effect on cortical-cell responses was not quite as severe. Only 27 per cent of the cells were driven by no stimulus; 32 per cent were abnormal in that they had no orientation, fatigued rapidly, and so on; and 41 per cent were normal. It was suggested that, when one eye is allowed normal vision and the other is not, the cortical cells tend to reorganize their connections so that the good eye takes over many of the synaptic connections of the unused eye.

These experiments suggest that some of the connections required to account for the properties of specific cortical cells are innate but that they are capable of modification by abnormal stimulation during the early stages of development. Some children (with "lazy eye") apparently have difficulty in coordinating the input from the two eyes and tend to use one eye only; Wiesel and Hubel's results suggest that a slight dominance of one eye may be magnified during the early months of life if steps are not taken to give both eyes a chance to maintain the initial connections to the cortex.

In an experiment to determine the effects of experience upon binocular interaction, Hubel and Wiesel (1965) reared two kittens with each eye occluded on alternate days, so that they were never able to use both eyes together. In these animals they found that fewer than 10 per cent of the cells in the visual cortex from which they made recordings could be driven by stimuli applied to either eye, compared with 80 per cent in the normally reared animal. Similar results were obtained from kittens raised with an artificial squint. In the least abnormal of these subjects fewer than half the cells responded to stimulation of either eye. It thus appears that in cats the convergence of afferents from corresponding retinal points onto single cortical neurons is not entirely brought about by early experience.

LESIONS OF THE VISUAL CORTEX

If, as seems indicated by the experiments of Hubel and Wiesel, an important part of the "epicritic" analysis of visual input is performed in the visual cortex in higher animals, we might expect that a large lesion in this area of the cortex would render the animal incapable of pattern vision—which appears to be the case. It has long been known that cortical lesions can produce "blindness" in animals (Munk, 1880), and it is also quite certain that pattern vision is lost after large lesions of the occipital lobe in man. In view of the connections from the retina to the tectal regions, however, it has been a matter of some interest to discover whether or not any degree of visual functioning remains after destruction of the cortical part of the visual system.

Lashley and Klüver worked on this problem at The University of Chicago in the early 1930s, Lashley with rats and Klüver with monkeys. Lashley (1930b, 1935) trained rats in a discrimination box in which they had to approach and pass through a lighted door for food. Errors were punished by shock. When the rats had learned this discrimination Lashley ablated the visual cortex as completely as possible and retested them. If any trace of visual cortex had been spared the rats retained the habit, but in those animals with complete retrograde degeneration of the lateral geniculate nuclei the habit was lost. The rats could be retrained, however, in about as many trials as initially. Increasing the size of the cortical lesion did not prevent relearning, but, when deeper lesions were made, so that the fibers passing through the lateral geniculates to the tectal regions were destroyed, the rats could not relearn the brightness discrimination.

Klüver (1936) did not train his monkeys to make brightness discriminations before the operations (which, incidentally, were performed by Lashley), but, by varying the size as well as the brightness of the lights to be discriminated, he was able to show that his subjects responded postoperatively to the light flux arriving at the eye and not to the absolute brightness. In other words, there was a breakdown of brightness constancy. This breakdown is what we would expect if pattern vision is completely eliminated. It is not possible to tell the difference between a small bright light and a large dim light if pattern vision is prevented by any means, including placing a diffusing screen over the eyes, because size information is thus lost.

This fact was used by Bauer and Cooper (1964) in an attempt to determine whether Lashley's rats had failed to transfer their brightness discrimination immediately after cortical lesions because the habit had to be relearned by some other structure (for example, the superior colliculus), as Lashley thought, or because of the disrupting effects of loss of pattern vision. Bauer and Cooper performed the initial training with light-diffusing cups sewn over the rats' eyes and found that there was only slight impairment of brightness discrimination after complete visual-cortical lesions, suggesting that the latter explanation is more likely.

The question of what the cortically blinded monkey can, or cannot, see is still open, and recent experiments by Weiskrantz (1963) have served to emphasize the fact. He showed that a monkey with extensive ablation of the visual cortex was capable of detecting whether a visual stimulus was moving or stationary and able to distinguish between two stimuli reflecting equal luminous flux but with different amounts of contour (as when one stimulus is a black stripe on a white card and the other a similar white card with the same area of black distributed in small pieces over the card). The monkey was thus capable of detecting the amount of edge in the visual field, even though it was not capable of analyzing the pattern.

In the cortically blinded monkey the detection of motion and of contour may each involve responding to gross changes in the amount of activity in the optic nerve. We know that either moving an object or moving the eye across a contour between dark and light will cause some retinal elements to give "on" or "off" responses, both of which augment the average level of firing in the afferent path. If the tectal region or some remaining part of the visual system were capable of detecting such changes and of supplying the information as a cue to the rest of the brain, the behavior of Weiskrantz's monkeys would be quite comprehensible. It would be interesting to know whether or not a monkey with striate cortical lesions would confuse a highly fragmented figure with a simple one moved at an appropriate rate.

According to P. M. Meyer (1963), several other visual functions survived complete ablation of the neocortex (including the visual cortex). She tested neodecorticate cats on the *visual cliff* (Gibson & Walk, 1960), in which the subject must descend from a narrow perch onto a glass plate, which on one side covers a deep hole, and found that they stepped down significantly more often on the shallow side than over the hole.

Animals held above a surface that they can see always stretch out their forelegs toward it, thereby demonstrating a reflex called "visual placing." This response might be expected to depend upon intact pattern vision, but, although P. M. Meyer, Horel, and Meyer (1963) were unable to obtain the behavior from neodecorticate cats under normal conditions, the visual-placing reflex was present in these animals when they were under the influence of the stimulant amphetamine.

These results indicate that some types of reflexive behavior, even those that require rudimentary pattern vision, are not entirely dependent upon the striate cortex. This area is presumably necessary for more complex pattern vision and especially for generating signals that allow complex visual stimuli to be associated with other aspects of behavior.

In humans, strangely enough, it is still not certain what effect complete loss of visual cortex has upon vision. The area lies deeply buried in the *calcarine fissure*, which is itself in an inaccessible part of the medial surface of the occipital lobe. It is quite possible that there has never been a case of pure loss of visual cortex from either accident or surgical operation. By the time a tumor, for example, has completely destroyed this region, it has almost inevitably done so much damage to other parts of the brain that the patient is too confused to be tested properly.

Partial lesion of the striate cortex or interruption of some of its afferent connections from the lateral geniculate is more common. Many such lesions have occurred as a result of penetrating head wounds in one war after another.

In such a case the patient is blind in part of his visual field. The blind patch is called a *scotoma*. If the scotoma is small and not too close to the area of central vision, the patient may be no more aware of it than we are of our monocular blind spots. He cannot see the outline of the defect; it must be plotted laboriously by means of an instrument known as a *perimeter*. The subject fixates the center of a hemisphere, and a small light or other object is placed at some known point on the surface. The subject has to report whether he sees it or not. The operation is repeated until an extensive map of the field, including the blind spot, has been developed. An alternative method, using a plane black screen (*tangent screen*), is often employed when only the central part of the field is of interest. The experimenter holds small white objects at various points around the fixation point and notes whether or not the subject sees them. This method is known as *campimetry*.

There are many unresolved problems involving the effects of partial lesions of the visual cortex in man, many of them discussed in a monograph by Teuber, Battersby, and Bender (1960). One problem is that, after complete destruction of the striate cortex of one hemisphere, many patients claim they can still see objects some three to four degrees inside the blind half-field around the point of central vision. Several hypotheses have been advanced, one of the more reasonable of which is that the phenomenon is caused by the mixing of fibers from both hemiretinas close to the midline. That is, the dividing line between the half of the retina whose fibers decussate and the other half is not a precise one; some of the fibers from one side of the line go one way, some the other.

Another long-standing problem about *hemianopic* patients (those with damage like loss of one hemisphere, which deprives them of vision in half the visual field) is the phenomenon of completion, discovered by Poppelreuter (1917) during an investigation of soldiers with head injuries. The patients were very vague about the nature of their impairment, most of them attributing it to weakness of one eye rather than to loss of vision in one field. When instructed to fixate the examiner's nose they might claim that they saw his whole face quite clearly. When a black card was then moved over his face until it covered the half in the patient's blind field, the patient still claimed to see the whole face until the card reached the fixation point or unless he moved his eye, at which time he was very surprised to find half the examiner's face obscured. Subsequently, in some patients, the card could be removed, and the patients would think it was still there (Gassel & Williams, 1963). Normal people think they see clearly over a wider angle than they actually do. This illusion is probably caused by an ability to store the impressions they obtain from frequent fixations and to use the total effect. The same mechanism seems to be available to patients; only when they are forced to maintain one fixation do they become aware of the limitation of their vision.

The phenomenon of completion is not confined to those with hemianopia. Lashley (1941), who suffered from migraine, which occasionally produced spreading scotomata, was talking to a friend one day and suddenly told him "I have beheaded you." The friend's head had disappeared in the scotomatous area, but the pattern of the wallpaper behind him then extended down to his necktie. The Gestalt psychologists thought that only regular shapes were completed, and by somewhat obscure reasoning regarded this "fact" as support for their notion of *Prägnanz*, or the innate dominance of certain features possessed by "good" figures. Empiricists, perhaps with better justification, have also regarded the phenomenon as support for the theory that there are neural representations (Hebb's "cell assemblies," for example) of familiar objects in the brain and that they will be activated by partial information as long as no conflicting information is received.

Apart from these problems, most investigators also have reported that the borders of scotomata are rarely well defined, but fluctuate depending upon the testing method, the attention of the patient, and so on (Pollack, Battersby & Bender, 1957; D. Williams & Gassel, 1962). Except near its borders, however, the scotoma is completely insensitive to light.

The case seems to be different in animals.

Cowey and Weiskrantz (1963) have constructed a device for performing perimetry with monkeys. It consists of a hemisphere with many small light bulbs arrayed on the inner surface. The monkey sits with its head at the center and looks at the lights through a peephole. The subjects were taught to press one of two levers whenever a buzzer sounded and the other when the buzzer was accompanied by a flash from any of the lights. At the instant of the flash the monkey's eye was photographed, so that the exact point of fixation could be calculated. When the monkeys reached criterion on this task, parts of the striate cortex were ablated and, after they had recovered from the immediate effects of the operation, the animals were retested in the same manner as before.

The results were somewhat surprising, in that they gave no absolute indication of any scotomata. In some parts of the visual field the monkeys missed more flashes than in others, but they never missed all the flashes. The animals seemed unaware of objects placed in those parts of the field, however. The effects of partial striate lesions in monkeys thus resembled those of complete ones in that detection of light changes was not entirely eliminated, even in the scotomatous areas, though pattern vision was abolished.

As a control for artifacts that might enable the monkey to detect the flash in some way without seeing it directly, Cowey (1967) has made small retinal lesions involving roughly the same visual angles as those of the cortical lesions. He has found that these lesions do produce complete insensitivity to flashes in the perimeter apparatus.

The evidence of substantial conservation of visual function in animals after destruction of the cortical projection area encourages speculation on the role of subcortical structures, especially the optic tectum, in vision. Most investigators have failed to detect any impairment of pattern vision after lesions of the superior colliculus alone (Rosvold, Mishkin & Szwarcbart, 1958; Sprague, Chambers & Stellar, 1961; R. Thompson, 1963), though Blake (1959) did report deficits from such lesions in cats. On the other hand, there have been many reports of visual impairment following lesions that penetrated farther into the core of the mesencephalon and posterior diencephalon. R. Thompson (1963) found that lesions in the posterior thalamus produced loss of simple visual-discrimination habits in rats. Adey (1962) described visual deficits in cats with lesions of the subthalamic nuclei, and Sprague and his colleagues (1961) found that cats with lesions in the subcollicular region behaved as if blind, though on further testing it turned out that the defect could better be described as almost complete inability to attend to visual stimuli. This finding is interesting because the region in question is continuous with the nucleus lateralis posterior of the thalamus, which projects to the parietal lobe and, as we shall see later, lesions in that part of the cortex also cause difficulties in visual attention.

It seems likely that the tectal region and the visual cortex work together in a rather complex way, at least in subhuman animals. Sprague (1966) has followed up his earlier findings and has reported that unilateral lesions of the superior colliculus produced temporary visual deficits, even though bilateral lesions did not. The cats in this experiment did not respond to moving stimuli or blink at the approach of stimuli in the contralateral field, and they circled towards the side on which the lesion had been made, presumably because that was the only way that they could see where they were going. The deficits were not confined to vision, however; the cats also had some contralateral tactual and auditory deficits, suggesting that an attentional system may have been involved.

Unilateral lesions of primary visual cortex also produced transient contralateral hemianopia, but in order to obtain a permanent deficit Sprague found it necessary to ablate all the posterior cortex down to the rhinal fissure. Such ablations included, of course, far more than the traditional visual cortex. On the other hand, a permanent hemianopia could readily be obtained when an area-17 (primary visual cortex) lesion was accompanied by a lesion in the ipsilateral superior colliculus. Other cortical lesions did not interact with the collicular lesions in this way.

These results seem to confirm the suspicion that each of these structures is capable of performing some of the functions of the other if one of them is damaged, but the situation is apparently still more complex. When cats that had been rendered completely hemianopic to clinical testing for a year by large unilateral lesions of the posterior cortex were given lesions of the *contralateral* superior colliculus, there was a dramatic recovery of vision in the previously hemianopic field. After the usual two or three weeks the deficit in the other visual field resulting from the collicular lesion also cleared up, leaving the animal with useful vision in both fields. The recovery from the first deficit was attributed to the removal of crossed inhibitory influences from the superior colliculus ipsilateral to the cortical lesion, so that it could perform some of the functions of the missing cortex.

Stimulation of the Visual Cortex

Doty and Rutledge (1959) have shown that cats can be conditioned to stimulation of the visual cortex as a CS, but, as the cat can be conditioned to stimulation in parts of the cortex other than the primary sensory areas, it is rather difficult to interpret this finding as indicating elicitation of sensory experience in the cat.

Mogenson (1962) determined the effect of early peripheral blinding upon the ease with which rats could be conditioned to electrical stimulation of the visual cortex. He found that it made no difference at what age the rats had been blinded, that all blinded rats were more difficult to condition than were those with intact eyes. Mogenson suggested that this finding might reflect degenerative changes conceivably occurring in the cortex after removal of the eyes. There is, however, no histological evidence of any such change.

The human visual cortex is very inaccessible, and consequently it has been stimulated less frequently than have areas on the lateral surface. Penfield and Rasmussen (1950) found that patients saw moving colored lights and areas of blackness in the contralateral field during stimulation of the visual cortex and that they were blinded to real visual stimuli in the affected parts of the field.

To summarize what is known about the striate cortex, then, it appears to be essential for form vision, but a small remnant can function quite effectively for that purpose, a phenomenon that has provided a long-standing puzzle for physiological theorists interested in vision. The visual cortex is probably not necessary for making discriminations based upon total luminous flux at the eye or upon movement or amount of contour of the stimulus, at least in some animals. All these stimuli affect the total amount of firing of the optic nerve. The effect of partial visual-cortical lesions is to produce blind spots, or scotomata, in humans, but this effect is apparently less pronounced in lower animals. At least some of the functions of the visual cortex can be carried on by structures in the tectal area.

LESIONS OF THE NONSTRIATE VISUAL CORTEX

Much of the work on the effects of cortical lesions has been inspired by the experiments reported by Lashley in his monograph *Brain Mechanisms and Intelligence* (1929). As was pointed out earlier, he thought that all parts of the cortex were equipotential for certain functions like maze learning and problem solving, and, as this view did not seem to be supported by evidence from human brain damage, many people immediately made attempts to demonstrate flaws in Lashley's reasoning and in his experiments.

It was pointed out that it would be difficult to devise a test worse than maze learning to detect specific effects of cortical lesions, or choose a less suitable animal than the rat. In the first place, many factors are involved in the successful performance of the maze; furthermore, the rat cortex is very undeveloped. Some rats in a group might use local visual cues to learn a maze; others might use distant visual cues or tactual, kinesthetic, or even auditory and olfactory cues. If each of these methods of solution involves a different part of the cortex, some rats would be impaired no matter where the cortical lesion was placed. If groups, rather than individuals, were compared, they might thus all show deficits after the lesions but for different reasons.

Even so, some subsequent work with rats in mazes did not entirely confirm Lashley's findings. C. J. Smith (1959), for example, showed that, although rats reared in the usual type of closed cage were equally impaired on maze running after lesions of the frontal and posterior cortex (excluding area 17), rats that had been reared in a "free environment," with much experience in a large maze-like living space, were more impaired after posterior than after frontal lesions. Smith's experiment did not fulfill the requirements of double dissociation (see Chapter 10), and it is possible that in his rats the posterior cortex was more important than was the frontal cortex for all aspects of behavior, but this possibility is not likely.

Visual Deficits in Monkeys

Earlier Lashley and some of his associates (including K. H. Pribram and Chow) had turned to the monkey as an experimental subject. Not only is the monkey's brain more like that of man, but it is also easier to teach monkeys more specific tasks like visual discriminations, tactual discriminations, delayed responses, and so on. One puzzling finding that created particular difficulty for believers in localization of function was that ablation of the *prestriate* cortex (Brodmann's *areas 18* and *19*), which neuroanatomical studies had shown contained the main terminations of fibers leaving area 17, did not interfere with visual discrimination to any significant degree except immediately after operation. Chow (1952) claimed that the visual cortex could be completely isolated from the rest of the cortex by removal of the prestriate cortex without producing any permanent deficit in form discrimination in the monkey. This claim was all the more surprising because postmortem examination of human patients seemed to implicate the prestriate cortex in visual impairments. Almost always, however, subcortical damage accompanied the cortical damage in these cases.

Later evidence casts doubt on the completeness of the isolation of area 17 from the rest of the brain in Chow's experiments. In some places the striate cortex borders the limbic system (Cuénod, Casey & MacLean, 1965), and in those regions the former is most inaccessible to the surgeon. Nevertheless, considering that the ablated cortex receives most of the known efferents from the visual cortex, it ought to play a major role in vision. Chow's results were therefore not very reassuring for those who thought that neural connections determined function.

Klüver and Bucy (1938, 1939) performed a series of experiments, however, that cast a different light on the matter. Klüver was aware that patients with epileptic activity originating in the temporal lobes were prone to visual hallucinations during their attacks, and he was at that time interested in the effects of mescaline and other hallucinogenic drugs. He wished to test the hypothesis that the drugs acted on the temporal lobe; he therefore prepared some monkeys with bilateral temporal lobectomies.

The behavior of these animals, even without drugs, was so peculiar that Klüver abandoned the drug study for a time and studied the effects of the lesions in more detail. Many of the effects were upon emotional and motivational behavior and will be mentioned later; what is of present interest is that the monkeys seemed unable to recognize objects by sight and had to touch them and put them in their mouths to find out what they were. Klüver thought this defect might be analogous to *visual agnosia*, sometimes found in human patients with brain lesions. These patients can see in all parts of the visual field, but the things they see mean nothing to them. Possibly because of his Gestalt and antilocalization leanings, Klüver seemed reluctant to explore the brain for a more precise localization of the phenomenon, and this task fell to others.

Chow (1952) and Mishkin and Pribram (1954) reported that a visual defect could be obtained from lesions of the temporal neocortex (as opposed to the whole lobe, which also contains subcortical and paleocortical structures), and Mishkin (1954) narrowed the crucial area to a small region in the ventrolateral part of the temporal lobe. After such lesions, monkeys did not retain difficult two-dimensional pattern discriminations they had learned before the operations, and in some cases they could not relearn them. Easier visual discriminations could be relearned but only slowly.

These monkeys had none of the other components of the *Klüver and Bucy syndrome* (tameness, hypersexuality, oral behavior, and so on), nor was the visual deficit quite so striking as in Klüver and Bucy's animals. They rarely, if ever, had difficulty in recognizing objects, a much easier task for normal monkeys than is the recognition of two-dimensional painted designs. Even difficult form discriminations (for example, between a cross and a square) were retained after the operation in those monkeys that had been thoroughly overtrained on the discrimination before (Orbach & Fantz, 1958). Nevertheless, under normal conditions loss of visual discrimination after ablation of temporal neocortex was clearly demonstrable, and all efforts to detect similar deficits in the auditory, tactual, or other modalities after similar lesions have failed. It therefore seems that we have conclusive evidence of cortical localization of visual function.

This conclusion was made more certain by the even more decisive double-dissociation experiments already mentioned in Chapter 10. M. Wilson (1957), working with Mishkin in K. H. Pribram's laboratory, tested monkeys with either parietal-lobe lesions (including the somatosensory area) or inferotemporal lesions on discrimination tasks. Some of these tasks were tactual, performed in the dark (discrimination between an "L" and an inverted "L" made of match sticks glued to the lids of food wells or between two dowels of different lengths similarly mounted). Other tasks were visual (the same "L" discrimination in the light and a cross and a square painted on the lids of the food wells). The tasks were presented in different orders to different monkeys in balanced design, some both before and after the operation and others only afterward. As previously mentioned, the subjects with parietal-lobe lesions had no trouble with the visual tasks but

did badly on the tactual tasks, and the subjects with inferotemporal lesions had difficulty with the visual tasks only.

In addition to the deficits on difficult visual discriminations, lesions of the inferotemporal cortex in monkeys have been shown to impair the formation of visual learning sets, for either object or form discrimination. Tests of learning set were devised by Harlow (1949), as mentioned in Chapter 10. The subject is given a few trials (six to ten, usually) with a pair of stimuli, one positive and the other negative, in the usual discrimination situation. Then, whether or not the subject has learned the discrimination, the first pair of stimuli is withdrawn and another pair substituted during the next series of trials. This procedure is continued through hundreds of different pairs of stimuli; in general, the subject improves until it can learn a new problem in one trial (that is, after one informing trial to discover which is the positive stimulus the subject makes no further errors). Normal monkeys reach this stage after several hundred problems, but monkeys with bilateral ablations of the temporal neocortex do not improve from problem to problem, though they may solve the first few problems as quickly as do normal monkeys if the discriminations are easy.

This type of deficit was first reported by Riopelle, Alper, Strong, and Ades (1953), who used monkeys with large, but unspecified, bilateral temporal-lobe lesions. The results were confirmed by Chow (1954b) and by W. A. Wilson and Mishkin (1959). The latter experimenters used monkeys with inferotemporal lesions, monkeys with lesions of the lateral occipital lobe that damaged the projection area for about the middle nine degrees of the visual field, and a control group of normal monkeys. They presented a number of visual tests, including the discrimination of patterns painted onto plaques, discrimination of the sizes of disks, object-learning set, and a "patterned string" test. In the last test two chains were arranged as shown in Figure 11.20, one of them baited with a peanut. The monkey had to pull the baited chain to receive the reward.

The "inferotemporal" monkeys were most

impaired on the object-learning set and painted-pattern discrimination tests, and the "lateral-striate" monkeys were most impaired on the patterned-string tests and size discrimination. The "lateral-striate" group was also impaired on the painted-pattern discrimination but not as much as was the "inferotemporal" group; the latter group was also impaired on size discrimination but not as much as was the former group. The double dissociation of tests and lesions has thus shown that these two visual areas perform different functions.

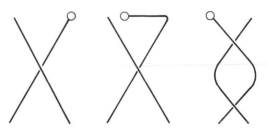

Figure 11.20 Three examples of "patterned string" tests for monkeys. The circle represents the peanut or other reward, visible to the monkey but accessible only by pulling the correct chain. (Used by W. A. Wilson & Mishkin, 1959.)

Visual Deficits after Cortical Lesions in Man

In man bilateral lesions of the temporal lobe are rare, but when they occur they do not seem to produce serious visual agnosia, like that which may arise from vascular accidents in the occipital lobe. Terzian and Dalle Ore (1955) performed a bilateral temporal lobectomy on a violent and dangerous homicidal psychopath; many of the features of Klüver and Bucy's syndrome resulted. The patient was subsequently unable to recognize individuals, including his parents, by sight, but he could tell the difference between men and women and had no difficulty in recognizing most objects.

Not surprisingly, unilateral temporal lobectomies produce much less impairment of visual proficiency than do bilateral lesions. In animals it is impossible, or at least very difficult, to detect any change after unilateral cortical lesions in association areas, but, owing to the functional asymmetry of the human brain (see Chapter 13) and possibly to the greater precision with which human abilities can be measured, such lesions in man can frequently be detected by behavioral tests.

Human subjects cannot be operated upon experimentally, however, and the unsuitability of neurological patients as subjects is clearly recognized. The locus and extent of the lesion are rarely known, and, even if the brain eventually comes to postmortem examination, further brain damage frequently takes place in the interval between psychological testing and death. Furthermore, it is usually impossible to test patients before and after the lesion is produced, and there is thus no base line against which to assess any impairment.

One type of patient is, however, rather less subject to these disqualifications: the epileptic patient who presents himself for surgery to relieve his symptoms. Epileptic fits are caused by uncontrolled discharge of brain cells, usually triggered by a region of malfunctioning tissue around a scar left by trauma or disease. If this scar is localized to a limited area of cortex, it can often be removed with beneficial results. If the scarring is subcortical, or diffuse as in some cases of epilepsy resulting from encephalitis, effective surgical treatment is usually not possible.

Although epileptic candidates for therapeutic surgery obviously cannot be regarded as completely normal, they have usually had normal childhoods (the symptoms typically do not begin until adolescence), they are of above-average intelligence (presumably a brighter-than-average selection elects to undergo surgical treatment), and they are usually young and cooperative. Furthermore, after the operation the nature and extent of their lesions are known as accurately as is possible in the absence of postmortem study.

One such patient, from whom part of the temporal lobe in the right hemisphere had been removed, was studied at the Montreal Neurological Institute by Hebb (1939); impairment on form-perception tests was found. Later B. Milner (1954, 1958) confirmed with a large group of patients that lesions of the right temporal lobe produce deficits on various visual tests. One of them is the "picture anomalies" test, originally designed by Hebb as a nonverbal test of social intelligence, in which the subject must point to a ridiculous feature (like a bird in a fish bowl) in each of a number of rough cartoons. Apparently patients with lesions of the right temporal lobe find many parts of the cartoons incomprehensible, for they point to objects that seem perfectly reasonable to normal subjects and to patients with other cortical lesions (left temporal lesions, for example). The few patients with right temporal lesions who achieve relatively normal scores on the test take much longer than do the normal patients; we therefore may assume that visual search is quite inefficient in these people.

Other visual tests on which patients with right temporal-lobe lesions show impairment are the picture-arrangement subtest of the Wechsler-Bellevue Intelligence Test (in which the subject must place sketches resembling parts of a comic strip in the correct order) and learning to recognize strange faces.

Doreen Kimura (1963) showed that patients with lesions of the right temporal lobe made poorer estimates of the numbers of dots on tachistoscopically presented cards, that they had more difficulty recognizing overlapping figures, and that they had poorer memories for nonsense forms than did patients with other cortical lesions. The visual-memory testing was done with a "recurring figures" test, in which the subjects were shown a sequence of cards with geometrical forms or nonsense squiggles on them. Some of the figures appeared only once, but others appeared repeatedly at intervals. The subject had to say, as each card appeared, whether or not he had seen it before.

Epileptogenic activity in the temporal lobes often engenders hallucinations, which are more frequently visual if the focus is in the right temporal lobe. Similarly, electrical stimulation of the brain during operation more often engenders visual phenomena from the right than from the left temporal lobe (Mullan & Penfield, 1959). We shall discuss the significance of these asymmetries in Chapter 13.

Connections to the Temporal Lobe

These results are interesting, but they do not explain why the temporal lobe, which has few if any direct connections from area 17, should be more important for vision than is the prestriate area (areas 18 and 19), richly supplied with connections from area 17. One possibility is that impulses are reflected back to the thalamus from the striate cortex and return from there to the inferior temporal region. The pulvinar is known to receive connections from the visual cortex, and it projects strongly to the temporal lobe.

Chow (1954a) tried to test this theory by making lesions in the pulvinars of monkeys but found no visual deficits. It must be noted, however, that the pulvinar was not completely destroyed in any of his subjects. In view of the astonishing degree of equipotentiality in parts of the visual system, the experiment did not therefore rule out the possibility that the pulvinar circuit is involved in vision.

A recent experiment by Mishkin (1966) strongly suggests that there is an important path through the striate cortex to the temporal lobe and that connections between the two prestriate areas through the corpus callosum allow information to flow to both temporal lobes from each side of the striate cortex. The implication of this experiment is that earlier experiments left enough remnants of the prestriate areas to maintain contact between area 17 and the temporal lobes. Again, this experiment did not exclude the possibility that the two regions are also connected through the thalamus.

Hypotheses Concerning the Role of the Temporal Lobe in Vision

It is usually assumed that the inferotemporal area constitutes a high-level analyzer of visual input and is perhaps the main locus of perceptual learning for this modality. If so, it is clearly not the only area capable of performing this function because total ablation impairs only difficult visual discriminations. It is interesting that well-established recognitions are less affected by the lesions than are recent acquisitions, suggesting that the area is most important in the earlier stages of visual learning. This finding is reminiscent of a suggestion about the frontal lobes made by Hebb (1949), and it receives some support, perhaps, from experiments reported by L. B. Flexner, Flexner, and Roberts (1967), who found that injections of puromycin, an inhibitor of protein synthesis, in the region of the temporal lobe eliminated recently learned habits but that the injections had to be delivered to the whole brain to interfere with habits of longer standing (see Chapter 21).

K. H. Pribram (1958) has put forth a completely different theory about the function of association cortex (or, as he prefers to call it, "intrinsic cortex"). He does not believe that afferent signals pass through these areas on their way to some efferent path or that engrams (neural representations of learned events) reside there. He believes that the paucity of connections to them from the sensory areas and the resistance of most habits to lesions there cast doubt on the conventional view of their function mentioned above.

The alternative, according to Pribram, is that the association areas produce their effects through centrifugal connections to the sensory pathways or to subcortical structures in which learning changes take place. At one time, he proposed that the superior colliculus was the crucial nucleus for visual learning and that input from visual afferents and from the inferotemporal cortex converged there. The results of lesions in the superior colliculus have not supported this particular hypothesis, but Pribram has continued to hold the general principle valid.

In support of Pribram's hypothesis, Spinelli and Pribram (1966) have shown that continuous electrical stimulation of the inferotemporal region in monkeys causes an increase in the interval before the visual cortex can respond to a second stimulus after the presentation of a first. This finding has been interpreted as demonstrating that inferotemporal activity keeps a signal active in the sensory system for a longer time and forces subsequent signals into other paths. Continuous stimulation of the temporal lobe during visual-discrimination learning did not produce any deficit; in fact the monkeys learned more quickly, though not significantly so, under these conditions. This finding suggests at least that the visual system

functions well in spite of activity in the temporal lobe that should preclude the establishment of complex specific patterns of firing there.

A weakness of Pribram's hypothesis as it stands is that it fails to explain how the inferotemporal cortex might receive any information capable of determining the pattern of its corticofugal modulation. It does seem surprising, furthermore, that this cortical structure, consisting as it does of an enormous number of highly interconnected neurons, should merely regulate in a gross way the much less complex afferent pathway.

Perceptual Extinction

Occasionally, unilateral cortical lesions produce a phenomenon known as "perceptual extinction" (not to be confused with the extinction of a conditioned response). The effect may occur in either the visual or the tactual sphere and possibly in other modalities. If a stimulus is presented on either side of the midline, the patient notices it and is able to report its presence. If another, similar stimulus is simultaneously presented on the other side of the midline, however, the one in the field contralateral to the lesion is not detected. The phenomenon is most frequently found after lesions of the right parieto-occipital lobe in man (Bender & Teuber, 1946), but it is also said to occur after frontal-lobe lesions, at least in lower animals. According to Teuber (1960), Loeb (1884) first described the phenomenon in dogs with either frontal- or occipital-lobe lesions.

More recently Kennard (1939) described a form of unilateral blindness following unilateral frontal-lobe lesions in monkeys. Bilateral lesions in the same area do not produce bilateral visual defects. Welch and Stuteville (1958) repeated this experiment and found that the effect was very transient and, furthermore, not confined to the visual modality. The monkey did not notice a peanut touching its mouth on the side opposite the lesion. Teuber interpreted this effect as a form of inattention similar to that presumed to be responsible for "extinction."

The frontal lesions in these experiments

included the frontal eye field, a region just anterior to the motor area in which stimulation generates movements of the head and eyes. There is strong projection from the striate cortex to the frontal eye fields, nevertheless the frontal cortex does not seem to be necessary for vision. Other effects of frontal-lobe lesions may make the evaluation of visual performance difficult, however, especially in animals.

Summary

Although it can hardly be claimed that we understand vision completely, we do now have a good idea of the parts of the brain that are most important for visual perception. The eye is an optical instrument for projecting an image of the environment onto a mosaic of light-sensitive receptors. The lens and iris are controlled by reflex connections to provide the sharpest image consistent with adequate brightness.

Above the layer of receptor cells are two layers of relay neurons, the bipolar cells and the layer of ganglion cells. There are also horizontal cells, with lateral connections between the dendrites of the bipolar cells, and amacrine cells occupying similar positions in relation to the ganglion cells. The axons of the ganglion cells form the optic nerve.

There are two main types of receptors, rods and cones. The rods are sparse in the center of the visual field, but they are more sensitive than are the cones when completely dark adapted. They are not effective in bright light because of excessive bleaching of the photo-pigment. The cones occupy the central part of the retinas of most diurnal vertebrates. They are less sensitive than rods, but they provide color vision when the light is bright enough. Individual cones have different spectral-sensitivity curves, but the average peak sensitivity of cones occurs at a longer wavelength than does that of the rods.

The effect of light upon the membrane potentials of visual receptors in many species is to produce hyperpolarization instead of the usual hypopolarization. Presumably this effect is accompanied by the release of a transmitter substance that modifies the membrane potential of bipolar and horizontal cells. Microelectrode recordings believed to come from these structures indicate that some of them are always hyperpolarized at the onset of light, whereas others are either hyperpolarized or hypo-polarized, depending upon the wavelength of the light. None has been observed to generate propagated impulses, presumably because the short distances involved do not warrant the use of this method of information transmission.

Cones have been isolated in the retinas of several animals with color vision and found to fall into three classes. Some absorb light maximally in the blue-violet region of the spectrum, others in the yellowish-green region, and a third group in the yellow or greenish-yellow region. Microelectrode recordings from fish retinas show three types of cones there with maximum sensitivity to light in the same regions of the spectrum as the maxima of absorbtion in the previous experiments.

Data from recordings taken in the bipolar- and ganglion-cell layers suggest that there are inhibitory interactions among the receptor outputs to convert the trichromatic color information into the form of a red-green, blue-yellow, and black-white opponents color code for transmission along the optic nerve.

Another characteristic of the responses of optic-nerve fibers to light is that the onset of light may produce a strong burst of firing, the burst may come when the light goes off, or there may be a burst on each occasion. If spots of light are used, the type of response may be determined by the location of the spot on the retina. This lability may be explained in terms of lateral inhibition, the "off" response being a rebound of the ganglion cell after a period of inhibition caused by the activity of neighboring pathways excited by the spot. Increased activity in the optic nerve during changes in light intensity results in vigorous firing of cells near a border between two levels of brightness as slight movements of the eye carry the corresponding receptors from the light to the dark zone and back again at frequent intervals. Stabilizing an image on the retina leads to rapid fading of the perception of the image.

Other experiments on the output of the retina suggest that the retina is capable of analyzing various properties of the visual stimulus. In frogs some optic-nerve fibers respond only to dark spots (bug detectors), others only to movements in various directions, and so on. Edge and movement cells have also been found in the optic nerves of birds, rabbits, ground squirrels, and other animals. Very complex receptive fields have been plotted for fibers of the cat's optic nerve through the use of a scanning technique.

Optic-nerve fibers decussate completely in animals with lateral eyes and no binocular fields. In animals with binocular vision the fibers from the temporal parts of the retinas (which "see" objects in the nasal fields) do not cross over but join those "seeing" the same regions from the nasal part of opposite retina. The fibers terminate in the lateral geniculate nuclei the pretectal nuclei, and the superior colliculi (tectum). Many of the last group of connections subserve reflexes for focusing and orienting the eyes, but some perceptual processes apparently also occur at that level. The tectal nuclei constitute the main perceptual system in animals below the mammal, and it is therefore not surprising that they still perform some of these functions in the mammal. The input to the lateral geniculate nuclei is relayed to the visual cortex, where it subserves complex perceptions of form and the like.

Microelectrode studies have revealed cells with differential color sensitivity in the lateral geniculate and cortex of the monkey, and cells with elongated fields oriented in many different directions have been found in the visual cortex

of cats and other animals. Cortical cells that fire only when suitably shaped stimuli are presented in the correct orientation have also been found. The organization appears to be innate, and the selectivity of these cells is no doubt a starting point for more complex, probably learned, analyses of visual input.

In behavioral studies it has been found that the visual cortex is necessary for form perception but not for the detection of total light falling on the eye. Monkeys have also been found able to detect movement and the amount of contour in a stimulus after extensive ablation of the visual cortex.

Partial lesions of the visual cortex in man produce blind spots, but the effect is not as severe in monkeys or presumably in other lower animals. Loss of one hemisphere in man results in loss of vision in the opposite field (hemianopia), but some central vision is spared, and patients tend to complete familiar objects into their "blind" field. This completion is probably only a more clear-cut form of our normal tendency to "see" things that are so peripheral as to be unrecognizable without knowledge derived from previous fixations. A case could be made for the idea that much normal perception is hallucinatory, the total perception being pieced together at any moment from a series of fixations, and it is not therefore too surprising that hallucinations are also relatively common under abnormal conditions of vision.

In man a right temporal lobectomy often results in mild but detectable deficits of visual learning and of comprehension of visually presented material like cartoons. Left temporal damage has little effect upon visual performance, except in the case of verbal material; no cases of bilateral temporal lesions confined to the neocortex have been reported.

It has been suggested that the temporal lobe has a general modulating influence on lower visual centers like the superior colliculus and that perception takes place only in the lower centers. A weakness of the theory is that it does not explain how the temporal lobes are supplied with the information they would need to provide any useful corticofugal input to lower perceptual mechanisms.

CHAPTER 12

THE VESTIBULAR AND AUDITORY SYSTEMS

The eighth cranial nerve (see Chapter 3) innervates receptors in a complex, fluid-filled structure called the *labyrinth*, which is embedded in the dense petrous (stony) part of the temporal bone (see Figure 12.10). The vestibular component of this structure provides information about the direction and intensity of forces acting upon it through gravity or accelerations of the head. The other part, the *cochlea*, is the organ of hearing.

THE VESTIBULAR SYSTEM

Simple invertebrates receive information about their orientations toward the gravitational field from small sacs, called *statocysts*, which are lined with mechanoreceptors and contain small solid particles called *otoliths*. The otoliths stimulate the receptors upon which they rest and thus indicate the downward direction. If the animal is changing speed or direction, the statocysts will not indicate the true direction of the gravitational pull, but they will nevertheless indicate the direction in which the animal needs support to avoid falling or rolling over, that is, the direction of the resultant of gravitational and other forces acting upon the animal.

The labyrinths of vertebrates have evolved from this simple indicator, and, along with other, more complex receptor apparatus, they still contain organs similar to statocysts. There are two, the *utricle* and the *saccule*, in each labyrinth. They are part of the membranous labyrinth, which lines the bony labyrinth and is separated from it by a cushion of fluid called the *perilymph*. The fluid inside the membrane is *endolymph*. The utricle and saccule each have a sensitive region called the *macula* (Figure 12.1), consisting of receptors (hair cells) whose hairs are embedded in a gelatinous mass loaded with calcium-carbonate crystals (otoliths) to make it heavy. The macula of the utricle is almost horizontal when the head is in its normal orientation; in the saccule it is vertical in the sagittal plane, with the hair cells pointing laterally away from the center of the head.

The receptor cells are sensitive to pull on their hairs; in normal orientation of the head little activity is generated in the utricular macula, but there is a steady flow of impulses along the nerve from the saccule. Some receptors fire for long periods if tension is maintained on the hairs; others apparently adapt after about half a minute (G. M. Jones, 1966). As the orientation of the head changes, different firing patterns are set up in the nerves from the four maculae (two in each labyrinth). These patterns can presumably be interpreted centrally as indicating the orientation of the head in space, but in higher vertebrates this information is largely redundant. We can tell which way up we are through vision and the tension in muscles and joints, especially those of the neck. People with congenital absence of the labyrinths have little difficulty in maintaining their balance or adequate postures, and, according to Walsh (1957), citing Beck (1912), deaf-mutes with nonfunctioning labyrinths can even swim and dive blindfolded with no trouble, though this claim was denied by Gernandt (1959), who stated that without visual cues they were liable to become disoriented under water. Presumably the otolithic organs are much more important for fish and birds, who have no other means of orienting themselves in space when visibility is poor and they are not resting on a surface.

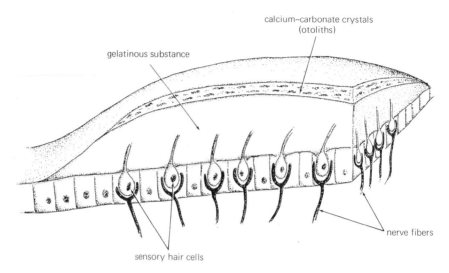

calcium–carbonate crystals
(otoliths)

gelatinous substance

nerve fibers

sensory hair cells

Figure 12.1   Section through the macula of either a utricle or a saccule, showing sensory hair cells embedded in a gelatinous substance containing otoliths. (After Geldard, 1953.)

The main function of the labyrinth in higher animals is to assist vision. All optical equipment needs a stable platform from which to function effectively, and the eye is no exception. A movie camera attached firmly to the head of a walking or running man would take very blurred pictures, but the eye works quite well under these conditions because head movements are automatically and accurately canceled out by compensatory movements of the eyes. You can easily confirm this point by looking at your hand held before your face and shaking your head vigorously up and down or from side to side. Then try shaking the hand at roughly the same rate and through the same visual angle and compare the clarity with which you see it under the two conditions. The head-movement sensors largely responsible for generating the compensatory signals are in the other vestibular structures, the *semicircular canals.*

There are three semicircular canals radiating from the utricular space in each labyrinth, as shown in Figure 12.2. One of the three is nearly horizontal when the head is oriented normally; the other two are vertical and at right angles to each other. They are not parallel to the principal axes of the head, however, but at an angle of about 45° to them, in the form of a

V pointing to the middle of the head, as shown diagramatically in Figure 12.3.

There is an enlargement, called the *ampulla,* at one end of each canal, just before it joins the utricular space. Each ampulla contains a *crista* (Figure 12.4), in which the receptor cells are located. The cristae follow the general design of all the receptors in the labyrinth; they consist of hair cells, with the hairs embedded

Figure 12.2   The right labyrinth partly cut open to show the membranous labyrinth inside the bony labyrinth. (After Geldard, 1953.)

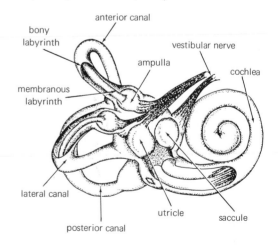

anterior canal

bony labyrinth

vestibular nerve

ampulla

cochlea

membranous labyrinth

lateral canal

utricle

posterior canal

saccule

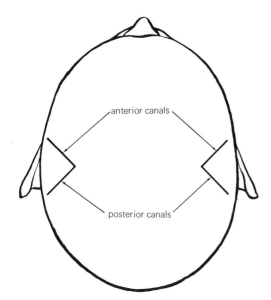

Figure 12.3 View from the top of the head, showing the planes in which the anterior and posterior canals of the labyrinths are located.

Figure 12.4 Section of a crista, showing sensory hair cells embedded in a gelatinous cupula.

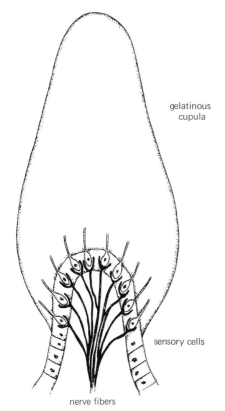

in a gelatinous substance. In this case the gelatinous substance is in the form of a *cupula*, or flap, which fits snugly across the ampulla like a valve or piston.

The slightest trace of movement of the fluid in the canal will push the cupula one way or the other in the ampulla, modifying the pull on the hair cells and thus changing the flow of impulses down the nerve. The endolymph does not move spontaneously, of course; in fact, it is usually the canal that moves (along with the head), and the fluid, because of its inertia, tends to lag behind. If the head is turned suddenly, the cupulas of the horizontal canals will thus be deflected, somewhat as a flag or a sheet of paper that is waved through stationary air. The analogy is not exact, however, because the air slips past a flag, whereas the endolymph cannot move past the cupula. Furthermore, the friction between the fluid and the walls of the narrow canal (only about 0.25 mm in diameter in the human) is so great and the mass of the fluid so small that in less than a tenth of a second the fluid attains the velocity of the canal wall, and no further displacement of the cupula is produced. If the head then stops rotating, as would normally happen within a fraction of a second, the reverse process occurs. Before the braking action of friction stops it the fluid moves back to where it started from relative to the canal. It can be shown both mathematically (Mayne, 1950) and experimentally (Löwenstein & Sand, 1940b) that for short intervals the displacement of the cupula is closely proportional to the angular velocity of the head in the plane of the canal. After a sudden angular acceleration the inertial flow of the fluid relative to the canal is great but of short duration; after a more gentle acceleration to the same velocity the flow is less rapid, but it continues longer, so that the same displacement is finally produced.

This relationship breaks down when motion is very slow because the cupula is elastic and a weak, though not insignificant, force tends to restore it to the central position. If the inertial force of the endolymph is very small, it cannot overcome this restoring force, and the cupula does not move. For the same reason, the output of the crista fails to provide an accurate measure of the angular velocity if the rotation continues for more than a few seconds. Once the endolymph is moving at the same speed as the canal wall, it is no longer acted upon by any inertial force, and the cupula will slowly return to its central position. Because the endolymph is viscous and the canal narrow, this return takes a long time, 20–30 seconds, so that it becomes a problem only during whirling dances, carousel rides, and so on. When prolonged rotation stops, the momentum of the endolymph carries it on briefly and causes a new displacement of the cupula in the opposite direction. It then takes another 20–30 seconds with the head stationary for the cupula to force the fluid back and return once more to its central position. During that time the crista is mendaciously indicating that the head is rotating in the direction opposite to its previous motion. The disparity between this information and that from the eyes and other senses produces postrotational vertigo.

False feelings of rotation can also be produced by irrigating the external auditory meatus (see Figure 12.10) with hot or cold water to produce temperature gradients in the petrous bone (Bárány, 1907). The liquid in the warmer segment of a vertical canal will be lighter than the liquid in the opposite segment and will therefore rise until it has displaced the cupula sufficiently to produce a counterbalancing force. According to Gernandt (1949), apart from this hydrostatic effect heating also increases the firing rates of some receptors, and cooling slows them down.

One of the features of this mechanism that most puzzled early investigators was how the cristae could indicate the direction in which the cupula was deflected and hence the direction of the head's rotation. It is now known from the experiments of Adrian (1943), Löwenstein and Sand (1940a, 1940b), and Gernandt (1949) that the afferent fibers are spontaneously active when the cupula is in the central position and that displacement of the cupula in one direction increases the firing, whereas displacement in the other direction decreases it.

The tonic (steady) flow of impulses along the vestibular part of the eighth cranial nerve during resting conditions seems to be important for maintaining the tone in postural muscles. As we have already learned (Chapter 6), destruction of the vestibular nuclei of the decerebrate animal reduces extensor rigidity.

Anatomy of the Vestibular System

Starting with the receptors, we find that both in the cristae of the semicircular canals and in the maculae of the utricle and saccule there are two distinct types of hair cells (Engström & Wersäll, 1958). Similar cells are also found in the cochlea. Type I cells are flask-shaped and are almost completely enclosed in a chalice-like nerve ending, an example from the guinea-pig is shown in Figure 12.5. Around the base of the chalice are a number of granulated nerve endings that are believed to be synapses of efferent neurons. Type II hair cells are cylindrical in shape and are innervated at their lower ends by a number of bud-like nerve endings. Some of these endings are also granulated and may be efferent synapses (Figure 12.5).

It is not known what purpose these efferent endings serve. They are usually assumed to be inhibitory, in which case they could cut off the signal from the vestibular receptors when it was

Figure 12.5 Type I and type II sensory hair cells in the vestibular receptor organ of the cat, guinea pig, or rat. (After Wersäll, 1960.)

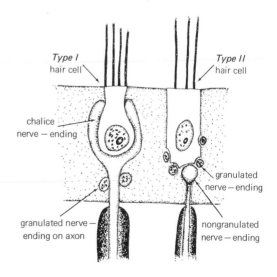

not required, during sleep perhaps. Alternatively, it is possible, though not likely, that the hair cells act as modulators for a stream of impulses that arrives through the efferent fibers and leaves again through the afferents. The efferent fibers appear to originate mainly in the nuclei that receive the afferent fibers, namely the vestibular nuclei and the *fastigial nuclei* of the cerebellum (Carpenter, 1960).

The cell bodies of the bipolar afferent nerves are in *Scarpa's ganglion*, close to the labyrinth, and the axons form the vestibular part of the eighth cranial nerve. This nerve enters the brainstem just below the pons; the main branch of the vestibular part then passes medial to the *restiform body* (one of the peduncles of the cerebellum) to end in the vestibular nuclei, which lie just below the posterior part of the fourth ventricle.

Not all the first order afferent fibers end in the vestibular nuclei, however; one branch joins the restiform body and ends in the cerebellum, and other branches go into the reticular formation to end either there or in the nucleus of the solitary tract (see Figure 9.2) and in the *dorsal motor nucleus of the vagus* (Carpenter, 1960). These latter connections may account, in part, for the dire effects of vestibular stimulation upon the digestive system, but other factors must also be involved, because in animals ablation of the *flocculonodular lobe* of the cerebellum (see Figure 10.3) eliminates motion sickness (Bard, Woolsey, Snider, Mountcastle & Bromiley, 1947).

There are four main pairs of vestibular nuclei: the *medial, lateral (Deiters'), superior (Bechterev's)*, and *inferior vestibular nuclei*. The input from the semicircular canals terminates in the superior and medial and in the lateral part of the inferior nuclei, whereas afferents from the utricle and saccule end mainly in the lateral and inferior nuclei, according to Lorente de Nó (1933a). Endings from the vestibular nerve are found only in the rostroventral parts of the lateral nucleus (Brodal, 1960).

Some efferents from the vestibular nuclei descend into the spinal cord; others ascend to higher levels of the brainstem. The deiterospinal tract connects the lateral nucleus to the ventral-horn cells of the cord with a somatotopic organization: that is, the rostroventral part of the nucleus projects to the forelimb motor pools and the caudodorsal part to the hind-limb pools. The medial nucleus contributes to the descending limb of the medial longitudinal fasciculus, which descends close to the ventral corticospinal tract and presumably also has motor functions. These motor connections are not surprising in view of the influence of the vestibular input upon posture and balance.

Brodal (1960) reported some return fibers from the caudal part of the spinal cord, ascending in the spinocerebellar tracts, which in turn terminate in the parts of the lateral vestibular nuclei where the efferents to the lumbar cord originate (that is, in the caudodorsal part). Other spinal afferents go to parts of the medial and inferior nuclei that do not receive primary vestibular-nerve afferents.

Another tract from the vestibular nuclei goes to the cerebellum, along with the twig of the vestibular nerve that goes there directly. They end in the most posterior part of the *vermis (uvula* and flocculonodular lobe) (see Figure 10.3) and around the fastigial nuclei. S. Andersson and Gernandt (1954) picked up potentials evoked by stimulation of the vestibular nerve in the anterior lobe of the cerebellum of cats, that is, in the region of somatosensory projection (see Figure 10.3).

Most of the vestibular connections to the cerebellum come from the inferior and medial nuclei. In return there is a somatotopic projection from the cerebellar cortex to the lateral vestibular nucleus. It corresponds to the pattern of efferents from the nucleus to the cord; that is, the part of the cerebellar cortex on which the forelimbs are projected projects to the rostral part of the lateral nucleus, and the part representing the hind limbs projects to the caudal part of the lateral nucleus. There are also connections to the vestibular nuclei from the fastigial nuclei of the cerebellum (Brodal, Pompeiano & Walberg, 1962).

The most important efferent pathway, to which all the vestibular nuclei contribute, is the ascending limb of the medial longitudinal fasciculus. Most of the ascending fibers end in the *oculomotor nuclei*; degeneration studies suggest that some of them continue beyond, though their ultimate destination is still in doubt. As stimulation of the vestibular nerve gives rise to short-latency evoked responses in the cortex, however, (S. Andersson & Gernandt, 1954; Mickle & Ades, 1952), it seems likely that the fibers synapse in the thalamus.

In the cat the cortical area in which maximum responses to vestibular stimulation are detected is near the second somatosensory area, located on the anterior bank of the suprasylvian gyrus. Andersson and Gernandt, who succeeded in separating the nerves to the various components of the vestibule, claim that the lateral ampulla projects to the suprasylvian and the utricle to the ectosylvian gyrus (Figure 12.6). The cortical projection is apparently not a very strong one compared with the auditory and somesthetic projections that overlap in the same area (see discussion of evoked potentials later in this chapter). The evoked potential can be picked up only under near-ideal conditions of anesthesia.

Oculomotor Control

At first sight, the relationships between the semicircular canals and the muscles of the eyes necessary to produce compensatory eye movements might seem fairly straightforward. Szentágothai (1943), on the basis of anatomical studies, concluded that there are short reflex paths from each of the cristae to the oculomotor nuclei such that the horizontal canals excite the ipsilateral *medial rectus* muscles and the contralateral *lateral rectus* muscles, the superior canals excite the ipsilateral *superior rectus* and the contralateral *inferior oblique*, and the posterior canals excite the ipsilateral *superior oblique* and the contralateral *inferior rectus*, as shown in Figure 12.7.

The functional importance of these connections was confirmed by a further study (Szentágothai, 1950) in which each canal was stimulated in turn by injecting a minute quantity (about 0.01 μl) of fluid into one side of the ampulla while recordings were taken from the

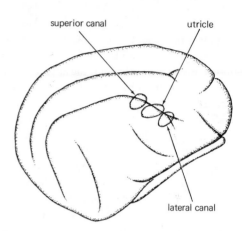

Figure 12.6 Regions in which evoked potentials are picked up in the cortex of cat after stimulation of branches of the contralateral vestibular nerve ending in the structures indicated. (After S. Andersson & Gernandt, 1954.)

individual eye muscles. Substantially identical connections can be inferred from other experiments in which the nerves to the different ampullae were stimulated electrically, one at a time, and the activity of eye muscles recorded (B. Cohen, Suzuki & Bender, 1965).

Taking into account that turning the head to the left, for example, fires receptors in the left horizontal canal and inhibits those in the right horizontal canal (Adrian, 1943; Gernandt, 1949), we can readily deduce that such a head movement causes contractions of the left medial rectus (which pulls the left eye toward the nose) and the right lateral rectus (which pulls the right eye toward the temple). Both eyes will thus turn to the right relative to the head, that is, will continue to look in the same direction as before.

Complicated though this process may sound, our analysis is nevertheless highly simplified. In the first place, if the eye muscles received the output of the cristae without modification, the eyes would immediately move to a *position* determined by the angular velocity of the head but not at a *rate* determined by the velocity. Furthermore, the eyes cannot rotate indefinitely at a constant velocity. What happens in fact is that, after turning through a small angle, they make a saccadic flick back in the same direction as the head movement and start the slow com-

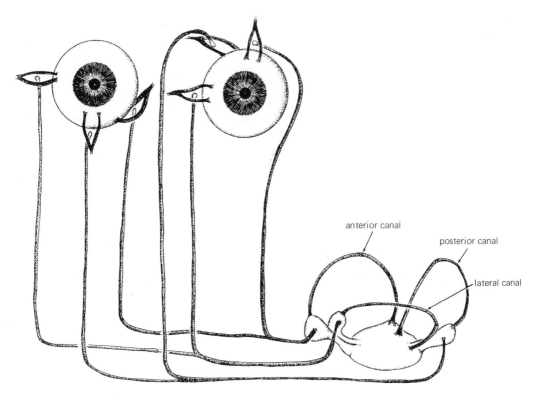

anterior canal

posterior canal

lateral canal

Figure 12.7 Connections between the ampullae of the three semicircular canals and the extrinsic muscles of the eyes. The semicircular canals on the other side of the head make corresponding ipsilateral and contralateral connections to the eye muscles. (After Szentágothai, 1950.)

pensatory sweep once again. This saw-toothed oscillation of the eyes is called *nystagmus*. The occurrence of nystagmus indicates that there is a difference between the signals from the two labyrinths produced either by rotation, by thermal or electrical stimulation, or by some pathological state like destruction of one labyrinth.

Lorente de Nó (1933b) pointed out the basic similarity between nystagmus and the scratch reflex or any of the other reflexes in which steady input is converted into phasic movements. He thought that recurrent collaterals and loops of short-axon neurons were the basis of all these reflexes and that part of the sensory input was conducted directly to the motor nuclei involved in producing the contraction phase and another part through a long inhibitory loop to produce intermittent relaxation of the muscles.

The mechanism postulated in Chapter 5 (see

Figure 5.17) to account for the scratch reflex would also fit the oculomotor reflex. In fact, the postulated decay of inhibition could perhaps convert the "velocity" signal from the semicircular canals into a steadily rising motor-nerve signal.

Lorente de Nó (1933b) inferred that the neurons responsible for the fast phase of nystagmus were located in the reticular formation because he could eliminate this phase in cats by lesions separating the vestibular nuclei from the reticular formation in acute experiments. Subsequently, however, Spiegel and Price (1939) made similar lesions and found that full nystagmus returned in a day or two. They concluded that the neurons responsible for the reflex lay entirely within the vestibular nuclei.

The problems of constructing a model of the vestibulo-ocular reflex become even more severe for head movements about horizontal axes, that is, nodding (pitching) and rolling, because these movements involve all four vertical canals. Pitching movements cause the eyes of animals like ourselves that have forward gaze to deviate up and down. In animals with lateral eyes, pitching movements cause the eyes to rotate about their optical axes, driven by the oblique muscles. Rolling causes the reverse movements; forward eyes rotate, and lateral eyes deviate up and down.

Trying to derive the connections required to bring about accurate compensation for such head movements is made even more difficult by interaction among the effects of the different eye muscles. When the eyes are deviated to the right by lateral and medial rectus muscles, for example, the superior and inferior rectus muscles pull obliquely on the eyeball and tend to rotate it about its optical axis besides moving it up and down.

Despite the extraordinary computational problem that results, however, the mechanism provides remarkably good compensation for small, rapid head movements. Continued rotation in the same direction causes the mechanism to break down, partly because, as we have seen, the sense organs begin to "slip" after a few seconds and partly because of adaptation of the central neural components. This effect is of little importance under the conditions that have prevailed during the more recent stages of our evolution, but it can have more serious consequences now that we have taken to the air and to space. As Jones (1966) has pointed out, when an aircraft rolls or spins, the pilot's eyes are stabilized at first, so that he sees his environment fairly clearly and also receives vestibular information about what goes on. If movement continues, however, this information fades; worse still, if the pilot succeeds in pulling out of a spin he experiences an aftereffect that tells him he is spinning in the opposite direction, which can be extremely confusing and has almost certainly proved fatally so on a number of occasions.

It seems possible, from the results of B. Cohen, Suzuki, and Bender (1965), that there is a mechanism that partly compensates for the decline in signals from the receptors during the first few seconds of rotation. If the ampullar

nerves are stimulated electrically at a constant rate, the velocity of eye movements during the slow phase of nystagmus increases steadily for about six seconds. Presumably this increase means that during the normal decay of ampullar nerve activity over time, there will be a tendency for the rate of eye movement to remain constant.

Apart from the short-term changes in vestibular function, there are medium and long-term changes that, though interesting, are not understood. Most people become adapted to the motions of a ship after a few days, for example, and acquired resistance to motion sickness often lasts for some time. After a rough sea voyage passengers experience strong hallucinations of motion when they first arrive on firm land, similar to the sensations they experienced on board. These aftereffects may last several hours. Possibly the rocking motion has been "learned," and the counteracting signals generated centrally continue for some time after the genuine movement ceases. It is difficult to imagine how such an erratic motion as that of a ship can be learned, however.

Another example of vestibular adaptation is that shown by ballet dancers and figure skaters. It has been established (McCabe, 1960) that there is permanent suppression of vestibular function in people who frequently spin themselves, even though they minimize the effect of rotation by making intermittent rather than continuous head movements. They experience no sensation of turning, and no nystagmus is produced, either during mild rotations or during irrigation of the external auditory meatus with warm or cold water.

In an experimental study Collins (1964) exposed normal subjects to many mild clockwise angular accelerations in the dark while they were performing tasks that demanded all their attention. Although they were not aware of the rotations, there was a decline in the nystagmus to clockwise rotation but not to counterclockwise rotation. After the session there was an increase in the threshold for detection of clockwise accelerations. The aftereffects were still present one month later, though the effect on nystagmus was more persistent than was that on the subjective estimates of rotation.

Adaptation of vestibular stimulation may become an important issue if it becomes desirable to rotate space vehicles to provide centrifugal force as a substitute for gravity. It is also conceivable that the vestibular system may provide a simple learning model for the study of fundamental processes in learning. Hydén and Pigón (1960) have already used this system in their search for the neurochemical basis of learning. They claim that there are changes in the composition of RNA in cells of the lateral vestibular nucleus as a result of training a rat to balance on a rope but no detectable changes from steady rotation of the animal. It seems unlikely, however, that the adaptations required for improved balance take place in the first sensory relay, and this finding must be viewed with caution.

THE AUDITORY SYSTEM

In conjunction with the development of external sound-collecting and sound-transmitting structures (*pinnae*), the cochlear part of the labyrinth has evolved great sensitivity to vibrations of the air or surrounding medium. Most animals can distinguish a variety of different sounds. A sustained cyclical pressure change within a frequency range that for man is about 20 Hz to 20 kHz constitutes a note. The pitch of such a note is determined by the frequency with which the cycle is repeated, high frequencies producing treble notes and squeaks, low frequencies bass notes and rumbles.

The wave form, or shape of the pressure wave plotted against time, determines the *timbre* or tonal quality of the sound. A sine wave (pressure a sinusoidal function of time) produces what we call a "pure" tone; other wave forms produce more "colored" notes and shrill, nasal, or buzzing sounds. The differences in the same note played by different instruments of an orchestra result from the different wave forms that they produce, as do the differences among vowel sounds.

It can be shown mathematically (Fourier's theorem) that any wave form can be analyzed into a series of *harmonically* related sine waves. A square wave, for example, consists of a fundamental sine wave; a sine wave of three times the fundamental frequency (the third harmonic) and of one-third the amplitude; a fifth harmonic of one-fifth the amplitude; a seventh harmonic of one-seventh the amplitude and so on to infinity. Figure 12.8 shows the almost sinusoidal wave form of the violin and the very complex wave form of the piano with harmonic analyses of both. The highest significant harmonic of the violin is the sixth, and that is very small; the piano has harmonics going up to the eighteenth.

In theory, if the response to sine wave input is known for any acoustical system, including the ear, its response to any other wave form can be found by analysing the wave and calculating the responses to each sinusoidal component separately. In most cases the higher, weaker harmonics can be neglected in the calculations because the ear is relatively insensitive above about 10 kHz (see Figure 12.9) and cannot detect them.

The shape of a wave synthesized from harmonics depends on when the peaks of the components occur in relation to one another (phase relationships). To form the square wave in the above example, all the component sine waves must start together, from zero, but it is part of the lore of sound engineers that a change in the phase relations of harmonics makes no difference to the sound of a note. The wave may look different when plotted but if it has the same harmonics in the same proportions it sounds the same. If this is so, the auditory system must analyze the complex wave into its harmonics and make use of only their relative amplitudes and not their phase (or timing) as cues for timbre. In view of the implications of this point for the theory of audition it would be useful to have an accurate determination of the effects of changing the phase relations of harmonics upon the timbre of a sound.

The ear of the average young person is sensitive to frequencies in the range of 20–20,000 Hz, the maximum sensitivity being to frequencies in the region of 2,000 Hz (2 kHz). The sensitivity curve is shown in Figure 12.9. To give an idea of the amplitudes of movement involved, at its most sensitive point the human ear can detect vibrations of the eardrum of 0.01 nm amplitude, less than 0.0001 of the wavelength of blue light. The amplitude of vibration of the basilar membrane, on which the auditory hair cells are located, may be thousands of times smaller still.

The human ear can handle a very wide range of intensities without becoming saturated or overloaded. In the middle frequency range a sound becomes painful only when its energy is about 10^{12} times that of threshold. Such astronomical ratios result in inconveniently large numbers unless a logarithmic scale is used and engineers have adopted a scale in which a ratio of ten to one (in energy) is called a *bel*. A ratio of 100 to 1 is therefore 2 bels, and the full range of hearing, from threshold to pain, is 12 bels. The bel is too large for most measurements, and the decibel (db) is the standard unit (1 bel = 10 db). The decibel scale is not used for sound measurements exclusively; any energy ratio can be expressed in decibel units.

As it is based on ratios, the decibel scale has no fixed zero; it merely indicates how many times more intense one sound is than another. It is often convenient to convert the scale into an absolute one by the use of some conventionally accepted arbitrary reference level of energy. The level now used for acoustical work is the energy delivered by a sound-pressure level (SPL) of 0.0002 dynes per square centimeter (or 0.0002 μ bar), which is close to the auditory threshold. This level then becomes the zero of a *phon* scale.

In order to deliver energy, a pressure wave must produce a movement (which would normally be proportional to the pressure). The energy level (which is determined by multiplying force times the displacement) will thus increase with the square of the pressure level; a tenfold increase in the SPL will generate a hundredfold increase in sound energy. As phons and decibels are based on energy ratios, not pressure ratios, they will be given by 20 times the logarithm of the ratio of sound-pressure levels: 2 μ bars = 80 phons (80 db above the arbitrary reference level), and a source of

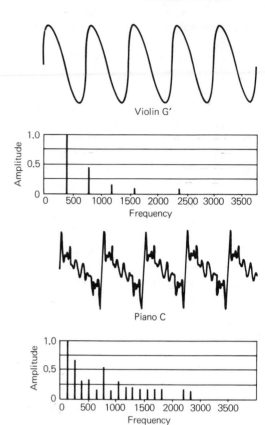

Figure 12.8 Wave forms of a violin playing the note G above middle C (384 Hz) and of a piano playing C below middle C (128 Hz). The histogram below each curve shows the amount of each harmonic relative to the fundamental note. The richer tone of the piano contains many more harmonics than does the violin tone. (After Fletcher, 1929.)

Figure 12.9 The sensitivity of the average human ear. The threshold sound level (phons) is plotted against frequency. (Data from Sivian & White, 1933.)

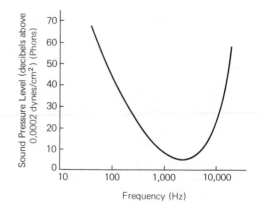

$0.00002\ \mu$ bar $= -20$ phons (20 db below the reference). Under optimal conditions a human subject can detect a change of about 1 db in the intensity of a steady note.

Apart from pitch, timbre, and intensity, we are also able to discriminate the direction of a source of sound. Binaural cues are normally necessary for this discrimination, though it can be made monaurally if head movement is permitted and even, it is claimed, without movement in some cases, thanks to multiple reflection of the sound from a familiar configuration like the folds of the external ear (pinna).

The physical properties of the sound that provide cues for localization are phase (or time) differences and intensity differences at the two ears. An intensity difference is the most straightforward and easily understood cue for direction. Obviously, if the sound originates on one side of the observer, the ear on his other side will be in the shadow of his head and will receive a weaker signal than will the one facing the source. In addition to being weaker, however, the sound will also arrive later, because of the time it takes to travel around the head. The delay may be nearly a millisecond if the sound source is on the axis passing through the two ears. It will be zero, of course, if the source is equidistant from the two ears. The delay, or phase difference, between the waves arriving at the two ears thus provides information about the angle between the interaural axis and the sound source. Additional information is required to determine the actual direction (whether in front, above, behind, or below). When the head is held still, this extra information must be provided by echoes from surrounding objects or by the shadowing effect of the head and pinnae. Animals that have mobile pinnae no doubt derive extra information from such adjustments.

Frequency, intensity, wave form, and binaural time differences are the only parameters of steady auditory stimuli to which the ear is sensitive, but most of our auditory information is gleaned from fluctuations in these parameters. For example, the human auditory system is sensitive to very subtle transient modifications in the harmonic content of vowel sounds, in-terpreting them as different consonents (see Chapter 13), and the complex transients produced by sound reflections tell us a great deal about our immediate surroundings. In animals like the bat and porpoise they form an essential part of the sensory equipment for piloting and catching prey. Investigations of responses of the auditory system to steady-state inputs must therefore be regarded as only a necessary preliminary to more comprehensive research, very little of which has been done so far.

Anatomy of the Auditory System

THE STRUCTURE OF THE EAR. The first necessity in our study of how the auditory system responds to the physical parameters outlined in the preceding pages is to examine the structure of the peripheral transducer (Figure 12.10). The ear is a complex organ consisting of an external sound collector or deflector, the pinna, leading to a tube called the *external auditory meatus*. At the end of this tube is a diaphragm called the eardrum, or *tympanic membrane*, which seals the rest of the ear from the outside air. (For pressure-equalizing purposes a narrow passage, the *Eustachian tube*, connects the middle ear to the back of the mouth. The tube is normally closed, except during swallowing and yawning. As the eardrum vibrates, it moves a chain of three very small bones or *ossicles*, the *malleus, incus,* and *stapes,* located in the middle ear. These bones transmit the motion to the *oval window* of the cochlea, or inner ear, which contains the neural transducing mechanism. Each of these parts will be described in turn.

In man, the pinna probably serves to shield the ear from extraneous noise from behind the head, and, as has been mentioned, it may play a role in providing directional cues. In some animals the pinnae may also be useful in concentrating the sound from a particular direction and funneling it into the external auditory meatus. It may also enable the animal to reduce the sound input when it is resting, as the eyelid blocks light.

The transmission mechanism of the middle ear serves two main functions. The first is to match the airborne pressure waves to the liquid

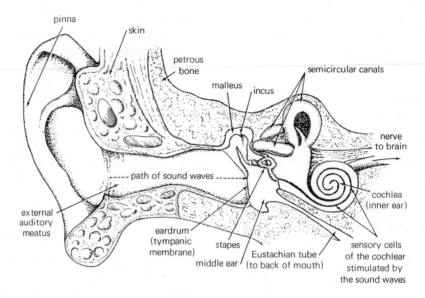

pinna

skin

petrous bone

malleus

incus

semicircular canals

nerve to brain

---- path of sound waves ----

external auditory meatus

eardrum (tympanic membrane)

stapes

middle ear

Eustachian tube (to back of mouth)

cochlea (inner ear)

sensory cells of the cochlear stimulated by the sound waves

Figure 12.10 The ear and the vestibular system. (After H. Davis, 1947.)

in the cochlea. If the waves were to impinge directly upon the window into the cochlea, most of the energy would be reflected back into the air because of the greater density of the liquid. (If a Ping-Pong ball hits a billiard ball, it bounces back, taking most of its energy with it, whereas if the colliding balls are of equal mass the moving one stops and the other acquires most of its energy.) The mismatch can be overcome by collecting the pressure exerted on a large surface by the air and concentrating it on a liquid surface of smaller area. This concentration occurs in the middle ear; the eardrum is about 15 times larger in area than the oval window. In addition, there is a slight leverage effect through the ossicle chain, so that a greater force is applied to the oval window by the stapes than is applied to the malleus by the eardrum.

The bones of the middle ear also help to regulate the sensitivity of the ear. Their relative positions, and thus the efficiency of sound transmission, can be varied by two small muscles, the *tensor tympani* and the *stapedius* (though according to Galambos the stapedius does most of the work; see discussion of Neff, 1961). Under the influence of a loud sound these muscles contract reflexively and dislocate the bones. The resulting deterioration of trans-

mission protects the delicate hair cells and other parts of the cochlea from damage. The effect is somewhat analogous to that of the iris in the eye.

The cochlea is a spiral tube divided lengthwise into three ducts or scalae, the *scala vestibuli* and the *scala tympani*, which contain perilymph and are therefore outside the membranous labyrinth proper, and the *scala media*, or cochlear duct, which contains endolymph and is the extension of the membranous labyrinth into the cochlea. The ducts are separated from one another by the *basilar membrane* and *Reissner's membrane* (Figure 12.11). The scala vestibuli and the scala tympani are not completely sealed off from each other; there is a small connecting hole through the apex of the basilar membrane, called the *helicotrema*, which links them.

The scala vestibuli opens up at the basal end of the cochlea into the vestibule of the labyrinth, where the oval window is located. A second window, the *round window*, opens into the basal turn of the scala tympani. This second opening through the bone is necessary because liquid is incompressible and the petrous bone is unyielding. When the oval window is moved by the stapes, the displaced liquid must be provided with somewhere to go. It should be

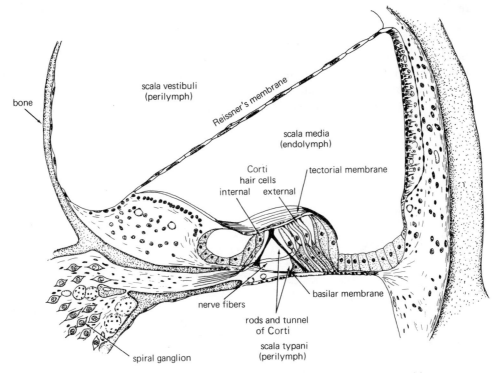

Figure 12.11 Cross-section of the second turn of the guinea-pig cochlea showing receptor structures on the basilar membrane. (After Davis and his associates, 1953.)

noted that Reissner's membrane and the basilar membrane lie across the route between the two windows, so that they are also displaced by any sudden motion of the fluid.

The hair cells of the auditory system lie in a structure called the *organ of Corti*, which rests on the basilar membrane in the scala media (Figure 12.11). It has a trapezoidal cross section, with a single row of internal hair cells forming one side and a triple row of external hair cells forming the opposite side. The inner hair cells resemble vestibular cells of type II, according to Engström (1960), whereas the outer cells are of a different type again and each may have up to 15 small, slightly granulated endings and 8–10 large, richly granulated nerve endings upon its surface. The hairs of these cells are, as usual, embedded in gelatinous tissue, in this case called the *tectorial membrane.* When a sound wave bulges the basilar membrane, the hair cells, which are standing upon it, are rocked from side to side, and their hairs,

embedded in the relatively stationary tectorial membrane, are pulled or bent. This pulling is believed to be the stimulus that gives rise to generator potentials in these cells. The motions at the threshold of hearing must be extraordinarily small. Even allowing for the fact that the tips of the hair cells may move many times as far as does the basilar membrane, the distances must be several orders of magnitude less than the diameter of the smallest atom.

One reason for the high sensitivity of these cells may be that the scala media is held at a positive potential of about 80 mv relative to the surrounding perilymph. As the inside of the hair cell is negative with respect to the perilymph, it is clear that the potential available for driving ions through any leaks in the membrane is about twice that available in other sensory cells (H. Davis, 1966).

THE AUDITORY PATHWAYS. The principal ascending pathways of the auditory system are shown in Figure 12.12. The hair cells of the organ of Corti are innervated by dendritic processes from the bipolar cells of the spiral ganglion, which runs up the middle of the cochlea. The axons of the bipolar cells constitute the afferent part of the acoustic branch of the eighth cranial nerve, a very short branch that enters the cochlear nuclei just caudal to the pons at the lateral extremity of the floor of the fourth ventricle. In man there are about 25,000 fibers in each auditory nerve.

The nerve divides as it enters the brainstem, one branch going to the *dorsal cochlear nucleus* and the other to the *ventral cochlear nucleus*.

Figure 12.12   Some of the more important auditory pathways.

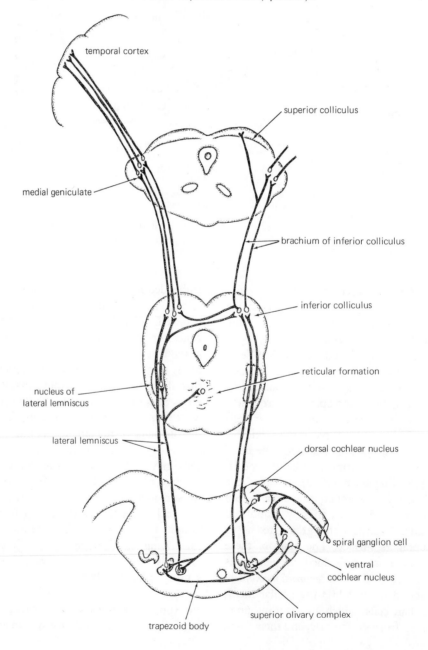

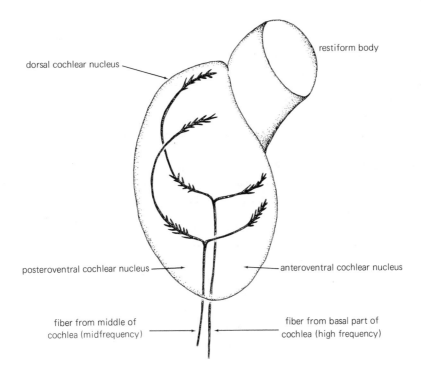

restiform body

dorsal cochlear nucleus

posteroventral cochlear nucleus

anteroventral cochlear nucleus

fiber from middle of
cochlea (midfrequency)

fiber from basal part of
cochlea (high frequency)

Figure 12.13 Tonotopic organization in three parts of the cochlear nucleus; high frequencies are represented in the more dorsal part and low frequencies in the more ventral part of each division. (After Rose, Galambos & Hughes, 1959.)

Rose, Galambos, and Hughes (1959) have explored these nuclei with microelectrodes and have reported that there are three separate regions, each with a tonotopical arrangement of neurons. The tuning point, or most sensitive frequency, is high for cells in the more dorsal part of each division and low for cells in the more ventral parts, as indicated in Figure 12.13.

Some axons of cells in the cochlear nuclei terminate in the surrounding reticular formation, but most of them pass to the *superior olivary complex*. This complex of cells can be divided into at least five separate nuclei, some of which are believed to subserve specialized functions. According to Tsuchitani and Boudreau (1966), the tonotopically organized pathway goes to the conspicuous S-shaped part of the complex on the same side. Low frequencies are represented by cells in the dorsolateral arm of the S and very high frequencies by cells in the ventromedial arm, with intermediate frequencies spread out in an orderly

sequence between. The *accessory nucleus* of the superior olivary complex receives afferents from both ears and has no tonotopic organization; most of the cells respond only to low-frequency sounds (Galambos, Schwartzkopf & Rupert, 1959). It is believed that this part of the complex is involved in processing binaural time-disparity cues for sound localization. About half the axons of the S-shaped nucleus cross over in the trapezoid body and ascend in the contralateral lateral lemniscus; the other half ascend in the ipsilateral lateral lemniscus (Stotler, 1953). Some fibers from the cochlear nucleus pass through the olivary complex and ascend mainly in the contralateral lateral lemniscus, where they synapse with cells in the *nuclei of the lateral lemniscus*.

A few fibers originating in the olivary complex return to each cochlea through the crossed and uncrossed *olivo-cochlear bundles of Rasmussen* (Rasmussen, 1946). About 500 fibers go to each ear, where they branch profusely and terminate on the hair cells and on the dendritic terminals of bipolar cells. Some olivary fibers also return to the cochlear nuclei, where they synapse extensively (Rasmussen, 1960).

Branches of those fibers that ascend in the lateral lemniscus go to the cerebellum, to eye-movement and pinna reflex centers, and to the reticular formation. The main body of fibers continues to the level of the inferior colliculus, however, where it partly decussates through the *inferior collicular commissure*. The fibers synapse with cells of both contralateral and ipsilateral inferior colliculi.

The tonotopical organization is preserved at the collicular level. According to Rose, Green-wood, Goldberg, and Hind (1963), there is an external nucleus, which does not have a very clear-cut tonotopic organization, and a central nucleus whose very clear tonotopic arrange-ment has low-frequency cells at the lateral extreme and high-frequency cells in the most medial part. A small percentage of cells in the inferior colliculus respond to all frequencies indiscriminately.

Some fibers of the lateral lemniscus do not terminate in the colliculus but continue with axons of the inferior-collicular neurons to the thalamus through the *brachium of the inferior colliculus*. The classical auditory-relay nucleus in the thalamus is the medial geniculate body, but, as has already been mentioned, responses to auditory stimuli can also be found in the posterior group of nuclei (see Chapter 10). Further evidence that auditory transmission is not confined to the medial geniculate is the finding that a cortical ablation large enough to produce a marked deficit in auditory-discrimi-nation learning results in retrograde degenera-tion not only in the medial geniculate but also in the anterior portion of the posterior group of thalamic nuclei and probably in the pulvinar as well (Rose & Woolsey, 1958). Although there is much crossing back and forth at various auditory commissures, the projection to the thalamus and cortex is stronger from the contralateral ear (Rosenzweig, 1961).

There is a strong presumption of tonotopical organization in at least some parts of the audi-tory thalamus, but it has not been confirmed by the sort of painstaking work that has been done on the lower nuclei. Galambos (1952) recorded the activity of medial-geniculate neu-rons in the cat to pure tones, but, although he found nothing to contradict the idea of tono-topic distribution, his data were too sparse to enable us to draw a map; furthermore, he used a somewhat restricted range of frequencies.

The projections from the auditory thalamus to the cortex are complex and have not yet been completely unraveled. The technique of retro-grade degeneration is not easy to use in ana-lyzing this system, and interpretation requires great skill and experience because most parts of the auditory cortex, when individually ab-lated, do not produce any marked change in the thalamus. If, however, lesions are large enough to include several areas, thalamic degeneration does occur. It is assumed that the axons of the thalamic neurons concerned branch and provide input to several cortical areas. If the termi-nation of only one branch is destroyed, the remaining branch (or branches) is able to sus-tain the neuron, which degenerates only if the projection areas of all its branches are ablated. Rose and Woolsey (1958) called the branching axons *sustaining projections*, as distinguished from *essential* projections, destruction of which always results in degeneration of the thalamic cell.

According to Rose and Woolsey, the only part of the auditory cortex that has essential projections is the first auditory area, A I, lo-cated in the *medial ectosylvian gyrus* of the cat (Figure 12.14). These essential projections originate in the anterior part of the medial geniculate, though A I appears to receive sustaining projections from much of the remainder of the auditory thalamus.

The method of evoked potentials is the most informative and most extensively used means of plotting the projections of the thalamus on the auditory cortex. It is more direct than are anatomical techniques and has the added ad-vantage that it will reveal any tonotopical or-ganization in response to suitable stimuli. As recording techniques have improved, a bewil-dering array of areas responding to sounds or electrical stimulation of the auditory nerve has

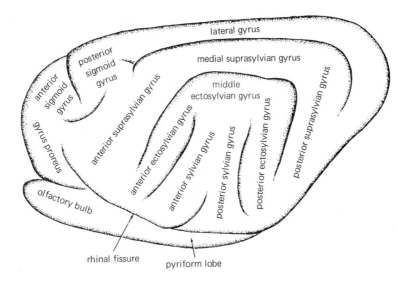

Figure 12.14   A lateral view of a cat cortex.

been discovered. Figure 12.15 is a recent map by Woolsey (1960, 1961), summarizing the data from a number of experiments on the cat. In this animal high frequencies are represented at the anterior end of A I and low frequencies at the posterior end. This representation was first shown by Woolsey and Walzl (1942), who recorded during electrical stimulation of different parts of the cochlea. Tunturi (1944) and later Hind (1953) confirmed this arrangement, using tone pips as stimuli.

Evoked potentials are also found just ventral to A I in the area known as the "second auditory area," A II. One of the features distinguishing A II from A I is the reversed direction of tonotopic representation. In A II the low-frequency end of the spectrum is represented in the anterior and the high-frequency end in the posterior part. A II appears to receive sustaining projections from the posterior part of the medial geniculate body. The farther a cortical lesion is extended down from A I, the farther posterior the thalamic degeneration extends.

Another large auditory area lies posterior to the two just mentioned, in the *posterior ecto-sylvian gyrus*. It is usually called "Ep." The tonotopic representation in Ep is easy to remember because the high notes are represented at the top and the low notes at the bottom. According to Rose and Woolsey (1958), this area receives sustaining projections from much the same region of the thalamus as does A I, with the more ventral regions receiving connections from the more posterior parts of the medial geniculate.

Tunturi (1945) discovered that auditory stimuli produced evoked potentials in an area at the anterior end of the suprasylvian gyrus of the dog, in what was already known as the "second sensory area," S II. He called it the "third auditory area," A III. It is quite small, perhaps too small for any tonotopical arrangement to be detected by the usual gross recording electrodes. Retrograde-degeneration studies suggest that this area has sustaining connections from the posterior group of nuclei, where the somatosensory and auditory inputs overlap in the thalamus (Rose & Woolsey, 1958). Berman (1961) has found that the overlap of S II and A III is not simply a mixture of neurons with different functions. In the cat, at least, sensory and auditory afferents interact in this region, though just what this interaction means for behavior is difficult to imagine. It has been found necessary to ablate A III, as well as A I, A II, and Ep, in order to obtain any lasting deficit of auditory discrimination.

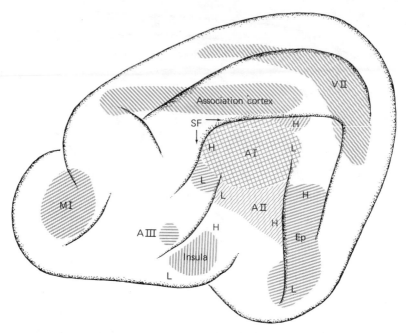

Figure 12.15 Areas on the cat cortex where evoked potentials have been recorded from click stimuli. In areas where tonotopic representation has been found the high-frequency end is labeled H and the low-frequency end L. The middle extent of the suprasylvian fringe area (SF) is buried in the suprasylvian sulcus. The responses in the second visual area (V II) are very late, on the order of 100 msec, and those in the association cortex have a latency of about 15 msec. Other areas giving evoked responses to auditory stimuli are the primary auditory cortex (A I), second and third auditory cortices (A II and A III), the posterior ectosylvian cortex (Ep), the motor cortex (M I), and the insula. (After Woolsey, 1960.)

Careful inspection of evoked-potential records in an area that used to be considered the anterior part of A II revealed that the frequency representation was running in the direction opposite to that in the rest of A II (Tunturi, 1952; Hind, 1953). Hind also noted an area just dorsal to the low-frequency end of A I that responded to high frequencies. Woolsey has suggested that these two areas belong together and are parts of another auditory area, which he calls the *suprasylvian fringe* (SF), whose middle part is buried in the depths of the suprasylvian sulcus.

Yet another cortical area with some tonotopic representation is found in the insular region. According to Diamond, Chow, and Neff (1958), the posterior part of the medial geniculate body projects to both the insular and temporal cortex. In addition, Buser, Borenstein, and Bruner (1959) demonstrated definite evoked responses in a region (Assoc. in Figure 12.15) above A I in the suprasylvian gyrus and extending rostrally into the anterior lateral gyrus in cats under *chloralose anesthesia* (which depresses the cortex less than do the more common *barbiturates*). Similar responses are also found in the motor area.

The responses in the suprasylvian and lateral gyri and in the motor cortex have latencies of about 15 msec, almost twice those of responses in A I, A II, A III, and Ep, but they can still be elicited after all these areas have been ablated (R. F. Thompson & Sindberg, 1960). They therefore cannot result from corticocortical connections from the shorter-latency areas. Degeneration studies suggest that these long-latency responses may be projected from the pulvinar. No tonotopic organization is apparent.

The only remaining area that has been shown

to respond to sound stimuli is the second visual area, V II, where the sound-evoked response has an exceedingly long latency, of about 100 msec. We do not know at present where the auditory projections to this area originate, but such long latency suggests that they may well pass through a nonspecific multisynaptic pathway like the reticular activating system.

In contrast to the wealth of information about the auditory cortex of the cat, next to nothing is known about the auditory system in other animals, including primates. Heschl (1878) traced the auditory fibers in man to a region in the posterior part of the superior temporal convolution (or gyrus), which is now called *Heschl's gyrus*. Stimulation of the monkey cortex had even earlier led physiologists to suspect that the main primate auditory area was located in the temporal lobe, within the sylvian fissure, and Polyak (1932) confirmed, using the Marchi degeneration technique, that the medial geniculate projects to that area. Since then retrograde-degeneration studies have led to the same conclusion.

Because of its awkward location and the proximity of the middle cerebral artery, the auditory area in the monkey has not been explored by the evoked-potential method nearly as fully as it has in the cat. K. H. Pribram, Rosner, and Rosenblith (1954) were able to pick up evoked responses to click stimuli at all points in the posterior part of the sylvian fissure, including the insula, and in the adjacent parietal lobe in the region of the second sensory area, S II.

According to Licklider and Kryter (1942) and Bailey, Bonin, Garol, and McCulloch (1943), high frequencies are represented in the most posterior part of the auditory area and low frequencies at the anterior end; this arrangement is the reverse of the tonotopic representation in A I of the cat. Although the primary auditory area in primates does not extend to the rostral part of the superior temporal gyrus, the latter area is homologous to the insulartemporal area in the cat. Extending a lesion forward from A I causes increased degeneration in the posterior part of the medial geniculate body.

The tonotopic representation in man is usually given in textbooks as being the same as that in the monkey, but we do not yet have satisfactory experimental evidence for this assumption. Stimulation of the temporal lobe in man often produces auditory phenomena, depending to some extent upon the locus of stimulation. With electrodes in Heschl's gyrus, the patient sometimes reports sounds like ringing, chirping, humming, clicking, booming, and so on (Penfield & Rasmussen, 1950). He may say that he is deafened by the stimulation or that such other disturbances of hearing as changes of pitch in the sound of his own and other voices occur. The patient almost always refers the effect to the ear contralateral to the stimulation, a further indication that, despite the intermingling of the pathways from the two ears, the crossed pathway is the dominant one.

Ventral to Heschl's gyrus, in the first temporal convolution, stimulation produces more complex phenomena, some visual, many auditory. The latter take the form of hallucinations of voices, often those of relatives or friends; sometimes the voices make clear and meaningful statements, and at other times they simply utter an indistinct jumble. Some patients hear music, again with varying degrees of clarity, during stimulation. Very occasionally effects of the same sort have been obtained from the undersurface of the temporal lobe, but normally auditory hallucinations are obtained exclusively from the part of the lateral surface just below the sylvian fissure. The response may be elicited from either the left or the right temporal lobe (Penfield & Perot, 1963).

It is interesting that nowhere does stimulation elicit a report of pure tones' being heard, as might be expected if the notion of tonotopic localization were taken to mean that each frequency is represented by the firing of cells in a particular area.

Electrical Responses of the Cochlea

We shall return now to the transducer organ to find out what is known about the ways in which the various parameters of the auditory stimulus are converted into nerve-impulse patterns.

Potentials believed to be the generator potentials of hair cells can be recorded from the region of the cochlea (Wever & Bray, 1930). One component has the same wave form as the impinging sound and is known as the *cochlear microphonic* (CM). Another, less sensitive component, which is best recorded with an electrode in the scala media, is a unidirectional (DC) potential that follows the envelope of the sound wave (the line joining the peaks) quite closely. It has been called the *summating potential* (SP; see H. Davis, Deatherage, Eldredge & Smith, 1958). It usually takes the form of a reduction of the positive potential in the scala media, though with small signals the polarity is sometimes reversed, suggesting that it may originate in more than one source.

The cochlear microphonic and the summating potential are picked up simultaneously by electrodes in the scala media, as shown in Figure 12.16. H. Davis (1961) thought that most of the CM was produced by the inner row of external hair cells, which are more sensitive than the rest. That it is an alternating potential suggests that these hair cells resemble some of those in the vestibular system in that they are hyperpolarized by movements of the hairs in one direction and hypopolarized by movements in the other direction. The summating potential, which Davis attributed mainly to the inner hair cells, seemed to indicate that the latter were hypopolarized by movements in either direction. The hair cells do not generate impulses themselves, but presumably they release transmitter substance (in amounts proportional to degree of hypopolarization) onto the dendritic terminals of the bipolar cells, where the nerve impulses originate.

Coding Intensity

It is apparent that the pattern of impulses transmitted by the bipolar cells at any instant must indicate the intensity, pitch, tonal quality, and location of the auditory input. We are certainly far from having cracked all the codes, but recordings from whole nerves and from individual fibers indicate, as might be expected, that the overall firing rate increases with sound intensity. This general rule does not apply to all fibers at all intensity levels; the firing rate in some of the more sensitive fibers increases with increase in the sound level up to a point and then begins to decrease. The amplitude of the cochlear microphonic behaves similarly.

This phenomenon may be explained by the action of the recurrent olivo-cochlear bundle of Rasmussen (see discussion of auditory pathways earlier in this chapter), which is believed to deliver inhibitory feedback to the cochlea (Desmedt, 1962; Desmedt & La Grutta, 1963) and to desensitize the most sensitive hair cells in the presence of strong signals. (In the eye, a combination of inhibition from the cones and slow recovery from bleaching serve an analogous purpose by eliminating the sensitive rod system in bright light.)

The code for intensity in the auditory nerve therefore appears to be a matter partly of the rate at which fibers are firing and partly of which fibers are firing. A small increase in the activity of sensitive fibers, with no change in the others, indicates a weak sound, and a large increase of activity in high-threshold fibers with reduced participation of the sensitive fibers indicates a much louder sound.

As we ascend the auditory pathway, the

Figure 12.16 Cochlear microphonic and summating potential (top curve) recorded simultaneously from an electrode in the scala media of the guinea pig in response to a strong tone burst at 7,000 Hz. The action potential (lower curve) is picked up by the same electrode; it can be isolated by filtering both the cochlear microphonic (7,000 Hz) and the summating potential (DC) from the signal. (After H. Davis, Deatherage, Eldredge & Smith, 1958.)

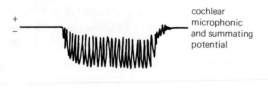

cochlear microphonic and summating potential

action potential

maximum firing rate of individual fibers is much reduced, and the increase in rate proportional to sound intensity is also much less. Figure 12.17 shows typical curves for activity of neurons in the auditory nerve, the trapezoid body, the medial geniculate and the cortex of a cat in response to sounds of varying intensity (Katsuki, 1961).

The cortex seems to play very little part in discriminating intensity. After bilateral ablation of all the areas from which evoked potentials to clicks can be detected under barbiturate anesthesia, cats had an unchanged threshold to sound and could learn to respond to slight changes in intensity as well as they had been able to before the operations (Kryter & Ades, 1943; Raab & Ades, 1946; Neff, 1961a). Only a slight change in the threshold was produced when the auditory pathway was completely cut at the brachium of the inferior colliculus.

In man there was a just detectable change in the ability to discriminate intensities, as measured by the "loudness" subtest of the Seashore Test of Musical Abilities, after ablation of the right temporal lobe (B. Milner, 1962b). The deficit was the same whether Heschl's gyrus was removed or spared. No change occurred after lesions of the left temporal lobe. Swisher (1967) found, paradoxically, that patients who had undergone left temporal-lobe excisions that included Heschl's gyrus had *lower* thresholds for intensity changes than before the operation. She attributed this result to interference with a descending inhibitory regulatory mechanism, postulated to originate in the auditory cortex.

Landau, Goldstein, and Kleffner (1960) have reported the case of a boy who had a perfectly normal audiogram (that is, whose auditory sensitivity was normal at all frequencies) yet who was found upon autopsy to have complete bilateral destruction of auditory cortex with almost complete degeneration of the medial geniculate. On the other hand, W. E. L. Clark and Russell (1938) described a woman with similar lesions who was deafened by the damage. It seems probable, however, that her lesions were not confined to the auditory system.

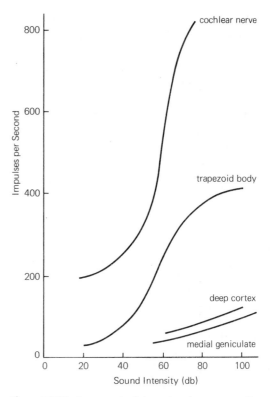

Figure 12.17 Increase in firing rate of neurons with increase in sound intensity at different points along the auditory pathway. (After Katsuki, 1961.)

Coding Pitch

The coding of intensity in the early stages of the auditory system is complicated by the influence of input frequency upon the firing rates of the units. When the input frequency is below about 2 kHz many afferent fibers fire in volleys of one or more impulses in step with the peaks of the sound waves. Furthermore, thanks to the geometry of the cochlea, about which we shall learn more in the next section, some fibers that fire vigorously at low frequencies do not respond at all to input of the same intensity at higher frequencies. This property no doubt constitutes a basis for coding pitch.

For many years there have been two schools of thought on how pitch information is transmitted. One theory, originated by Rutherford (1886) and revived by Wever and Bray (1930), stated that the frequency of the impulses in the nerve was the same as that of the sound, just as in a telephone wire; hence the name *telephone theory*. As individual nerve fibers cannot transmit impulses at more than about 1,000 per second, it was postulated that a number of them collaborated to transmit higher frequencies, one firing at one cycle, another at the next, and so on. The theory is incomplete, however, without some specification of how this type of message could be used by the higher centers of the nervous system, and no such decoding mechanism was suggested until much later, when Licklider (1959) proposed a model based on the principle of autocorrelation.

Licklider's model is shown diagrammatically in Figure 12.18. It is based on the obvious fact that there is a longer interval between successive wave peaks at low frequencies than at high frequencies. If the signal is sent along two paths, one with a higher conduction velocity than that of the other, a wave (or impulse generated by the wave) traveling in the faster path will eventually catch up with the previous wave (or impulse) in the slower path. A short, high-frequency wave will, of course, catch up sooner than will a long, low-frequency wave because it has a shorter distance to travel. To provide a measure of frequency, a mechanism is required to indicate the points on the paths where the impulses are in step again after one

has fallen a wavelength behind the other. This indication is given in Licklider's model by a chain of cells upon which collaterals from the fast and slow paths converge. Cells in the chain fire only when there is a coincidence of input to them from both paths.

Despite the ingenuity of this model, the telephone (or frequency) theory is still open to several objections. Measurements have failed to detect any synchronization between nerve impulses and sound waves at frequencies higher than about 3 kHz, even in the cat, which can hear frequencies of more than 40kHz, and the time relationship between the wave peak and the impulse is none too stable at frequencies above a few hundred Hz. We would therefore predict, in view of the workings of the autocorrelation analyzer, that low frequencies would be readily discriminated and that there would be steady deterioration of pitch acuity in the middle-and high-frequency ranges. Exactly the reverse is true. Pitch discrimination in man is about twenty times better at 2 kHz than at 60 Hz (Shower & Biddulph, 1931).

Furthermore, the autocorrelation mechanism would give false responses at high frequencies because of coincidences between impulses more than one wavelength apart. At 1 kHz such a coincidence would fire cells representing 500, 333, 250, 200 Hz and so on. If the wave form

Figure 12.18 Licklider's autocorrelation pitch analyzer. Each impulse in the fast path catches up with the previous impulse in the slow path at a point that indicates the time interval between the waves that originally generated the two impulses. In the example shown the interval is long, indicating a fairly low frequency. (After Licklider, 1959.)

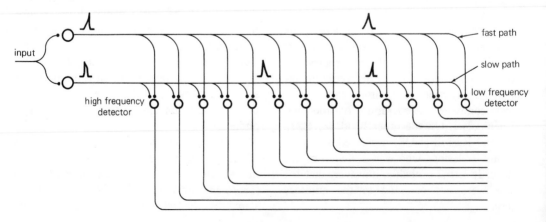

is complex or if several frequencies are present at once, which is common, the autocorrelation frequency analyzer would give so many false outputs as to be quite useless.

The other important theory of pitch coding is the *place theory*. In its early form (Helmholtz, 1862) it proposed that each receptor of the cochlea was tuned to a different frequency and had its own nerve fiber to the brain. The nerves innervating different places along the basilar membrane would thus represent different frequencies of sound input; their firing rates would indicate the strength of the sound at that frequency. This theory was one of the more extreme examples of the "specific energy of nerves" hypothesis.

Although there now seems to be little alternative to some form of place theory, at least to account for high frequencies, the researches of Békésy (1949; Békésy & Rosenblith, 1951) have demonstrated that there is no sharp tuning of the parts of the basilar membrane (Helmholtz had suggested that the membrane consisted of a number of strings, as in a harp, in which sympathetic vibrations were set up by the sound). Furthermore, Tasaki (1954), among others, has shown that individual fibers of the auditory nerve respond to a much wider range of frequencies than would be predicted by the early place theory.

Nevertheless, these same investigations have proved that the cochlea is capable of a rough kind of mechanical frequency analysis and that the fibers of the auditory nerve do respond preferentially to different frequencies. Some of the response curves for single fibers of the auditory nerve measured by Katsuki, Watanabe, and Suga (1959) are shown in Figure 12.19. There is one frequency at which each nerve is fired with a minimum input. As the frequency of the sound departs from this optimum value, a greater intensity is required to fire the nerve. In most fibers the sensitivity falls off more rapidly as the frequency is increased from the tuning point than as it is reduced, but there are some, believed to have widespread connections with many outer hair cells, that have more symmetrical response curves (Katsuki, 1961).

As we have seen in other modalities, it is not

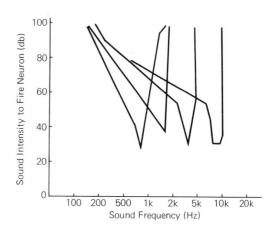

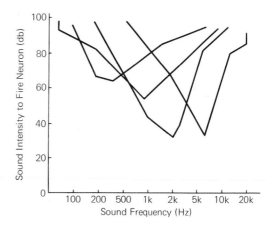

Figure 12.19 Curves showing minimum sound intensities required to fire a sample of primary neurons at different frequencies. The upper curve shows a number of neurons with asymmetrical characteristics; the lower curve shows those more nearly symmetrical. (After Katsuki, Watanabe & Suga, 1959.)

necessary for the peripheral organ to perform as complete an analysis of the stimulus as the discriminating capacity of the organism might lead one to expect. A slight differentiation between inputs at the periphery can be magnified by lateral inhibition and other sharpening circuits in the pathway until the required discrimination is achieved. Such circuits in the auditory pathway could perfectly well account for the accuracy of pitch discrimination without recourse to the telephone theory, but there are one or two phenomena that force us to consider the possibility of a combined frequency and place theory.

One is that pulsation or modulation, at a low

frequency, of noise or a high-frequency note causes the subject to hear a low frequency, which should not be possible, according to the place theory, because no low-frequency waves reach the apical turns of the cochlea, where the nerves representing low frequencies originate. The slightest distortion of the sound by the mechanical transmission system would, however, generate a true low-frequency component and invalidate the assumption upon which this objection to the place theory is based.

The effects of stimulating the auditory nerve are sometimes also cited in support of the telephone theory, but they would certainly not be predicted from that theory. When the auditory nerve is stimulated at a low frequency, we would expect the subject to hear that frequency, but Simmons, Epley, Lummis, Guttman, Frishkopf, Harmon, and Zwicker (1965), who implanted six electrodes in different parts of the auditory nerve of a man who was deaf in that ear, found that stimulation at 4–10 pulses per second (below the audible range) was heard as buzzing, at 10–20 pulses per second as a telephone ringing, at 30 pulses per second as an automobile horn, and at 100–300 pulses per second as steady whistles and high-pitched ringing. Above 300 per second, changes in the frequency of stimulation had no further effect upon the reported sensations. Different effects were produced from differently located electrodes, as the place theory would predict; when several electrodes were used simultaneously the subject heard sounds different from any that could be elicited by single electrodes. These findings strongly suggest that the coding of pitch depends upon the overall pattern of activity in the nerve. As has also been found in other modalities, the effects of stimulating peripheral nerves are surprisingly similar to those produced by cortical stimulation.

The question of coding pitch has not been finally answered, but, although there is no evidence that the higher levels of the auditory system are capable of interpreting signals coded according to the telephone theory, even in the low-frequency range where that theory is still considered valid by some, we do know that the cochlea can act as an adequate frequency ana-lyzer to form the basis for a system operating according to the place theory. Before considering the coding of other parameters it is useful to look more closely at how this analysis is carried out.

Acoustical Properties of the Cochlea

As shown in Figure 12.20, the basilar membrane is not of constant width along its length, and, just as the retina surprises us by being "inside out," the basilar membrane is peculiar in being wider and thinner at the apex of the cochlear coil than at the base. It is about 40 μ wide at the base and gradually widens to about 500 μ at the apex, where it is also 100 times less stiff than at the base.

This difference means, of course, that under pressure the basilar membrane bends farther at the apex than it does lower down. At very low frequencies, below about 20 Hz, the basilar membrane does not move appreciably, even with quite large inputs to the ear, because the perilymph leaks through the helicotrema as rapidly as it is displaced by the movements of the oval window. As the frequency increases, however, the fluid cannot flow quickly enough through the small hole, pressure builds up in the scala vestibuli, and the basilar membrane is deflected. Naturally this deflection is greatest near the apex, where the membrane is most flexible, but the whole membrane is deflected to some extent.

As the frequency rises further, the fluid must accelerate more and more rapidly to deliver pressure at the remote apical end of the coiled tube, and this acceleration produces a back pressure toward the basal end. The wave thus finds it easier to deflect the stiffer part of the basilar membrane than to force its way to the apex of the cochlea, where the membrane would be easier to bend; the peak of deflection occurs lower down the coil. At the highest audible frequencies, the pressure wave will take the shortest possible path between the oval and round windows, even though it involves bending the membrane at the point where it is stiffest; the inertia of the column of liquid in the cochlea effectively filters the high-frequency pressure waves from the middle and apical parts of the cochlea.

This mechanism was suggested by Békésy and Rosenblith (1951) on the basis of Békésy's very elegant measurements of the mode of vibration of the basilar membrane in various animals. The measurements were performed by drilling small "observation windows" in the cochlea and watching, through a microscope, the motion of fine particles of silver sprinkled on the basilar membrane (which would otherwise be transparent). The preparation was illuminated by a stroboscopic light flashing at the same frequency as the applied sound. By adjusting the phase of the flash, it was possible to observe the specks of silver at any point on their oscillation as if they were stationary. They were first observed at one end of their travel and then at the other; the experimenters were thus able to determine the peak-to-peak amplitude of the deflection of the membrane at that point. Békésy performed these measurements for various frequencies and at several different points along the membrane, obtaining the curves shown in Figure 12.21. They agree closely with the results to be expected from a knowledge of the physical properties of the system, as already described. At low frequencies the whole membrane vibrates, with the greatest deflection at the apex; at high frequencies only the basal region vibrates.

There is a further complication, however; the pressure wave does not travel at infinite speed,

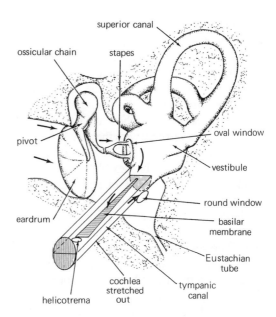

Figure 12.20   The middle and inner ear, showing the cochlea uncoiled. The basilar membrane is wider at the apex than at the base of the cochlea. (From Békésy, 1962.)

and therefore all parts of the basilar membrane do not reach their peak deflections at the same instant. A wave of peak deflection travels along the basilar membrane from the basal end toward the apex. Energy losses from the viscosity of the fluids and the internal friction of the basilar membrane are such that virtually no energy is stored from one wave to the next (as occurs, for example, in the resonant strings or air columns of musical instruments); thus no

Figure 12.21   Amplitude of peak displacements of the basilar membrane at different distances from the oval window. Values for low-, middle-, and fairly high-frequency sound input are shown. The membrane displacements shown on the ordinate are not to the same scale as the length measurements shown on the abscissa. (After Békésy & Rosenblith, 1951.)

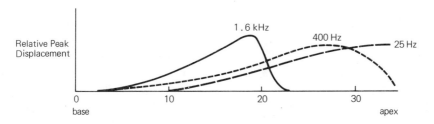

standing waves are established in the cochlea. Each sound wave produces an individual disturbance that travels along the cochlea a certain distance and is then dissipated.

The velocity of the wave depends partly upon the stiffness of the basilar membrane. (If it were completely solid the wave would travel along the scala vestibuli with the speed of sound in the fluid, approximately 1.5 km per second. If it were completely flexible the velocity would be more like that of surface ripples, which travel at about .0001 the speed of sound in the fluid. The actual stiffness lies between these extremes and is not constant, as we have seen. The velocity of the wave is thus actually about 5 m per second at the base and 50 cm per second at the apex.) As the wave approaches the apex, therefore, it slows down (which means that the wavelength grows shorter) and loses energy, as shown in Figure 12.22, which is an instantaneous picture of the traveling wave for a sound of about 400 Hz. The Békésy curves (Figure 12.21) represent the envelopes traced out by the peaks as they advance up the cochlea.

Because the wave travels rather slowly in the final stages of its progress along the membrane, there is usually more than one wave present on

Figure 12.22 Traveling waves (a) in a membrane unsupported at the edges and (b) in a membrane similar to the basilar membrane, in which the edges are fixed. (From Tonndorf, 1960.)

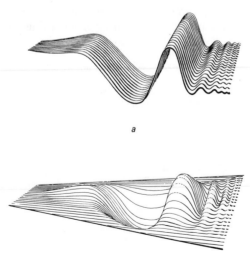

a

b

the membrane at any moment, as shown in Figure 12.22. This train of waves would actually provide a more satisfactory basis for an autocorrelation pitch analyzer than does Licklider's neural model if the necessity for such a mechanism should ever be definitely established. The cochlea stores low-frequency input for about 15 msec and high-frequency input for a shorter time. At any instant several points along the basilar membrane are passing through displacement maxima, and may therefore be generating nerve impulses in the fibers innervating the hair cells there. A few microseconds later the maxima will have moved a short distance toward the apex to fire new fibers. The spacing of the fibers that are firing simultaneously in this way will depend upon the wavelength of the disturbance, which is, of course, a function of pitch.

The decoding of pitch in such a model would be quite complex. Both the timing of the impulses and their points of origin would have to be taken into account. It could involve the convergence onto higher-order "pitch" cells of afferents from points various distances apart on the basilar membrane. Activity originating at two or more points would then summate to fire the particular cells on which the impulses arrived at the same instant. These cells would represent the frequency that caused the basilar membrane to have peak deflections at those points simultaneously.

The only experimental evidence that gives any hint that such a mechanism may exist is that of Simmons and his colleagues (1965) in the experiment with human auditory-nerve stimulation already cited. It will be remembered that simultaneous stimulation of different parts of the nerve caused the subject to report frequencies not reported when those parts of the nerve were stimulated separately.

Although this mechanical version of the autocorrelation model escapes a few of the criticisms leveled against the neural version, it is still open to many of them. At present, the evidence against the place theory is not compelling enough to warrant abandoning it in favor of even less convincing alternatives.

As predicted according to the place theory,

the "tuning" of single elements becomes sharper as the signals ascend the system to the cortex; there, for some reason, the curves become flatter again (Katsuki, 1961). Auditory neurons are also relatively more sharply tuned at the higher frequencies than at the lower frequencies (Tsuchitani & Boudreau, 1966).

It might be imagined, by analogy with the visual system, that lesions in the auditory cortex might produce sound "scotomata" or gaps in the sound spectrum, but none has been observed. One reason may be the multiple tonotopic representation at the cortex. As can be seen in Figure 12.15, there are at least five areas in which frequency is separately represented, and so far no one has attempted to ablate the locus for a particular part of the sound spectrum in all five areas.

In general, even lesions that destroy all the known auditory cortex are not followed by any loss of pitch discrimination. D. R. Meyer and Woolsey (1952) obtained a deficit of pitch discrimination in cats after lesions that included A I, A II, Ep, and A III, but R. F. Thompson (1960) and others have criticized this finding as an artifact of the testing method. The experiments of Thompson and those of Butler, Diamond, and Neff (1957) demonstrated that cats with very extensive lesions of the lateral cortex, including all the auditory areas (with the possible exception of parts of V II, the second visual area, see Figure 12.15) can learn to discriminate pitch to avoid shock.

Butler and his colleagues used a single note repeated at intervals to indicate safety and an alternation between that note and a new one as a warning of impending shock. The cats with large ablations could learn to make an avoidance response to this signal but not if the warning was a repeated note at a frequency different from the safe one. Apparently discrimination is possible only with repeated presentation of both notes in close juxtaposition. Although it is clear that a mechanism for pitch discrimination is still functional in cats with extensive cortical lesions, it is equally clear that the time over which a pitch comparison can be made is more limited than before operation.

In these experiments the difference in fre-quency between the two notes was quite large, 20 per cent or more. No attempt seems to have been made to determine whether or not the threshold for pitch discrimination was changed by a lesion.

Bilateral transection of the brachium of the inferior colliculus does not prevent pitch discrimination either, but, if the lesion is extended outside the pathway until auditory stimuli no longer evoke cortical potentials, frequency discrimination is lost. Presumably there are pitch-sensitive cells in the medulla and mesencephalon, but they need some communication with the cortex in order to become associated with an avoidance response. The classical auditory pathways are not necessary for this communication.

Monkeys have more difficulty with auditory discriminations under laboratory conditions than do cats, perhaps because they prefer to depend upon vision as far as possible. Weiskrantz and Mishkin (1958) were unable to train normal monkeys to press a lever for one tone and to refrain from pressing it for another in order to obtain food, but when one of the stimuli was changed to *white noise* (noise distributed with approximately equal energy in all parts of the auditory spectrum) normal animals learned to discriminate it from a 1 kHz tone.

Bilateral lesions were then placed in the inferior temporal lobes, the posterior sylvian areas, or the lateral frontal lobes. It was expected that monkeys with lesions of the posterior sylvian areas would show deficits in performance on auditory discriminations but not on visual ones, whereas the inferior temporal-lobe lesions would produce deficits in the visual tasks but not in the auditory ones. The frontal lesions were for control purposes and were not expected to influence either task. What actually happened was that neither the posterior sylvian nor the inferior temporal lesions had any significant effect upon auditory discrimination, but the frontal lesions completely eliminated it and prevented relearning.

As we shall see later, lesions of the lateral surface of the frontal lobe produce deficits in delayed-response tasks, but Gross and Weiskrantz (1962) and Gross (1963) were able to show that lesions in the *sulcus principalis* (which produced maximal effect on the delayed response) had less effect upon auditory discrimination than did other frontal-lobe lesions that had little effect upon delayed response. It proved impossible to obtain the auditory deficit by electrical stimulation of the frontal cortex, though very striking deficits of delayed response were obtained during stimulation of the *sulcus principalis* region (Gross & Weiskrantz, 1964); Weiskrantz, Mihailović & Gross, 1960).

It is uncertain to what extent it is valid to extrapolate from animal to human hearing. Chorazyna and Konorski (1962) found that dogs learned to discriminate absolute pitch much more easily than they learned relational discriminations. If a dog was trained to discriminate a high note from a low one, with the two notes changed from day to day, it soon became confused and refused to perform. Human subjects, on the other hand, found absolute-pitch judgments difficult but could easily learn a relational discrimination. This difference may indicate a fundamental difference between the two auditory systems or, possibly, only that man is capable of a higher level of concept formation than the dog.

Right temporal-lobe lesions in man possibly produce slight deterioration in performance on a pitch test (part of the Seashore Test of Musical Abilities), especially if Heschl's gyrus is spared, but the deficit does not approach statistical significance (B. Milner, 1962b).

Coding Timbre

The tonal quality of a note depends, as stated earlier, upon its harmonic content. In theory, therefore, the frequency analysis used for pitch discrimination should suffice to provide all the information required for discrimination of timbre. The actual discrimination would then be performed by a circuit capable of comparing the relative intensities of the various frequencies present in the input.

A slight complication arises, in that the output of the cochlea when more than one frequency is present is not simply the sum of the activity elicited by each frequency alone; there

is also a nonlinear interaction. Such interaction effects have been studied in the cochlear nucleus and the medial geniculate by Katsuki, Wantanabe, and Suga (1959). Figure 12.23 shows the response of a cell in the cochlear nucleus of a cat. Normally it responds strongly to tone pips in the region of 5 kHz, but a strong background stimulus of 10 kHz fires it continuously at a moderate rate. When tone pips of various frequencies are superimposed upon this continuous high-frequency stimulation, the activity is inhibited by some frequencies and increased by others. Even when the tone pip causes an increase in the continuing activity, however, the cell does not fire as vigorously as it would have done in the absence of the 10 kHz background; it is therefore true that in the cochlear nucleus the interaction among inputs is mainly inhibitory. In the cortex, on the other hand, the interaction between two tones on single neurons is often facilitatory, particularly when the two tones bear a harmonic relation to each other (Katsuki, 1961).

Unfortunately, our rather sparse information on the effects of multiple stimulation does not permit us to guess what sort of patterns are produced in the whole nerve by sounds rich in harmonics, chords, or other complex wave forms, but it does seem likely that there is first a frequency analysis and then a further mechanism to synthesize the product in a timbre signal.

Some support for this theory is given by the fact that lesions in the higher auditory centers have much greater effects upon the discrimination of timbre than upon that of loudness or pitch. Dewson (1964) has found that cats with lesions of the auditory cortex, in some cases confined to the insular-temporal region, failed to discriminate vowel sounds ("ū" and "ī" were used in the experiment). Normal animals can learn this discrimination and can transfer it readily from a male voice to a female voice.

In man, unilateral temporal-lobe lesions cause a highly significant deficit in ability to discriminate timbre on the Seashore Test of Musical Abilities. Even before operation, patients with temporal-lobe epilepsy do badly on the test. After left temporal ablation there is little change; in fact those whose lesions include Heschl's gyrus may improve slightly, but after right temporal-lobe ablations there is further severe and highly significant deterioration. The additional deficit is significantly greater in those cases in which Heschl's gyrus is spared by the operation than in those with larger lesions that include it (B. Milner, 1967).

These deficits after cortical lesions are consistent with the hypothesis that there are neurons in the temporal lobe analogous to the complex visual cells described by Hubel and Wiesel (1962). Afferents from cells tuned to different frequencies synapse with them so that each fires to a particular combination of input frequencies. It should be mentioned, however, that the boy with bilateral auditory-cortex lesions studied by Landau and his colleagues (see "Coding of Intensity" earlier in this chapter) was able to understand speech and had a vocabulary of about 175 words. This accomplishment is probably an example of the plasticity of the cortex early in life. Scharlock, Tucker, and Strominger (1963) have shown that cats undergoing large excisions of the auditory cortex during the first few days of life are later capable of making most of the auditory discriminations that are impossible for cats that sustain similar lesions later in life.

Sound Localization

There are two main cues for the localization of sound: the relative intensity of the input to the two ears and the difference in time of arrival at the two ears. This information is almost always augmented in practice through head and pinna movements, but this additional information requires comparison of sounds originating at different times, and thus involves some form of storage; we shall therefore not consider it at this point.

As the important cues for localization are binaural, it is clear that they cannot be interpreted until the paths from the two ears meet and interact. We have already seen that at low frequencies each wave generates a synchronous volley of impulses in the auditory nerve. Similar volleys are also produced by the onset of

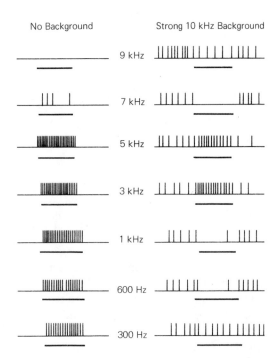

Figure 12.23 Responses of a neuron in the cochlear nucleus of the cat to tone pips of various frequencies with and without a strong, continuous 10 kHz background stimulus. The duration of the tone pips is indicated by the line below each oscilloscope tracing. (After Katsuki, Watanabe & Suga, 1959.)

high-frequency sounds or such other transients as clicks. According to Rosenzweig (1961), Bowlker (1908) was probably the first to suggest that the time difference between the volleys from the two ears could be converted to spatial coding by feeding the impulses through paths of different length before allowing them to converge on higher-order cells. Jeffress (1948) made the model more explicit, and Licklider's (1959) autocorrelation model for frequency analysis incorporated a cross-correlation component for sound localization.

The essentials of the mechanism are illustrated in Figure 12.24. If a signal arrives at one ear 100 μsec, let us say, before it arrives at the other, then, in order for the two volleys to summate most effectively, the one in the nerve from that ear must arrive at a higher-order convergence cell with a transmission delay of 100 μsec more than that of the volley from the other ear. In a circuit like that shown the earlier signal will go more than halfway to meet the

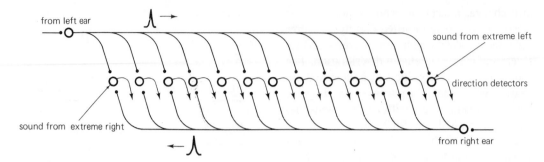

Figure 12.24 The cross-correlation mechanism postulated to explain a sound localization. Impulses produced by a source to the right of the observer start along the lower path before those from the left ear start along the upper path; they thus converge on the detector cells to the left of center. Impulses from a source straight ahead leave the two ears simultaneously and meet in the middle of the detector chain. (After Licklider, 1959.)

later one, and the impulses will converge through collaterals onto the higher-order cell whose location is determined by the temporal disparity of the two volleys and thus by the angle between the source of the sound and the sagittal plane of the head.

It would clearly be advantageous to have the interaction between the two signals take place as close as possible to the origin in the cochlea, because uncertainty of timing is introduced at each synaptic junction. It is not impossible that some interaction takes place in the cochlear nuclei, as there are connections from each to the other, but at present the evidence suggests that the most important loci of interaction are the medial superior olivary nuclei. Stotler (1953) has shown anatomically that fibers from the two cochlear nuclei converge on cells of the medial superior olivary nuclei, and Rosenzweig and Sutton (1958) have determined that the interaction between impulses from both ears has already taken place by the time they reach the lateral lemniscus. The medial superior olivary nuclei appear to have afferents mainly from the low-frequency parts of the cochlea (Galambos, Schwartzkopf & Rupert, 1959), where the impulses have more precise temporal relations to the peaks of the waves.

Because loud sounds produce impulses in the auditory nerve with shorter latencies than weak sounds, we might suspect that a single mechanism sensitive to time disparities would work for differences of both length of path and loudness, but apparently it does not. That there

are separate mechanisms for the interpretation of loudness and temporal differences is apparent from the experiments of Masterton, Jane, and Diamond (1967), in which cats were trained in an avoidance apparatus to differentiate between signals presented through earphones to either the right or the left ear. When this discrimination had been learned, the cats were presented with clicks of equal amplitude in both ears, with a brief interval (usually 0.5 msec) between them. When the first click went to the right ear the cat behaved as if it had an input to that ear alone and vice versa. The normal cat can thus transfer immediately from loudness to time-delay cues for localization.

After lesions had been made in the trapezoid body, however, the cats could no longer learn to discriminate on the basis of time cues, though they could still learn on the basis of intensity. This difference suggests that intensity cues can still be processed by bilateral interaction at levels higher than the olivary complex (in the inferior colliculus or the cortex, for example, Rose, Gross, Geisler & Hind, 1966) but that the temporal cues are lost forever if they are not analyzed at an earlier stage.

Using the same earphone technique on cats with large auditory-cortex ablations, Masterton and Diamond (1964) confirmed earlier findings (Neff & Diamond, 1958) that localization was severely impaired by such lesions. It was almost impossible for the cats with cortical lesions to relearn the discrimination on the basis of time differences alone, but discrimination on the basis of intensity was less impaired. Axelrod and Diamond (1965) found that after lesions of the auditory cortex, cats had difficulty distinguishing between sounds fed to the right or left ear.

The investigators concluded that the basic mechanisms for analyzing directional cues were located in the medulla but that the processed information was transmitted to the auditory cortex, where it could be used to construct a representation of auditory space. Such a representation is essential for learned behavior dependent upon sound localization.

Teuber (in discussion of Neff, 1961) has stated that damage to the right parietal lobe in man will produce a deficit in sound localization. He suspects that some patients have greater deficits for time-disparity cues and others for loudness cues.

Echolocation

Most animals can make use of sound reflections from nearby objects to guide them about in the dark or when blinded. Supa, Cotzin, and Dallenbach (1944) showed that the "facial vision" of the blind was an auditory phenomenon. Subjects sat still wearing earphones connected to a microphone carried by the experimenter; they could tell by the sound when the microphone was approaching an obstacle. The investigators also showed that blind subjects lost their facial vision when their ears were plugged.

Rats have similar abilities, as was shown by Riley and Rosenzweig (1957), and, of course, the skill has evolved to an extraordinary degree in bats (see Griffin, 1953, 1958) and porpoises (Kellogg, 1961) for the purposes of pilotage and catching prey. These animals emit pulses of sound and detect the returning echoes. In this way they can determine the distance, as well as the direction and size, of the reflecting objects (Kellogg, 1959).

These abilities depend upon the discrimination of short time intervals between successive signals presented to the same ear. It thus seems likely that the initial analysis is performed as close as possible to the periphery, perhaps in the cochlear nucleus. The cortex is probably necessary for the incorporation of the echo information into the general picture of auditory space. Certainly the auditory cortex of the porpoise is very large. Unfortunately the vascular system of the *cetacean* (aquatic mammal) *cortex* imposes a great technical obstacle to the making of lesions, so that research on the physiological basis of echo ranging has not yet made much progress.

Discrimination of Tonal Patterns

With the exception of a few threshold tests, all auditory discriminations require some form of storage to allow one signal to be compared with a subsequent one. Even pitch discriminations require such storage, and it is for this reason perhaps that cortical lesions interfere with performance when there is a long interval between the two notes.

When storage capacity is limited, interference effects can be very important, and it is not surprising that the comparison of sequences of notes should be particularly susceptible to cortical lesions. Using the shuttle-box avoidance technique, Goldberg, Diamond, and Neff (1957) found that bilateral lesions of the insular and temporal auditory areas produced severe deficit in the ability of cats to discriminate between patterns of notes (for example, A-B-A versus B-A-B).

Oder (see Neff, 1961b) has demonstrated deficits of discrimination of tonal patterns in monkeys after ablations of the anterior temporal cortex that have had no effect upon visual pattern discrimination. Ablation of the right temporal lobe in man produces a severe deficit of tonal memory as measured by the Seashore Musical Abilities Test (B. Milner, 1962b, 1967). Lesions of the left temporal lobe have no significant effect upon this measure. We have already seen that right temporal-lobe lesions produce no effect upon pitch discrimination; apparently these patients can tell one note from another without difficulty, but they have the greatest difficulty in learning simple tunes.

Lesions of the auditory cortex also impair discrimination of the duration of a sound, both in cats (Neff, 1961b) and in human patients with right temporal lesions (B. Milner, 1962b), though in the latter the deficits are slight except in patients with sparing of Heschl's gyrus. The explanation for the paradoxically bad effects of leaving the auditory area intact may be that it is usually removed only when that part of the brain is already not functioning well because of the epileptic lesion. Such malfunctioning may force some other structures (perhaps the contralateral temporal lobe) to take over auditory functions, thus tending to protect the patient from the severest effects of the ablation.

Interaural Rivalry in Man

The Broadbent test reveals a deficit after left temporal-lobe lesions in man. In this test Broadbent (1954) made ingenious use of a stereophonic tape recorder, playing different sets of digits simultaneously into the two ears of his subjects. When three pairs of digits were presented at intervals of a second or less, the subjects could usually recall all six, repeating all the numbers heard in one ear before giving the other three. Doreen Kimura (1961) used a special version of this test on patients with brain lesions and found that those with seizures originating in the left temporal lobe performed significantly worse than any other group. After lobectomy for the relief of the seizures, the left-temporal group became worse still. The performance of other groups, on the average, remained unchanged after operation, but the right-temporal patients recalled fewer of the digits presented to the left ear and more of those presented to the right ear than they had before the operation. This effect upon the contralateral ear was very marked after left temporal lobectomies also, suggesting that, when there is competition between inputs from two sources, the loss of one temporal lobe puts the input going mainly to that hemisphere at a disadvantage. On the intact side the signals from the contralateral ear are stronger and apparently suppress the input from the ipsilateral ear when both inputs arrive simultaneously.

The disparity between performance on this test and on the various Seashore Musical Abilities subtests, which, when they show deficits at all, do so only after right temporal lobectomies, appears to arise from the type of material presented. The Broadbent test uses words, and in most people the left hemisphere is dominant for speech. Possibly as a consequence the right side is dominant for some nonverbal material. This assumption is supported by the fact that substituting snippets of music for digits in the Broadbent test caused patients with right temporal lobectomies to do worse than those with left temporal lobectomies (Doreen Kimura, 1964b).

Summary

The labyrinth has two main divisions: the vestibular apparatus, which provides information about the orientation and movements of the head, and the cochlea, which contains the auditory receptors.

In most mammals the main function of the vestibular system is to assist vision by keeping the eyes steady while the head is being joggled, as during running. The utricle and the saccule are developments of simple statocysts in which heavy otoliths rest upon a sensitive surface and indicate by their positions the orientation of the head.

The vestibular system also contains three semicircular canals, each of which indicates the velocity of the head's rotation in one of three planes. During head turning, the inertia of the fluid in the canals causes it to lag behind the head and to flow into one side or the other of the ampulla, displacing the cupola as it does so.

Movements of the cupola bend hairs of the

hair cells in the crista and, depending upon the direction of movement, either hypopolarize or hyperpolarize the cells.

The receptors fire neurons whose axons form the vestibular branch of the eighth cranial nerve and end mostly in the vestibular nuclei. From there the output goes to motor nuclei in the spinal cord and medulla and to sensory areas in the cerebellum and cortex. There is a particularly strong pathway to the oculomotor nuclei to provide for compensatory eye movements.

The cochlea is a coiled tube divided longitudinally by the basilar membrane, upon which rests the organ of Corti with its sensitive hair cells.

Airborne pressure waves are transmitted to the fluid in the cochlea through the eardrum, a chain of small bones (malleus, incus, and stapes), and windows into and out of the cochlea (the oval and round windows).

Low-frequency waves are able to reach all parts of the cochlea and produce the greatest vibration of the basilar membrane at the apex of the coil, where the membrane is most flexible. High-frequency waves cannot reach the apex, however, because of the inertia of the fluid in the tube, and they must therefore bend the basilar membrane where it is stiffer, near the basal end.

When the basilar membrane vibrates, it displaces the hair cells of the organ of Corti. This displacement generates impulses in bipolar cells of the spiral ganglion, whose axons form the acoustic branch of the eighth cranial nerve.

Because different parts of the basilar membrane are displaced maximally by sounds of different frequencies, the nerves innervating the hair cells in different parts of the organ of Corti have maximum output for sounds of different frequencies.

This tonotopic arrangement is maintained throughout the ascending pathway of the auditory system, and in the cat there are at least four different cortical areas, each with a separate representation of the sound spectrum. There are several other auditory areas without known tonotopical organization.

In general, an increase in the intensity of sound causes an increase in the firing rate of cells in the auditory system and an increase in the number of cells firing, but there are exceptions. Some sensitive fibers become less active at high intensities because of inhibitory feedback.

Corticothalamic participation does not appear to be required for intensity discriminations in animals. There is some doubt whether or not cortical lesions impair loudness discrimination in man.

Two main types of theories have been advanced to explain pitch discrimination. The more satisfactory so far is the place theory, which is based on the differential responses of different points on the basilar membrane to sounds of different frequency. The coarse tuning of the membrane can be improved by subsequent neural processing to provide the required degree of discrimination. Pitch discriminations can be made by animals that lack auditory cortex.

Timbre is a quality of sound that depends upon harmonic content. The ability to discriminate sounds with different timbre is seriously impaired by lesions of the auditory cortex in animals and man. Such impairment suggests that the harmonic analysis is performed at the thalamocortical level.

Cortical lesions also impair the ability to locate the source of a sound, using differences in both time of arrival and intensity of sound at the two ears as directional cues.

Lesions of the trapezoid body prevent the use of time-disparity cues but still permit the animal to locate the sound by loudness differences at the two ears. The main analyzer of the time-disparity cues seems to be the medial superior olivary nucleus; more central areas are able to use loudness cues.

The discrimination of sequences of notes is impaired by lesions in the auditory cortex in animals and man, although the discrimination of single notes, played one after the other at close intervals of time, is not impaired by the same lesions. Probably the storage capacity of the cortex is necessary to prevent interference between the traces of the notes in a sequence.

In man, no doubt because of the functional asymmetry of the cortex, unilateral lesions can produce deficits of auditory discrimination. In almost all cases the deficits are produced by right-hemisphere lesions.

An exception is revealed by an interaural-rivalry test involving verbal material. After ablation of the left temporal lobe patients have difficulty in recalling different sequences of digits that have been presented simultaneously to both ears. When the material consists instead of snatches of music similarly presented, the patients with right temporal-lobe lesions show the greater deficits.

In both cases the material presented to the ear contralateral to the lesion is recalled less well than material presented to the other ear, confirming other indications that the crossed pathway from the ear to the cortex dominates the uncrossed one.

CHAPTER 13

LANGUAGE AND CEREBRAL DOMINANCE

Verbal communication is a uniquely human achievement, which means, among other things, that there are limits to the types of experimental procedure we can use to study its physiological mechanisms. It is true that some animals can imitate human speech sounds (and other sounds also) with astonishing fidelity, but they cannot rearrange the words in conformity with grammatical rules in order to convey new meanings; their performance is not therefore a linguistic one.

Only a few animals have the necessary vocal structures to imitate human speech, but most mammals can learn the meanings of many words or phrases by rote, just as they can learn the meaning of other auditory stimuli. Such understanding does not represent true linguistic communication either. The animal can never learn the rules of order, inflection, and so forth that enable one who understands a language to know immediately upon hearing a new sentence which word represents the actor, which the action, and which the thing acted upon.

It is even possible, if the theory of Liberman and Cooper to be discussed shortly is correct, that most animals do not have invariant perceptions of *phonemes* (elements that make up words) in the way that we do. Sound-spectrographic analysis has shown (see, for example,

Liberman, Harris, Hoffman & Griffith, 1957; Liberman, Delattre & Cooper, 1958) that most consonants cannot be represented by single physical sounds. As will be explained more fully, the sounds that we perceive as "d" in the syllables "dee," "du," "ud," and "eed" are all quite different from one another, and we have no idea whether an animal like the dog hears the sounds veridically (differing according to the accompanying vowel) or as invariant in the same way that we do.

Possibly the closest approach to true linguistic comprehension in infrahuman animals is the ability to transfer a cue from one situation to another. For example, if reward for pressing a bar is withheld in the dark and as a result the animal learns to stop responding in other situations when light is turned off, we may assume that darkness has acquired the general meaning of "no reward," in the same way that certain qualifying words like "not" are used in a language.

Animals are able to communicate with one another quite effectively through gestures and sounds, each with a different stereotyped meaning. In most cases the sign is an innate response to a particular situation, and the reaction of the other animal to the sign is also innately determined. As far as we know at present, no animal other than man has evolved a motor system with the hierarchical complexity necessary to manipulate the order of responses in such a way as to multiply the number of different messages that can be emitted. The porpoise has an unusually rich repertoire of vocalizations, and it has been suggested that some of them may involve syntactical language (Lilly, 1963). There is no satisfactory evidence of such an ability, however, and, if the porpoise or any of its cetacean relatives has a language, we have not been able to decode it or to learn its grammar. Lilly (1965) has paid the bottlenosed dolphin the compliment of trying to teach it English, but if we cannot cope with the dolphins' language (if they have one) it is optimistic to hope that they can learn ours.

In a phylogenetic progression of nervous systems with increasing degrees of motor complexity, the one that can produce speech and writing will certainly rank as the most complex. We may suppose that the effectors of the very simplest systems can be moved in one innately determined order or not at all. The first stage of progress would permit more than one arrangement of effector firing, depending upon some central state like level of excitement (leading perhaps to the alternatives of going forward or backward). With further development, relatively subtle changes of central state acquire the ability to switch control of effectors from one to another of a variety of differently programmed motor patterns, so that the "mood" of the animal may be expressed by different vocalizations, gestures, and other activities.

After the next advance, perhaps, the control no longer requires a change of mood or emotional state; a special part of the nervous system evolves to regulate the switching of motor patterns according to learned requirements. The animal may thus press a lever in one situation and turn a wheel in another. Some birds have performed extraordinary feats of rote learning; for example, a budgerigar learned eight nursery rhymes, along with a great deal of occasional poetry, telephone numbers, and other items. Presumably the bird has one neural state corresponding to the motor sequence that produces "Baa, baa, black sheep," another for "Little Jack Horner," and so on.

At least one further level of complexity is introduced, however, when man speaks · or writes. The movements necessary to produce the individual words may be organized in a stereotyped way, as in the talking birds (though, in fact, certain aspects of a spoken word, like intonation, vary with its position in the sentence and the meaning it conveys), but the word *order* is under the control of yet another neuronal high-speed switching system, which works according to complex learned patterns that we know behaviorally as the rules of grammar. Chomsky (1967) apparently believes that the rules of grammar are not learned, but this claim can be valid only to the extent that everything we learn is dependent upon innate structures and upon the innate ability to learn.

TRANSMISSION AND RECEPTION OF SPEECH

Lashley (1951) has discussed the problem of how stereotyped serial orders, including those for words, might be programmed by the brain, and a simplified but more specific model for this has been outlined by P. M. Milner (1961b). But the mechanisms of grammatical speech are almost too complex to contemplate. Even such relatively mechanical details as how each part of the sentence or word, as it is emitted, erases the underlying neural activity that produced it and clears the way for the next unit to be emitted, a process that seems to be defective in stutterers, is still a complete mystery.

One thing that contributes to the complexity of the production of speech sounds is that they are transmitted not over a single channel but over three or four channels simultaneously. As Liberman, Cooper, Shankweiler, and Studdert-Kennedy (1967) have pointed out, speech can be followed at rates of up to about 30 phonemes per second. Because of the redundancy of most languages (elements not essential for the meaning) it is unlikely that all the phonemes are being used, but even so the rate of information input in normal speech is very high, much higher than the rate at which the nervous system can normally process sequential input.

The explanation for this high efficiency, according to Liberman and his colleagues, is that several information channels are transmitting and receiving in parallel, each carrying information at a more normal rate. This ability is achieved by a process analogous to *multiplexing* in electronic communication. The vocal apparatus includes a number of resonant cavities, each of which can be tuned relatively independently of the others by adjustments of the muscles of the tongue, lips, and face; by opening and closing apertures to the nasal cavity; and so on.

Pulses of air produced by vibration of the vocal cords excite these resonant cavities and produce bands of sound concentrated in different parts of the auditory spectrum, as· shown in the sound spectrogram (Figure 13.1). These different bands are called *formants*, the first formant being that of lowest frequency, the

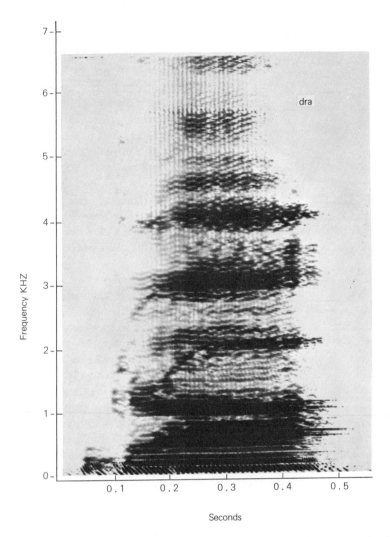

Figure 13.1   Sound spectrogram of the speech sound "dra," showing the multiple-frequency bands, or formants, generated during the pronunciation of the vowel "ah." (Photograph provided by Dr. A. M. Liberman and the Haskins Laboratory.)

second formant that above the first, and so on. The combinations of formants that make up some consonant-vowel pairs are shown in the simplified spectrograms of Figure 13.2. Each formant constitutes a parallel channel of communication that can be varied independently of the others, just as many telephone conversations can be carried along a single telephone line by combining them with carriers of different frequencies and providing suitable filters to separate the different signals at the receiving end (after which the carrier frequencies are removed). The multiplexing of stereophonic

programs by FM radio transmitters is a better analogy, however, because then, as in speech, the multiple signals are recombined after having been received.

Telephone lines are expensive, and telephone systems use multiplexing techniques to reduce the number they must lay, but the nervous system is accustomed to the luxury of many parallel nerve fibers for its connections. It compensates for relatively slow conduction rates by using many paths simultaneously. When one person is speaking to another, however, a bottleneck would be imposed if the

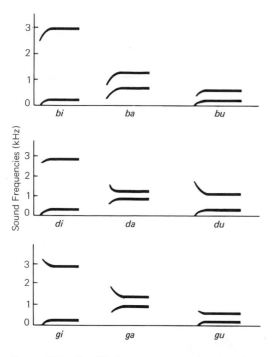

Figure 13.2 Simplified spectrograms showing the first two formants only, for a number of syllables. (After Delattre, Liberman & Cooper, 1955.)

parallel paths had to funnel down to a single one as the information passed between the two nervous systems. The evolution of a simple multiplexing mechanism for speech counteracts to some extent this threatened slowing of transmission rate.

One unsuspected consequence of this process is that phonemes cannot in general stand on their own. It is impossible, for example, to cut a segment from a tape recording of speech that can be used to represent consonants like "d" or

Figure 13.3 Spectrograms of transitions that produce the consonant "d" before different vowels. (After Liberman, 1957.)

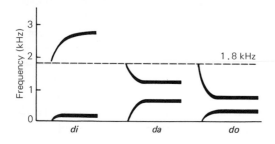

"b." The sound that represents "d" in front of the vowel "a" is quite different from the sound that represents "d" before the vowel "u," as is shown in Figure 13.3. What seems to be invariant about the phoneme "d" is that, just before the vocal cords are activated for the succeeding vowel, the cavity for the second formant is tuned to about 1,800 Hz. The sound one hears as "d" is the rapid slide of the second formant resonance toward the frequency necessary for the vowel, which may be as high as 2,600 Hz in an "ee" sound or as low as 700 Hz in an "oo" vowel sound. When the consonant follows a vowel, the slide of frequency is in the opposite direction, toward 1,800 Hz (Liberman, Ingeman, Lisker, Delattre & Cooper, 1959).

Liberman, Cooper, Shankweiler & Studdert-Kennedy (1967) considered it likely that we perceive these different stimuli as similar because the auditory signals of speech are decoded by the same neural mechanism that generates the sequences of instructions to the vocal muscles. The sounds from the "d" phoneme thus somehow excite the neurons that direct the tongue and mouth muscles to produce a resonant cavity of 1,800 Hz.

The arguments for this theory were presented clearly in the report by Liberman and his colleagues (1967), but the difficulties of testing it are formidable. Recordings from the muscles of some speech organs have been made during speech, in an effort to see whether or not the muscle contractions are invariant for the same phonemes in different contexts. The findings seem generally to agree with the hypothesis, but even if it were absolutely certain that phonemes have invariant representation at the motor level the question of how the sounds are decoded at the receiving end would still be completely open.

One way in which the decoding system might be organized, though this possibility is not made explicit in the 1967 paper cited, is for an association between the activity in the auditory system and that in the motor system to occur during the babbling phase of infant development. Cortical activities that result in the production of the sound "da," for example, when fed to the motor system will overlap in time with another cortical activity evoked by the auditory input from the sound. Similarly, a neural activity resulting in the pronunciation of the syllable "dee" will overlap the auditorily evoked activity of that sound. If we assume that the motor instructions for the consonant are the same in each case, even though we know the resulting sounds to be different because of the influence of the different vowels, the two auditory inputs will both have the opportunity to become associated with the same motor activity. If we further assume that while listening to our own speech we attend only to what is going on in the region of the brain where the speech instructions originate and not to more peripheral parts of the auditory pathway, we would be unaware of the different sounds, perceiving only the invariant speech instructions that they are associated with.

The theory, if it holds at all, must certainly be an oversimplification. A person can distinguish more phonemes than he can pronounce, and the ability to detect a foreign or regional accent does not depend upon the ability to mimic it. There is also reason to believe, as we shall see, that the mechanism for speech production can be quite seriously impaired by brain damage without a corresponding failure in comprehension of speech; but the theory is a challenging one and has already led to some important findings.

LANGUAGE DISTURBANCES RESULTING FROM BRAIN LESIONS

In view of the number of brain functions that are called upon in the production and comprehension of language, it is surprising that verbal behavior is not seriously impaired by any cortical disturbance, however slight, but the fact is that only part of one hemisphere, usually the left, appears to be indispensable.

The absence of functional symmetry in the human brain has already been remarked in connection with perception. We saw in Chapters 11 and 12 that the perception and retention of music, geometrical forms, and the like are impaired more by damage to the right hemi-

sphere than to the left and that the reverse is true of the perception and learning of verbal material.

The association of the left hemisphere with speech was probably first suspected by Dax, who in 1836 noted in a paper (which he wrote but did not present or publish) that speech disorders frequently accompanied paralysis of the right side of the body resulting from brain damage but were rarely found in patients with paralysis of the left side. Twenty-five years later, Broca described two patients who had lost almost all speech before they died and whose brains he had subsequently examined. He found that both brains had sustained multiple lesions but that there was a common area of damage in the third frontal convolution of the left hemisphere (Figure 13.4). Although the evidence was really quite inadequate, Broca (1861) concluded that this area controlled speech. Subsequent findings have confirmed that this part of the frontal lobe is indeed involved in verbal behavior, and it is now known as "Broca's area."

Broca suggested several possible reasons for loss of language ability (*aphasia*) after a brain lesion. One was that the patient had lost his ability to ideate or form concepts; a second was that he could no longer form the connections between his concepts and the words for them; and a third was that, although the patient could think of the words, he could not connect them to the motor system. It now appears that one or another of these mechanisms may predominate in different patients.

Figure 13.4 The left hemisphere of a human cortex, showing some areas that have been implicated in language behavior. (After Penfield & Roberts, 1959.)

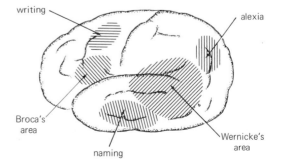

writing

alexia

Broca's area

naming

Wernicke's area

Ogle (1867) discovered a patient who could write but could not speak, suggesting that in some cases, at least, motor involvement is the most important factor. Bastian (1882) saw many aphasic patients, some of whom were "word blind" or "word deaf," that is, could see objects and had no disturbance of speech yet could not read (*alexia*) or could hear sounds but could not understand speech. These perceptual deficits of language are sometimes called *receptive aphasias*. Patients who can understand speech but cannot produce it are said to have *expressive aphasia*.

Wernicke (1874) concluded that word deafness was produced by lesions in the posterior part of the first temporal convolution (Figure 13.4). He suggested also that Broca's area was concerned with the movements necessary for speech and that there was a writing center in the second frontal convolution just anterior to the motor area for the hand (Figure 13.4), a view shared by Exner, whose name is sometimes attached to that area. Dejerine (1914) thought he had evidence that word blindness was caused by lesions in the angular gyrus of the parietal lobe, and he later decided that this area was another writing center.

Many other papers appeared toward the end of the nineteenth century and early in the twentieth claiming various localizations for particular aspects of language, in most cases with very tenuous or no anatomical justification. More systematic study has since made it apparent that, although aphasia (or, more accurately, *dysphasia*, as "aphasia" means total loss of language ability) manifests itself in various forms, pure examples of any of these forms are extremely rare, and some may not exist at all.

Types of Dysphasia

Despite the paucity of pure examples, it is still convenient for descriptive purposes to classify the different manifestations of dysphasia. The two basic categories of expressive and receptive aphasia have already been mentioned. The former includes difficulties in speaking or writing, the latter difficulties in reading or understanding the spoken word.

Speech disturbances can result from damage to the muscles or peripheral nerves connected to the tongue, the vocal cords, and so on or from lesions in the motor centers of the medulla. A severe lesion completely precludes speech; milder lesions may produce speech that is thick or slurred, uncontrolled in loudness or intonation, or disturbed in timing. This complex of symptoms is known as *dysarthria*. When it is caused by peripheral lesions it is not of great interest to the psychologist, but similar symptoms can be caused by cortical lesions, in which case they are usually accompanied by other language disturbances.

Stuttering is another form of expressive speech disturbance that sometimes results from brain lesions. It is sufficiently common among the normal population to require no description.

Aphasic anarthria is complete loss of the ability to speak in the absence of any muscular weakness of the speech apparatus and with preservation of the ability to write and to understand speech and writing. This impairment is sometimes called *aphemia* or "word dumbness," but it probably never occurs in pure form.

Verbal aphasia is the inability to communicate either by speech or writing, though sometimes simple ideas can be conveyed by gestures or by nonverbal vocalizations. It is sometimes called "Broca's aphasia" because it was the form most apparent in the patients whom he studied. His patient Leborgne, for example, was able to utter only "tan" and "Sacré nom de Dieu." Frequently a patient is able to pronounce nothing but his name or a common word like "no" or "yes." The preservation of a swear word or profane phrase by the patient is not uncommon. After a time such patients often learn to communicate many meanings with whatever words or pseudowords are left to them, through changes in stress, intonation, and the like, somewhat after the fashion of an intelligent dog. They are often assumed to be able to understand what is said to them because they obey simple commands, but in most cases their comprehension of complex verbal material is undoubtedly impaired.

In less severe cases the patient may have a fair vocabulary, but some words are mispronounced. Usually the patient is at least partly aware that the words are not right and may show irritation at not being able to produce the sounds intended. Lenneberg (1967, p. 195) quoted a recording of a woman who had been an accomplished speaker before suffering a stroke:

I am taking —ah—Sherriks ah Sherring's mixture (laugh). It's easier for me to—stalk—talk staccato and breaking up each word—into sentences—breaking up sentences into words provided they have ah—not many syllables. Ah, syllable is hard.—Precise words that I have trouble with are Republican and Epics—Epis—copalian.

Reversals of order at all levels are conspicuous in this quotation. Other patients are unable to count in sequence or to give the days of the week and the like in the correct order.

Writing may be similarly affected. The patient makes spelling mistakes, leaves words out, and so on. Again he may recognize that he has made mistakes and try, usually unsuccessfully, to correct them. B. Milner, Branch & Rasmussen (1964) illustrated this problem with a patient's note to a member of the hospital staff (Figure 13.5).

In some forms of dysphasia grammatical mistakes occur, as in Head's *syntactical aphasia* (1926). An example given by Brain (1961) was "I haven't been headache troubled not for a long time." Another example, this time in writing, from Penfield and Roberts (1959) was a patient's attempt to describe his operation:

Well, I thought thing I am going to the tell is about my operation and it is not about all I can tell is about the preparation the had was always the V time was when they had me to get ready that is they shaved off all my hair was and a few odd parts of pencil they pf quive me in the fanny.

Another difficulty that often accompanies other expressive dysphasias is the unavailability of certain words to describe objects, which is called *nominal aphasia*. All of us suffer from this difficulty to some extent, especially when we are working near the limits of our vocabulary or making introductions, but in severe nominal dysphasia the patient may be unable to name such common objects as a pen, scissors, comb, and so on. Sometimes he attempts a circumlocution. A shoe may be described as

Figure 13.5 A note from a dysphasic patient. (From B. Milner, Branch & Rasmussen, 1964.)

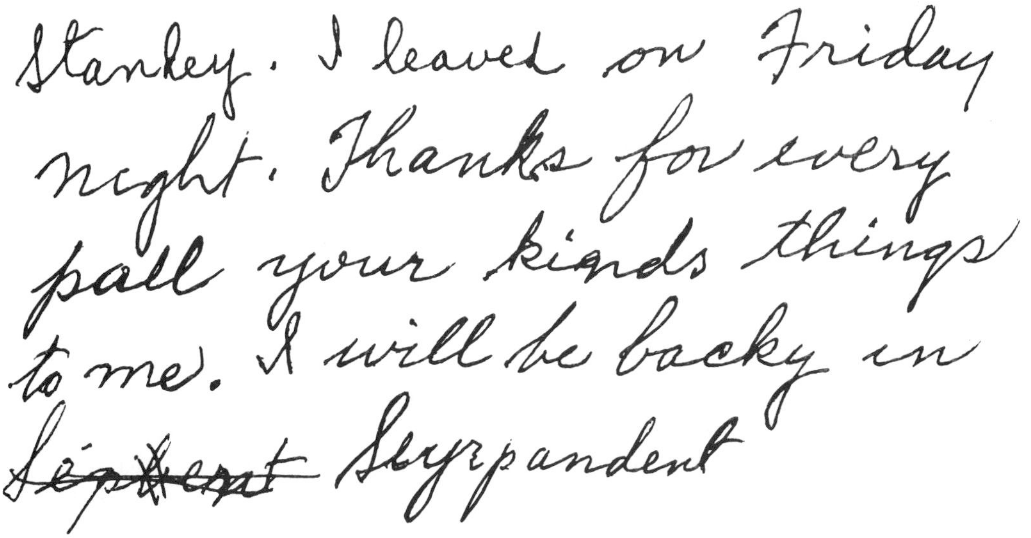

something to put one's foot in. In one case mentioned by Penfield and Roberts, a comb elicited the response "I comb my hair," but the patient still could not give the noun. This differential availability of nouns and verbs, even when they have identical forms, is interesting to students of linguistics.

Another example of naming difficulties, taken from Brain (1961), was that of a man asked to name a bunch of keys. He responded, "Indication of measurement of piece of apparatus or intimating the cost of apparatus in various forms." Production of unintelligible statements of this sort is called *jargon aphasia*. Sometimes the patient will chatter for long periods, making no sense and perhaps not even producing recognizable words.

A difficulty that often complicates nominal aphasia is *perseveration*. A patient may correctly name a pen at the beginning of a test session and then call everything that he is subsequently shown "a pen." The example of jargon given probably involved some perseveration, as the patient had been shown a tape measure just before being shown the bunch of keys.

Brain gave another example, in which the patient called a pair of scissors a "nail-file." When the word "scissors" was suggested to him, he said: "Yes, that's it! Of course it is not a nail-file, it's a nail-file." He did not recognize his mistake. Sometimes in nominal aphasia the word substituted for the proper word has a similar sound; for example, a comb may be called a "camel." Many patients suffering from the types of dysphasia described here also have obvious receptive dysphasia.

As previously mentioned, pure word deafness involves loss of meaning of spoken language, with retention of normal ability to read, write, and speak. A patient cannot repeat what is said to him or obey commands but is otherwise normal. A patient considered by Hemphill and Stengel (1940) to be suffering from word deafness described his state: "Voice comes but no words, I can hear, sounds come, but words don't separate. There is no trouble at all with sound. Sounds come, I can hear, but I cannot understand it." Judging from this quotation, it seems likely that there was at least a suggestion

of an expressive disorder also present in this patient, but this disorder was clearly not of the same magnitude as was his comprehension difficulty.

Brain mentioned a patient who suffered transient dysphasia during migraine headaches. During his attacks he was under the impression that he was speaking nonsense, though he was, in fact, speaking quite sensibly.

Alexia, or the inability to read, accompanied by no other disturbance of vision or of comprehension of the spoken word, was mentioned earlier in this chapter. *Dyslexia* is a less severe disturbance of reading ability.

This list by no means exhausts the different types of dysphasia that have been described by investigators in this field, but, as is probably clear from the examples given, the types tend to merge into one another. Most of these examples may be taken as illustrating more than one dysphasic phenomenon.

Cortical Localization of Lesions Resulting in Dysphasias

Hécaen and Angelergues (1964) attempted to rate a series of 214 patients with lesions in different parts of the left hemisphere on the severity of their disorders of articulation, fluency, comprehension, naming ability, ability to repeat spoken sentences, reading, and writing. Their conclusions, representative of those arrived at by many contemporary investigators, were that lesions of only one of the classical speech areas (Figure 13.4) produced relatively mild residual dysphasic symptoms, lesions in the posterior temporal and parietal areas being more disabling than those in anterior areas. Several cases have been reported in which complete removal of Broca's area produced only transient dysphasia.

Frontal-lobe or posterior lesions can result in difficulties either of speech articulation, or writing, or both. Naming difficulties also result from lesions of any of the speech areas but occur most frequently after injury to the temporal lobe. Comprehension of spoken or written language does seem to be localized in the more posterior areas as a rule; it is very rarely disturbed after lesions of the frontal speech areas.

Hécaen and Angelergues (1964) found that after larger lesions, involving more than one area, the dysphasias were more severe and deficits of many language components occurred. In general, the relationship between the locus of the lesion and the type of dysfunction was no more clear-cut than after smaller lesions, a conclusion previously arrived at by Weisenberg and McBride (1935) and others. Nevertheless, occasional patients do turn up with remarkably specific dysphasias, similar to some of those described in the classical literature.

One result of the increased use of surgical treatment of human brain injury and disease has been to make possible the study of effects upon verbal behavior of electrical stimulation of exposed cortex. A surgeon stimulates the brain during an operation for several reasons, one of the most important being to plot the speech areas so that the surgical lesion will not encroach upon them unnecessarily.

Electrical stimulation at moderate frequencies (usually about 60 Hz) and intensities appears to prevent normal functioning in the cortex near the electrode, probably by inducing an unnatural firing pattern in it. If the cortex in that region is necessary for speech, the patient will reveal some form of speech disturbance during stimulation.

Stimulation produces much the same types of dysphasic phenomena as lesions; it was therefore hoped that the data collected during brain operations could be used to arrive at a much more accurate picture of the functions of the various speech areas than had been obtained from postmortem examination of the brains of dysphasic patients. With stimulation, many points can be sampled in each patient, and the points can be accurately localized.

As Penfield and Roberts (1959) discovered after analyzing many such data, however, the stimulation technique merely confirmed what had been suspected on the basis of lesion analysis: There is a great deal of overlap in the functions of the different speech areas. The dysphasias resulting from stimulation were often quite specific, but there was little tendency for one type to appear exclusively or even

predominantly in response to stimulation in a particular area (Figure 13.6). It is possible, however, that somewhat more evidence of a differentiation between expressive and receptive areas might have been found if more complete testing had been possible. Very often the conditions of the operation did not permit sufficiently thorough testing to warrant firm negative conclusions.

Penfield and Roberts classified the language difficulties produced during stimulation as vocalizations (grunts and vowel sounds—stimulation has never been known to produce involuntary speech), slurring or hesitation, stuttering, difficulties in counting (the patients were asked to count, and then stimulation was applied), inability to name common objects, misnaming of such objects, and complete arrest of speech. Ability to comprehend spoken language or to read during stimulation was inadequately sampled.

Apart from vocalization, which was obtained primarily from stimulation of the motor cortex of either hemisphere, maps of the stimulation points at which the various effects were obtained do not differ very much from one another. They all correspond closely to the known speech areas (Figure 13.6).

Careful psychological testing of verbal ability usually reveals subtler deficits than can be detected by routine neurological examination like

Figure 13.6 A lateral view of the left hemisphere, showing points at which electrical stimulation produces repetition (dots) or naming difficulties (lines) without harming the ability to speak. (After Penfield & Roberts, 1959.)

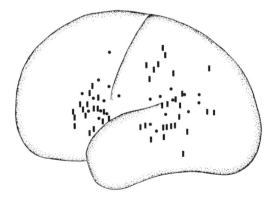

that just described, in which the patient is asked to repeat words or sentences, name objects, respond to verbal or written commands, read, write, and so on. Luria (1964) was among the first to test the idea that interference with the complex decoding mechanism implied by the theory of Liberman and his colleagues (1967) (see discussion earlier in this chapter) was a major cause of receptive dysphasia. In patients who had no impairment in the hearing of pure sounds but who could not understand speech, Luria thought that the auditory system might be incapable of resolving the rapid changes of frequency occurring during formant transitions, which would make the discrimination of consonants difficult or impossible. His tests showed that patients with lesions of the posterior temporal lobe of the dominant hemisphere for speech were impaired on consonant discriminations.

Another indication that the decoding of formant transitions involves the speech areas of the brain to a greater extent than does the decoding of other sounds like vowels has been provided by Shankweiler and Studdert-Kennedy (1967). It will be remembered that Doreen Kimura (1961) showed, in her adaptation of the Broadbent test, that when different stimuli were fed simultaneously into the two ears each signal was dealt with preferentially by the contralateral hemisphere (see "Interaural Rivalry in Man," Chapter 12). Words presented to the right ear thus reached the speech areas more directly than did words presented to the left ear. Shankweiler and Studdert-Kennedy found that in this test, syllables differing only in their vowels were recognized equally well through either ear but that syllables differing in their consonants had a distinct advantage when they arrived at the right ear.

Another type of language disability described by Luria (1964) was what he called *dynamic aphasia*, in which the patient could speak accurately enough but was incapable of making spontaneous statements of more than a few words. Milner (1964) has also remarked upon the absence of spontaneous speech in some otherwise nondysphasic patients and has quantified the impairment, using the Thurstone

Word-Fluency Test. In one part of the test the subject had to write down in five minutes as many words beginning with a certain letter as he could think of. There were other, similar parts to the test. Patients with lesions anterior to Broca's area in the dominant frontal lobe showed marked impairment on this test. The same patients were also very taciturn in everyday life.

There is unusually good evidence of the localization of the word-fluency deficit, as it can be "doubly dissociated" from the impairment of verbal learning. V. Meyer and Yates (1955) and B. Milner (1958, 1967) found that patients with left temporal lobectomies were impaired on such verbal-learning tasks as recalling stories and paired-associate learning. Meyer and Yates considered this impairment to be an auditory loss, but B. Milner (1967) has shown that it was equally severe when words were presented visually. The evidence for double dissociation is that patients with temporal lobectomies whose verbal learning is impaired are completely normal on the word-fluency test and that patients with frontal-lobe lesions whose fluency is impaired have completely normal verbal-learning scores.

CEREBRAL DOMINANCE AND HANDEDNESS

Dysphasic symptoms and interference with speech by brain stimulation at operation present opportunities for studying the relationship between the laterality of speech and handedness, a subject shrouded in controversy and misunderstanding. At one time it was assumed that in right-handers the left hemisphere was dominant for motor activity, speech, perception; almost everything in fact, and that in left-handers the dominance was the opposite.

We have already had occasion to note that many nonverbal functions are carried out more efficiently by the hemisphere not dominant for speech. The persistence of the idea that the right hemisphere is usually dominant for speech in left-handers is a classical example of how scientists can neglect data that do not conform to current theory or to common sense.

As late as 1935 Weisenberg and McBride

found very few exceptions to the rule that dominance for speech was the same as that for motor activity. The view was hardly challenged by anyone until Humphrey and Zangwill (1952) made a careful study of ten case histories of left-handed patients, five with injuries in the right hemisphere and five with injuries in the left hemisphere. Those with left-hemisphere injuries had the greater incidence of linguistic deficits, but four of those with right-sided injuries also had some dysphasia. The investigators concluded that the left hemisphere is still most important for speech in left-handers but that there is reason to believe their speech is not as strongly lateralized as is that of right-handers, a conclusion that further research has strengthened. It has been suggested that this finding results from the fact that left-handers (including most of those in the study) used to be forced to write with their right hands. Humphrey and Zangwill pointed out that there should then be an increase in "right-brainedness" among younger left-handers, as the practice of forcing such children to become right-handers has fallen into disrepute. This prediction has not been borne out, however; in the more recent studies to be reported here there was an even lower proportion of right-brained left-handers than in the earlier literature, presumably because of better experimental design and not because of any real change in the population.

One study of this problem, in which a large enough series of patients was used to allow statistically valid conclusions, was that of Penfield and Roberts (1959). Transient dysphasias of varying degrees of severity are likely to develop following brain operations if the borders of the lesions are anywhere near a speech area. Such dysphasias are believed to result from swelling and irritation of the tissue around the lesions during the first few days of recovery. Such transient dysphasias are less common nowadays because the patients are given cortisone to prevent *edema* (loss of fluid by the cells), but the data used by Penfield and Roberts came from patients operated upon before this refinement was introduced.

These investigators were able to demonstrate

transient speech disturbances in roughly 70 per cent of their right-handers operated upon in the left hemisphere and in only 0.4 per cent of those operated upon in the right hemisphere. In left-handers, the speech of 38 per cent was disturbed after operations on the left hemisphere and the speech of 9 per cent after operations on the right hemisphere. The remaining patients had no postoperative dysphasias; the operations were presumed to have been so far removed from the speech areas (or to have produced so little edema) that no disturbance ensued, but the alternative possibility remains that speech was bilaterally represented in some of these patients and that the undamaged side was able to maintain speech during the dysfunctioning of the side operated upon.

The patients in this sample were not normal people, of course. Had they not all suffered brain injury or disease, they would not have been on the operating table. It is considered likely that in those patients in whom such injuries occurred during birth (a relatively common cause of focal epilepsy) or soon afterward, both handedness and the laterality of speech may have been influenced by the injury. Some left-handers with speech in the right hemisphere may thus have acquired both these characteristics as a result of damage to the left hemisphere at an early age. When patients with clinical evidence of left-hemisphere injury suffered before the age of two years were eliminated from the sample, the chance of dysphasia after a left-hemisphere operation was found to be nearly the same for right- and left-handers, but left-handers still had a much greater chance than did right-handers of becoming dysphasic after a right-hemisphere operation. The figures cannot be considered as representative of the general population, but they do suggest the hazards of attempting to predict the dominant hemisphere for speech in left-handed subjects.

B. Milner, Branch & Rasmussen (1964, 1966) used a different technique to investigate the same problem. It is possible to anesthetize one hemisphere, leaving the other functioning almost normally, by rapidly injecting a fast-acting barbiturate (usually *Sodium Amytal*) into the *carotid artery* (which supplies blood to a large part of the brain) of that side (Wada, 1949). The patient abruptly loses all motor power in his contralateral limbs, a sign used to determine the effectiveness of the anesthetic.

This procedure is sometimes carried out on patients about to have brain operations, in order to determine beforehand the possible effects of a unilateral ablation on memory or speech. When the injection is made in the dominant side for speech, the patient is rendered aphasic for a few minutes, thus providing information on the laterality of his speech.

When, for reasons mentioned earlier, patients offering clinical evidence of early brain damage were eliminated from the sample, Milner and her colleagues' results were as shown in Table 13.1.

High as it is, the number of right-handed patients with speech on the left is probably lower than in the normal population because the test was given mainly to patients suspected on the basis of their clinical history of having atypical cortical representation of speech. The figures for left-handers may also be unrepresentative, but even of those patients (excluded from the table) who showed evidence of early damage to the left hemisphere, about a third still had speech localized there. It seems therefore that the normal left-hander is much more likely to have speech on the left, like nearly everybody else, than to have it on the right. At the same time, his chance of having speech on the right is much higher than is that of the normal right-hander.

It is interesting that about 13 per cent of the ambidextrous and left-handed patients showed milder signs of dysphasia than usual from in-

jections of Sodium Amytal into either corotid and that in these cases the dysphasia from each side was of roughly the same intensity. The presence of clearly lateralized neurological signs (for example, loss of tone in the contralateral limbs) indicated that the target hemisphere was adequately anesthetized and that there was no significant leak of anesthetic from one side of the brain to the other. It offered a strong indication, therefore, that these ten patients (see Table 13.1) have some representation of speech in both hemispheres. Only one right-handed patient showed evidence of bilateral speech representation.

In about half the bilateral patients it was noted that there was a disturbance of naming ability when one hemisphere was anesthetized and a disturbance of ability to count, recite the days of the week, and to perform other serial tasks when the other hemisphere was anesthetized. One such patient, who had difficulty naming objects after a left-carotid injection and made mistakes in serial tasks after right-carotid injection (the more frequent pattern) had her right parietal lobe removed; afterward she had difficulty with counting, spelling, and other serial tasks but none with naming.

The investigators suggested that left-handed and ambidextrous people may have less strongly lateralized speech mechanisms than do right-handed people, a conclusion previously arrived at by Humphrey and Zangwill (1952) on much more slender evidence. Subirana (1958) also found that the prognosis for recovery from dysphasia after a stroke was much better for left-handed people than for right-handers. The implication is that in some left-handers the undamaged hemisphere is more

TABLE 13.1 Number of Patients with Speech Disturbed by Amytal Injections into Right and Left Carotids

			SPEECH	
	N	Left	Bilateral	Right
Right-handers	95	87	1	7
Left-handers and ambidextrous	74	51	10	13

able to perform the speech functions previously carried out by the damaged hemisphere than is true with most right-handers.

During the last few years another surgical technique for the treatment of some types of epilepsy has been developed, involving the sectioning of the corpus callosum, anterior and hippocampal commissures, and sometimes the *massa intermedia* (midline thalamic nuclei). The operation produces subjects whose hemispheres have been isolated from each other except through the lower brainstem, permitting the functions of each hemisphere to be investigated separately through suitable testing.

Sperry and Gazzaniga (1967) have devised various ingenious tests for these patients, and their results are of great interest in connection with the localization of speech. Because the optic chiasm is intact, visual stimuli pass from each eye to both hemispheres, but the right visual field is projected only to the left occipital lobe, and the left field is projected only to the right occipital lobe. If an image is flashed into one or the other field and removed before an eye movement can take place, visual information can be presented to one or the other of the separated hemispheres. Similarly, tactual information from the left hand goes only to the right hemisphere and from the right hand only to the left hemisphere.

Sperry and Gazzaniga made use of these anatomical facts in their tests, which were mostly performed in an apparatus similar to that shown in Figure 13.7. When a picture is flashed on the right side of the screen the patient can immediately tell the experimenter what it was, but he can say nothing about a picture flashed on the left side of the screen

Figure 13.7 An apparatus for testing patients with sectioned corpus callosum. Words or pictures can be flashed tachistoscopically on either the left or the right side of the screen (with a central fixation point), and objects can be placed upon the table out of sight of the subject. (From Sperry & Gazzaniga, 1967.)

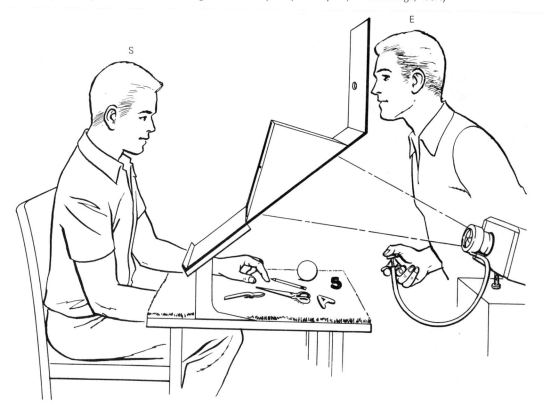

except that there was a flash. Similarly, he can tell what object has been placed in his right hand, but he cannot tell what is in his left hand. In fact, he can report nothing about stimuli presented to his left side and appears at first to have a serious sensory impairment on that side. An experienced neurologist actually diagnosed such an impairment in one of these patients after careful neurological testing.

When we take into account the fact that the right hemisphere has no speech mechanism, however, another explanation is apparent. The right hemisphere "knows" what it has seen or felt but cannot verbalize the information. When it is provided with other means of communication, this explanation proves to be correct.

An amusing, but not very rigorous, way to demonstrate that the right hemisphere can see is to flash a picture of an emotionally arousing subject, like a nude girl, in the left field. The patient then gives an unmistakable emotional response, though he (or she) is still unable to tell the experimenter what caused it. A more conclusive demonstration is to have the patient pick out an object similar to one that has been flashed in his left field from a collection of objects placed out of sight behind a curtain. He can do so but only with his left hand. If he is forced to use his right hand, he performs at chance level. After he has located the object he is still not able to tell what it is unless he is also allowed to feel it with his right hand.

This finding is what we might expect on the basis of what is already known about speech and the connections of the sensory systems; what is surprising in these experiments is that the patient can also pick out an object the *name* of which has been flashed on the left screen. He can also find with his left hand any object named by the experimenter, even when the name is not given in a straightforward way but by a description like "writing instrument" for a pen, "inserted in slot machines" for a coin, and so on. Of course, the verbal information goes to both hemispheres because the sound goes to both ears (even if the words were presented to the left ear only, the signals would be projected to both hemispheres because of the merging of the auditory pathways in the brain-

stem), but the left hemisphere, although it knows what is to be sought, cannot tell the right when the correct object has been found because it has no idea what object the left hand is holding at any time.

These and other experiments show quite conclusively, therefore, that the right hemisphere can mediate the comprehension of simple speech and writing; the very fact that it "understands" the instructions for the tests seems to make this conclusion unavoidable. Tests have also shown that patients can even spell simple words like "hat" with large cut-out letters manipulated out of sight by the left hand.

These abilities should not surprise us unduly if we consider that many mammals can understand simple commands, learn their names, and the like. It would, in fact, be more surprising if the right hemisphere of a human being turned out to be less intelligent than that of a dog or a monkey. What is puzzling about these results is the difficulty of reconciling them with the fact that many patients suffer receptive aphasias (word deafness or alexia) after lesions confined, as far as can be determined, to the left hemisphere. Possibly the presence of the remaining part of the damaged hemisphere has an inhibitory or interfering effect on the intact hemisphere when the commissural fibers are intact.

Each hemisphere can control the motor system of both sides through the interaction of the motor paths in the brainstem and spinal cord. If the patient with separated hemispheres is allowed to see what he is doing he can write with his left hand, though not very well. Facial grimaces and gestures can also be controlled from either hemisphere, and the patient will assume an expression of irritation or disgust if one side is making errors when the other side knows the correct answer but cannot communicate it. Such cues can be used to reach the correct answer through a process of trial and error in some cases if the patient is allowed enough time.

These experiments raise intriguing philosophical questions about the definition of the self. In many ways the patient with the split brain seems to be two people, one dumb but not unintelligent and both engaged in competition for control of a single motor system. The casual observer may regard the nonspeaking half as having no independent identity because it cannot express its personality in words, but more thorough study reveals that it has a will of its own and that it can do some things better than the speaking half.

Summary

Human beings are the only animals we know of that have developed the use of grammatical language as a means of communicating with one another. Ability to mimic speech obviously does not constitute linguistic ability (though the performances of some birds reflect remarkable development of neural mechanisms for the storing and emission of long sequences of motor activity), nor does the ability of some animals to respond appropriately to verbal cues; such performance shows merely that the animal can learn to discriminate certain features of the stimulus.

The infinite variety of messages that can be conveyed through language depends upon the adoption by those using it of common names for things and actions and of common ways to modify such names (through inflections, word order, and the like), so that each can carry a number of meanings.

Speech is by far the most efficient form of communication so far evolved by animals. Writing and typing are not only slower but are also more difficult to learn, as is reading. This efficiency seems strange, for it is easier to make a machine that will decode writing than to make one that will decode speech, suggesting perhaps that human beings possess complex, largely innate mechanisms for the production and analysis of speech.

The results of accidental or surgical interference with brain functioning also indicate that part of the brain is specialized for language ability. In most people, disturbance of language (dysphasia) follows damage to the lateral surface of the left hemisphere, especially in the region of the third frontal convolution (Broca's area) and the posterior temporoparietal area (Wernicke's area). Frontal lesions tend to produce deficits in speech production (expressive dysphasia), and posterior lesions tend to produce difficulties in comprehension (receptive dysphasia), but the distinction is far from clear-cut. Lesions or electrical stimulation in or near any part of the speech system are likely to produce any of a number of types of dysphasia or, more often, several types at once.

These varieties include impairment of speech (dysarthria), loss of speech and writing ability (verbal aphasia), and difficulties with grammar (syntactical dysphasia) or with finding names (nominal dysphasia). In some instances combinations of these difficulties produce jargon aphasia; the problem may also be aggravated by a tendency to perseverate. Most dysphasic patients have further disturbances of language comprehension, and in a few such disturbances are the major symptom. Alexia is the inability to read, and incomprehensibility of speech to the patient is called "word deafness."

A few impairments of language ability do seem to be more distinctly localized than most of the types just listed. Luria's "dynamic aphasia," in which the patient has reduced spontaneous speech and poor word fluency, seems to be caused by injury to the frontal lobe (on the side dominant for speech). Verbal-learning deficits result from dominant temporal-lobe, but not from frontal-lobe, lesions.

Investigations during the last ten or twenty years have shown that left-handedness does not necessarily indicate that the right hemisphere is dominant for speech. The left hemispheres of most left-handers and ambidextrous people and almost all right-handers are dominant for speech. Evidence is accumulating to indicate that the lateralization of speech is less complete in left-handers, however, and some of them have been shown to have speech mechanisms roughly equally divided between the two hemispheres.

Patients with split brains (that is, in whom the corpus callosum and other forebrain commissures have been sectioned) provide interesting data on lateralization of language. It has been shown that these patients cannot make any sort of verbal report about stimuli applied to their left side (and thus projected to their right hemisphere), but they are able to understand simple phrases presented either visually or auditorily to the right hemisphere. The right hemisphere can even spell simple words under conditions in which participation by the left hemisphere is impossible.

It is not clear how these abilities of the right hemisphere can be reconciled with the receptive dysphasias resulting from left-hemisphere lesions. Possibly, in the normal person or one whose left hemisphere is damaged, the language functions of the right hemisphere are inhibited or interfered with by activity of the intact part of the left hemisphere transmitted through the commissures.

PART FOUR

ALERTING MECHANISMS

Organisms are not passive objects upon which stimuli impinge to produce behavior; the activity of the nervous system of most animals is in a state of constant flux, and the fate of a stimulus is largely determined by the pattern that happens to be present in the nervous system when it arrives.

When an animal is asleep it is very insensitive to most stimuli. Not that the brain is inactive; cortical cells may be as active in sleep as during waking. We also know from electrographic recording that afferent impulses reach the cortex during sleep, but the pattern of cerebral firing is such that very little input is stored at that time and the motor system has a very high threshold. At least two distinct phases of sleep exist in the mammal, but as yet we can only guess what function either of them serves and how they are normally induced. Some findings and speculations about these states are presented in Chapter 14.

When the animal is awake the situation is more complex. The waking animal responds to some of the stimuli that excite its sense organs, but most of these stimuli still produce no more effect than they did when the animal was asleep. This fact is often neglected by experimental psychologists because we are very skillful at manipulating conditions so that our subjects (human or otherwise) respond to the stimuli that we intend them to respond to. Again we must assume that, unless the pattern of brain activity is propitious, an input is not stored and produces no response.

Several factors influence the probability that a particular stimulus will be used. One is the motivational state of the subject, which may be determined by a primitive drive like hunger or sex or by a more sophisticated drive like a desire to solve a problem. Another factor is the familiarity or unfamiliarity of the stimulus; repeated stimuli eventually fail to attract attention. Perhaps the most important determining factor is what is currently being perceived. There is continuity of attention most of the time, so that a person who is reading will tend to go on reading, a person who is watching a play continues to watch the play, and so on. This continuity tends to be overlooked because investigators of attention are usually more interested in the transitions from one state to another than in the persistence of a particular state.

Much of the neurophysiological research on attention has been based on the idea that the neglected input never passes beyond the first relay point on the sensory path. The results of some experiments may even appear to support this hypothesis, but the methodology has often been very poor and the findings of doubtful validity. On the other hand, it seems logical that the higher levels of the central nervous system must have access to as much information about the environment as possible in order to make the best possible adjustment to it. Furthermore, there is no lack of experimental evidence that far more information reaches the perceptual system than we are immediately conscious of or able to speak about.

The study of attention by physiological methods is fraught with difficulties, but perhaps more progress would be made if investigators were to abandon the idea that selection or filtering is carried out in the sensory pathways and were to entertain instead the hypothesis that the process is a consequence of competition among central processes for control of the motor system, which can deal with only one response sequence at a time. In Chapter 15 these problems and possibilities will be discussed more fully.

CHAPTER 14

SLEEP
AND
AROUSAL

EARLY THEORIES OF SLEEP

It seems likely that sleeping has stirred the curiosity of our ancestors from the earliest times. The contrast between sleep and waking must have led the more articulate among them to speculate about consciousness, and it seems likely that the resemblance between sleep and death, combined with the phenomenon of dreaming, did much to mold primitive ideas about mortality and the afterlife. It is easy to see how, once the idea of a spirit or soul as the conscious part of the individual arose, primitive animists would consider sleep and death as the absence, temporary or permanent, of this part. One idea that persisted into historical times was that during sleep the spirit left the body to frolic on its own, thus accounting for dreams.

Since spirits have been banished from theories of body functioning and more mechanistic explanations have been sought, other theories of sleep have been proposed. One that was popular for a time was that the body, including the nervous system, "ran down" or became worn out after a certain amount of activity and had to recover during a period of quiescence. Exhaustion was considered by some to be caused by the accumulation of toxins produced by muscular and nervous activity. For example, Legendre and Piéron (1912) reported reversible changes in the inclusion bodies of cortical cells in dogs kept awake for a week or more; they also found that cerebrospinal fluid from such a dog, injected into the fourth ventricle of a rested dog, would induce in the recipient an overwhelming desire to sleep.

Another theory was that the natural, undisturbed state of the brain was sleep and that sensory input was necessary to maintain wakefulness. Strümpell (1877), who attributed the theory to Pflüger, cited as support the example of a patient who was completely lacking in somatic sensibility and whose only channels of sensory input were one ear and one eye. When those channels were shut off, the man invariably fell asleep in two or three minutes and could be awakened only by removing the blindfold or earplug. It would be unwise to make much of this evidence, however, as the patient probably had serious abnormalities of the nervous system, in addition to those that deprived him of most of his senses.

The theory that attributes sleep to fatigue does not explain satisfactorily why people who sit around doing nothing all day do not sleep significantly less than do those who engage in strenuous physical, or even mental, work. The theory that input is necessary to maintain wakefulness founders on the opposite problem. A combination of the two theories has been proposed as a way to overcome these objections. This combination postulates that, during waking, the brain becomes progressively fatigued so that more and more intense sensory stimulation is necessary to maintain arousal. If the sensory input cannot overcome the increased threshold at any time, the animal falls asleep, and a further increase in the arousal threshold automatically ensues. During sleep, however, there is a gradual recovery of brain cells so that the arousal threshold is reduced and eventually a small stimulus can wake the animal. Once awake, a further sudden reduction in the arousal threshold takes place so that the animal stays awake for a considerable time.

This type of theory is sometimes called a "passive" theory of sleep, because it suggests that the brain must be driven into activity by external stimuli. An alternative theory suggests that the brain is normally active but that there is an inhibitory system that from time to time depresses the parts required for conscious behavior and thus brings about sleep. This theory is the "active" theory of sleep.

Brown-Séquard (1889) argued for an active theory on the grounds, first, that certain parts of the brain were more active during sleep than waking and, second, that hypnosis implied inhibition of active intellectual processes. Pavlov (1927) was led to a similar conclusion by his observations that sleep appeared during experiments on conditioned inhibition. He proposed that sleep resulted from cortical inhibition spreading from certain inhibitory centers. Economo (1918) postulated a "sleep center" on the basis of clinical observations of patients with sleep disturbances, and, also in keeping with the theory, W. R. Hess (1931) located an area in the diencephalon of cats in which electrical stimulation apparently induced sleeping.

Activity Cycles

An extension of the active theory that is widely accepted at present is that of the biological clock as sleep-inducing mechanism. Richter (1967) has shown that rats, blinded to eliminate the influence of the diurnal light cycle, continued to have periods of activity and rest roughly once a day (*circadian*), as before (Figure 14.1). The exact period of the "decoupled" activity cycle varied from rat to rat, but it rarely deviated from 24 hours by more than 20 minutes. For each rat the period was quite consistent and independent of external influences. The interval between activity periods could not be altered by adrenalectomy, castration, pregnancy, hunger, thirst, hypophysectomy, removal of the pineal gland, anoxia, electroshock, or a variety of drugs including tranquilizers, anesthetics, atropine, or LSD, though, of course, the amount of activity was often influenced by the treatment. In some rats the daily onset of activity did not vary by more than a few minutes from the predicted time over a period as long as seven months, a better performance than most mechanical clocks deliver.

The timing of the activity cycle did not depend upon previous conditioning to the 24-hour light-dark cycle; it appeared in congenitally blind rats and in rats blinded at birth. It could not depend upon some unknown outside influence (like cosmic radiations), for, as soon as they were blinded, the rats fell out of step not only with the terrestrial day but also with one another, even though they were all in the same room. After a few weeks some rats were starting activity at all hours of the day and night. Apparently the only stimulus that could slightly modify the intrinsic timing of the "clock" was the diurnal change of illumination acting through the intact visual system.

Although most of Richter's data were based on running-wheel activity, rather than sleep, presumably there is a high correlation between the two. Certainly rats do not run when they are asleep, and for a long-term study of this nature it is reasonable to assume that a highly periodic activity cycle is paralleled by a highly periodic sleep cycle. Only when we want to know whether an animal is awake or asleep at a particular instant does it become important to have a more exact criterion (or set of criteria) for sleep. Finding such criteria has not proved easy. Often the best that can be done is to say that an animal is "asleep" when it has its eyes closed and does not respond to mild stimuli yet is aroused by strong ones.

The discovery that characteristic patterns of electrocortical activity usually accompany sleep was consequently of great value and has given considerable impetus to research in this area.

Spontaneous Electrical Activity of the Brain

The first reports on the fluctuations of electrical potentials in the brain were made by Caton (1877) in England and Danilewski (1891) in Russia. Their discoveries resulted from the introduction of very sensitive galvanometers into physiological research. Both investigators were trying to detect electrical currents evoked in the cortex by sensory stimuli, and both found it impossible to achieve a steady base line. Despite all efforts to eliminate sensory input, a galvanometer connected to electrodes on the cortex recorded a persistent wobble.

This phenomenon was rediscovered several times subsequently, but it remained a neglected

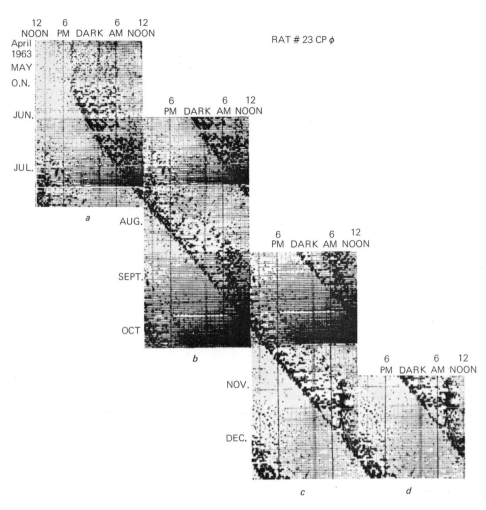

Figure 14.1 Activity cycles of a rat blinded at the time indicated at point O.N. (early in May). Each horizontal line represents a period of 24 hours. Activity produces a thickening of the line. Before the rat is blinded the activity takes place mainly during the hours of darkness. After blinding the activity becomes more intense and the period lengthens from 24 hours to about 24 hours and 20 minutes, resulting in a daily drift of the onset of activity. By July the rat was thus active during daylight, in early August at night again, and so on. The average interval between periods of activity remains remarkably constant for many months in the absence of any light or other diurnal cues from the environment. (From Richter, 1967.)

curiosity until Berger (1929) rediscovered it once more. That time, however, further improvements in the apparatus enabled him to record the oscillating brain potentials through electrodes placed on the scalp of human subjects, rather than from the cortical surface. The potentials were much attenuated by passing through the skull and tissues of the head, the average amplitude being of the order of 10–100 μv.

The ability to record the *electroencephalogram* (EEG) from human subjects without surgical intervention and with little discomfort or inconvenience to them encouraged the development of this technique as a research tool and soon led to many clinical applications.

One very early discovery was that the character of the brain potentials changes with the alertness of the subject. A very alert or frightened subject has a low-voltage, rapidly fluctuat-

EXCITED

RELAXED

DROWSY

ASLEEP

DEEP SLEEP

COMA

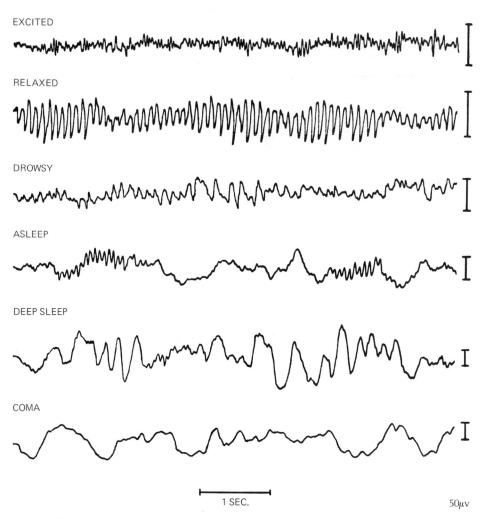

1 SEC.   50μv

Figure 14.2 Typical EEG records from normal subjects in different states of arousal and from a comatose subject. (From Jasper, in Penfield & Jasper, 1954.)

ing potential, sometimes called a "desynchronized wave." As he relaxes the voltage grows, and lower frequencies appear in the record until, as he falls asleep, very large, slow waves predominate (Figure 14.2). The correlation is not perfect; slow waves may be present in waking subjects, but they are rare and usually indicate some pathological condition; as we shall see, low-voltage fast waves regularly occur in certain stages of sleep.

ELECTROPHYSIOLOGY OF SLEEP

Before the correlation between the EEG and sleep had been established it was impossible to learn anything about the state of consciousness

of a paralyzed animal, but Bremer (1935) was able to show that the electrical activity of the brain of a cat whose brainstem had been transected at the level of the colliculi (producing a *cerveau isolé*) was like that of a normal sleeping animal. When the transection was more caudal, at the level of the gracile and cuneate nuclei (producing an *encéphale isolé*), the head did not register sleep continuously (Figure 14.3).

These observations revitalized the passive theory of sleep. Bremer (1936) interpreted them to mean that input arriving along the nerves that enter the brainstem between the two sections (principally the fifth and eighth cranial nerves) were responsible for maintaining wakefulness and that sleep was caused by the

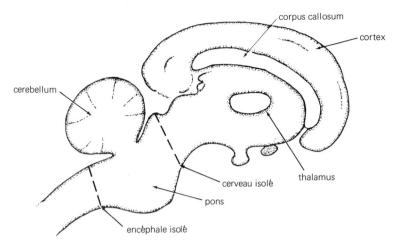

Figure 14.3 A section of the brainstem of the cat, showing the location of cuts producing the *cerveau isolé* and the *encéphale isolé*.

reduction of sensory input after the more rostral transection.

The weakness of this interpretation should have been clear from the possibility of producing brief periods of arousal in the *cerveau isolé* through olfactory or visual stimulation, periods that do not outlast the stimuli. In the *encéphale isolé*, on the other hand, similar stimulation produces long-lasting arousal. It thus appears likely that there is a central mechanism for maintaining arousal during the intervals between stimuli in the normal animal and in the *encéphale isolé* but that this system has been eliminated in the *cerveau isolé* preparation.

Reticular Activating System

The next advance in understanding arousal mechanisms was the discovery that stimulation of part of the brainstem during sleep could produce a high-frequency, low-voltage EEG resembling that of an awake animal (Jasper, Hunter & Knighton, 1948; Moruzzi & Magoun, 1949).

Moruzzi and Magoun investigated the phenomenon in great detail and found that the region from which such arousal could be produced corresponded to the reticular formation (Figure 14.4). Stimulation of the lemniscal sensory pathways was not a necessary factor in the arousal. The investigators interpreted these findings as showing that the reticular formation

Figure 14.4 Sections through (a) the posterior thalamus, (b) the mesencephalon, and (c) the lower medulla of the brainstem of a cat. The areas from which low-threshold arousal responses can be elicited by electrical stimulation are hatched. (After Moruzzi & Magoun, 1949.)

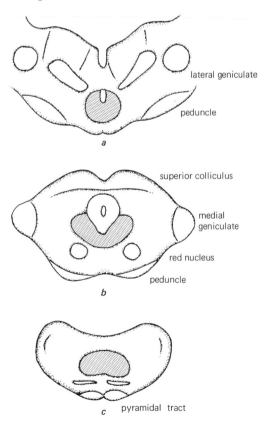

was the structure responsible for maintaining arousal in the normal animal. This previously enigmatic network of cells, which some anatomists seemed almost to regard as only packing for the more distinct nuclei and tracts of the brainstem, suddenly came into the limelight and remained the center of attention (in more ways than one) for many years.

Although the discovery has turned out to be less enlightening than was originally hoped, it had a very valuable side effect in promoting an era of fruitful cooperation between physiologists and behavioral scientists. Before that time most physiologists were working on systems not very closely related to behavior, and psychologists found little in physiology, apart from the peripheral parts of the sensory systems, to interest them. Even the sensory psychologist was not entirely satisfied with what the physiologists had found, for it was clear to him that perception involves more than the conduction of impulses from receptors to the cortex. Some principal of selection, or attention, was clearly required to explain why, at any particular time, one set of sense data predominates in the control of behavior to the exclusion of the rest. As the news about Magoun's experiments spread, some psychologists saw in the reticular formation the structure they needed to explain the selectivity of attention.

Such speculation went considerably beyond the data, encouraged perhaps by the ambiguity of the word "consciousness." Physiologists often use the word to mean a state of normal activity, the opposite of unconsciousness, or sleep. But to the psychologist "consciousness" implies consciousness *of* something, that is, attending to something. The idea thus arose that the mechanism that keeps the organism aroused may also determine to some extent the content of its waking experience.

This kind of reasoning is open to the usual arguments against the existence of "centers" in the brain. In addition, some of the less restrained speculations came close to endowing the reticular formation with the properties of a soul, of a "little man inside" who could recognize every input immediately, decide whether or not it should be noticed, and know which part of the brain it should be addressed to if

it was allowed through. The obvious objection to this view is that, if the reticular formation has these capabilities and can make such important decisions, why do we need the rest of the brain at all? If the reticular formation does indeed play a role in determining the focus of attention, it presumably does so only as a link in a complex network and not as an autonomous center; but we shall leave further discussion of this point until the next chapter and return now to the question of sleep.

The reticular formation, as its name implies, consists of a network of interconnected neurons, and Magoun (1952) somewhat tentatively suggested that activity persisting in loops of the network after presentation of a stimulus was responsible for maintaining wakefulness during the intervals between stimuli. If that were the case, lesions of the reticular formation could be expected to result in somnolence. A frequently cited experiment by Lindsley, Schreiner, Knowles, and Magoun (1950) did partially confirm this prediction. One group of cats sustained lesions in the medial reticular formation and central gray, and another group had lesions of similar size in the lateral sensory pathways. Most of the cats in the first group were somnolent, at least for a few days after the operation; the cats in the other group were not (Figure 14.5). Cats with lesions in the central gray alone were not somnolent either.

Strong auditory or tactual stimuli would produce transient arousal of the animals with medial lesions, but the EEG returned to a sleep pattern almost immediately after the stimulus was removed (Figure 14.6a). The cats whose lateral pathways had been cut could be awakened by a sound, and they would then stay awake for some time, as normal cats would (Figure 14.6b). It was concluded that the arrival of sensory impulses at the cortex through the lemniscal pathways did not result in maintained arousal but that, if the reticular formation was intact, impulses arriving there through collaterals from the sensory pathways resulted in prolonged activity that would keep the cortex activated for some time.

Some of the results did not support such a tidy conclusion, however. In almost all cats allowed to survive a week or more, the sleep-waking cycle returned to normal. A lasting increase in somnolence occurred only when the lesion encroached upon the posterior diencephalon. Large lesions of the mesencephalic reticular formation that spared the diencephalon did not produce lasting somnolence, and later experiments have shown that, when the mesencephalic reticular formation is carefully removed by suction instead of being destroyed by the usual electrolytic or burning methods, there may be no somnolent phase at all.

It therefore seems impossible to attribute control of sleep and waking solely to the reticular formation; a region in the posterior diencephalon may be more important.

Magoun's view of sleep and waking, like those of Bremer and many other physiologists, overemphasized the role of sensory input. It is true that sensory input can usually awaken an animal, but it is not true that absence of sensory input automatically results in sleep. A quiet, dark place can be very disturbing to some animals. Conversely, very strong and varied stimulation eventually fails to keep an animal awake. The cyclical nature of sleep attests to the much greater influence of intrinsic factors than early physiological theories allowed for.

Lindsley and his colleagues were not the first to implicate the posterior diencephalon in waking. The relationship had long been suspected on the basis of clinical studies, and Ranson (1939) had already shown that a comatose state resulted from lesions in the posterior hypothalamus. The same phenomenon had also been observed by Nauta (1946) in wild rats (the only experimental animals available in occupied Holland during the war).

More recently Feldman and Waller (1962) have shown that the hypothalamus is important in behavioral arousal and that the reticular formation is more important for electrographic arousal. These experimenters compared the effects of lesions in the midbrain reticular formation with those of lesions in the posterior hypothalamus. They found that posterior hypothalamic lesions resulted in somnolent behavior, which persisted even when stimulation of the reticular formation (or strong peripheral stimulation) produced low-voltage, high-frequency EEG potentials similar to those of

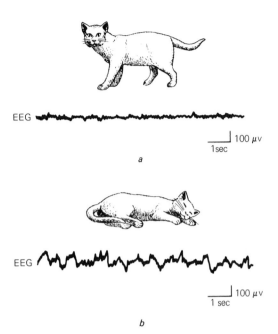

a

Figure 14.5 (a) A cat with a lesion of the lateral sensory paths in the midbrain on the twenty-first postoperative day. The cat is awake and shows a waking pattern in its cortical EEG. (b) A cat with a lesion of the midbrain tegmentum "asleep" on the twelfth postoperative day, with a sleeping cortical EEG. (After Lindsley, Schreiner, Knowles & Magoun, 1950.)

Figure 14.6 EEG tracings from cats: (a) The arousing effect of a buzzer upon a cat with a tegmental lesion on the seventh postoperative day. The cat is asleep again in about 2 seconds. (b) The arousing effect of the experimenter's walking in the room upon a cat with a large lateral mesencephalic lesion cutting all lemniscal paths. The cat remained awake about a minute. (After Lindsley, Schreiner, Knowles & Magoun, 1950.)

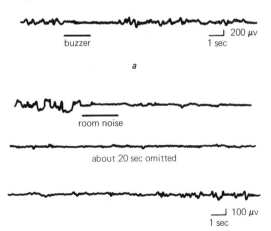

b

alertness. On the other hand, cats with lesions of the reticular formation were not unduly somnolent, although the EEG records showed a predominance of high-voltage slow waves. This "sleep" pattern sometimes persisted throughout experimental sessions during which the animals were clearly alert and their eyes were following visual stimuli.

A patient described by Lhermitte, Gautier, Marteau, and Chain (1963) demonstrated a

Figure 14.7 Recordings from the cortex of a cat (a) before, (b) during, and (c) after cooling the mesencephalic reticular formation with an implanted thermode. (After Naquet, Denavit, Lanoir & Albe-Fessard, 1965.)

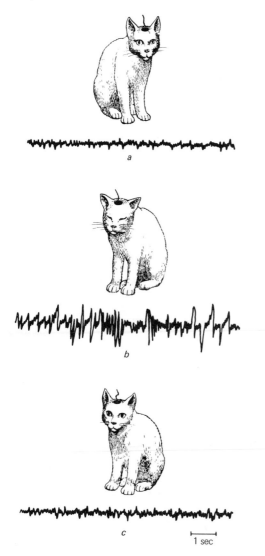

similar dissociation. She had severe damage to the mesencephalic reticular formation and appeared comatose, yet she was able to answer quite complex questions by using her only remaining response, a slight forearm flexion.

Naquet, Denavit, and Albe-Fessard (1962) found that cooling the mesencephalic reticular formation to produce a temporary lesion provoked cortical slow waves and spindles (runs of moderately slow waves indicative of drowsiness or sleep), two of which appear on the "asleep" record of Figure 14.2. However, in animals with permanently implanted cooling probes (thermodes), spindles were most readily produced by cooling the subthalamic region near the *zona incerta* (see Figure 16.7). Even in this area, however, deep sleep was not produced; the cat closed its eyes and appeared drowsy, but it did not usually lie down in the typical sleeping posture (Figure 14.7; see also Naquet, Denavit, Lanoir & Albe-Fessard, 1965).

Shinshu Nakajima (1964) used a different technique to make temporary lesions in the brainstem. He found that injecting very small quantities of calcium salt or procaine (a local anesthetic) into the mesencephalic reticular formation of rats produced great excitement and hyperactivity, which, at higher dosages, suddenly gave way to coma. He concluded that delirium and coma were two stages of a single syndrome quite different from sleeping, one that resulted from abnormality in the reticular formation.

The theory that sleep is a passive reaction to reduced sensory input received a further setback with the discovery by Batini, Moruzzi, Palestini, Rossi, and Zanchetti (1958) that sectioning the brainstem of cats at the midpontine level permanently established cortical fast waves and, as far as could be determined from the slight motor functioning still available to these preparations, permanent wakefulness as well. These preparations had no more sensory input than did the cat with *cerveau isolé*, which slept all the time; there thus seems little doubt that the elimination of sleep is caused by loss of signals to the brain from the pontine reticular formation.

The possibility that permanent arousal is

produced by irritation of tissue just rostral to the lesion seems to be ruled out by the finding that perfusion of the medulla and pons with the anesthetic Thiopental through the vertebral artery will awaken a sleeping cat, though perfusion of more rostral parts of the brain through the carotid artery will put an awake cat to sleep (Magni, Moruzzi, Rossi & Zanchetti, 1959). Unless we make the improbable assumption that there are peculiar neurons in the pons that are excited by Thiopental, it seems that we must accept the conclusion that there is a midpontine system exerting a synchronizing influence on the cortex either directly or through the more rostral mesencephalic reticular formation.

Attempts to produce cortical synchronization by electrical stimulation of this system have not been very successful, though Magnes, Moruzzi, and Pompeiano (1961) have triggered cortical spindles by stimulating the vicinity of the rostral end of the medulla (near the solitary tract) at frequencies of between one and six pulses per second. There are also examples of hypnogenic (sleep-producing) peripheral stimulation like rocking (which stimulates the vestibular system) and rhythmic sounds and movements that might produce bursts of low-frequency firing in the medulla. Pompeiano and Swett (1962) claimed to have induced sleep in cats by stimulating cutaneous nerve fibers with low-voltage shocks at three to eight per second, but this method works only on drowsy cats which have already been habituated to the shocks.

These experiments recall those of W. R. Hess (1931, 1957), who decided many years ago, on the basis of his finding that low-frequency electrical stimulation of the thalamus sent a cat to sleep, that sleep must be an active process. Many experiments of this type are open to doubt because cats spend so much of their time asleep or dozing even without help from the physiologist. Surprisingly few of these experiments have employed proper statistical controls for spontaneous sleeping. Both Hess and Pompeiano, for example, have stated that their stimulation would not put the cat to sleep unless it was already relaxed and in a condition compatible with normal sleep. The findings

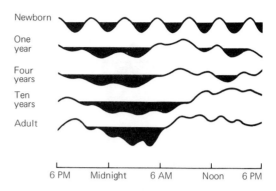

Figure 14.8 Kleitman's representation of polycyclical sleep in the infant and its residual effects in the adult. The black troughs represent sleep. (After Kleitman, 1939.)

would be more convincing if the stimulation made the cat go to sleep again just after it had awakened from a long sleep or if it significantly increased the total duration of sleep over a 24-hour period.

Sleep with Low-Voltage, Fast-Wave EEG

Although the onset of sleep is usually accompanied by high-voltage spindles and slow waves, investigators studying electrical activity of the brain during sleep soon observed that there are periods when the sleeping subject has an EEG quite similar to that when he is awake. These periods were usually accompanied by disturbed breathing and restlessness and were taken to indicate very light sleep. Kleitman (1939) noticed that these periods of "light" sleep were cyclical, occurring three or four times during the night, and suggested that they were vestiges of an infantile polycyclical type of sleep (Figure 14.8).

Some time later Aserinsky and Kleitman (1955), working on the sleep of infants, noticed a great deal of eye movement under their closed lids as they slept. Sleeping adults were therefore also investigated to see whether or not they also experienced such eye movements (Dement & Kleitman, 1955). As it is not easy to see the eye movements of adults through their eyelids (especially in the dark), an electrical method (see Chapter 11) was used to pick up the movements and record them on the same chart that the EEG was recorded on. It was clear from these charts that not only did adults have pe-

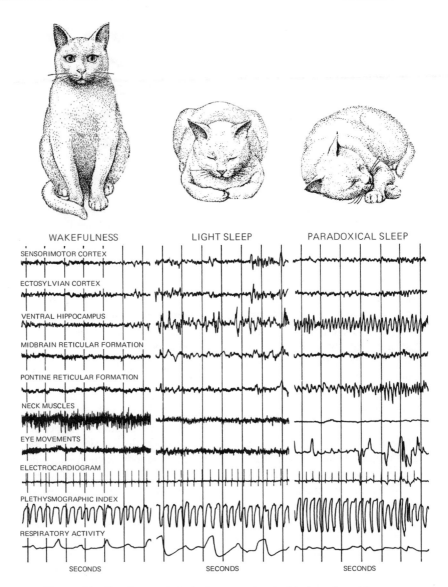

WAKEFULNESS   LIGHT SLEEP   PARADOXICAL SLEEP

SENSORIMOTOR CORTEX

ECTOSYLVIAN CORTEX

VENTRAL HIPPOCAMPUS

MIDBRAIN RETICULAR FORMATION

PONTINE RETICULAR FORMATION

NECK MUSCLES

EYE MOVEMENTS

ELECTROCARDIOGRAM

PLETHYSMOGRAPHIC INDEX

RESPIRATORY ACTIVITY

SECONDS   SECONDS   SECONDS

Figure 14.9 The characteristic rhythms associated with deep sleep (the group of traces at right) are so much like those associated with wakefulness (the group at left) and so different from those of light sleep (the middle group) that M. Jouvet has applied the term "paradoxical" to deep sleep. Normal cats spend about two-thirds of their time sleeping. They usually begin each sleep period with 25 minutes of light sleep, followed by 6 or 7 minutes of paradoxical sleep. In the latter state they are hard to awaken, and their muscles are relaxed. The electrical activity of other brain structures and records of bodily activity during waking, normal sleep, and paradoxical sleep are also shown. From Jouvet, "The states of sleep" Copyright © 1967 by Scientific American, Inc. All rights reserved.

riods of rapid eye movement during sleep but also they took place only during periods of low-voltage, fast-wave EEG. More careful observation of the subjects revealed that, during periods of desynchronized EEG, the trunk muscles were very relaxed, though in addition to eye movements there were twitches of the extremities and some irregularity of breathing and heart rate (see Figure 14.9, which shows similar phenomena in the cat).

The idea that the subject might be dreaming during the periods of rapid eye movement occurred to several people, and this idea was confirmed by Dement and Kleitman (1957). When subjects were awakened during these periods they reported dreaming on about 80 per cent of the occasions, whereas they reported dreaming on only about 7 per cent of the arousals at other times.

The phenomenon has been given many names; one of the most common is "rapid eye movement" (REM) sleep. Others include "low voltage, fast wave" (LVFW) sleep, "desynchronized" sleep, "low muscle tone" (LM) sleep, and "dreaming." Jouvet (1967) uses the term "paradoxical sleep" (PS) to describe the phenomenon in his experimental cats because of the paradox of sleep accompanied by a waking EEG, and this term will be used in this chapter because it does not refer to a single symptom (as does REM, for example), which may for one reason or another be absent in particular cases. Normal sleep is often called "slow-wave sleep" (SWS), but again the term "normal sleep" will be used here because it is less specific.

Rather surprisingly, despite the aroused EEG, subjects are often not as easy to awaken during paradoxical sleep as during normal sleep. The periods of paradoxical sleep occur at roughly 90-minute intervals and last on the average about 20 minutes. In normal adults about 20 per cent of sleeping time is spent in paradoxical sleep. In infants the proportion is much higher. About 80 per cent of their longer sleeping time is spent in paradoxical sleep during the first few weeks of life.

Although there is a statistical relationship between rapid eye movements and dreaming, it seems unlikely that these eye movements are caused by the subject's "following" the objects in his dreams, as some have suggested. In the first place, the movements do not resemble those of normal vision very closely, and the fact that the eye movements occur in decorticate animals and newborn infants, who presumably have little visual imagery, is also difficult to explain on this basis.

At about the same time that Dement and Kleitman were investigating paradoxical sleep

in humans, Jouvet and Michel (1958) discovered a similar phenomenon in cats. They were taking continuous records of the brain activity of sleeping cats and noticed that after about an hour of sleep with slow waves the EEG would revert suddenly to the waking pattern for a few minutes and the cat would make restless movements of the extremities, whiskers, tail, and eyes. Breathing also became unsteady and the heart rate irregular (Figure 14.9). This phase would last an average of six minutes and would recur at half-hour intervals.

As in human subjects, this phase arose from the deepest sleep (when the EEG showed the largest and slowest waves). Jouvet found, however, that any attempt to wake the animal when it was in this phase put it back into the slow-wave state, and it was more difficult to awaken the cat during paradoxical sleep than during normal sleep. He also found that the trunk muscles were relaxed during paradoxical sleep and that there was a loss of monosynaptic (tendon jerk) reflexes. Loss of tone in the neck muscles is regarded as one of the better indicators of paradoxical sleep. Other characteristics of paradoxical sleep are *theta waves* (regular waves of about 4–8 Hz) in the hippocampus and other limbic structures, including the mesencephalic reticular system, and curious spike activity in the pons, lateral geniculate, and occipital cortex (*PGO spikes*; see Figure 14.10). Paradoxical sleep has been observed in many mammals and even in some birds. The percentage of total sleep spent in paradoxical sleep tends to increase with the degree of corticalization.

Jouvet (1962) investigated the structures responsible for paradoxical sleep, making lesions at different levels of the nervous system. He found that lesions of the *nucleus reticularis pontis caudalis*, part of the reticular formation in the dorsal midpontine part of the brainstem, drastically reduced the percentage of paradoxical sleep for as long as the animals survived, usually several weeks.

When a lesion was made somewhat rostral to this level, leaving the whole of the pontine region intact but eliminating all higher structures, the cat would sit in a rigid posture for about half an hour at a time, alternating regu-

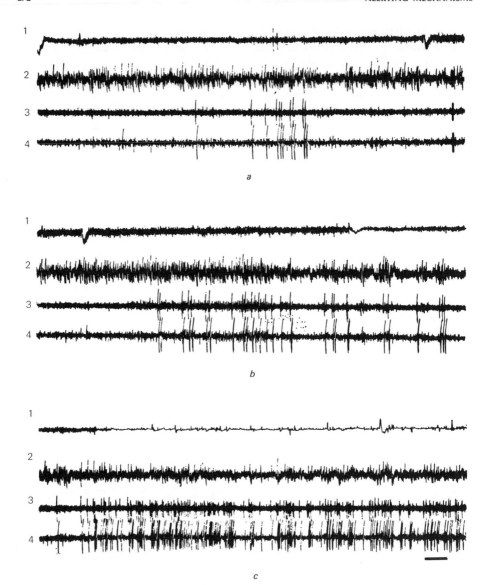

Figure 14.10 Recordings (1) of muscle activity from the neck and (2) of EEG activity from the occipital cortex and (3) the right and (4) left lateral geniculate bodies of the cat during normal and paradoxical sleep. The records are continuous and represent a total of six minutes. The frequency of the spikes in the geniculate bodies increases as the onset of paradoxical sleep (indicated by loss of tone in the neck muscles) approaches. Although they are difficult to distinguish from waves at the slow paper speed employed, there are also spikes in the cortical record during the paradoxical stage of sleep. (From M. Jouvet, 1967.)

larly with periods of about six minutes during which the tone in the trunk muscles disappeared. Jouvet regarded this finding as evidence of a paradoxical-sleep mechanism in the pontine region, one that is triggered about every half-hour in the decerebrate cat and inhibits the main postural muscles. Because the cerebral hemispheres had been removed in these animals there was no way of telling what sort of EEG would be present during loss of tone, but it seems likely that they would correspond to low-voltage, fast-wave episodes.

During normal sleep cats have synchronized EEGs not only in the cortex but in most of the brainstem as well. In the "pontine" cat, however, no slow waves are ever recorded from the pons or medulla. M. Jouvet regarded this absence as evidence that pontine cats have no normal sleep but only paradoxical sleep. He also assumed that the mechanism for generating slow waves must be rostral to the mesencephalon. The evidence seems to point to a synchronizing mechanism in the orbital frontal cortex (M. Jouvet, 1967).

Several investigators, including Dement (1960) and D. Jouvet, Vimont, Delorme, and Jouvet (1964), have selectively deprived human and animal subjects of paradoxical sleep by rousing them whenever rapid eye movements occurred or the tone of the neck muscles disappeared. A simple way to awaken small animals is to confine them to a small platform in the middle of a bath of water. The animal can sleep, but as soon as its neck muscles relax its head droops into the water, and the animal is awakened.

These experiments have revealed that such deprivation leads to a gradual increase in the tendency to fall into paradoxical sleep. After a few days the subject goes straight from waking into paradoxical sleep with no intermediate stage of normal sleep, and thus starts being deprived of all sleep. It is then difficult to interpret any changes in the subject. On the first undisturbed night after a week or two of deprivation of paradoxical sleep the subjects spend about twice the normal time in this kind of sleep.

Dement has suggested that paradoxical sleep is produced by an agent that builds up during waking and normal sleep and is used up during paradoxical sleep. The accumulation of a deficit in paradoxical sleep is difficult to explain on any other basis. Attempts have been made to transfer the effects of deprivation from one animal to another by exchange of cerebrospinal fluid but with inconclusive results (Dement, Henry, Cohen & Ferguson, 1967). These workers did, however, report a number of changes produced by deprivation of paradoxical sleep that did not occur in animals deprived of similar amounts of normal sleep. Cats tended to be restless when awake, and they tended to be both *hyperphagic* (that is, to eat more) and hypersexual; there was also a rise in the heart rate.

Deprivation also seems to increase the excitability of the nervous system, as measured by the amount of electric current necessary to induce convulsion. It is interesting that convulsions in nondeprived subjects seem to reduce the amount of paradoxical sleep that occurs, as if the substance that triggers paradoxical sleep and is used up by it is also used up by convulsions. In connection with the hypersexuality of deprived cats, it is interesting that, according to Snyder (1967), one of the autonomic effects that accompanies paradoxical sleep in primates is penile erection.

Evarts (1964) has recorded from pyramidal-tract neurons in the motor cortex of monkeys during waking and sleep. He found that when the monkey was awake but not moving the Betz cells (identified by the short latency of antidromic conduction from the bulbar pyramids to the cortex) were relatively silent, whereas pyramidal-tract cells with small-diameter axons fired tonically at high frequencies. When the animal slept the activities evened out: the large cells fired more frequently and the small ones more slowly. There was also a change in pattern. Instead of firing at regular intervals the small cells began to fire in short bursts, so that, although the average rate was reduced, the peak rate during the bursts may actually have been higher during sleep. During paradoxical sleep the bursts occurred more frequently, and the average firing rate was usually higher than during quiet waking (Figure 14.11).

During the eye movements of paradoxical sleep it is possible to pick up sharp waves or spikes in the pons, geniculate, and occipital cortex, as mentioned earlier. These waves persist for a time after blinding or removal of the eyeballs. Bizzi (1966a, 1966b) has performed experiments consistent with the idea that spikes in the lateral geniculate correspond to bursts of presynaptic inhibition on optic-nerve terminals, timed to prevent visual transmission dur-

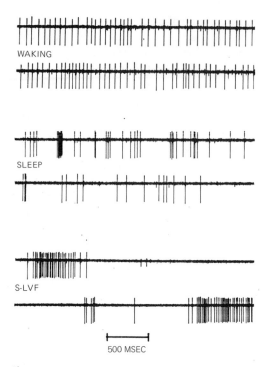

WAKING

SLEEP

S-LVF

500 MSEC

Figure 14.11 Firing patterns of a small pyramidal-tract neuron during waking, normal sleep, and paradoxical sleep. (From Evarts, 1964.)

ing eye movements. This inhibition may be part of a mechanism that serves the same purpose during waking.

Unit recordings of geniculate cells show that many emit bursts during eye movement. These bursts do not originate in the optic nerve; some other input is apparently feeding into the geniculate body, possibly from the pontine or vestibular region. It has even been suggested that this input may have something to do with the production of dream images.

Pompeiano (1967) presented evidence implicating presynaptic inhibition in the loss of spinal reflexes during paradoxical sleep. The motoneurons themselves must not be inhibited at the time; as the limbs twitch in response to centrally generated activity. Evarts (1967) has pointed out that this finding illustrates the value of presynaptic inhibition. It can block input to neurons from one source while leaving the pathway open to signals from other sources.

HUMORAL FACTORS IN SLEEP AND WAKING

As mentioned at the beginning of this chapter, humoral theories of sleep have a long history. Some experiments have suggested that substances carried in the bloodstream can induce sleep; others have cast doubt on these results. For example, that double-headed monsters or Siamese twins with common circulation may sleep independently of each other is difficult to explain. Possibly the concentration of "hypnotoxin" does not rise to a level adequate to overcome the average arousal level when each head obtains adequate sleep. Nobody seems to have done the experiment of keeping one head awake and seeing whether or not the other head sleeps more.

Monnier and Hösli (1964) were apparently able to dialyze (filter through a membrane) a substance from the blood of a rabbit that had been put to sleep by thalamic stimulation and then to induce sleep in recipient rabbits with the substance. On the other hand, these investigators were not able to transmit natural sleep in this way; it may be that thalamic stimulation produces some substance, either in the brain or in other parts of the body, that is hypnogenic but has little or nothing to do with spontaneous sleep.

Other investigators have made more direct attempts to determine what changes occur in the metabolism of the brain during sleep. Kety and his colleagues have used various methods of measuring oxygen consumption and blood flow through the brain in a variety of circumstances, including natural sleep. In human subjects there is a slight but significant increase in blood flow, with no significant change in oxygen consumption, as the subject goes into natural sleep. No measurements were made during paradoxical sleep (Mangold, Sokoloff, Conner, Kleinerman, Therman & Kety, 1955). Using a radioactive-tracer technique with cats, however, Kety (1967) found that the cerebral blood flow apparently doubled during paradoxical sleep, a magnitude of change not otherwise observed except during convulsions. Metabolism measures also tended to confirm the finding of Evarts (1964) that there was more neural activity during paradoxical sleep than at almost any other time.

Jasper, Khan, and Elliott (1965) have studied the release of some amino acids by the cortex during sleep and waking. Approximately three times the quantity of *gamma aminobutyric acid* (GABA) was released during sleep (mostly normal sleep) as was released during waking. At the same time the quantity of glutamic acid collected was reduced about one-third, and there was no change in the amount of other amino acids, eliminating the possibility that the results were caused by a general change in circulation or metabolism. GABA is an inhibitory substance at some synapses, but, in view of the relatively small change in overall neural activity in the brain during normal sleep, it is not clear what the change in GABA release means.

Sodium butyrate and other short-chain, fatty-acid compounds induce unconscious states resembling sleep. According to Matsuzaki, Takagi, and Tokizane (1964), an increase in the dose will cause a rapid shift to paradoxical sleep; with continuous infusion paradoxical sleep can be maintained as long as 70 hours.

Hernández-Peón and his coworkers (Hernández-Peón, Chávez-Ibarra, Morgane & Timo-Iaria, 1963) have reported sleep in cats following the introduction of a cholinergic agent like *carbachol* into the *medial forebrain bundle*, a pathway in the limbic system that leads from the region of the precommissural fornix and the olfactory bulb through the preoptic area and the lateral hypothalamus into the central mesencephalon. As with injections of fatty acid, increasing the dose is supposed to lead to an early transition into paradoxical sleep.

Hernández-Peón and his colleagues reported having performed all the necessary controls (failure to obtain sleep from the introduction of other chemicals into the medial forebrain bundle or from injection of cholinergic substances into other parts of the brain), but the results of these controls were not presented in any detail in the paper (1963), which is unfortunate because other investigators have not

been able to replicate the main finding. Myers (1964a) found that crystals of carbachol introduced into the lateral hypothalamic part of the medial forebrain bundle of the cat (where Hernández-Peón and his colleagues had observed sleep) produced "nervousness" and, in larger doses, fierce attacks upon the experimenter. Carbachol in the ventricles did, however, produce a comatose state, and it is possible that the earlier results were obtained because the carbachol solution leaked into the ventricular space. Myers' use of solid crystals avoided this possibility. MacPhail and Miller (1968) do not seem to have had this problem when injecting carbachol solutions, for they were unable to obtain sleep from any of the injection sites used by Hernández-Peón and his colleagues. Like Myers, they elicited only fear or rage from their cats. As we shall see, there are surprising species differences in response to transmitter substances injected into the brain; even if cholinergic substances do produce sleep in cats it would therefore not be possible to draw general conclusions from the fact. Rats, for example, are induced to drink by injections of carbachol into the limbic system (Fisher & Coury, 1962).

Further doubts about the cholinergic theory of sleep have been raised by M. Jouvet's finding that large doses of *atropine* (a cholinergic blocking agent) injected into cats induced a form of slow-wave sleep. The cats also showed periods of rapid eye movements but none of the tonic changes involved in true paradoxical sleep (no desynchronization of the EEG and no relaxation of the neck muscles).

The fact that sleep induced by fatty acids may pass to the paradoxical stage more or less quickly, depending upon the amount of drug injected, suggests there is a continuum of sleep, the paradoxical phase being more intense than is the slow-wave phase. On the other hand, some of M. Jouvet's experiments appear to have disproved this hypothesis by showing that one or the other phase can be selectively eliminated by drugs. Not only has Jouvet argued that the two phases of sleep can be dissociated, but, as just pointed out, he has also gathered evidence that the phasic (rapid-eye-movements for example) and tonic components of paradoxical sleep can be separated from each other and must therefore have different mechanisms.

Most of Jouvet's work has involved the role of *monoamines* in sleep. Dahlström and Fuxe (1964) have observed the fluorescence of tissue under ultraviolet light and demonstrated that there are *serotonergic* and *catecholaminergic* neurons in the brainstem. Jouvet (M. Jouvet & Delorme 1965; M. Jouvet, 1967) noted that these systems correspond closely to the brainstem regions implicated in sleep by lesion and other studies and decided to investigate the effects of monoamines on sleep.

According to the fluorescence studies, there is a concentration of *serotonin* (5-hydroxytryptamine, or 5-HT) in the complex of central tegmental nuclei sometimes called the *nucleus of the Raphé* and of catecholamine (mainly norepinephrine) in and around the *locus coeruleus*, darkly staining nuclei at the anterior end of the floor of the fourth ventricle (Figure 14.12).

Jouvet found that any treatment that increased the amount of serotonin in the brainstem (for example, injection of a precursor or of a monoamine-oxidase inhibitor like *nialamid*, which prevents serotonin from being broken down after release) increased the amount of normal sleep but absolutely prevented paradoxical sleep for hours, even in cats that had been deprived of such sleep for several days beforehand.

Injection of a precursor of norepinephrine induced a state of "quiet wakefulness" lasting several hours. *Reserpine*, a tranquilizer that depletes the monoamines in the brainstem, caused a state resembling sleep, but for many hours there were twitches, continuous fast cortical activity, continuous rapid eye movements, and PGO spikes but no relaxation of the neck muscles.

In other experiments Jouvet made lesions in the Raphé or in the locus coeruleus (which consists almost exclusively of catecholaminergic cells). He found that after the former lesions cats did not sleep for several days but lay on their sides and made walking movements; they had a fast-wave EEG and rapid heart rate. Later both normal sleep and paradoxical sleep reappeared.

After lesions of the locus coeruleus cats had short periods of relatively normal slow-wave

Figure 14.12   (a) The brainstem of the cat at the level of the inferior colliculus (mesencephalon), showing the location of the anterior end of the nuclei of the Raphé. (b) The brainstem of the cat at the level of the fourth ventricle (upper medulla), showing the location of loci coerulei and the more posterior part of the nuclei of the Raphé.

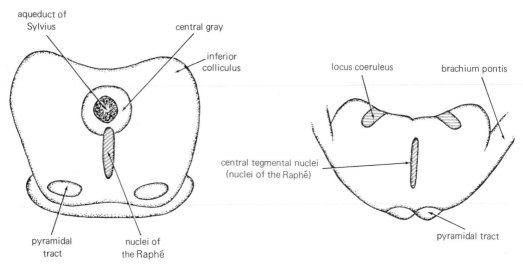

a

b

sleep for a few days, but then jerks, twitches, and rapid eye movements began to occur during the slow waves, and eventually the animals had violent episodes while asleep, during which they would stand up and attack imaginary objects. During these attacks, the cats were unresponsive to actual objects placed in their visual fields.

The meaning of these observations is not immediately obvious, but in conjunction with the results of many other experiments, Jouvet has interpreted them as showing, first, that serotonergic neurons are involved in normal sleep; second, that monoamine oxidase is necessary for the transition from normal to paradoxical sleep; and, third, that there are different mechanisms for the phasic and tonic components of paradoxical sleep, the tonic components (desynchronized EEG and loss of muscle tone) being cholinergic and noradrenergic and the phasic components (eye movements and twitches) being related in some way to the depletion of monoamines from brainstem structures.

The complex patterns of excitation and inhibition during sleep revealed by these experiments suggest that, whatever the reason for the intense bursts of cortical activity during paradoxical sleep, a mechanism normally prevents them from having much effect upon the motor system. Without this inhibitory mechanism we might be in a state similar to that of Jouvet's cats with lesions of the locus coeruleus, and we might get into a great deal of trouble during paradoxical sleep.

Furthermore, if we really dream as much as the experiments of Dement and others suggest, we must also have an effective mechanism for shutting off the learning and memory systems during the episodes of fast-wave cortical activity. If the dreams we do remember (presumably by awakening before some "primary" trace has faded) are typical, it is just as well that storage is normally poor. If we were regularly faced with the problem of distinguishing waking memories from a vast collection of dream memories, life would be even more difficult than it is.

One of the reasons that experiments on sleep

seem so inconclusive may be that sleep involves many areas of the brain, each capable of independently modifying the arousal level. Although there seems little doubt that brainstem structures have a strong influence on sleep in the normal animal, Villablanca (1965) has shown that the EEG of the isolated telencephalon (*cerveau isolé*) reverts to a relatively normal sleep-waking cycle after a few days. After a week or ten days the cortical EEG of the animal may even be aroused for a greater percentage of the time than is that of an intact cat. Experiments show that the low-voltage, fast-wave activity of these cats does not correspond to paradoxical sleep but to a genuine aroused state.

Routtenberg (1968) has proposed that there are two arousal mechanisms, one in the brainstem that energizes responses and tends to be involved in aversive processes and another in the limbic system that is involved in arousal of vegetative processes. Villablanca's finding accords with this hypothesis, but it seems likely that there are more than two subsystems capable of organizing cyclical behavior in parts of the brain. Normally the subsystems are synchronized by their interconnections, but, if they are isolated, the rhythm of each persists independently.

Discussion

The experimental evidence on sleep does not present a clear picture of what occurs, but it does seem consistent with the theory that sleep depends upon specific patterns of neural activity and is not simply absence of activity. The neural patterns of sleep, furthermore, seem to be triggered by activity in limbic and brainstem intrinsic pathways or, in some cases, by external stimuli like rocking. In this sense, as we shall see, they bear some resemblance to certain drive states. The main difference between sleepiness and most other drives is that the goal-directed activity required to satisfy the drive is minimal and that the consummatory behavior consists for the most part of no overt behavior at all. Nevertheless, sleep competes with other drives for the time of the organism; a migrating bird, an inspired artist, or a frightened student may sleep very little or not at all for several days. Some organisms sleep excessively when they have nothing else to do, just as others eat or drink excessively.

It is easy to see how neural mechanisms for the regulation of eating and similar behavior might have evolved. Individuals lacking the required systems would not have survived when food became scarce. If they completely lacked a food-drive mechanism they would not have survived more than a day or two under any conditions. The survival value of sleep mechanisms is not quite so clear, perhaps, but several possibilities come to mind. A certain amount of exploratory activity is valuable to an animal, especially when it needs food, water, or a mate, for example, but when none of these fulfilments is lacking random muscular activity is wasteful, interferes with efficient digestion of food, and increases exposure to predators. A mechanism to subdue overt behavior when

other drives are satisfied would thus have survival value.

Those animals that have become adapted to nocturnal hunting and similar habits are at a disadvantage during the day because they do not see well in bright light and their coloration may make them conspicuous; they are better off tucked away quietly unconscious during that time. The opposite is true of animals adapted to daylight activity. The mechanism is thus influenced by light and eventually is controlled by diurnal "clocks."

The almost continuous sleep of infants also has survival value. Until they are capable of reacting effectively to danger they are less of a hazard to themselves and to their parents when they are asleep. No doubt sleeping slows down their mental development, but perceptual and other mental skills developed before the physical strength required to make use of them would be more a disadvantage than an advantage.

Summary

According to the earliest physiological theories, sleep resulted from the accumulation of toxins during activity. Other theories of sleep can be classified as either "passive," claiming that the normal state of the brain is sleep, and that sensory input is necessary for wakefulness, or "active," postulating a sleep center, or mechanism, that shuts off the brain periodically.

Passive theories usually overemphasize the sensory control of sleep and cannot explain its strongly cyclical, or circadian, character. With constant sensory input day and night, rats continue to sleep at regular intervals of about 24 hours.

Normal sleep is accompanied by an increase in the voltage of the electrical activity of the cortex and a decrease in the predominant EEG frequency, a relationship that has proved useful as an index of sleep, especially in animal experiments.

Section of the brainstem at the intercollicular

level (producing a *cerveau isolé*) was found to produce sleep in the isolated head, as indicated by the EEG and the appearance of the eyes. More caudal section (producing an *encéphale isolé*) did not have this effect, which was interpreted as meaning that sensory input from the fifth and eighth cranial nerves is responsible for maintaining arousal.

Subsequently it was found that stimulation of the reticular formation arouses a sleeping or even an anesthetized animal, and the theory was therefore modified. It was then assumed that all sensory paths sending collaterals into the reticular formation, rather than only the fifth and eighth cranial nerves, contribute to keeping the animal awake. Furthermore, reverberating loops of neurons in the reticular formation were believed able to maintain arousal during short periods when no sensory stimulation was present.

This model represented the zenith of the

passive theory. As more evidence has been collected and examined, the role of internal factors in producing sleep has been given more prominence. It is now known that the *cerveau isolé* will revert to an electrographic sleep-waking cycle after a few days if it can be kept alive by careful maintenance.

The hypothalamus, a structure important in many drive states, has been shown to be important for behavioral (as opposed to electrographic) sleep and waking. Lesions in the posterior hypothalamus produce a comatose state, which persists even when arousal activity is induced in the cortex by reticular stimulation. Animals with lesions of the reticular formation recover from their somnolence after a few weeks but may still show EEG slow waves when they are behaviorally awake.

The existence of a midpontine inhibitory system capable of inducing sleep has been postulated on the basis of experiments in which lesions of that area or its perfusion with anesthetic have resulted in sleeplessness. The hypothesis of a sleep-inducing mechanism in this region is somewhat weakened, however, by failure to induce clear-cut sleep by bulbar or midpontine stimulation.

Stimulation of the intralaminar nuclei of the thalamus has been claimed to produce sleep in cats, lending support to the active theory of sleep, but in the absence of stringent controls for spontaneous sleep such results must be accepted with caution because cats fall asleep very readily under laboratory conditions.

Much work has been done in the last few years on the different levels of sleep. It has been found that humans and animals spend about 20 per cent of their sleeping time in a state characterized by low-voltage, high-frequency EEG similar to that of arousal; reduced muscle tone; and rapid eye movements. Humans awakened during these episodes, which last 10–30 minutes and occur three or four times a night, usually report that they have been dreaming. They rarely report dreaming when awakened during normal sleep.

These episodes are variously called "low voltage, fast wave," "rapid eye movement," "low muscle tone," and "paradoxical sleep." Animals are more difficult to awaken from paradoxical sleep than from normal sleep, and human beings probably are too. During paradoxical sleep theta waves are registered throughout much of the limbic system, and spike activity appears in the pons, the lateral geniculate, and the occipital cortex. The spikes do not originate in the eyes; they are probably involved in inhibiting visual input during eye movements. Changes in heart rate, respiration, and movements of the extremities and facial muscles also accompany rapid eye movements. Spinal reflexes, on the other hand, are blocked.

Subjects deprived of paradoxical sleep incur a sleep debt that accumulates over periods of days. There is at the same time a lowering of the seizure threshold. These changes have led to speculation that a humoral agent is responsible for paradoxical sleep, but attempts to isolate it or to transfer the effects of deprivation from one animal to another by exchanging cerebrospinal fluid have so far been inconclusive.

The average firing rate of cortical neurons does not change greatly from waking to sleep, but there is a change in the firing pattern. Small cells in the motor cortex fire in bursts during sleep but at a lower average rate than during waking. Larger cells fire at a higher rate during sleep. During paradoxical sleep the firing rates of all cells are greater than during quiet wakefulness.

It now seems certain that very complex humoral changes are correlated with sleep, but the study of these relationships is still in its infancy. During sleep more gamma aminobutyric acid (GABA) is released at the cortex than during waking, though the release of other amino acids is either reduced or not affected. Short-chain fatty acids induce states closely resembling natural sleep; increasing the dosage produces more paradoxical sleep.

Cholinergic perfusion of the limbic system has been reported to produce sleep in cats, though this finding has been disputed by other investigators who have found only rage. Similar injections in rats produce drinking. Atropine, which blocks acetylcholine, does not cause wakefulness in normal cats, as might have been predicted if the sleep system were cholinergic. The tendency is in the other direction; atropine generates slow waves in the cortex, and large doses apparently result in a state similar to sleep.

Monoamines have also been shown to have complex relationships with sleep. Normal sleep seems to increase and paradoxical sleep to disappear with excess serotonin. Norepinephrine causes wakefulness. Lesions in the principal serotonergic nuclei prevent sleep for some time, though both forms of sleep eventually return. Lesions in the important catecholaminergic nuclei increase the amount of paradoxical sleep but seem to interfere with the motor inhibition that usually accompanies it.

In many ways the events leading to sleep resemble those leading to eating and other consummatory activities, and we are probably justified in regarding sleep as a form of drive. It is possible that it has evolved, not because of any physiological necessity for rest periods, but because sleeping during either the dark or the light part of the day has survival value, resulting in evolutionary selection of the requisite neural mechanisms.

CHAPTER 15

ATTENTION

A response is never determined by all the physical stimuli impinging on an organism at a given moment. Some stimuli are ineffective because the animal has no receptors for them; others may be lost because the receptors are not adjusted, or oriented, to receive them. Even among those that succeed in stimulating receptors the majority fail to make contact with the response mechanism for one reason or another. A stimulus that elicits a strong reflex will pre-empt the motor pathways for the reflex and thus prevent other stimuli from gaining access to them. In the higher levels of the nervous system a similar competition for pathways exists, and, when, as usually happens, one set of stimuli controls responses to the exclusion of others, we attribute the selection to attention.

It is clear that there must be a close relationship between attention and motivation. Very often an animal's immediate goal will determine what stimuli it attends to. If there is no immediate goal, as when the animal is exploring, for example, attention is more likely to be influenced by environmental stimuli than by central factors.

Introspectively attention seems to act on perceptual processes; we attend to things by looking at them, listening to them, sniffing them, and so on. This experience has led to the common definition of attention as something that selects what is to be perceived, but the definition may lead to difficulties because different people have different ideas of what constitutes perception. If by perception we mean conscious awareness of sensory input and if we expect the perceiver to be able to describe or react appropriately to the stimulus, then

attention is certainly involved. But, if we use perception in a more restricted sense to refer only to the processes of analysis and classification that are assumed to take place in the sensory systems, it would be unjustified to assume that attention is essential for perception. On the contrary, the evidence, as we shall see, indicates that even high-level sensory analysis of stimuli can take place when attention is directed elsewhere. A simple example is the attention-getting property, when one is reading or thinking, of one's own name spoken among other surrounding conversation. The sounds that constitute the name have to be analyzed and compared with stored patterns *before* attention is attracted. No doubt several mechanisms combine to promote attention, but the most important level of selection seems to be the point of transfer from the perceptual analyzing systems to the motor and memory systems.

Not that attention has no effect at all on sensory mechanisms; we cannot see with our eyes closed, nor can we see what is behind our backs. Movements of the fingers are necessary to help determine the texture of a surface, and, if peripheral receptors have become adapted and no longer generate impulses, adjustments must be made to bring fresh receptor surfaces to bear upon the stimulus. We thus see that receptor orientation is an important aspect of attention, but it is by no means the only aspect. Changes also take place in the central nervous system, and it is these changes that are of greatest interest to the physiological psychologist.

PHYSIOLOGICAL MECHANISMS OF ATTENTION

A clear formulation of the physiological problem of attention did not appear until about twenty years ago. Earlier it had been speculated that the intensity of a stimulus determined its chances of being selected for further processing. It was believed that the sensory pathway having the greatest concentration of afferent impulses gained control of central mechanisms and prevented other inputs from doing so. Other theorists had stressed the importance of the already-mentioned mechanisms for receptor adjustment.

One of the first to attempt an explanation in terms of the central nervous system was Hebb (1949), who developed the theory that a percept was the firing of a particular spatio-temporal pattern of neurons. Central facilitation of one such pattern would render it more likely than other patterns to be fired by input. Facilitation thus constituted attention in Hebb's theory.

This idea was valuable but difficult to test physiologically, and there was still the problem of precisely what caused facilitation of one pattern rather than of others. Consequently, the theory was rather overshadowed at the time by the experiments of Magoun, Jasper, and others described in Chapter 14, which seemed to implicate the reticular formation and other parts of the arousal system in attention.

Even before these investigations, Penfield (1938) had postulated a brainstem mechanism for maintaining consciousness and directing attention to particular aspects of the total sensory flux. He reasoned that, as stimulation or ablation of the cortex of a patient never produced loss of consciousness during a brain operation (such operations are normally carried out under local anesthesia), the "center of consciousness" must be subcortical. Furthermore, on one or two occasions when he had probed the hypothalamus or lower brainstem during operations, he had produced loss of consciousness and was therefore inclined to locate the "center" there.

Later Penfield labeled his hypothetical system the *centrencephalic* system and attributed to it many of the qualities attributed to the pineal gland by Descartes. He suggested, for example, that when a man wants to perform some act his centrencephalon directs impulses to the parts of the cortex where instructions for that behavior are stored. When the performance is no longer required, the impulses are shut off (Penfield, 1952).

Unfortunately, neither Penfield nor any other proponent of this type of theory has clarified the relationship between the "man" and his "centrencephalon" or indicated how one com-

municates with the other. If, as seems the only possible nonmystical interpretation, the activity of the centrencephalon *is* what can be called the ego of the man, then we have the paradox already raised in Chapter 14: that a small region, probably consisting of relatively undifferentiated neurons, in which the specificity of most of the sensory input is degraded by convergence, must be capable of making rapid, precise discriminations; of generating expectancies; of directing the traffic of sensory and motor impulses; and, in fact, of behaving as a tiny replica of the whole organism. These accomplishments are highly improbable, though not yet completely ruled out by neurophysiological data.

Peripheral Sensory Blocking and Attention

One of the ways in which the reticular formation is supposed to influence perception is by inhibiting receptors, or the early stages of sensory transmission, so that only selected information is allowed to pass through to the center. Interest in this type of control stems from a by now classical experiment of Hernández-Peón, Scherrer, and Jouvet (1956). Recordings of evoked potentials to clicks were taken in the cochlear nuclei of unanesthetized cats. It was found that any disturbing stimulus, like the smell of fish, the sight of mice, or shock to the feet, produced marked reduction in the size of the evoked potentials (Figure 15.1). Stimulation of the reticular formation had a similar effect.

This experiment appeared to confirm the speculations of a number of people on the function of the centrifugal sensory-system pathways. The investigators were no doubt aware of the work of Galambos (1956), who had just shown that stimulation of the efferent fibers of the olivocochlear bundle depressed the sensitivity of the auditory receptors. This and other similar experiments had encouraged the belief that the reticular formation might modulate the input, besides influencing the central analyzing structures, during attention.

Unfortunately, both the results of Hernández-Peón's experiment and their interpretation are open to criticism. The recordings were taken with gross electrodes, which do not measure individual cell activity but probably do measure the dendritic potentials produced by the partial depolarization of many neurons. It is now generally recognized that such potentials, like those of the EEG, are usually larger in the relaxed animal, possibly because during arousal more cells are already partially depolarized and cannot be depolarized much further without firing. The brief potential of the nerve impulse, followed immediately by complete repolarization, has little effect upon gross electrodes. Reduced evoked potential may not, therefore, be an indication of a reduced transmission of auditory impulses through the cochlear nucleus; the opposite is more likely to be the case.

Even if the evoked potential could be taken at its face value, however, such other factors as movements of the head and pinnae might alter the signal strength, as has been pointed out by Horn (1965).

On logical grounds alone it seems unlikely that stimuli are blocked at or near the receptor level. In the first place, if the signal were cut off before it reached the central nervous system, it would be impossible for the attentional mechanisms to determine whether or not the signal was still there or whether or not it had changed to something important. Furthermore, this experiment implies that attention operates by changing the sensitivity of a particular sensory mode, but normally attention must operate on objects not on modalities. We are able both to watch and to listen to an orchestra, at the same time ignoring the hat of the lady three rows ahead and the occasional cough or the noise from the ventilation system. The cat alerted to mice is probably keenly sensitive to olfactory and auditory, as well as to visual, cues pertaining to mice, though it may well ignore stimuli in those modalities from other sources.

It is impossible to account for intermodal attention in terms of the blocking of one or more modalities suggested by Hernández-Peón. Even the suggestion that attention blocks only selected parts of some modalities runs into serious difficulties. What retinal cells would it be necessary to suppress, for example, in order

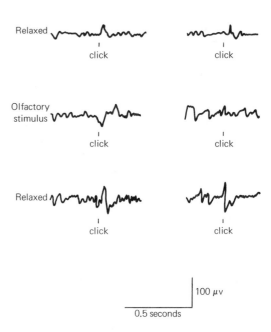

Figure 15.1 Responses evoked in the cochlear nucleus of a cat by clicks before, during, and after presentation of an olfactory stimulus that aroused the cat. (After Hernández-Peón, Scherrer & Jouvet, 1956.)

to ignore trees and clouds while walking in the country? The answer would obviously depend upon the shape, size, distance, posture, and color of the objects and upon their location in the observer's field of vision. A slight movement of his eye, or of the object, would require a new pattern of centrifugal inhibition. By the same token, facilitation of retinal elements or other receptors, to enhance the effects of a particular category of stimuli, like dogs, would not be a practical proposition either. It is conceivable that centrally induced changes in peripheral sensitivity play a minor role in attention under some conditions, but we must look elsewhere for the important mechanisms.

If Hernández-Peón and his colleagues had wished to demonstrate convincingly that one sensory modality was inhibited when the cat was attending to another, they should have measured the evoked potentials in both modalities at once. Then, as attention was directed to one or the other of the modalities, the changes in evoked potential in that modality could have been compared with changes in the other, to ensure that the change was not simply a general effect of arousal. This type of control was employed by Horn (1960), who used cortical evoked potentials, however, rather than those in sensory nuclei.

Flashes and clicks were presented continuously to cats, and recordings of evoked potentials were taken from electrodes in the visual and auditory cortices. From time to time the cats were shown a mouse; at other times an auditory signal that had previously been paired with shock was presented. Instead of increased visual evoked potentials when the mouse was shown and increased auditory evoked potentials when the auditory warning was sounded, as would be predicted by the peripheral-gating (or blocking) theory, both stimuli produced reductions in both visual and auditory evoked potentials.

The result was perhaps what one would expect if the arousal elicited by interesting stimuli of any sort had a general effect upon the size of all evoked potentials. It is nevertheless interesting that, although the average visual evoked potential was reduced 20–30 per cent during mouse watching, the EEG voltage was reduced 50 per cent at the same time. The ratio of evoked potential to background fluctuation was therefore increased during attention.

A similar but more elaborate experiment was performed by Jane, Smirnov, and Jasper (1962); cats were fitted with electrodes in the lateral and medial geniculate nuclei as well as in the visual and auditory cortices. Evoked potentials to very bright flashes and loud clicks presented synchronously once every second were recorded in these structures. Usually 50 stimuli were presented without any distraction and the evoked potentials recorded; then another 50 stimuli were accompanied by either a visual distractor (a rat in a plastic box) or an auditory distractor (tape-recorded rat squeaks). Finally another 50 stimuli were presented without distraction.

One result that was clear from this experiment was a lack of any difference between the effects of the visual and auditory distractions upon either the visual or the auditory evoked potentials. In most instances there was a positive correlation between the evoked potentials

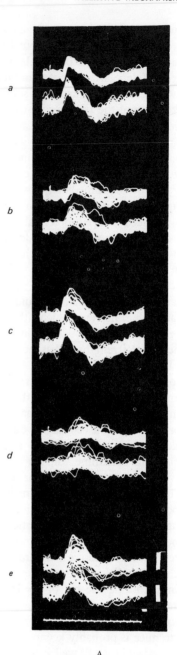

A

in the two modalities (they went up and down together), but the direction of the change varied from animal to animal. In two of the cats the evoked potentials were usually reduced by distractions (Figure 15.2A), and in the other three they were usually increased and made less variable in latency (Figure 15.2B).

The multiple-trace photographs used by Jane

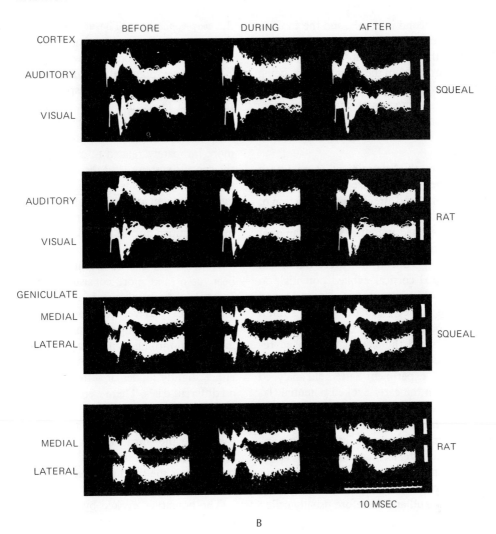

BEFORE   DURING   AFTER

CORTEX

AUDITORY   SQUEAL

VISUAL

AUDITORY   RAT

VISUAL

GENICULATE

MEDIAL   SQUEAL

LATERAL

MEDIAL   RAT

LATERAL

10 MSEC

B

Figure 15.2 (A) Fifty superimposed sweeps of evoked-potential records from auditory (above) and visual (below) cortex in the cat to simultaneously applied visual and auditory stimuli: (a) no distraction; (b) visual distraction; (c) no distraction; (d) auditory distraction; (e) just after auditory distraction. The time marker was 10 msec, and the calibration marks are 100μV. (B) Fifty superimposed evoked-potential records from the auditory and visual cortex (top two frames), and from the medial and lateral geniculate bodies (lower two frames) before, during, and after distraction by auditory (rat squeal) or visual (rat in plastic box) distracting stimuli. Calibration marks, 100μV. (From Jane, Smirnov & Jasper, 1962.)

and his colleagues and shown in Figure 15.2 represent an early application of averaging methods in experiments on attention. Later applications of this technique have employed computer averaging (see Chapter 4), an advance that has made possible the measurement of evoked potentials from the scalp of human subjects. Much more reliable and convenient

control of attention can, of course, be obtained with human than with animal subjects, and this fact has been exploited by many investigators.

Satterfield and Cheatum (1964) recorded cortical evoked potentials to somesthetic stimulation of the wrists (produced by painless, low-voltage stimulation of the ulnar nerves). The shocks were given alternately to each wrist at about one-second intervals, and the subjects were asked to attend to one wrist for a time and then to the other. In most of the subjects evoked potentials from the wrist that was being attended to were smaller than those from the ignored wrist. There was no change in the size of the potentials recorded from the ulnar nerve itself, ruling out the possibility of peripheral artifacts.

Although in this experiment there was a correlation between the size of the cortically evoked potential and attention, the direction of the change suggested an inverse relationship between the evoked potential and the amount of central activity elicited by the signal. In a subsequent experiment, however, Satterfield (1965) recorded cortical evoked potentials to clicks and shocks to the ulnar nerves and found that in most subjects (40 of 47) the stimuli attended to produced *larger* evoked potentials. Attention reduced the size of the evoked response in the other seven subjects.

In the latter experiment Satterfield analyzed separately both the early evoked potential (latency about 20 msec), which was picked up from the lateral surface of the scalp over the sensory cortical areas, and a later, larger component (latency greater than 100 msec), which was picked up from anywhere on the scalp but most easily recorded from electrodes on the vertex of the skull and therefore usually called

the *vertex potential*. The vertex potential was the only one influenced by changes in attention; the short-latency potentials were not affected.

The vertex potential is evoked by any type of stimulus and is very widespread, making it reasonable to assume that it is the result of activity in the nonspecific sensory system. As we shall see later, the nonspecific system seems more intimately related to attention, than are the specific systems, and the fact that most experiments on humans have concentrated on the late component of the evoked potential may well account for differences between the findings in human and in animal experiments.

In some recent human experiments more objective methods of controlling attention have been used, and more consistent results have sometimes been obtained. H. Davis (1964) recorded evoked vertex potentials during the presentation of groups of four tone pips. The first was a warning signal at a frequency lower than that of the other three. The third was either slightly louder or softer than the others on different trials. There were three conditions: In the first the subjects read during the recordings, in the second they had to press a button each time the third pip was louder than the second, and in the third they had to press the button after the third pip every time, whether it was louder or softer.

The potentials evoked by the first, second, third, and fourth pips were added and averaged separately from one another, and the results for the three conditions are shown in Figure 15.3. The third potential was enhanced only when a decision about its size had to be made. Davis did not find that instructions to attend to the pips had any effect upon the size of the vertex potential, nor, apparently, did the subject's rather close attention to the standard pip, in order to compare it with the test pip, in the decision series have an effect.

Spong, Haider, and Lindsley (1965) performed an experiment somewhat similar to that of Satterfield, using as stimuli alternate flashes and clicks at one-second intervals and recording evoked potentials. Attention to one mode or the other was ensured in some cases by having the subjects detect weak clicks or dim flashes; in

Figure 15.3 Average evoked responses to tone pips from the vertex of the human scalp. The test pip was sometimes either 3 db softer or 3 db louder than the standard, and in the decision series the subject had to press a button when he thought the test tone was louder than the standard. In the response series the subject had to press the button to every test pip, whether he thought it was louder or not. The evoked potential appears to be larger when a decision has to be made. (After H. Davis, 1964.)

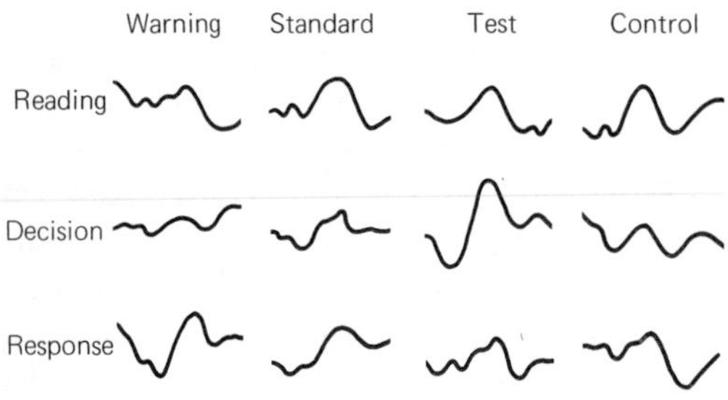

other cases the subjects had to press a key after each stimulus in the selected modality or count the stimuli and press a key after each 50.

The late components of the evoked potentials were influenced by attention in the vigilance condition, that is, when the subjects were trying to detect weak stimuli. The visual responses were increased by attention to the visual stimuli, and to a lesser extent the auditory responses were increased by attention to weak clicks. These investigators did not find any consistent change with pressing the key or counting; some subjects had decreased and others increased evoked potentials under these conditions.

Habituation

The electrophysiological changes that occur during habituation to a frequently presented stimulus have been studied in the hope that they might tell us something about attention. Hernández-Peón (1961) claimed that after many hours of continuous exposure to clicks the evoked response at the cochlear nucleus was diminished or eliminated. If the sound quality of the click was changed suddenly or a shock was paired with the click, the evoked potential returned to its original value. Similar results had previously been reported by Galambos, Sheatz, and Vernier (1956).

Further investigation of this phenomenon by others has yielded equivocal results. In some cases, changes in size of the evoked potentials have occurred, but they have been shown to be caused by changes in the position of the ears or eyes or by pupillary constriction. Fernández-Guardiola, Roldán, Fanjul, and Castells (1961) showed that the average potential evoked from a regularly occurring flash did not change over a period of three hours if the cat's pupils were maintained in a dilated state by atropine. Worden and Marsh (1963) tested cats that had been permanently provided with electrodes in the auditory pathways and failed to record any consistent change in the amplitudes of evoked potentials to clicks over a period of six hours. Cats tested continuously for five days gave similar negative results. Decreases sometimes occurred, only to be followed later

by a return to the original level, or even an increase (Figure 15.4). Worden and Marsh attributed these erratic fluctuations to head movements and especially to the burying of the ears when the cats curled up to sleep. The reciprocal changes shown by evoked potentials in the right and left cochlear nuclei in some animals (for example, subject 24 in Figure 15.4) lend support to this view.

Even if the phenomenon proved to be replicable, it is difficult to see what relevance such electrophysiological habituation could have for behavioral habituation (that is, for the loss of an orientation response to a stimulus) because the disparity between the times of onset is so extreme. Behavioral habituation usually takes place after only a dozen or so presentations of a stimulus; those who have observed electrophysiological habituation in peripheral sensory nuclei have claimed that it occurs only after tens of thousands of presentations.

Those, like Hernández-Peón, who attribute the blocking of input during habituation to activity in the reticular formation have even less excuse for accepting any relationship between the effect and behavioral habituation, for in other experiments described below it has been observed that changes in the activity of the reticular formation are highly correlated in time with the onset of behavioral habituation.

As we saw in Chapter 14, a novel or interesting stimulus will produce desynchronization of the cortical EEG. After repeated presentation of the same stimulus, the effect disappears, as demonstrated in dramatic fashion by Sharpless and Jasper (1956). Cats equipped with cortical electrodes were allowed to rest quietly until the EEG showed large synchronized waves, and then a loud raucous note was turned on for a few seconds, causing a startle response and a long period of low-voltage, fast-wave EEG (Figure 15.5). When the cat had settled down and was dozing once more, the sound was presented again, causing a second arousal, and so on. There was a rapid decline in both the intensity and duration of the EEG arousal, and after 10-30 presentations of the sound it caused no more than a slight flattening of the EEG while it was on and later not even that (see the

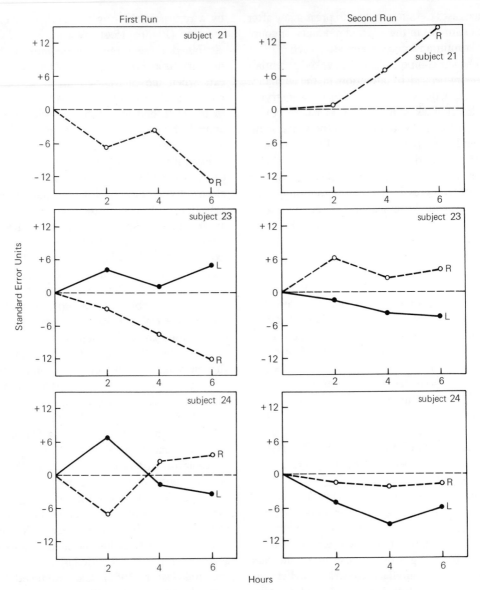

Figure 15.4 Changes in mean auditory evoked potentials from the cochlear nuclei of three cats during two separate "habituation" runs. Dashed lines represent the right cochlear nuclei; solid lines represent the left cochlear nuclei. Often the change is in different directions for the two runs and for the two ears, suggesting that orientation with respect to the source of the sound is an important factor in the variation. (From Worden & Marsh, 1963.)

first stimulus in Figure 15.6). When habituation was complete, presentation of a tone of different frequency or loudness would again arouse the cat (see the second stimulus in Figure 15.6), but the generalization gradient was quite flat. After habituation to 500 Hz, for example, a tone of 600 Hz would not produce arousal,

though a normal cat can learn to discriminate between those two frequencies when awake. To produce dishabituation the frequency change had to be on the order of two to one. There was always a close correspondence between EEG arousal and behavioral arousal.

Cats also habituated, though more slowly, to

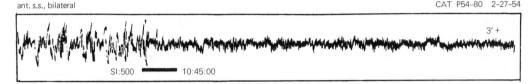

Figure 15.5 A recording from the anterior suprasylvian gyrus of a cat, showing an arousal response to a single presentation of a 500 Hz tone. The arousal lasted more than 3 minutes. (From Sharpless & Jasper, 1956.)

complex auditory stimuli like a tone sliding in about four seconds from 200 to 5,000 Hz. When the cat had become habituated to such a rising glissando, it was still aroused by the same range of frequencies sliding downward at the same rate. A change in the stimulus pattern, even though it involved the same receptors, could thus be arousing, indicating that the signal had undergone some analysis before it reached the synapses at which habituation took place.

Lesions in the auditory cortex had no effect upon habituation to single tones and only a slight effect upon habituation to patterns, but cutting the brachia of the inferior colliculus, thus depriving both the thalamus and the cortex of specific auditory input, made the animals very difficult to arouse, and dishabituation to new frequencies no longer occurred.

Sharpless and Jasper conclude that there were two sources of arousal, the thalamus and the reticular formation. The former was more difficult to habituate, was frequency- and pattern-specific, but generated only short periods of arousal. The reticular formation was quickly habituated, showed hardly any frequency or

Figure 15.6 Recordings from a cat with almost complete ablation of the lateral and posterior cortex. The sixty-first presentation of a 700 Hz tone failed to produce any arousal, but a 200 Hz tone, presented for the first time immediately afterward, produced arousal. A few minutes later 700 Hz still failed to arouse the animal, but a 1,200 Hz tone presented for the first time was effective. Frequency-specific habituation thus occurs even in a cat with no auditory cortex. (From Sharpless & Jasper, 1956.)

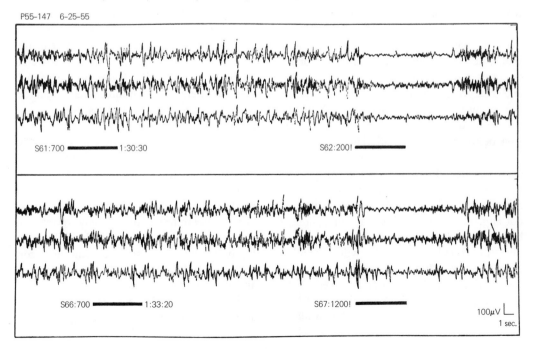

pattern specificity, but produced vigorous and long-lasting arousal to novel stimuli.

Horn and Hill (1964) and Hill and Horn (1964) have obtained evidence at the single-cell level that the nonspecific sensory system is more susceptible to habituation than the specific sensory pathways, in which only occasional habituating cells are found (Horn, 1963). Rabbits were used in the experiments, and habituating cells were most frequently found in the tegmentum, ventral to the superior colliculus. The neurons were tested for responsiveness to a variety of stimuli such as whistles, rattling coins, animal noises, spots of light, animal silhouettes, and air blown on the rabbits' fur. Many cells in the tegmentum gave a strong response to the first of a series of identical stimuli but smaller responses to subsequent presentations a few seconds apart. After a rest of 5–10 minutes the cells usually recovered, at least to some extent. Adaptation to one stimulus did not affect the cell's response to another stimulus, though, of course, not all stimuli would fire a particular cell.

It is a little surprising that so few sensory neurons in the cortex should show habituation, in view of the very consistent changes in cortical EEG during arousal. It is further evidence, if any were needed, of the dissociation between EEG and neuronal firing. The relative abundance of habituating cells in the tegmentum underlines the importance of that area for the orienting response (or general arousal) to novel and unexpected stimuli.

It seems likely that in some cases habituation to a stimulus is caused by failure of transmission between the active afferent neurons and neurons in the arousal system. This failure could be caused by some change at the synapses involved, possibly fatigue or depletion of transmitter substance. The arousal system itself is not appreciably fatigued, but it can no longer be influenced by input from the familiar stimulus. Any stimulus change that will cause other afferent paths to fire will provide renewed access to the arousal system and trigger a full-sized response there. The same thing occurs at the moment when a steady stimulus to which the animal is habituated is turned off (Weinberger & Lindsley, 1964). In such cases it is reasonable to suppose that "off" impulses, traveling in different afferent fibers from those of "on" impulses, are invading the arousal system.

PERCEPTION WITHOUT ATTENTION

Although the hypothesis that "raw" sensory input is prevented from reaching the arousal system during habituation satisfactorily explains the data of many experiments like those just described, it is not adequate for more complex situations. We become habituated to street noises, the decor of our rooms, the feel of our clothes, and so on, despite the fact that the receptors and presumably the afferent paths fired by the stimuli are continually changing. It seems that we can adapt to objects or generalizations almost as easily as to particular stimuli. In order to habituate to an object, we must have activity, representing that object in the brain, to which the arousal system can become unresponsive. The elicitation of such an activity demands sensory processing at a high level of complexity. Once habituation is complete, therefore, it follows that this perceptual processing must go on in the absence of attention. The results of the sensory analysis of input are fed into the arousal system only when a new or unexpected percept is detected. Activity in the higher levels of the sensory pathways may thus determine attention, rather than the other way round, as is frequently assumed.

Sokolov (1960) proposed that a model of familiar stimulus patterns is formed in the cortex during the habituation process. If the incoming stimuli are in accord with the internal model, their collateral input to the arousal system is inhibited, though any specific response appropriate to the stimulus will probably be elicited. If the stimulus is not in accord with the model, the arousal paths are opened, and the orienting response results.

The evidence for some such "gating" of arousal by a continuously operating perceptual mechanism is largely behavioral. It is difficult to see how physiological confirmation of the theory can be obtained until we have a clearer understanding of what the neural basis of a concept is and can measure it.

One of the most convincing demonstrations of perception in the absence of attention has been provided by the dichotic listening experiments of Broadbent (1954, 1956). He showed that subjects could pay attention to material being presented to one ear and then switch attention to the other ear or even to another modality like vision and retrieve material that had been presented there during the preceding few seconds. If we assume that attention is unitary, that is, that we cannot simultaneously attend to several disparate stimuli we are forced to conclude that complex sound or light patterns can be associated with their previously learned meanings and stored in correct sequence for a brief time, all without benefit of attention. Attention does, however, seem to be necessary for the transfer of briefly retained material to the motor system or for storing it in more permanent form. If attention is not directed to the trace within a few seconds of its being laid down, little or nothing is remembered.

The function of attention in this situation seems to be to put a complex perceptual trace into contact with the motor system, where it can either produce a spoken or written response or be "rehearsed" at a premotor level, which facilitates permanent storage (see R. L. Cohen & Johansson, 1967).

The reticular formation has long been known to have important motor functions. It regulates muscle tone, and some investigators use the electromyogram, which records the firing of muscle cells, as a measure of arousal. It would be a reasonable extension of the reticular formation's role at spinal motor centers if part of its centrally directed output were to alert the upper levels of the motor system to significant changes in the environment that could necessitate adopting a different "set" or the use of a different array of stimuli in the generation of responses.

THE RETICULAR FORMATION AND ATTENTION

Lesion studies certainly support the idea that an important component of the attention mechanism is located in the mesencephalon. Sprague, Chambers, and Stellar (1961) found that cats with subcollicular lesions were unresponsive to visual and olfactory stimuli in the contralateral fields, even though the main sensory pathways were not damaged. The difficulty was believed to result from inattention rather than from loss of sensory input because, with long training and adequate motivation, the cats could eventually be induced to respond to stimuli in the affected fields.

The animals were apathetic and silent, resembling human patients suffering from "akinetic mutism," a condition usually resulting from damage to the brainstem. The cats showed hardly any rage, fear, or pleasure. Social and sexual behavior were greatly curtailed and abnormal. The fact that the cats showed no interest in stimuli does not mean they failed to perceive them, however; akinetic human patients occasionally demonstrate by slight movements, often of the eyes, that they are receiving external stimuli.

Various degrees of inattentiveness also occur in human beings suffering from petit mal, a form of epilepsy in which attacks are accompanied by an electrographic spike-and-wave discharge occurring synchronously over the whole cortex (Figure 15.7). There may be no motor involvement, or there may be jerks of the limbs (*myoclonic jerks*). It is inferred from the EEG pattern that the primary site of the epileptic discharge is somewhere in the nonspecific projection system, for example, in the thalamus or the reticular system.

The effects of the discharge upon consciousness vary considerably. Cornil, Gastaut, and Corriol (1951) measured reaction times to sound at various stages of spike-and-wave EEG triggered by a flickering light (in patients who were susceptible to such *photic driving* of the epileptic discharge). During short bursts of spike-and-wave activity there was often no loss of consciousness and no increase in reaction

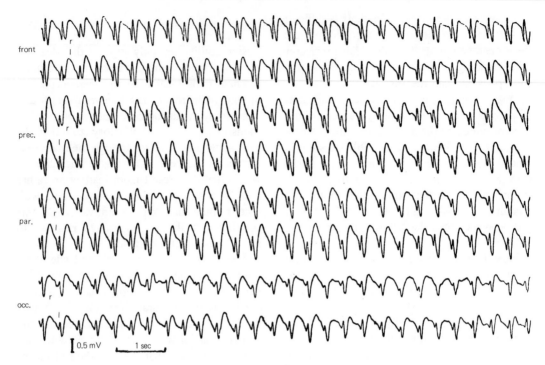

front

prec.

par.

occ.

0.5 mV   1 sec

Figure 15.7   Spike-and-wave activity recorded from the right and left frontal, precentral, parietal, and occipital cortices during a petit mal attack. (From Jung, 1954.)

time, especially in those patients who showed some jerking of the muscles. When a long burst of spike-and-wave activity was elicited the patient often demonstrated an increased reaction time, though he would still be able to discriminate different sounds. Automatic rhythmic movements, which the patient had been instructed to keep making, continued undisturbed throughout the seizures, but the patient sometimes did not remember anything about them. Similar findings have been reported in the research of Jung (1954) and by Courtois (1954).

Johnson, Davidoff, and Mann (1962) took autonomic measures of a group of petit-mal patients, many of whom were so unaffected by their seizures that they could not tell when they were taking place. In general only those patients whose spike-and-wave seizures were accompanied by changes in skin resistance, heart rate, or other autonomic effects were able to detect their seizures. Very few showed any disturbance of tapping or counting behavior during the discharge, indicating that a grossly abnormal

EEG, presumably caused by a malfunctioning arousal system, is not incompatible with more or less normal consciousness.

More demanding tests can detect impairments of behavior during petit-mal attacks, however. Mirsky, Primac, Ajmone Marsan, Rosvold, and Stevens (1960) and Lansdell and Mirsky (1964) devised a vigilance task known as the *continuous performance test* (CPT) and used it to demonstrate lapses of attention in such patients.

The apparatus consists of a window in which a series of letters appear, one at a time. The subject has a key that, during the first part of the test, he must press each time he sees the letter X. In the second part he must press only when the sequence A-X occurs.

Mirsky and Van Buren (1965) recorded the EEG while patients were performing on the CPT. They found that patients with clear-cut spike-and-wave bursts were more severely impaired during seizures than were those with less well-defined EEG patterns, even though the amplitudes and durations of the seizure discharges were matched. They also found a significant fall in performance on the CPT a few seconds before the seizure could be seen on the EEG record, and recovery on the test took place before the electrographic seizure ended, suggesting that some precursor of the seizure has an adverse effect upon attention (Figure 15.8).

In another experiment with epileptic subjects, Doreen Kimura (1964a) found that patients with petit mal and no myoclonic jerks were significantly slower than other epileptic patients in arranging groups of four letters in alphabetical order. There was some evidence that these nonjerking patients had lesions in the thalamic part of the arousal system, whereas those with jerks may have had more posterior lesions, in the mesencephalon or cerebellum, for example.

Spontaneous electrical discharge of the reticular formation in human patients thus has little effect upon behavior, though any effects it does have are deleterious. Experimental electrical

stimulation of the reticular formation in animals also usually seems to produce slight impairment of behavior (Chiles, 1954), though in one experiment improvement has been claimed. Fuster (1958) trained monkeys to make visual discriminations for food rewards in a Wisconsin General Testing Apparatus (WGTA) and then presented the task tachistoscopically, running the experiment in the dark except for single flashes. When low-voltage stimulation of the mesencephalic reticular formation was applied two seconds before each flash, the animals made fewer errors and had shorter latencies of response than in the absence of such stimulation. At higher stimulation voltages the performance deteriorated, possibly because of distracting motor effects.

This experiment has been criticized on the grounds that stimulation may have served to inform the animals that flashes were about to occur (though an auditory warning signal was also given to all groups just before the flash). The improvement would thus have resulted

Figure 15.8 Performance on the Continuous Performance Test just before and just after the onset of a burst of cortical spike-and-wave activity and just before and just after the end of the burst. (After Mirsky & Van Buren, 1965.)

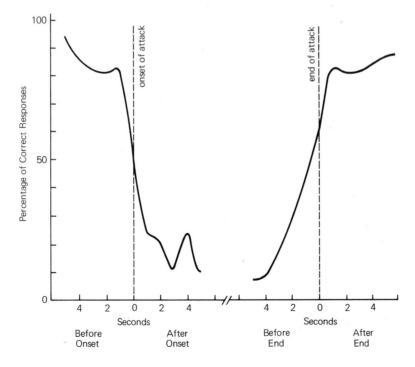

from the subjects knowing when to look and not from improved functioning of the nervous system. The results would certainly be more conclusive if control stimulations had been given in other structures.

Fuster (1961) has since shown, with microelectrode recordings, that stimulation of the reticular formation may facilitate some cortical neurons and inhibit others, which he thinks could lead to better discrimination; but, of course, many factors other than sensory acuity enter into attention.

In conclusion, we may say that there is reason to believe that the reticular formation is an important component of the attentional mechanism. After severe damage to the structure, attention is impaired or, in some cases, entirely lacking. Just how the reticular formation fulfills this role is still a mystery, but it seems likely that it has less control over the input to primary sensory projection areas than is usually assumed and that its main effect is upon the switching of motor "set."

The maintenance of attention to a particular stimulus or concatenation of stimuli is less difficult to explain, perhaps, than are sudden changes of attention. During attention to one theme, we may assume that an activity in central perceptual networks (a cell assembly, in Hebb's terminology) generates expectancies and facilitates related neural activities. It also provides inhibition to deprive other "cell assembly" activities from gaining access to the motor system or to those premotor and memory processes that appear to be related to conscious awareness. In other words, a continuing "set" maintains itself and in so doing ensures the continuity of attention.

It may be that the role of the reticular system in attention is to help to break up this dominance when necessary and to allow a new "set" to establish itself. A sudden general wave of inhibition or unorganized firing could dislodge the entrenched activity, and during the subsequent free-for-all another set of perceptual activities could take over.

The source of the disturbance could be a strong stimulus that invades the reticular system through the diffuse sensory pathways, a novel or unexpected stimulus that arouses the system through the cortex, or a stimulus that has strong associations with arousal because of its relationship to some drive. The peculiar features of the stimulus that cause it to fire the arousal system would no doubt also give it an advantage in supplanting the previous "set" after the disrupting wave has passed.

This outline of a model of attention, which incorporates the ideas of Hebb, Sokolov, Sharpless, and others, has been introduced not so much because the evidence leads inevitably to it as because it serves as an antidote to the suggestion, mentioned earlier, that the reticular formation is the embodiment of the self or, still less credible, that some "little man" inhabits the region and sweeps his searchlight around to reveal to consciousness the goings-on in one or another of the normally dark recesses of the brain, at the same time manipulating doors to keep out distracting stimuli.

Summary

Although attention is often defined as the selective factor in perception, a more behavioral definition and one that accords better with some of the facts of perception is that it is a process by which certain percepts attain access to the motor and long-term memory systems.

This result is achieved through various mechanisms, ranging from the control of receptor orientation to central facilitation and inhibition of different levels of the sensorimotor paths.

Because physiologists find it easier to study peripheral than central mechanisms, experiments tend to be concentrated there. One process that has received a great deal of attention involves the inhibition of receptors through centrifugal sensory fibers. Despite some supporting experiments, the evidence at present suggests that this mechanism is not important for attention. On logical grounds alone, it is difficult to see how most of the phenomena of attention could be explained if sensory signals never reached the central nervous system in the first place.

One interesting but still unexplained outcome of these experiments is the discovery that what might be regarded as perceptual effort has an enhancing effect upon the size of the nonspecific evoked response to a stimulus. Less surprising is the fact that the novelty or unexpectedness of a stimulus increases this component of the evoked potential.

Another line of research, also at the peripheral level, that of measuring habituation to repeated stimuli (on the assumption that familiarity reduces attention to the stimuli), appears to be expiring in a welter of inconclusive results. It now seems likely that, except for receptor fatigue or adaptation, which occurs in some sensory modalities, habituation does not involve the peripheral parts of the sensory systems. It does occur, however, between the sensory system and the arousal system, and it occurs rapidly, after only a few dozen presentations of the stimulus as a rule.

Habituation is not entirely explicable in terms of blocking sensory afferents to the arousal system; it also occurs with complex stimuli like traffic noises, which are not repeated predictably. It seems that the classifying powers of the higher levels of the perceptual system must be called upon to process the input before it is fed into the arousal system. This finding introduces the interesting idea that perceptual analysis takes place quite normally in the absence of attention or while attention is directed to different aspects of the perceptual field.

Further evidence for this hypothesis comes from the dichotic-listening experiments of Broadbent, in which simultaneously arriving auditory signals to the two ears are both decoded, though attention is directed to only one at a time.

Finally, the importance of the arousal system for attention is illustrated by a number of experiments showing that lesions in the system have deleterious effects upon attention and result, in extreme cases, in complete failure to pay attention to anything. Epileptic discharge in the arousal system has been shown to impair performance on certain tasks that demand vigilance, though not as severely as might be expected.

In studying attention, we come very close to such difficult psychological problems as that of the ego, or "self." The temptation to attribute attention to the control by some undefined "little man" must be resisted or we are faced with the task of investigating his mechanisms. Avoidance of this pitfall is made more difficult, however, by the lack of any reasonable hypothesis as to how attention can be controlled without him. An attempt was made in conclusion to show that attention is self-maintained as long as nothing happens in other spheres to demand a change of "set." It is postulated that the role of the arousal system in attention might be to facilitate the shift of attention from one object to another.

PART FIVE

MOTIVATION AND EMOTION

The study of motivation brings us to the heart of the problem of behavior. Motivation means literally that which produces motion, but in psychology the term is given a narrower interpretation; it is applied not to the metabolic and mechanical features of the motor systems but to certain hypothetical states of the nervous system that determine what actions the organism will perform at any moment.

A dog that is eating is presumably doing so because it is hungry. Hunger is thus a form of motivation. Hungry organisms perform various actions to obtain food, according to their sensory, motor, and intellectual capacities, and this tendency can serve as an operational (or behavioral) definition of the state. The hunger drive is considered to be absent or inactive if the animal ignores food.

In everyday language, "hunger" can mean either readiness to eat or the sensations associated with need for food, which are expected to disappear after eating. When someone says, "I am hungry," we either understand his statement in its behavioral sense ("I would like to eat"), or we are reminded of how hunger feels and assume that he is experiencing such feelings.

This mixture of operational and introspective meaning is typical of the everyday vocabulary of motivation, and to use the same vocabulary for scientific purposes can be quite confusing. It is too much to hope that the subjectivism introduced into the language through thousands of years of nonscientific expression of needs, desires, and the like—our most important subjects of conversation—can be swept away by a paragraph of explanation, but it is nevertheless worthwhile to discuss the terminology briefly, if only to draw attention to possible pitfalls.

Some motivational states are so closely tied to peripheral stimuli that in common usage they are spoken of simply as "sensations." Foul odors, pain, excessive heat or cold, and the like are highly motivating, but we have no separate words to describe the motivational states they elicit. On the other hand, motivational states that are not always accompanied by obvious external stimuli have names like "fear" and "anger." We call these states (which we are aware of mainly through introspection) "emotions," rather than "sensations," though the difference is apparently not in the state but in the way in which it is elicited. Fear motivates behavior that, if we neglect the reflexive components, is much the same as that motivated by such noxious stimuli as foul odors.

The main force of the words for emotions, however, is directed not to the behavior they produce but to some introspected central state, an emphasis that applies even more strongly to emotions like joy, grief, boredom, and anxiety, than it does to fear and anger. It is true that we can usually detect these states in others by autonomic measures and involuntary patterns of facial expression, but these clues hardly constitute motivated behavior in the usual sense. It is quite possible, incidentally, as the James-Lange theory of emotion states (James, 1890), that at least part of the discrimination of our own emotions involves recognition in ourselves of the signs that we use to judge emotional states in others.

Another reason that the special name "emotion" has been given to some motivational states seems to be that they occur irregularly and are slightly out of the normal routine of life. They depend upon chance external factors or arise spontaneously (in which case they may be regarded as verging on the pathological). Hunger, thirst, and sexual desire, on the other hand, recur at frequent intervals and, with luck, can be satisfied at early stages before they reach distressing proportions. For these reasons they may be called merely "needs." Sometimes they are also called "sensations," even though the stimuli come from internal states of the body. As physiological psychologists, we must avoid the assumption that distinctions among motivational states based on introspection necessarily imply different neural mechanisms.

A general introduction to motivation should make some mention of the theories about its origin. Until quite recently many philosophers took for granted that man ate because he was reasonable enough to understand that if he did not he would perish. All human activities—working, begetting and bearing children, protecting the home and raiding the homes of others, and so on—were believed to occur with the conscious and premeditated aim of benefiting self and family. If a person came eventually to enjoy doing what was good for him, it was because the effects produced pleasure and the anticipation of pleasure became attached to the actions. Beasts seemed to behave similarly and were assumed to do so for similar reasons. The result was a highly anthropomorphic view of animal motivation, though an alternative explanation in terms of instinct was also popular.

This rationalistic theory may not have been entirely convincing to everybody, but like many of today's theories it was accepted for lack of a more reasonable alternative. The theory of evolution eventually provided such an alternative. Animals, including man, certainly tend to act in ways beneficial to themselves and their group but not necessarily because they have thought it all out beforehand. They behave this way because they have inherited nervous systems that strongly urge them into the appropriate activities, and the reason they have inherited such convenient nervous systems is that their forebears would not have ventured into their *ecological* niche or survived in it with less effective motivational equipment. In other words, the principle of natural selection applies to behavior as well as to structure.

All organisms must absorb nutrients and avoid damaging environments if they are to prosper. The simplest organisms can survive quite well by sitting in a nutritive environment and reproducing rapidly when conditions are good, so that at least some of their progeny have a chance to reach other suitable environments and to survive and reproduce in their turn. Such organisms still need, as a minimum, a reproductive system and enzyme systems for extracting energy and structural materials from their environment. Any mutation that deprived the offspring of these systems would be lethal.

In order to flourish in less benign environments, animals depend upon mutations that provide them with more complex motivational systems, and only those animals that acquire or inherit such systems can survive in certain environments. Motivational systems arise by chance and are found in present-day animals precisely because animals without them have been weeded out in the process of natural selection.

The "rational self-interest" theory of motivation required only that the individual be able to distinguish good effects from bad and to learn. Most learning theories of the early behaviorist era (for example, that proposed by Hull, 1943) were based on these principles. It was argued that to attribute motivation to "instincts" explained nothing, and there is a good deal of force to this argument as long as no attempt has been made to explain how instincts work. But to say that instincts explain nothing is no justification for pretending they do not exist.

It may sound silly to say that animals have instincts to avoid cold draughts, spit out poisonous food, eat salt when sodium depleted, and so on, which is one reason why the word is used with restraint these days, but the fact remains that such self-preservative mechanisms are found in many animals and can, in most cases, be shown not to depend significantly upon learning. Physiologists studying the neural and hormonal bases of motivation and *ethologists* studying species-specific behavior in the natural habitat (for example, Tinbergen, 1951) are steadily undermining the argument against invoking instinct, but as the instinctive mechanisms are better understood the need to call them "instincts" diminishes.

With our increasing knowledge of underlying mechanisms we must not, however, be tempted to attribute too much to innate processes. "Pure" instinctive behavior is rare, except in very primitive or very naïve animals, and it is usually crude and inefficient. Most animals can fulfill their needs in a blundering way by instinctive mechanisms if they have had no previous experience, but they continually improve upon their performance by learning.

Improvement implies that learning is directed in some way. Such direction may well come from a simple "better-worse" indicator that provides appropriate reinforcement, as postulated in many learning theories, in which case we must assume that the various motivational systems, despite their separate reflexive and instinctive mechanisms, feed into a common system capable of influencing higher-level goal-directed behavior and learning.

Such a common system would be of more interest to psychologists than are the individual regulatory circuits that activate it, just as the higher perceptual integrating systems of the sensory systems are more interesting than the receptors and peripheral pathways. But, as with the sensory systems, we know much less about the central mechanisms of motivation than about the more reflexive systems of regulation. At this stage in the history of physiological psychology, therefore, we must reconcile ourselves to the study of those parts of the nervous system that are accessible to our present research methods and hope that this study will provide us with hints to how the central mechanisms work or how to investigate them.

There are, of course, innumerable physiological mechanisms by which the body is maintained in an optimum state. Most of them—for example the beating of cilia in the lungs to expel fluid and foreign matter—operate below the level of consciousness and hardly require mention here except as examples of one end of a "continuum" of mechanisms, ranging from the very simple and automatic to the most complex and intellectual, on which our lives and well-being depend.

When we take a single requirement of the organism, we usually find a hierarchy of mechanisms involved in its fulfillment, some at the reflexive level and others at higher levels. Even in the case of the beating pulmonary cilia, malfunctioning recruits behavioral mechanisms, at first reflexive coughing perhaps. The animal eventually feels ill and this feeling elicits certain nonreflexive behaviors (finding a sheltered place to lie down or, in man, calling a physician) that may sometimes be helpful in combating the condition. This pattern is typical: The automatic regulatory mechanism operates within its range, but once the unbalance or disturbance becomes too great for correction at that level a higher level is brought into play. It is the higher levels that we usually regard as motivation, but if we are to understand the system as a whole it is necessary to consider the lower levels also. One good reason is that the detectors of imbalance are often common to the various hierarchical levels.

In Chapter 16 we shall consider the systems involved in the day-to-day regulation of some of the more important needs like those for stable temperature, various nutrients, and water. (The need for oxygen is almost too urgent to have ever evolved complex motivational mechanisms; the animal usually dies before any high-level behavior can be aroused. Sublethal increases in the concentration of carbon dioxide will produce avoidance behavior, however, as demonstrated by Sommers, 1963.)

Later chapters deal with reproductive mechanisms, including parental behavior and motivations like love (or attachment), fear, and curiosity that maintain group cohesion, help to preserve the animal from danger, and ensure that it becomes informed about its environment.

After examining the individual aspects of some motivational systems, we shall finally consider the interactions among them and between each and the common evaluative system that determines how motivation influences "voluntary" behavior. This evaluative system has sometimes been called the *hedonic system* and credited with producing "pleasure" and "pain," (or "displeasure.") The strict behaviorist prefers to place less emphasis upon subjective impressions and to think of the system as producing approach or avoidance or simply as a "stop-go" system. We shall see how such a system might fit into an overall picture of animal motivation and learning.

CHAPTER 16

SOME REGULATORY MECHANISMS

TEMPERATURE REGULATION

Metabolic processes necessary for life operate best within a rather narrow range of temperatures (usually 30–40° C.); large deviations from this optimum range are lethal. Cold-blooded animals (*poikilotherms*) adopt nearly the temperature of their surroundings, but birds and mammals (*homoiotherms*) have evolved physiological mechanisms for maintaining their body temperature at a relatively constant value, which of course, allow them to function at optimum efficiency in a wider range of environments.

Nevertheless, cold-blooded animals do regulate their body temperatures to a considerable extent. The simplest method is to move toward regions of optimum temperature. According to Mendelssohn (1902) paramecia will move into a region where the temperature is 24–28° C. from either warmer or cooler regions, and other poikilotherms also have "preferred" temperature zones. Figure 16.1 shows Rocky Mountain ticks congregating in a zone where the temperature is about 30° C., avoiding warmer and cooler places.

Social insects have very elaborate means of keeping their larvae at optimum temperature, and the temperature of the brood combs of a beehive is maintained within a degree of 35° C., which is as nearly constant as the body temperature of many homoiotherms. When the hive temperature falls below 35° C., workers gather on the combs and generate heat by muscular exertion. If the temperature rises much above 35° C., air is fanned through the hive; when the outside air is no longer cool enough for this method to be effective, the workers spread dilute nectar or water on the combs and blow air over it with their wings to evaporate it. On hot days foraging bees bring in very dilute nectar or even pure water, and most of the workers are engaged in cooling the hive (Lindauer, 1961).

Homoiotherms use the same principles of temperature control. When the animal is cold it generates heat by muscular action, including shivering, and when it is warm it loses heat through evaporation of water. In some mammals most of the water is evaporated from saliva, in others from the secretion of sweat glands in the skin.

In a cool environment animals equipped with hair or feathers fluff them out to trap air; still air is a very good thermal insulator. In addition, blood is shunted away from the surface of the body, which deprives the skin of some heat, of course, but also reduces the heat loss from the core of the body. A moderate fall in skin temperature is uncomfortable but not as dangerous as a fall in the temperature of the blood would be.

When the core temperature is high, the peripheral blood vessels dilate to give the blood access to the surface, which is where most of the heat is removed. Animals with few sweat glands salivate profusely when they are overheated, and evaporation of saliva is increased by protrusion of the tongue and panting, which moves air rapidly over the wet surface. Many small animals (opposums, rats, guinea pigs) do not pant, but they spread saliva over their fur to increase the area from which evaporation can take place (Higginbotham & Koon, 1955; Hainsworth & Epstein, 1966).

Hormones are also important in thermoregulation. Prolonged cooling increases the release of *thyrotropic hormones* from the anterior pituitary, (Figure 16.2) and thus of *thyroxine* (a substance that increases the metabolic rate) from the thyroid glands (Andersson, Ekman, Gale & Sundsten, 1963). The release of epi-

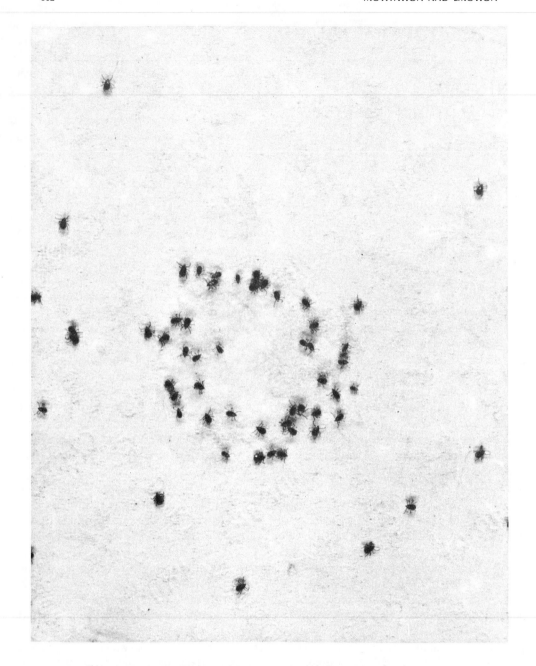

Figure 16.1 Demonstration of temperature preference of Rocky Mountain ticks. The back of the paper was illuminated with a lamp so that the middle was hot and the outer regions cool. The ticks congregated in the zone that was at an intermediate temperature. (Photograph by Dr. J. Nowosielski, after Fraenkel and Gunn, 1961.)

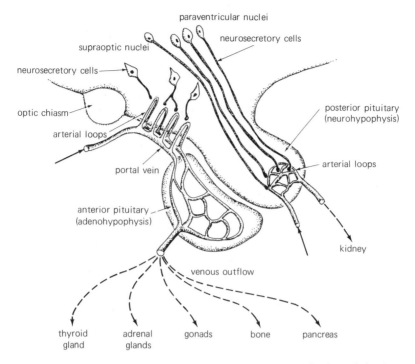

Figure 16.2 The pituitary activation substances secreted by hypothalamic neurosecretory cells are picked up through loops of the artery that supplies the anterior pituitary and stimulate the cells of that organ to produce hormones. These hormones enter the venous outflow and are carried to other glands and organs of the body to control their secretions. The secretions of cells in the paraventricular nucleus are picked up by loops of another artery in the posterior pituitary and are carried directly to the target organ in the bloodstream, bypassing the anterior pituitary. (After Bargmann & Scharrer, 1951; Scharrer & Scharrer, 1963.)

nephrine is another cause of heat production by increasing muscular activity and releasing glucose into the blood. The hormones are controlled by hypothalamic neurosecretory cells through the blood supply to the anterior pituitary (Figure 16.2).

These effector mechanisms are the most important ones for reflexive heat regulation; the next question is how they are brought into and out of action as circumstances demand.

Location of Thermoreceptors

Clearly, any compensatory response depends upon the body temperature, which must be measured in some way. For a long time it was assumed that the temperature receptors in the skin were the only ones responsible for providing the feedback to heat-regulatory mechanisms, but that theory encountered a number of difficulties. We know that most peripheral receptors adapt fairly quickly to changes in temperature but that the core temperature of the body remains constant to within a fraction of a degree. Obviously there must be receptors that continuously indicate the true temperature and not just the rate of temperature change.

It was already known in the last century that damage to what we now call the hypothalamus interfered with temperature regulation, and this finding has been confirmed many times since (for example, Ranson, 1940). Electrical stimulation of the preoptic region also indicates that this area is important for temperature regulation. B. Andersson, Grant, and Larsson (1956) elicited panting, cutaneous vasodilation, and other cooling responses in goats by electrically stimulating a restricted region between the anterior commissure and the optic chiasm (Figure 16.3).

This finding shows that the anterior hypothalamus is involved in autonomic responses to overheating but does not prove that there are thermoreceptors there. The region is well supplied with blood, however, which maintains its temperature close to that of the heart and lungs; it would thus be a suitable place to register temperature.

One way to test the hypothesis that there are thermoregulatory receptors in the hypothalamus is to heat or cool the region locally. This procedure is equivalent to blowing hot or cold air on the thermostatic element of a home furnace or an air-conditioning unit. If the element is cooled below room temperature, the furnace will be turned on, and it will stay on because it will fail to warm the element to the temperature it was set to maintain. The rest of the house may become very hot in the process. It has been found that warming the anterior hypothalamus in cats causes sweating and panting (Magoun, Harrison, Brobeck & Ranson, 1938) and that cooling causes huddling and reduces the threshold for shivering, though, according to Freeman and Davis (1959), it does not itself cause shivering. Hammel, Hardy, and Fusco (1960) reported, however, that in dogs, cooling the hypothalamus causes peripheral

vasoconstriction and shivering. The trunk becomes overheated, but, because of the vasoconstriction, the extremities cool down.

Nakayama, Eisenman, and Hardy (1961) and Nakayama, Hammel, Hardy, and Eisenman (1963) have been able to locate neurons in the preoptic region of the cat that increase their firing rates when the hypothalamus is heated, but they have found none that responds to cooling. Hardy, Hellon, and Sutherland (1964), who made similar recordings from the anterior hypothalamus of the dog, found that about 30 per cent of the cells sampled in the region between the optic chiasm and the anterior commissure responded to heating of the region and that about 10 per cent of the sampled cells increased their firing rates when the region was cooled. None of these cells showed any change of activity when only the skin of the face was heated.

There has been a suggestion that the "cold" receptors are serotonergic and that the "warm" receptors are adrenergic, though it has not been tested by direct measurement. Feldberg and Myers (1963) injected epinephrine and norepinephrine into the third ventricle of cats made feverish by *pyrogen* injections and found that shivering was abolished and that temperature was reduced for several hours. Injections of 5-HT (serotonin) into the third ventricle of

Figure 16.3 Sagittal section of the diencephalon of the goat, showing the region between the anterior commissure and the optic chiasm that is sensitive to heat.

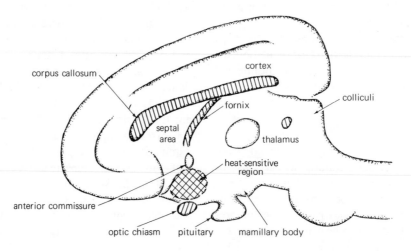

normal cats produced temperature rises of up to 2° C.

Another way of testing the theory that temperature-controlling receptors are located in the hypothalamus is to see how closely the hypothalamic temperature is correlated with sweating, panting, shivering, and the like. Forster and Ferguson (1952) found a high correlation between panting and hypothalamic temperature in five cats, but in two others they found panting more closely correlated with skin temperature.

These experiments indicated that there are thermoreceptors in the hypothalamus but did not compare the proportion of regulation provided by hypothalamic receptors with that of peripheral receptors, though most experiments suggested that both are involved. Benzinger (1962) made a very careful series of heat-transfer measurements in man, using a specially constructed calorimeter. He took the temperature of the eardrum, which shares the arterial supply of the hypothalamus and has been shown to be at nearly the same temperature, and found that above a temperature of 37° C. there was a perfect correlation between temperature and the rate of heat loss through sweating.

This relationship held only when the skin temperature was above about 33° C., however; at lower skin temperatures the rate of sweating was proportionately lower (Figure 16.4). Above 33° C. skin temperature had no effect upon the rate of heat loss. An ice cube held against the roof of the mouth, where it cools the anterior hypothalamus, reduced the sweating rate drastically, even though there was a sharp rise in skin temperature as a result.

Benzinger could find no simple relationship between eardrum temperature and the rate of heat generation in a cold environment, and he argued that skin temperature controlled this response. In support of the theory that heat loss depends upon hypothalamic temperature and heat generation upon skin temperature, Benzinger recalled that the effects of local cooling of the hypothalamus in animals are less impressive than are the effects of heating (some investigators found it impossible to elicit shiver-

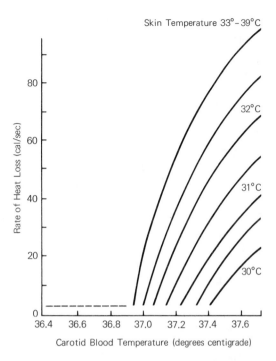

Figure 16.4 Rates of heat loss in a man at various skin temperatures, plotted against blood temperature. (After Benzinger, 1962.)

ing, for example), but at least one investigator (Satinoff, 1964) has since shown that cooling the hypothalamus is effective in eliciting regulatory behavior. It is therefore probably safer to assume that both central and peripheral receptors are involved in responses to cold.

One factor that may complicate the interpretation of these experiments is the formation of conditioned reflexes involved in heat regulation. It is almost certain that after a time such responses as tensing the muscles and vasoconstriction occur in anticipation of changes in the core temperature. They may occur at the sight of snow or ice, for example, or when skin temperature changes, even if skin receptors have no innate connections to the heat-regulatory system.

Although peripheral receptors may play a subsidiary role in initiating thermoregulatory reflexes, they are probably important in eliciting such behavioral adjustments as the search for a warmer or cooler resting place, and they are of primary importance in guiding the animal to such a place. It would be inefficient for the animal to wait until the temperature of the whole body had changed before being able to judge whether it had made a favorable or unfavorable move.

Behavioral Thermoregulation

Under a broad enough definition of "behavior," all thermoregulatory responses can be called "behavioral," but we exclude such autonomic and reflexive responses as sweating, salivating, shivering, and *pilo-erection* (hair fluffing) from the behavior to be considered here. Temperature regulation in poikilotherms depends entirely upon behavioral adjustments, some of which have already been mentioned. Protozoa and many other organisms congregate in regions of optimum temperature, and presumably when they try to move into hotter or colder regions some inhibition or redirection of movement occurs. The mechanism could be reflexive, depending upon some action of temperature upon propulsive mechanisms in simple organisms or controlled by sensory input from receptors in the feet, antennae, or other parts of the body in higher organisms.

If only one part of an animal is heated or cooled excessively, that part will be withdrawn, just as if it had been hurt. This response suggests that local thermoregulation involves a close link between pathways for temperature and for pain. Such localized protective mechanisms are not usually considered part of the thermoregulatory system, but they do, in fact, play a role under some circumstances, and it is well to recognize that most motivational systems have many relatively independent subsystems that cooperate to benefit the whole animal.

When we come to study more complex behavior, it is necessary to introduce some form of evaluating mechanism, like the "better-worse" circuit mentioned earlier, that can bring a more general influence to bear upon behavior. In higher animals, this aspect of the motivational system not only helps to steer activity toward the goal of optimum body temperature; it also helps to ensure learning of successful responses.

Although it is not very useful to consider the subjective correlates of neural activity, some people may find it helpful to view activity in such evaluative circuits as the basis of "pleasure" (or "comfort") and "distress" (or "discomfort"). It must be recognized, of course, that these terms cannot be used in *neural* explanations of behavior.

As a hypothetical example of how an evaluative system might refine and extend a purely reflexive system of heat regulation, let us consider again the rat's saliva-spreading response to heat. It is possible that the first time a rat is exposed to excessive heat it does no more than salivate profusely and dribble onto the fur of its chin and neck; if, however, it should chance to groom at this time and thus to wet a greater area of fur, the feedback of coolness would excite the "better" circuit, which would then maintain and perhaps intensify grooming behavior. The activity of this circuit would also encourage learning of the response for use under similar circumstances in the future. Higginbotham and Koon (1955) reported that two-month-old raccoons could cool themselves by licking their feet and tails but did not say whether or not any learning appeared to be necessary.

Building nests and seeking shelter are other behavioral responses to extremes of temperature. Nest building may also involve learning of the sort described. Possibly there is a basic tendency among some animals to pick things up and drag them around, and if this behavior accidentally results in the construction of an insulating mat on a cold floor, for example, the increased comfort may direct such activity into more effective constructions. If the animal is lactating, the same basic response tendency (dragging objects around) may be directed to retrieval of its young.

Under laboratory conditions it is possible to show that rats are capable of learning to make any arbitrarily determined response to regulate their temperatures. Weiss and Laties (1961) trained cold rats to press a bar to obtain a short period of heat from a heat lamp placed above them (Figure 16.5). The rats were shaved so that their normal protection against the cold was less effective. Even so, bar pressing did not start for several hours after the rats had been placed in the cold, presumably because the first effect of the cold was to make them huddle into a ball and shiver, a response incompatible with bar pressing.

More recently Epstein and Milestone (1968) have shown that rats will learn to spray water over themselves when they are placed in a hot box fitted with a bar-operated shower. They will do so in preference to spreading saliva, a finding that suggests that the saliva-spreading response is not entirely innate.

Learned thermoregulatory responses provide another means of investigating the location of the receptors and control mechanisms of the system. Satinoff (1964) demonstrated bar pressing for heat in response to hypothalamic cooling in rats, even though the animals were not cold. There seems to be no good reason to assume that the corresponding experiment of training rats to press a bar to obtain a water spray or a flow of cool air when the hypothalamus is heated would not work also. Electrical stimulation of the anterior hypothalamic region would probably have the same effect. In the experiments of B. Andersson, Grant & Larsson (1956), electrical stimulation of the region between the anterior commissure and the optic chiasm in the goat led to behavior similar to that produced by overheating.

There seems to be little doubt, then, that stimulation of the hypothalamus, electrically or by heat, not only activates the motor mechanisms for heat regulation but also produces the total thermoregulatory response, including the firing of evaluative (or hedonic) circuits.

Once it has been established that certain modes of hypothalamic firing can have general effects upon behavior and learning, the only limitations to regulatory behavior are those imposed by the abilities of the animal. As might be expected, therefore, human beings do many more things than animals do to maintain comfortable temperatures. We must spend proportionally as much time and energy upon this task as bees do—and with less excuse, being homoiothermic. The clothing and housing industries spring, at least partly, from man's desire to

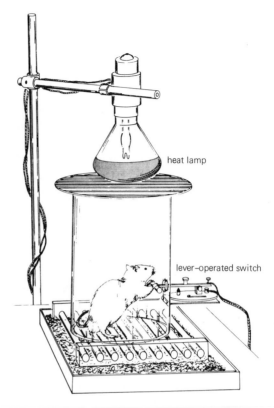

Figure 16.5 A heat-reinforcement apparatus. The rat can turn on the heat lamp by pressing the lever in its plastic cage. (After Weiss & Laties, 1961.)

avoid extremes of temperature. So do the search for fuels and other sources of energy; their transportation, sometimes halfway across the world; and their use in ever more complex heating and cooling devices, the design, manufacture, and installation of which are also flourishing industries. Although it may be too much to claim that research into the basic properties of matter has been motivated by the "thermoregulatory drive," certainly no time is lost in applying the fruits of such research to the design of thermostats, air-conditioners, and the like.

Apart from these efforts to provide ourselves with model environments, many of us try to spend as much time as possible in places where the natural climate is pleasanter than where we work. There is no doubt that, measured in terms of the amount of money and time spent satisfying it, the thermoregulatory drive would rank not far behind that for food among most inhabitants of the earth.

WATER REGULATION

Although the receptor and effector systems are different, the same general principles apply to water regulation as to thermoregulation. The primary requirements for both these—and for other regulatory systems—are, first, a detector (or detectors) of deviations from optimum conditions and, second, effectors capable of remedying such imbalances. Both internal reflexive adjustments and behavioral mechanisms are usually involved in the restoration of optimum conditions.

In water balance the main internal adjustment is the release of an *antidiuretic hormone* (ADH) to reduce the rate of water excretion. This hormone, which is synthesized by cells in the supraoptic and paraventricular nuclei of the hypothalamus, passes along the axons of these cells to the posterior pituitary (or *neurohypophysis*), where it is stored until the cells fire (Bargmann & Scharrer, 1951). It is then released into the bloodstream (Figure 16.2) and carried to the kidneys, where it increases the reabsorption of water from the tubules, thus increasing the concentration of the urine.

This control is negative, however, we do not know whether or not water depletion encourages production of water by oxidation of hydrogenous material like body fat, but it is not likely that this mechanism is important except in some desert animals that rarely or never drink.

With that possible exception, the only way to make more water available to one part of the organism internally is by transfer from another. The cells of the body constitute a large reservoir of water (about 50 per cent of body weight), and, as extracellular water, including that in the blood, is lost, some of it is replaced from this source.

In thermoregulation, there has never been any doubt that the receptors of the system are sensitive to temperature, even though there may have been doubt about their location, but what

physical parameter or parameters are being monitored by the receptors of the water-balance system is not so obvious. According to Descartes (see Adolph, 1964):

When we stand in need of drink, there arises from this want a certain parchedness in the throat that moves its nerves, and by means of them the internal parts of the brain; and this movement affects the mind with the sensation of thirst, because there is nothing on that occasion which is more useful for us than to be made aware that we have need of drink for the preservation of our health.

The physiologist Cannon (1929) espoused this venerable theory, but the experimental investigations that resulted from his interest killed it. It was found that dogs without salivary glands actually drank more often, but no more, than did normal dogs (M. F. Montgomery, 1931), and, as we shall see, most subsequent research has indicated that internal receptors are responsible for eliciting drinking. Water balance is too vital to be entirely dependent upon so vulnerable a signal as dryness of the mouth, though it would be surprising if such dryness were not one of the factors involved.

Verney (1947) suggested that the brain contains *osmoreceptors*, which measure the concentration of solutes in the extracellular fluid. The flow of water through cell membranes (or any semipermeable membrane) is under the influence of *osmotic pressure*. If the concentration of a dissolved substance is greater on one side of the membrane than on the other, molecules of the solute bombard the membrane more frequently on that side (that is, they exert a greater fraction of the total pressure). This bombardment reduces the chances that water molecules will hit and penetrate the membrane from that side; more water then diffuses from the dilute side, and this process continues either until the two solutions become equally concentrated or until excess pressure builds up on the concentrated side of the membrane to resist further flow. The excess pressure necessary to prevent water from flowing into a solution through a semipermeable membrane is called the "osmotic pressure of the solution." If cells lacking the special reinforcement of cutaneous cells are placed in water, the osmotic pressure of the intracellular fluid is demonstrated dramatically by the rupture of the membrane.

The same molar concentrations of different substances have different osmotic pressures because of the different sizes and mobilities of the molecules and the different strengths of their interactions with water molecules. Solvents that pass through the membrane produce no osmotic pressure because no concentration difference can be maintained. For these reasons it is inaccurate to say that the loss of water from cells depends only upon the concentration of the extracellular fluids; it depends upon the *osmolarity* (as the effect of the concentration upon osmotic pressure is called), but unless there are significant changes in the constitution of the fluids osmolarity will be closely related to concentration.

Verney's idea was that some large cells, or vesicles, that he saw in sections of dog hypothalamus would swell or shrink under the influence of extracellular osmolarity and in doing so would stretch the dendrites of neighboring neurons and thus signal the osmolarity.

Special structures for transducing osmotic pressure into mechanical deflections for detection by "microstretch" receptors may not be necessary, however. The neurons themselves undergo changes as a result of variations in extracellular fluid concentration, and these changes may have a direct effect upon the neurons' firing rates.

The theory that osmolarity is the most important parameter involved in water regulation has received much experimental support. The osmolarity of the blood can be increased by injections of hypertonic saline, known to be a powerful stimulant for drinking and other responses of the water-balance mechanism. If a potassium salt of the same concentration is substituted, there is no immediate effect upon drinking (Falk, 1961) because the cell membranes are more permeable to potassium and no change in osmotic pressure results.

If water balance were to depend entirely upon the osmolarity of the extracellular fluid, however, we would expect sodium depletion,

by reducing extracellular osmolarity, to inhibit drinking, but that does not appear to happen. McCance (1936) induced sodium depletion in volunteer subjects by making them sweat profusely and feeding them a low-salt diet. Most of them drank more water than normally. Two of the three said they had a funny taste in their mouth not quite like thirst, but nevertheless they drank to try to eliminate it.

As sodium was eliminated, body weight fell, for, in order to maintain constant osmolarity of extracellular fluid, water had to be lost. After a fall in weight of about 3 kg, however, no further loss occurred, and the osmolarity of the extracellular fluid fell instead. At that point the volume of the blood was low and its concentration of proteins, cells, and the like high. Only the sodium concentration was low. As increased drinking was not caused by increased osmolarity, it has been suggested that blood volume may be a factor.

Animals can conveniently be depleted of significant quantities of sodium by injecting a glucose solution into the *peritoneal space* (in the abdomen) and removing an equal volume of fluid several hours later. The glucose is absorbed by the body, and the electrolytes from the blood (mainly NaCl) diffuse into the dilute fluid, the membranes separating the peritoneal space from the bloodstream being permeable to sodium ions (Figure 16.6). This method of producing acute sodium loss was first employed by Darrow and Yannet (1935), who claimed, on the basis of its immediate effects, that it produced the inhibition of drinking that was to be expected. Later experimenters have shown, however, that, if the animals are subsequently maintained for several days on a low-salt diet, their drinking increases after the initial transient depression (Cizek, Semple, Huang & Gregerson, 1951; McCleary, 1953). This result was confirmed by Falk (1961), who introduced modifications in the technique to establish more definitely that loss of sodium ions from the extracellular fluid produces the drinking.

As may be seen in Figure 16.6, *dialysis* results in swelling of the cells; it has been suggested that perhaps osmoreceptors fire stretch

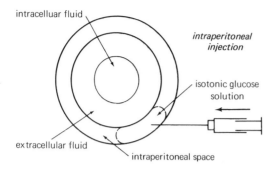

intracelluar fluid

intraperitoneal injection

isotonic glucose solution

extracellular fluid

intraperitoneal space

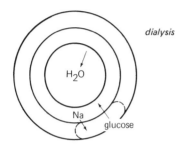

dialysis

H₂0

Na

glucose

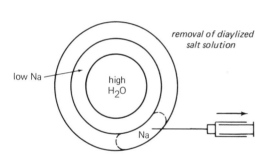

removal of diaylized salt solution

low Na

high H₂0

Na

Figure 16.6 Exchange of glucose for sodium chloride in the intraperitoneal space to produce rapid sodium depletion in the animal. Glucose solution is injected into the peritoneum from where the glucose is absorbed into the blood-stream and utilized by metabolic processes. The excess water in the peritoneum then attracts sodium salts from the extracellular fluid to help maintain tonicity and the peritoneal fluid, now consisting mainly of salt solution, is withdrawn. As the extracellular fluid becomes more dilute, the cells of the body absorb some of the excess water and swell. (After Falk, 1961.)

receptors both when they shrink and when they expand. This possibility seems unlikely, however, for several reasons. The first is that it would lead to positive feedback if the animal ever became accidentally overhydrated. The more the animal drank, the thirstier it would

become, and it would probably die of water intoxication.

Another objection to the theory is that it does not explain the further finding that removal of extracellular fluid without change of osmolarity also increases water intake. The simplest way to demonstrate this phenomenon is to remove whole blood from the animal. Hemorrhage has classically been found to make people thirsty; Holmes and Montgomery (1951, 1953) were therefore surprised to discover that blood donors never complained of thirst. They followed up this observation by letting up to 40 per cent of the blood of dogs and reported that the dogs did not increase their drinking. A similar result was obtained with rats by Schnieden (1962), but Fitzsimons (1961) and Oatley (1964) both found that rats did drink more after having been bled.

Fitzsimons (1961) also reduced extracellular volume by another technique; he attracted extracellular fluid into the peritoneum by injecting a colloid like gum acacia or polyethylene glycol. A similar result can be obtained by implanting in a body cavity a cellulose sac containing a colloid. This procedure sequesters isotonic fluid; that is, the extracellular fluid along with its dissolved salts moves into the space and is held there by the colloid.

In the short run this technique produces no change in osmolarity of the extracellular fluid and no change in the fluid content of cells, yet the treated rats drink far more water than normally. These results have been confirmed by Stricker (1966), and the name *hypovolemia* has been given to the state of reduced extracellular fluid volume, which is assumed to be the stimulus for the drinking that occurs.

Further evidence that normal thirst does not result solely from changes of osmolarity was provided in an experiment by Novin (1962). He measured the electrical conductivity of brain tissue (from which an estimate of the osmotic pressure can be made) and found that, although injection of a certain quantity of hypertonic saline might produce the same change in tissue conductivity as did a period of water deprivation, the amount of drinking it produced was considerably less. This finding probably means that reduced volume, as well as increased osmotic pressure, is a factor in stimulating drinking in dehydrated rats.

In addition to these factors, which are primarily involved in maintaining water balance, it has also been found that temperature and emotional changes can influence drinking.

Receptors for Water-Balance Mechanisms

Having determined some of the stimuli that appear to be involved in water balance, we turn next to the receptors. The cells that secrete antidiuretic hormone are located in the supraoptic and paraventricular nuclei of the hypothalamus (Figure 16.2), and Verney (1947), on the basis of experiments in which he injected saline into the carotid artery, inferred that the osmoreceptors must be near the vessels flowing directly from the carotid. He therefore looked for osmoreceptors in the hypothalamus and, as mentioned earlier, found the small cysts or vesicles to which he tentatively allocated that function.

This allocation has never been verified experimentally, but there is further evidence that some cells in the supraoptic region are sensitive to changes in osmolarity. B. Andersson (1953) found that injections of minute quantities of hypertonic saline into the anterior hypothalamus of goats produced copious drinking. Similar injections into the nearby optic chiasm or the lateral hypothalamic nuclei had no effect upon drinking.

Electrical stimulation of the supraoptic nucleus also produced drinking (B. Andersson & McCann, 1955). This finding reveals less about the location of the receptors, of course, because the electrical stimulation could also fire pathways and other neural elements of the water-balance system. It is difficult otherwise to explain the finding that electrical stimulation of the supraoptic region elicits both drinking and antidiuresis, whereas electrical stimulation of the more caudal part of the anterior hypothalamus elicits only drinking.

In rats the region producing the greatest amount of drinking during electrical stimulation is a part of the lateral hypothalamus dorsolateral to the fornix (Figure 16.7), as has been shown by Greer (1955), Mogenson and Stevenson (1966, 1967), and many others. It seems likely that the neural mechanisms responsible for drinking rather than the osmoreceptors are in this area. Hypertonic solutions do not produce drinking when injected there, but in the rat injections of the neural transmitter acetylcholine do (S. P. Grossman, 1960, 1962). Stimulation of the area has no effect upon diuresis (Mogenson, 1969).

It is still not known exactly what receptors are stimulated by changes in blood volume, if blood volume is indeed a factor in drinking. One suggestion that has received experimental support is that of Henry and Pearce (1956). They found that forcing animals to breath air at reduced pressure (which sucks blood into the thoracic space) induced diuresis (it reduced ADH secretion). Other maneuvers that increased the volume of blood in the region of the heart had the same effect, which could, however, be abolished by cutting the vagus nerve.

Recording from the vagus nerve, Henry and Pearce found fibers that responded to increase in the volume of an atrium of the heart as it filled with blood. Blowing up a balloon inside the atrium increased the firing of these fibers; removing blood decreased the firing rate (Figure 16.8). It is believed that the primary purpose of this signal is to provide feedback for the cardiovascular center in the brainstem that controls circulation, but Henry and Pearce made a good case for the idea that some of the signal also goes to the water-regulation system. Changes of 5 per cent in the volume of circulating blood produce a detectable change in the firing rate of vagal fibers. An interesting test of the theory would be to find out whether or not vagotomy has any effect upon drinking in salt-deficient or bled animals.

Disturbance of the blood supply to the kidney has been found to increase drinking in rats. Fitzsimons (1966, 1967) has suggested that this might be the mechanism for hypovolemic drinking. One of the substances secreted by the kidney when its blood supply is reduced is *angiotensin*, which increases blood pressure.

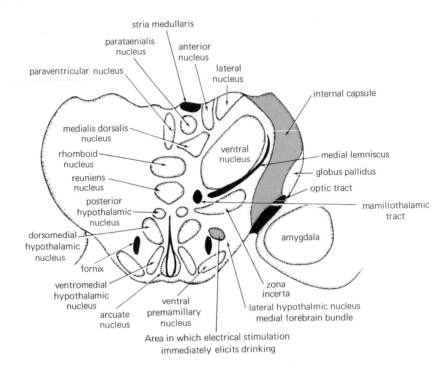

stria medullaris

parataenialis
nucleus

anterior
nucleus

lateral
nucleus

paraventricular nucleus

internal capsule

medialis dorsalis
nucleus

rhomboid
nucleus

reuniens
nucleus

posterior
hypothalamic
nucleus

dorsomedial
hypothalamic
nucleus

fornix

ventromedial
hypothalamic
nucleus

arcuate
nucleus

ventral
premamillary
nucleus

ventral
nucleus

medial lemniscus

globus pallidus

optic tract

mamillothalamic
tract

amygdala

zona
incerta

lateral hypothalmic nucleus
medial forebrain bundle

Area in which electrical stimulation
immediately elicits drinking

Figure 16.7 Coronal section through a rat diencephalon, showing major nuclei
and tracts. The region from which drinking can be elicited by electrical stimulation is indicated by the shaded area just dorsolateral to the right fornix. There
is a similar region on the left, but, in the interest of clarity, it is not shown.
(After Mogenson & Stevenson, 1967.)

Fitzsimons and Simons (1968) have shown that angiotensin also increases water consumption in the rat, probably by its action on hypothalamic chemoreceptor cells connected to the drinking system.

The water-balance system receives input from other parts of the brain besides osmolarity and volume receptors. It is well known that emotional disturbance has an antidiuretic effect, and Verney (1947) used mild electric shock in some of his experiments to induce the release of ADH. Although the hypothalamopituitary system is activated by such stimuli, drinking is not. In fact, drinking is usually inhibited by emotional stimuli or by injection of epineph-rine. Even the injection of ADH is reported to inhibit drinking, paradoxical as this finding may seem.

Under some circumstances, however, emo-tional states can increase drinking. Falk (1961, 1964) investigated a very curious phenomenon in rats, which he considered to be analogous to *psychogenic polydipsia* (excessive drinking for no apparent physiological reason). Hungry rats, trained to press a bar for small food pellets on various schedules of reinforcement that involved a good deal of waiting, tended to drink large quantities of water during the wait-ing periods if given the opportunity. Falk found, for example, that a group of rats whose average daily water consumption was about 27 ml would drink an average of more than 90 ml during a 190-minute session of bar pressing for food on a variable interval, average 1 minute, (VI-1) schedule.

It is possible that this behavior was a form of "superstitious" behavior, adopted because the chance of receiving a pellet was greater after the rat had paused to drink, but in some cases rats became polydipsic on schedules that made drinking disadvantageous in obtaining food. For example, they showed polydipsia on a schedule that never delivered a pellet less than 15 seconds after the last lick at the water bottle, which rules out the suggestion that drinking becomes a pseudoinstrumental response.

It seems more likely that the generally exciting but frustrating situation of having food doled out in tiny quantities over a long period of time leads to drinking as what ethologists call "displacement behavior." It is possible that the phenomenon is related to the finding, discussed in more detail later, that animals stimulated electrically in an area that elicits eating will switch to drinking if the food is taken away and vice versa (Valenstein, Cox & Kakolewski, 1968).

The involvement of the emotional system in water metabolism may explain the finding that cholinergic stimulation of many parts of the limbic system will increase drinking in the rat. Fisher and Coury (1962, 1964) found that injections of carbachol into the structures listed in Table 16.1 produced drinking in water-satiated rats. Similar injections into the posterior hippocampus, lateral hippocampus, midbrain tegmentum, amygdaloid nuclei, lateral thalamic areas, ventromedial and paraventricular hypothalamus, frontal cortex, subiculum, entorhinal areas, pyriform cortex, and caudate nucleus did not influence water intake.

The responses of rats stimulated in positive drinking areas were specific to water; the animals ignored stimuli associated with other primary drives. Some of the structures found by Fisher and Coury to be associated with drinking gave the same effect when stimulated electrically. B. W. Robinson (1964) found particularly strong drinking effects after stimulation of the cingulate cortex in monkeys.

The ineffectiveness of chemical stimulation of the amygdala in satiated rats was confirmed by S. P. Grossman and Grossman (1963), but these investigators found that introduction of carbachol crystals into the anterior amygdala greatly increased water consumption in water-deprived rats. Intermittent electrical stimulation in the same region had a similar effect. Electrical stimulation of the posterior amygdala decreased both eating and drinking in rats deprived of both food and water, an observation that had also been made by Fonberg and Delgado (1961) in cats.

Small lesions in the anterior amygdala of the rats produced a significant decrease in water intake, and small lesions in the posterior ventral amygdala increased drinking very significantly for several weeks after the operation. Lesions of the hypothalamus also produced changes in water consumption consistent with the stimulation results. Lesions of the anterior hypothalamus and preoptic area made by conventional techniques are almost invariably fatal (Nauta, 1946; B. Andersson, Gale & Sundsten, 1964), but Andersson and his colleagues were able to produce nonfatal lesions in this area in goats by proton irradiation. The lesions completely

Figure 16.8 Recordings from a single fiber in the vagus nerve after successive removals of 50 ml of blood from the animal and after replacement of 200 ml of the loss. The top trace in each record shows the burst of firing during the filling of the left atrium at each heartbeat. The traces on the left are for one heartbeat during inspiration, showing the maximum firing; those on the right were taken during expiration and show the minimum firing. The second trace in the two upper records is the electrocardiogram (ECG). The sharp wave accompanying the contraction of the ventricles does not appear; it was used to trigger the time base at the beginning of each beat. In the lower records the second trace shows the blood pressure in the left atrium. Each dot represents $\frac{1}{60}$ second. (From Henry & Pearce, 1956.)

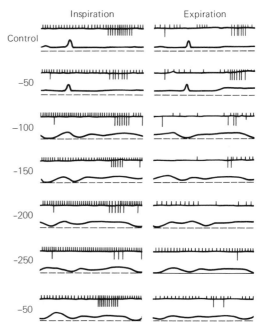

TABLE 16.1   Brain Areas in which Injected Carbachol Induced Drinking

| BRAIN STRUCTURE | N | WATER INTAKE (ML)* | |
		MEAN	MAXIMUM
Dorsomedial hippocampus	6	20.7	56
Septal area	6	14.0	31
Diagonal band area	3	17.5	40
Midline thalamic nuclei	5	13.7	45
Perifornical area	5	9.7	16
Preoptic area	5	10.0	19
Lateral hypothalamus	6	8.5	17
Mamillary bodies	4	10.2	17
Anterior thalamic nuclei	5	8.9	15
Cingulate cortex	3	12.5	22

*During the hour following carbachol injection.
Data from Fisher & Coury, 1962.

eliminated drinking, besides seriously interfering with heat-loss mechanisms.

Goats with lesions of the anterior hypothalamus continued to eat despite dehydration, but they refused to touch water. They had to be given water through stomach tubes to keep them alive. Lesions in the lateral hypothalamus also produce *adipsia* in many animals, as well as transient *aphagia* (refusal of food). This result was first noted by Witt, Keller, Batsel, and Lynch (1952), and later Epstein and Teitelbaum (1964) showed that the adipsia is always longer-lasting than the aphagia. In some cases it was permanent. The interesting thing about the rats that recovered from lateral hypothalamic adipsia is that they drank only with food. If they were deprived of water overnight and then offered water with no food in the morning, most would not drink, though normal rats drink avidly under these conditions. Neither hypertonic saline nor heat stress could induce drinking; it appears that after lateral hypothalamic lesions rats lose their ability to regulate water balance, though they still drink in response to such peripheral factors as dryness of the mouth.

Lesions in the midbrain at the posterior extremity of the third ventricle near the posterior commissure have been shown to reduce drinking. Gilbert (1958, 1964) has suggested

that this reduction results from destruction of a group of secretory cells called the *subcommissural organ*, which is located on the dorsal wall of the third ventricle, where it joins the aqueduct of Sylvius. Others have suggested that it results from lesions of the dorsal longitudinal fasciculus, part of the efferent path from the hypothalamus (Crow, 1964). Taylor and Farrell (1962) believed the subcommissural organ might have something to do with sodium balance, in which case it might affect water intake indirectly.

Lesions that damage the tract leading from the supraoptic nucleus to the posterior pituitary produce *diabetes insipidus*, a condition in which the animal excretes large quantities of dilute urine. It is caused by interference with the ADH release mechanism. Diabetes insipidus is accompanied by polydipsia (excessive thirst), which has usually been attributed to an excessive loss of water from the kidneys. R. W. Smith and McCann (1964) have shown, however, that lesions of the base of the olfactory tubercle, which normally produce both polyuria (excessive urination) and polydipsia in the typical syndrome of diabetes insipidus, increased drinking even in rats whose kidneys had been removed, preventing excretion of water. This finding indicates that at least some of the additional drinking is not secondary to the polyuria and supports the idea that there is a water-satiation mechanism in the medial basal hypothalamus. Such a mechanism would respond to excess extracellular water by inhibiting the secretion of ADH and at the same time inhibiting drinking.

If an adequate supply of water is provided, thirsty animals will usually drink amounts commensurate with their body deficits and then stop. The question of what stops the drinking at the right point is important. In extreme cases it may be that the capacity of the stomach limits the intake, but this factor cannot be the deterrent to further drinking when the deficit is relatively small.

Some water is absorbed from the stomach before drinking stops, but even in the rat, which drinks rather slowly and in short bursts, drinking usually stops long before the volume of extracellular fluid and the osmolarity have returned to normal. In any case, drinking stops eventually, even when no water reaches the stomach. Bellows (1939) showed that neither stomach distension nor water absorption was necessary for some degree of intake control to occur. Dogs were provided with *esophageal fistulas* (the esophagus is cut and the two ends brought out separately to the skin of the neck) so that none of the water that they drank entered their stomachs. The dogs were made thirsty and then allowed to "sham drink." They took amounts proportional to their deficits (usually about double) before stopping for a time. If no water was put into the stomachs through the other opening in the neck they would sham drink similar amounts an hour or so later.

There are several possible explanations for the cessation of drinking in the absence of rehydration. The simplest is that the motor system for drinking becomes fatigued. If the water deficit is severe it will generate a strong input to the motor system, which will force drinking to persist until a high level of fatigue has built up. A lower level of fatigue will prevent drinking when deprivation is more moderate.

This theory appears to be ruled out by an experiment by Hendry and Rasche (1961),

however. They found that rats would lick at a tube that delivered a puff of air to the tongue. This behavior appeared to be related to drinking because water-satiated rats did not exhibit it; yet in thirsty rats the licking persisted at a high rate (up to 3 licks per second) for an hour with no sign of fatigue. Normal drinking slowed down very considerably after a few minutes. Presumably no swallowing takes place during "air drinking," and possibly it is only the swallowing response that fatigues.

Another possibility is that feedback from receptors in the mouth (many animals have receptors that respond to water, as noted in Chapter 9) "meters" the amount of water swallowed, balancing the total against the firing rate of osmoreceptors and other indicators of dehydration. When the meter indicates that the deficit has been made up, an inhibitory signal is turned on, and drinking stops.

The experiments of S. P. Grossman and Grossman (1963) mentioned earlier provided evidence for this view. They found that carbachol injections into the amygdala had no effect upon satiated rats but increased the water consumption of thirsty and hungry rats. The only reasonable explanation for this finding is that carbachol interferes with the early inhibition of drinking by input from mouth receptors or motor feedback.

In addition, there are other grounds for thinking that the amygdala may be involved in the sensory control of satiation: It receives sensory input from the olfactory system, and, being located very close to the part of the cortex that receives gustatory and proprioceptive input from the mouth and throat, it probably receives such information also. Furthermore, stimulation experiments have shown that some parts of the amygdala strongly inhibit eating and drinking.

Other experiments suggest moreover that temporal summation in the amygdala (as well as in some other parts of the limbic system) can occur over periods of many minutes, which would make it an effective integrator of input. A constant sensory input would thus generate a steadily increasing output from the amygdala. When the output had built up to a level at which it could inhibit the excitatory signal from dehydration detectors to the drinking system, drinking would stop. The duration of a bout of drinking would thus be determined by the intensity of the deprivation signal.

The peripheral satiation mechanism produces temporary inhibition of drinking only, but some such mechanism is necessary to prevent the animal from becoming bloated before it has absorbed enough water into the bloodstream to provide more permanent satiation. Students of feedback networks will recognize the device as a form of "phase advance" stabilization in which a signal that anticipates the correction of an error is used to prevent overcompensation.

Water-Seeking Behavior

Drinking, like all other motivated behavior, has reflexive components. Water placed in the mouth of a thirsty animal is swallowed reflexively. Animals that have been deprived of water may also display taxic (orientation and approach) behavior toward it, using such cues as smell and vision. Naïve recently hatched chicks find water by approaching and pecking at moving reflecting surfaces (Rheingold & Hess, 1957), presumably an innate response.

In order to explain such taxes, we must invoke once more the evaluative circuit that was postulated in connection with the attractiveness of optimum temperatures. In this case the system is connected in such a way that, when the thirsty animal is approaching water, the system signals "better" and encourages the response. If the stimulus from the water recedes or becomes less intense, the response is inhibited, and another is tried instead. Stimuli from needed objects (or stimuli normally associated with such objects in the animal's natural habitat) attract the animal by their modulation of the motor system through the evaluative circuits.

Only the inexperienced animal would have to find what it needed in this way, however. In its home environment an animal soon learns where and when its requirements are to be found. The complexity of this learning depends more upon the abilities and learning capacity of the animal than upon the drive the learning serves. Animals can learn equally difficult paths whether they are finding food or water, so it is parsimonious to assume that the various drives feed into a common system implicated in all aspects of goal seeking.

If we accept the sort of model outlined here (and described in more detail in Chapter 18), we should not be surprised to find that artificial methods of eliciting drinking also evoke learned, as well as taxic and reflexive, responses. In fact, even the simplest experimental arrangement, in which for example the tested animal must drink from a dish or spout to demonstrate its thirst during brain stimulation, elicits some learned responses: The animal must find the water promptly and use the correct drinking technique.

B. Andersson and Wyrwicka (1957) felt compelled nevertheless to elaborate on the simple situation by teaching water-deprived goats to climb two steps to obtain water; they were then able to show that the goats would perform the same learned maneuvers to obtain water when they were satiated and stimulated in the drinking area of the hypothalamus. S. P. Grossman (1962) showed that rats also can perform complex learned responses to obtain water when drinking is elicited by carbachol injections into the hypothalamus. His rats would press a bar to obtain water on a VI-15 second schedule, just as they did when motivated by normal thirst.

B. Andersson and Larsson (1956) tried a very different type of conditioning. They paired a light and a tone with electrical stimulation of the drinking area in goats, in an attempt to condition thirst. One goat was subjected to 110 pairings to no effect whatever; it never started to drink or even to show the slightest interest in water at the presentation of the CS (light and tone), though it always drank when electrically stimulated. This result may seem rather surprising, especially to those who think the brain is a hodgepodge in which any two neural activities that occur at the same time become associated, but it would be unfortunate if our regulatory mechanisms could so easily be conditioned to signal false deficits. The situation is different in externally aroused drives like fear, of course. In such instances it is important to use all the advance information available, in order to avoid, as far as possible, stimuli that are innately capable of arousing the drive.

The brain has evolved through millions of generations, and the capacity to learn, like all other capacities, has developed only in systems in which it confers an advantage to the animal or at least in which it is not immediately disadvantageous.

SALT BALANCE

The regulation of sodium-ion concentration in the extracellular fluid is, as we have seen, closely related to water balance, and strikingly similar mechanisms are involved in the two. Blood plasma contains a relatively high concentration of sodium chloride, and, as this solution filters readily through the kidney tubules, a mechanism has evolved for preventing excessive loss. The hormone that facilitates reabsorption of sodium is produced by the adrenal cortex and is called *aldosterone*. When the level of blood sodium is low, aldosterone is released; when excess sodium is present, no aldosterone is released, and sodium is rapidly excreted.

An aldosterone-release factor to control the activity of the secreting cells in the adrenal cortex has been postulated, and Taylor and Farrell (1962) have gone so far as to suggest that the factor is secreted by the subcommissural organ (see discussion of water-balance receptors earlier in this chapter), but this suggestion is almost pure guesswork. Presumably there *are* receptors for the feedback mechanism somewhere, but, as the sodium level has profound effects upon the functioning of all neurons, it is difficult to pin down where the receptors might be.

When the adrenal cortex is destroyed, animals lose sodium rapidly and, if maintained on a low-sodium diet, will soon die. Richter and

Eckert (1938) discovered, however, that adrenalectomized rats survived in a healthy state if they had access to plentiful supplies of salt. As in the case of water, a behavioral mechanism is brought into action when the internal regulation breaks down.

Richter (1947), in accordance with the emphasis on peripheral mechanisms at that time, was inclined to attribute increased sodium intake to innate changes in the sensitivity of the taste receptors for salt during the deficiency. This theory can be dismissed on logical grounds, however, as the adrenalectomized rats consumed sodium at high concentrations that normal rats avoided, as well as at low concentrations that normal rats ignored. Further evidence cited by Richter in support of his theory—that cutting the taste nerves abolished the compensatory increase in salt intake—is not crucial to the argument; this operation would prevent development of any taste preference, whether as a result of learning or of any other internal changes. Pfaffmann and Bare (1950) and Nachman and Pfaffmann (1963) finally disproved the theory experimentally by showing that neither the thresholds of single salt fibers nor the total activity of the gustatory nerve varied with salt deficiency.

Richter's experiments did not establish with certainty that salt-deprived rats are innately attracted by the taste of salt. As each of his tests lasted a number of days, it is quite possible that the rats learned that salt prevented them from feeling ill. This point was settled by Nachman (1962), who gave adrenalectomized, salt-deprived rats brief preference tests between sodium and various other salts and found that they showed a clear-cut preference for sodium within 15 seconds (Figure 16.9). Nachman (1963) also found that sodium-deprived rats showed a preference for lithium salts (rats cannot discriminate between lithium and sodium by taste), even though lithium is poisonous and made the rats feel sicker than ever. This finding rules out the possibility that the preference is learned on the basis of beneficial aftereffects.

Subjectively salt deprivation appears to

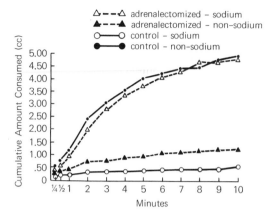

Figure 16.9 Mean cumulative consumption of sodium and nonsodium solutions by 41 adrenalectomized and 41 control rats in a 10-minute preference test. (From Nachman, 1962.)

render food "tasteless" (although different tastes can still be discriminated). McCance (1936) reported that rinsing the mouth with salt solution after a salt deficiency had been established was immediately very refreshing.

Oakley and Pfaffmann (1962) found, as might be expected from Richter's denervation experiments, that rats with lesions of the thalamic taste nuclei lost their normal preference for dilute sodium-chloride solutions. Wolf (1968) repeated these observations on salt-deprived animals, and he also found that lesions of the lateral hypothalamus abolished the salt preference. Degeneration from both these lesions could be traced as far as the ventral tegmentum, and Wolf found that lesions in this convergence area also eliminated the response of the deprived rat to sodium. Lesions in the septal area have also been found to influence the drinking of sodium-chloride solution, but these lesions produced an increase in the preference for dilute salt solution over water (Covian, 1967).

It is not yet possible to build up an anatomical picture of the salt-balance system from these experiments, but it is clear that when the blood-sodium level is low an innate connection between salt receptors in the mouth and the response-facilitation ("better") circuits that we have mentioned is activated. The animal will

then persist in whatever responses produce stimulation of salt receptors and will learn them for future use.

REGULATION OF OTHER MINERALS

Another important chemical element in the structure and function of the body is calcium. Calcium is used in the formation of bone, and the calcium level in the blood must be closely regulated, for if it falls too low, nerves and muscles begin to fire spontaneously, and permanent contraction of the muscles of respiration will lead to death. Regulation depends to some extent upon the *parathyroid glands*, though the exact mechanism is not clear. Probably parathyroid secretion causes the excretion of phosphates; if the parathyroid gland is removed phosphates build up in the bloodstream and precipitate the calcium in the form of calcium phosphate. Parathyroidectomized animals thus have low blood calcium and suffer fatal convulsions.

Richter and Eckert (1937) found that parathyroidectomized rats compensate for reduction in blood calcium by increasing their intake of calcium if it is available. Richter, naturally, considered this response another example of an innate change in receptor sensitivity in the service of homeostasis, but further research has aroused doubt that the behavior is even innate, let alone that it involves changes in receptors.

Scott, Verney, and Morissey (1950) confirmed Richter and Eckert's finding that calcium-deprived rats choose a calcium-rich diet, but they found that if, after a few days, the calcium were placed in the nonpreferred diet the rats would continue to eat the diet in which they had first found the calcium, suggesting that they cannot recognize the calcium but can learn only which food is associated with improved health.

M. Lewis (1964) showed that calcium-deprived rats would learn to bar-press for calcium reward, but she also cast doubt on the theory that selection of calcium is innate by showing (M. Lewis, 1968) that calcium-deprived rats were more interested in sodium-chloride solution than in calcium lactate if they had to choose between them. Rodgers (1967) showed that calcium-deprived rats preferred a novel calcium-deficient diet to their old calcium-deficient diet to which calcium had been added. When this trick is played with sodium on sodium-deprived rats, the rats continue to eat the supplemented old diet, presumably because they immediately find the taste improved, but the calcium-deprived rats have no such immediate recognition of the taste of calcium.

The objection that has been raised to the alternative theory (that rats learn to eat the diet containing calcium because they feel better after they have done so) is that classical learning theory has not prepared us to accept the idea that rats can learn anything with such a long delay in reinforcement. Nevertheless, the evidence for the learning of delayed aftereffects involving taste and gastric sensations is now overwhelmingly strong.

Most of the evidence comes from experiments on "bait shyness" in rats (Barnett, 1963) and from related experiments in which rats have avoided the taste of food that they had been given several hours before being made sick by X-radiation (Garcia, Kimeldorf & Hunt, 1961, Revusky & Bedarf, 1967), but Garcia, Ervin, Yorke, and Koelling (1967) have also demonstrated the converse phenomenon. Vitamin-deprived rats will learn to increase their intake of flavored water when they receive an injection of the vitamin some time after drinking the solution.

It has also been shown that rats that have eaten several substances, some of them with novel tastes, in the period just before X-radiation will subsequently avoid those with novel tastes. Presumably such tastes or smells make a stronger impression and are remembered more clearly when sickness develops. It seems reasonable to assume that simple senses like taste and smell, which do not involve complex temporal patterning as do vision, hearing, and so on and are less frequently bombarded by stimuli, produce information that can be stored for much longer periods.

In calcium hunger, for example, it seems very

likely that we must consider a behavioral mechanism completely different from those previously encountered. Instead of a sensory apparatus innately connected so that encountering the required object immediately excites approach mechanisms, or "better" circuits, animals rely on a mechanism that establishes new connections to such circuits from any gustatory pathway whose stimulation is followed within a few hours by beneficial effects.

This adaptation exemplifies the presence in animals of innate connections that make some learning very easy, whereas other learning is very difficult if not impossible. The rat could never learn, for example, to approach a triangle or to avoid a circle for food presented several hours after it had made the response. Presumably there are special mechanisms for long-term storage of gustatory and olfactory input, and the potential connections between them and motivational circuits are easily converted into actual connections.

P. M. Milner (1950) and P. M. Milner and Zucker (1965) found that on a brief preference test potassium-deprived rats would immediately choose a potassium salt rather than another novel solution. This finding was interpreted as indicating an innate specific hunger for potassium in the potassium-deprived animal, but this conclusion now seems unjustified as it has been discovered that the animals prefer sodium-chloride solution to potassium-chloride solution over a wide range of concentrations (Zucker, 1965). It is known that potassium deprivation disturbs sodium metabolism, and it is possible that the rats may develop a specific hunger for sodium. As potassium salts taste something like sodium salts to human beings, and possibly also to rats, the rats may have immediately taken the potassium in the early experiments because it most resembled sodium.

The experiments did show, however, that rats that had recovered from their deficiency had a long-lasting preference for potassium solutions, which was not present in normal rats, suggesting that the same kind of learning mechanism postulated for calcium also works for potassium.

Magnesium deprivation is a special case. Magnesium-deprived rats fed a diet containing magnesium acquire an aversion to it and may die of magnesium deprivation with plenty of magnesium-rich food in the cage (Scott, Verney & Morissey, 1950). Normal rats do not, however, avoid magnesium salts in an immediate preference test (P. M. Milner & Zucker, 1965). Rodgers (1967) confirmed the observations of Scott and his colleagues, pointing out that, as the recovery phase is accompanied by depression of activity and diarrhea, the rats probably feel worse immediately after eating the magnesium diet than they felt before and so behave as if they have been poisoned (a "bait shy" response).

These observations confirm that there is no innate mechanism for producing a specific preference for the taste of magnesium in the magnesium-deprived rat. Even the learning mechanism does not work to the advantage of these rats, but it must be pointed out that the probability that a magnesium deficiency will arise in a natural environment is negligible.

OTHER SPECIFIC HUNGERS

The idea that animals will select an adequate diet if given the opportunity to do so is not new. According to H. H. Green (1925), the explorer Le Vaillant used to estimate the quality of the grazing in regions of Africa through which he passed in 1780 by noting to what extent the cattle raided his camp for bones. Agricultural research on diet in the early part of this century also leaned heavily on the notion that animals have "instincts" for selecting optimum diets, and experiments on spontaneous selection in pigs, fowl, and cattle were performed (Evvard, 1916; Pearl & Fairchild, 1921; Nevins, 1927). C. M. Davis (1928, 1939) extended this work to human infants and showed that they would select foods that maintained them in good health if they were allowed to feed cafeteria style.

In these experiments normally prepared foods were used. Richter, Holt, and Barelare

(1938) showed that animals could still choose a balanced diet when provided only with purified food components (protein, starch, sugar, fat, salts, vitamins, and so on), most of which they had not met before in those forms. The complexity of the learning that would be required to accomplish this feat on the basis simply of beneficial results persuaded Richter that the ability must be innate.

In the case of vitamins, however, the role of learning had already been established beyond reasonable doubt by L. J. Harris, Clay, Hargreaves, and Ward (1933), and it was later confirmed by Scott and Quint (1946a) and Scott and Verney (1947). Harris and his colleagues showed that rats with vitamin-B deficiencies chose a diet that contained vitamin-B complex when supplied with two new diets in addition to the old one. Only one of the new diets contained the vitamin, but no matter which it was the rats ate only that one and ignored the other two. As the tests lasted several days, this result does not tell us whether the food was immediately attractive or the preference had to be learned. When provided with many (up to 10) new diets, only one of which contained the vitamin, however, very few rats found the right one.

Scott and Quint (1946a) demonstrated that rats are able to detect thiamine, riboflavin, and pyridoxine (components of the vitamin-B complex) by taste or smell, though they cannot detect a fourth component, pantothenate. It is clear, therefore, that the inability to choose the correct diet from a large number in Harris' experiment did not result from lack of cues. It must have been that the smell and taste of vitamins were not innately attractive to the deprived rats. After a short period of "training," during which they received the supplemented diet alone and were able to experience its beneficial effects, the rats were all able to find the correct diet when it was presented among many other diets.

In another experiment, Harris and his colleagues switched the vitamin from the new diet to a second new diet after a preference had developed for the first. The rats all continued to eat the food that contained no vitamin and ignored the vitamin-supplemented diet. This result also shows that rats have no innate way of telling that the vitamin is what makes them feel better.

Much of this work has been confirmed and further quantified by Rozin (1965, 1967), Rodgers (1967), and Rodgers and Rozin (1966), who have drawn particular attention to the rat's rejection of a diet that has been associated with a developing deprivation syndrome. After recovery on another diet, rats will starve themselves rather than go back to the deficient diet. The investigators suggest that the behavior resembles "bait shyness," by which rats made sick with poison acquire a strong aversion to the taste of the poisoned food.

It is clear, then, that the appetite for foods containing vitamins is acquired, as is that for most of the salts, and that the rapid association of taste and smell with delayed beneficial or noxious aftereffects is a most important mechanism in the regulation of food intake in the rat. How far these data can be generalized to animals other than rodents is at present unknown.

Almost no attempt seems to have been made to discover the neural basis of this type of learning, but the experiment by Fonberg and Delgado (1961) mentioned earlier may throw some light on part of the mechanism. They found that stimulation of the amygdala of the cat during eating would inhibit eating and produce avoidance of the particular food eaten for some weeks afterward. This finding supports the theory that the amygdala is involved in (among other things) the effects of taste upon eating. The amygdala's proclivity toward long-term changes in sensitivity could account for the persistence of the traces of gustatory stimulation that enables these traces to become associated with later discomfort. It would be interesting to discover whether amygdalectomized animals can learn adaptive food preferences and avoidances.

Hunger for Proteins

In addition to minerals and vitamins, most animals need a plentiful supply of amino acids with which to build proteins; these chemicals are largely derived from plant and animal protein, which the animal eats and breaks down. Proteins also supply a significant fraction of the caloric requirements of animals, though normally the main source of energy is carbohydrate.

When rats are allowed to select their own diets, they consume quantities of protein adequate to maintain health, according to Richter, though Scott (1946) and Pilgrim and Patton (1947) found that they ate barely enough. This discrepancy may have been a function of the type of protein offered; some proteins are unappetizing to rats (Scott & Quint, 1946b). Rozin (1968) repeated some of these studies, using liquid foods, and found that each rat maintained a very stable intake of sugar solution, protein (amino-acid solution), and oil, though the ratios were different from rat to rat. When the amino-acid solution was diluted, the rats drank more of it, so that they almost compensated for the dilution, even when the solution was made less palatable by the addition of quinine. When the sucrose solution was diluted, no such increase took place, and the missing calories were obtained by increased intake of protein and fat.

It thus appears that protein intake is regulated separately from the total caloric intake in the normal rat. If carbohydrates are in short supply or available only in unpalatable form, rats will increase their protein intake to compensate, but even when a highly palatable carbohydrate (like sucrose) is available, protein intake does not fall below a certain minimum.

It is impossible to say whether or not rats learn to take protein in the same way that they learn to take vitamins, but it seems unlikely because the rats in Rozin's experiment were never seriously deprived of protein before the selection trials, and even when they were later deprived of protein for a few days they showed no compensatory increase in intake when protein was made available again.

Hunger for Calories

All animals must absorb substances from which they can derive energy, though the requirements may be quite low in poikilothermic or hibernating animals when activity and body temperature are low or in animals that have large energy stores in the form of fat.

Most protozoa and other primitive forms ingest food particles they encounter by chance, either through their own swimming movements or those of water currents. If food is plentiful the animals grow and multiply quickly; if it is not their growth and metabolism slow down, but they do not necessarily die. In some of these animals, movement and ingestion of food particles may be inhibited for a time during the digestion of previously ingested food, a process that resembles food satiation in higher animals.

More complex food regulation is found in adult insects. Butterflies, bees, and flies of various kinds respond to contact with a sweet solution by extending their proboscises and imbibing the solution. The threshold for this reflex varies with food deprivation. After a meal the response cannot be elicited in intact insects even by solutions of high sugar concentration, but after a long fast very dilute solutions will elicit it.

Dethier and Bodenstein (1958) set out to discover the cause of this rise in threshold. They established that the level of sugar in the blood is not responsible by transferring blood from sated flies to starved flies without producing any consequent reduction in threshold of the reflex. Furthermore, they showed that the severed head of a well-fed fly would immediately start to feed on dilute sugar solution long before the composition of the blood in the head had had time to change. This experiment also proved that the increased threshold is not caused by long-term adaptation of taste receptors in the proboscis.

Loading the hindgut and midgut with sugar solution by anal injection had no effect upon the feeding threshold, but injecting liquid into the foregut apparently did increase the threshold. The next step was to denervate the foregut, which had a dramatic effect. The flies continued to feed at frequent intervals as long as food was present and became extremely bloated. Dethier pointed out that these flies resembled "honey pot" ants which imbibe great quantities of honey and act as living honey stores for the ant colony.

In most invertebrates, then, eating is a reflex that takes place reliably in the presence of an adequate stimulus unless it is inhibited by signals indicating the presence of food in part of the digestive system.

In higher animals the situation is probably not very different in principle, though the systems are considerably more complex. In particular, homoiothermia places a heavier responsibility on the feeding mechanism. Most homoiotherms die if they cannot generate enough calories to maintain their body temperature; the level of blood sugar, the primary source of energy, must therefore be well regulated. If the level falls below about 0.4 mg/ml in a mammal, the animal suffers from muscular weakness, sweats, shivers, salivates, urinates, defecates, and ultimately becomes comatose and dies. The level is normally prevented from falling below about 0.6–0.8 mg/ml by various regulatory mechanisms.

Blood sugar (glucose) is absorbed from the blood by the muscles, brain, and other organs during activity, and it is replaced from digested food through the stomach and intestinal walls. The concentration of glucose in the blood cannot rise much higher than about 2 mg/ml without excessive loss through the kidneys; the amount that can be stored in the blood is thus quite limited. In order to avoid the necessity of almost continuous eating, therefore, much of the glucose that is absorbed from a meal is converted into *glycogen* and stored in the liver and muscles. As the blood-glucose level falls again, the glycogen is reconverted into glucose and returned to the blood to maintain an adequate level.

If long-term food intake exceeds the rate of energy expenditure, so that glycogen remains unused for some time, some of it is converted into fat, which is carried in the blood and deposited in various parts of the body for future reconversion to sugar if necessary. These reactions are carried out under the control of hormones, *insulin* being one of the most important and thoroughly studied.

Insulin seems to facilitate the passage of glucose through the membranes of some cells. Without it glucose is not converted into glycogen, nor can it be used very effectively by the muscles. Destruction of the insulin-producing cells in the pancreas (which can be done experimentally by injections of *alloxan*) produces *diabetes mellitus*, in which the blood-glucose level is excessively high and considerable quantities of glucose are excreted in the urine. In spite of the high level, the body reacts as if it were starved for glucose, and all the mechanisms for releasing glucose into the blood are operating in high gear. The reactions for breaking down fats are maximally activated, and protein is also broken down to provide energy. The subject usually has a craving for sugar and high-energy foods.

It seems clear that without insulin the receptors that signal the blood-sugar level cannot function properly and indicate too low a value. The situation is quite analogous to that in which temperature receptors are misled by fever toxins into firing at a rate that does not correspond to true body temperature, causing the regulatory mechanism to try to compensate for a nonexistent deficit.

In normal animals the release of insulin is under the control of a diabetogenic factor released by the anterior pituitary, presumably under the influence of secretory cells in the hypothalamus (Figure 16.2). Little is known about the control of hormones that regulate fat and protein metabolism, but they probably also depend upon hypothalamic mechanisms and require detectors of blood glucose, lipoids (fats), and so on. If no food is available, the body will consume most of its substance (sparing the heart and nervous system) in order to stave off the fall in blood glucose that would lead to fatal hypothermia.

The replacement of energy, even in the simplest animals, involves interaction with the environment and overt behavior. In many higher animals (most vegetarian primates, for example), a significant fraction of waking life is devoted to feeding; we should not be surprised to find that it is a very complex process.

MECHANISMS OF FEEDING

Feeding in most animals is a periodic activity. It often starts at certain times of the day and stops after a few minutes or, in some cases, hours. Early investigations of hunger concentrated on the question of what causes eating to start, probably because these investigations were introspective and it is easier to "introspect" about hunger than about satiation. To most observers sensations in the stomach region, usually called "hunger pangs," seemed to provide an immediate answer to the question.

Cannon and Washburn (1912) showed that hunger pangs were correlated with stomach contractions and claimed that they were the physiological basis of hunger. The theory obviously does not go far enough, however; next we must know what causes stomach contractions (Mayer & Sudsaneh, 1959). The theory has also been undermined by the discovery that people without stomachs can still feel hungry (Wangensteen & Carlson, 1931).

When we take a less introspective look at the problem, it begins to appear that the question of what stops eating is at least as interesting as that of what starts it and more amenable to experimental investigation. Presumably all animals that have nervous systems at all have circuits, basically innate, that are capable of initiating food-seeking and eating behavior. It is quite likely that food-seeking and eating are the natural behavior of the system and that satiation is caused by blocking of the system by certain stimuli (a full stomach or high blood sugar, for example). The major problem then, as in the case of the blowfly example given earlier, is to determine what internal states are responsible for the pauses between meals.

Many mechanisms have been proposed, but none has received overwhelming support, probably because all, or most, contribute to the inhibition of eating but none crucially. It is also likely that some mechanisms are more important for one species than for another, which adds to the confusion.

A fairly obvious possibility is the one that we have already met in the invertebrate: When the stomach is full it signals the fact to the brain, which inhibits food-oriented behavior. There is, in fact, some evidence that stomach distension inhibits eating, especially in dogs. Share, Martyniuk, and Grossman (1952) found that the presence of an inflated balloon in the stomach cut down eating. If the balloon was inflated to about 75 per cent of the volume of the usual meal, the dog would eat only half as much as usual. Filling the stomach with some inert substance like celluflour also decreased the amount of food ingested.

Towbin (1955) showed that dogs on an *ad libitum* feeding and drinking regimen (food always available) ate and drank more at each meal after section of the vagus nerve, which conducts the afferent stretch signals from the stomach to the brain (Paintal, 1954). Inflation of an intragastric balloon not only fires sensory fibers in the vagus; it also alters the electrical activity of the ventromedial nucleus of the hypothalamus (VMH; see Sharma, Anand, Dua & Singh, 1961). As we shall see later, the VMH appears to be implicated in the inhibition of eating.

Dogs tend to eat greedily and probably regulate their food intake (as they do their water intake) by varying the intervals between meals rather than by varying the size of each meal. This behavior may be an evolutionary adaptation to the fact that many *canidae* hunt in packs; the best-fed wolf, for example, is the one that can put away the most food in the shortest time. The capacity of a dog's stomach may therefore be an important factor in determining the size of a single meal. But this factor cannot operate as a long-term energy-balancing mechanism, as meals vary in nutritional value and animals' energy requirements change. The important factor in the dog may be the duration of satiation following each meal, which is usually believed to depend upon some change in the composition of the blood.

Humoral Factors in Feeding

Certainly some factor in the blood seems to be important in the regulation of food intake. J. D. Davis, Gallagher, and Ladove (1967) have

shown that blood from satiated rats, when transfused into deprived rats, inhibited the latters' eating, whereas control transfusions of blood from deprived rats did not.

McCleary (1953) pointed out that when food enters the stomach it usually dehydrates the rest of the body by attracting water into the gut. This change elicits a response from osmoreceptors, and it has been found that their activity can inhibit eating. Mook (1963) has shown that rats with esophageal fistulas stop "sham drinking" strong sugar solution when the extracellular fluid is artificially made hypertonic, even though the solution "drunk" by the rat does not enter the stomach.

The dehydration after eating may last for some time, until most of the food is digested, and may thus account for the delay before eating starts again. Energy regulation cannot be performed by the mechanism, however, any more than by stomach distension, as the degree of dehydration bears no relation to the caloric value of the food ingested. Injection of water into the bloodstream of rats during feeding increases the amount eaten, but not by as much as the dehydration theory would predict (M. H. Smith, 1966).

The level of glucose in the blood is very important, and it is known to be regulated hormonally within certain limits; it therefore seems reasonable to speculate that it may have a major influence upon the size and frequency of meals. Again we find some evidence favoring the hypothesis and some that does not support it. Measurements of blood glucose show that under normal conditions it is low when eating begins and rises rapidly as food is digested, but in some abnormal conditions like diabetes mellitus eating occurs when there is a high level of glucose in the blood. The most direct test of the hypothesis, injection of glucose into hungry animals to see what effect it has upon eating, sometimes yields results in accordance with the hypothesis (for example, Stunkard & Wolff, 1954; M. H. Smith, 1966) and sometimes does not (for example, Hanson & Grossman, 1948; Janowitz, Hanson & Grossman, 1949).

Mayer (1953), one of the principal exponents

of the *glucostatic theory* of food regulation (as he has called it), has suggested that the rate of use of glucose is more important than is its actual level in the blood. This parameter can be estimated by determination of the difference in glucose levels of arterial and venous blood; a large difference would indicate that glucose is being used at a high rate, at which time eating does not occur. When the use of glucose falls, either because it is unavailable or because of some difficulty in metabolizing it, eating or food-oriented behavior is elicited.

There are two hormones that increase both the level of blood glucose and the rate of its use. One is epinephrine, which is known to suppress eating (Mayer & Bates, 1952) but which has a number of other autonomic effects that make this finding difficult to interpret. The other is *glucagon*, a substance secreted, like insulin, by the *islands of Langerhans* in the pancreas.

Stunkard, Van Itallie, and Reis (1955) injected glucagon into hungry human subjects and found that it suppressed both hunger and gastric contractions, besides elevating the general level of blood glucose and its rate of use (Figure 16.10). J. L. Schulman, Carleton, Whitney, and Whitehorn (1957) followed up subjective reports of reduced hunger by showing that injections of glucagon ten minutes before each meal produce a highly significant fall in caloric intake and a loss of weight of several pounds over a two-week period.

Mayer argued that the receptors for glucose utilization rate are located in the ventromedial hypothalamus (VMH). Intraperitoneal injections of glucagon do increase the neural activity of this nucleus (Sharma, Anand, Dua & Singh, 1961), as do infusions of glucose (Anand, Dua, & Singh, 1961; Anand, Chhina, & Singh, 1962.) This result is not caused by any direct effect of the hormone upon the hypothalamus; small quantities of glucagon injected into the ventricles, from where it could diffuse into the hypothalamus, do not affect eating (Herberg, 1962).

The VMH is further implicated by the experiments of N. B. Marshall, Barrnett, and Mayer (1952), in which it was found that in-

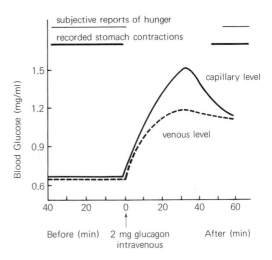

Figure 16.10 The effect of an intravenous injection of 2 mg of glucagon upon the blood-glucose levels in the capillaries and veins of a fasting subject. The upper lines represent times when the subject reported being hungry and when stomach contractions were detected by means of a balloon in the stomach. The indexes of hunger are more closely correlated with the difference in capillary-venous glucose levels (rate of use) than with the absolute levels of glucose in the blood. (After Stunkard, Van Itallie & Reis, 1955.)

jections of *aurothioglucose* (a preparation containing gold) caused selective damage to cells in this nucleus in mice and that the mice then became obese. The argument was that the glucose part of the molecule was preferentially absorbed by glucoreceptors, which were then killed by the gold part of the molecule. After the receptors were killed the mice behaved as if glucose use had fallen to zero, and no inhibition of eating occurred.

This hypothesis is attractive, for, as we shall see, there are many other reasons for believing that the VMH is important in food regulation. If the receptors were located there they would also be conveniently placed to control the secretion of hormones by the anterior pituitary. Nevertheless, the experimental evidence is not very favorable to the idea. Epstein (1960) was unable to inhibit eating in hungry rats by injections of isotonic glucose into the VMH, though injections of a local anesthetic through the same cannula increased eating and injections of hypertonic saline solution did inhibit eating. The concentration of isotonic glucose is several hundred times that in the blood, and, although it seemed unlikely that too high a concentration of glucose was the reason for the lack of effect, Epstein also tried lower concentrations in isotonic saline; they had no effect either.

Wagner & DeGroot (1963) also injected glucose into the VMH with similar negative results. Herberg (1960) reported that injections of isotonic glucose into the ventricles of rats reduced their eating, but considering the concentration of the solution, in comparison with normal levels of glucose in the blood, the reduction was trifling. Although neither glucagon nor glucose separately has any effect upon the VMH, it is possible that both together do. The glucose may not be used by the receptor cells in the absence of the hormone. Apparently no one has yet injected the combination into the VMH.

Another puzzling aspect of the theory of VMH glucoreceptors is that one would expect their destruction to abolish the hormonal regulation of blood sugar. Mice with no glucoreceptors should become diabetic and metabolize fats and proteins at a high rate, rather than becoming fat. That they do not suggests that glucoreceptors are located elsewhere and transmit to the VMH either neurally or by hormonal messenger to influence feeding.

Kennedy (1953) has proposed fat as the substance that regulates eating, on the grounds that normal animals tend to maintain a constant amount of fat. Older animals are usually stabilized at a higher level of body fat than young ones, but when they have reached a certain degree of obesity they eat just enough to maintain that level. This *lipostatic theory* implies that the feeding system is provided with information about the quantity of body fat, but no suggestions have been forthcoming as to how this information is transmitted. Although the theory is very speculative, it would explain why there is usually a time lag between a change in diet or energy use and the adjustment to it and why weight is usually relatively stable under these variable conditions.

Temperature Regulation of Feeding

Another hypothesis about the rate of energy input and how it is balanced against the rate of energy use has been put forward by Brobeck (1948). He has suggested that heat generated during digestion produces a rise in temperature that inhibits the eating system. If the animal is already warm the temperature will soon reach a level at which eating stops, but if the body temperature is low, either because of low environmental temperature or starvation, the animal will eat for a longer time.

It has been confirmed that there is an interaction between the temperature of the anterior hypothalamus and eating. B. Andersson and Larsson (1961) found that heating the area with an implanted thermode made goats stop eating and start to drink. The temperature had to be several degrees above normal, however, for these effects to be fully manifested.

Attempts to correlate natural changes in hypothalamic temperature with eating have been less encouraging for supporters of this theory. Rampone and Shirasu (1964) found that the temperature of the hypothalamus started to rise within 5 seconds of the onset of eating, probably as the result of changes in circulation to the brain, too soon, certainly, to result from assimilation of nourishment by the animal. Eating usually continued with unabated vigor for some time after the temperature had passed its peak and was beginning to fall again. S. P. Grossman and Rechtschaffen (1967) confirmed this finding and also showed that animals eating cold food became satiated just as readily as those eating warm food, even though the hypothalamic temperature fell.

That rats stop eating when the environmental temperature rises to near body temperature has also been cited as evidence for Brobeck's theory, but Kennedy (1953) showed that when rats became acclimatized to the heat they again began to eat at a rate that allowed them to maintain their weight. Rats placed in a cold room also lost weight for some days before they became adjusted to the greater energy requirements.

The Influence of Learning upon Feeding

Some of the conflicting results of the many experiments devised to find out what variables regulate food intake may be explained by the influence of learned eating habits. Share,

Martyniuk, and Grossman (1952) and Janowitz and Hollander (1953) introduced extra food into the stomachs of dogs each day through permanently implanted cannulas and found that it was several weeks before the dogs reduced their intake, even though they were sometimes receiving more than twice their normal amount of food. After they had adjusted, it took them several more weeks to readjust when the extra feeding was stopped.

Presumably the dogs were in the habit of taking so much food each day, and this habit overrode any other form of regulation for a time. The learning theory of feeding presupposes that the animals have some way of estimating, from oral (and perhaps visual) stimuli and feedback from motor activities like chewing and swallowing, how much food they have consumed. Again the evidence is conflicting. It has been shown that dogs with esophageal fistulas will "sham eat" many times their usual amount of food before stopping. Hull, Livingston, Rouse, and Barker (1951), for example, had a 10 kg dog that "sham ate" 8 kg of dog food and milk at one meal, and Janowitz and Grossman (1949), in a similar experiment, found that dogs "sham ate" more than five times as long as they had eaten when the food entered the stomach.

Further evidence that oral factors are not necessary for the regulation of food intake has come from an experiment by Epstein and Teitelbaum (1962). They found that rats adapted remarkably well to never eating but injecting food directly into their own stomachs through implanted cannulas by pressing a bar in a Skinner box. When the food was diluted, the rats immediately increased the number of bar presses to maintain a constant caloric intake, and they did the same if the amount of food delivered for each press was reduced.

That this compensatory reaction is much prompter and more accurate than that of the dogs in Janowitz and Hollander's experiment suggests that it is an advantage to be in a completely new situation in which old eating habits cannot introduce confusing information and the animal is forced to use postingestional cues only.

The general conclusion from all these experiments is that the basic regulator of eating is some factor in the blood, possibly glucose but more likely some substance related to metabolism of fats, but that many other factors like stomach distension, temperature, oral factors, and habit may have powerful effects in the short run.

NEURAL PATHWAYS OF SATIATION

Whatever stimuli inhibit eating, it seems certain that many of them act through the ventromedial nucleus of the hypothalamus. It has been known for more than a century that tumors in the base of the skull can cause symptoms of excessive eating and obesity, though it has not always been clear whether they damaged the pituitary or the hypothalamus. Fröhlich (1901) described a boy who became rather fat and had undeveloped genitalia, both of which symptoms he attributed to pituitary damage (which the boy undoubtedly had). The syndrome has since become known as "Fröhlich's syndrome."

Animal experiments, on the other hand, tended to support the idea that obesity was caused by hypothalamic damage, and this idea was conclusively established by a series of experiments by Hetherington and Ranson (1940, 1942). They showed not only that lesions confined to the hypothalamus could produce obesity in rats but also that they could do so in rats that had previously been hypophysectomized without consequent obesity.

These findings have since been replicated many times, and obesity has been produced in many species, including monkeys (Brooks, Lambert & Bard, 1942), cats (Wheatley, 1944), and mice (Mayer, French, Zighera & Barrnett, 1955). More precise localization of the lesions has usually shown that the greatest effect is produced by lesions in the ventromedial nuclei (Hetherington & Ranson, 1942; Brobeck, Tepperman & Long, 1943), though Kennedy (1950) reported on the basis of a very large series that his most obese rats had lesions slightly ventrolateral to the nucleus that sometimes did not encroach on it at all.

Reynolds (1963) claimed that nonirritative lesions of the VMH produced by thermocoagulation did not produce obesity in rats and suggested that the obesity caused by electrolytic lesions may in many cases have resulted from irritation, by toxins released from the electrode, of lateral hypothalamic nuclei responsible for initiating eating. This explanation is improbable on many grounds. Lesions bordering on the lateral nuclei in other directions do not cause obesity, but injections of local anesthetic into the VMH do cause eating and can hardly be suspected of exciting neighboring nuclei. Hoebel (1965) has since shown that hyperphagia and obesity can be produced by the method that Reynolds used unsuccessfully, and Reynolds (1965b) has replied that he never went so far as to say there was no satiety system in the hypothalamus but still maintains that it cannot be in the VMH.

These controversies illustrate the fact that the production of syndromes from lesions is not always as routine as it sometimes seems in textbooks (and even in some original papers). I know someone who made lesions in the VMH region of many male rats of the hooded variety without producing hyperphagia or obesity in any of them. It was not until he started to use female albino rats that he began to have some success. Singh and Meyer (1968) also noted that female rats showed more pronounced hyperphagia than did males after VMH lesions, and a search through the literature reveals that female rats were used in most of the classical experiments. It is possible that females have a more active feeding mechanism than males do in order to cope with the increased demands of pregnancy and lactation, making the inhibitory mechanism more important under normal circumstances. Kennedy (1953) found that lactating rats with VMH lesions did not become obese until after the pups were weaned. Infant rats with VMH lesions did not become overweight until they reached the age at which their growth would normally slow down.

It has been suggested from time to time that VMH lesions cause increases in fat synthesis, besides increasing food consumption, but VMH rats gain no more than do normal rats when they are restricted to the same amount of food. A recent experiment in which this control was reversed, and the normal rats were force-fed the same amount of food as the hyperphagic animals ate (Han, 1967) apparently showed that weight gain was less in the normal rats; the question of whether or not the lesion affects more than eating thus remains open.

Electrical stimulation of the VMH has the expected effect of inhibiting eating in food-deprived animals (Margules & Olds, 1962; Hoebel & Teitelbaum, 1962), and, as has already been noted, various treatments that stop eating—increased rate of glucose use and stomach distension, for example—cause increased electrical activity in VMH, as measured by either gross electrodes (Sharma, Anand, Dua & Singh, 1961) or microelectrodes (Oomura, Kimura, Ooyama, Maeno, Iki & Kunioshi, 1964; Anand, Chhina, Sharma, Dua & Singh, 1964).

These data have been used to support Mayer's glucostatic theory, on the assumption that the glucoreceptors are located in the VMH and inhibit eating when they are fired. This interpretation is by no means certain, however, especially as intraperitoneal glucose has been reported to inhibit eating even in rats made hyperphagic by hypothalamic lesions (Russek & Morgane, 1963). Other *anorexigenic* (hunger reducing) agents like amphetamine, which may induce *hyperglycemia*, suppress eating even more effectively in hyperphagic rats than in normal animals (Stowe & Miller, 1957; Epstein, 1959; Mogenson, Cinnamon & Stevenson, 1967).

Most experimenters report that rats with VMH lesions start to eat voraciously immediately upon recovering from the anesthetic, though Kennedy (1950) pointed out that the rats that eat most on the first day after the operation are not necessarily those that will become obese. During this dynamic phase, the rats behave as if they were very hungry. They compensate for dilution of the diet with kaolin or other nonnutritive materials by increasing their intake still further and continue to gain weight.

After a few weeks their weight begins to level off at a new value, sometimes two or three times the previous value, and at that stage (static phase) they eat only slightly more than normal rats do. They are, of course, very lethargic, presumably because of the effort required to move their great bulk, and it was believed at one time that the low activity contributed to the obesity. It seems, however, that the activity level immediately after the lesion depends upon the size and location of the lesion; some hypothalamic lesions make rats inactive without causing obesity, and others have little effect upon activity at first but do cause obesity.

When rats have reached the static phase they no longer show signs of a strong hunger drive. Kennedy (1950) found that they did not compensate for diluted diet and sometimes refused the less palatable diet altogether until they had lost a good deal of their excess weight. N. E. Miller, Bailey, and Stevenson (1950) found that obese rats with VMH lesions would eat more food if it was easily accessible but that if some impediment was placed in the path to food they ate less than normal hungry rats. The hyperphagic rats ran more slowly down an alley, pulled less strongly on a harness that restrained them from reaching food, and ate much less food from containers with weighted hinged lids. They also pressed less frequently than did controls when food pellets were delivered on an FI-5 minute schedule in a Skinner box (a phenomenon demonstrated even more dramatically by P. Teitelbaum (1957), who used various fixed ratio (FR) schedules (Figure 16.11). When 1 per cent quinine was mixed with the food, the hyperphagic rats reduced their intake from more than 26 g to 2.8 g per day, whereas controls reduced intake from 16.3 g to 10.8 g per day. Hyperphagic rats are not abnormally sensitive to quinine (Mook & Blass, 1968); presumably they are simply less attracted by bad-tasting food.

P. Teitelbaum (1955) confirmed most of the findings of Kennedy and of Miller and his colleagues, he used cellulose as a diluting agent, however, and did not find the same degree of compensation for low nutritional value in dynamic hyperphagics as Kennedy had found. This finding may have resulted from strain or sex differences (Teitelbaum used only females) or from the fact that, depending upon the site of the lesion, some hyperphagic rats are less

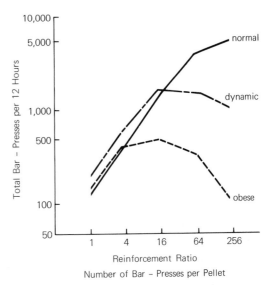

Figure 16.11 The relationship between the fixed-ratio (FR) schedule and the rate of bar pressing for normal and hyperphagic rats. The "dynamic" rats are those in the early phase of hyperphagia before they have become obese. (After P. Teitelbaum, 1957.)

finicky about the taste and texture of their food than are others (Graff & Stellar, 1962).

One of Teitelbaum's most important findings (1955) was that in obese, hyperphagic rats, eating was determined primarily by the palatability and not by the nutritional value of their food. Sweetening the diet with dextrose, for example, caused them to overeat even more than when they were on a standard diet, and they ate more when the food was in pellet form than when it was powdered.

The VMH is not the only part of the brain that has a restraining influence upon eating, but we shall postpone discussion of other areas until we have taken a look at what is known about the positive side of the eating system.

Neural Mechanisms for Eating

In the rat, at least, most of the basic motor components of eating are located at the mesencephalic level and below. Woods (1964) reported that rats decerebrated at the upper mesencephalic level would lick drops of water or milk from their face and swallow them. After a few weeks recovery the rats would immediately groom if a few drops of water were sprinkled anywhere on their bodies. They would also lick water or milk from a spout placed in contact with their lips and grasp a pellet between their forepaws and gnaw it in typical rodent fashion. They did not differentiate between edible and inedible objects, however, and would just as readily gnaw a pencil as a food pellet.

As might be expected from the separation of the eating mechanism from the hypothalamic regulatory mechanisms, the feeding behavior of these rats was not regulated in any way by food intake. They would drink milk or gnaw on pellets just as enthusiastically after having been fed (through a tube) as before. They were never observed seeking food.

Higher animals, like the cat, when deprived of forebrain connections, are not capable of such well-integrated drinking or eating behavior as these rats. The mesencephalic cat will swallow food placed in its mouth but will not attempt to bite food or to take it into its mouth when it is placed in contact with its face. It seems likely, nevertheless, that even in the higher animal many of the basic coordinating centers for eating are located in the mesencephalon; they presumably need more facilitation from forebrain activity in order to function than do those in the rat. Even in the rat it is clear that the forebrain is necessary to initiate the search for and approach to food, to inhibit the ingestion of noxious substances, and to regulate intake in accordance with need.

While observing the effects of stimulating the diencephalon of the cat, W. R. Hess and Brügger (1943; cited by Gloor, 1954) discovered that stimulation of the medial forebrain bundle between the olfactory tubercle and the anterior part of the lateral hypothalamic nuclei elicited sniffing along the ground, as if the cat were seeking food. Stimulation slightly farther back, in the part of the lateral hypothalamus around the fornix bundle, produced voracious eating of food or gnawing of inedible objects, even though the cat had shown no desire to eat before the stimulation (Brügger, 1943). Presumably this part of the brain is a main center for controlling the mesencephalic eating circuits.

Some years later Anand and Brobeck (1951) made lesions in the same part of the lateral hypothalamus in rats and cats, producing complete cessation of eating and drinking (aphagia and adipsia). The animals eventually starved to death with plenty of food available to them. P. Teitelbaum and Steller (1954) discovered that, when the aphagic rats were kept alive for a time by tube feeding, they eventually recovered, taking very palatable foods like evaporated milk at first and later ordinary laboratory feed. As mentioned earlier in this chapter, sometimes rats with such lesions never recover completely from adipsia, though they will take water with dry food, presumably to keep the mouth moist.

The cause of the recovery from aphagia is not known, but the immediate aftereffects of most types of lesions are more severe than the later effects, because of the disturbance of many neurons that eventually recover their functioning. P. Teitelbaum and Epstein (1962) showed that additional lesions made near the sites of the original ones would reinstate the aphagia, which lends support to the idea that only part of the system had been permanently damaged by the lesions. On the other hand, the evidence of P. Teitelbaum and Cytawa's experiment (1965) points to cortical participation in the recovery. These investigators found that if recovered "lateral hypothalamic" aphagic rats were subjected to cortical spreading depression, they became aphagic again not only during the period of cortical depression but also for many days afterward. Possibly the remaining cells of the eating system require more facilitation from cortical activity in order to function normally, but the long duration of the effect makes it seem that some learned adaptation is eliminated by the spreading depression.

When animals with lateral hypothalamic lesions have completely recovered, they tend to become hyperphagic and even somewhat obese (D. R. Williams & Teitelbaum, 1959). This tendency may result from some interference with the inhibitory input to the remaining part of the eating system from the VMH.

Brügger's original stimulation experiments on cats have been repeated on sheep and goats by Larsson (1954) and on rats by Coons (1964),

Hoebel and Teitelbaum (1962), Margules and Olds (1962), and many others. It is interesting that effective stimulation sites are usually just lateral to the fornix, in the general region that also produces drinking (Greer, 1955). Roberts and Carey (1965) have recently shown that gnawing unrelated to hunger can be elicited from this same region by electrical stimulation.

Chemical stimulation of the lateral hypothalamus in rats has also been found to elicit eating. S. P. Grossman (1960, 1962) showed that adrenergic stimulation through implanted cannulas would elicit eating but not drinking in rats satiated for food and water, whereas cholinergic stimulation would have the opposite effect (drinking without eating).

The optimum points for eliciting eating by chemical stimulation do not coincide with those for eliciting it by electrical stimulation. Booth (1967) found that injections of norepinephrine into the region of the lateral hypothalamus, where bilateral lesions produce aphagia, did not evoke eating; the chemically excitable sites

were more anterior, in the septal area and along the path of the stria medullaris (Figure 16.12). The implications of this finding are not entirely clear, but it does seem to rule out the theory that all neurons of the eating system are adrenergic. It may even be that epinephrine is blocking transmission in inhibitory circuits.

Sommer, Novin and LeVine (1967) elicited eating by injecting carbachol into the lateral hypothalamic nuclei, the lateral preoptic area, and the area dorsal and anterior to the medial preoptic nuclei of rabbits. Drinking was obtained only from the region near the supraoptic nuclei and only with low concentrations of carbachol solution. Norepinephrine injections into these cholinergic eating sites did not elicit eating, but other sites were not explored.

Adrenergic stimulation of the cat hypothalamus has never been observed to elicit eating. Usually a drowsy or stuporous state is produced; injection into the lateral hypothalamus often produces vomiting (Myers, 1964a). Sleep or fear has been observed after injections

Figure 16.12 Coronal section of a rat brain at the level of the anterior diencephalon. The cross-hatched area is that in which injections of norepinephrine elicit eating. The area extends about 1 mm anterior into the septal area and about an equal distance posterior into the medial part of the zona incerta at the level shown in Figure 16.7. (After Booth, 1967.)

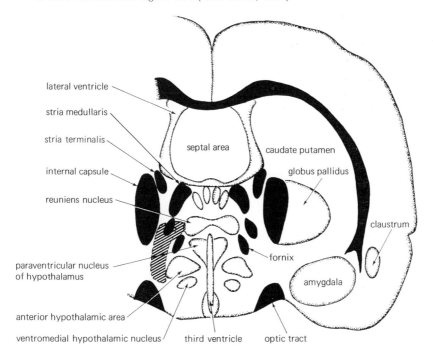

of epinephrine into the hypothalamus of monkeys (Myers, 1964b). This observation possibly means that there are profound species differences in the chemical nature of various drive systems, but it may also mean that in some species there is a greater overlap of incompatible systems using the same chemical transmitter than in others. Another possibility is that in one species one drive dominates when both are simultaneously activated chemically and that in another species a different drive dominates.

Competing drives are even more likely to be evoked simultaneously by electrical stimulation, which is presumably less specific than chemical stimulation. Valenstein, Cox, and Kakolewski (1968) have found that, when the normal effect of electrical stimulation in the lateral hypothalamus is blocked by the absence of the appropriate goal object, rats will eventually produce an alternative response to the stimulation. If, for example, the stimulation at first produced eating and food was not provided, the rat might after several hours drink or gnaw wood during stimulation. After a period of such "training" with an alternative goal object, the stimulation would continue to elicit the trained behavior when the original goal object was replaced. Presumably competing drives are normally elicited by the electrical stimulation, and the one that dominates depends upon a number of factors, including the presence of certain peripheral stimuli and learning.

Stimulation of the lateral hypothalamic eating area elicits a true motivation to eat, in the sense that the animal not only chews and swallows food placed near it but also searches for food if none is present. Wyrwicka, Dobrzecka, and Tarnecki (1959) showed that satiated goats would perform a learned movement (placing the forefoot on the food tray) in order to be fed during stimulation of the lateral hypothalamus. The response was extinguished if no food was given.

Coons, Levak, and Miller (1965) carried the demonstration a step further by showing that satiated rats would learn to press the correct one of two bars for food during stimulation of the lateral hypothalamus and would then transfer the response to naturally induced hunger. The reinforcement of electrically induced motivation to obtain food thus promotes discrimination learning, as does the reinforcement of natural motivation.

It is a truism among psychologists that there are no "centers" in the brain for various activities like eating and drinking; these behaviors are very complex and must require the organized interplay of many parts of the brain (Ehrlich, 1964). It was therefore puzzling, and somewhat disconcerting, to find that the areas from which eating and drinking can be elicited by stimulation are so discrete. The difficulty of successfully implanting electrodes that reliably produce the desired effect attests to the fact that stimulation of pathways into and out of a particular region does not have the same effect as stimulation of the region itself.

Morgane (1961c) showed more systematically that stimulation anterior and posterior to the lateral hypothalamic eating area did not elicit eating. He also showed that cutting the medial forebrain bundle, an important pathway from the forebrain limbic system through the middle of the eating area and into midbrain limbic nuclei (Figure 16.13), did not prevent elicitation of eating by lateral hypothalamic stimulation. Nor did the lesions have any effect upon the normal eating pattern of the animals (Morgane, 1961a).

Extrahypothalamic Sites for Initiating and Inhibiting Feeding

The eating area is at the confluence of a number of other fiber tracts in addition to the medial forebrain bundle; they include the fornix and the pallidohypothalamic tract, which joins the globus pallidus to the hypothalamus. Morgane (1961b), on the basis of lesions made in the globus pallidus, argued that it is the interruption of connections between the globus pallidus and midbrain through the hypothalamus that causes aphagia, the implication being that it results from a motor deficit. The dysfunction is certainly more than an inability to ingest food, however, as has been shown by Rodgers, Epstein, and Teitelbaum (1965). Using their technique for passing a cannula into the stom-

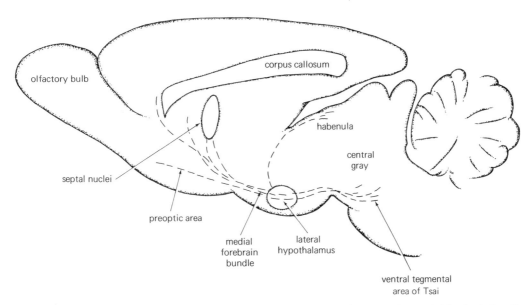

olfactory bulb

corpus callosum

habenula

central
gray

septal nuclei

preoptic area

medial
forebrain
bundle

lateral
hypothalamus

ventral tegmental
area of Tsai

Figure 16.13 Sagittal section of a rat brain, showing fiber pathways contributing to the medial forebrain bundle. (After Wolf & Sutin, 1966.)

ach, they found that rats would not press a bar to inject food into the stomach during the period of lateral-hypothalamic aphagia. When they were recovering, the rats would start to eat before they pressed the bar. There can be little doubt that after lateral hypothalamic lesions rats lose all interest in food; they do not fail to eat merely because of some motor impairment.

That aphagia can be produced by lesions in the globus pallidus does not explain away the absence of stimulation effects there and in other parts of the presumed eating circuit upon food-motivated behavior. Perhaps there are many mutually inhibitory paths intertwined in all parts of the pathway except the lateral hypothalamus. Even there, as we have seen, the distinction is somewhat precarious, and one type of "stimulus-bound" activity may easily be replaced by another if electrical stimulation is used.

Furthermore, in spite of Morgane's negative results, evidence is accumulating that eating can be elicited from sites other than the lateral hypothalamus. B. W. Robinson and Mishkin (1962, 1968), exploring the brains of conscious monkeys with movable stimulating electrodes, found various points in the posterior hypothal-

amus and medial preoptic and olfactory-tubercle areas from which eating could be elicited. The proportion of successful stimulations in these areas was usually much lower than in the lateral hypothalamus (though not in the posterior hypothalamus), and often there were neighboring points where the stimulation caused hungry monkeys to eject food from their mouths. Stimulation of some other structures, in particular the amygdala, septal area, and anterior thalamic nuclei, evoked vomiting. Some eating points were found in the cingulate cortex and midline thalamus. Fonberg and Delgado (1961) and Egger and Flynn (1963) also found that eating was inhibited by stimulation of the amygdala.

Coury (1967) explored the rat brain with norepinephrine and carbachol-crystal implantations and found that norepinephrine elicited eating responses from dorsomedial hippocampus, mamillary body, anterior thalamus, cingulate gyrus, lateral septal nucleus, some midline thalamic nuclei, and one point in the fornix. It is interesting that regions that most frequently give vomiting upon electrical stimulation can cause eating when stimulated with norepinephrine. Coury did not obtain eating from adrenergic stimulation of the amygdala in satiated rats, confirming S. P. Grossman and Grossman's finding (1963) that such stimulation increased eating only when the animal was already hungry.

Morgane (1961c) elicited eating as a "rebound" effect after stimulation of the VMH. Presumably the inhibitory cells of this nucleus became fatigued or refractory after the intense activity engendered by the stimulation and released the eating system from inhibition for a time. Milgram (1968) obtained similar post-stimulation eating from the dorsolateral hippocampus in rats.

Wyrwicka and Doty (1966) found that stimulation of the ventral tegmental area of Tsai (see Figure 6.13) in cats caused eating. It was in this area that Wolf and Sutin (1966) found strong projections from the lateral hypothalamus. We thus see that the feeding system is not as exclusively concentrated in the lateral hypothalamus as was at one time believed.

In view of the widely held theory that the reason animals become satiated is that the ventromedial hypothalamic nucleus or some nearby structure is inhibiting a critical pathway, it would be interesting to know whether eating elicited from extrahypothalamic structures is produced by facilitation of an eating system, by inhibition of the satiation system, or by bypassing the hypothalamic part of the system altogether. Except for stimulation posterior to the eating area of the lateral hypothalamus, inhibition of the satiation system seems the most likely mechanism.

The effects upon food intake of lesions in most of the extrahypothalamic eating systems are slight, which is consistent with B. W. Robinson and Mishkin's finding that most of those systems contained points from which both negative and positive responses to food could be elicited. There have been a number of reports, however, that lesions in the amygdala, where stimulation produced mostly negative responses, also produced mild hyperphagia. S. Brown and Schäffer (1888) found that monkeys with bilateral temporal-lobe ablations ate more than normal, and Klüver and Bucy (1938) reported that monkeys with similar lesions

ate indiscriminately. A human patient with bilateral ablation of the temporal lobe was also reported to be hyperphagic, eating whatever he could scrounge from the hospital kitchen (Terzian & Dalle Ore, 1955).

Anand and Brobeck (1952) found a slight decrease in food intake in rats with lesions of the amygdaloid nucleus, but it is possible that their lesions encroached on the lateral hypothalamus. S. P. Grossman & Grossman (1963) obtained mild hyperphagia from small amygdaloid lesions in rats. Morgane and Kosman (1957, 1959, 1960) found that in cats amygdaloid lesions produced less weight gain than did VMH lesions but that combined lesions were more effective than either alone. They inferred from this result that the amygdala does not regulate food intake through the hypothalamic inhibitory system, but there are loopholes in the argument. The new level of regulation after VMH lesions presumably depends upon how much of the system escapes the lesion. The remnants would perhaps become even less effective if they were deprived of some of the input they received from the amygdala.

Several investigators have reported that lesions of the mesencephalic tegmentum produce voracious and indiscriminate eating or at least some weight gain. Very large ventrolateral lesions in the mesencephalon of cats prevented voluntary eating for a time (Sprague, Chambers & Stellar, 1961), but when the cats began to eat they did so voraciously. Ehrlich (1963) found a slight increase in food intake in some rats with lesions near the red nucleus and central gray of the tegmentum. Like rats with VMH lesions, these rats were not highly motivated to seek food. Ehrlich also found that rats with fornix lesions tended to eat more than normal rats. Singh and Meyer (1968) obtained a similar effect from septal lesions, which were, in fact, quite similar in extent to Ehrlich's lesions.

We thus see that the eating system is organized in such a way that accidental damage to the brain or the natural loss of cells with aging is more likely to increase appetite than to eliminate it. The parts of the brain that have a net inhibitory effect upon eating are much more widespread than are those essential for motivating hunger. No doubt this arrangement improves the chances of survival after brain injury, but it also means that there is a greater chance of becoming obese as forebrain structures deteriorate.

Summary

In this chapter we have studied some aspects of three important forms of motivation: temperature regulation, thirst, and hunger. In each case we have seen that internal receptors are necessary to indicate departures from optimum conditions, though we have not yet been able to identify all of them. Before any overt compensatory behavior is elicited by the firing of these receptors, internal changes usually occur to counteract the disturbance as far as possible. Behavioral regulation is brought into play if the imbalance persists or becomes more serious.

On the basis of artificial heating and cooling of parts of the brain, it has been concluded that there are thermoreceptors in the anterior preoptic area of the hypothalamus that control heat loss by the autonomic mechanisms of sweating or salivating and by peripheral vasodilation. This system also inhibits such mechanisms in the posterior hypothalamus as pilo-erection, increased muscle tone and shivering, mobilization of blood-sugar release (by epinephrine and glucagon), and so on that warm the animal. The evidence for hypothalamic cold receptors, which would have effects opposite to those of the warmth receptors, is conflicting, but it seems likely that there are at least some central cold receptors in some species. Most excitation of the heat-generating mechanism appears to be from cold receptors in the skin, however, and a very regular relationship has been plotted between skin temperature and inhibition of the sweating response at temperatures below about 33° C.

Firing of either heat or cold receptors, besides eliciting reflexive compensatory action, also establishes a drive to find a more comfortable environment. If the animal has not learned any way to reduce the drive it will perform exploratory responses until one of them brings relief.

It is important to note that separate receptors may be involved in the establishment of the drive state and the signaling of escape from that state. In an overheated animal, for example, the heat receptors are in the hypothalamus, but cooling the temperature receptors in the skin may inform the animal that his responses are having the desired effect; the signal innately elicits more vigorous performance of the beneficial response.

In higher animals performance of a response that warms a cold subject or cools a hot one will not only be encouraged, it will also be learned, and the response will thus be more likely to occur quickly if the situation should arise again. Various learning experiments have shown that stimulation of hypothalamic mechanisms by artificial means will cause animals to learn compensatory responses, even though the responses may not be necessary under the circumstances. For example, a rat with a cooling probe in the hypothalamus will learn to press a bar to obtain heat, even though the rest of its body is quite warm.

Hunger and thirst reflect even more clearly the dissociation between internal drive-inducing receptors and the peripheral receptors that innately indicate the presence of the drive-reducing objects. Water deprivation is indicated by osmoreceptors in the anterior hypothalamus and possibly by blood-volume receptors in the atria of the heart. The stimuli that attract animals when these receptors are firing are the smell and taste of water, which are detected by receptors in the nose and mouth. Responses that increase these peripheral stimuli are both encouraged when they occur and learned for future reference.

Firing the central receptors for water deprivation elicits increased secretion of antidiuretic hormone (ADH) to reduce the water loss from the kidneys, besides initiating behavioral responses to replenish the body's water supply. If a response for obtaining water has previously been learned, it will probably be elicited; if the animal is naïve or in a strange environment, it will explore and will learn any successful response.

Central osmoreceptors can be fired by microinjections of hypertonic solution into the anterior hypothalamus, and the drinking system can be stimulated electrically or chemically at a site near the fornix in the lateral hypothalamus. Cholinergic stimulation of much of the limbic system in the rat elicits drinking, but this effect does not occur in the cat or the monkey and occurs only slightly in the rabbit.

Hunger is a motivational system more complex than, though essentially similar to, that of thirst. Certain substances like sodium appear to be regulated by hormones that limit excretion and by innately steered behavioral mechanisms for replenishment. A sodium-deprived rat can immediately recognize food containing sodium and will eat it. Animals do not appear to have such innate recognition of most other salts and vitamins when they are deprived of them, but they do have a mechanism that ensures rapid learning about the effects of different foods upon their health. If rats are made ill as late as several hours after taking food, they will avoid that kind of food for some time. On the other hand, if eating a new food makes them feel better, they will quickly establish a preference for it.

Animals do not use up salts or vitamins very quickly; even amino acids can be used over and over again to manufacture different proteins. Animals can thus survive for weeks without replenishing their supplies of most of these substances. Energy is being used up continuously, however, especially by homoiothermic animals, so that the most urgent hunger is that for calories. Calories are provided mainly by starches, sugars, fats, and proteins.

The muscles and organs of the body receive their energy through the bloodstream in the form of glucose, and it is vital that the level of blood glucose be maintained above a minimum value at all times. Although the exact mechanism by which the level is detected for purposes of regulation is at present still in doubt, it seems likely that there are glucose-sensitive neurons in the hypothalamus and possibly in other parts of the body as well.

When the glucose level is low, epinephrine and glucagon are released into the bloodstream to convert glycogen in the liver into glucose. When blood glucose is high, insulin is released to allow it to be converted to glycogen and stored in the liver and muscles. A prolonged excess of glucose results in the formation of fat, which is stored in various parts of the body for future conversion to glucose if needed.

It is tempting to assume that the receptor system for blood-glucose level is also involved in the control of eating, but there is little solid evidence on this point. Many factors can stop eating in the short run: distension of the stomach, absorption of water into the stomach and intestine from the extracellular fluid, increased temperature in the preoptic heat-regulatory system, and the activity of various forebrain structures like the amygdala, but none of these factors provides the long-term regulation of intake necessary to prevent either excessive fat deposit or wasting away of body tissue. It is believed that long-term energy balance may depend upon some substance or substances in the blood that depend in turn upon the amount of fat deposited and inhibit eating if that amount exceeds a certain value.

Inhibition of eating is effected through the ventromedial nucleus of the hypothalamus (VMH). It has been shown that lesions in this nucleus cause hyperphagia and obesity; stimulation there stops eating in hungry animals. Many of the stimuli that reduce eating (stomach distension, anorexic drugs, and so on) increase the firing of cells in the VMH.

Although it seems reasonable that glucoreceptors should be located in the VMH, where they could easily influence hormonal glucose-balancing mechanisms through the pituitary as well as through the inhibitory circuits for eating, it has never been possible to produce any effect upon eating by injecting glucose into this nucleus, though injections of glucose into the bloodstream sometimes do reduce eating.

Animals that have been made hyperphagic by VMH lesions do not work harder than normal animals to obtain food; in fact, once they become obese they are less motivated by food. If more work is demanded or if the food is diluted or made less palatable, obese hyperphagics reduce their intake dramatically for a time and lose some of their fat. Normal rats on the other hand, will eat more of a diluted diet to compensate for its lower nutritional value.

The basic motor control of eating is probably organized at the mesencephalic level, but this system is useless without the direction and regulation provided by diencephalic and telencephalic structures. Both stimulation and lesion studies point to the importance of the lateral hypothalamic area in the control of eating, as well as of drinking. Animals with lesions in this area starve to death unless fed by stomach tube for days or weeks. Stimulation in the area forces the animal to eat or drink and sometimes elicits other stimulus-bound instinctive patterns of behavior. Chemical stimulation with norepinephrine has been found to elicit only eating, and never drinking, in rats. In most other species it produces reduced activity, rather than eating, and it is assumed that several motivational systems with different chemical transmitter substances overlap in the region.

Animals can learn responses that satisfy the hunger aroused by lateral hypothalamic stimulation just as easily as they learn them when hunger is produced by deprivation, indicating that stimulation arouses the full motivational pattern, rather than only the motor component.

Attempts to induce eating by stimulating pathways leading to and from the lateral hypothalamus have not been very successful, though it has recently been reported that stimulation in the ventral tegmental area of Tsai, which lies on the main pathway from the nucleus, causes eating in cats. Eating has also been observed during stimulation of various other points in the brain, but in most of these experiments it has been found that stimulation of adjacent points in the same structure either has no effect or even produces rejection of food.

The amygdala is an interesting structure, in that it seems to be part of the pathway through which sensory stimuli inhibit eating. Stimulation of parts of the amygdala while an animal is eating will not only stop the eating, it will also give the animal a long-lasting aversion to the particular food. It has been suggested that this effect may be part of the mechanism required for learning the aftereffects of eating poisonous and beneficial foods. The amygdala may also be involved in metering food intake, so that eating stops when the required amount has been eaten and before postingestional factors can have any controlling effect.

CHAPTER 17

NON-REGULATORY MOTIVATIONAL SYSTEMS

Regulation of the internal environment is essential for life in higher organisms, but other needs must also be taken into account. We shall now turn to motivations having to do primarily with effective relations with other animals—mates, offspring, enemies, and so on—and to some extent also with inanimate objects in the environment.

The behavior associated with these motivations is not basically different from that already described. Under the influence of internal changes the animal is attracted (or repelled) by stimuli from certain objects. If contact is made with the attracting object, as for example a receptive female, further stimuli from the object trigger a sequence of consummatory responses.

REPRODUCTIVE BEHAVIOR

In unicellular organisms reproduction can be relatively simple. A mature cell undergoes *mitosis*, in which the two resulting daughter cells separate and go their ways as individuals. From time to time these organisms engage in a form of sexual activity in which conjugation of two individuals takes place, and each receives half the other's supply of chromosomes. Higher animals effect a merger of chromosomes and then provide for their offspring during early

development as well. These aspects will be discussed separately under the headings of sexual and parental behavior.

Sexual Behavior

In sexually reproducing organisms, special cells in the gonads undergo *meiosis*, a division in which only one of each pair of chromosomes is passed on to each daughter cell. In the female these *haploid* cells form eggs, or ova; in the male they become spermatozoa. The fusion of a sperm with an ovum produces a *zygote* cell, with the full complement of chromosomes; by repeated mitosis the zygote can develop into a full-sized member of its parents' species. The growth process requires nourishment, and usually a supply adequate to the needs of the embryo is incorporated in the ovum.

The behaviors by which sperm and ova are brought together in different species are almost infinitely variable. Observation of these techniques constitutes a popular branch of several biological disciplines, and the comparative literature is extensive, ranging all the way from paramecia (Wichterman, 1953) to man (Masters & Johnson, 1966). In some of the simpler aquatic animals, eggs and sperm are released into the water at more or less the same time and place; male and female behavior is synchronized by some external stimulus like the phase of the moon or the height of the tide. In most animals, however, sperm are introduced into the genital tract of the female by the male during copulation, and fertilization of the ova takes place there.

The contact between the animals during mating requires that the usual escape behavior of the pursued and the predatory tendency of the pursuer be held in abeyance at that time. Most insects copulate only once, after which the male is superfluous and in the thriftier species is sometimes eaten by the female as her sex drive wanes and her food drive reasserts itself. After copulation most female insects lay their eggs on something that the hatchlings can eat when they emerge; a female social insect stores the sperm and uses it to fertilize each egg as she lays it during her lifelong confinement as queen.

Most animals below the phylogenetic level of the bird mate once a year during a season that will ensure suitable temperature and food supply for the young. Birds and mammals are more variable, for, although many species are still dominated by the annual breeding cycle, others have reached a state of adaptation to the environment that makes them relatively independent of the seasons for reproduction. In such species the female may ovulate at intervals varying from every few months to every few days. Some females ovulate not on a regular schedule but in response to cues from sexually active males; various combinations of environmental and internal factors regulate ovulation in other species.

FEMALE HORMONAL MECHANISMS. Ovulation is controlled by hormones, which, in birds and mammals at least, are produced in the anterior pituitary (*gonadotrophic hormones*) and in the gonads (*gonadal hormones*). As is usual with pituitary hormones (see Chapter 16), gonadotrophins are ultimately controlled by hypothalamic secretory cells (G. W. Harris, 1964), and it is through neural pathways terminating on these cells that length of daylight (Rowan, 1938), stimulation from the smell (Bruce & Parrott, 1960) or sight (Harper, 1904) of the male, the effects of copulation (Brambell, 1944), and the like are able to influence gonadal functioning.

The cycle of ovarian development (estrous cycle) usually starts with the secretion of *follicle-stimulating hormone* (FSH) by the neurohypophysis and follows the course illustrated in Figure 17.1.

If the eggs are fertilized, another gonadotrophic hormone, *lactogenic hormone* (*luteotrophin* or *prolactin*), is secreted by the pituitary. This hormone prevents the regression of the corpora lutea, induces it to secrete *progesterone*, and, in mammals, stimulates production of milk. It also promotes maternal behavior, as we shall see later.

In mammals the gonadal hormones estrogen and progesterone act upon the uterus to prepare it to receive the fertilized ova. In birds they organize the production of egg nourishment (yolk and albumin) and shell and modify the blood supply to the breast to form the bare, highly vascularized "brood patch" for the incubation of the eggs. These hormones also have marked effects upon behavior.

Because the development of the eggs in the female determines when fertilization must take place, the female usually regulates mating behavior. She may do so in a variety of ways. Many receptive females have glands that emit a sexual scent attractive to males. Some female moths, for example, can attract males from a mile or more downwind (C. V. Riley, 1895); male rats prefer the odor of receptive female rats to that of nonreceptive females (Carr, Loeb & Wylie, 1966), and dogs are attracted by the odor of urine from receptive bitches (Beach & Gilmore, 1949). Readiness to mate can also be indicated visually, as by the conspicuous "sex skin" of the chimpanzee and certain other primates or the swollen abdomens of female fish ready to spawn.

The receptive female usually displays behavioral changes in addition to the changes in smell or appearance. They may include vocalization, restless movements, rubbing, and so on, as in members of the cat family, or more overt solicitation, as in many female primates, who when in heat adopt the copulatory position ("presenting") before males. Female rats become hyperactive when in heat, and this hyperactivity increases their chances of encountering males (Wang, 1923). Bolles, Rapp, and White (1968) claim that female rats do not actively seek out males because they do not run faster to an active male than to a sexually inactive one. Gorzalka (1970) has shown, however, that in a choice situation estrous females do in fact prefer the active male. There is also a good deal of evidence that female rats are positively reinforced by copulation and learn to approach a sexually active male in preference to an inactive one.

All these changes are brought about by the high level of estrogen and the onset of progesterone production that occur at about the time the follicles rupture (at, or just after, ovulation), and this combination of hormones also has a profound effect upon the way the

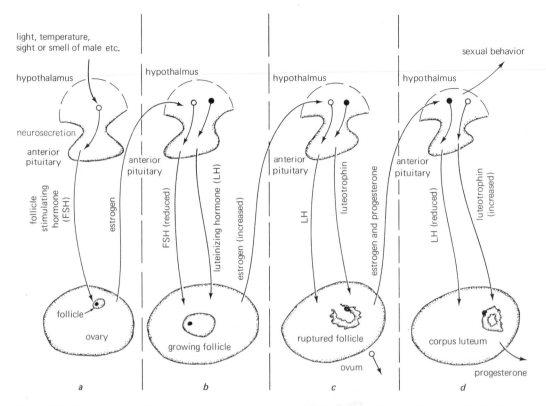

Figure 17.1 Four stages in the estrous cycle of the female. (a) The action of an environmental stimulus (or in many instances internal timing mechanisms) on the hypothalamus produces neurosecretions that are carried in the blood to the anterior pituitary. The anterior pituitary then produces follicle-stimulating hormone (FSH), which causes the growth of follicles in the ovary. The follicles produce estrogen, which is carried back to the hypothalamus. (b) In the hypothalamus estrogen stimulates increased production of neurosecretions that induce the pituitary to secrete luteinizing hormone (LH); it also suppresses FSH secretion to some extent. (c) The LH accelerates the growth of the follicle until it finally ruptures, releasing an ovum, or egg; meanwhile the higher level of estrogen acts upon the hypothalamus to stimulate production of luteotrophin by the anterior pituitary. This hormone acts upon the ruptured follicle to produce progesterone, which, combined with estrogen, acts upon hypothalamic neurons to facilitate sexual receptivity. (d) The ruptured follicle becomes a corpus luteum, and under the influence of increased luteotropin it produces progesterone. If the ovum is fertilized, the corpus luteum is maintained to produce the progesterone needed during pregnancy or hatching. If the ovum is not fertilized, the corpus luteum regresses, and the ensuing fall in progesterone level allows another cycle to begin.

female reacts to the sexual advances of the male once she has aroused his interest. With few exceptions, an anestrous female mammal resists attempts by a sexually aggressive male to mount her, but when in heat she reacts by adopting a posture that makes it possible for the male to insert his penis into her vagina (intromission). This posture may involve arching the back downward (*lordosis*), elevating the hind quarters, and shifting the tail to one side. Elephants and primates with prehensile appendages may use them to guide the penis into the vagina (Beach, 1949).

That these behavioral changes depend upon hormones can easily be shown by injecting estrogen into anestrous or gonadectomized females. After several days they will develop estrous behavior. In some cases progesterone is also required after a period of estrogen priming to bring on the estrous condition.

The females of a few species, like the rabbit, remain in the preovulatory phase of the estrous cycle for considerable lengths of time and only ovulate in response to vaginal stimulation. For this reason they will accept the male most of the time. The sexual behavior of primates also tends to be less rigidly dependent on the hormonal cycle, but not for the same reason as in the rabbit. Female monkeys will sometimes present during anestrus to divert attacks from aggressive males or to obtain preferential treatment, and apes do so even more readily. The emancipation of sexual behavior from gonadal hormones seems to have reached its ultimate stage in the human female, whose receptivity bears little relation to ovulation or the level of circulating estrogen. Money (1961) described several women who were receiving estrogen-replacement therapy after loss of their ovaries and who discontinued the treatments for various reasons. They found that lack of estrogen made no difference to their sexual behavior, erotic imagery, sensitivity, or frequency of orgasm. Disturbance of normal sexual behavior occurred only when there were regressive changes in genital morphology. The same conclusions may be derived from observations of the effects of menopause, when the levels of circulating estrogen and progesterone fall.

If there is any evolutionary significance in this development, it may be that the advantage to a female and her offspring of constant male help and protection has survival value and that a good way to ensure such protection is to be more continuously interesting than other females are. At the human level sexual behavior has thus acquired social as well as strictly reproductive function, and the survival of certain sexual traits may not depend on their effectiveness for reproduction as much as on their contributions to group organization and cohesiveness.

Beach (1949) regards it as inevitable that increased corticalization of function will render sexual behavior less dependent upon basic humoral or hormonal mechanisms, but there is reason to believe that what has happened in the human female is an increasing dependence of sexual behavior upon male sex hormones (*androgens*) secreted by her adrenal glands, rather than upon estrogen, as in lower animals. In three ovariectomized women with normal sex drive, the drive was abolished by subsequent removal of the adrenal glands. It has also been reported that women receiving androgen

therapy experienced increased sex drive as a side effect (Money, 1961).

MALE HORMONAL MECHANISMS. The male gonads in seasonally mating species undergo similar changes to those described for the female of these species. Environmental stimuli like length of daylight initiate the production of FSH and LH by the anterior pituitary (LH in the male is called *interstitial cell-stimulating hormone,* or ICSH, because it stimulates the secretion of testosterone by interstitial cells in the testes). Increasing secretion of testosterone brings about growth of the genitals and secondary sexual characteristics, as well as changing the animal's behavior in relation to territory, other males, and females. After the mating season is over, gonadotrophin and testosterone levels fall again, and the genitals regress.

In nonseasonal breeders there is an increase in the secretion of gonadotrophins at puberty; testosterone rises to the adult level and stays relatively constant, apparently stabilized by negative feedback through the hypothalamus. If the androgen level increases, it acts on hypothalamic cells to suppress the production of gonadotrophic hormones until it falls again to normal.

Removal of the testes (castration) eliminates that source of androgens and causes a reduction in the sexual behavior of males of most species, as well as some regression of accessory genital structures. It is curious that the decline in sex drive may take many months, though the fall in androgen level after castration is almost immediate, which suggests that the main effect of androgen upon behavior is produced through changes in the structure of neural pathways for sexual activity. Other data, which we shall encounter later, suggest, however, that the hormone can also act as a neural transmitter in pathways involved in reproductive behavior.

Castration before puberty is likely to prevent the establishment of adult sexuality unless testosterone injections are subsequently given. The normal onset of puberty will then be mimicked whatever the actual age of the subject. Much has been made of the fact that sexually experienced male animals, and particularly men, continue to be sexually active long after loss of testes (sometimes for ten or twenty years), and it has been suggested that once sexual behavior has been learned, it becomes independent of hormones. It should be pointed out, however, that the adrenal glands constitute a significant source of androgen that is not eliminated by loss of the gonads and that in any case there is almost always a considerable diminution in the intensity of the drive. It may not fall to zero, but it usually falls enough in a man to annoy his wife, who is liable to complain quickly enough if her husband fails to obtain his regular testosterone injections (Money, 1961). The difference in behavior of experienced and inexperienced animals after castration is interesting, but it may mean only that less motivation is required to perform an act than to learn it. On the whole the evidence that male sexual behavior can persist indefinitely in the total absence of circulating androgens is not completely convincing.

SEXUAL DIFFERENTIATION. Birds and mammals not infrequently exhibit the mating behavior of the opposite sex under certain conditions. Females of almost all species have been seen to mount other females or even males. According to Beach and Rasquin (1942), mounting and pelvic thrusting in female rats was not correlated with estrus; ovariectomy had no effect upon this behavior. They attributed it to androgen from nonovarian sources (for example, the adrenals). On the other hand, doses of synthetic estrogen in the heifer led to a great increase in male sexual behavior, and in one experiment implanted estrogen pellets induced such vigorous pelvic thrusting that the pelvis was fractured in about 20 per cent of the treated herd (Cowie, 1944; Folley & Malpress, 1944). It is somewhat difficult to interpret these and many other experiments involving injected hormones, because the fate of hormones in the body is usually unknown. Most of the sex hormones are closely related to one another in chemical structure (Figure 17.2), and they are deactivated or converted from one form to another by some of the tissues that absorb them.

Male animals do not exhibit female behavior

as often as females show male behavior, but such behavior is nevertheless frequently observed. Beach (1949) reported that it was more likely to occur in highly sexed individuals, especially when they have already been excited by the presence of a receptive female.

That male and female behavior can be elicited from either sex indicates that nervous structures for both types of behavior must be present; it has been suggested that the predominant behavior is determined by the type of hormone rather than by the type of nervous system. Beach (1947) suggested that the neural structures responsible for female behavior are sensitized by estrogens and that the structures responsible for male behavior are sensitized by androgens. Females, who normally have more circulating estrogen than androgen, thus show female behavior; males, who normally have more androgen than estrogen, show male behavior.

This hypothesis certainly does not explain human sexual behavior, which, as we have seen, is relatively independent of estrogen levels in either sex. Homosexual men do not become heterosexual as a result of testosterone injections; they merely become more actively homosexual. Homosexuality, as opposed to the bisexuality found in most mammalian species, may be the price we pay for the noncyclical androgen-controlled female sex drive. If the female drive is indeed controlled by the same hormone as that of the male, the differences in sexual behavior must depend entirely upon the neural structures of males and females, and neural structure is susceptible to modification by many factors, including prenatal hormone levels (see discussion later in this chapter) and learning.

Even in birds and subprimate mammals, however, there are reasons for thinking that Beach's hypothesis is an oversimplification. It has been known for some time that girls born to mothers who were receiving hormone therapy (usually a form of testosterone) during pregnancy, occasionally have masculine external genitalia (Wilkins, Jones, Holman & Stempfel, 1958). These females have almost always been raised as boys and have preferred to continue as boys even when the increased ovarian activity at puberty has begun to induce secondary feminine characteristics.

Phoenix, Goy, Gerall, and Young (1959) used the technique of androgen injection into pregnant female guinea pigs to produce *pseudohermaphrodite* female offspring and attempted to find out whether their behavior, as well as their external genital morphology, had been changed. The hermaphroditic females were ovariectomized in order to eliminate the effects of endogenous gonadal hormones; as adults they were injected with estradiol (a type of estrogen) followed by progesterone, a combination that produces estrous behavior in normal females. The hermaphroditic females showed even less female sex behavior after this treatment than before; usually the effect was an increase in mounting and male sex behavior.

After receiving male hormones, the hermaphrodites showed as much male behavior as did castrated males receiving the same hormone treatment. The investigators therefore concluded that at a critical stage in the growth of the nervous system the presence of androgens will produce circuits potentially capable of organizing male sexual behavior.

These observations were confirmed and extended to rats and monkeys in subsequent investigations (for example, G. W. Harris & Levine, 1965; Gerall, 1966; Gerall & Ward, 1966; Levine & Mullins, 1964; Goy, Bridson & Young, 1964; and Young, Goy & Phoenix, 1964). Pseudohermaphroditic female monkeys have been produced by androgen injections into their mothers during pregnancy (Young, Goy & Phoenix, 1964), and in preliminary tests it appeared that these animals' play behavior as infants was much closer to that of normal males than to that of normal females. There was more frequent display of threat, initiation of play, and rougher play than among normal females. The hermaphrodites also showed greater frequency of mounting behavior and demonstrated pelvic thrusting and phallic erection even in the absence of male hormone injections.

Rats are born at an earlier stage of development than are guinea pigs or monkeys; hormone injections can thus be given directly to the

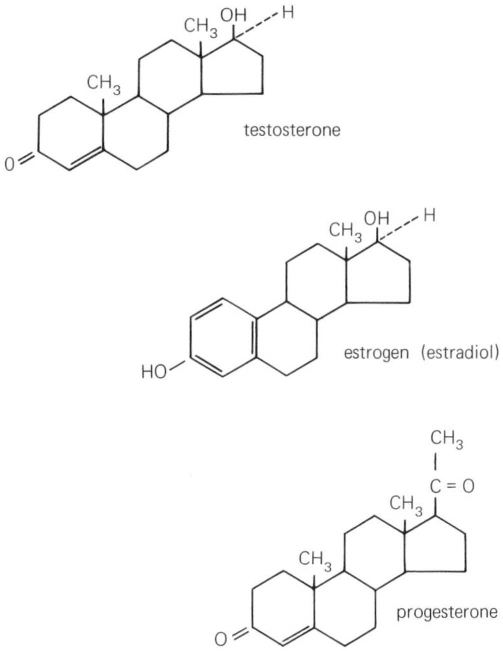

Figure 17.2 The chemical structures of three sex hormones to illustrate underlying similarities.

neonates instead of to the mothers. G. W. Harris and Levine (1965) found that testosterone injected into four-day-old female rats masculinized their subsequent behavior. Grady, Phoenix, and Young (1965) have shown that male rats castrated at birth or within ten days of birth displayed weak masculine behavior as adults and that under the influence of estrogen and progesterone they displayed more estrous behavior than did males castrated at a later age and similarly treated with hormones. Feder and Whalen (1965) found that feminization of castrated male rats was not increased by estrogen injections during infancy; the effect of the injections was rather the reverse, and the investigators concluded that either androgen or estrogen at birth tends to masculinize subsequent behavior.

Such a conclusion also seems indicated by the experiments of Levine and Mullins (1964), who found that large doses (100 μg) of estrogen injected into neonate female rats caused atrophy of the ovaries; as adults these animals could not be brought into heat with injections of estrogen and progesterone.

It must be emphasized that, from the behavioral point of view, animals are never all male or all female, whether they are normal or hormonally modified pseudohermaphrodites. The "sex changing" experiments do not completely rule out the idea that neural circuits for both male and female behavior are present in animals of either sex. They do, however, force us to conclude that the circuits for male behavior have higher thresholds in the female than in the male and vice versa; we also conclude that these differences do not result directly from gene action on the nervous system but depend upon the presence or absence of testicular secretions at a critical stage in the development of the nervous system. (In the guinea pig the critical period is about the thirtieth day after conception, according to Goy, Bridson, and Young, 1964; in the rat, whose gestation period is only about three weeks, the critical period seems to be at about 25 days.)

Although androgens may be a necessary condition for the development of male behavior, they are apparently not sufficient. Valenstein, Riss, and Young (1955) raised male guinea pigs either in groups or in isolation and found that those isolated very early in life (before they were about 10 days old) were not able to copulate effectively as adults. Many components of mating were present, but were not properly organized. The males became excited in the presence of receptive females and pursued them, but they attempted to mount from the side or the head end and did not clasp the female but rested their forepaws on her back, whereupon she jumped away. Injections of androgen did nothing to remedy this disorientation and merely served to increase the diffuse excitement (Valenstein & Young, 1955). Social rearing, whether with other males or with females, even for a short time just after weaning, allowed the male to learn whatever behavior is necessary for effective mating as an adult.

Similar results were obtained by H. D. Gerall, Ward, and Gerall (1967) in the rats. The rats did not have to be completely isolated; separation from other groups by wire mesh sufficed to disturb the response. The isolated male became highly excited in the presence of

a receptive female, climbing over and tunneling under her, leaping in the air, but failing to mount with the correct orientation or to grasp her. As the female rodent plays a subordinate role in mating, it has presumably not been considered worthwhile to test the effect of isolating females.

Monkeys raised in isolation also show severely impaired sexual responses. Males are very interested in females but are extremely inept and rarely succeed in achieving intromission (Mason, 1960). In this species isolated females are as severely disturbed as males. As Harlow stated in a delightful article (1962):

When the laboratory-bred females were smaller than the sophisticated males, the girls would back away and sit down facing the males, looking appealingly at these would-be consorts. Their hearts were in the right place but nothing else was. When the females were larger than the males, we can only hope that they misunderstood the males' intentions, for after a brief period of courtship, they would attack and maul the ill-fated male. Females show no respect for a male they can dominate.

According to Zingg (1940), the records of several humans raised during infancy in isolation or away from human society (*feral men*) showed that they had little interest in sexual matters, though in one instance the presence of women was likely to evoke a good deal of excitement. It seems that sexual behavior, though it does not have to be learned, is nevertheless dependent upon nonspecific social experience in early life.

NEURAL BASES OF MATING BEHAVIOR. Most of the autonomic and skeletal reflexes involved in mating depend upon motor pools located in the lumbar and sacral segments of the spinal cord. Semans and Langworthy (1938) were able to reproduce all stages of the copulatory response in cats by sequential stimulation of the sacral nerves. In some animals, transection of the cord above the lumbar region produced erection and ejaculation within a few minutes (Bacq, 1931). Erections have been reported after death by hanging (breaking the neck) in man. Bacq also stated that section of the *hypogastric nerve* leading from the lumbar part of the sympathetic chain to the genital regions prevented ejaculation in rabbits and resulted in prolonging of mating until both partners were physically exhausted. In the male cat, Root and Bard (1937) state that normal copulation occurs despite removal of all sacral and the two lowest lumbar segments of the cord. Destruction of the inferior mesenteric ganglion prevented erection and abolished copulatory behavior.

After recovery from spinal shock, genital stimulation will produce what Riddoch (1917) called the "coitus reflex" (erection and ejaculation) in men with completely transected spinal cords. The patient, of course, experiences nothing and, if prevented from seeing, is unaware of what is happening. There are varying reports as to the sexual potency of patients with spinal transection. Many factors like the patient's general health, the amount of damage to the lower parts of the spinal cord, and so on must be taken into account. Money (1961) reported that about 66 per cent of a group of 500 *paraplegic* and *quadriplegic* patients were capable of erection and about 20 per cent were capable of coitus. Monro, Horne, and Paull (1948) stated that 74 per cent of their group of 84 patients had erections from time to time but that only 8 per cent were capable of ejaculation. Two of the latter succeeded in impregnating their wives. It was possible to stimulate emission of semen (for purposes of artificial insemination) by electrical stimulation of the genital area in many of the other patients.

Although Herman (1950) claimed that patients with spinal transections lost all libido as a result of the loss of genital sensation, his descriptions of their behavior toward nurses was not entirely consistent with that conclusion. Money (1961) found a dissociation between "mental" and "phallic" sexual arousal. Some of his patients reported having sexual dreams culminating in hallucinations of orgasm but with no genital involvement, or they reported that a woman's kiss would produce a "phantom" erection with no corresponding penile erection. At other times an actual erection

might occur with no mental involvement or even awareness.

Bard (1940) has studied the effects of hormones upon sexual responses (treading, rolling, and the like) to vaginal stimulation in the spinal female cat, and he has found that the reflexes are completely unaffected by hormone level or estrus. This independence appears to rule out a theory that had been put forward earlier: that the reflex pathways or the erogenous-zone receptors were sensitized by hormones.

Bard also discovered that decerebrate cats and dogs (with brainstem transected at the medulla and pons) were very unresponsive to genital stimulation. There was no erection in the male and no treading or rubbing in the female. Vaginal probing did, however, produce complete loss of decerebrate rigidity in the female cat, though not in the bitch. This difference may have been related to the estrous crouch, which is part of the sexual response of the cat but not of the bitch. The normal cat in estrus, however, crouches long before the vagina is stimulated by the male.

These results suggest that there is an inhibitory system in the lower brainstem that antagonizes the spinal reflexes for sexual behavior, a suggestion supported by Hart (1967) who found it possible to induce an "intense ejaculatory reaction" in spinal but not in normal male dogs by artificial stimulation of the penis. Lesions in the hypothalamus profoundly depress sexual behavior and excitability (Bard, 1940; Brookhart & Dey, 1941; Dey, Fisher, Berry & Ranson, 1940; G. Clark, 1942; Law & Meagher, 1958). Lesions of the medial anterior hypothalamic area between the optic chiasm and the stalk of the pituitary were most effective in abolishing sexual behavior. These lesions also disturbed the female sexual cycle in many cases, but such disturbance was not a necessary concomitant of the loss of sex drive. The females still refused to mate even when brought into estrus with hormone injections. It is odd that histologically indistinguishable lesions left some females in permanent estrus (as indicated by vaginal condition) and some in permanent anestrus. The lesions did not affect the estrous cycle at all in still other females. In all instances, however, the behavioral effect of the lesion was the same; the females became unreceptive. Male animals also became impotent after hypothalamic lesions, though the testes and the level of circulating testosterone remained normal.

Electrical stimulation of the hypothalamus also indicates that it contains a system for organizing male sex behavior. Vaughan and Fisher (1962) elicited male sexual behavior in rats by stimulating the lateral anterior hypothalamus. This stimulation produced continuous erection and greatly increased the frequency with which the rats mounted estrous females. The refractory period after ejaculation, during which sexual behavior ceased, was shortened from the normal 5 minutes or more to an average of 27 seconds. Copulation stopped immediately after the stimulating current was turned off. One rat was stimulated (five minutes on and five minutes off) for seven and a half hours, during which time it mounted the female 155 times, 81 times with intromission and 45 times with ejaculation.

Herberg (1963a) obtained emission of seminal fluid, though without erection, from stimulation of the hypothalamus of the rat just above the mamillary body near the fornix. He does not appear to have determined how the stimulation would affect the rats' behavior toward females, but Caggiula and Hoebel (1966) implanted bilateral electrodes in similar places and found that stimulation induced vigorous sexual behavior if a female was present (Figure 17.3).

Like Herberg, they obtained only seminal emission with no other signs of sexual activity in the absence of the female. Although the electrodes were in the medial forebrain bundle (MFB) close to the fornix, the rats did not eat during stimulation; in fact if they were already eating, stimulation stopped them. As eating is obtained from an area slightly anterior to this one, this finding indicates how closely packed along the MFB the critical areas for different motivational systems are.

Roberts, Steinberg, and Means (1967) obtained exaggerated male sexual behavior from hypothalamic stimulation in the opossum. Both male and female animals, when stimulated in the medial part of the anterior hypothalamus between the anterior commissure and the optic chiasm, not only mounted female opossums but also persistently attempted to copulate with a woolly toy dog. They would learn a T maze to reach the dog during stimulation and would also demonstrate a preference for a furry mat (which they would rub against) as compared with a wooden platform of similar dimensions. That the response was identical (except for penile erection) in males and females is further evidence in favor of the presence of fully developed neural circuits for both types of sexual behavior in animals of either sex.

Chemical stimulation has also been found to produce sexual behavior. None of the usual transmitter substances has so far proved effective, but minute injections of testosterone or other hormones of similar form into the lateral preoptic area of the hypothalamus in rats pro-

Figure 17.3 A record of the copulations of a male rat during stimulation of the posterior hypothalamus. Stimulation was administered during three-minute periods, as shown by the heavy black lines. (After Caggiula & Hoebel, 1966.)

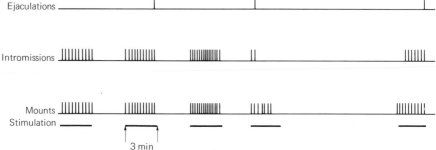
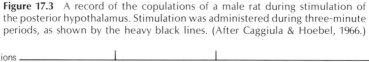

duced a great increase in the vigor and frequency of mounting, pelvic thrusting, and so on within a few minutes (Fisher, 1956). Exaggerated sexual behavior persisted for an hour or more after the injection.

Electrical activity recorded at the site of the injection indicated that the hormone produced neural discharges during the period of heightened sexual activity, but injection of other substances that also induce neural firing in the region did not produce sexual behavior. These results were obtained in both male and female rats.

G. W. Harris and Michael (1964) also stimulated the hypothalamus with hormones, but instead of injecting them in aqueous solution as Fisher had done they implanted a wire with a small quantity of hormone fused to its tip. The hormone dissolved very slowly and diffused into the surrounding tissue. Estrogen implants in the mamillary or premamillary region in ovariectomized female cats produced continuous receptivity lasting for months, or until the hormone had dissolved. The latency of onset of the behavior varied between 4 and 106 days in different preparations, presumably depending to some extent upon the proximity of the implant to the critical area. The gross difference between the minimum latency in this experiment (4 days) and the maximum in Fisher's experiment (about 10 minutes) is difficult to explain. It may have resulted partly from the difference in solubility of the hormones used; differences between the organization of male and female sexual behavior may also have been a factor.

In neither of these experiments could the hormone have been acting upon any part of the sexual system except the neural tissue in the immediate vicinity of the cannula or implant because the same quantities injected nearby had no effect. In the ovariectomized cats it was possible to confirm that the hormone produced no change in the anestrous state of the vagina. R. P. Michael (1962) used radioactive estrogen in some cats and then made autoradiographs of sections of the hypothalamus to determine the amount of diffusion. The radioactivity was detected no farther than about .5 mm from the implant. It is interesting that there were a few scattered clusters of blackened grains in the autoradiographs corresponding to neurons that had apparently absorbed the hormone preferentially. There were more of these neurons in the sections from cats that had shown good sexual responses than in those that had not; it was therefore assumed that the radioactive cells were the ones that had been sensitized by the hormone and had produced the change in sexual behavior.

These experiments suggest that hormones have a dual effect on the nervous system. One function is to stimulate the growth of connections in circuits for sexual behavior and the other is to act as a transmitter substance or facilitatory agent in such circuits.

RECORDING STUDIES. Recording of electrical activity in the brain during genital stimulation also implicates the lateral hypothalamus in sexual behavior. Porter, Cavanaugh, Critchlow, and Sawyer (1957), for example, found that probing the vagina of estrous cats elicited electrographic discharges resembling seizures in the lateral hypothalamic area (Figure 17.4). This activity did not spread to other parts of the hypothalamus, and it never occurred in anestrous cats. It usually persisted several minutes after stimulation had ceased and was apparently related to the pronounced "after-reaction" shown by estrous cats immediately after copulation.

Barraclough and Cross (1963) recorded from single units in the lateral hypothalamus just lateral to the fornix of estrous and anestrous rats. Sixty-four per cent of all the cells from which they were able to record showed some change (usually an increase in rate) in response to painful stimuli (pinching the tail), and 60 per cent responded to cold (ethylchloride sprayed on the tail for one second). Forty-seven per cent of the cells responded to probing of the cervix with a tapered glass rod lubricated with liquid paraffin, but no significant differences were found in the number of cells firing to stimuli at different phases of the estrous cycle, except that in *proestrus* (the period just before estrus) about 40 per cent of the cells

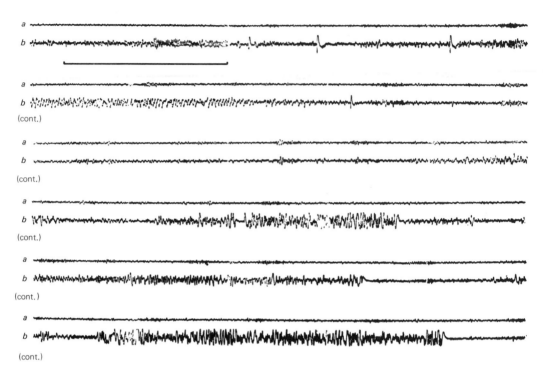

Figure 17.4 A continuous recording from (a) the medial hypothalamus and (b) the lateral hypothalamus of a cat. During the 15-second period underlined at the beginning of the record the cat's vagina was stimulated with a blunt glass rod 4 mm in diameter. From (Porter, Cavanaugh, Critchlow & Sawyer, 1957.)

responded to an odor presented to the rat, whereas fewer than 20 per cent responded to the same stimulus at other stages of the cycle.

Injections of progesterone rapidly inhibited the response of many cells in the hypothalamus to genital but not to other forms of stimulation (Figure 17.5). The inhibition reached a maximum after about 30 minutes and disappeared again after an hour, hardly what one would expect, considering that progesterone is used to bring rats into estrus after a period of priming with estrogen. But presumably hormones can affect behavior either by increasing or decreasing neural activity, just as other transmitters do. It is puzzling, however, that progesterone can influence receptivity many hours after it is injected, at a time when it no longer influences the activity of hypothalamic cells and after it has, in all probability, been cleared from the bloodstream.

Although species differences complicate the problem of localization within the hypothalamus, the experiments described indicate that there are two regions with predominately sexual functions: an anterior region, which can be stimulated medially in the opossum with electrodes and more laterally in the rat with either electrodes or injected hormones, and a posterolateral region lateral to the fornix at the level of the mamillary bodies from which the behavior may be elicited by electrical stimulation in rats. In estrous female cats, afterdischarge occurred at many points along the medial forebrain bundle, from the preoptic to the lateral hypothalamic nucleus, following vaginal probing, though estrous behavior was produced by hormone implants in a more posterior location, lateral to the mamillary bodies. Lesions most frequently interfere with sexual behavior when they are in the medial part of the anterior hypothalamic area just anterior to the ventromedial nucleus. We may therefore speculate that the sex mechanisms are diffusely organized along the hypothalamic path of the MFB, with nodes at various points where effective stimulation may be delivered.

Extrahypothalamic sites that can influence sexual behavior, or components of it, have also been found. In a series of experiments on the squirrel monkey, MacLean and his colleagues have explored the brain for points that give penile erection upon stimulation (Dua & MacLean, 1964; MacLean & Ploog, 1962). It should be pointed out, however, that it is rather easy to elicit erection in this species; in fact, erection appears to be a form of greeting or dominance display (Ploog & MacLean, 1963), as well as a component of mating.

Electrical stimulation of the anterior preoptic area of the hypothalamus or of the septal area produced erections. Another such zone was found along the path from the cingulate gyrus through the anterior thalamus and mamillo-thalamic tract to the mamillary bodies (MacLean & Ploog, 1962). Dua and MacLean (1964) found sites in the frontal cortex and the medialis dorsalis nucleus of the thalamus at which stimulation gave penile erection. It was reported that hippocampal afterdischarge usually accompanied the erections, but very few hippocampal points were found from which erections could be obtained by direct stimulation.

Unfortunately, these experiments were all carried out on monkeys immobilized in a monkey chair, so that it was not possible to determine whether or not stimulation would

Figure 17.5 Responses of a single neuron in the lateral hypothalamus of a proestrous female rat at various times after administration of 400 μg progesterone. The top record, taken 27 minutes after injection, shows no response to light or to probing of the cervix but does show a strong response to pain. The middle record, taken 40 minutes after injection, shows no response to light, partial recovery of the response to probing of the cervix, and a strong response to pain. The bottom record, taken 60 minutes after injection, shows no response to light and strong responses to both cervical probing and pain. (From Barraclough & Cross, 1963.)

Effect of 400 μg. progesterone

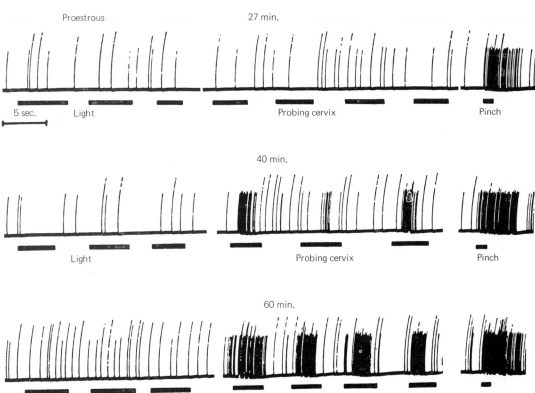
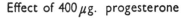

produce any changes in behavior toward female squirrel monkeys.

Kim (1960) claimed that lesions in the dorsal hippocampus and overlying cortex increased the frequency of mounting in the male rat. Control lesions in the cortex alone decreased sexual activity. These results have not been confirmed in experiments by Kimble, Rogers, and Hendrickson (1967), who found no significant effects of hippocampal lesions upon sexual behavior in either male or female rats. Impaired maternal behavior was found in females, however.

Gol, Kellaway, Shapiro, and Hurst (1963) reported that sexual behavior ceased after hippocampal lesions in cats, monkeys, and baboons. The lesions were made without damaging the amygdala and with minimal damage to the cortex, which may account for the difference between these results and those reported by Klüver and Bucy (1939) from monkeys whose temporal lobes had been amputated. Both male and female monkeys became hypersexual and increased their frequency of copulation and masturbation after the complete lobectomy. Similar behavior was also found in one monkey with a bilateral medial temporal-lobe resection, which removed both amygdalas and parts of the hippocampi but did not disturb the temporal neocortex (Orbach, Milner & Rasmussen, 1960). Kling (1968) reported an increase in the sexual activity of juvenile monkeys after amygdalectomy.

Cats also become hypersexual after temporal-lobe lesions, but some controversy has arisen over exactly which structure is the crucial one. Schreiner and Kling (1953) made lesions confined to the amygdala in male cats, producing a variety of bizarre sexual behaviors, which included mounting other species and inanimate objects and engaging in tandem copulations in which a hypersexual animal would mount the hindmost of a pair of already copulating animals. All these effects have been observed in presumably normal, male cats, however, once they have become used to mating with receptive females in a particular room (J. D. Green, Clemente & De Groot, 1957; Hagamen, Zitman & Reeves, 1963), and the

interpretation of Schreiner and Kling's experiments is thus open to question.

J. D. Green and his colleagues pointed out, however, that male cats are very reluctant to mate in unfamilar territory, and in their studies of the effects of temporal-lobe lesions they used male willingness to copulate in a strange place as a criterion of hypersexuality. Their results indicate that small bilateral lesions confined to the pyriform cortex can produce hypersexual behavior as intense as any produced by combined lesions of amygdala and cortex. They found, as had Schreiner and Kling, that castration eventually eliminated the hypersexual behavior of these animals.

Although Green and his colleagues believed that the amygdala was not involved in the suppression of sexual behavior in the cat, it would be surprising if this structure, with its close connections to the hypothalamus, had nothing to do with sex. Shealy and Peele (1957) have, in fact, reported that stimulation of the amygdala produced erection, copulatory movements, and ejaculation in male cats. Ovulation could be triggered in females, and in pregnant females amygdaloid stimulation produced abortion. Lissák and Endröczi (1961) reported hypersexuality as an aftereffect of stimulation in the medial amygdaloid nuclei and in the pyriform cortex.

The data from human patients with lesions of the temporal lobe are as confusing as are those from animals. Terzian and Dalle Ore's (1955) patient with bilateral temporal ablations, whom we met in Chapter 16, exhibited many of the same symptoms as did Klüver and Bucy's monkeys, including a form of hypersexuality. Several weeks after the second temporal lobe was removed he became sexually aroused by the sight of an anatomical chart in one of the rooms at the hospital and proudly demonstrated his erection to the doctor present. His exhibitionism gradually became more persistent over the next few weeks, and he frequently made homosexual advances to the doctors. He showed no particular interest in nurses or other females, however—in marked contrast to his behavior before the operation.

Other patients, in whom only medial temporal-lobe structures were damaged bilaterally (Scoville, 1954; B. Milner, personal communication), became or remained hyposexual. The patient described by Scoville had been suffering very severe seizures; apparently he had never shown any interest in sexual activity before the operation, and this aspect of his behavior did not change afterward, although his seizures became much less frequent. Another patient, operated upon by Penfield for temporal-lobe seizures, had an atrophic lesion of the hippocampus contralateral to the surgical ablation. This patient was married and seems to have led a normal sex life before the operation, but it ceased after the operation. He received testosterone treatment, which does not seem to have restored his sex drive.

The effects of unilateral temporal lobectomies seem equally unpredictable. Epileptic seizures originating in the temporal lobe very frequently decrease libido in the human patient (Gastaut & Collomb, 1954), apparently because of active inhibition from epileptiform "spiking" in the amygdala or nearby limbic structures. After a successful operation in which the source of the seizures was removed, Gastaut claimed that normal sexuality returned and that some patients even became hypersexual.

Blumer and Walker (1967) have provided evidence to support this view; one of their patients was described as a very religious man who abhorred "low talk" and had intercourse with his wife about once a year before being operated on for temporal-lobe epilepsy. About a month after the operation he became sexually aroused, and his arousal intensified during the next few weeks until he had an almost continuous erection, became totally preoccupied with sex, and used obscene language. He then began to have seizures again and promptly returned to his former condition.

Despite the cases described by Gastaut and Collomb and Blumer and Walker, temporal-lobe patients at the Montreal Neurological Institute more often seem to be hyposexual, even after seizures are surgically abolished. Hypersexuality is a more frequent sequel to ablations that involve the orbitofrontal cortex. This correlation is interesting in view of the notion current early in this century that there was a "sex center" in the frontal cortex. This idea followed an earlier guess by the phrenologist Gall (1810–1819), who had put the sex center in the cerebellum.

The theory of the frontal center quietly faded out as a result of a number of experiments on animals. Rogers (1922) showed that the cortex was not necessary for mating or rearing the young in the pigeon, and Stone (1925) found that male rabbits with large cortical lesions in the area suggested as the sex center showed unabated sexual vigor. Brooks (1937) later made "complete" cortical removals in buck rabbits without diminishing their willingness or ability to copulate immediately upon being presented with a doe. He found, however, that when the olfactory bulbs were cut the animals no longer mated. Removal of the olfactory bulbs in rabbits with intact cortex had no effect upon mating, however, even when visual and auditory receptors were also destroyed.

C. D. Davis (1939) claimed that some completely decorticate male rats were also capable of mating, but Beach (1940), on the basis of rather more detailed experiments (though some of his lesions certainly included more than the cortex) disputed this claim. There is little doubt that complete cessation of sexual activity results from bilateral cortical ablations in the male cat, though hemidecortication has little effect upon mating (Beach, Zitrin & Jaynes, 1956). The decorticate cat does not even show any diffuse excitement in the presence of an estrous female, nor can any increase in sexual interest be produced by injections of testosterone. No decrease in female sexual activity occurs after cortical lesions in the cat or in the rat (Beach, 1944).

MECHANISMS OF SEXUAL SATIATION. Motor fatigue does not seem to be an important aspect of sexual satiation, as animals rendered hypersexual by lesions are capable of almost continuous sexual activity and animals that have stopped copulating can be induced to start again by electrical or chemical stimulation of the brain. Furthermore, just as hibernators become seasonally hyperphagic, seasonal breeders tend to be sexually insatiable during the mating season. In several respects, sexual satiation is similar to satiation for food.

One similarity is that (in the rat at least), after transection of the *neuraxis* (brainstem-spinal cord axis) above the level of the motor pools for the sexual or eating responses, reflexes can be elicited independently of the state of deprivation or hormonal level. This independence can be explained only if satiation normally results from an active suppression of motor activity, originating in some part of the brain.

We have seen that satiation for food and water are determined by many factors, but long-term regulation apparently demands that the composition of the blood exert a dominant role in controlling the frequency and duration of consummatory behavior. There is no such regulatory function for sexual activity, and the only benefit to be derived from sexual satiation is that excessive preoccupation with sex may expose the animal to predators or prevent it from obtaining enough food. Furthermore, in some animals fertility is reduced by excessive sexual activity.

Satiation could nevertheless be the result of humoral or hormonal factors. For example, orgasm may influence the hypothalamic cells that regulate the release of gonadotrophins. We know that it does so in females of those species that ovulate after mating, but there seems to be no information on the effect of sexual activity upon the androgen level in males.

One argument against the theory that testosterone level is a factor in satiation is that supposedly weeks or even months are required before the loss of testosterone occasioned by castration has a noticeable effect upon the strength of the sex drive; on the other hand we have the evidence of Fisher's experiment that hormone level in the hypothalamus can produce immediate change in the intensity of sexual activity.

Another possible satiation mechanism, which may operate in parallel with a hormonal one, is similar to that suggested for the short-term satiation of feeding. Neural activity associated with orgasm may change the activity or the sensitivity of an inhibitory structure like the amygdala or the pyriform cortex, so that excit-atory pathways for sex are suppressed for a time. This structure either could exert a tonic inhibitory effect, or it could be part of a sensory path that delivered inhibition to sexual mechanisms whenever a stimulus that would normally be sexually exciting was encountered. In the latter case, a synaptic change resembling that of short-term memory would suffice to reduce the attractiveness of sexual stimuli for a time.

Parental Behavior

The type and degree of infant care vary enormously from species to species. In some animals the only parental behavior consists of depositing eggs where they will have a better-than-average chance of survival and where the emerging young will be able to find food. Social insects, on the other hand, make elaborate provisions for the care of eggs and larvae. Cells to accommodate them are constructed of wax or paper and stocked with food. Workers assigned to nursemaid duties feed and groom their larval siblings, "air-condition" the nurseries, and so on.

Some sort of care of eggs and young is necessary in most higher animals, and these duties may be performed by either parent or by both. Foster parents may adopt the offspring of other animals of either the same or related species, and sometimes adoption is the rule, as among cuckoos and cowbirds. In mammals, arrangements for nourishment of the young by the female both before and after birth dictate that most parental duties fall to the mother.

An excellent and very comprehensive review of comparative parental behavior in birds and mammals and its relations to hormones has been published by Lehrman (1961). With various colleagues he has also made a detailed study of the hormonal basis of the sexual and parental behavior of the ringdove. As pointed out by Harper (1904) and Craig (1911), the reproductive cycle of the dove family, which includes pigeons, is initiated by the male's courtship of the female. After several days of "bowing and cooing" on his part, both birds begin to construct a nest, and copulation takes place. About a week later, when the nest is completed, the female lays two eggs, and both birds take turns sitting on them. The eggs hatch after about two weeks, and the young birds (squabs) are fed by the parents on "crop milk," a fluid secreted in the crops of both parents at that time. The squabs are able to look after themselves in another two or three weeks, and the parents start the courtship ritual again (Lehrman, 1958a).

L. H. Matthews (1939) put a glass partition between the two birds during courtship and found that nest building still occurred; it did not continue, however, if the partition was opaque. It was similarly shown by Patel (1936) that secretion of crop milk by the male took place only if he could see his mate sitting on the eggs.

Following an early experiment by Riddle and Lahr (1944), who found that implantation of either progesterone or testosterone pellets would induce incubation in ringdoves, Lehrman (1958b) determined that injecting progesterone into isolated birds once a day for a week would induce them to incubate immediately when presented with a nest of eggs (Figure 17.6). Estrogen injections during a similar period made some birds sit on the eggs earlier than normal but had the opposite effect upon other individuals. All estrogen-injected birds immediately started to build nests, even though a nest with eggs had been provided. Often a new nest was built on top of eggs.

These results suggest that courtship stimulates estrogen secretion (through hypothalamic pathways), which motivates the birds to build nests. The nest-building activity and perhaps the sight of the nest then stimulate progesterone secretion, which triggers ovulation in the female and motivates incubation behavior in both birds.

Injection of prolactin into ringdoves causes crop growth and prepares the adult birds to feed squabs but does not have a strong influence upon incubation. It is assumed that the sight of the mate sitting on the eggs can stimulate secretion of prolactin. In other birds (the dove is almost unique in producing milk) this hormone presumably motivates the parents to bring food back to the nest and to feed it to

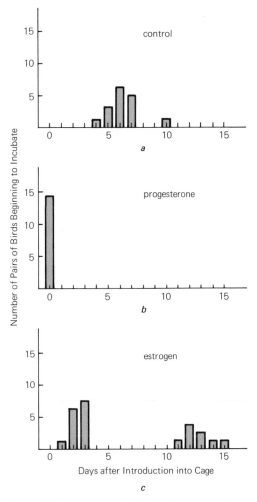

Figure 17.6 Latency of incubation in groups of ringdoves that (a) had no hormonal injections, (b) had injections of progesterone, and (c) had injections of estrogen for seven days before being placed in pairs in cages with nests and eggs. (From Lehrman, 1958b.)

the nestlings. Nalbandov and Card (1945) reported that in the domestic hen prolactin injections produced a broody response to chicks (calling them, hiding them under wings, leading them to food, and so on). Similar responses are obtained in cocks after prolactin injections, though they do not otherwise participate in rearing chicks (Figure 17.7).

A start has been made on the difficult task of determining the sites of hormone action in the nervous system controlling parental behavior. Komisaruk (1967) implanted small quantities of progesterone into the brains of

Figure 17.7 A broody response to chicks induced in a cock by an injection of prolactin. The cock would normally ignore or even attack chicks that approached him. (From Nalbandov & Card, 1945.)

ringdoves. When the implantations were in the preoptic nuclei or the supraoptic decussation, both males and females incubated if presented with eggs and nest. Some of the males continued to show courtship behavior, however, although it always stops during normal incubation. When progesterone was implanted in the anterior hypothalamic nuclei, male courtship was suppressed, but incubation was not usually produced. Male behavior can be produced in castrated male birds by testosterone implants (Barfield, 1965) or by electrical stimulation (Åkerman, 1966) at the sites where progesterone blocks such behavior in the intact bird.

In mammals the main components of parental behavior are building nests or finding secluded places in which to deliver the young, feeding the young, and protecting them from predators and other dangers. These duties are more commonly performed by the female.

Many animals build nests for shelter independently of their reproductive status, but there is usually an increase in such activity just before parturition. Some female animals, like the rabbit, lose hair a few days before a litter is due and use it to line their nests or lairs. There is a sudden rise in nest-building activity in the

pregnant laboratory rat four or five days before it gives birth, and such activity remains at a high level until the pups are weaned. In some rodents injections of progesterone have increased nest building by nonpregnant females (see Lehrman, 1961). Fisher (1965) found that injections of soluble steroid hormones into the medial preoptic nucleus of either male or female rats would immediately induce very active nest building, as well as other components of maternal care like retrieving scattered pups.

Although hormonal action is necessary to facilitate immediate maternal care for newly born or newly hatched young in most animals, Rosenblatt (1967) found that nonpregnant, ovariectomized, or hypophysectomized rats—and even castrated male rats—displayed maternal behavior after one or two weeks of exposure to pups. Hormones are thus not strictly necessary for eliciting maternal behavior, but they certainly reduce the latency with which it is evoked by offspring.

Rather surprisingly there seems to be no available information on the effects of hypothalamic lesions upon maternal behavior, but there is every reason to suppose that such lesions, suitably placed, would interfere both with neural circuits and with the production of the hormones involved in maternal behavior. Nest building, suckling, and retrieval of the young are impaired by extensive lesions of the medial cortex in rats but are unaffected by more lateral cortical lesions (Stamm, 1955). Kimble, Rogers, and Hendrickson (1967) confirmed that lateral cortical lesions have no effect upon maternal behavior and discovered that dorsal hippocampal lesions have effects somewhat similar to those observed by Stamm in the medial cortex. This finding is not altogether surprising in view of the important connections between the cingulate cortex and the hippocampus (though in avoidance behavior the two structures apparently play different roles). It seems clear that some of the innate circuits activated by hormones for the organization of maternal behavior lie in these anterior limbic structures.

In Stamm's experiment, although the rats with medial cortical lesions did not suckle their young immediately (and many of the infants died), when pups that had already learned to nurse with normal mothers were substituted, nursing began; the rats with lesions thereupon improved in such other aspects of maternal care as retrieving. Stamm suggested that this improvement might have resulted from learning based on relief of tension in the mammae as milk was removed. That may be, but such learning is not necessary for nursing behavior to develop in rats without cortical lesions, as was demonstrated by Moltz, Geller, and Levin (1967). Pregnant rats whose mammary glands had been removed gave birth normally and adopted a normal nursing posture over their litters as frequently as did control mothers.

It is remarkable that the *primiparous* (giving birth for the first time) mammal can perform all the complex and specific behaviors necessary for the successful delivery and rearing of her young, with no possibility of having learned them beforehand. At least some of these behaviors must be initially dependent upon gonadal hormones, for when the ovaries are removed just before parturition only about 50 per cent of the rats will accept the pups and attempt to rear them. *Multiparous* rats (rats with previous maternal experience) treated in the same way almost all accept litters and rear them successfully (Moltz & Wiener, 1966). This finding indicates that, as with sexual behavior, previous experience makes an animal less dependent upon circulating hormones.

The effects of nonspecific experience upon maternal behavior have also been recorded in various animals, most interestingly in the monkey. Harlow (1962) found that female monkeys reared in isolation, with *surrogate mothers* constructed of wire or cloth, were very deficient in maternal feelings when they themselves became mothers. Their infants had to be very agile and resilient to survive the cruel treatment they received. It is not clear precisely what had gone wrong with the development of the nervous system in these animals, but in view of the wide-ranging behavioral deficiencies it was probably not specific to the innate pathways regulating maternal behavior.

Harlow (1962) was critical of those students of reproductive behavior who confine themselves to investigations of sex drive and the like and show no interest in what he calls "affectional systems," or attachment. In most species, attachment develops between offspring and parent or foster parent, often on the basis of very early experience. Many *precocial* birds (capable of a high degree of independence from birth), for example, follow any moving object that they see soon after hatching and henceforth regard it as the mother, running to it when disturbed (Heinroth, 1910). This learned attachment is called *imprinting*. Imprinting is also found in lambs and other hoofed animals that can walk soon after birth. In most species the parent rapidly becomes attached to the offspring and is highly possessive toward it (Thorpe, 1956).

Similar bonds are often formed between mating pairs of animals, but species differ greatly in this respect. Animals that live in groups, in which the mothers do most of the rearing, tend to be sexually promiscuous; their main attachment is to the group as a whole. Some males may show selectivity in the females they court and vice versa, but individuals usually pay no special attention to each other except during sexual activity. In other species pairs raise the young together and may stay together for life. Herring gulls, despite their gregariousness during the breeding season, form lasting pairs, and each can recognize its mate among a vast throng of other gulls at great distances, either by sight or by call (Thorpe, 1956).

In the absence of the true mother, most infants become attached to some surrogate. In birds, as we have seen, the substitute is usually something that moves; primates become attached to furry objects that they can cling to. Harlow's infant monkeys preferred a terry-cloth surrogate to a wire one, and human infants frequently become attached to a soft toy or a blanket.

At a later stage human beings may form attachments to a great variety of toys, pets, and sporting equipment and still later to objects like motorcycles, guns, musical instruments, and articles of clothing or adornment. Their reluctance to part with these objects, even temporarily, and their grief if the objects are lost or broken can be very intense during the early stages of the attachment, though adaptation usually sets in before long. In all these respects the phenomenon is similar to falling in love and may well involve the same physiological mechanisms. Unfortunately, although we know a great deal about the hormonal and physiological bases of sexual arousal and behavior, next to nothing is known about the physiological mechanisms involved in enthusiasms and attachments to particular objects or individuals. Such mechanisms clearly evolved as an aid to successful rearing of offspring, in order to bind family units together, but there is no reason to suppose that they have much else in common with the sex drive. In other words, loneliness is not the same type of motivation as that produced by sexual deprivation, and we would expect different neural circuits to be involved.

ACTIVITY, EXPLORATION, AND SENSORY SELF-STIMULATION

If animals responded only to stimuli directly related to satisfaction of needs, they would be lucky to survive for more than a few days, for the objects they require are not usually within range of their sensory receptors. Animals must explore or at least move about, in order to find what they need at any given time. Learning reduces the need to explore, but not much useful learning can take place without exploration.

Few domestic animals, including the laboratory rat, seem to indulge to any great extent in activity for its own sake, though the female rat will run great distances when in heat (Wang, 1923). Wolves and other wild members of the dog family, which range over wide hunting areas, seem to have a need to locomote unrelated to their need to explore. In zoos and other confined spaces they adopt stereotyped running patterns and soon beat visible paths in their paddock as they lope back and forth hour after hour.

In the laboratory it is not always easy to make a sharp distinction between pure activity and exploration. Both involve the same

responses and are recorded by the same types of apparatus, but we usually assume that the animal becomes satiated with exploration as it becomes familiar with its environment, whereas it becomes satiated with activity after it expends a certain amount of muscular energy. If an animal becomes active in an environment familiar to it, we can never be sure, however, that it is not making an inspection tour to see whether or not any changes have taken place or that it has not forgotten some details of the environment.

If the function of random or exploratory activity is to improve the animal's chances of reaching necessary commodities, we might expect positive correlations between hunger, thirst, and the like, on one hand, and locomotor activity, on the other. Increased running in the receptive female rodent is an example of such a correlation, but the relationship between activity and hunger seems less clear, at least under laboratory conditions. B. A. Campbell and Sheffield (1953) found that rats confined to activity cages did not become more active as they become hungrier but that hunger did make them respond more actively to a stimulus change. It seems that, once the rat has fully explored the cage and made sure that there is no way to obtain food, it conserves its energy until some disturbance that might be a signal that food is available takes place. DeVito and Smith (1959) found that hunger had no effect on activity in monkeys. Temperature of the environment had only slight effects on activity.

There are conflicting reports on the effects of hunger and thirst upon exploration in more complex environments like mazes. K. C. Montgomery (1953) found that deprivation of food and water reduced the amount of exploration by rats in an empty Y maze, but W. R. Thompson (1953) and Glickman and Jensen (1961) found increased exploration in male rats under some conditions of food deprivation. The differences may reflect differing amounts of previous experience in the apparatus, as Fehrer (1956) has suggested. True exploratory behavior can occur only if the animal has had no appreciable opportunity to become familiar with the places it can visit; when this criterion has been met, hungry animals explore more than do satiated ones.

Aside from locomotor exploration, some higher animals can be motivated by sensory stimuli not obviously related to need. Rodents will press a bar to obtain a change in illumination (Marx, Henderson & Roberts, 1955; Kish, 1955), but the drive for stimulus change is not strong at this phylogenetic level. In primates visual and auditory stimuli have proved to be very effective incentives. Monkeys will work for hours to obtain short glimpses of a toy train, for example, and will learn to make discriminations in order to perform the viewing response (Butler, 1953, 1954). Auditory stimuli will motivate similar performances (Butler, 1957). At the human level most of us know from personal experience the kinds of strong emotional arousal that can be produced by music, paintings, and other forms of sensory stimulation not immediately related to survival.

It is possible that these motivations are by-products of other neural developments and have no survival value in themselves, but it is also conceivable that, in animals that depend heavily upon learning, they serve the purpose of exposing the animals to the widest range of stimuli possible, so that a useful supply of concepts can be built up. A similar explanation might be offered for the drive to manipulate objects, which is also very much more evident in primates than in lower animals (Glickman & Sroges, 1966).

Less is known about the physiological bases of these nonregulatory drives than about those studied above. Bianchi (1895) mentioned that some monkeys with damaged frontal lobes that he tested were hyperactive, and he described the stereotyped pacing so characteristic of such animals: "She runs incoherently from one end of the room to the other; when she reaches the wall she stops, returns to the opposite angle." Other pioneers of experimental brain surgery also noted similar behavior after frontal lesions in some animals, though quite frequently exactly the opposite effect—dullness and lethargy—was observed.

Richter and Hines (1938) attempted more precise localization of the area involved in the

monkey's hyperactivity and concluded that increased movement was associated with lesions in what they called "area 9" in the frontal cortex, a saddle of cortex extending from the dorsomedial surface just posterior to the frontal pole over the dorsal surface and part way down the lateral surface (Figure 17.8). Ruch and Shenkin (1943), on the other hand, consistently produced increases in "methodical pacing" when their lesions included the orbital frontal surface just lateral to the olfactory bulb (A. E. Walker's area 13, 1940). Zubek and De Lorenzo (1952) demonstrated increased running-wheel activity in rats after removal of the whole frontal pole but none in rats with partial frontal lesions or lesions of other cortical areas. They considered their results to be in accordance with the findings of Ruch and Shenkin.

Figure 17.8 (a) A lateral view of the monkey brain, showing the location of area 9. (b) A ventral view, showing the location of area 13.

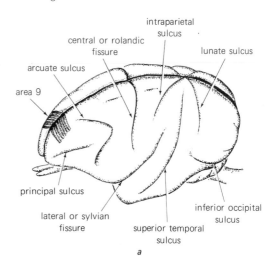

a

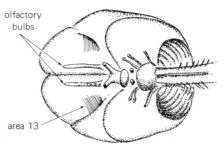

b

All the experimenters have agreed that when a lesion encroaches upon the caudate-putamen there is a great increase in pacing activity and *obstinate progression* (walking movements that continue even when the animal is stuck in a corner or otherwise prevented from advancing) also appears (Mettler & Mettler, 1942).

Ruch and Shenkin mentioned that their hyperactive monkeys became even more active in the presence of an experimenter, and Isaac and DeVito (1958) measured the effect of light and noise upon the activity of monkeys with frontal-lobe lesions. As can be seen in Figure 17.9, activity was greatly increased during sensory stimulation. In the dark it was hardly greater than that of normal control animals.

Frontal-lobe lesions in man often give rise to increased walking, and even after unilateral frontal lesions patients are said to be very fidgety, engaging in compulsive finger snapping, foot tapping, and the like. The explana-

Figure 17.9 The average activity, of normal and frontal-lobectomized monkeys under different conditions of stimulation, as measured by interruptions of a light beam. The intensity of room illumination was 1.6 footcandles (ft-c), the noise about 70 phons. All cortex anterior to the arcuate sulcus was removed six months to a year before testing. (From Isaac & DeVito, 1958.)

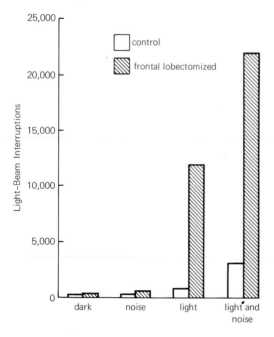

tion sometimes offered is that inhibition has been removed from lower motor pathways. Sensory input increases the general activity of the brain, including the activity of motor systems, but in the intact animal a counteracting inhibition operates through frontal regions. When those regions are ablated the motor responses are evoked unchecked.

A different form of hyperresponsiveness, related more to exploratory or manipulatory behavior than to "pure" activity, occurs in monkeys after temporal-lobe ablation. Klüver and Bucy (1939) called the effect *hypermetamorphosis*; the animal does not move around excessively, but it follows every movement of the experimenter or other objects very closely with its eyes. It also repeatedly picks up and mouths any small objects near it.

Rats with dorsal hippocampal lesions also persist in exploring for an abnormally long time. The running and sniffing in corners exhibited by a normal rat in a strange cage fall to a low level after 10–15 minutes, but in rats with damage to the dorsal hippocampus they continue for at least an hour (H. Teitelbaum & Milner, 1963; Leaton, 1965), and probably for more than 12 hours (Sengstake, 1968). Sengstake suggested that hippocampal lesions increase activity rather than reduce habituation, but this claim is based on the finding that hippocampals already showed more activity than did normal rats during the first 20 minutes. Many normal rats would have been almost completely habituated before that, however. Rats with hippocampal lesions also moved farther in an open field and made many repetitive errors in mazes (Kimble, 1963).

There is ample evidence that the hippocampus can inhibit movement. MacLean (1957) found that hippocampal stimulation produced "arrest" of locomotion, and Flynn and Wasman (1960) found that conditioned avoidance responses were suppressed during hippocampal afterdischarges in cats.

Investigatory motivation probably resembles other motivational systems we have discussed in consisting of a basic neural mechanism through which every stimulus elicits approach, sniffing, manipulation, and the like, but which is, however, inhibited by other systems after satiation. Satiation of exploration is assumed to take place when the animal has learned enough about the environment to be able to predict the stimuli that a given response will reveal. The effect of hippocampal lesions suggests that familiar stimuli arouse more hippocampal activity than unfamiliar stimuli and that this increased activity tends to inhibit any approach or manipulatory response generated by the basic circuit before it is emitted. After hippocampal ablation, the basic approach and exploratory behavior is less inhibited by familiar stimuli, and satiation is delayed.

ESCAPE AND AGGRESSIVE BEHAVIOR

The systems we have discussed so far involve approach as a basic behavior. In order to survive, however, animals not only must find sustenance but must also escape or avoid various destructive situations and agents like fire, drowning, falling, poison, and predators.

Specific escape mechanisms have evolved for most of these dangers. One of the simplest is the withdrawal reflex, which operates at the spinal and bulbar level to produce movement away from damaging (or potentially damaging) stimuli. Stimulation of high-threshold receptors almost always elicits the response, but nearly any unexpected stimulus will elicit escape or avoidance in an intact animal. An explosive reaction can be obtained by blowing quite gently on the vibrissae, or guard hairs, of a dozing animal; a harmless insect walking about on a man's skin may produce a similar effect. Even a sudden sound can, if unexpected, produce a protective flinching or startle response.

Taste receptors that respond to bitter substances elicit a spitting reflex as a protection against some poisons, and we have already encountered the more involved mechanism by which animals learn to avoid smells and tastes that have previously been followed by nausea or illness.

Rapidly approaching objects or rapidly expanding ones (which produce a similar effect upon the retina) elicit blinking, startle and running away in most animals. An advancing lion may be warded off by opening an umbrella quickly in its face, so it is said, and Melzack (1952) has used this stimulus or rapidly inflated balloons to evoke "fear" in dogs.

At a less reflexive but still innate level most animals avoid heights as soon as they are old enough to see and walk (Walk & Gibson, 1961), an attribute that no doubt saves many of them from falling out of nests, over cliffs, out of bed, and so on. Dislike of getting wet is also common among animals not endowed by nature for an aquatic existence.

Darkness, with its nocturnal predators, produces signs of distress or fear in many diurnal animals; nocturnal animals, on the other hand, appear to suffer from *photophobia* (fear of light). Small birds are very upset by the sight of a stuffed owl, almost all animals display innate defensive reactions to snakes, and innumerable other examples of specific evasion of predators by their prey have been reported by ethologists.

Human beings retain many of these innate fears, though they appear less rational now (especially during the last few generations of urban civilization) than they must have seemed in the past. Usually fear becomes attenuated by adaptation (as in animals), but severe and persistent fears are quite common, and overcoming them requires more intensive training. Many psychiatrists still seem to believe that phobias are learned from traumatic experience, but, although an unpleasant experience may intensify a phobia in some people, the ease with which certain stimuli (like water, blood, or darkness) can be associated with fear, in comparison with the difficulty of establishing such associations for others that are more objectively dangerous (cigarettes, for example), makes it very likely that potential circuits for such associations are innate.

Lesion Studies

As we pointed out in the introduction to Part Five, fear and anger are states of mind, and we have no right to attribute them to organisms that cannot speak. We do not know at what phylogenetic level or at what level of neural complexity emotional states accompany attempts to escape attack and the like, and it is doubtful that we shall ever find out. Men with spinal transection do not, of course, report sensory or emotional experiences when withdrawal reflexes are elicited in a limb below the level of the transection, but this fact does not constitute evidence that simple neural systems are incapable of emotional experience. Probable as this conclusion may be, we must recognize that the disconnected neural remnant is no longer in communication with its brain, and, like the right hemisphere of a split-brain patient, can therefore communicate only by signs. Withdrawal and thrashing around could be interpreted as signs of emotion (and probably would be if observed in an intact mammal), but, even if disconnected neural structures or intact lower animals do experience emotions, they must be very different emotions from our own. In the following discussion the expressions "fear," "anger," and so on are used in connection with animals only as a convenient shorthand for patterns of autonomic responses combined with withdrawal or aggressive behavior.

DECEREBRATE ANIMALS. More nearly complete expressions of behavior associated with fear and anger than can be elicited from the spinal cord are observed when the neuraxis is severed above the mesencephalon. Cats and dogs decerebrated at the pontine level growl, spit, scratch, and bite when handled roughly. They also show sympathetic discharges (pilo-erection, changes in heart rate, and so on; see Woodworth & Sherrington, 1904; Bazett & Penfield, 1922), but the stimulation must be definitely nociceptive (injurious) to elicit attack. Loud high-pitched sounds evoke arousal, sympathetic discharge, and running away from the source of the noise. The reactions of these preparations are sometimes called *pseudaffective* or *sham rage*, presumably on the shaky assumption that "real" emotion cannot be experienced unless the cortex or forebrain structures are involved (Keller, 1932; Macht & Bard, 1942; Bard & Macht, 1958).

Cats decerebrated above the hypothalamus have much lower thresholds for sham rage; they become violent at the slightest touch, and their attacks are much better integrated, including running, biting, and well-timed and well-aimed clawing (Bard, 1928).

We are therefore led to conclude that the mesencephalon contains motor circuits for attack, which are capable of being fired by strong sensory input from the body or, even more effectively, by input from a hypothalamic system that amplifies and organizes the sensory input. Normal animals, however, do not respond with automatic rage to every tactual stimulus, and tame animals will tolerate a considerable amount of handling without resentment. Once more, therefore, we are confronted with the probability that a basic system (this time for self-preservation) is suppressed by forebrain structures when it is not needed.

FOREBRAIN LESIONS. Some of the inhibitory influence is apparently conducted through the anterior hypothalamus and rostral pathways like those through the septal area. Lesions in these areas produce, at least for a time, as dramatic a drop in the rage threshold as does removal of the entire brain rostral to the hypothalamus (Fulton & Ingraham, 1929; Spiegel, Miller & Oppenheimer, 1940; Brady & Nauta, 1953). Complete decortication has a similar effect (Goltz, 1892; Cannon, 1928), and this finding led to the speculation that part of the cortex inhibits the hypothalamic system for rage through rostral pathways.

Bard and Mountcastle (1948) found that removal of neocortex alone, leaving limbic structures (olfactory bulb and tubercle, hippocampus, amygdala, pyriform cortex, cingulate cortex, retrosplenial and presubicular cortex) intact (see Figure 17.10), made cats more placid than before; they naturally inferred that the limbic cortex was responsible for the suppression of rage.

The limbic cortex was then subjected to more detailed study. Lesions of the cingulate and retrosplenial cortex did not lower the threshold for angry behavior and may even have increased "friendliness." Cats with hippocampal lesions also appeared friendlier. Cats

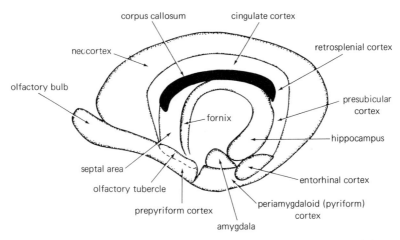

corpus callosum   cingulate cortex

neocortex   retrosplenial cortex

olfactory bulb   presubicular
                                                              cortex

                          fornix

                                                              hippocampus

septal area

olfactory tubercle   entorhinal cortex

                                              periamygdaloid (pyriform)
prepyriform cortex   cortex

                          amygdala

Figure 17.10 A schematic view of parts of the limbic system. Some of the structures, like the amygdala and the hippocampus, are laterally placed and would not show in any sagittal section that would show such midline structures as the fornix, septal area, and cingulate cortex. (After Nauta, in Brady, 1958a.)

with damaged amygdalas, on the other hand, slowly developed a low threshold for rage, and two or three months after the operation most were very dangerous to handle. The slightest touch or approach by the experimenter would provoke savage and well-directed attack. The tail and back appeared to be the most sensitive regions, and one cat still purred if stroked gently on the head, though the slightest touch elsewhere on its body produced a raging attack.

These results are still something of a mystery. Klüver and Bucy (1939) had already shown that removal of the temporal lobes, including the amygdalas, had a taming effect upon wild monkeys, and subsequently Schreiner and Kling (1953) failed to observe the development of low rage thresholds in 18 of 20 cats with amygdaloid lesions, though it did occur in the other two. Four of their cats became unusually docile after the lesions, and, of course, almost all became hypersexual. Agoutis, lynxes, and monkeys have also been tamed by amygdalectomy, and Adey, Merrillees, and Sunderland (1956) were able to tame *phalangers* (savage marsupials) by ablation of entorhinal cortex (see Figure 17.10). Rosvold, Mirsky, and Pribram (1954) found that in social situations two of three amygdalectomized monkeys became less dominant, though they

seemed to have lost their timidity toward humans as a result of the lesion.

Bard and Mountcastle suggested that the inhibitory effect of the cortex upon rage is funneled through the amygdala, but, apart from the uncertainty of the data, this theory is impossible to reconcile with the fact that for several weeks even their animals were more friendly than before, becoming hyperirritable only weeks or months after the operation. The delayed onset is more likely to indicate secondary degeneration or the development of denervation hypersensitivity in other structures. J. D. Green (1958) suggested that irritative lesions may have caused the low rage thresholds.

THE ROLES OF SPECIFIC HYPOTHALAMIC NUCLEI. Hypothalamic lesions also produce paradoxical effects. Although in decerebrate animals the rage threshold is lowered when the hypothalamus is spared, in normal cats the rage threshold is lowered by a lesion of the ventromedial nucleus of the hypothalamus (Wheatley, 1944). Again the change is not immediate but takes several weeks to achieve maximum effectiveness, suggesting that other hypothalamic pathways are being sensitized and that the effect is not caused by loss of an inhibitory pathway.

The low rage thresholds produced by pre-chiasmal lesions of the olfactory tubercle (Fulton & Ingraham, 1929), of the fornix (Spiegel, Miller & Oppenheimer, 1940), of the septal area (Brady & Nauta, 1953), or of the anterior cingulate gyrus (Brutkowski, Fonberg & Mempel, 1961) appear immediately after the lesion and in most cases slowly disappear, suggesting genuine loss of inhibition followed by slow compensatory changes.

Although various lesions are said to produce a "lowered rage threshold," the real nature of the change has never been fully investigated, and it is quite likely that different lesions have fundamentally different effects. Bard and Mountcastle's description of the behavior of some of their amygdalectomized cats is consistent with the view that the cats became hypersensitive to pain in some parts of the body, as sometimes happens to patients after thalamic damage. (This thalamic-pain syndrome also develops slowly.) This theory would explain the behavior of the cat that liked having its head stroked but resented being touched anywhere else and the fear shown by most of the cats at the experimenter's approach.

Other lesions, like those in the septal area for example, may produce more fundamental changes in the motivational system, making the animal more aggressive and bad-tempered in the same way that various factors like hunger, lack of sleep, hormones, or bacterial toxins may.

Electrical Stimulation

Although there is universal agreement that hypothalamic stimulation can evoke behavior indicative of fear and rage, there are some differences of opinion as to the localization of these effects within the hypothalamus. Ranson (1937) found that stimulation of the hypothalamus evoked rage responses in lightly anesthetized cats during acute experiments. W. R. Hess and Brügger (1943) confirmed this finding on awake and unrestrained cats and claimed that the responses were elicited from the perifornical area of the lateral hypothalamus.

Roberts (1958a) differentiated between a "flight" response, in which the cat looked frantically for a way to escape, and an "alarm"

response, which was more similar to the behavior of a cat confronted by a dog. The former was obtained by stimulating a small area of the posterior hypothalamus near the mamillary bodies, the latter from stimulating scattered points in a wider hypothalamic and thalamic field. Glusman and Roizin (1960) reported that in their experiments true attack was evoked only from the ventromedial hypothalamic nucleus, whereas fear and flight reactions were obtained from more dorsal and posterior points. Some of the disagreement may result from confusion of defensive and predatory attack. Wasman and Flynn (1962) and Egger and Flynn (1963) found that stimulation in the region of the lateral hypothalamus, from which W. R. Hess and Brügger had reported attack behavior produced not rage but quiet stalking and deadly attack on smaller animals. Stimulation of more medial points produced a noisy defensive attack—with arched back, erect hair, spitting, and hissing—in which the cat would ignore a rat but spring viciously at the experimenter if he came too close.

Roberts and Kiess (1964) also obtained two types of attack: biting from stimulation of the dorsomedial and anterior lateral hypothalamus and clawing from more ventral and medial areas (except the ventromedial nucleus itself, which produced only defensive display without attack). Roberts, Steinberg, and Means (1967) also found separate regions for defensive and aggressive behavior in the hypothalamus of the opossum. Biting attacks on other animals were elicited by stimulation of the dorsolateral midhypothalamus and the dorsolateral preoptic area and defensive threats from a ventral zone in the midhypothalamus including the ventromedial nuclei.

Roberts and his colleagues drew attention to the fact (also noted by other investigators) that the response occurs mainly when an appropriate object is present. Significantly more attacks were made on live rats and mice than on dead ones and far more attacks on either than on shoes or blocks of wood. The response can also be suppressed if the attacked object puts up a fight; an electrically stimulated opossum will not attack another opossum of equal size unless the latter has been put at a disadvantage (by having its mouth taped shut, for example).

Stimulation in the biting system elicits a true drive to hunt and kill. Cats selected for their lack of interest in rats when not stimulated learned during stimulation to run through a maze to find and kill a rat. Without stimulation they wandered aimlessly in the maze (Roberts & Kiess, 1964). The cats were not motivated by induced hunger, for they would leave food at the onset of stimulation to kill a rat they did not then eat, but it is clear that predation in the cat is indirectly related to eating, and strictly speaking we should perhaps have classified it as a regulatory mechanism. Hunting behavior is quite probably facilitated by food deprivation.

AMYGDALOID STIMULATION. Another region from which affective responses can be elicited by electrical stimulation is the amygdala. Gastaut, Vigouroux, Corriol, and Badier (1951) reported that amygdaloid stimulation produced defensive reactions in cats quite similar to those produced by hypothalamic stimulation:

"Halloween" posture, bared teeth, pilo-erection, and so on.

Magnus and Lammers (1956) also obtained autonomic and "emotional" responses from the amygdala, with localization of the effect in the anterior part of the medial nucleus. Fernandez de Molina and Hunsperger (1959, 1962) plotted an extensive system, including the amygdala, stria terminalis, hypothalamus, and central gray, from which defensive reactions could be obtained by electrical stimulation in the cat (Figure 17.11). As the stria terminalis is a heavy fiber connection between the amygdala and the hypothalamus, they naturally assumed that it was the pathway along which "rage" impulses reached the hypothalamus from the amygdala.

In order to test this idea more thoroughly, Zbrożyna (1960) and Hilton and Zbrożyna (1963) cut the stria terminalis between the amygdala and the hypothalamus and found that amygdaloid stimulation still evoked defensive reactions. Furthermore, stimulation of the hypothalamic end of the transected stria produced no such response, but stimulation of the end leading to the amygdala did. Hilton and

Figure 17.11 The amygdala, stria terminalis, hypothalamus, and central gray, forming the pathway from which defensive reactions are obtained by electrical stimulation in the cat. The stippled region is the amygdala and stria terminalis from which flight is obtained. The lower hatched area is the hypothalamic mesencephalic zone from which flight is obtained. The solid zone is where stimulation elicits hissing. (After Fernandez de Molina & Hunsperger, 1959.)

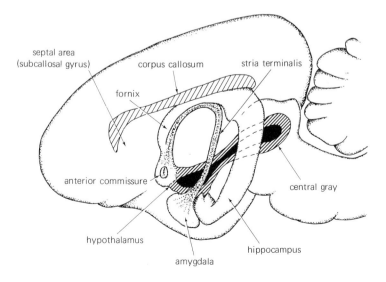

Zbrożyna eventually showed that the relevant connection between the amygdala and the hypothalamus is a flat band of fibers lying just above the optic tract, the ventral amygdalofugal path of Nauta. When this path was completely cut, stimulation of the amygdala no longer generated defensive reactions.

Stimulation of the amygdala does not arouse the hunting response that can be obtained from parts of the hypothalamus; in fact, amygdaloid stimulation suppressed hunting, both in natural "mousers" and in cats that were being motivated to kill rats by hypothalamic stimulation (Egger & Flynn, 1963). This finding is consistent with the fact that amygdaloid stimulation produces "fear," which inhibits aggressive attack. Fear induced by natural causes, as when an attacked rat bites back, would often lead cats to abandon the hunt in spite of continued hypothalamic stimulation.

THALAMIC STIMULATION. Roberts (1962) evoked crouching and escape behavior by stimulating the medialis dorsalis nucleus of the thalamus in cats. The cats quickly learned to avoid this type of stimulation if given the opportunity. MacDonnell and Flynn (1964) found points in the medialis dorsalis and lateralis dorsalis nuclei of the thalamus in the cat from which biting attacks, quite similar to those from the lateral hypothalamus, could be elicited by stimulation; other thalamic points produced defensive reactions. All but one of the "hunting" points in the thalamus facilitated hypothalamically induced attack. The remaining one had an antagonistic effect; if current was passed through both thalamic and hypothalamic electrodes the cat was quiescent but alert, but it launched an attack if either was switched off. Stimulation of points along the midline of the thalamus between the habenular interpeduncular tracts, though it did not produce attack by itself, facilitated hypothalamically induced attack.

Noxious stimulation, the sight of a predator, and the like disrupt ongoing behavior by producing typical fear responses, which usually include massive sympathetic discharge and may include crying, grimacing, and running or leaping. In most animals these responses can readily be conditioned to neutral stimuli presented just before or during fear-evoking stimuli. This ability confers a great advantage, as the animal can acquire new and useful fears on the basis of nonlethal encounters with noxious events. Animals incapable of acquiring conditioned avoidances have to rely entirely on inherited connections between olfactory, visual, and other danger cues and the avoidance system. New dangers from a changing environment continually catch such animals by surprise and could soon wipe out a large fraction of the population.

CONDITIONING ELICITED "RAGE." The motivational system for escape differs from regulatory motivational systems, at least in the ease with which new stimuli can acquire the ability to evoke activity in it. Stimuli associated with hunger do not evoke hunger in a thoroughly satiated animal, for example, though they may augment hunger in a moderately deprived one. The conditionability of natural fears might lead us to expect that fear produced by brain stimulation would also be amenable to conditioning, and several experiments have tested this hypothesis. The first such experiments (Masserman, 1941, 1943) showed that very little conditioning took place when sham rage was evoked by hypothalamic stimulation. Some slight conditioning of pupillary responses occurred in some cats after 80–160 trials. Other cats showed no conditioning at all after 480 trials, although the response to hypothalamic stimulation was very violent. Masserman concluded that the stimulation tapped only the motor outflow of the emotional system; the animal did not "experience" any emotion despite the display and thus exhibited no sensory or central activity that could be associated with the CS.

AVOIDANCE BEHAVIOR

Besides his attempts to condition autonomic responses, Masserman also tried unsuccessfully to train cats to make an instrumental avoidance response with hypothalamic stimulation as the punishment. B. D. Cohen, Brown, and Brown

(1957) decided that the failure resulted from inadequate opportunities to learn an escape response and modified the experimental procedure so that the cat could turn off the hypothalamic stimulation by crossing the hurdle of a shuttle box. The CS was a warbling tone presented for 16 seconds before the onset of the stimulation. In contrast to Masserman's findings, all the cats learned to avoid the stimulation in fewer than 200 trials.

These contradictory findings were reconciled to some extent by Roberts (1958a). He placed electrodes in different hypothalamic nuclei of cats and observed that those whose electrodes produced a "flight" reaction quickly learned to *escape* the stimulation as soon as it was applied, by jumping a hurdle or running to the correct arm of a T-maze but never learned to *avoid* it (to respond before the stimulation was applied). Cats that showed an "alarm" reaction to stimulation not only learned to escape but also learned to avoid. Grastyán, Karmos, Vereczkey, Martin, and Kellényi (1965) also found that cats would press a pedal to escape hypothalamic stimulation and that some of them would learn to avoid by remaining on the pedal when the stimulation had been turned off.

It now seems possible that the onset of stimulation in certain hypothalamic nuclei may not be aversive, and may even be attractive (Roberts, 1958b), though the animal may escape from the stimulation after it has been on for a short time. This possibility would explain the failure of cats to avoid some types of stimulation that appear at first sight to be aversive.

Delgado, Roberts, and Miller (1954) were able to elicit clear-cut avoidance learning in cats with stimulation of the tectal area, lateral thalamus, and hippocampus as the UCS. The first two of these areas may well have involved pain pathways; the third may have evoked central activity corresponding to fear, though it is rare if not impossible to elicit fear from the hippocampus. Delgado, Rosvold, and Looney (1956) varied this experiment by first training monkeys to make a discriminatory response to avoid shock and then stimulating one of various neural structures. Transfer of the shock-avoidance response was obtained with electrodes in the amygdala and rhinal fissure, central gray, and several sensory structures that probably included pain pathways. There was no effect from the hippocampus.

Hypothalamic stimulation in human beings has been found to cause various autonomic effects like sweating and changes in blood pressure, but it also has emotional concomitants. In one study some patients felt overwhelming anxiety, and one had a fit of uncontrollable sobbing. None of the patients felt anger during stimulation, though others with tumors of the hypothalamus sometimes became very combative and had hallucinations (Grinker, 1939).

Stimulation of the amygdaloid region in man generates a variety of responses. In some cases only motor effects (usually involving the face and mouth) are observed; in others there is complete amnesia for the period of stimulation and a cloudy hallucinatory state during it (Feindel, 1961). Great anxiety may be evoked in some patients, and in one case reported by King (1961) the patient said that she felt very aggressive and wanted to tear things or slap the interviewer's face during the stimulation. She also said that she did not like the experience, though it was not painful.

Avoidance Learning After Lesions

The effects of lesions upon the learning of avoidance responses provide a further aid to determining what role different brain structures play in "fear" motivation. Brady and Nauta (1953), after observing the viciousness and exaggerated startle responses of rats with septal lesions, attempted to measure the change more objectively by observing how quickly the rats learned a conditioned emotional response (CER).

The rats were placed in a box with a grid floor through which shocks could be administered. The CS was a clicking noise presented for three minutes before each shock. After a few trials in this situation, normal rats crouch and become immobile at the sound of the click. They may defecate and show other signs of autonomic discharge. Brady and Nauta found no differences in the rate at which normal and septal rats acquired these responses. Rats trained before operation, however, lost their CER for some time after septal lesions, though not after lesions of the cingulate cortex. When the "septal" hyperactivity wore off, the CER spontaneously returned. Rats with septal lesions showed complete retention of a preoperatively learned CER when tested for the first time 60 days after the operation (Brady & Nauta, 1955).

These results are somewhat surprising; they suggest that during the period when the rats are hypersensitive to an unconditioned stimulus like touch, the avoidance system is less accessible to conditioned stimuli. This suggestion would make sense if pathways both for learned inhibition and learned facilitation of emotional responses passed through the septal area and anterior hypothalamic region, but it is perhaps more likely that the lesion interferes with the expression of the CER, which predominantly involves freezing.

Using a different measure, King (1958) was able to demonstrate enhancement of avoidance learning in rats with septal lesions. In the shuttle box these rats learned to avoid shock more quickly than either normal rats or rats with amygdaloid lesions. Levine and Soliday (1960) obtained very similar results with rats in the same apparatus after lesions of the anterior hypothalamus.

Passive and Active Avoidance

At first sight these data might be regarded as confirmation that septal lesions increase fear, but this simple theory does not survive more complete analysis of the phenomenon. McCleary (1961) was the first to state clearly the important principle that we cannot lump all types of avoidance training together; the type of response called for has an important bearing upon the effect produced by a lesion. We have already seen that the shuttle box gives different results from those of the CER situation; McCleary demonstrated that the passive-avoidance situation gives still different results. Each cat in this experiment had to go to a part of the apparatus to obtain food and, after this

approach response had been well established, a shock was administered there. The reluctance of the hungry subject to return to the feeding place after the shock was a measure of the strength of passive avoidance.

McCleary's cats had lesions in the medial limbic system, either in the cingulate gyrus or in its rostral extension into the subcallosal gyrus (which corresponds to the septal area in the rat; see Figure 17.11). These areas were chosen because Kaada (1951) had shown in acute experiments that the subcallosal area was inhibitory and the cingulate area facilitatory for motor functions.

The results of the experiment conformed to expectations based on Kaada's data. Cats with subcallosal lesions were deficient in passive avoidance, but they performed normally (or, as had King's rats, slightly better than normally) in the shuttle box; those with lesions of the cingulate gyrus, on the other hand, showed normal passive-avoidance behavior but were impaired on active avoidance in the shuttle box. The avoidance deficits resulting from either lesion can hardly be attributed to inability to acquire conditioned fear motivation, because the performance was adequately motivated when a different response was required.

(It should be noted, before describing the next experiment of this series, that recent findings by Lubar, Perachio, and Kavanagh, 1966, and Lubar, Schostal, and Perachio, 1967, indicate that cingulate lesions have little effect on avoidance learning in the cat but that lesions of the adjacent lateral gyrus produce severe deficits. They have suggested that McCleary's cingulate lesions and those of Lubar in the experiment to be described next damaged fibers passing below the cingulate gyrus on their way to the lateral gyrus.)

Lubar and Perachio (1965) found that cingulectomized cats (in which the lateral gyrus was involved) learned with no difficulty a one-way active avoidance (in which the subjects were always shocked in one compartment and the other was always safe), though they performed poorly in the usual two-way shuttle box (in which they were alternately shocked in each compartment and on each new trial had to return to the place where they had been shocked on the previous trial).

There is little doubt that one-way avoidance learning is simpler than shuttle-box avoidance, and this difference may account for the absence of impairment on the former after lesions. Lubar and Perachio's alternative explanation is that the lesion enhances the cats' tendency to freeze, which is already much greater in the shuttle box than in the one-way avoidance situation. Fear is innately associated with two types of skeletal response: freezing and running away. Both can have survival value, and both, though antagonistic, are probably highly facilitated during the elicitation of conditioned fear. Depending upon what parts of the nervous system have been damaged, the balance may be thrown in favor of one response or the other.

Septal Area Lesions

Just as lesions of the lateral gyrus impair only two-way shuttle-box avoidance, this type of avoidance is uniquely enhanced by septal lesions. King's demonstration that rats with septal lesions improve on this test has already been mentioned, and the finding has been confirmed by Krieckhaus, Simmons, Thomas, and Kenyon (1964) and by Kenyon and Krieckhaus (1965a), but Kenyon (1962) and Kenyon and Krieckhaus (1965b) showed that septal lesions produce a deficit in simple one-way avoidance learning.

The impairment of passive avoidance found in septal cats by McCleary (1961) has been confirmed by Zucker and McCleary (1964) and demonstrated in rats by Kaada, Rasmussen, and Kveim (1962). Kasper (1964) found that continuous stimulation of the septal area, especially of the lateral nucleus, had much the same detrimental effect upon passive avoidance as did lesions, though the stimulation reduced the emotional response to the shock, rather than increasing it as septal lesions did.

McCleary's notion that septal lesions interfere with response inhibition seems to explain most of the data. As already mentioned, freezing is probably a greater source of difficulty in the two-way shuttle box than in the one-way

apparatus, even for normal animals, because the directional cues are weaker. The animal does not have such a clear idea what it is running away from, and uncertainty encourages freezing. After septal lesions, the animal is more likely to run, and therefore its performance on the test is improved. The same loss of inhibition impairs performance in passive-avoidance experiments.

The perseverative behavior of septal animals (Zucker & McCleary, 1964) or of animals during septal stimulation (Kasper, 1965), in habit-reversal tests can also be explained in terms of impaired learning to inhibit the no longer appropriate response. Until the animal has stopped responding to the wrong stimulus it cannot begin to learn the correct response.

Hippocampal Lesions

Somewhat similar effects have been observed in rats as a result of lesions in the hippocampus and fornix, though additional damage to overlying cortex, which is difficult to avoid, makes interpretation of some of the data uncertain. Differences between the functions of the dorsal and ventral hippocampus compound the confusion in experiments involving this structure.

Brady, in his valuable review of the limbic system (1958a), mentioned that he and his colleagues had completely abolished a conditioned emotional response by large hippocampal lesions, but the extent of the lesions seems never to have been reported. Thomas and Otis (1958) tried to determine the effect of hippocampal lesions upon shuttle-box avoidance, but their lesions turned out to be mostly in the cingulate cortex, and they finished by demonstrating in the rat what McCleary later demonstrated in the cat, that cingulate lesions produce a deficit in avoidance learning. (In the rat the deficit really *is* caused by the cingulate lesion and not by interference with the adjacent cortex.)

Douglas Kimura (1958) observed the effect of hippocampal lesions upon passive-avoidance learning in the rat. Rather small selective lesions were made electrolytically in either the anterodorsal or the posteroventral hippocampus, with minimal damage to other structures. The rats were trained to run down an alley to obtain food, and when they repeatedly reached the food in less than two seconds they were given a single strong shock on one occasion as they ate. The strength of the passive avoidance was measured by the length of time that it took the rat to resume running and eating in the apparatus after the shock. Kimura found that the posteroventral lesions significantly interferred with both acquisition and retention of the avoidance; that is, they caused the rats to return more readily to the food after the shock.

Isaacson and Wickelgren (1962) produced an even more impressive passive-avoidance deficit with large lesions of the hippocampus and overlying cortex produced by aspiration. Isaacson, Douglas, and Moore (1961) also used large aspiration lesions of the hippocampus and observed an improvement in shuttle-box avoidance learning in rats. Kimura's and Isaacson's data on the rat hippocampus thus parallel those of McCleary on the subcal-

losal gyrus, in the cat. R. H. Green, Beatty, and Schwartzbaum (1967) have recently confirmed that hippocampal lesions enhance two-way avoidance learning in rats.

In the cat the effects of hippocampal lesions seem a little less clear. Brady, Schreiner, Geller, and Kling (1954) found no change in the rate of acquisition of a two-way shuttle-box avoidance in two cats with hippocampal lesions (Figure 17.12), though it is possible that enhancement would have been noticeable if more animals had been used. H. F. Hunt and Diamond (1957), on the other hand, claimed that hippocampal lesions impaired acquisition of the shuttle-box avoidance. Andy, Peeler, and Foshee (1967) reported deficits of retention but not of acquisition of two-way avoidance after hippocampal lesions in cats.

In monkeys the situation is even more confused. K. H. Pribram and Weiskrantz (1957) did not test acquisition of avoidance after lesions but found that extinction of a previously learned two-way avoidance response was very

Figure 17.12 Effects of limbic lesions in cats upon learning a conditioned avoidance. (After Brady, Schreiner, Geller & Kling, 1954.)

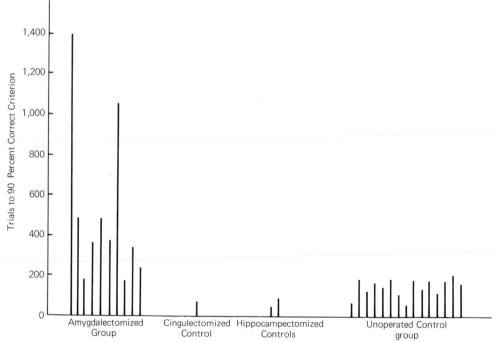

rapid after hippocampal lesions. Unfortunately, the investigators did not differentiate between anticipatory errors and failures to respond to the CS, and it is therefore impossible to say whether the hippocampectomized monkeys were showing deficits of response or of response inhibition.

Hippocampectomized rats, like septal rats, are perseverative. When trained to press a bar for food on continuous reinforcement, for example, they find it impossible to transfer to a schedule that differentially reinforces low rates of response (DRL). They have no difficulty with the DRL schedule, however, if they are trained on it from the start (C. V. H. Clark & Isaacson, 1965; Schmaltz & Isaacson, 1966). The severe maze-running deficits found in hippocampectomized rats may also be caused by the difficulty these animals have in extinguishing a useless response so that a more adaptive one can take its place.

One of the many controversies about the function of the hippocampus involves whether it specifically inhibits learned responses that are no longer being reinforced (or are being negatively reinforced) or is implicated in inhibition of both learned and unlearned responses. Kimble, Kirkby, and Stein (1966) found that hippocampectomized rats had no difficulty inhibiting their untrained tendency to step through a hole in order to escape from a small illuminated ledge high above the floor; later D. G. Stein and Kirkby (1967) found that hippocampectomized rats were not impaired on a passive-avoidance task if they had run for food only a few times before shock and were therefore not overtrained on the approach response.

These results suggest that only learned responses are subject to inhibition through the hippocampus during extinction; however as we saw earlier, the natural tendency to explore is extinguished very slowly after hippocampal lesions. Furthermore, H. Teitelbaum and Milner (1963) found that hippocampectomized rats would repeatedly jump off a small safe platform onto an electrified grid, another example of failure to inhibit a natural escape tendency that was being punished. (It was also observed, however, that "suicidal" jumping was much

aggravated by one or two shocks that left the rats in a highly aroused state.) Isaacson, Olton, Bauer, and Swart (1966) also found that hippocampectomized rats could not be trained to stay on a shaking platform.

The position adopted by R. J. Douglas (1967) and others, that the hippocampus is part of a mechanism for withholding active responses, learned or unlearned, appears to have the weight of the evidence on its side. As J. Kaplan (1968) has pointed out, however, the situation is reversed if we consider "freezing" to be a response, as in the conditioned emotional response. The hippocampus is apparently responsible for generating such "stop" responses, rather than for inhibiting them.

Not all the results of experiments on hippocampal lesions fit into the rather simple response-inhibition model suggested here. Nadel (1968), for example, found that dorsal hippocampal lesions improved the acquisition of conditioned emotional responses and caused no impairment of passive avoidance. Nor did ventral hippocampal lesions impair passive avoidance in his experiments. The reasons for these discrepancies are obscure at present. They may have been caused by differences in the lesions (size, locus, involvement of extrahippocampal structures, and so on) or in the test situation. As we have seen, quite subtle differences in the amount of training or the strength of the response tendency may completely change the outcome.

Hippocampal lesions in man produce few, if any, of the changes found in animals. The most conspicuous feature of the human syndrome is a general inability to learn anything new (see Chapter 20). The perseverative tendency and loss of response inhibition do not appear to any appreciable extent; in man they seem to be associated with lesions of the frontal cortex. In some animals hippocampal lesions and frontal-cortex lesions appear to produce equivalent behavioral effects (H. Teitelbaum, 1964).

Thalamic Lesions

Medial thalamic lesions have been found to produce a deficit in the learning of one-way avoidance in the rat and cat. Vanderwolf (1962, 1963a) observed that these deficits were caused by the long response latency of these animals in aversive situations. When the rats were allowed 5 seconds in which to run from a grid compartment to an adjacent safe compartment before the shock current was turned on (ample time for a normal rat to make the avoidance), those with medial thalamic lesions never learned the response, but when they were allowed 15 seconds all mastered the problem. The rats were certainly not indifferent to the CS, even when they failed to run in time; they would squeak and freeze as soon as they were placed in the apparatus. Replogle (1960) showed that rats with similar lesions acquired a conditioned emotional response as readily as did normal rats.

The deficit was not caused by general motor slowness either, because the rats ran along an alley for food more quickly than normal rats, and in an open field they explored more. Only in aversive situations were they slower to respond, which supports Vanderwolf's hypothesis that the medial thalamic nuclei are part of a motor-facilitation system that normally tends to counteract freezing induced by fear.

Very similar results were independently obtained in the cat by Roberts and Carey (1963), who were led to study the medial thalamus (medialis dorsalis nucleus) by the observation that stimulation there elicited expressions of fear (Roberts, 1962). These investigators also came to the conclusion not that poor avoidance learning was caused by deficits in the learning of fear but rather that the medial thalamic system facilitated movements in aversive situations.

A complication was introduced by Olton and Isaacson (1967), who found that rats trained before operation to make either a one-way or a two-way avoidance showed no impairment during extinction after medial thalamic lesions. These rats, in fact, made slightly more extinction responses than did normal rats or "lateral thalamic" controls. As soon as shock was reintroduced during postoperative reacquisition training, however, the performance of the "medial thalamic" animals deteriorated. Pos-

sibly the milder aversiveness of the conditioned fear during extinction was not enough to elicit the severe freezing that interfered with the performance of the avoidance response when a more immediate threat of shock was evident. Once an animal had mastered an avoidance problem, the quality of the motivation seemed different from that which had motivated the early, less successful responses, and the experiment by Olton and Isaacson may indicate differences in neural participation under the two conditions.

Amygdaloid Lesions

Amygdaloid lesions also seem to produce deficits in most types of avoidance, and in this instance there is a possibility that the deficits are really caused by some disturbance of fear motivation and not by a more immediate effect upon motor activity.

Following Klüver and Bucy's reports of emotional changes after temporal-lobe injuries in monkeys, Brady, Schreiner, Geller, and Kling (1954) trained cats with amygdaloid lesions to make avoidance responses in a shuttle box. As can be seen in Figure 17.12, the animals were significantly impaired. Cats with control lesions in the cingulate cortex or hippocampus were not impaired, as mentioned earlier. Amygdaloid lesions in cats that had already learned the avoidance produced some loss of retention, compared with the performance of cats with control lesions in the frontal cortex.

King (1958) found that rats with lesions in the amygdala required no more trials than normal rats to learn a shuttle-box avoidance, but his lesions were quite small, and the avoidance responses had longer latencies in the amygdalectomized group. If a shorter CS-US interval had been used, the experimental animals might well have shown impaired learning.

With more complete amygdaloid lesions in monkeys, Weiskrantz (1956) observed deficits in learning a shuttle-box avoidance. The amygdalectomized monkeys also extinguished the response more quickly than controls if they had been trained before the operation. A conditioned emotional response (depression of the rate of panel pushing to obtain food pellets during the presentation of a stimulus associated with a loud noise or shock) was also extinguished more quickly in the experimental monkeys than in the controls.

These results may be interpreted as indicating that amygdaloid lesions reduce the intensity with which animals experience "fear." Possibly unconditioned aversive stimuli generate smaller autonomic responses (Bagshaw, Kimble & Pribram, 1965, found that amygdalectomized monkeys had reduced GSR, for example), and the reduced feedback from visceral sensory input could make the conditioning of fear more difficult. In this connection, Solomon and Wynne (1954) found that eliminating peripheral autonomic motor functioning through a combination of surgical and drug procedures led to slower acquisition and faster extinction of a conditioned avoidance response in dogs.

This theory is perhaps too simple to explain all the effects of amygdalectomy on avoidance learning. Hearst and Pribram (1964) reported that amygdalectomized monkeys learned to avoid shock as successfully as did normal monkeys in a Sidman (1953) avoidance situation (brief shocks delivered every 20 seconds unless the monkey resets the timer to zero by pressing a bar) and are speeded up to the same extent by the introduction of occasional unavoidable shocks. Horvath (1963), influenced by McCleary's demonstration (1961) that the type of avoidance training cannot be neglected, trained cats with lesions of the basolateral part of the amygdala on both one-way and two-way shuttle-box avoidance and on passive avoidance. He found that his cats were impaired on all these measures of avoidance, but, compared with the deficit on the two-way shuttle box, the other impairments were not impressive.

Goddard (1964b) found that electrical stimulation of the amygdala in rats would interfere with the acquisition of shuttle-box avoidance and conditioned emotional response. For the latter the stimulation was effective when it was applied either continuously or for a few minutes immediately after the shock; stimulation applied during the CS and during the shock had no effect upon the establishment of the CER.

Although there are differences in the degree to which interference with the amygdala produces deficits in avoidance learning, most of the results are consistent with the hypothesis that the establishment of contact between neutral sensory input and the systems that facilitate avoidance behavior normally involves some part of the amygdala. Avoidance behavior is, of course, only one of the aspects of behavior influenced by this very complex structure (Gloor, 1960; Goddard, 1964a); Horvath's results suggest that the basolateral amygdaloid complex is more closely involved in aversive responses than is the corticomedial part.

HUMORAL FACTORS IN AGGRESSIVE, ESCAPE, AND AVOIDANCE BEHAVIOR

As has been mentioned earlier, it is well known that hormones can affect the reaction of animals to aversive stimuli. Most male animals become less aggressive after castration, and female mammals usually become more aggressive when they have young. Endröczi, Lissák, and Telegdy (1958) found aggressiveness of mother rats correlated with lactation. Administration of estrogen, which antagonizes the effects of lactogen, abolished the tendency of the mother to attack a frog introduced into her cage.

There are indications that other hormonal secretions are involved in avoidance behavior. Noxious or stressful situations result in release by hypothalamic cells of neurosecretions that are carried to the anterior pituitary where they cause the release of adrenocorticotrophic hormone (ACTH). The steroids released by the adrenal cortex under the influence of circulating ACTH have been shown to have various effects upon brain excitability and behavior (Lissák & Endröczi, 1961; Woodbury, 1952, 1954).

Escape learning is not affected by adrenalectomy, which removes the source of adrenocortical steroids (Moyer, 1958), and injections of ACTH have not been found to influence the rate of active avoidance learning (Murphy & Miller, 1955), though extinction of the response was retarded. Levine and Jones (1965) reported a highly significant increase in the persistence of passive avoidance as long as injections of

ACTH were continued. ACTH by itself did not produce passive avoidance.

Endogenous ACTH is released during the presentation of shock and is present in all animals while learning is taking place. It may be that maintaining the level of ACTH by injection preserves the learned response by keeping the nervous system in the same state that it was in during learning. Dissociation of learning in different drug states has been observed in several situations. Girden and Culler (1937) found that a response conditioned under a partially paralyzing dose of curare in dogs disappeared as the drug wore off but reappeared if more drug was administered. The converse was also true; responses learned in a normal state were not performed under the drug. In fact, two different responses could be conditioned to the same stimulus, one when the animal was under curare and the other when it was in a normal state.

A similar dissociation was observed by Overton (1964) in rats in a T-maze. Rats could be trained to run to one of the goal boxes to escape shock when under a subanesthetic dose of barbiturate and to the other goal box after an injection of saline.

Brush and Levine (1966) found that the decay of the level of circulating corticosterone during the hours following fear conditioning was roughly parallel to the decay in the number of avoidances made to the CS in different groups of rats given avoidance training at different intervals after fear conditioning. There has been some suggestion, in several experiments on the effects of pituitary and

adrenal secretions upon avoidance, that ACTH is more important than are the steroids it releases from the adrenal cortex. R. E. Miller and Ogawa (1962), for example, found that extinction of an avoidance response was delayed by ACTH injections even when the rats had been adrenalectomized.

Weiss, McEwen, Silva, and Kalkut (1969) compared hypophysectomized, adrenalectomized, and normal rats on passive-avoidance and other fear tests, in order to determine the relative importance of the various hormones. The hypophysectomized rats cannot produce ACTH; the adrenalectomized rats cannot produce corticosterone and other adrenal steroids. The investigators found that hypophysectomy resulted in rapid extinction and that adrenalectomy had the opposite effect, delaying the onset of extinction, especially when the intensity of fear was not unduly strong. They suggested that ACTH enhances fear responses and that one or more of the steroids released by the adrenals counteract this effect.

The effects of ACTH and cortisone upon people are extremely variable. They have no effect on emotion in about half the patients, but increased irritability or euphoria develops in others. Many patients swing violently from euphoria to depression. In this respect, these hormones resemble gonadal, thyroid, and some other hormones. It is clear that steroids of all sorts have profound effects upon the activity of hypothalamic circuits related to "mood" or emotion but that the effects upon a particular individual are quite unpredictable (Goolker & Schein, 1953).

Summary

In this chapter we have studied several types of motivation not directly involved in regulation of internal states of the body. They have many characteristics in common with regulatory motivations; sexual, parental, and exploratory motivations involve systems like those of the regulatory systems for attracting the animal to various stimuli and for satiating or habituating responses. Escape behavior is produced by a mechanism that is connected differently from those of the other motivational systems. The response to stimuli that excite the escape mechanism is retreat rather than approach—turning away rather than toward. Habituation occurs in this system just as in others, however, so that the animal eventually becomes indifferent for a time to many innately frightening stimuli if they have been presented often.

An essential component of reproduction in all but the most primitive organisms is fertilization of the eggs. Ovulation is controlled by various factors, depending on the species. In many species environmental factors like temperature, length of day, sight of a mate, or vaginal stimulation fire receptors that initiate ovulation through a multistage pathway involving hormones. Neurosecretory cells in the hypothalamus are fired by the sensory input and release substances that are carried by a portal vein to the pituitary gland. There the substances cause the release of gonadotrophic hormones (the follicle-stimulating hormone and the luteinizing hormone) into the blood. When the gonadotrophic hormones reach the ovaries they stimulate the secretion of still another hormone, estrogen, and eventually cause eggs to be released. Not all species ovulate in response to external stimuli; some ovulate cyclically under the control of an endogenous hypothalamic rhythm.

The estrogen, along with progesterone, which is secreted at about the time of ovulation, acts on the nervous system to make the female sexually receptive. Only when these hormones are present in adequate amounts do the females of most species become attractive to males and participate cooperatively in mating activity. Sexual receptivity can be induced by injections of estrogen and progesterone in females whose ovaries have been removed, showing that the hormones act directly on the brain to produce the behavior.

Female primates are less dependent upon gonadal hormones for receptive behavior than are lower animals, and in human females the relationship seems to have almost disappeared. It has been suggested that the sexual responsiveness of women depends on androgens (male hormones) produced by the adrenal gland and not on the cyclically fluctuating levels of estrogen and progesterone.

In species that mate once a year, male sexual activity is seasonal like that of the female. The same stimuli that elicit ovulation in the female initiate growth of the testes in the male and produce a great increase in the amount of circulating androgen. The androgen acts on the male nervous system to produce behavior changes that often include establishing territory, antagonism toward other males, and pursuit of receptive females. After the mating season is over the gonads regress, and behavior reverts to normal. In other species the male is sexually active throughout adult life, and the testosterone level is maintained relatively constant through a negative-feedback circuit that includes the hypothalamus, the pituitary, and the gonads. Reduction of the level of testosterone by castration diminishes sexual behavior; subsequent injections of testosterone revive it. There is a time lag of weeks or longer in the behavioral effect of a change in the hormone level, suggesting that the hormone produces a growth of neural connections rather than acting as a transmitter or facilitator of neural transmission.

Castration before puberty prevents the onset of sexual behavior; it has less effect upon the behavior of a sexually experienced animal, perhaps because a stronger drive is required to elicit unlearned behavior than to elicit long-familiar behavior.

Most species exhibit bisexual behavior to some degree; that is, females sometimes engage in mounting and other masculine activity, and males sometimes submit to being mounted. This bisexuality implies that both males and females have the neural circuits necessary for performance of either sexual role. It has been suggested that both brains are identical but that female behavior is preferentially elicited by female hormones and male behavior by male hormones. Experiments do not support this view; androgen injected into adult ovariectomized females does not produce predominantly male behavior, nor do estrogen injections significantly increase female behavior in castrated males. It is true that hormone injections into the lateral preoptic area of the hypothalamus produce male sexual behavior in rats of both sexes, but these results can be obtained with either male or female hormones. The experiment thus proves that circuits for male sexual behavior exist in the female, but it does not prove that the structure is normally as sensitive in the female as it is in the male.

The theory that in male brains the circuits for male behavior are intrinsically more sensitive than are the circuits for female behavior and vice versa in female brains is supported by "sex change" experiments in which testosterone is injected into pregnant animals to produce masculinized female offspring. These pseudohermaphrodites are most likely to exhibit male sexual behavior as adults. On the other hand, male rats castrated at birth or shortly after are feminized and cannot be made to exhibit male behavior even with testosterone injections as adults. It appears that in the absence of testosterone the brain develops with a dominant circuit for female behavior and in the presence of testosterone at the critical stage of growth (20–30 days after conception in the rat and guinea pig) dominant circuits for male behavior are formed.

In addition to receiving the correct hormone at the critical time, male sexual development depends upon social contacts in infancy. Male rats reared in isolation from an early age do not learn to copulate properly as adults. Monkeys of both sexes are even more crippled sexually by having been reared in isolation.

The reflex circuits for sexual behavior lie in the lumbar and sacral segments of the spinal cord. They are normally inhibited by activity originating in the medulla; animals with transections of the neuraxis above the medulla show no reflex response to genital stimulation, as "spinal" animals do.

Central activating circuits for mating behavior are present in the hypothalamus. Lesions of the hypothalamus alone produce complete failure of sexual responsiveness, and stimulation of anterior nuclei elicits or increases male sexual behavior in a number of species. Persistent receptivity has been induced in female cats by implants of estrogen in the hypothalamus but not elsewhere. Changes in the electrical activity of parts of the hypothalamus have been recorded during sexual stimulation. The data of many lesion, stimulation, and recording experiments suggest that the anterior hypothalamus is a focal area for sexual behavior, with more diffuse areas arranged along the path of the medial forebrain bundle.

Hypersexuality is produced in monkeys by bilateral ablations of the temporal lobe; the effect seems to be localized in the region of the amygdala. In cats the crucial area may be the pyriform cortex lying close to the amygdala. It is suggested that the amygdala plays a role in the satiation of sexual behavior somewhat similar to that attributed to it in feeding. Sensory input from sexual activity, orgasm, and the like may establish temporary circuits there that inhibit hypothalamic sex-drive systems.

The effects of neocortical lesions on sexual behavior depend upon the species and sex of the animal. Quite large cortical excisions have little effect upon copulation in male or female rats or rabbits, though it is claimed that total decortication eliminates mating in male rats. Decorticate male cats show no interest in estrous females, but female behavior is relatively unaffected by decortication.

There is probably more variation in parental behavior from one species to another than in any other motivated behavior. Any genetically induced addition to the repertoire that leads to a better survival rate among the offspring will obviously spread throughout the species as more offspring with the requisite genes survive and outnumber those of "inferior" parents.

Nest building, incubation of eggs, feeding and defending the young, retrieving them when they stray, and in higher animals playing with and thus training infants are some common forms of parental behavior. These behaviors are modulated by hormones, just as is sexual behavior. Progesterone injections will induce doves to sit on eggs immediately, though they do not normally do so until they have spent time in courtship and nest building. Preliminary research into the sites of hormone action suggests that progesterone acts on the preoptic nucleus to produce incubation and on the anterior hypothalamus to suppress courtship behavior. Nest building will start without preliminary courtship in doves that have had estrogen injections. Prolactin injections produce protective behavior and feeding, as well as lactation in mammals and manufacture of crop milk in some birds like the pigeon.

Lesions of the medial cortex or hippocampus of rats appear to interfere with maternal behavior, but strangely little work has been done on the effect of hypothalamic or other subcortical lesions upon such behavior.

As with sexual behavior, abnormal rearing has a very deleterious effect upon maternal behavior in monkeys. "Motherless" mothers seem intent on doing away with their infants.

Attachment of the young to the parent or a surrogate (imprinting) and vice versa are important aspects of rearing in many species. The tendency to form attachments to infants, to mates, or to various other objects appears to be widespread, but the relevant physiological mechanisms have not been studied.

Animals can usually attain a goal that is under their nose, but they are often faced with the problem of finding remote goals, which requires intrinsically generated activity or exploration. Some animals range over considerable distances with little or no facilitation from environmental stimuli. Even those animals that are not normally very active are attracted by unfamiliar stimuli. In the laboratory it is not always easy to differentiate between pure activity and exploration, but the former is assumed to be operating when animals move about in a familiar environment and the latter when continued exposure to the same environment leads to a steady decline in the amount of activity.

There are conflicting reports on whether or not exploration is facilitated by hunger or other drives, possibly because in most experiments the animals have not been completely unfamiliar with the apparatus when they became hungry. In any case exploration does not show any dramatic change with drive state.

Not all exploration involves locomotion. Some animals will manipulate levers that produce changes in environmental stimulation. Primates are especially motivated to see what is going on around them. Monkeys will work for hours for the opportunity to look out of their cages.

The frontal cortex is predominantly inhibitory for locomotion. After lesions these animals usually become more active and may pace continuously or indulge in other stereotyped repetitious activity. The effect upon locomotion is even more drastic following lesions of the caudate nucleus; walking movements persist in these animals even when forward motion is prevented by an obstacle.

In many species the satiation or habituation of exploratory behavior appears to involve the hippocampus, though there is no evidence that it does so in man. After temporal lobectomies monkeys engage in persistent exploratory and manipulatory behavior, and hippocampectomized rats continue to explore their environment long after normal rats would have become habituated.

Systems that enable animals to escape or avoid common dangers have survival value and thus become part of the neural equipment of the species. Reflex withdrawal from painful stimuli, spitting out bitter and therefore potentially poisonous substances, and locomotion away from fire, heights, and many other threatening situations are incorporated into the repertoire of a species in this way. Defensive reflexes are present at the spinal level in the form of circulatory changes, withdrawal of the affected limb, and, if the noxious stimulation persists, movements of the limbs that resemble running. More elaborate reactions occur when the medulla is intact, but in cats and dogs with pontine sections aggressive behavior is not elicited except by quite rough treatment. The threshold for vicious attack is dramatically reduced, however, if the cut is above the hypothalamus.

It thus appears that the mesencephalon and spinal cord contain circuits for escape and attack but that they are relatively insensitive without some facilitation from structures at the hypothalamic level. Intact tame, or domesticated, animals do not react to every touch with violent attack, as do hypothalamic preparations; it therefore seems clear that there are inhibitory structures in the forebrain. Initial indications that the amygdala was the main source of such inhibition have not been confirmed. In fact, the reverse usually seems true; amygdaloid lesions have a taming effect upon wild animals.

It now seems likely that the inhibitory pathways from the forebrain descend through the septal area and the medial part of the anterior hypothalamus. Lesions there produce immediate, but transient, lowering of the rage threshold. Lesions in the ventromedial nucleus of the hypothalamus slowly give rise to longer-lasting reduction in the rage threshold. This gradual onset cannot be reconciled with the idea that the ventromedial nucleus is the primary source of inhibition; perhaps the lesion sensitizes adjacent rage systems in some way.

In man some lesions of the thalamus lead to slowly developing hypersensitivity to pain over large areas of the body. If amygdaloid or ventromedial hypothalamic lesions have a similar effect in animals, it could explain much of the behavior that has been described as "sham rage" following such lesions. Lesions of the septal area in normally tame animals may cut off forebrain activity that suppresses the hypothalamic and spinal defensive reactions when an "expected" stimulus is presented.

Stimulation of the hypothalamus evokes responses indicative of fear or rage; the locus of the stimulation is important in determining just what behavior will occur. Medial stimulation produces a noisy defensive clawing attack or flight; lateral stimulation may lead to stalking and predatory killing. The behavior in each case is most likely to be directed toward an appropriate object, the experimenter or other large animal in the first instance, a smaller and relatively innocuous and defenseless animal in the second.

Fear and escape responses similar to those from the medial hypothalamus can be obtained by intense stimulation of the amygdala. Lower currents elicit an attentive or "orienting" reaction and will usually stop predatory behavior.

Thalamic stimulation may also provoke either defensive or predatory attacks, depending upon the location of the electrode, and these effects often summate with similar effects evoked from hypothalamic points.

Attempts have been made to condition hypothalamic "rage" by pairing hypothalamic stimulation with a signal like a light or a buzzer but with little success. Escape from hypothalamic stimulation can sometimes be conditioned to a neutral stimulus, but, when the animal fails to respond to the warning signal and waits for the stimulation before escaping, there is reason to suppose that the onset of the stimulation is rewarding and that the stimulation becomes aversive only after it has been on a short time. Cats have also been trained to avoid stimulation in the tectal area, lateral thalamus, and hippocampus. Hypothalamic stimulation in man causes various emotional responses; amygdaloid stimulation sometimes induces anxiety or aggression.

Although septal lesions in the rat increase startle responses, they do not enhance a conditioned emotional response. When such a response has been learned preoperatively, it is eliminated for as long as the rat remains hyperreactive, but "septal" rats can learn a conditioned emotional response as quickly as can normal rats.

"Septal" rats have learned a two-way shuttle-box avoidance in fewer trials than it takes normal rats, but they are slightly poorer at learning a simple one-way avoidance. They are also much worse at learning passive avoidance. These data suggest that septal lesions, besides producing slight learning deficits, interfere with the freezing response to frightening situations that normally makes two-way avoidance learning very difficult.

Both septal and hippocampal lesions also cause perseveration and delay extinction, perhaps because the areas are involved in the inhibition of responses that are no longer rewarded. It will be remembered that hippocampal lesions also interfere with the inhibition of exploration.

Lesions of the cingulate cortex or lateral gyrus produce opposite effects from those of septal and hippocampal lesions. Active avoidance is severely impaired and passive avoidance enhanced. Medial thalamic lesions also lead to excessive freezing in frightening situations. These lesions have no effect upon rate of approach to a reward, but the subjects are paralyzed with fear in the simple one-way avoidance test.

Amygdaloid lesions impair all types of avoidance to some extent, though the effect upon active shuttle-box avoidance is most pronounced. It is believed that the amygdala may be involved in the analysis of motivating stimuli and their association with other stimuli.

As in other motivational states, hormones play a part in aversive reactions to stimuli. In addition to the previously mentioned effects of gonadal hormones, it appears that adrenocorticotrophic hormone (ACTH) and perhaps the steroids that it releases from the adrenal cortex influence the motivation to escape or avoid stressful situations. Injections of ACTH have not been found to affect the rate of avoidance learning, except in hypophysectomized animals, which lack an endogenous source of the hormone, but continued injections of ACTH after avoidance training will delay extinction of the response. Adrenalectomy is reported to have a similar effect to that of ACTH injections, from which it has been inferred that corticosterone either counteracts the effect of ACTH on hypothalamic "fear" circuits or suppresses the production of ACTH or both.

Therapeutic administration of ACTH or cortisone to human patients sometimes produces violent changes in mood, as do other steroid hormones. The effect is quite unpredictable and seems to bear no relation to the patient's previous personality.

CHAPTER 18

SELF-STIMULATION AND MECHANISMS OF MOTIVATION

As we have seen in earlier chapters, it is possible to produce a whole hierarchy of responses through brain stimulation. Simple muscle twitches or tonic movements can be elicited from some parts of the motor system; more complex phasic (but still entirely stimulus-bound) movements like chewing or ear wiggling are obtained from other motor sites. In areas that may be considered as belonging to motivational systems, stimulation may elicit responses that vary with the environmental situation. The response may depend, for example, upon where a goal is located in relation to the animal. From some of these sites it is even possible to elicit complex behaviors outside the animal's normal repertoire: rat killing in gentle cats or maternal behavior in male animals of various species for example.

During such motivational stimulation it is usually possible, as we have seen, to train the animal to attain a goal that is not immediately accessible. For example rats stimulated in the "eating" system will learn to press a bar to get food, which encourages us to assume that the stimulation may artificially elicit or augment one or more drives. It is therefore of consider-

able theoretical interest to discover that some of the effects of goal *achievement*, or *consummation*, can also be reproduced through brain stimulation, paradoxically enough in many animals from the same sites that give rise to goal-seeking behavior.

The rewarding effect of brain stimulation is not usually dependent upon the presence of any normal drive, though, as we shall see later, such drives may influence the phenomenon; we must therefore assume that the stimulation, or rather an aftereffect of the stimulation, is capable of inducing the necessary drive state or motivation to maintain the behavior.

The first demonstration of the phenomenon was made by J. Olds and Milner (1954), who stimulated the septal area in rats. Although not reported at the time, the first hint of what might be happening was that a rat would return persistently to a place where it had been stimulated and when presented with short bursts of stimulation it would show very active searching and sniffing behavior in the vicinity.

The attractiveness of the stimulation for the rat was demonstrated more objectively by so connecting a Skinner box that the rat delivered stimulation to itself whenever it pressed the bar. Rats with suitably placed electrodes then stimulated themselves with remarkable vigor and persistence (Figure 18.1).

MEASURES OF THE REWARDING EFFECTS OF STIMULATION

In the early experiments J. Olds took as a measure of the relative strength of a reward the percentage of time that a rat spent pressing the bar during a self-stimulation session. Later average rates of bar pressing were used, but this measure was criticized by Hodos and Valenstein (1962), who found that the rates at which a rat pressed a bar to obtain stimulation through different electrodes did not correlate highly with the preference shown by the rat when it could choose which electrode would be stimulated. The same conclusion applied to the relationship between the rates of bar pressing at different current levels and choice of current level.

48 Hours
Anterior Hypothalamic Electrode # 253

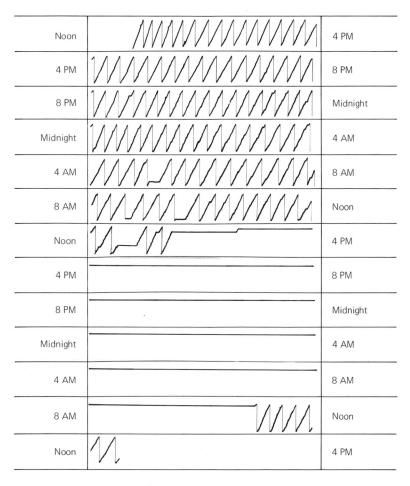

Figure 18.1 A cumulative bar-pressing curve for a self-stimulating rat with an electrode in the anteroventral hypothalamus. Each sweep of the curve represents 500 responses. The rat responded almost continuously at about 2,000 presses per hour for 24 hours and then slept most of the next day. (From J. Olds, 1958b.)

Valenstein and Meyers (1964) developed a platform-choice test to give a more reliable measure than pressing rate. As long as the animal stood on one side of a shuttle box it received stimulation with the parameters (current strength, wave form, frequency, duration, and so on) under investigation; on the other side no stimulation was delivered. The percentage of time spent on the stimulated side was taken as the measure of reward value.

Another measure of reward strength may be derived from the two-bar response-chaining situation used by Pliskoff, Wright, and Hawkins (1965; see "Extinction and Intertrial Decrements" later in this chapter). Pressing one bar gave the rats access to the other bar, which would deliver a few bursts of stimulation before being withdrawn again. The rate of pressing on the "instrumental" bar is a measure of the attractiveness of the "consummatory" bar.

ANATOMICAL PLOTTING OF REWARD SYSTEMS

Having established that intracranial stimulation could be rewarding, the investigators' next task was obviously to explore as fully as possible the anatomical distribution of the points that would yield self-stimulation. Olds and Milner obtained significant rewarding effects from the cingulate cortex, the mamillothalamic tract, and the tegmentum, as well as from the septal area. Stimulation of the medial lemniscus apparently produced avoidance of a lever that delivered stimulation.

More complete mapping studies were subsequently performed by J. Olds (1956a) and M. E. Olds and Olds (1963); their main findings were that stimulation was rewarding in much of the limbic system and especially in parts of the hypothalamus (Figure 18.2). Very few structures in which some points are not at least mildly rewarding have been found in the rat. In some structures, however, punishing points are found along with rewarding ones; even in the most consistently rewarding parts of the

Figure 18.2 (a) Medial and (b) lateral sagittal sections of a rat brain, showing areas where stimulation is rewarding (shaded) or punishing (stippled). (After J. Olds, 1958c.)

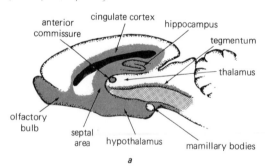

a

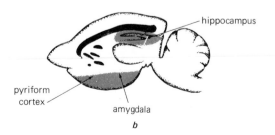

b

brain a fraction of the sites investigated have turned out not to be rewarding.

Because of incomplete and sometimes conflicting data from the earlier studies, several structures have been investigated in more detail. For example, J. Olds and Peretz (1960) found that in the dorsal region of the tegmentum (in the lower layers of the superior colliculus) stimulation caused unambiguous escape behavior but that at points below the medial lemniscus, probably near the ventral tegmental area of Tsai and ventral tegmental decussation (see Routtenberg & Malsbury, 1969), stimulation was often rewarding.

The amygdala was explored in more detail by Wurtz and Olds (1963) in an effort to resolve the apparent discrepancies between observational studies (mostly in cats), in which only aversive effects were seen, and self-stimulation studies, in which some rats with amygdaloid electrodes sought stimulation. Their results suggested that the more medial nuclei (nearer to the hypothalamus) tend to be rewarding, whereas the lateral nuclei tend to be punishing. On the basis of these results and taking into consideration the effects of amygdaloid lesions, Wurtz and Olds suggested that the amygdala is a receptive area for such reinforcing stimuli as pain, food, and so on.

The hippocampus is another somewhat ambiguous region, which has been the subject of special study by Ursin, Ursin, and Olds (1966). These investigators found that slow but steady self-stimulation could be elicited from the more lateral part of the hippocampus (field CA3, which has direct connections to the lateral septal area). Stimulation in the dentate gyrus appeared to be punishing. On the other hand, Milgram (1968) has observed self-stimulation from electrodes in all parts of the hippocampus, though the more medial placements yielded very slow rates (Figure 18.3).

M. E. Olds and Olds (1963) noted great differences between the effects of stimulating the medial and lateral hypothalamus. In the region through which the medial forebrain bundle passes (lateral to the fornix), the rat stimulated itself very energetically and would tolerate relatively long bursts of stimulation before attempting to turn the current off. More ambivalent behavior appeared when the medial hypothalamus was stimulated. The rat stimulated itself more slowly, taking only short bursts, and turned the current off very promptly when it was turned on by the experimenter. These findings have been confirmed by Poschel (1966) also using rats, and on cats by Wilkinson and Peele (1963). Medial-hypothalamic stimulation in the cat often yields purely aversive responses, but the reward system in the cat appears to be much weaker and more difficult to excite than in the rat or in most other animals.

The thalamus has been explored by Cooper and Taylor (1967). In addition to the limbic component in the anterior region, more caudal midline nuclei have been found to support self-stimulation in the rat. Grastyán and Ángyán (1967) also obtained reliable self-stimulation from the anterior thalamus in cats.

Although the limbic system certainly contains some very important circuits for self-stimulation, many investigators have found that stimulation of the extrapyramidal system, which is closely related in many ways to the limbic system, is also rewarding. Brady, Boren, Conrad, and Sidman (1957) and Justesen, Sharp, and Porter (1963) have found that cats will self-stimulate at points in the caudate nucleus; Brady (1960) has reported self-stimulation from the globus pallidus in monkeys. Routtenberg and Kramis (1967) were able to elicit self-stimulation most successfully from the substantia nigra in gerbils, and Routtenberg and Huang (1968) obtained self-stimulation in rats from the *lenticular fasciculus*, a subthalamic pathway from the globus pallidus to the tegmentum ending in the region of the red nucleus. Routtenberg and Malsbury (1969) elicited self-stimulation from the region of the *brachium conjunctivum* (which contains mainly fibers leaving the cerebellum) also in rats. Many other extrapyramidal reward points were discovered by M. E. Olds and Olds (1963) in the course of their thorough mapping study, but the self-stimulation rates at these points were usually rather low.

Although the rat has been studied far more

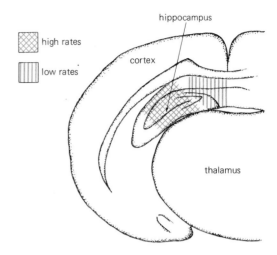

Figure 18.3 Coronal section of a rat brain, showing the areas of the hippocampus in which higher rates and lower rates of self-stimulation may be obtained. (After Milgram, 1968.)

thoroughly than any other animal, self-stimulation has been observed in many other species. In addition to the previously mentioned cats, monkeys, and gerbils, self-stimulation has been observed in dogs (Stark & Boyd, 1963), pigeons (MacPhail, 1966; Goodman & Brown, 1966), dolphins (Lilly & Miller, 1962), goats (Persson, 1962), goldfish (E.S. Boyd & Gardner, 1962), and man (Sem-Jacobsen & Torkildsen, 1960; Bishop, Elder & Heath, 1963). Apparently there is no species in which serious attempts to produce self-stimulation have been completely unsuccessful.

As far as can be ascertained from the few data available, the distribution of points from which self-stimulation has been obtained seems relatively constant among species. There are, however, some differences in the ease with which the effect can be obtained. Such areas as the septal region and the medial hypothalamus, which are moderately rewarding in the rat, do not reward the cat at all. Nevertheless, the regions of negative and positive reinforcement plotted for the cat by Wilkinson and Peele resemble those plotted for the rat fairly closely.

There is little anatomical evidence from human studies but Sem-Jacobsen and Torkildsen have suggested that their patients found stimulation in the mesencephalon (presumably in the ventral region near the termination of the medial forebrain bundle) most pleasurable or rewarding. Other rewarding sites were found in the medial thalamus or hypothalamic region, and weaker effects were also obtained from the medial frontal lobe and parts of the temporal and parietal lobes.

LESION STUDIES

The emergence of the medial forebrain bundle (MFB) as the most highly rewarding locus of stimulation in many of the animals tested suggested to some investigators that this pathway was, or led to, a reward center. Lesions were therefore combined with stimulation in an attempt to discover the significant structure into which the MFB activity was being fed.

Morgane (1962) reported abolition of self-stimulation after lesions of the MFB. Schiff (1964) found that ventral tegmental lesions reduced rates of bar pressing for septal stimulation, but Valenstein and Campbell (1966) were quite unable to eliminate bar pressing for stimulation of the septal area or olfactory tract by lesions in the MFB or by anterior limbic lesions that almost severed the subcortical parts of the brain (Figure 18.4). In some cases the response rates rose after the lesions. The investigators concluded that the conduction might be through dorsal limbic connections too diffuse to be affected by sectioning. Ablations of dorsal limbic structures (cingulate cortex and hippocampus) were, however, carried out by Asdourian, Stutz, and Rocklin (1966), and usually produced an increase in the rate of bar

Figure 18.4 A lesion in the rat brain anterior to the electrode site, which had no effect upon the rate of self-stimulation. (From Valenstein & Campbell, 1966.)

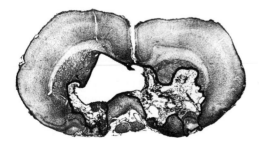

pressing for septal stimulation. Only in a few instances was a decrease observed.

Lorens (1966) obtained very similar results from rats bar-pressing for lateral hypothalamic stimulation. Lesions in the septal area increased the pressing rate, and lesions in the MFB posterior to the stimulating electrode had no effect upon it. Molnár and Grastyán (1966) found an increase in the rate of lateral hypothalamic self-stimulation in several cats after hippocampal lesions. A few cats pressed at a lower rate after the lesion.

It seems that deficits are usually found only when the animals are retested within a few days after the lesion has been made; when sufficient time is allowed for the tissue surrounding the lesion to recover from the operation no impairment is seen, as a rule. Corcoran (1968) has traced the course of recovery of bar pressing after tegmental lesions and has found a transient slowing in the rate of bar pressing for lateral hypothalamic stimulation.

BRAIN ACTIVITY DURING SELF-STIMULATION

Porter, Conrad, and Brady (1959) recorded from various structures in the monkey during self-stimulation in the septal area, anterior hypothalamus, anterior thalamus, hippocampus, and amygdala. Six of eight monkeys with stimulating electrodes in the medial forebrain bundle showed spike-and-wave activity in the septal areas during stimulation at the beginning of the session. When this activity was no longer elicited by the stimulation the monkeys responded only sporadically or stopped (Figure 18.5). Monkeys pressing for stimulation of the anterior thalamus also revealed spike-and-wave activity in the septal and anterior hypothalamic areas. This activity was not, however, essential for the occurrence of self-stimulation; the other two monkeys with good self-stimulation rates showed no abnormal septal or hypothalamic activity.

Electrographic seizure activity frequently accompanied self-stimulation in the monkey hippocampus, and the investigators were of the opinion that such activity was a necessary component of reward. This hypothesis is in-

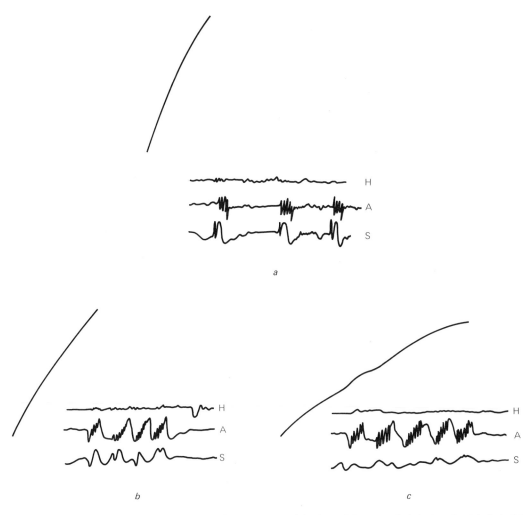

Figure 18.5 Cumulative response curves for bar presses and brain activity recorded during the (a) first, (b) second, and (c) fourth hours of self-stimulation in the medial forebrain bundle of the monkey. H, hippocampus; A, amygdala; S, septal area. (After Porter, Conrad & Brady, 1959.)

consistent with later experiments, in which higher self-stimulation rates have occurred in rats when they have been given anticonvulsant drugs (Mogenson, 1964; Reid, Gibson, Gledhill & Porter, 1964). Bogacz, St. Laurent, and Olds (1965) have also shown that seizure activity can be dissociated from self-stimulation.

Grastyán, Karmos, Vereczkey, and Kellényi (1966) have found a reliable relationship between hippocampal activity and the reinforcing effect of hypothalamic stimulation in cats (Figure 18.6), consistent with Grastyán's hypothesis that slow hippocampal theta rhythm is associated with approach (or "pull") behavior and that fast theta or desynchronized hippocampal activity is associated with avoidance (or "push") behavior. The records of hippocampal activity in monkeys presented by Brady and his colleagues, however, provide no support for the idea that any particular hippocampal activity is essential for the reward effect, and, of course, the findings that some animals stimulate themselves more rapidly after hippocampal lesions means that the hippocampus is not an essential link in the self-stimulation circuit. It may be that the correlation observed by Grastyán and

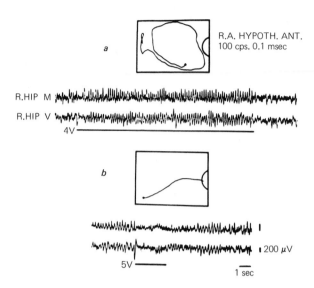

Figure 18.6 Effects of hypothalamic-stimulation behavior and hippocampal electrical activity in cats. (a) With moderate stimulation the cat makes diffuse searching movements and avoids the goal (at the right of the box), to which a stable approach response has previously been established. Theta waves are produced in the hippocampus. (b) With higher stimulating voltage the cat moves quickly to the goal, and there is desynchronization in the hippocampus. (From Grastyán, Karmos, Vereczkey & Kellényi, 1966.)

his colleagues is more apparent in cats than in other animals. Theta rhythm is difficult to distinguish in the activity of the primate hippocampus, whereas in lissencephalic (smooth brained) animals like the rat and the rabbit theta rhythm is more prominant than in the cat and, according to some observers (for example, Vanderwolf, 1968), its presence is correlated with voluntary movements of any sort in these animals.

Another possible method of exploring the anatomy of the reward system is to stimulate at two or more points simultaneously and to determine what the interaction between them is. This method has hardly been exploited, but Albino and Lucas (1962) showed that septal stimulation could be potentiated by simultaneous stimulation in the posterior part of the brain near the red nucleus and substantia nigra, and Routtenberg and Olds (1966) inhibited hypothalamic and septal self-stimulation by concurrent chemical or electrical stimulation of the dorsal midbrain region.

BEHAVIOR ELICITED BY BRAIN-STIMULATION REWARD

Psychologists who had read about but had not personally seen self-stimulation sometimes suggested that the animals might be caught up in a motor loop so that each stimulation forced it to make the movements that resulted in another bar press. This explanation obviously did not account for the original observation that rats would seek out a place in which they had received stimulation; partly to answer speculations of this sort J. Olds (1956b) formalized the locomotor-approach situation by having rats run a maze to receive brain stimulation. He found the behavior of the stimulated rats very similar to that of hungry rats running the same maze for food (Figure 18.7). The first runs of the second and third days were a little slower than were those of food-rewarded rats, but the daily improvement was considerable.

Another demonstration that motivation for self-stimulation is strong was obtained by running rats in an obstruction box in which they had to cross an electrified grid in order to reach a pedal that would deliver brain stimulation. Rats tolerated stronger foot shocks when rewarded by brain stimulation than when rewarded by food after 24 hours of fasting (J. Olds, 1960).

It is possible that in the latter experiment one effect of stimulation might have been to reduce the animals' fear of electric shock. Brady (1958) found that animals failed to stop pressing a bar for brain stimulation during the presentation of a sound that had been associated with foot shock (the conventional "conditioned emotional response"), though the same rats would stop at the signal when they were pressing the bar for water.

The results from both the obstruction box and the conditioned emotional response could be interpreted as indicating either that brain stimulation is so rewarding that the rat is willing to accept a great deal of unpleasantness in order to obtain it or that the stimulation suppresses for

a time activity in brain pathways concerned with aversion. The latter explanation seems more likely in view of the findings of Cox and Valenstein (1965) that rats apparently do not notice mild foot shock during stimulation. They do not discriminate between a place where they receive both shock and brain stimulation and another place where they receive brain stimulation alone, though if the stimulation is not presented they avoid the shock area. Valenstein (1965) has shown that rewarding stimulation can also counteract the effect of punishing brain stimulation.

INTERACTION OF REWARDING STIMULATION WITH NATURAL REWARDS

After the discovery that brain stimulation can be rewarding an obvious question was how the phenomenon is related to natural drives. Morrison (1955) determined the effect of self-stimulation upon eating in food-deprived rats and of 24-hour food deprivation upon bar pressing for brain stimulation. He found that

Figure 18.7 Mean maze-running times for seven rats with food as goal are represented by the broken line and for eight rats with short periods of self-stimulation as goal by the solid line. The rates of acquisition and extinction are very similar for the two groups.

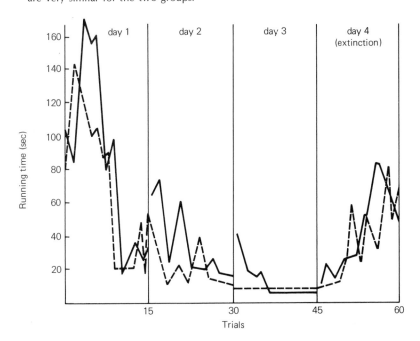

stimulation significantly reduced eating but that satiation for food had no significant effect upon self-stimulation in rats with electrodes in the septal area. Brady, Boren, Conrad, and Sidman (1957) found, however, that rats and cats deprived for 48 hours of both food and water showed significantly higher rates of self-stimulation; increases of 100 per cent or more were obtained in some animals. Satiation for food and water did not, however, abolish self-stimulation completely in any animals.

The enhancement of self-stimulation could have been caused by a general effect of deprivation upon activity, rather than by a specific summation of biological drive with drive for brain stimulation, especially as the rates in the experiment of Brady and his colleagues were initially very low. This question was settled by manipulating more than one drive at a time (J. Olds, 1958a). Castrated male rats were used and their sex drive increased by injections of androgen. Olds found that some rats showed increased self-stimulation when hungry and others when injected with androgen; there was a negative correlation between the effects of the two treatments, showing that drive per se is not always facilitatory. The hunger-sensitive rats had electrodes in medial areas; those sensitive to androgen level had more laterally placed electrodes.

Hodos and Valenstein (1960) attempted to determine the influence of artificially induced estrus on bar pressing in female rats but found no relationship. Later, however, Prescott (1966) found such a relationship with natural estrus in rats with electrodes in the lateral posterior hypothalamus.

A more consistent clue to the relationship between drives and self-stimulation comes from the fact that most of the electrode sites that elicit goal-seeking behavior also reward the animal. Margules and Olds (1962) and Hoebel and Teitelbaum (1962) showed that rats would stimulate themselves through electrodes in the lateral hypothalamus that also induced eating. Herberg (1963a) noticed that some rats had seminal emission during self-stimulation, and Caggiula and Hoebel (1966) showed that self-stimulation could be obtained from a region in the posterior hypothalamus where, as mentioned in Chapter 17, sexually satiated male rats could be induced to copulate by stimulation.

Mogenson and Stevenson (1966) found that drinking and self-stimulation could be obtained from the same electrodes in the anterior hypothalamus. The two effects could be dissociated, however, by varying the duration of the stimulation. With bursts of less than one second the rats engaged in more bar pressing than drinking, but when the bursts were longer than one second the rats drank more than they pressed the bar (Figure 18.8).

Recent experiments have explored still more directly the interactions of self-stimulation with other motivations. Mogenson and Morgan (1967) showed that, when the current was just above reward threshold, rats that both drank and self-stimulated would stimulate themselves at a higher rate if water was available. At higher levels of stimulation current, the rate was not influenced by the availability of water. This result has been extended by J. Mendelson (1967), who showed that, when the current was reduced to the threshold for eliciting drinking, rats

Figure 18.8 Lever presses and licks during two-minute periods of self-stimulation in one rat. Similar results were obtained from three other "stimulus-bound" drinkers. (From Mogenson & Stevenson, 1966.)

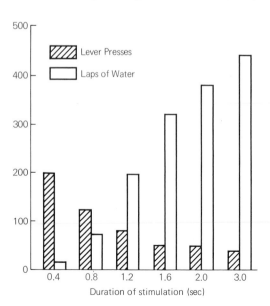

would not stimulate themselves at all unless water was present.

Coons and Cruce (1968) found a similar relationship in rats that engaged in stimulus-bound feeding. The rats did not stimulate themselves significantly when currents were just above the threshold for eating unless food was present, though at higher currents they would stimulate themselves vigorously, even in the absence of food.

The possibility that interaction of this type would occur was presaged by J. Mendelson's demonstration (1966) that food-satiated rats would run to the goal box of a T-maze in which stimulation produced stimulus-bound eating. The rats would avoid the other goal box in which they were stimulated but not provided with food. Rats that were stimulated during the run but not in the goal box containing food did not learn the maze (Figure 18.9).

Mendelson differentiated between the effects of biological drives (like hunger), which in his opinion, can induce only consummatory behavior, and *incentives* (secondary drives based on the expectation of consummatory activity; see Bindra, 1968), which can induce the appropriate instrumental goal-seeking activity. This differentiation is important and will be discussed later in this chapter. It may roughly be expressed as that the rats are attracted by the idea of eating (for example), even though they are not hungry, as long as they expect to eat when they reach the food. They will not, however, continue to visit a place where food is to be found, even when they are hungry, if they lose their appetite when they arrive there or if they are prevented in some way from eating.

It should be emphasized that the phenomenon observed by Mogenson and Morgan and Coons and Cruce is manifest only when the stimulation current is near threshold level for eating and drinking and in animals that have a lower threshold for stimulus-bound consummation than for self-stimulation. That these two thresholds can vary independently, depending upon the exact location of the electrodes (J. Mendelson, 1967) and that many self-stimulation points produce no known drive indicate that, although the rewarding effects of

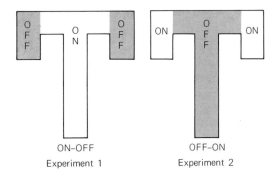

ON-OFF
Experiment 1

OFF-ON
Experiment 2

Figure 18.9 The conditions in the different stages of Mendelson's experiment. Rats did not learn to run the maze for food when the stimulation was turned off in the goal box (Exp. 1) but did learn to run when no stimulation was presented during the running if stimulus-bound eating was elicited in the goal box (Exp. 2). (From J. Mendelson, doctoral dissertation, M.I.T., 1965.)

stimulation are intimately bound up with the effects of feeding, drinking, sexual behavior, and the like, they do not depend upon these drives completely. The electrodes must usually stimulate a considerable tangle of motivational and other systems simultaneously; the different effects thus may well be mediated by different but interacting systems.

A number of reports (for example, J. Olds, 1958b) have suggested that rats with hypothalamic electrodes will stimulate themselves to the neglect of all other drives. This suggestion was confirmed by Routtenberg and Lindy (1965), who allowed rats with electrodes in various self-stimulation sites access to food and stimulation for only one hour each day. Some of the hypothalamic animals ate very little and lost more than 10 gm per day during testing. The effect was highly correlated with the distance of the electrodes from the medial forebrain bundle. The "septal" animals and those with electrodes in hypothalamic sites remote from the medial forebrain bundle distributed their time between eating and self-stimulation and lost no weight.

EXTINCTION AND INTERTRIAL DECREMENTS IN SELF-STIMULATION PERFORMANCE

One of the first things to strike the experimenter watching rats stimulate themselves is that, despite an apparently insatiable and desperate need for electrical stimulation, many lose interest as soon as the current is turned off. The rate of extinction is quite impressive to anyone used to observing rats pressing a bar for food or other natural reinforcers. With some of the first rats trained to press a bar for brain stimulation, J. Olds and Milner found that the only way to initiate responses again after they had been extinguished was to "show that the current was turned back on" by giving a free stimulation. Later this procedure became known as *priming*, and, as we shall see, more careful analysis indicates that it does more than simply provide information to the animal, as was at first assumed.

In his maze experiment, mentioned earlier, J. Olds (1956b) found that on each day the first run through the maze for brain stimulation was slower than later runs and slower than the later runs of the previous day. When the rats were running for food, however, the first run of the day was, if anything, faster than the later runs. He also reported that some rats with anterior electrodes could not be taught to run the maze for stimulation, although the same rats would bar-press for it in a Skinner box. Wetzel (1963) also reported that rats running down an alley for stimulation once a day usually failed to run without being primed by a pre-session stimulation period in the goal box.

Sidman, Brady, Boren, Conrad, and Schulman (1955) had some difficulty in training rats

and cats on ratio and interval reinforcement schedules that cut down the number of stimulations the animals received per minute. They were able to train cats to reach a variable interval of 16 seconds and a fixed-ratio schedule of 8:1, but they found it necessary to increase the strength of the stimulation to maintain regular responding at the highest ratio (Figure 18.10).

Further evidence that some rats perform poorly when the intervals between stimulation are long was provided by an experiment of Seward, Uyeda, and Olds (1960). They ran rats down a runway for hypothalamic stimulation in either massed trials or trials spaced 15 minutes apart and found that the spaced trials produced absolutely no improvement either during daily sessions or from day to day. Massed trials produced considerable improvement in speed both during sessions and from day to day. As spaced trials usually lead to greater improvements than do massed trials when conventional rewards are used, the investigators suggested that some sort of "warm-up" was needed with brain-stimulation reward and that the immediate aftereffects of stimulation upon drive strength might be important for maintaining response.

This idea was elaborated by Deutsch (1960), who postulated that brain stimulation established a quickly decaying drive state, which would motivate the next response. If the re-

Figure 18.10 Cumulative-response curves for a cat pressing a pedal for caudate-nucleus stimulation (0.1 msec pulses at 100 per second, delivered for 0.5 seconds per press) on an 8:1 fixed-ratio schedule with current levels as shown in the figure. (After Sidman, Brady, Boren, Conrad & Schulman, 1955.)

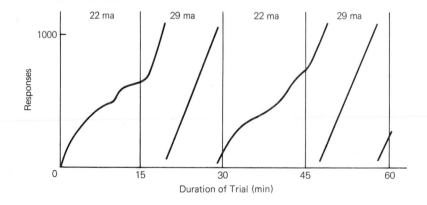

sponse were prevented for more than a fraction of a minute (or no stimulation were given for responding), the motivation would soon be too weak to elicit further responses.

To test this hypothesis, Howarth and Deutsch (1962) trained rats to stimulate themselves and then removed the lever for periods of up to 10 seconds. When the lever was reintroduced into the box, it delivered no current. According to most theories of extinction, the number of responses to extinction should not be greatly affected by a short period of enforced lack of responding at the beginning of the extinction period, but Howarth and Deutsch found that the response rate depended upon the time since the last stimulation and not upon the number of unrewarded responses (Figure 18.11). This result supports the drive-decay theory.

Herberg (1963b) tested other predictions based on the theory. One was that, as a natural drive like hunger increases the rate of self-stimulation, the response would be extinguished more slowly in hungry rats than in satiated rats because the natural drive (which does not decay) would be added to the drive induced by the stimulation. But hunger level was found to have no effect upon extinction rate in Herberg's experiment, though Deutsch and DiCara (1967) found that on the first few extinction trials hunger did retard extinction. Herberg also showed that training on a partial-reinforcement schedule increased the number of responses to extinction, though strict application of the theory might predict more rapid extinction under that condition because the initial drive level would be lower.

Howarth and Deutsch's experiment was replicated by Pliskoff and Hawkins (1963). They found that if the lever was present during extinction almost all the responses took place in the first 22 seconds and that if the lever were removed for that length of time at the onset of the extinction period very few responses were made later when it was put back. If the experimenter delivered stimulation several times during the time that the lever was unavailable, in order to reestablish the drive, the number of responses made when the lever was

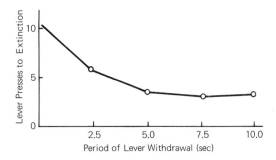

Figure 18.11 The effect of an enforced pause in self-stimulation upon the rate of extinction. (After Deutsch & Howarth, 1963.)

put back increased, as might be expected from the theory. Pliskoff and Hawkins trained another group of rats somewhat differently, however. During initial training the lever was withdrawn for 22 seconds every 5 minutes, but it remained connected when it was returned. The rats trained in this way were then put through the extinction procedure exactly as before; this time a great many responses were made during extinction. If the current was merely turned off without notice, however, these rats extinguished very quickly.

Serious doubts have thus been cast upon the generality of Deutsch's hypothesis, and in fact every experimenter who has observed self-stimulating rats is able to recall examples of subjects that did not show the rapid extinction and daily decrement on which the hypothesis is based. Even the fact that most rats do stop responding promptly when stimulation is turned off is open to alternative explanations, as was very nicely illustrated by W. E. Gibson, Reid, Sakai, and Porter (1965). Their experiments made the point that, when an animal presses a bar for brain stimulation, the reinforcing effect is coincident with the response, so that pressing is more nearly equivalent to a consummatory response than to an instrumental response in the usual sense.

Gibson and his colleagues compared the extinction rates of rats licking a dipper to obtain brain stimulation with those of hungry rats licking a dipper for sugar water. When the supply of sugar water was cut off, the rats stopped licking just as quickly as did the self-stimulators when current was cut off. Nobody is very astonished to discover that rats stop drinking when no liquid is present. Why, then, should anyone be mystified by the rapid decay in responding for brain stimulation when it is withheld?

To complete their experiment, Gibson and his colleagues performed the complementary test of making the self-stimulation situation resemble more closely that for food reward. Rats were trained to press a bar in order to gain access to a dipper, which delivered a small number of stimulations to one group and sugar water to another. When pressing the bar no longer gave access to the dipper both groups had normal rates of extinction on the bar.

A rather more elaborate study of the same sort was performed by Pliskoff, Wright, and Hawkins (1965), who chained responses in a two-bar Skinner box. Pressing the first lever caused a second lever to be introduced into the box, and the second lever was programmed to deliver a fixed number of stimulations (usually 20) and then to withdraw. This procedure separated instrumental responses from "consummatory" responses in the same way that they are separated for conventional rewards in the Skinner box.

The investigators were able to maintain smooth response curves in rats with posterior hypothalamic electrodes on schedules of FI 8 minutes and DRL 3 minutes applied to the first (instrumental) lever. The performance of "septal" rats was more erratic as a rule, and on a fixed ratio none of the rats behaved quite like the normal conventionally rewarded rats. Nevertheless, the investigators claimed that their results showed no basic difference between the reinforcement provided by brain-stimulation and that provided by food. It is apparent, however, that they may have overstated the case against the drive-decay theory as strongly as Deutsch overstated the case for it. None of these workers has laid enough emphasis upon the many individual differences in the degree of motivational decrement that follows a bout of stimulation in self-stimulating rats with different electrode placements.

This point is made clear in an experiment by Wetzel (1963). As mentioned earlier, she ran rats down a runway once a day for self-stimulation reward. In one group, which received no priming before the run, seven of the nine rats not only did not run but even had to be pushed the length of the alley into the goal box, where they still would not stimulate themselves until primed. The other two rats, however, ran quickly down the alley and were clearly motivated to stimulate themselves 24 hours after a previous stimulation. Control rats that received neither stimulation nor food in the goal box did not avoid it; after being gently pushed there a few times they usually went spontaneously when placed in the start box. The behavior of the seven reluctant self-stimulators was so different that Wetzel concluded that stimulation had long-term aversive effects upon them. Once primed, these rats would press rapidly for more stimulation, but after the effect of the stimulation had worn off the rats made every effort to avoid the situation.

Other investigators, including the author, have often observed self-stimulating rats that would react to being placed in the Skinner box each day by freezing at the end of the box remote from the lever, usually with their backs to the lever, where they would remain indefinitely unless primed. After priming they might stimulate themselves at the rate of thousands of responses an hour for many hours. It seems, therefore, that many rats fail to respond after an interval not because the drive has merely decayed but because it has reversed itself. J. Olds and Olds (1965) found that many ambivalent rats actually tried to escape in the midst of pressing the bar and were unwilling to return to the box.

A possible explanation is that the stimulation excites both positive and negative reinforcing mechanisms, and, although the effect of the former overwhelms that of the latter in the short run, the negative system forms the more durable associations with the situation. This question will be discussed more fully later in this chapter.

Various other experiments have indicated that the effect of brain stimulation is not always unalloyed reward. In the earliest experiments, the apparatus was connected in such a way that stimulation was maintained as long as the lever was held down. The rat could therefore have had continuous stimulation if it so desired, but it almost never chose it. Most rats took the stimulation in quite short bursts, each lasting less than a second. There are several possible explanations for this behavior. One is that forced movements might throw the rat off the bar. Another is that the rewarding effect of stimulation rapidly habituates and that the bar is released in order to produce the rewarding effect of another onset of stimulation. A third possibility is that an aversive component builds up, causing the rat to terminate the stimulation deliberately.

Again the evidence suggests that more than one explanation may be valid. Some rats apparently become too active to be able to hold onto the bar during stimulation; when allowed to stimulate themselves by standing on one side of a shuttle box, they manage to take much longer periods of stimulation than when they must press a bar. Other rats definitely escape the stimulation after it has been on for a very short time. In the shuttle box such rats (with electrodes in the medial hypothalamus, for example) stand on the divider and rock back and forth, with the result that they receive only short bursts of stimulation (Poschel, 1966).

Roberts (1958b) was first to set up an objective situation to demonstrate that stimulation could be initially rewarding and then could become aversive with no change in parameters other than duration of the stimulation. In his experiment cats learned to run to one place to obtain stimulation and then to run to another place to have it turned off. L. Stein (1962b) concluded that hypothalamic stimulation might elicit punishing effects when he found that the preferred duration of the stimulation burst became shorter as the intensity of the stimulation became greater. Septal and forebrain stimulation, on the other hand, elicited longer bursts at higher intensities, which was interpreted as demonstrating the effect of adaptation. The animal adapts to more intense stimulation more slowly, thus the stimulation must be turned off and on less frequently. L. Stein

(1965) also showed that rewarding brain stimulation could facilitate avoidance of punishing brain stimulation in rats.

M. E. Olds and Olds (1963), in plotting escape and approach points in the rat, found many points where both phenomena were elicited in sequence. They attributed these findings to the proximity of avoidance and reward systems, and they assumed that, when the electrode was near the border of an aversive region, temporal summation would eventually arouse that system and drive the animal to turn off the stimulation.

This explanation was challenged by Valenstein and Valenstein (1964), who tested rats in a two-lever box (one lever turned on the stimulation; the other turned it off). They found that at higher intensities all rats shortened both the stimulation periods and the intervals between stimulations. They considered it very unlikely that all their electrodes were near aversive systems and suggested that rats terminated the stimulation to obtain respite from the excessive autonomic activity it produced. If so, recovery from this discomfort must be quite rapid, for the average duration of pauses with high-intensity stimulation of the hypothalamus was only 1.6 seconds. Certainly most self-stimulation does produce marked autonomic effects. These include slowing of the heart as an immediate aftereffect of stimulation in the lateral septal nucleus (Malmo, 1961, 1964) and a tendency to overall acceleration of the heart rate during periods of hypothalamic stimulation (Perez-Cruet, Black & Brady, 1963; Meyers, Valenstein & Lacey, 1963). When more detailed analysis has been conducted, however, it has revealed that the heart rate also slows immediately after each hypothalamic stimulation of rewarding sites in many rats.

Grastyán, Czopf, Ángyán, and Szabó (1965) commented that their cats showed rage (growling, hissing, pilo-erection, and so on) during self-stimulation. They agreed with Roberts (1958a, b) that the early stages of the stimulation may be attractive (pull) and the later phase repellant (push). There seems little doubt that almost all stimulation of the motivational systems can arouse aversion if it is intense and maintained for a long time. It is not unreasonable to suppose, therefore, that in some instances an animal may acquire overall avoidance of a self-stimulation situation.

SECONDARY REINFORCEMENT

The question of the long-term aftereffects of self-stimulation brings us to the problem of secondary reinforcement. By "secondary reinforcement" learning theorists usually mean the transfer of reinforcing properties to normally neutral stimuli by association of the stimuli with a primary reinforcer. In Skinner boxes the lever and the sound of the food-delivery mechanism acquire secondary reinforcing properties and can be used to motivate further learning. There are conflicting accounts of the effectiveness of rewarding brain stimulation in producing secondary reinforcement.

In an early study L. Stein (1958) implanted electrodes in septal and anterior hypothalamic reward areas in rats. Then he measured the rates of pressing in a two-lever box; one lever turned on a sound, and the other did nothing. The sound was then paired 100 times with stimulation delivered by the experimenter through the electrode. The rats were next put back in the Skinner box and their rates of pressing for tone again measured. Finally the second lever was connected to deliver brain stimulation, and the rats were sorted into self-stimulators and non-self-stimulators according to their behavior in this situation. Once it was known which were which, it could be seen that the self-stimulators had pressed the tone bar significantly more often after the pairing procedure than had the non-self-stimulators. This result was considered evidence that the tone had acquired reinforcing properties by being paired with rewarding brain stimulation. Unfortunately, Mogenson (1965) found it impossible to replicate this result.

Another method of measuring secondary reinforcement is to have a discriminative stimulus like a light present during reinforced responses but absent when no reinforcement is given. If the discriminative stimulus becomes a secondary reinforcer, extinction will take longer when each response is accompanied by the stimulus than when both the primary reinforcer and the discriminative stimulus are withheld.

Seward, Uyeda, and Olds (1959) reported no significant differences in extinction rates as a result of presenting a discriminative light stimulus during extinction of a response acquired to brain-stimulation reward, but the investigators presented no relevant data, making it difficult to determine whether the lack of significance resulted from great variability or from genuine absence of secondary reinforcement. It is clear that animals whose motivation had decayed to zero or had become negative early in the extinction process would produce so much variability that very large groups would be necessary to demonstrate secondary reinforcement.

EFFECTS OF PHARMACOLOGICAL AGENTS UPON SELF-STIMULATION

J. Olds and Travis (1960), L. Stein (1962a), and others have studied the effects of various drugs upon self-stimulation. Injections of tranquilizers like chlorpromazine and reserpine very effectively inhibit self-stimulation, though other depressants like meprobamate and pentobarbital are relatively ineffective. In some cases, as mentioned earlier, barbiturates actually increase bar-pressing rates unless the doses are so large as to produce loss of consciousness (Mogenson, 1964; Reid, Gibson, Gledhill & Porter, 1964). The investigators suggested that this effect might result from reduced incidence of seizures.

The technique used by L. Stein (1962a) to assess drug effects involved a two-lever Skinner box. One of the levers provided a short burst of brain stimulation at each press but at the same time caused the current level to be set slightly lower for the next press; pressing the second lever delivered no stimulation, but it reset the current level delivered by the first lever to its maximum value. The trained rat would therefore press the reward lever until the current had been reduced to about the threshold value and would then reset the current by pressing the second lever. By this method, sometimes called *titration*, a continuous record of the threshold current can be obtained (Figure 18.12).

Injections of chlorpromazine (2 mg/kg) elevated the threshold for self-stimulation (the rats reset the current level after fewer responses on the reward bar), and response ceased altogether for minutes at a time. Small doses of reserpine had an even more drastic effect, causing long-lasting inhibition of self-stimulation and elevating the threshold for several days.

The stimulant amphetamine, on the other hand, lowered the threshold considerably and eliminated pauses in rats that did not otherwise press continuously. Persson (1962) also noted increased rates of self-stimulation in goats after amphetamine injections. It was expected that another stimulant (or antidepressant drug), imipramine, would have a like effect, but it did

not. Imipramine had an effect similar to that of chlorpromazine except that a larger dose was required (10 mg/kg). When the effects of these two inhibitory drugs on the enhancement of the response caused by amphetamine were investigated, however, a difference between them became apparent. The chlorpromazine counteracted the effect of the amphetamine, but the imipramine potentiated (strengthened) it (Figure 18.13).

These results have possible implications for mechanisms of human mental disorders. Stein has suggested, for example, that clinical depressions may be caused by high thresholds in parts of the reward system, so that even in the presence of normal rewards the patient behaves as if he were on extinction. Agitation, in this view, is caused by excessive activity of the reward system, so that various meaningless activities are pursued. These conditions can be

Figure 18.12   The titration method for determining self-stimulation thresholds used by L. Stein. The level of stimulation current is plotted on the ordinate and time along the abscissa. When the rat presses the "reset" lever, the setting of the stimulation current returns to the maximum value. It is stepped down by a small amount every time the rat stimulates itself by pressing the "stim" lever. (From Stein, 1962a.)

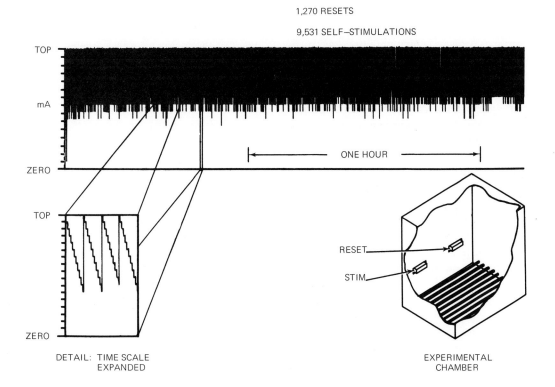

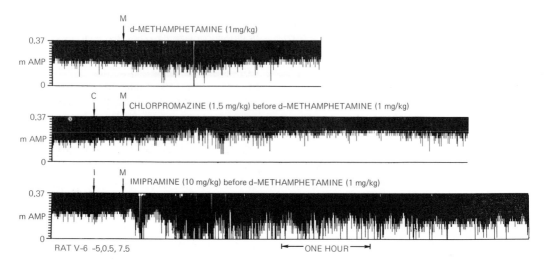

Figure 18.13 Records from titration experiments. The top record shows the reduction in threshold produced by injection of the stimulant *d*-methamphetamine into the self-stimulating rat. The next two records show the interaction between methamphetamine and first chloıpromazine, then imipramine, each of which elevates the threshold when administered alone. The chlorpromazine partly counteracts the amphetamine effect and subsequently produces a long-lasting rise in the threshold. The imipramine produces a very long-lasting potentiation of the amphetamine effect. (From Stein, 1962a.)

"mimicked" by drugs, the chlorpromazine acting to depress the reward system and the amphetamine to excite it.

Amphetamine facilitates the rapid release of norepinephrine from sites in the brain, chlorpromazine blocks adrenergic transmission, and reserpine depletes norepinephrine, as mentioned in Chapter 14. Imipramine is now known to prevent the rebinding of released norepinephrine, so that its potentiating effect upon amphetamine may result from the more effective use of norepinephrine released by the amphetamine. L. Stein (1966) concluded from these data that reward depends upon an adrenergic system located along the medial forebrain bundle. Dahlström and Fuxe (1964) have described adrenergic neurons in the ventromedial part of the mesencephalon with fibers ascending in the medial forebrain bundle and terminating in the lateral hypothalamus, among other places. As this route appears to be the only adrenergic pathway in the self-stimulation system, Stein assumed that it must play an important part in reward and in clinical depressions and agitated states.

The effect in the dog of *physostigmine*, which has a central cholinergic action, is to elevate self-stimulation thresholds and to reduce response rates (Stark & Boyd, 1963). Atropine blocks this effect but by itself has little effect upon self-stimulation. Presumably cholinergic systems normally do not inhibit self-stimulation, but if they are sensitized (possibly to the extent of increasing afterdischarge and seizure activity), such an effect becomes apparent. It seems clear that the cholinergic systems play a less important role than the adrenergic systems in self-stimulation.

PHYSIOLOGICAL THEORIES OF REINFORCEMENT AND MOTIVATION

The tone of discussion of "the physiology of motivation" seems to have been set by Stellar (1954) in a paper bearing that title. Stellar pointed out the importance of the hypothalamus, which is acted upon by humoral, sensory, and experiential factors, in determining motivational states. He also discussed the reciprocal relationships between "centers" of motivation and satiation that had been noted. But he made no serious attempt to explain how the output of the motivational systems influenced behavior, commenting that, as nothing was known about the relationship, it would be premature to consider the question. Many papers on motivation written since have also been more detailed about the anatomical and physiological interrelationships of different parts of the motivational system than about what the final output of the system might do.

J. Olds (1962) and J. Olds and Olds (1965) were more explicit about the ways in which reinforcement might modify behavior than are most writers. In their model the motivational system was divided into two opposing parts: a medial, adrenergic, tactual, inhibitory, aversive system and a lateral, cholinergic, olfactory, facilitatory, approach system. These systems were supposed to have evolved from a primitive nervous system capable only of tactual reflex activity, primarily of a defensive nature, to which was later added a mechanism for generating spontaneous activities for feeding and other trophotropic (nutritive) behavior. Next came a "reward" sensory system (initially olfactory), which was capable of inhibiting the aversive-reflex system and finally a mechanism for generating operant responses. Provision was made for operant responses to be superimposed upon spontaneous behavior if the responses had previously led to activation of the sensory reward system.

The systems were postulated as interconnected in higher animals as shown in Figure 18.14. Rewarding sensory input can inhibit the tactual-avoidance reflex, which, in turn, can inhibit the spontaneous trophotropic system. J. Olds and Olds have suggested that the lateral hypothalamic motivation system (which apparently corresponds to the "spontaneous" system of the more primitive organism) has a special relationship with the operant motor system such that, when a reward is presented just after the operant system has performed a response, the neurons responsible for the response become more sensitive and are thus more likely to fire on subsequent occasions.

J. Olds and Olds' suggestion for how this effect is achieved is apparently that the neurons of the operant system become permeable to a substance x for a time after they have fired. Excess substance x inside the membrane lowers

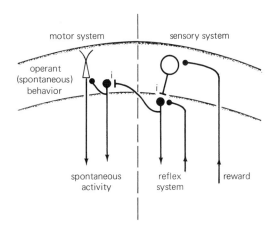

Figure 18.14   A neural model of the release of operant (or spontaneous) behavior during presentation of a reward. The reward inhibits the reflex system, which was previously inhibiting the spontaneous activity. (After J. Olds & Olds, 1965.)

the neuron's threshold, but if there is more x inside the membrane than outside it there will be an outward flow each time the neuron fires and the response threshold will thus rise. If a reward is presented during the permeable phase after firing, however, the neurons of the motivational system will deposit excess x on the outside of the operant motor neurons, and the flow through the permeable membrane will be reversed. The x will enter the recently fired neurons and will lower their firing threshold, but it will have no effect upon unfired motor neurons. In this way the successful responses will tend to occur more often. Self-stimulation results, of course, from the firing of motivational systems by an electrode, so that x substance is deposited in the motor system, where it is absorbed by the neurons active during the response that turned on the current.

This ingenious mechanism conforms to the definition of reinforcement derived from Skinner's theory of operant conditioning (that it increases the probability of a response), but certain types of behavior are very difficult to explain by this simple principle. In latent learning or learning by watching others, for example, a reward subsequently introduced will increase responses that have never been reinforced by that reward, and J. Olds and Olds did not attempt in their brief exposition to grapple with these problems.

The reward and aversive systems postulated by J. Olds and Olds (1965) resemble to some extent the "pull" and "push" mechanisms postulated by Grastyán that have been mentioned on several occasions earlier in this chapter. Grastyán, Czopf, Ángyán, and Szabó (1964, 1965) described a model in which these two opposing systems are interconnected so that both are usually activated by stimulation at any point in the motivational system. The pull system is normally elicited first, followed by dominance of the push system, though in some instances the push system presumably dominates from the outset.

The theory is based on a number of experiments carried out by Grastyán and his colleagues. In one it was found that conditioned approach and avoidance responses could both be elicited by identical stimulation of some points in the brainstem motivational system (Grastyán, Czopf, Ángyán & Szabó, 1964). Cats were first conditioned by the usual techniques to avoid cold water at the onset of one CS and to approach food in another part of the apparatus on presentation of a different CS. With certain electrode placements it was found that the cats would make either of these responses during electrical stimulation (in the absence of either CS), depending upon various factors like intensity of hunger, how recently one or the other of the responses had been made, the direction the cats were facing at the onset of stimulation, and so on.

If the stimulation was turned off when the response was completed, the responses were not extinguished either to the stimulation or to the original conditioned stimuli, even though neither food nor cold water was presented during the stimulation trials. If, however, the stimulation was turned off at some arbitrary point either before or after the cat had reached the goal, the response was extinguished. It is obvious from this result that the termination of the stimulation must have been rewarding.

The level of stimulation seems to be an important variable in this effect, however, as pointed out by Grastyán, Karmos, Vereczkey,

Martin, and Kellényi (1965). If low-level hypothalamic stimulation was turned on when the cat was in a particular part of its cage, the cat would soon learn to avoid a pedal that would turn the stimulation off. But, if the stimulation was made stronger, the cat would learn to go directly to the pedal and would soon refuse to be dislodged from it. Grastyán compared this result with those of Roberts (1958b) and Bower and Miller (1958), in which cats and rats turned rewarding stimulation off after it had been on for some time. In another experiment Kopa, Szabó, and Grastyán (1962) found that thalamic stimulation produced either agitation or calming depending on whether or not the cat was in a place where it had previously received shock.

These effects were believed to have been caused by excitatory connections from the initially active pull system to the push system and inhibitory connections in the opposite direction, so that electrical stimulation of the pull system, if strong enough, eventually established push activity and inhibited itself. Neural connections for self-inhibition of hippocampal pyramidal cells were cited by Grastyán (1968) as an analogy for this asymmetrical feedback effect.

Grastyán's conception of reinforcement is close to that of classical drive-reduction theory. He is aware, however, of the paradox that, whereas learning may require increased neural activity, drive reduction appears at first sight to reduce such activity, and he has presented evidence that drive reduction is actually accompanied by a momentary increase in neural firing. At the termination of motivating stimulation, administered by either the experimenter or the cat itself, sharp phasic movements, or motor rebounds, were usually observed. They were believed to be caused by the release from inhibition of neurons belonging to the pull system. Grastyán has postulated that the vigorous rebound of previously inhibited neurons produced the increased activity necessary for learning at the moment of drive reduction (Grastyán, Szabó, Molnár & Kolta, 1968).

Glickman and Schiff (1967) have presented what they call a "biological theory of reinforcement," but they also appear to have been more interested in how reinforcement is produced than in explaining what it does. They have drawn upon a large body of evidence to demonstrate that specific behavior is generated by the play of hypothalamic, sensory, and cortical systems on preconnected response pathways, and they have suggested that motor facilitation during the elicitation of consummatory behavior, whether it results from natural input or from brain stimulation, is itself reinforcing. It is not altogether clear, however, whether the authors consider reinforcement necessary to increase the probability that the same consummatory response will occur again or whether they consider its function as to encourage the ongoing response. Their statement that "the learning of new responses would take place by contiguity" (presumably contiguity with reinforcement) suggests that

their views on the influence of reinforcement upon operant responses are somewhat similar to those of J. Olds and Olds.

Another model of motivation that stresses fixed action patterns, but in quite a different way, is that of Tinbergen (1951). His model is really one of instinctive behavior, and reinforcement does not enter into it. He has suggested that motivational energy accumulates in neural centers until it is released by a stimulus from a goal object or reward. The energy then flows through a series of paths to the motor system and produces the appropriate behavior directed toward the goal object. Sensory feedback from the object acts upon the flow of energy at various levels of the motor system to ensure that the final responses are not stereotyped but are at all times guided by the location and behavior of the goal object (Figure 18.15).

If the animal never encounters a releasing

Figure 18.15 Tinbergen's model of the hierarchical system of innate release mechanisms controlling instinctive goal-directed behavior patterns. (After Tinbergen, 1951.)

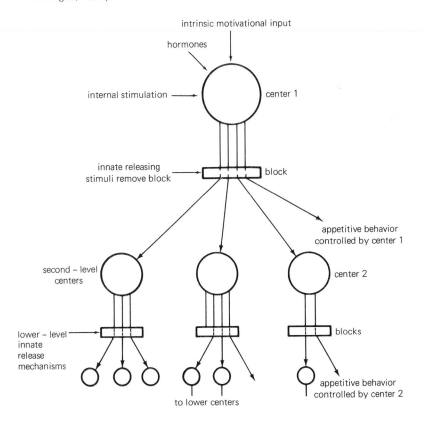

stimulus, a distorted or incomplete form of the response may eventually appear as the motivational energy forces its way past the inhibitory blocks separating it from the motor system. This activity is known as "vacuum activity."

Deutsch (1960) and Deutsch and Deutsch (1966) have refined and extended this model to incorporate learned behavior. Hypothalamic motivational systems are assumed to have innate connections to various species-specific response systems, as in Tinbergen's model, but, in addition, new pathways can be formed through which the motivational neural activity can be conveyed to motor patterns that will bring the animal to objects that have been associated with a primary goal, or that will allow manipulation of unfamiliar apparatus like Skinner boxes.

The new connections are supposedly formed when the motor neurons for the response are active (and receiving sensory guidance) just before sensory input from a reward is presented. The motor neurons and the neurons of the motivational system then exchange messages along a set of connections, the outcome of which is to provide a path from the source of motivation to the motor neurons responsible for the successful response. This path is then used by motivational impulses on subsequent occasions. In this model, therefore, response neurons each have two potential connections to each motivational system. Normally these connections do not function, but, if the motivational system receives information that a reward is presented at about the time certain response neurons fire, the "reinforcement" paths are activated, and they in turn make the "motivational" paths available.

Deutsch has assumed that, when an animal stimulates itself, the arrival of brain stimulation in a motivational path during the motor activity for the self-stimulation response results in the firing of the "reinforcement" connections between the motivational system and the response neurons. The motivation aroused by the stimulation thus flows to the response and elicits a repeat performance. The theories of J. Olds and Deutsch are somewhat similar except in the hypothetical processes of association and

Deutsch's greater emphasis upon sensory feedback to guide the responses.

As we saw earlier in this chapter, Deutsch and his colleagues have conducted experiments to show that during self-stimulation motivation is elicited through brain stimulation but decays rapidly during periods of no stimulation. It is not clear how crucial this point is for Deutsch's theory. It would be very easy to modify the theory to explain the behavior of those rats that acquire long-lasting motivation for brain stimulation, by introducing the idea that some motivational systems can be conditioned to environmental stimuli. Then, whenever such an animal was reintroduced into a self-stimulation apparatus, enough motivation would be aroused by association to start the response again.

A more intriguing consequence of the model is that it might be possible to stimulate only one of the separate motivational and reinforcement pathways and to compare the actual effects with those predicted by the theory. Deutsch (1964) has performed a number of experiments in which he claims to have separated these two pathways by making use of the slightly different *refractory periods* (the time following the transmission of an impulse during which a neuron is unresponsive to further stimulation) of each.

If these results are confirmed they will certainly challenge other theories of motivation and reinforcement, but the experiments are quite difficult to perform, and efforts by Szabó to replicate some aspects of them at McGill University have yielded results different from those reported by Deutsch. The refractory periods found by Deutsch (about 0.6 msec for reinforcement neurons and 0.8 msec for neurons of the motivational pathway) are remarkably short for neurons of that system if the optimum frequency for stimulation (60–100 Hz) is any guide.

MOTIVATION AS A RESPONSE SELECTOR

As most of the authors whose theories have been discussed here have pointed out, it is instructive to consider how motivational mechanisms may have evolved in phylogenesis.

The evolutionary process ensures that all existing organisms are equipped to behave in ways that improve their chances of survival. Finding sources of nourishment and avoidance of injury are the most important requirements for individual survival; adequate opportunities for reproduction are the requirement for species survival, assuming that individuals survive.

Plants are so constituted that their roots turn toward the depths where they are most likely to come into contact with moisture and minerals; their leaves turn to provide maximum absorption of light, their source of energy. Some primitive animals are attracted by chemicals (odors) given off by the organic material that they feed on; others like the paramecium are not drawn toward food and oxygen so much as deterred from leaving a region in which these commodities are plentiful. This deterrence is achieved through a "backing" reaction triggered whenever there is a deterioration in the chemical nature of the environment. At a higher phylogenetic level some insects that would fall easy prey to birds or other animals in the light are photophobic; when exposed to light they run to the nearest dark place.

These examples are only a few of the mechanisms known as *tropisms* or *taxes*; they invariably involve feedback of some sort. That of an insect escaping a light or approaching an odor (from food or a female, for example) is straightforward enough, as illustrated in Figure 18.16. If light falls on the right eye of this hypothetical creature, there is greater excitation of the motor system on the right side of the body than on the left, which causes the animal to swing around until its back is to the light. The light then falls equally on both eyes, and both sides of the motor system are equally excited. The animal then pursues a more or less straight course away from the light.

An insect with crossed connections from the antennae, where the olfactory receptors are located, will approach an odor because a source nearer to the right antenna provides more excitation to the left side of the motor system; the left legs will thus have a stronger kick than those on the right and will turn the animal toward the source of odor on the right.

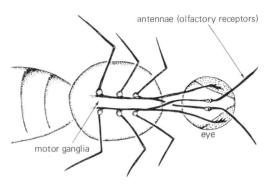

Figure 18.16 A hypothetical photophobic food-seeking insect. It turns away from the side with most motor facilitation from the receptors, providing an example of feedback steering.

The feedback loop in these examples consists of the following links: the asymmetrical stimulus produces a "difference" signal in the bilaterally paired receptors; this signal is fed to the motor system, and the response modifies the sensory input to minimize the sensory imbalance. Any subsequent error of response produces a new sensory imbalance that feeds a correction signal to the motor system, and guidance is thus exerted until the goal is reached.

Even at this low phylogenetic level we find some taxes that vary in strength from time to time (for example, those for food and sex) and some that are relatively constant (for example, defensive reactions). In order to incorporate such variability into the model, we can interpose "gates" or modulators in the paths between the receptors and the motor system. Each gate is selective for the particular impulses generated in the sensory systems by the relevant goal stimuli, so that the animal will approach food when it is hungry, a mate when it is sexually mature, and so on. The gates are transmission elements in which the influence of a goal stimulus is modulated by what C. T. Morgan (1957) has called a *central motive state*. Central motive states depend upon deprivation, concentration of hormones, and so on; they correspond to what are usually called "drive states."

There are several ways in which a central motive state might modulate the signal from a goal stimulus. Changes in the chemical or physical nature of the internal environment might act directly to change the thresholds of relay cells in the pathway between the stimulus and the motor system, or the changes could actually fire special drive-receptor cells (like osmoreceptors), and their activity could then facilitate or inhibit cells in the goal-stimulus pathway. In either case it is clear that the control of motor activity by a goal stimulus is a function of the intensities of the goal stimulus and of the corresponding central motive state. For example, a strong food smell coupled with moderate food deprivation could be as effective as a weaker smell presented to an animal more severely deprived.

If more than one goal and more than one central motive state were to act simultaneously on an animal like that in Figure 18.16, the guidance system would be upset, and the animal might be left suspended between two goals, unable to reach either. To prevent this dilemma, it is necessary to postulate mutual inhibition among the motivational pathways, ensuring that the strongest activity acquires sole control and eliminating the effects upon the motor system of weaker activities.

The "steering" type of approach behavior illustrated by this model is completely under stimulus control at all times, which makes it rather less interesting psychologically than the cruder but less stimulus-bound "backing" reaction of the paramecium. The paramecium swims an erratic path, and each time it backs up it starts again in an essentially random direction. With only two responses in its repertoire, swimming and backing when an obstacle or a deterioration of the environment is encountered, the organism can nevertheless eventually reach anyplace in its environment, and, more to the point, it can cruise around in the more salubrious parts of it.

It is possible to imagine an elaboration of this mechanism in which more complex animals, with larger repertoires of responses, could switch from one response to another when no beneficial stimuli were detected but could "lock on" to any response that fired a motivational pathway. A simple model based on this hypothetical principle is shown in Figure 18.17. Like the models of J. Olds and Deutsch, it has a mechanism for spontaneously generating response patterns. This generator is considered to be located in high-level central motor struc-

Figure 18.17 A trial-and-error model for goal seeking. The response arises spontaneously in the response-pattern generator (RPG) and is either maintained by the response-hold mechanism (RHM) when the response produces an increase in the goal (or "good") input c_g or is changed to another response by the response-switch mechanism (RSM) when it produces a noxious input or a reduction of goal input, c_n. The variable gate transmits the goal signal to the motivating system more strongly when the need for the goal is greater.

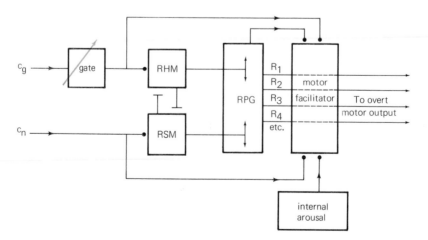

tures, and its activity interacts with sensory input (not shown in the diagram) to play upon preconnected motor pathways in the lower hierarchical levels.

The activity of the response generator is modified by two structures considered to have widespread connections with it, the *response-hold* and the *response-switch mechanisms*. As the names imply, when the response-hold mechanism is active, the pattern in the response generator is maintained; when the response-switch mechanism is active, the response pattern changes to a different one at frequent intervals. These two auxiliary elements have reciprocal connections, so that, as the activity of one increases, the activity of the other is inhibited.

Input to the response-hold mechanism comes from the sensory system involved with "good" or attractive stimuli; such stimuli are, of course, filtered through drive gates similar to those described for the "insect" of Figure 18.16, so that food, for example, fires the hold system only when the animal is hungry. For simplicity only one goal-stimulus system, c_g, is shown in Figure 18.17, but in practice there would be many for different positive motivations (sex, food, water, temperature, and so on), each with its own gate and feeding into the common hold system. Mutual inhibition among the different goal systems would prevent more than one from controlling the rest of the motivational system (and thus the animal's behavior) at any one time.

The response-switch element is fired primarily by noxious stimuli, which override other inputs and do not depend upon the internal state of the animal, thus requiring no gate. When there is no input from either "good" or "bad" stimuli, the response-switch mechanism is probably slightly dominant over the response-hold mechanism, resulting in periodic shifts in response pattern.

"Good" and "bad" stimuli are biologically defined by the connections of the model. Any stimulus that encourages a response to continue is, from the point of view of the behaving system, good. It is taken for granted that in the course of evolution animals inheriting connections leading them to approach the necessities of life have tended to survive long enough to reproduce, whereas those inheriting connections that allowed them to approach damaging stimuli or forced them to avoid necessities did not live long enough to transmit their ineffective nervous systems to subsequent generations. In any existing animal, therefore most good stimuli (as defined) are those from objects necessary for survival or reproduction, and most bad stimuli arise from dangerous objects. This rule is not absolute, however; changing environmental conditions may even result in acceptance of some noxious stimuli as good by the nervous system (cigarette smoke in humans, for example) or vice versa.

In addition to being fired by good sensory inputs, the response-hold mechanism is assumed to be fired by rebound when inhibition from the response-switch mechanism suddenly stops, and the response-switch mechanism is also fired by rebound when response-hold activity is reduced.

The other control imposed upon the activity of the motor system is that of general facilitation, which is applied by a *motor-arousal mechanism*. This mechanism receives input from both positive and negative motivational pathways, as well as from a periodically active general-arousal system. The response-hold, response-switch, and motor-arousal units may well represent different aspects of the behavior of a single physiological system, but it is convenient to distinguish among their functions for the purpose of exposition. The three units, along with the pathways for motivational sensory input are collectively called the "motivational system" in the following discussion.

The "trial and error" model differs radically from that of the "insect" illustrated in Figure 18.16, in that there is no direct control of the motor system by sensory input; the animal is not steered toward the goal by elicitation of species-specific responses. (In this respect it also differs from real organisms. Fixed action patterns like freezing, for example, have been omitted from the model to allow us to concentrate on the more significant variable mechanisms that come into play when stereotyped responses fail in their object.)

Assuming that there is enough motor arousal to allow patterns of motor activity generated in the higher motor centers to become overt, we find that the animal will make random movements as the dominant response-switch mechanism acts on the response generator. When the animal eventually comes within range of a goal, the response-hold mechanism will fire, and the successful response will be maintained for as long as it continues to increase the input c_g. The connection between the response-hold and motor-arousal mechanisms will also increase the vigor with which the approach response is made. If no further improvement in c_g occurs at any stage, adaptation of neurons in the motivational system will cut down the output of the response-hold unit, and the latter will no longer be able to maintain its inhibition of the response-switch unit; the response will thus be changed to a different one. If the c_g signal decreases further, the response switch will fire even more vigorously as it rebounds from inhibition, and further new responses will be emitted.

Any response that brings the animal nearer to a goal will thus be maintained, but any response that carries it away will be discouraged immediately, as in the children's game of "hunt the thimble." On the average, therefore, approach will predominate over withdrawal, and the animal will usually arrive at its goal. If one path is blocked, new responses will be tried, or a return to random behavior will allow the animal to make a fresh start from a different point in order to bypass the obstacle.

If in the course of its explorations the animal encounters a noxious object, the response will immediately be modified as the response-switch mechanism is fired, and alternative responses will be vigorously pursued.

The model described here, like its predecessor in Figure 18.16, is completely devoid of learning ability. Having found food on one occasion it must find it all over again the next time it is hungry. Assuming that it has an active response system and that food is never very scarce, an organism designed along these lines might survive. But in an environment where food is difficult to find animals that can store information about the route to food obviously

have a great advantage over those that cannot. Learning ability is thus a valuable development in conjunction with motivational mechanisms.

Probably the most primitive sort of learning that can confer some advantage is the ability to associate neutral stimuli with goal stimuli when both are present at the same time. The animal may then be attracted by an object like a bottle, a food dish, or a door leading to food when it has previously been guided only by the smell of food, for example. Figure 18.18 illustrates how such learning might be added to the basic mechanism of the previous model (see Figure 18.17).

The units labeled c_1 and c_2 represent "cell assemblies" (see Chapter 7), groups of cells that fire whenever the concept of a particular environmental object is aroused (normally by sensory input from the object). c_g and c_n are similar central structures, fired by goal stimuli and noxious stimuli respectively. As Hebb (1949) postulated, activity can persist in these assemblies for some time after the stimulus has gone. Potential connections exist between every pair of assemblies, but the only ones shown in this simplified model are those between the neutral assemblies and the motivational assemblies c_g and c_n. Potential connections are shown as lines with no synaptic knob at the end.

If c_1 is fired just before c_g on several occasions, as might be the case if c_1 represented the visual stimuli at the entrance of a goal box and c_g the smell or taste of food, the potential connections become effective (indicated on the diagram by a synaptic knob). It is obvious that, when such an association has been formed, presentation of the stimulus c_1 will elicit all the central effects of reward. Similarly, if c_2 precedes a noxious stimulus on one or two occasions, presentation of c_2 will elicit all the central effects of punishment. Central effects are specified because there are reflexive effects of reward and punishment (ignored in the present account) that cannot always be elicited through association with neutral stimuli.

As the rest of the model is identical with that in Figure 18.17, it is clear that the organism will approach signs of reward (or subgoals) using the same mechanisms it uses to approach the reward itself. When the subgoal has been reached, there is a good chance that the true goal will then be within range, and, by virtue of its greater effectiveness in firing the motivational system, it will take over control of the approach behavior. In a similar way the animal will avoid objects that have become associated with the firing of c_n and will thus be able to take evasive action before being subjected to actual punishment.

With this rather primitive form of learning, the organism must always make overt movements in relation to the goal or subgoal, in order to produce the changes in sensory input required as feedback to encourage or discourage the response being made. The most significant advance in goal-seeking ability takes place when learning relieves the animal of the need to make overt trial-and-error responses on every occasion. This learning involves storage of information about the usual outcomes of various responses in different environmental situations, acquiring a *cognitive map* as Tolman (1932) called it. Our basic model can be modified to include a simple form of cognitive learning with surprising ease, though complications arise when we try to incorporate more realistic behavior (species-specific responses to rewarding and punishing stimuli, for example).

Instead of going on immediately to describe the final model, however, it is helpful to pause and discuss the characteristics of cognitive-behavior theories and to review the alternative possibilities. With the aid of a cognitive map the organism can predict whether a contemplated action is likely to lead to improvement or deterioration in the environmental stimuli, and, depending upon the verdict, the contemplated action may occur or not. This sort of model was popular among psychologists in the days before behaviorism swept all before it, but the mentalistic language in which it was couched made it an easy target for mechanistic theorists.

Thorndike (1931), who was one of the earliest and most influential critics of the cognitive theory, summed it up:

"This theory, which we may call for convenience the representative or ideational theory, would explain the learning of a cat who came to avoid the

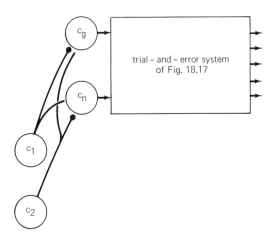

Figure 18.18 Simple stimulus-associative learning applied to the goal-seeking model of Figure 18.17, so that stimuli frequently present with innately determined goals or punishments acquire attractive or repulsive qualities.

exit S at which it received a mild shock and to favor the exit F which led it to food, by the supposition that the tendency to approach and enter S calls to the cat's mind some image or idea or hallucination of the painful shock, whereas the tendency to approach and enter F calls to its mind some representation of the food, and that these representations respectively check and favor these tendencies.

He then went on to dismiss the theory largely on the ground that in most learned behavior there would not be time to compare different responses and evoke images of likely outcomes.

This is a valid criticism of any attempt to use the theory to explain all learned behavior, but it is not a good reason for dismissing the theory in all circumstances. In fact, Thorndike's argument could well be turned around and the hesitations of animals and people in the early stages of learning used as evidence in favor of some sort of internal trial-and-error process.

It is true that many responses seem to be elicited in conformity with the stimulus-response association paradigm proposed by Thorndike (1898), Pavlov (1927), and many others, but some behavior is very difficult to reconcile with the theory. Unfortunately, psychologists have been so impressed during most of this century by the successes of the stimulus-response association theory that they have either ignored its failures or papered them over with rather unconvincing additions (many of which turn out on close inspection to be clumsy substitutes for the cognitive map). In order to show why it is necessary to look again at the "representative" theory, we should perhaps investigate briefly some of the less successful aspects of the stimulus-response theory of learning.

The simplest principle of association is that of pure contiguity: If two events, a stimulus and a response, let us say, occur at roughly the same time, the stimulus, according to this theory, becomes able to elicit the response. A simple contiguity theory, however, predicts that errors, especially frequent ones, become stronger or more probable, which is not true. Contiguity seems only to effect the association of correct (that is, rewarded) responses.

Most theorists therefore accept the need for some additional principle of association to account for the preferential acquisition of successful responses. Thorndike spoke of correct responses as "stamped in" by reward and of incorrect responses as "stamped out" by punishment. Learning theorists later adapted the term "reinforcement" to describe these effects upon associations of reward and punishment. Presumably the hypothetical neural bonds between the stimulus and the responses were directly or indirectly strengthened, or reinforced, by the stimuli encountered by the animal after making a correct response.

This selective mechanism satisfactorily explains the behavior of animals learning a response for a reward, but it is less satisfactory as an explanation of the behavior of punished animals. Negative reinforcement is supposed to weaken such connections as already exist between the stimulus and the response, but the weakening process is difficult to understand physiologically, especially as punishment effectively "stamps in" some autonomic and reflexive responses at the same time that it supposedly "stamps out" voluntary skeletal responses. Shock increases the probability that a rat will show changes in heart rate, defecate, or squeak in response to environmental cues, but it will definitely not increase the probability of the locomotor response that brought the animal into contact with a shock.

Latent-learning experiments also throw doubt on the idea that stimuli become associated with responses as a result of reinforcement. A hungry animal will soon stop exploring a simple maze if no food is to be found there, but, if food is placed in one part of the maze and the animal is informed of the fact by being fed there, stimulus-response connections apparently appear out of thin air. The animal will make responses to reach the food that have never been followed immediately by a reward.

Similarly, a naïve person wandering into a gambling hall and seeing "one-armed bandits" for the first time might deposit coins and pull levers for a few minutes from curiosity, but, if he were rewarded by nothing more than the sight of rotating pictures of fruit, he would soon give up. If he were then informed that from time to time these machines deliver small fortunes to lucky operators, he might, depending upon his credulity, return to manipulating the machines with great persistence and vigor.

In these examples, the mere expectation of a reward would apparently strengthen the stimulus-response connections, and this result is also difficult to explain by simple reinforcement theory. It is more parsimonious to assume that the connections are there all the time but are used only when the animal calculates that the response will lead to a reward.

The quotation from Thorndike describes in clear but not very scientific terms a model in which expectancy can determine whether or not a response is made. Tolman (1932), in more obscure—and from the point of view of the more conservative behaviorists—hardly less objectionable language, expressed a similar idea. His attempts were considerably clarified and tidied up by MacCorquodale and Meehl (1954), but none of these models gave any suggestion of what physiological mechanisms might be involved in the control of responses by expectancy.

The idea that the motor system might be a dual structure, one part involved with the elaboration of complex patterns and the other converting into overt responses the response patterns established by the first part, suggests a mechanism by which the prediction of the outcome of a contemplated response could determine whether that response would or would not be made. This idea and others already mentioned in connection with the models shown in Figure 18.16, 18.17, and 18.18 were incorporated into a model of motivated behavior by P. M. Milner (1960; 1961a). A more recent version of the model is shown in Figure 18.19 and will be described here.

The most important difference between this model and that in Figure 18.18 is the addition of a bank of "predictor" cell assemblies (r_1c_1, r_1c_2, ... r_2c_1, r_2c_2, ... r_3c_1, r_3c_2 ...), which receive input both from sensory analyzers c and from the central response-determining assemblies r. It is postulated that simultaneous input from both sources is necessary to generate significant activity in these predictor assemblies. When one of them fires it therefore means that a particular response has been made (or contemplated) in the presence of a particular stimulus.

Assuming that an overt response is made by the animal as it explores its environment, the rc assembly so fired will "reverberate" for a time, and its activity may become associated (in accordance with Hebb's principle that cell assemblies acquire connections with one another by firing together) with sensory cell assemblies fired by any new stimuli revealed by the response. In this way the animal will slowly build up a cognitive map of its environment, each association preserving the information that a response (x) made in the presence of a stimulus (a) will lead to another stimulus (b, for example). On a subsequent occasion when a is present, if x is contemplated the predictor $r_x c_a$ will fire again, and by association it will fire c_b, thus predicting that, if response x is made overtly, b will appear.

If at any time a reward is encountered the animal will acquire an association between the predictor fired by the stimulus-response combination and the neural activity aroused by the reward, which, as in the earlier models, includes motor facilitation and a tendency to hold the response.

Once this type of association has been formed, an interesting feedback situation arises. Suppose that the organism has had the experience of making response r_2 in situation c_1 and

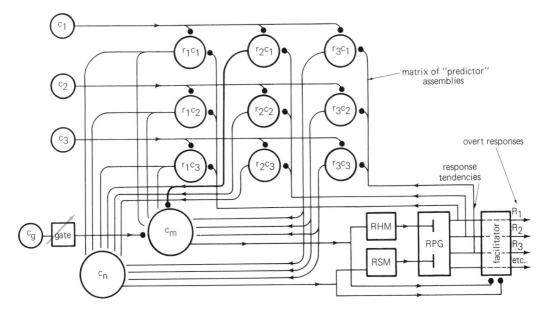

Figure 18.19 A trial-and-error model with an internal-feedback loop for making trials without overt responses after a "cognitive map" has been learned. The heavy line connecting r_2c_1 and c_m indicates an association between those networks formed on the basis of contiguity. Subsequent firing of r_2c_1 by a combination of input and response tendency will fire the motivational system and result in facilitation of the response tendency that is present, r_2.

has then found a goal object c_g. This sequence will result in an association of the assembly r_2c_1 with c_g and with the motivational activity accompanying the presentation of c_g. (There will also be a tendency for an association to form between the stimulus c_1 and the response pattern r_2, but it is assumed that, in order to avoid the undesirable association of every stimulus with every response during the course of exploration, many contiguous firings are required to produce significant associations between such activities. We can therefore neglect stimulus-response associations at this stage of learning.)

When the organism is next placed in the situation c_1 no immediate evocation of response r_2 is to be expected; rather, a variety of response patterns, or tendencies, will appear at random in the response generator (possibly, though not necessarily, producing such small overt movements as oscillations of the head or eyes). If r_2 happens to appear among the series of patterns, it will cause the assembly r_2c_1 to fire (c_1 being already present), and this predictor will, in turn, fire the motivational pathway through its recently acquired connections. "Holding" and motor arousal will immediately result, and the previously rewarded response pattern will thus be converted into an overt response. The boost to the motor system is not directed to any specific neurons or response elements; any response pattern active in the response generator at the time of motor facilitation would receive the same treatment, but the feedback connections ensure that the facilitation appears only when the previously rewarded response pattern is active.

The organism is, at this stage of learning, unable to *produce* the correct response immediately, but it can *recognize* it if it appears spontaneously and will behave appropriately. Eventually, after the correct response has been made a number of times, the direct connections between c_1 and r_2 will become strong enough to ensure that r_2 appears promptly whenever c_1 is presented. According to this theory, therefore, well-established learning is primarily stimulus-response association (though the response still must be released by motor facilitation), but this final state must not cause us to

lose sight of the essential transition phase of learning during which the animal must weigh the possibilities of alternative responses.

Latent learning is easy to explain with this model. Exploration of an unrewarded situation allows the animal to acquire a stock of predictor associations (indicating which response leads to which stimuli, starting from many points), but, as none of the responses ever leads to the prediction of anything but other neutral stimuli, the motivational system is not activated, and the animal does nothing or wanders aimlessly.

As soon as food is presented in one part of the apparatus, however, the stimuli in that part acquire connections to the neural activity aroused by food, including the activity of the motivational system. When the animal is placed at some other point in the apparatus, it will hesitate at places where it has a choice of responses and will eventually choose (more often than by chance) the response that gives rise to a prediction of the stimulus associated with food.

INCENTIVE MOTIVATION AND THE PROBLEM OF EXTINCTION

An interesting question whether the predictors acquire connections with the part of the motivational system peripheral or central to the "drive gates" arises. If the association were with c_g, the feedback would be blocked when the animal was not in the proper drive state. This conclusion seems reasonable; animals do not usually perform learned responses to obtain food when they are not hungry. Under some conditions, however, behavior can be elicited in the absence of biological drive; it is then considered to be elicited by "incentive motivation" (Bindra, 1968). This phenomenon could be explained by the model, assuming that the predictor assemblies acquire connections to the parts of the motivational system beyond the drive gates, for example to the response-hold and motor-arousal mechanisms.

It is clear, however, that incentive motivation cannot sustain behavior indefinitely. If the organism reaches the reward and then ignores it, it is the same as if it had reached the goal and did not find the expected reward there. In both cases a process of extinction ensues.

Extinction is perhaps the most puzzling of all learning phenomena. We know that with partial reinforcement the number of responses made during extinction can be increased far beyond the normal, which contradicts the idea that extinction is a depletion process like the loss of x substance from operant motor cells in the theory of J. Olds and Olds (1965; see "Physiological Theories of Reinforcement and Motivation" earlier in this chapter). An alternative possibility is that functional groups of neurons occur in antagonistic couples, each system having an "antisystem" bound to it by reciprocal inhibitory connections. The hold and switch units of the present model constitute such a complementary couple.

If a cell assembly y has acquired an association with an activity corresponding to a reward, y will induce some of the reinforcing activity normally evoked by the reward, but if the reward does not appear there will be a rebound activation of the "antireward" (switch) system, and, if this rebound occurs frequently, the assembly y will start to acquire an association with that activity instead of, or as well as, with reinforcement. When the associations with the switch system outweigh those with reinforcement, extinction is complete.

A discriminative stimulus (one that is present when a reward is not presented) will acquire connections only with the antireward system and will thus contribute to more rapid extinction. On the other hand, there will be at least partial recovery of the association on trials when the discriminative stimulus is omitted. When an incentive motivation is extinguished because the drive state does not allow the goal stimulus to fire the central motivational pathways, the absence of the drive state may also act as a discriminative stimulus, so that the animal soon learns not to make responses when the appropriate drive state is absent. Drives may thus act as cues indicating whether or not an instrumental response will be rewarded by consummatory behavior.

Mendelson (1965) has suggested that it may be possible to reverse the normal significance of drive cues. He succeeded in training rats *not* to respond when the appropriate drive was elicited by brain stimulation yet to respond on those trials when the drive was absent, as described in "Interaction of Rewarding Stimulation with Natural Rewards" earlier in this chapter. His experiments showed that incentive motivation was all that was necessary to induce a rat to run a maze. His animals were satiated, yet they consistently ran the maze if they were made to eat by hypothalamic stimulation in the goal box after each successful run. Although the rats were not hungry as they ran, they nevertheless did eat at the goal, and thus the incentive motivation was not allowed to become extinguished. As Mendelson has remarked, the predictor cell assemblies in the model under discussion would not be able to control behavior when the animal was satiated if they had associations only with goal-stimulus cell assemblies or with parts of the motivation path peripheral to the drive gates.

ESCAPE AND AVOIDANCE BEHAVIOR

The behavior of the punished animal requires that we take some account of fixed action patterns like freezing or backing and spinal reflex-withdrawal activity. In Figure 18.20 two environmental situations are represented: The term c_p represents the stimulus present before the punishment, and c_a represents the stimulus present during the punishment. In conjunction with the response r_p that led the animal into trouble, c_p fires the $r_p c_p$ predictor assembly which, of course, acquires an association with the motivational activity elicited by the punishment c_n. As there are no gates in the aversive system, it does not matter where the association occurs, and for convenience we shall assume that it is with the assembly c_n.

Assembly c_n has innate connections that produce responses like vocalization, freezing, jumping, and so on, but the punishing input also evokes reflex responses that may at first override the motor signals originating more centrally. Let us suppose, however, that some response r_t eventually does manage to break through the reflexive behavior and terminates

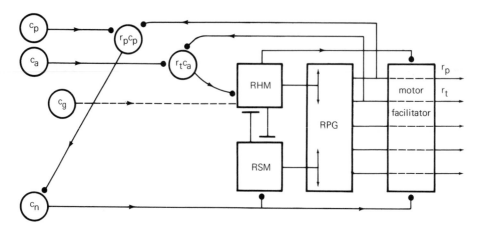

Figure 18.20 Connections involved in escape and in passive and active avoidance in a model including internal trial-and-error learning. To avoid complicating the diagram unnecessarily, only the relevant elements of the "predictor assembly" matrix are shown.

the punishment. The $r_t c_a$ predictor will be fired by this response, and it will acquire connections with the hold mechanism, which is in the process of rebounding after having been strongly inhibited by the firing of the switch mechanism. (It should perhaps be emphasized again that only *realized* connections are shown in the diagram. Each predictor assembly has *potential* connections with other organized groups of cells in all parts of the brain.)

Consider now the behavior of the hypothetical animal represented by the model when it is placed again in situation c_p. Any tendency for the response r_p to occur will fire $r_p c_p$, which will result in the firing of the aversive motivation pathway and elicit freezing or backing, vocalization, defecation, or the like; it will also activate the switch mechanism, which will eliminate that response tendency and induce the response generator to replace it with another. This entire process constitutes passive avoidance of a dangerous situation.

If the creature is placed in the punishing situation once more, it will again make reflexive withdrawal responses, and, as before, there will be rapid switching of patterns in the response generator thanks to strong activation of the switch mechanism. If the previous escape response r_t should appear in the generator, thus firing $r_t c_a$, there will be some activation of the hold mechanism and suppression of the switch mechanism, with the result that the previously

successful escape response will have a better chance than others of becoming overt.

If the hypothetical animal is returned to the situation c_a, but with the punishment turned off, the association between c_a and the aversive system will again produce freezing and similar responses and will again activate the switch mechanism. Response tendencies will be generated at random but will not be able to compete with the innate freezing response until r_t appears in the generator. Then the association from the $r_t c_a$ assembly will fire the hold mechanism, which will give the response a better chance of overcoming the freezing response and eventually will lead to an active avoidance response. As with approach learning, associations between c_a and r_t will gradually be acquired by contiguity if the pair occur together frequently, and then the avoidance response will occur promptly.

REINFORCEMENT IN THE EXPECTANCY MODEL

As mentioned earlier, the concept of reinforcement was originally applied to the hypothetical process of strengthening stimulus-response bonds. The opposite process of weakening the bonds was called "extinction." Later, presumably in an attempt to avoid basing the definition on hypothetical constructs like neural bonds that could be neither seen nor measured, reinforcement was redefined as a stimulus that increased the probability that antecedent responses would be emitted again later. No doubt this definition was originally believed to be an operational equivalent of the "strengthened stimulus-response bond" definition previously described, but from the point of view of the expectancy theorist, who does not accept strengthening of stimulus-response bonds as the source of all behavior, the two definitions of reinforcement appear to apply to different processes.

In the model of Figure 18.19, it is possible to increase the probability that a response will be emitted by manipulating the value of the goal without changing the strength of any stimulus-response bonds. The only connection undergoing modification may be one between a cue stimulus like a tone and a reward stimulus like a food pellet. After contiguous presentation of tone and food, an animal that had lost interest in pressing a bar to obtain the tone alone would start pressing again in the expectation of obtaining food as well. In classical learning theory such effects are attributed to secondary reinforcement.

The presentation of reward or punishment may thus be reinforcing because it results in contiguous firing of cognitive (c_1 and so on in Figure 18.18) and motivational (c_m in Figure 18.19) cell assemblies. At the same time, reinforcement may also affect the rate of formation (or *consolidation*) of neural connections (see Chapter 20), in closer accordance with the earlier meaning of the word. This function may result from the increased firing rates of neurons during the arousal that usually accompanies presentation of reward or punishment. If an association depends upon contiguous firing, it should occur more rapidly and more effectively when the firing rate of the whole system is increased by arousal.

MECHANISMS OF SELF-STIMULATION

According to the evidence on the organization of the motor system and to the hypotheses advanced in this book, all responses depend upon adequate firing in a facilitatory system. In learned behavior it is assumed that central motor patterns produce responses that lead to a reward more or less accidentally on the first occasion; then any subsequent tendency for the pattern to fire elicits motor facilitation through an acquired association, forcing the central pattern of response activity to become overt.

According to this model it should make no difference whether the motivational path leading to response facilitation is fired by a normal reward or by electrical stimulation of the pathway. Any response preceding or accompanying such stimulation should tend to be repeated because the rc cells fired by the combination of the response and the environmental stimuli will acquire associations with the motivational system. When the same response pattern fires in the response generator again, it will refire its rc circuit and elicit the facilitation it requires to emerge as an overt response.

If the electrode were so placed that it could fire only the part of the motivational path lying ahead of a drive gate the effect of stimulation would depend upon the presence of the appropriate drive. As we have seen, self-stimulation has never been found to depend entirely on food or water deprivation or other drive manipulation, and we must assume either that the animal is never completely satiated for all biological drives or that it is impossible to stimulate the reward path in such a way that the activity can neither break through the gates nor bypass them. Possibly the activity elicited by stimulation can always be made strong enough to overcome the inhibitory block if the stimulating voltage is high enough, or perhaps there is always a mixture of pregate and postgate fibers in the self-stimulating areas, so that the current will always spread to both.

Stimulation of the motivational pathways might fire a variety of fixed action patterns in addition to the hold and motor-arousal mechanisms. These patterns could include eating, gnawing, copulating, and so on, depending upon the part of the path maximally stimulated. Such behavior can often be elicited from self-stimulating animals, but it does not appear to be essential.

Stimulation of the brain to fire the motivation system and especially of the part involved in motor facilitation would be expected to make animals active, and such activity is usually observed in animals that stimulate themselves. Christopher and Butter (1968), for example, found that locomotor exploration was evoked from all 28 self-stimulation points in their sample and from none of the points that did not furnish self-stimulation. Other evoked behaviors like grooming, burrowing, and feeding, also observed by these investigators, were not exclusively associated with self-stimulation points, but they did occur at many of those points. Plutchik, McFarland and Robinson (1966) considered the behavior evoked by brain stimulation in monkeys to be related to the motivation generated.

It has been shown (Coons & Cruce, 1968; J. Mendelson, 1967; Mogenson & Morgan, 1967; see also "Interaction of Rewarding Stimulation with Natural Rewards" earlier in this chapter) that some rats will stimulate themselves more vigorously at lower levels of current if they are provided with a goal object for consummatory behavior that the stimulation elicits. That is, if the stimulation makes a satiated rat drink, the rat will press a bar for stimulation when water is present, but if the voltage is near the threshold for drinking it will not press when water is absent. This result may be explained on the assumption that sensory input from the presence of a reward like water lowers the threshold of motivational neurons, even though it cannot normally fire them when the animal is satiated for water. Electrical stimulation near the threshold also lowers the threshold of the pathway, and the combination of both inputs causes the system to fire, although either input alone could not. Firing the system has the usual effects of eliciting consummatory behavior and repetition of responses that occurred just before the system fired.

Because of the mutual inhibition postulated between parts of the approach and avoidance

systems, strong stimulation of one will suppress the activity of the other. The central parts of the avoidance system are no doubt more easily fired by peripheral stimulation of an unpleasant nature than are the central parts of the approach system by attractive peripheral stimuli; avoidance would thus normally take precedence over approach responses. Electrical stimulation of the pathway to the hold mechanism, however, may well reverse the dominance, so that the switch mechanism may remain inhibited during mildly noxious input. This effect would explain the results of Cox and Valenstein (1965) and others who have found that rats ignored mild shock during self-stimulation.

Mutual inhibition may also explain why rats will press a bar for stimulation that fires both approach and avoidance parts of the motivational system. If the neurons of the approach system adapt to continued stimulation more quickly than do those of the aversive system, (which would probably have survival value), the rewarding effect may change to a punishing one as the hold mechanism loses inhibitory control over the switch mechanism.

The proposed model cannot account in any simple way for the behavior of those self-stimulating animals that either avoid or show no interest in brain stimulation without having recently been "primed." Priming apparently is necessary to induce what amounts to a drive, possibly a state of discomfort or fear that can be alleviated by the onset of another burst of stimulation. Such discomfort could arise from the rebound of part of the aversive system that is inhibited during the stimulation, another way of expressing the old idea that some rats continue to self-stimulate "because it hurts to stop." The idea is not inconsistent with the model, but its detailed incorporation would be even more speculative than the material presented so far.

Summary

Electrical stimulation of many parts of the limbic and extrapyramidal systems has been found to act as a reward, so that animals will perform a response that turns on the stimulation (self-stimulation). In general the best self-stimulation results have been obtained from electrodes in the medial forebrain bundle in the lateral and posterior hypothalamic regions in all mammals so far tested; in pigeons the best results come from parts of the striatum, though hypothalamic stimulation is also effective.

More detailed mapping studies in the rat and cat have shown that self-stimulation can be elicited from the ventral part of the tegmentum, the more medial nuclei of the amygdala, and the lateral part of the hippocampus, though stimulation of other parts of these structures may engender avoidance of the stimulation.

It has proved extremely difficult to influence the rate of self-stimulation other than transiently by making lesions in pathways leading from the electrode site. Sometimes a lesion in a more anterior structure even increases the rate of self-stimulation. It thus seems likely that the effect of the stimulation is distributed to other parts of the brain through very diffuse paths.

No very clear relationship between self-stimulation and the electrical activity recorded in various limbic structures has been observed. In some studies it appeared that self-stimulation occurred only during spike-and-wave or other forms of seizure activity, but it is now believed that this correlation was incidental and, in fact, it seems that animals respond better when seizure discharges are controlled by anticonvulsant drugs.

It has proved possible to motivate all forms of instrumental behavior by using brain stimulation as a reward. Rats will learn mazes, make discriminations, cross electrified grids, and press levers for brain stimulation reward. During stimulation at rewarding points, animals are less sensitive to shock and to fear-provoking stimuli.

Degree of deprivation of food or water and so on has no profound effect upon self-stimulation, though detectable changes in performance have been reported as a result of food and water deprivation and of manipulation of the sex drive by castration and hormones.

A more impressive demonstration of the relationship between self-stimulation and other drives is the frequency with which eating, drinking, copulation, grooming, and other species-and drive-specific behavior can be evoked from electrodes for self-stimulation. Although self-stimulation and drive elicitation can be obtained from the same electrode sites, they can be dissociated in various ways: Frequently the thresholds for the effects are different, and it is sometimes possible to obtain only self-stimulation by using short trains of stimulation and only consummatory behavior by using longer trains of suitable intensity.

Additive effects of goal objects and brain stimulation have also been noted. Rats that eat or drink when stimulated may be induced to stimulate themselves at currents that are normally below threshold if food or water is available. Rats with electrodes in the medial forebrain bundle often fail to eat if they are given the choice of eating or stimulating themselves with a strong current.

One of the puzzles of self-stimulation is the rapid rate of extinction when the stimulation is withheld; after only a few minutes many animals show no revival of interest in the situation, which makes it relatively difficult to run many self-stimulating animals on schedules that result in spaced reinforcement (for example, interval schedules or DRL). Spaced trials are also ineffective with some animals. If "free" stimulation (or "priming") is given just before a run, however, the drive may be reestablished.

A number of experiments have tested various hypotheses about this effect. It has been shown, for example, that rats stop drinking from a dipper when it runs dry as quickly as they stop pressing a bar when it no longer turns on brain stimulation, suggesting that rapid extinction is caused by the immediacy of reinforcement. Other experiments suggest that self-stimulation is motivated by a drive that itself depends upon brain stimulation. When the stimulation is withheld, the motivation to obtain more stimulation rapidly ebbs. A variant of this theory is that stimulation produces an aversive aftereffect in some rats, which is abolished during further stimulation. In the absence of stimulation the aversive aftereffect soon dies away.

Some evidence that may be considered to support the latter suggestion has been provided by experiments showing that some rats have an ambivalent or outright antagonistic attitude toward the self-stimulation situation except when they are "primed." A similar conclusion may be drawn from many animals' toleration of rewarding stimulation only for short periods. If the stimulation is turned on and left on by the experimenter, the animals learn to turn it off.

Experiments to determine the secondary-reinforcing properties of rewarding stimulation have yielded inconclusive results; it is clear that the effect, if it exists at all, is not very great. In any case secondary reinforcement would be difficult to observe if many animals in the sample acquired a negative attitude toward the situation during periods when they were not receiving stimulation.

The effects of drugs upon self-stimulation have been widely studied. In general, the results indicate that the self-stimulation system is adrenergic. The threshold is elevated by chlorpromazine and other drugs that interfere with adrenergic transmission and lowered by adrenergic drugs like amphetamine. It is known that there is an adrenergic pathway along the medial forebrain bundle. Drugs that enhance cholinergic transmission have an adverse effect upon self-stimulation as a rule, but anticholinergic drugs have little effect, suggesting that the cholinergic system normally plays little part in the phenomenon but that, when it is overactive, it has an inhibitory effect.

Behavior depends upon motivation, but the exact relationship between them has never been elucidated, at least from a neurophysiological point of view. Theories of motivation have tended to concentrate on the relationship between such anatomical structures as the hypothalamus and motivational states like hunger and fear. There is practically no experimental evidence on the ways in which the activity of these structures might control goal-directed behavior.

J. Olds and Olds have speculated that certain innate approach and avoidance responses are elicited by activity in opposing motivational systems and that instrumental responses can be added to the repertoire as a result of a reinforcement process that sensitizes neurons whose firing has led to a successful response. They have paid little attention to the role of sensory input in their model.

Grastyán and his colleagues have also proposed a dual motivational process, in which the approach mechanism is called a "pull" system and the avoidance mechanism a "push" system. A successful instrumental response is incorporated into the animal's behavior because when it is made there is a rebound burst of neural activity in the motivational system as parts of it that were previously inhibited by the drive state are released. The response thus becomes conditioned to any stimuli present in the environment at the time when drive reduction occurs.

Several theories have been devoted to showing that motivation can elicit species-specific behavior aimed at achieving appropriate goals, and Deutsch has gone farther to suggest that new responses can be linked to the motivational energy that, according to these theories, normally flows in the channels leading to the species-specific behavior. In Deutsch's model the addition of new responses is achieved through activity in certain postulated pathways, called "reinforcement paths," leading from motivational to motor neurons.

Finally, a model has been presented that incorporates the idea that motivational activity can make use of a "cognitive map," in which the animal stores information on the usual outcomes of various responses in different situations. When a response-stimulus combination leads to firing of the motivational system (by leading to reward or punishment), this information is also stored in the form of a connection from the active "cognitive" elements to the active motivational elements. If the possibility that the previously successful response will be made again in the same situation subsequently arises, the motivational system is excited by the acquired link, and the response tendency is facilitated.

CHAPTER 19

THE FRONTAL-LOBE SYNDROME

Throughout most of this book we have dealt with systems defined in terms of behavioral function, rather than anatomically, but the effects of frontal-lobe lesions are not understood sufficiently well to be treated in this way. In fact, the deficits produced by such lesions probably result from interference with several different systems, and to lump them together under the title of "frontal-lobe syndrome" may itself be somewhat misleading.

Most other lesions of the neocortex produce relatively well-defined deficits of cognitive or perceptual function; lesions of the frontal lobe, however, influence complex motivational processes, and we can perhaps regard this area as a link between the cortex and subcortical systems involved in motivation.

EARLY THEORIES OF FRONTAL-LOBE FUNCTION

For many years the frontal lobes were believed to serve the very highest intellectual functions. Gall, the anatomist turned phrenologist, considered intelligence to be localized in that area, ostensibly because that is where his intelligent friends had bumps on their skulls, but he was undoubtedly influenced in his choice by the fact that the frontal lobes constitute a much greater fraction of the brain of the primate and especially of *Homo sapiens*, than of apparently less intelligent animals. Gross and Weiskrantz (1964) have provided a summary of nineteenth-century experimental work on the effects of frontal ablations. Many of the results were inconsistent or contradictory, and it is clear from our present vantage point that some resulted from faulty surgical procedures. According to these early experiments, the frontal lobes were variously implicated in attention, volition, motor functioning, personality and emotion, perception, and association. There was no strong evidence from animal experiments to support the idea that intelligence was localized there, but neither this lack nor the fact that nobody had any clear idea of what intelligence was could deter some people from believing that the human frontal lobes were the seat of intelligence.

Jacobsen, in the late 1930s, launched a more systematic investigation of the relationship between the frontal lobes and intelligence, using primates as experimental animals. His most important finding was that lesions in what used to be called the "prefrontal cortex" (the anterior frontal cortex and not, as might be supposed, some tissue anterior to the frontal lobes) produced marked impairment on *delayed-response tasks*. In the typical delayed-response procedure the animal is shown a piece of food, which is then hidden under one of two (sometimes more) identical cups. After a delay the animal is allowed to choose one of the cups. Jacobsen's "frontal" monkeys were able to perform normally on discrimination tasks but failed whenever a task involving delay was introduced. Chimpanzees that had learned to use sticks to reach for food before ablation of the anterior frontal cortex could perform the response after operation only if both food and sticks were in the visual field simultaneously (Jacobsen, 1936). On the basis of these experiments, Jacobsen concluded that the anterior frontal lobes were necessary for immediate memory or for the use of symbolic memory images.

Before operation one of Jacobsen's female chimpanzees had a temper tantrum every time it made a mistake and eventually developed a severe experimental neurosis, but after the operation it became much calmer and made many mistakes with perfect equanimity. Hearing of this change, the courageous neurosurgeon Moniz had the idea of cutting the connections between the frontal lobes and the rest of the brain (*frontal lobotomy*) for the relief of human psychosis, a procedure that the advent of psychoactive drugs has fortunately rendered almost obsolete.

DEFICITS IN DELAYED RESPONSE

Before turning to the numerous experiments that have been done on impairments produced by the frontal-lobe lesions, we should first note that this area is the only part of the neocortex—and almost the only part of the brain—that seems indispensable for delayed-response behavior in monkeys (Rosvold & Szwarcbart, 1964). Although large lesions in any part of the lateral frontal cortex will produce the deficit, in the rhesus macaque monkey the greatest effects are obtained from lesions near the *sulcus principalis* (see Figure 17.8A). The impairment is much less, even negligible, from lesions of the medial or ventral parts of the lobe.

A variant of the delayed-response test, often used because of its convenience, is the *delayed-alternation* test. The reward is alternated from side to side with a fixed delay between the trials, but the subject does not see the cup being baited. He must remember where food was found on the previous trial and choose the other cup. This problem appears to be more difficult than a simple delayed response. Deficits in the delayed-alternation test occurred after lesions in the cingulate cortex (K. H. Pribram, Wilson & Connors, 1962) and in the hippocampus (Orbach, Milner & Rasmussen, 1960), as well as after *principalis* lesions, in monkeys. Both delayed alternation and delayed response are impaired in monkeys after lesions (or during stimulation) of the head of the caudate nucleus (Rosvold & Delgado, 1956; Battig, Rosvold & Mishkin, 1960), a region that receives connections from the lateral surface of the frontal lobe (Nauta, 1964), and after subthalamic lesions in the cat (Adey, Walter & Lindsley, 1962). The subthalamic nuclei receive connections from the caudate nucleus. In the cat, however, frontal-lobe lesions produce only a slight impairment of delayed response (Warren, 1964), but hip-

pocampal lesions are supposed to produce a more severe deficit (Karmos & Grastyán, 1962).

Very large lesions in the medial thalamus also impair delayed response in monkeys (S. Schulman, 1964), but they must extend well beyond the borders of the *medialis dorsalis* nucleus, which projects to the frontal cortex. Several earlier attempts failed to demonstrate any deficit when the lesion was confined to the *medialis dorsalis* (Peters, Rosvold & Mirsky, 1956; Chow, 1954a). The value of Schulman's finding is somewhat diminished by the fact that his large lesions also produced other deficits. After the operation, his monkeys required several times as many trials to reacquire a simple black-white discrimination as they had required during the initial preoperative learning. The thalamic lesions are difficult to understand because lesions near the *sulcus principalis* produce retrograde degeneration in only part of the *medialis dorsalis* nucleus, but destruction of either that part or the whole nucleus has no effect whatever upon delayed-response performance.

CONNECTIONS OF THE FRONTAL LOBES

Nauta (1964) has pointed out that most of the places from which delayed performance can be disturbed are part of a frontolimbic system. He has demonstrated that many of the cortical neurons dorsal to the *sulcus principalis*, and in the depths of the sulcus itself contribute to a bundle of fibers that runs through the cingulate region and ends in the cingulate, retrosplenial, and presubicular cortex (see Figure 17.10). These regions in turn send connections to the hippocampus. There are also projections from the anterior frontal cortex to the head of the caudate nucleus and to the hypothalamus, thalamus, and midbrain tegmentum. Nauta has suggested that the anterior frontal region constitutes a neocortical extension of the limbic system, the dorsal part being more closely associated with the hippocampus and the ventral part with the amygdala. It has been suggested that the limbic system has something to do with the production of innate species-specific behavior or motivation of learned responses. If the frontal lobe should be considered part of the same system, we might speculate that it has something to do with the learned regulation of motivation. There have been frequent suggestions that it has an inhibitory effect upon innate motivational patterns and that people deprived of frontal-lobe function are impulsive, uninhibited, irascible, euphoric, or otherwise emotionally labile.

FURTHER EXAMINATION OF DELAYED-RESPONSE DEFICITS

Jacobsen's simple hypothesis that the delayed-response deficit was caused by impairment of immediate memory was called into question quite soon by Malmo (1942) and Finan (1942). Malmo found that "frontal" monkeys could succeed on the delayed-response test if they were kept in the dark during the delay interval, suggesting that the animals were very susceptible to retroactive inhibition (erasing of recent memories by new stimuli). This view is supported by the fact that monkeys with lesions of the anterior frontal lobe are both hyperactive and hyperreactive (French & Harlow, 1955), and therefore may find it more difficult to concentrate on the stimuli when the food is being hidden and may be more vulnerable to distracting stimuli during the delay interval.

Finan found that, when "frontal" monkeys were allowed to make one rewarded response before the delay, they showed no deficit in delayed response. This finding too may indicate that the "frontal" monkey fails because it does not normally pay enough attention to the stimuli during their presentation. In any event, it is clear that the animal's short-term memory is still capable of functioning.

Other experiments that seem to support the hypothesis that the deficit results from hyperactivity and distractability have involved the effects of sedatives upon delayed-response performance. Wade (1947) and K. H. Pribram (1950) gave small doses of barbiturate to monkeys and baboons and found that the performance of the "frontal" groups improved. Prib

ran also found that increased food deprivation helped the "frontal" animals. The idea that normal monkeys learned the delayed response by maintaining a body orientation toward the correct food well and that the frontal monkeys were not able to stand still long enough to do so has not received experimental support. Some "frontal" monkeys are not hyperactive and still cannot learn the delayed response.

Mishkin and Pribram (1956) tried other variants of the delayed response and found that monkeys with lateral frontal lesions were not impaired when only one food well was used and food was sometimes placed there and sometimes not. A monkey saw (and heard) the peanut dropped into the cup on the "go" trials and was shown an empty hand on the "no-go" trials. If the subject responded within five seconds after the screen went up in a "no-go" trial, the trial was repeated until the monkey waited the full time. As long as spatial concepts like right and left were not involved, these "frontal" monkeys were not seriously impaired on delayed-response tasks. When the peanut was placed in one cup as a signal to "go" and in another cup as a signal to "stay," however, they could not learn; it was not therefore the "go"-"no-go" aspect of the problem that made it easier for them. Presumably it was easier to remember whether or not a peanut had been presented than to remember where it had been presented.

These results led to another experiment in which, instead of having to remember where the bait was put, the monkeys had to learn the object under which it was hidden. In the alternation version of this test, the food was placed first under one object and then under the other; the position of the objects was varied randomly. "Frontal" monkeys were just as bad at this task as at the standard spatial delayed alternation.

In another experiment Mishkin and Pribram (1955) compared monkeys on the standard left-right delayed-alternation test, an up-down delayed-alternation test, and a "go"-"no-go" delayed-alternation test. Those with lateral frontal lesions failed all tests when the limit was set at 600 trials, but they did reach 88 correct in the last 100 trials for the "go"–"no-go" test, compared with chance scores on the spatial (right-left and up-down) tests. Although in most experiments ventral frontal lesions have interfered with "go"–"no-go" tests, one animal with ventral frontal lesions in this experiment showed little impairment on any of the delayed-response tasks.

The deficit in delayed response is a highly reliable consequence of lesions of the lateral frontal lobe in monkeys, but it may not be the deficit that will tell us most about frontal-lobe function. For one thing, it is quite mild in some animals, like the cat and the chimpanzee, and it does not appear at all in man, presumably because of the possibility of verbal mediation. Other frontal-lobe deficits appear more regularly in all species and can sometimes be dissociated from the delayed-response deficit.

Perseveration After Frontal-Lobe Lesions

K. H. Pribram (1960) compared monkeys ablated in the frontal and temporal lobes on a very complex learning task. The first problem was a straightforward object discrimination, except that, instead of the tray having only the usual 2 food wells, it had 12, and the two objects were placed over different wells randomly from trial to trial. When a monkey had learned the correct object, the problem was reversed, and the monkey had to learn to choose the other object. Then another object was introduced, and each of the three became the positive object in turn until it had been learned by the monkey. Then a fourth object was introduced and the process repeated until 12 objects were on the board. Pribram found that the "frontal" monkeys made more repeated errors than did normal or "temporal" monkeys; they would choose the same wrong object many times. This result suggests that perhaps they found it more difficult to eliminate previous learning than normal or temporal monkeys.

In another experiment that points in the same direction, K. H. Pribram (1958) used a Skinnerian bar-pressing situation. Monkeys learned a 40 : 1 fixed-ratio schedule when a red light was

on and a four-minute fixed-interval schedule when a green light was on. Then the light cues were discontinued, and the two schedules were alternated (that is, when the monkey had received a reward for pressing 40 times, it had to wait four minutes for its next reward; then it would return to FR 40 and so on). Normal and "temporal" monkeys adapted to the alternation by pressing faster during the fixed-ratio schedule and pressing only toward the end of the fixed-interval schedule; the monkeys with frontal ablations did not.

In an early experiment with "frontal" dogs, Lawicka (1957) demonstrated impairment of inhibition that could not be ascribed to hyperactivity. She noticed that dogs with frontal lesions barked much less than normal dogs, and she therefore taught them to bark for food when a metronome sounded. A bell was then introduced as an inhibitory stimulus; the bell plus the metronome meant no food for barking. Other metronome rates were also given as negative stimuli. Normal dogs could master these discriminations and barked only when the correct metronome rate was presented, but the "frontal" dogs persisted in barking to all stimuli.

Warren (1964) has found considerable deficits in spatial-reversal learning in cats following lesions in the frontal lobe. The cats had to learn to go to a black object on the right and to ignore a white object on the left; the criterion was 11 correct in 12 consecutive trials. Then the reward was placed under the white object on the left and the cat had to learn the reversal according to the same criterion. An even greater impairment was found in "frontal" cats if the two objects were identical instead of black and white, especially if several reversals were made on the same day. If a new pair of objects was used each day, the difference between "frontal" and normal cats disappeared; all the subjects did even better when different objects were introduced at each left-right reversal.

Another test that brought out the differences between normal and "frontal" cats was one in which, on each day, one object was correct for 15 trials (regardless of position), then the other object was correct, then the right side was correct (regardless of the object on that side), and finally the left side was correct, each for 15 consecutive trials. In order to perform well on this test the animal had to be able to change its "set" rapidly.

Mishkin (1964) and various coworkers, have also found reversal-learning deficits in frontal-lobectomized monkeys. Brush, Mishkin, and Rosvold (1961) found, rather to their surprise, that monkeys with lateral frontal lesions were seriously impaired on object-discrimination learning sets. They attributed such impairment to difficulty in relinquishing an initial preference for certain objects. Such perseverative behavior did not make much difference on the first few problems, when all animals make many errors, but later, when the normal monkey had learned to switch to the correct object in one trial, the reluctance of the "frontal" monkey to give up its preference put it at a great disadvantage.

The hypothesis was tested by inducing a preference or an aversion for one object by presenting it alone, either with or without reward, for five trials before the discrimination trials. When a preferred object was correct in the later discrimination test, the "frontals" made very few errors, but when it was the negative object they made more errors than the normal monkeys. Similarly, when an aversion had been induced, the "frontal" monkeys did well later when it was the negative object but poorly when it was the positive object (Figure 19.1).

Mishkin, Prockop, and Rosvold (1962) then tried the effect of frontal lesions on one-trial learning or delayed matching from sample. This test is very similar to that just described, except that only one trial is given with the sample object alone (either baited or unbaited), followed by a single-choice trial between the sample and a new object. In this test it was found that baiting the sample had little effect, for the monkey nearly always chose the novel object. The normal monkeys learned to overcome this tendency, but the "frontal" monkeys never did. Mishkin (1964) also reported that

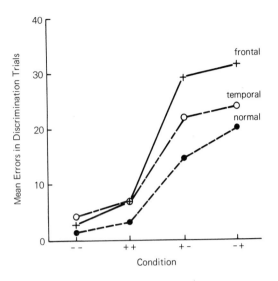

Figure 19.1 Mean errors under different conditions of pretraining and discrimination learning for monkeys with lesions of the frontal or temporal cortex and for normal monkeys. In the condition represented by − − the unrewarded object during pretraining was also the negative object during discrimination; + + means that the rewarded object during pretraining was also the positive object during discrimination; + − and − + were reversal conditions in which the previously rewarded objects were negative during discrimination and the previously negative objects were positive during discrimination. Errors on the first discrimination trial were not counted. (After Brush, Mishkin & Resvold, 1961.)

"frontal" monkeys suffered a deficit on spatial-reversal learning tests, much as the frontal-lobectomized cats in Warren's experiment had done.

These results led Mishkin to propose that the deficits of "frontal" animals could be explained in terms of a perseverative tendency. Whatever "set" the frontal subjects brought to the situation was more resistant to change by external rewards or punishments than was that of a normal animal. After comparing "lateral frontal" monkeys with "orbital frontal" monkeys (see Figure 19.2), however, Mishkin found that this explanation could not be extended to delayed-response performance because the "orbital" monkeys were much less severely impaired on this test than the "lateral frontal" monkeys, although on almost all the other tests—for example, "go"-"no-go" tests, ob-

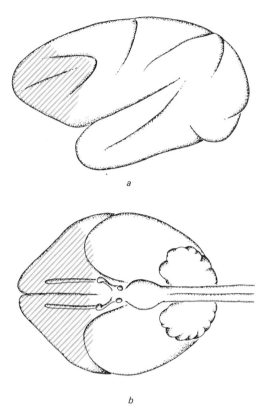

Figure 19.2 (a) Lateral view of a monkey brain, showing location of the lateral frontal lesion. (b) Ventral view of a monkey brain, showing location of the orbital frontal lesion.

ject-discrimination learning set tests, object-discrimination reversals, and delayed matching from sample—they were much more impaired. The only test on which the two groups of animals did not differ was a left-right reversal problem, suggesting to Mishkin that the "lateral frontal" monkeys showed perseveration of central sets in more attenuated form than did "orbital frontal" monkeys but had additional difficulty with spatial concepts that the "orbital" group did not have. Hence their more severe deficit on the normal spatial delayed-response problem.

Susceptibility of "Frontal" Animals to Distraction

Not all the evidence favors Mishkin's analysis, however. Buffery (1965, 1967) has shown that baboons with frontal-lobe lesions show deficits in nonspatial delayed matching from sample that cannot be attributed to perseveration. In one experiment the baboons were placed in a Skinner box with five panels that could be illuminated by various colored lights. First one panel was illuminated (the sample), and then two or more of the other panels were illuminated, one of them with the same colored light as the sample. Pressing this panel delivered a reward.

It was found that even when the sample panel remained illuminated until the animals made their response, the "frontal" baboons still had some difficulty choosing from four illuminated panels. This difficulty was much more severe, of course, if the sample panel was extinguished before the other panels were lit up. Buffery argued that the confusion of the "frontal" baboon when confronted with several discriminanda supports the hypothesis that animals cannot learn to pay attention to the relevant stimuli. In other words, the data support the old distractibility theory of frontal-lobe impairment.

In another test, slightly reminiscent of K. H. Pribram's multiple-discrimination test, Buffery gave the baboons first a simple discrimination and then on the next day added another negative object. This object was either a replica of the first negative object or a novel object; for some animals, both negative objects were novel on the second day. On the third day another negative object was added. Again it was either the same as the other two or different, or a complete set of three new negative objects was introduced. This process was continued until as many as seven negative objects were present. The baboons with lesions of the frontal lobe made many errors when there were many novel objects. As in Mishkin's experiments, the animals were more interested in exploring the novel negative objects than in obtaining food from beneath the familiar object. Clearly they had no serious memory loss because they could distinguish the new from the familiar. Their deficit arose from the operation of a motivation different from those of the normal or "temporal" control animals. The latter groups extinguished their exploratory tendency before the end of the experiment.

Although Buffery favored the distractibility hypothesis as an explanation for the delayed-response deficit in frontal monkeys, one of his own experiments did not support this conclusion. Buffery pointed out, as had Gross and Weiskrantz (1964), that keeping the monkeys in the dark during the delay interval or giving sedative drugs may make the problem easier for normal animals, as well as for "frontals," but that the former are already performing nearly perfectly and cannot therefore demonstrate improvement. In order to overcome this flaw in previous experiments, Buffery used a "titration" method of presenting the delayed-response test. If the animal made two successive correct choices, the delay interval was increased slightly; if it made a mistake the interval was decreased. In this way, the animals were all working at about their performance limit and any change in the experimental conditions that made the stimuli more confusing or distracting should have affected the "frontal" animals more than the other groups. This prediction was not borne out. When the number of discriminanda was increased from two to four, the "frontal" group (which was performing at much shorter intervals than were the normal and "temporal" control groups) was less affected than the other groups.

The sample of experiments with "frontal" animals summarized here is only a fraction of the total, but it seems representative and likely to give some idea of how the search for a parsimonious explanation of the deficits is progressing.

LESIONS OF THE FRONTAL LOBE IN MAN

Perhaps the most impressive finding in patients with frontal-lobe injury is that they make perfectly normal scores on most standard intelligence tests (Hebb & Penfield, 1940). There are, however, subtle and relatively unquantified personality changes. The patients are described as lacking initiative, planning ability, or foresight, and sometimes they are unreliable, rude

or tactless, frivolous, irascible, and so on. These characteristics may prevent them from holding a job for long, despite their normal "intelligence."

There are a few behavioral tests on which performance is impaired by frontal-lobe damage. Most of them seem to involve frequent shifting from one goal or set of responses to another. Others, including the one to be described next, seem to involve disturbances of perception.

Teuber and Mishkin (1954) tested a large number of men with gunshot wounds for ability to set a luminous rod into a vertical position in a dark room when the chair on which they sat was tilted at various angles to the vertical. Those with wounds of entry in the frontal part of the skull performed significantly worse on the test than did those with wounds in other parts of the head or with damage to peripheral nerves. Teuber speculated that the frontal lobes might be part of a frontostriatal mechanism for compensating the visual system during changes of posture. There may be some connection between this deficit and auditory impairments found in monkeys with frontal lesions (Weiskrantz & Mishkin, 1958; see "The Auditory System," Chapter 12). The cortical projection area for the vestibular branch of the eighth cranial nerve overlaps that of the acoustic branch to a considerable extent.

Many of these same patients were also given several short-term memory tests by Ghent, Mishkin, and Teuber (1962). The tests involved both verbal (for example, memory for digits) and nonverbal (for example, memory for visual forms) problems, but the "frontal" subjects were in no way inferior to the other subjects with head wounds.

On the other hand, Prisko (cited by B. Milner, 1964) did find a form of memory deficit in patients with large unilateral frontal lesions. She used a test similar to one developed by Konorski for use with animals. Verbal mediation (which human patients may use to overcome delayed-response deficits) is of no assistance in this test. Two stimuli—clicks or flashes at different rates, colors, tones, or nonsense figures—are presented one after the other with an interval of up to one minute between them; the subject must say whether or not they are identical. For the first three types of stimuli (rates of flashes or clicks and different shades or red), the "frontal" patients performed worse than patients with lesions of comparable size in the parietotemporal lobe. They did not perform significantly worse when the stimuli were two tones, and their performance was almost normal—and considerably better than that of "right temporal" patients—when the stimuli were nonsense figures. It is notable that a new pair of nonsense figures was used for each trial, whereas for the other tests each value of the stimulus was used for more than one trial, suggesting that the "frontal" patients far from having a short-term memory deficit, remembered the stimuli too well and confused earlier trials with the latest one, a form of *proactive interference*.

Nichols and Hunt (1940) studied one patient with large frontal lesions very intensively and formed the impression that he often had trouble switching from one task to another. The patient completely failed to solve a problem similar to the reversal tasks that give difficulty to "frontal" animals. Five playing cards were placed face down in front of him, and he had

to find the ace of spades. This card was placed twice at the extreme right and then twice at the extreme left, and so on in a double-alternation sequence. It does not take long for most other patients to catch on to this pattern, but the frontal patient did not do so.

B. Milner (1963) has established very clearly, with large groups of subjects, that frontal patients are significantly impaired on a card-sorting task developed by Grant and Berg (1948). In this test four cards are placed in front of the subject, one with a red triangle, the second with two green stars, the third with three yellow crosses, and the fourth with four blue circles printed on them (Figure 19.3). The patient was then given a pack of 128 cards to be sorted into piles below the sample cards. The cards in the pack had designs similar to those in the samples, varying along the dimensions of color, form, and number. For example, there might be a card with two red crosses, which would resemble the first sample in color, the second in number, and the third in form. If the subject placed the card below the first sample, the examiner would say "right" if the sorting principle was color, and the subject had to learn that all the cards were then to be sorted according to their color; the other features were to be ignored. When 10 successive cards had

Figure 19.3 The card-sorting test developed by Grant and Berg (1948). The subject has to sort the pack of cards into four piles so that they match the sample cards laid out as shown, either in color, number of symbols, or form of symbols. (From B. Milner, 1963.)

 red
green
yellow
blue

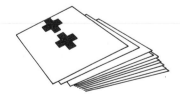

been correctly sorted, the principle was changed, without warning, to form. Color responses were then called "wrong," and the subject had to discover what the new sorting principle was. After he had again sorted 10 successive cards correctly, the principle was changed to number, once again without warning. The sequence of three sorting principles was then repeated once more. The subject continued until he had sorted 10 cards correctly in all three categories twice or until he ran out of cards.

Patients with unilateral lesions in the dorsolateral frontal lobe were significantly impaired on this test. They usually learned the first sorting principle (though some had an initial preference that they were never able to abandon) but then found it difficult or impossible to change when the second principle was required. They made more perseverative errors (choices that would have been correct if the principle had not been changed) and achieved fewer categories than did the control group of patients with posterior cortical lesions. Rather surprisingly, patients with orbital frontal lesions did not differ in performance from the controls. The "frontal" patients were not at all incapable of solving the problem intellectually; many of them in fact commented at the outset that the cards could be sorted to form, color, or number, but once they became fixated on one of the solutions they seemed to forget that any other was possible.

Luria and Homskaya (1964) have demonstrated a dissociation between the verbal and other motor responses of patients with large tumors in the frontal lobe (which probably damage much more than the frontal neocortex). If such a patient was instructed to press with his right hand when a green signal light came on and with his left hand when a red light came on, he would do it successfully a few times and then would press with only one hand to all signals or would press at random. If he was asked to repeat what he was supposed to do, he could repeat his instructions perfectly; he could say "right" when the green signal was presented and "left" when the red signal was presented, but he still did not press with the

correct hand. "Frontal" patients also had trouble with conflict situations in which they had to give a short press to a long signal and a long press to a short signal. They soon reverted to mimicking the signal. When they had to press weakly to one cue and strongly to another, the patients could succeed only for a few trials, and then they pressed strongly to every signal, even though they could still call out "strong" or "weak" appropriately to each cue. The verbal instruction just did not seem to penetrate to the motor system. This dissociation between verbal and other responses is sometimes found in normal people, who may say "left" yet turn right, for example.

B. Milner (1964) found that "frontal" patients were unexpectedly poor at the "bolt head" stylus-maze test compared with all other groups with cortical lesions except those with severe memory loss resulting from bilateral medial temporal-lobe lesions. During testing it became clear that the "frontal" patients were making different kinds of mistakes from those made by the other patients. Instead of returning to the previous point on the maze when they made an error, they would plunge ahead or move along diagonals (against the rules) or would retrace the path along which they had come. They knew that they should not do these things but appeared unable to control their impulsive actions.

It may be that the "frontal" patients had the one aim of reaching the end of the maze and found it difficult to inhibit this goal when it conflicted with some other value system like the rules established for the test. When the numbers of "broken rules" were counted for patients with different lesions, it was found that the "frontal" patients had very significantly more than any other group.

These findings augment the anecdotal evidence that "frontal" patients have difficulty in changing their behavior when it ceases to be appropriate. As with many animals with frontal-lobe lesions, the effect of external motivation seems to be weakened, or, more exactly, when several conflicting motivations must be taken into account the patients have difficulty in switching from one to another.

Summary

There has been no experimental support for the idea that the frontal lobes are the seat of intelligence, an assumption based on the fact that the most intelligent animals have the largest frontal lobes. In subhuman primates one of the most consistent effects of bilateral lesions of the frontal lobes is impairment of delayed-response performance. Lesions of the caudate nuclei or very large lesions of the medial thalamus that include the area projecting to the frontal lobes are almost the only other lesions that interfere with simple delayed-response performance. A more difficult variant of the test, delayed alternation, is impaired, in addition, by lesions of either the cingulate cortex or the hippocampus.

The delayed-response deficit was at first attributed to loss of immediate memory, but it was soon shown that monkeys with frontal lobectomies could remember well enough under some conditions. If they were kept in darkness during the delay interval, for example, they performed much better, as they did also when allowed to make one reinforced response before the delay test. Sedatives also counteracted the effect of frontal lesions upon delayed response. A simpler form of the test, which involves remembering not in which of alternative places food is hidden but only whether food has been presented or not, was not impaired by frontal-lobe lesions.

It has been found that the most important part of the frontal lobe for delayed-response performance is the lateral surface near the sulcus principalis; lesions of the more ventral orbital cortex have little effect.

A great many experiments have indicated that "frontal" animals, including man, are perseverative. The subjects find it difficult to change from one solution of a problem or one form of response to a different one. Probably this difficulty means that they are slow to extinguish a learned response, perhaps because of a higher frustration tolerance.

Perseveration shows up particularly in reversal-learning problems and in other problems in which a previously preferred response must be inhibited. Deficits in acquiring object-discrimination learning sets may also be related to perseveration. "Frontal" monkeys do not learn to abandon their initial preference for one object as quickly as do normal monkeys on each trial. This slow learning may help them slightly when their preference is for the correct object, but many errors result when their preference happens to be for the incorrect object.

In addition to this perseverative tendency, "frontal" animals perform badly when they are confronted with a choice of many stimuli. This confusion may result partly from a difficulty in learning to pay attention to relevant stimuli and possibly also from a failure to inhibit curiosity about unfamiliar objects.

Frontal damage in human patients has very little effect upon their performance on standard intelligence tests, but some deficits resembling those shown by animals can be detected by special tests. One such test involves the ability to change "set" (in this case a card-sorting principle) without warning whenever the tester pronounces the previously correct mode of responding incorrect.

Although there is no evidence of short-term memory impairment in "frontal" patients, they do perform badly on some tests that involve comparison of stimuli presented about a minute apart. When new stimuli are used for each comparison trial there is no deficit; the problem may thus be that the subject has trouble keeping recent memories separate. He may not be able to distinguish the traces of stimuli given during previous trials from the trace of the first stimulus of the current trial. Some such difficulty could also explain the deficits in delayed response and delayed alternation in the "frontal" monkey.

Frontal patients are often found to be impulsive and incapable of responding according to rules that they can nevertheless verbalize. It seems possible that, just as the motor cortex is important for increasing the flexibility of a well-organized subcortical motor system, the frontal cortex has the function of increasing the flexibility of a well-organized subcortical motivation system. In that case, the frontal lobes could be responsible for switching in and out the multiple and sometimes contradictory motivations required to adjust to the complex rules and regulations of social living. In support of this idea that the frontal cortex plays a role in motivation are its strong connections to many limbic structures, such as the hippocampus, amygdala, and hypothalamus. These structures are known to have important motivational functions.

PART SIX

MEMORY
AND
LEARNING

Since prehistoric times, man has been at least dimly aware that he remembers things, and when he has tried to explain the phenomenon it has usually been by analogy with physical information-storage methods familiar to him. For example, Aristotle in the fourth century B.C. apparently thought that in perception material particles entered the head from the perceived object and left impressions of themselves in the soft substance of the brain as a stylus does in clay or a seal in wax.

The early Greeks seem to have had no very clear appreciation of the relationship between memory and learning. Learning, for them, involved a deliberate effort to acquire information; memory was the incidental storage of everyday events. Plato considered that learning, or education, consisted of activating knowledge that was innately immanent. In other words, a student could learn only what was in a sense already represented in his mind; an idea that is not as preposterous as it sounds at first and that has its counterpart among present-day learning theories (those that attribute learning to the elimination of unsuccessful responses, for example).

There was no great advance in theories of memory or learning for the next 2,000 years until Descartes introduced his "hydraulic" model of the nervous system. Descartes thought that nerves were tubes or pores through which "vital spirits" flowed from the sense organs to the muscles, and he speculated that frequent use caused the tubes to become distended and reduced their resistance to flow, thus accounting for the formation of habits.

In more recent times, learning has been attributed to conductivity changes in a telephone-switchboard type of network and to wave-interference patterns (Lashley, 1942); with the advent of computers and tape recorders, it has even been suggested that cortical neurons form semistable "domains" like the iron molecules in a permanent magnet (Cragg & Temperley, 1955). The interference-pattern model has lately been revived following the discovery of the holograph, a method of three-dimensional photography using light-wave interference patterns (Longuet-Higgins, 1968; Gabor, 1968).

The most popular analogy for memory at present, however, is the mechanism of genetic storage, the elucidation of which has been the scientific success story of recent years. The analogy in this case is at least biological, rather than electrical or hydraulic, but that does not guarantee its validity, of course.

Experimental studies of learning and memory, as opposed to speculation, have a very short history. It is less than a century since Ebbinghaus (1885) published his pioneering work on the association of nonsense syllables. At about the same time, Lloyd Morgan (1894) and Hobhouse (1901) were exploring the possibilities of testing animal learning ability. Thorndike (1898) was probably the first to set up formal learning situations for animals in the laboratory, and very soon afterward Bechterev and Pavlov began to study conditioned reflexes, a limited but highly influential learning paradigm, in animals and man. The effects upon learning of physiological treatments like drugs and brain lesions were first taken up in a serious way by Lashley only about 50 years ago.

For many years after that, physiological learning experiments were strongly influenced by Pavlovian ideas. The cortex was systematically explored in an effort to find the loci of conditioning changes but with little success. During the last 10–15 years, however, a more fruitful line of communication has arisen between physiological psychologists and experimental psychologists working on problems of learning and memory. Physiological treatments that interfere selectively with different types of learning and forgetting have provided learning theorists with much information that is unobtainable from normal subjects.

In return, the more advanced learning theories that have emerged have been useful in shaping further physiological research. They have encouraged, for example, the shift in emphasis away from attempts to localize "engrams" and toward the investigation of basic changes that take place at the synaptic or metabolic level during the storage of information by the nervous system. These lines of investigation are proceeding in healthy fashion, but it will no doubt be several more years before any clear picture of the learning mechanism emerges from the data.

CHAPTER 20

PHYSIO-LOGICAL CONTRI-BUTIONS TO LEARNING THEORY

The growing mass of data emerging from experimental investigations of learning and memory during the last 80-90 years has revealed a number of phenomena that may now be regarded as well established and relevant to theories of learning. Ebbinghaus (1885) confirmed with his nonsense-syllable learning experiments what had been clear all along to "common sense," that it is easier to learn a short list of items than a long one. We are so familiar with this fact that it seems trivial, but it demonstrates clearly that the human memory is not like that of a computer or a tape recorder, which keeps storing information until the space is full or the mechanism stopped. If the brain does store all its input, it is difficult to explain why short lists of items can be recalled after one presentation, whereas longer lists can be recalled only after many repetitions.

It has since been established that most people can store about seven bits of information in a single isolated trial (see G. A. Miller, 1956) but that, when a second list is stored immediately

thereafter, the ability to recall the first list is lost. These phenomena have generated the notion of a two-stage (at least) memory mechanism in which items are first stored in "immediate" memory, from which some are later transferred to a more permanent store.

A good example of immediate memory is the looking up and dialing of a telephone number that we do not expect to need again. By some lucky foresight of evolution, most people can retain the necessary seven digits long enough to dial, provided they are not distracted, but soon after the number has been used it is forgotten, and new numbers can be stored in immediate memory with little interference from earlier ones.

There is some retention, however, even in these cases. Both Hebb (1961) and Melton (1963) have shown that, if the same number is stored in immediate memory on several separate occasions, it will later be remembered more easily than other numbers presented for the first time.

Another example of immediate memory is the storing of words that you are performing at this moment in order to extract some meaning from this sentence. At the end of the sentence some clearing process takes place; the parts of speech of one sentence do not leak through to the next, as a rule.

If we want to retain a complex input for a longer time, we "rehearse" it. Once a number has been put into a long-term store and tagged as someone's telephone number, for example, it can be recalled as a unit, even after much interpolated activity, and each time that it is recalled the trace seems to be further strengthened.

Melton called this process of converting elements into larger complexes "chunking." "Chunks" can then become the elements for more complex memories still. If we know seven telephone numbers "by heart" and someone reads them out to us in a particular order, we can store them in immediate memory and recite back all 49 digits in the correct order after only one hearing (if we recognize them and do the necessary transformations). Melton's chunks correspond, of course, to concepts, which are,

427

according to Hebb (1949) patterns of stimuli for which neural representations ("cell assemblies," see Chapter 7) have been acquired by the organism; we must therefore assume that the elements of short-term storage are cell assemblies.

Another phenomenon related to the theory of a two-stage memory mechanism is the way in which certain procedures interfere with the memory of recently learned material. Müller & Pilzecker (1900) drew attention to the fact that, if a subject learned a long list of items (much beyond the immediate memory span) and was then given another list of similar items to learn shortly afterward, his memory of the first list would suffer. He would remember the first list better if he waited a day or two before learning the second list.

In other words, even after the information had been successfully transferred into a long-term store, it was still vulnerable to interference from the addition of further similar material to the store. The process by which information becomes more firmly established with the passage of time and able to withstand the addition of more information is called *consolidation*. Müller and Pilzecker suggested that the consolidation process might involve subcortical reverberation.

McDougall (1901) reviewed Müller and Pilzecker's paper and added his own suggestion that the retrograde amnesia caused by head injuries and concussion might also result from disruption of incompletely consolidated memory traces. After a severe head injury there is usually a complete memory loss covering a period of a few seconds or minutes immediately before the injury and a transient amnesia covering a longer period. W. R. Russell and Nathan (1946) studied 1,000 cases of head injury and found that about 700 of the patients had suffered permanent amnesia covering several seconds to half an hour preceding the injury, 130 had suffered permanent amnesia for longer than half an hour, and about the same number had suffered no amnesia at all. Presumably the differences were mainly caused by variations in the severity or type of injury, but even so they

imply a puzzling variability in the time it takes to consolidate a memory.

Reminiscence is another phenomenon that may be related to consolidation. A list of items that has been incompletely learned may be more successfully recalled several hours after the learning session than immediately after it. An interesting and probably related phenomenon discovered by Kleinsmith and Kaplan (1963) is that recall of material learned under low arousal is initially better than that of material learned under high arousal, but that after a long interval (perhaps a week) the positions are reversed and the material learned under high arousal is recalled better than that learned under low arousal. This phenomenon is interesting, not only because it indicates that arousal has a beneficial effect upon long-term memory, but also because of the implications of the paradoxically deleterious effect of arousal upon early recall.

Other experiments have shown that learning is not an all-or-none affair. When a subject cannot recall something he previously knew, it is usually possible to show that he can recognize it, and when even recognition is impossible he can relearn it more easily than before (the difference in trials to learn being called *savings*).

The physiological significance of these findings will be discussed in more detail later, but it appears that gradations in memory result either from differences in the potency of some neural changes, or, if the changes are all-or-none, from differences in the number of such changes that occur.

It has also been found that the distinctiveness of an event has a strong influence upon the ease with which it is learned and upon the durability of the resulting memory trace (Restorff, 1933). If one word of a list is printed in a different color from the rest, for example, it will be learned very quickly. A distinctive item is one that can be classified on a different dimension from that of the others, and it may be that the trace of this dimension suffers less interference because of its isolation and is thus stored more effectively.

It is usually assumed that some sort of reward or punishment increases the learning rate, but the relationship is very complex and not altogether clear. The effect may be largely the result of an increase in the distinctiveness of the reinforced stimulus. Reinforcement also provides motivation for the subsequent display of whatever learning has taken place, a very important feature when animals are used as subjects.

PHYSIOLOGICAL BASES OF LEARNING

There are two broad aspects of the physiological study of learning. One is aimed at discovering what processes take place at the neural level during learning; the other involves the type of circuit necessary to ensure that the appropriate information is stored and read out at the appropriate time so that it can be used to produce adaptive behavior. These two objectives are, of course, mutually facilitative. The more we know about the properties of the neural change, the more certain we can be about the sort of circuit the "learning" neurons participate in and vice versa.

The physiological study of learning is not made easier by the range of behavioral changes that have been classified as learning. It seems impossible that a single neuronal mechanism can account for such disparate behavioral phenomena as learning to recognize objects, learning to ride a bicycle or to play a piano, salivating at the sight of a lemon, readjustment of hand-eye coordination while wearing distorting or inverting spectacles, learning a poem, remembering the words of a long sentence heard or read just long enough to be able to comprehend the sentence as a whole but no longer, and remembering the general content of an article or book. Some of these performances involve brief but complete storage with subsequent erasure; others involve changes that last a lifetime. Some involve voluntary effort; others occur involuntarily. We must thus be prepared, apparently, to find that different forms of learning involve not only different neural circuits but also different fundamental neural mechanisms.

It is unlikely, for reasons to be suggested later, that all neurons are equipped to participate in learning; among those that are, there may well be additional variability. For example, the two-stage theory raises the possibility that short-term storage takes place in one set of elements and persists there only long enough for the information to be transferred to other elements capable of more durable storage. A likelier alternative is that all the elements involved in the learning are initially changed but that the changes pursue different courses in the different elements. We shall return to these questions later.

Most attempts to relate learning to physiological mechanisms involve experiments with animals, but it is not at all clear to what extent animal learning resembles that of humans. Almost certainly animals do not have as great an immediate memory span; in many it may include no more than one item. Phenomena like one-trial learning and incidental (or latent) learning, which are very obvious characteristics of human learning, can be demonstrated in animals only with considerable difficulty and ingenuity of experimental design.

Rats have been used extensively in learning experiments, but, from the earliest days, it has proved astonishingly difficult to establish generally accepted facts about the learning of these animals. Bitter controversies absorbed the energies of learning psychologists during the 1930s and 1940s because, for example, the rats used by Hull's disciples learned according to stimulus-response association principles whereas those used by Tolman and his followers behaved somewhat more intelligently.

Rats subjected to brain lesions and other physiological treatments apparently show even less consistent behavior. The reason may be that the final performance of a rat in a complex learning situation is determined by many uncontrolled factors, each reflecting imperceptible differences in internal or external conditions.

Ablation Studies of Learning

The first thing a physiological psychologist usually tries to do when investigating a new problem is to find out which parts of the nervous system are important for the behavior at issue. In the study of learning, the neocortex seemed a likely place to begin the search. There were several reasons for adopting this hypothesis: First, learning ability is correlated phylogenetically, albeit not very precisely, with the relative size and development of the neocortex; second, the cortex receives a wide variety of sensory signals and has a region devoted to motor activity; and, third, the cortex is probably the only area that has enough interconnections, or potential interconnections, to store the required amount of information.

In Pavlov's original physiological model of conditioning, transcortical pathways from sensory to motor areas were postulated, and some early ablation experiments appeared to confirm that no conditioning was possible in the absence of neocortex (Pavlov, 1927).

Later, however, both Bromiley (1948) and Poltyrew and Zeliony (1930) demonstrated that learning is not limited to neocortical tissue by successfully training decorticated animals to perform discriminative conditioned responses. Nevertheless, such training was extremely difficult, indicating that under normal conditions the neocortex plays an important part in mammalian learning.

Attempts to establish even very simple conditioned reflexes in "spinal" dogs and cats have shown that, despite the considerable complexity of spinal circuits, no significant learning takes place in them. Kellogg, Deese, Pronko, and Feinberg (1947) were unable to demonstrate any learning of a classical leg flexion to shock in chronic spinal dogs. Shurrager and Culler (1940) were sometimes able to obtain "conditioned" muscle twitches in acute spinal preparations, but the absence of essential controls leaves the interpretation of these findings in doubt.

Temporary changes like habituation and post-tetanic potentiation have been observed in spinal systems (Eccles, 1953; R. F. Thompson & Spencer, 1966), but these processes are probably not closely related to learning (see "Learning in Simple Preparations" later in this chapter).

Early in his career Lashley started what turned out to be a lifetime project to discover more precisely where the neural substrate or underlying processes of learned habits (engrams) were stored (Franz & Lashley, 1917; Lashley, 1920, 1924). In most of his experiments he failed to interfere with such learned habits as maze running and latch-box opening by cortical ablations or cuts that should have prevented any transcortical communication between sensory and motor areas. About 30 years later Lashley (1950) summed up his efforts to locate the engram with the remark that he sometimes felt "in reviewing the evidence on the localization of the memory trace, that the necessary conclusion is that learning just is not possible." In a more serious mood, he declared that "it is not possible to demonstrate the isolated localization of a memory trace anywhere in the nervous system. Limited regions may be essential for learning or retention of a particular activity, but . . . the engram is represented throughout the region."

Lashley thought the explanation for the wide distribution of an engram was that it was represented many times throughout the region, and he used the analogy of interference patterns between waves originating at various points to illustrate how it might come about. He was never able to expand the analogy into a clear model, however, and there seems no good reason for making such complex assumptions. Multiple synaptic changes distributed more or less at random throughout a large population of neurons, so that the behavior would survive the loss of a moderate fraction of the cells, would provide a satisfactory explanation, as Hebb (1949) has suggested.

In earlier chapters on the sensory systems many examples of the effects of localized cortical lesions upon discriminative learning were given. In most of those examples it was not easy to decide whether the deficit following a lesion was caused by loss of acquired connections or by destruction of innate perceptual or motor mechanisms. In view of the importance of perceptual learning in the formation of concepts, it seems likely that tissue ablated from the neighborhood of sensory cortex will contain both innately determined and learned connections used in the analysis of sensory input. The behavioral deficits typically conform to Lashley's dictum that a small lesion within one system will produce a small impairment of all behavior related to that system and that a larger lesion will produce a more severe but equally general impairment.

When, as often happens, a lost ability is reacquired, it lends support to the idea that learned connections have been destroyed by the lesion, though in some cases a habit lost after a lesion returns without *specific* retraining, as a result of training on some quite different task. In such cases the deficit may have been one of motivation or of inability to adopt the required set rather than loss of specific connections. Also, it is possible that an initially innate ability can be reacquired through training after the original connections have been destroyed. Deficits after lesions may also result from changes in attention or motor organization; measures of learning or retention that depend upon performance measures are thus always difficult to interpret.

Electrophysiological Studies of Learning

An alternative to the ablation method of determining what structures are involved in learning is to record the electrical activity of the brain during learning. This method may also provide information about other aspects of the learning process, but up to now interpretation has generally proved difficult.

It was noticed very early in the history of electroencephalography (EEG; see Chapter 4) that "desynchronization" accompanying arousal can readily be conditioned to a neutral stimulus (Durup & Fessard, 1935). This phenomenon was studied more systematically by Jasper and Shagass (1941a, 1941b). The CS in these experiments was a faint sound that, after a few preliminary adapting presentations, did not by itself have any effect upon the alpha rhythm (the 10 per second waves from the occipital region) in most subjects. The UCS was a light that consistently blocked the alpha waves. By pairing the light with the CS according to the

usual Pavlovian schedules, Jasper and Shagass were able to demonstrate conditioning of alpha blocking to the previously neutral sound (Figure 20.1). During trace conditioning (in which a constant interval is interposed between the CS and the UCS as in the experiment shown in Figure 20.1) and temporal conditioning (in which there is no CS but the UCS is presented at regular intervals) the conditioned alpha blocking was more accurately timed than were the subjects' estimates of the time before the light would come on, which seems to rule out the possibility that blocking resulted from conscious expectation of the light.

Subsequently, with monkeys as subjects, Morrell and Jasper (1956) used a flickering light, which produced a train of evoked potentials in the visual cortex (photic driving) as the UCS and established discriminative conditioned responses to different auditory or tactual stimuli. The conditioned EEG response was a train of waves starting soon after the onset of the CS and at roughly the same frequency as was elicited by the flickering light (not always the same as the flicker frequency, but sometimes at a multiple of that frequency).

The sequence of changes during conditioning was similar to that noticed by Livanov and Poliakov (1945), who had done a very similar set of experiments using rabbits as subjects. Initially the CS produced a general arousal correlated with an orienting response. The monkey became alert and searched for the source of the stimulus. This response was eliminated by repeated presentation of the CS before the pairing of the CS and the flickering light began. After the first few pairings the CS once again elicited a general arousal and flattening (desynchronization) of the EEG. After more pairings (usually between 6 and 15) the CS began to elicit a burst of frequency-specific sharp waves in the visual cortex (similar in form to those evoked by the UCS) during the two-to-three second CS-UCS interval (Figure 20.2). Later, after about 20 more trials, the frequency-specific response disappeared and was replaced by desynchronization, this time confined to the visual cortex.

Yoshii and Hockaday (1958) performed a

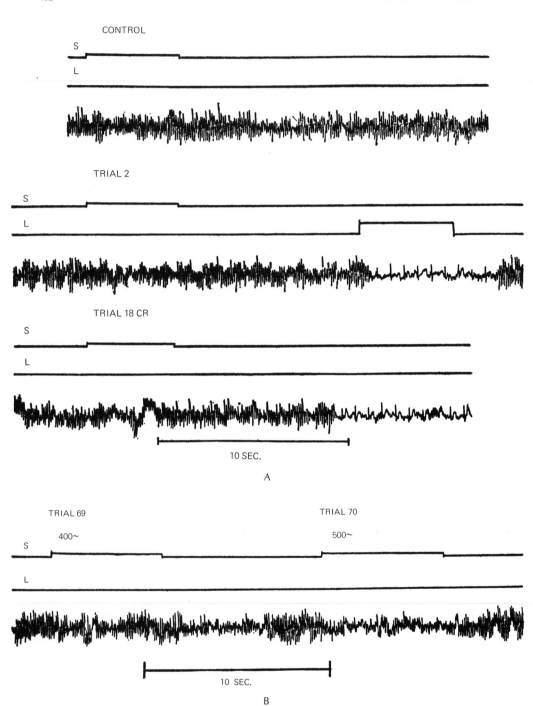

Figure 20.1 (A) EEG recordings from a human subject during establishment of trace conditioning of the arousal response. The top record is a control with the sound stimulus alone. The middle record shows an arousal response only to light following the end of the sound stimulus after an interval of 9.4 seconds, on the second trial. The bottom lower record shows a trace-conditioned arousal response when light was omitted on the eighteenth trial. (B) Differential conditioning of EEG in a human subject. Light has been paired with a sound stimulus of 500 Hz but not with a stimulus of 400 Hz. There is no arousal during the presentation of the 400 Hz signal (trial 69), but the response does accompany the 500 Hz signal (trial 70). (From Jasper & Shagass, 1941a)

LP - O

RP - O

S

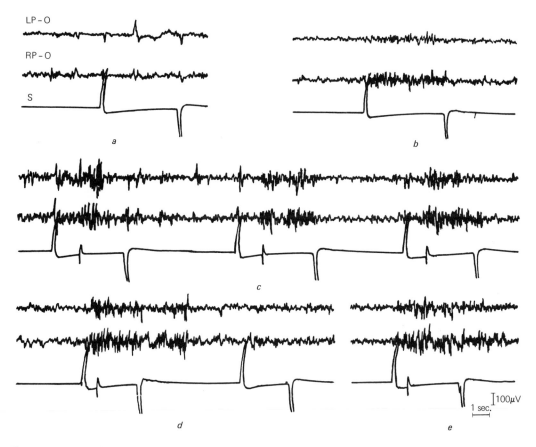

a

b

c

d

e

1 sec. $100\mu V$

Figure 20.2 Recordings from the left (upper trace) and right (middle trace) parieto-occipital cortex of a monkey before and during conditioning of visually evoked response to a tone. (a) Response to a 500 Hz tone before conditioning. (b) Response to flicker at 50 flashes per second before conditioning. (c) Response to a pairing of tone and flicker. The tone comes on at the large upward deflection of the marker pen (lower trace); about two seconds later the flicker starts at the small deflection of the marker, and about four seconds after that both go off at the downward deflection of the marker. Some increase in activity occurs during the sound before the flicker starts (d) A large response to a tone of 500 Hz with very little response to "unreinforced" 1,000 Hz tone presented a few seconds later. (e) Another example of a conditioned response, showing, as in (d), a long-lasting response continuing beyond the stimuli. (From Morrell & Jasper, 1956.)

very similar experiment on cats but with recording electrodes in many subcortical areas, as well as in the cortex. As is only too common in this type of experiment, however, there were great individual differences in the responses of different animals. In some it was found that the photic-driving response, which was at first weak in the frontal region of the brain, became stronger with repeated presentation, especially in the frontal cortex, amygdala, caudate nucleus, and internal capsule. In most of the cats the conditioned frequency-specific waves were much more stable than in Morrell's monkeys; furthermore, the waves were not confined to the

occipital cortex. In subcortical structures, however, the conditioning was unstable and disappeared after the first week of training.

The experiments mentioned here are representative of many in which the conditioned response has been a change in EEG. A more common approach is to train the animal in a normal learning situation and to record the changes in EEG or evoked response (usually to the CS) during the course of learning. One such experiment was that of Grastyán, Lissák, Madarász and Donhoffer (1959), who examined the electrical activity of the hippocampus (and, in some cases, of the mesencephalic reticular formation) in cats during the acquisition of alimentary and avoidance instrumental responses. In alimentary conditioning the cats learned to press a bar for food during the presentation of one sound and to refrain from pressing the bar during presentation of another sound. Avoidance training, also involving positive and negative auditory stimuli, took place in a double grid box.

Arousal of the cat with a familiar auditory stimulus ("puss, puss") elicited rhythmic theta waves (about six per second; see Figure 20.3) in the hippocampus, as had been reported previously by J. D. Green and Arduini (1954). These waves were accompanied by orienting responses. Completely unfamiliar stimuli like a tone in the test apparatus, which caused the animal to freeze, produced a flat, desynchro-

Figure 20.3 Responses of the reticular formation (R.F.), hippocampus (H.), motor cortex (M.C.), and auditory cortex (A.C.) in the cat to various stimuli. (a) A familiar sound elicits rhythmic theta waves (five per second) in the hippocampus and similar smaller waves in the reticular formation. (b) Theta waves are also evoked by showing the cat a mirror. (c) An unfamiliar stimulus of a 1,000 Hz tone produces freezing and desynchronization of hippocampal, as well as cortical, activity. (From Grastyán, Lissák, Madarász & Donhoffer, 1959.)

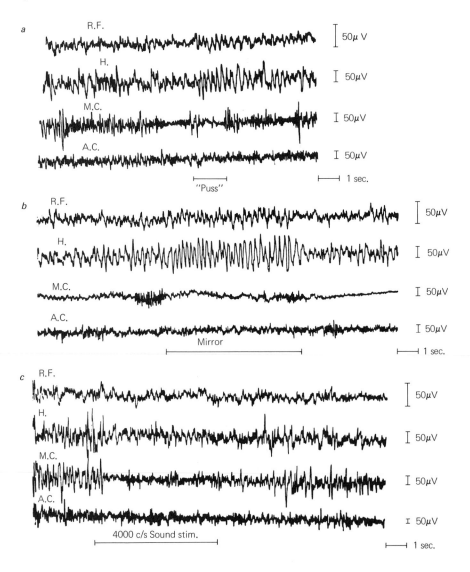

nized pattern in the hippocampus, as well as in the cortex.

As the freezing response to the stimulus abated and the cats began to show orienting responses, the hippocampus showed theta activity to the tone, which continued through the early stages of training, but when the response had been thoroughly learned the theta waves disappeared, and the hippocampus once more responded to the CS with fast waves. During differentiation training both positive and negative stimuli tended to elicit orienting responses, and the theta rhythm appeared again in the hippocampus, only to disappear as the cats learned to discriminate among the stimuli. During extinction the stimuli again elicited theta waves for a time but eventually produced no effect upon hippocampal activity. In some of the cats the activity of the mesencephalic reticular formation was found to be quite similar to that of the hippocampus at all stages of training.

Grastyán and his colleagues postulated that the rapid activity of the hippocampus was responsible for inhibiting the orienting reflex. The reflex was inhibited either when the stimulus frightened the cat and caused it to freeze or when the stimulus had a very well-established meaning and elicited a specific response or no response at all. During slow-wave theta activity the inhibitory effect was withheld. The investigators thought the hippocampus participated in learning by allowing orientation during the acquisition phase and suppressing it later, so that it would not interfere with the smooth performance of the adaptive response. On the other hand, Vanderwolf (1968) has presented strong evidence that in the rat hippocampal theta waves are correlated only with "voluntary" movements and are not influenced by learning.

Adey (1961) reported rather more subtle changes in hippocampal activity during learning. Cross correlation of activity from different recording sites indicated that during the early stages of learning the temporal relationship between waves in the hippocampus and those in the adjacent entorhinal cortex was altered. In his experiment cats learned to run a T-maze for food. Before learning started, the waves in the hippocampus were found to lead those in the entorhinal cortex, but when the cat learned where the food was the hippocampal waves lagged behind the entorhinal ones. Adey believed that the significance of these changes was that at first the input went to the hippocampus and was fed from there to the entorhinal area, where it was stored. Later the information stored in the entorhinal cortex provided a standard against which the input was compared to determine what action should be taken; the activity thus started there before the incoming signal reached the hippocampus.

One of the most elaborate experiments, in which activity of many parts of the cat brain was recorded during the acquisition and extinction of an avoidance response, was performed by John and Killam (1959). The CS was a light flashing 10 times per second (called a *tracer CS* because it allowed the investigators to trace the path of the signal through the brain by recording the evoked potentials at 10 per second or multiples thereof.

The cat had to learn to jump from one compartment of a double grid box to the other, to avoid shock whenever the CS was presented. Later a differential stimulus consisting of a light flashing 7 times per second was introduced. No shock followed the presentation of this stimulus.

The CS initially gave rise to photic driving at many points in the brain, but it faded out with repeated presentation during preliminary adaptation (Figure 20.4). (This finding does not conform to those of Yoshii and Hockaday, described earlier, but the disparity may arise from the difference in light intensity of the CS, rate of presentation of trials, or various other aspects of the experiments.)

As soon as the conditioning started (when shock was presented after the CS) the tracer potentials reappeared at all recording sites, including visual and auditory cortices, the reticular formation, nucleus ventralis anterior of the thalamus, the fornix, the septum, the hippocampus, and the amygdala (Figure 20.5). As the cat learned to avoid shocks, the tracer potentials disappeared again, except from the

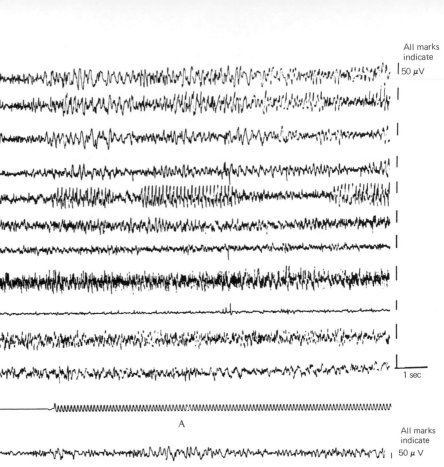

A

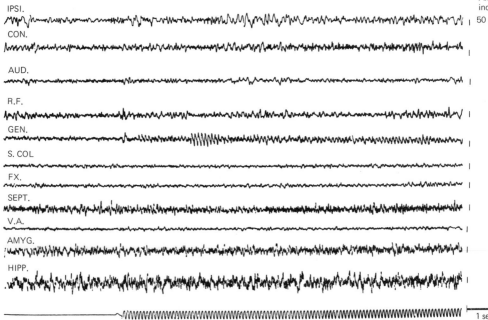

B

Figure 20.4 (A) Recordings from a cat during familiarization with flashes at 10 per second. IPSI., a record from two electrodes in the visual cortex of one hemisphere; CON., a record from two electrodes, one in each visual cortex; AUD., a record from the auditory cortex; R.F., a record from the reticular formation; GEN., a record from the lateral geniculate nucleus; S.COL., a record from the superior colliculus; FX, a record from the fornix; SEPT., a record from septal area; V.A., a record from the nucleus ventralis anterior of the thalamus; AMYG., a record from the amygdala; HIPP., a record from the hippocampus. The time marker on the bottom trace indicates the presentation of flashes. Responses at the frequency of the flashes are evoked in many structures. (B) Recordings from the same structures during presentation of the same stimulus at the end of the familiarization procedure. Frequency-specific responses to the flashes are much less apparent than in the previous set of records. (From John & Killam, 1959.)

visual cortex, hippocampus, and midbrain reticular formation. Later still, when the cat had completely learned the avoidance response, the tracer potentials also disappeared from the hippocampus but reappeared in nucleus ventralis anterior (a motor nucleus).

During differential training, it was found that the 7-per-second flicker first generated a 10-per-second evoked response in the visual cortex and that the cat would make its usual avoidance response. As the cat began to discriminate behaviorally, however, the cortical responses also became differentiated and the 7-per-second flashes evoked 7-per-second waves. During the intermediate phase the cat usually made an error when the frequency of the evoked potential was not that of the presented stimulus. In other words the behavior corresponded to the cortical activity rather than to the objective CS. Differentiation of the response using another discriminative stimulus at 13 flashes per second gave similar results.

At this point 10 clicks per second were presented instead of the light. They did not evoke responses in the visual cortex, nor did they elicit an avoidance response. The cat rapidly learned to respond to the auditory stimulus, however, and the cortical activity was then very similar to that occurring to light flashes at 10 per second.

John and Killam suggested that during learning there was active participation of those structures (hippocampus and visual pathways) that had large tracer potentials at the time and that, when the habit was well established, only the visual and motor pathways were involved.

It is possible, however, that the responsiveness of different structures reflects not changes in information processing by those structures, but a change in the general emotional state of the animal. To investigate this possibility, McAdam (1962) used 20 flickers per second as a stimulus, either paired with foot shock in a classical leg-flexion conditioning procedure or in random relation to shock, as a control. Many of the structures that responded during the avoidance learning in John's experiment also showed tracer potentials in the control animals, though the latter were not being conditioned.

The main difference between the conditioned and control groups in McAdam's experiment was that the control animals did not develop trace-evoked potentials in the sensorimotor cortex.

John, Ruchkin and Villegas (1964) have advanced the idea that learning involves changing relationships among the wave forms of evoked potentials in different parts of the brain. Applying factorial analysis to the average evoked-potential wave form produced by the CS in different structures at different stages of conditioning, these investigators have shown that, as learning proceeded, there was a tendency for the waves to become more similar in many regions, including sensory cortex, association cortex, sensory-relay nuclei, the thalamic and mesencephalic reticular formation and rhinencephalic structures.

The implication of their results is that there are a number of "sources" (corresponding to the various factors of the analysis), each sending a particular wave form to other regions whenever the CS is presented. The outputs of these sources are combined in various amounts at the different structures, and, as conditioning continues, the connections are strengthened so that all the structures tend to pull into step. Theoretically the factorial analysis should provide information on the location of the various "sources" and what connections are being formed during learning, but, because of individual differences and the general instability of the responses, this goal has not yet been realized.

Several investigations into the firing of single units during learning have been made. Experiments by Jasper, Ricci, and Doane (1958) have already been discussed briefly in Chapter 6. Recordings of unit activity in the motor and parietal cortex of monkeys were made during the establishment of an avoidance response to flickering light. As might be expected, some units changed their firing pattern during the CS, showing either increases or decreases in firing rates. As the monkey learned the response, there were further changes in some cases. Figure 20.6 shows the response of a cell in the parietal lobe, which increased in rate

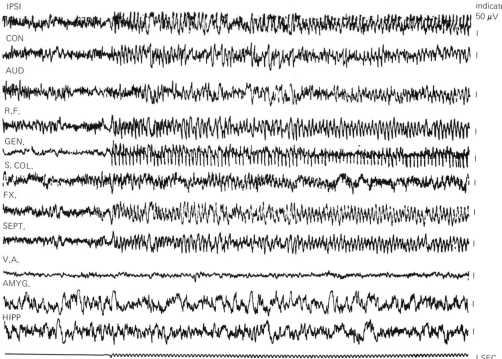

IPSI

CON

AUD

R.F.

GEN.

S. COL.

FX.

SEPT.

V.A.

AMYG.

HIPP

1 SEC

1 ST DAY OF TRAINING

A

Figure 20.5 (A) Recordings from the structures listed in Figure 20.4 during the first day in which the flashes signaled presentation of shock in the compartment occupied by the cat. Responses to the flashes reappeared in almost all the records. (B) Recordings when the cat was making 100 per cent avoidances in response to the signal. Frequency-specific responses are found mainly in the visual pathways and ventral nucleus, a motor nucleus of the thalamus. (From John & Killam, 1959.)

Figure 20.6 (a) A recording from a microelectrode in the parietal cortex of a monkey during the presentation of a flashing light (CS), which was followed during training by shock to the paw. The lower trace is the muscle response during the CR, which terminated the CS. (b) A recording from the same unit during the presentation of a discriminative stimulus (Δs), a flashing light of different frequency, which did not elicit a response. (Jasper, Ricci & Doane, 1958.)

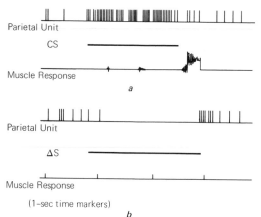

Parietal Unit

CS

Muscle Response

a

Parietal Unit

ΔS

Muscle Response

(1–sec time markers)

b

when the CS was presented but decreased when a differential stimulus (a higher frequency of flashing light not followed by shock) was presented. Before the differentiation was established the parietal unit was not inhibited, and the monkey responded to the differential stimulus.

Yoshii and Ogura (1960) studied units in the pontine reticular formation of cats under conditions of flashing-light CS and leg-shock UCS somewhat similar to those used by Jasper and his colleagues, except that the animals were immobilized with curare and could make no avoidance responses. Changes in responsiveness of units were found when the CS and shock were paired, especially in those units that normally responded to more than one type of stimulus (*polysensory units*).

J. Olds and Olds (1961) were able to modify the firing pattern of neurons in the rat brain with a paradigm similar to that for operant

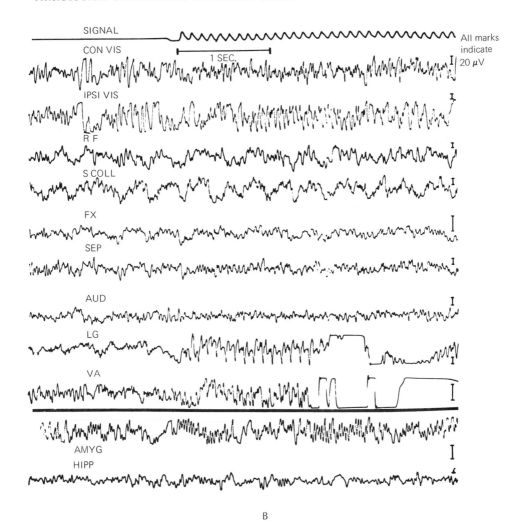

B

conditioning. In certain neurons of the hippocampal system, each spontaneous discharge was "rewarded" by a burst of stimulation at a site previously found to elicit self-stimulation. Under these conditions the cell's spontaneous firing rate increased very significantly and not as a result of general excitation: In control studies with the same amount of rewarding stimulation not contingent upon neuronal firing the neuron did not increase its firing rate.

Carmona has applied a similar technique in order to modify the EEG of curarized rats (see N. E. Miller, 1969). He increased the number of large waves in one group of rats and decreased it in another group by reinforcing changes in the desired direction with rewarding brain stimulation.

None of these experiments is easy to interpret. The difficulty may best be exemplified by considering what would happen if one placed a microelectrode in a motor pool involved in a conditioned response. Certainly one would expect to find changes in the activity recorded as learning progressed, but this change would not necessarily imply that the particular neurons were participating in the learning, except in a trivial sense. The cells in Yoshii and Ogura's experiment may have been involved in arousal, and there is no doubt that when a neutral stimulus has been paired with shock a few times it will produce arousal. We might postulate that the cells that "learned" an instrumental response in the Olds' experiment participated in some voluntary performance, sniffing, for example. If the rat learned to sniff in order to obtain hypothalamic rewarding stimulation, the cell would appear to be learning, but this appearance might be deceptive. So far, electrophysiological methods have added little to our knowledge about the location of learning processes in the brain. They have indicated that many parts of the brain are involved in learned responses, but we can still only guess to what extent their participation is secondary—reflecting changes in arousal, changes in motivation, or changes in motor activity—rather than directly in the process of information storage.

Learning in Simple Preparations

Although ablation and recording experiments have identified some relationships, between the brain and behavior, they have proved disappointing, as we have just seen, to the scientist interested in the basic mechanisms of learning. He would like to be assured that a particular learning change is taking place in a particular small volume of tissue or, better still, in a certain identifiable cell that he can subject to detailed scrutiny. As this requirement seems to be impossible to fulfill under conditions of normal mammalian learning, various methods have been adopted to force learning to occur where it can be conveniently observed.

One approach is to use very simple organisms; another is to isolate, surgically or otherwise, a small part of a more complex system. Both methods encounter difficulties. Systems simple enough to allow the "learning" tissue to be identified do not usually "learn" in the usual, mammalian sense. In many instances the changes are only transient, lasting a few minutes or hours at the most.

It has been suggested from time to time that learning can occur in protozoa, the simplest level of animal life (S. Smith, 1908; Day & Bentley, 1911; Gelber, 1952). Gelber observed clustering of paramecia around a sterile platinum wire on which food had previously been presented but no clustering in control groups that had not been fed on the wire.

This result has been questioned by Jensen (1957) on the ground that the medium in the region of the wire may still have been chemically attractive to the organisms. He suggested that the effect would not be observed if the sample of culture were thoroughly stirred between feeding and testing, but Gelber (1957) cited in reply experiments that cast doubt on this explanation. Even if a change in behavior could be established, however, few would be willing to class it as learning. It seems unlikely that paramecia are capable of perceiving the wire except by its chemical contamination from the surrounding fluid.

Learning has definitely been shown in worms. Yerkes (1912) trained earthworms to turn toward a dark chamber and away from a shock in a T-maze, and others (for example, J. S. Robinson, 1953) have repeated the experiment. This learning is not localized in the head ganglia; it survives amputation of the 12 anterior segments.

R. Thompson and McConnell succeeded in conditioning the even more primitive flatworm (planarian) to contract, or curl, at the onset of a light (CS) that had been paired with shock (UCS). Block and McConnell (1967) have answered criticisms of the controls in this experiment by showing that planarians can also be differentially conditioned. After vibration had been paired with shock the worms responded to vibration but not to light. Then when light was paired with shock the same worms could be made to respond to light but not to vibration. As we shall see later, planarians have been used to some extent in the biochemical analysis of learning (McConnell, 1962; Corning & John, 1961; John, 1967).

Another very simple preparation for which learning has been claimed is the abdominal ganglion of the sea slug (*Aplysia depilans*). Following the work of Fessard and Tauc (1960), Kandel and Tauc (1965) succeeded in "conditioning" single neurons of this ganglion. Intracellular potentials were recorded from micropipettes so that partial depolarization, as well as propagated spike potentials, could be detected. The preparation is a very convenient one to use for the study of relationships between single neurons because the cells are so large and sparse that they can be mapped and identified individually under the microscope.

There are two *connectives* (nerve trunks between ganglia) entering the abdominal ganglion (Figure 20.7), and it is possible to stimulate one of them electrically at such an intensity that only a small depolarization of the cell under observation is produced. The stimulation of the other connective is adjusted to a level strong enough to fire the cell. Some ganglion cells were found to be sensitized by being fired. After such cells had been fired a number of times via one connective, stimulating the other connective produced more depolarization in them than before and in some cases even fired them (Figure 20.8).

At first it was thought that there were two types of cell, some that were made more sensitive simply by being fired and others in which the change was produced only if the two connectives were stimulated almost simultaneously on a number of occasions, the latter type forming a good model for learning. It has since been found, however, that if the stimulation is strong enough in the connective that fires the cell it will sensitize any cell, pairing being unnecessary. Reduction of the stimulation intensity, on the other hand, ensures that the potentiation effect is greater when stimulation of the two connectives is paired rather than randomly presented (Kandel & Spencer, 1968).

The change in sensitivity does not last more than a few minutes, and it may therefore have nothing to do with behavioral learning. In fact,

Figure 20.7 A dorsal view of an abdominal ganglion of *Aplysia depilans*, showing stimulator input to each connective and a recording microelectrode in one ganglion cell. (After Kandel & Tauc, 1965.)

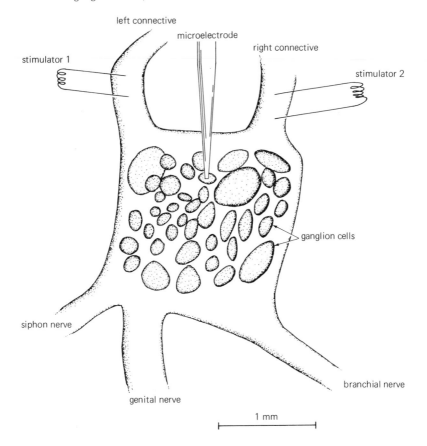

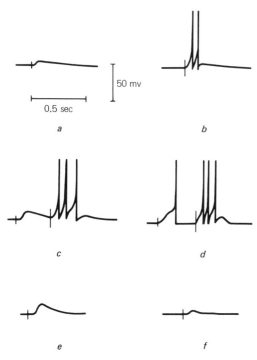

Figure 20.8 Oscilloscope tracings of intracellular potentials from a cell in an abdominal ganglion of *Aplysia* during stimulation of connectives, as shown in Figure 20.7. (a) Weak stimulation of the left connective alone. (b) Strong stimulation of the right connective alone. (c) Stimulation of the left connective followed by stimulation of the right one after 5.5 minutes of pairing the two stimulations. (d) The same sequence as in (c) after 10 minutes of pairing. (e) Weak stimulation of the left connective alone 2.5 minutes after pairing has been discontinued. (f) The same sequence as in (e) 10 minutes after pairing has stopped. (After Kandel & Tauc, 1965.)

it is not yet certain that *Aplysia* is capable of learning,[1] though other gastropods, water snails, have been conditioned to make mouth movements in response to touching the foot (E. L. Thompson, 1917).

Another simple preparation with interesting possibilities for the study of learning is the isolated ganglion and leg of the cockroach or locust. Horridge (1962) showed that, when the insect leg (with its nerve and part of the ventral nerve cord intact) is wired so that a shock is delivered to it every time it is extended, it remains flexed for longer and longer periods.

[1] But see Lickey, M. E. Learned behavior in *Aplysia Vaccaria*. *Journal of Comparative and Physiological Psychology*. 1968, 66, 712–718.

If a similar preparation is wired in series with the first so that it receives shock when the other does, independently of its own state of flexion or extension (Figure 20.9), the "yoked" control leg does not adopt any particular position. It is thus the pairing of extension and shock and not the shock alone that is responsible for the postural change. If the trained and control legs are later retested individually, the trained leg receives far fewer shocks than the control leg (Figure 20.10).

Hoyle (cited by Horridge, 1965) used the rate of neural activity in the motor nerve of the insect leg to control the delivery of shock and was able either to increase the firing rate by shocking every time the rate fell below a criterion level or to decrease the rate of firing by employing the opposite maneuver. The leg-ganglion preparation has also been used to study the effects of chemical agents upon "learning" (B. M. Brown & Noble, 1967).

A similar experimental arrangement has been used by N. E. Miller (1969) and a number of his colleagues to demonstrate instrumental changes in autonomic functioning, mostly in rats. In one experiment curarized rats could avoid shocks by reducing their heart rate whenever a warning signal was presented. Within a short time considerable drops in heart rate were produced by the signal. If the situation was reversed, the signal eventually produced an increase in heart rate.

The heart rate of curarized rats could also be significantly increased or decreased by presenting a burst of rewarding brain stimulation each time there was a spontaneous change in the desired direction. Intestinal contractions, urine formation, blood pressure, and blood flow in peripheral vessels could also be driven in either direction by rewarding the required response whenever it occurred. It even proved possible to make the curarized rat increase the blood flow to one pinna relative to the other by rewarding it with brain stimulation whenever the vessels in that ear underwent greater dilation than those of the other.

Morrell (1961b) has drawn attention to the potential value of secondary epileptic foci (*mirror foci*) for the study of cellular changes

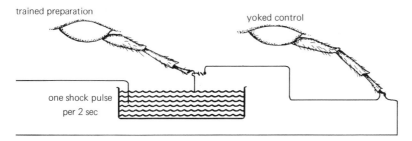

Figure 20.9   An experimental arrangement for avoidance conditioning of the cockroach leg-ganglion preparation with the control animal wired in series so that it also receives a shock each time the trained animal makes an error. (After Horridge, 1962.)

in learning. It has long been known that patients with epileptogenic lesions in the cortex often develop a secondary focus symmetrically located in the contralateral cortex, presumably as the result of frequent intense bombardment of the area through callosal pathways.

Similar mirror foci have been produced experimentally in animals. A few days after an electrographically discharging lesion has been produced by local application of ethylchloride spray, paroxysmal discharges occur in the opposite hemisphere. After several days to a week (in the rabbit) the new focus becomes independent (that is, it continues to show epileptic discharge after the original focus has been eliminated by ablation).

The process of establishing such secondary foci seems to have the characteristics of normal learning, the main difference being that in the former instance large numbers of neurons in a concentrated region are involved. It should thus be easy to discover changes in either morphology or biochemical constitution of the cells. Because the changes occur in mammalian cortex and appear to be permanent, there is a good chance that information derived from the preparation will be applicable to normal learning processes.

Changes in sensitivity of tissue exposed to daily electrical stimulation from an implanted electrode have been reported (Goddard, 1967; Racine, 1969) and presumably result from the same mechanism as do secondary foci. This method could also be used to provide localizable learning changes for detailed investigation.

Surprisingly little work has been done with either of these preparations, though Morrell (1961b) has shown with a staining technique that some cells in the region of a secondary focus have higher than normal concentrations of ribonucleic acid (RNA). As we shall see later, this is a common consequence of increased neural activity and may have nothing to do with the learning change itself.

Figure 20.10   The average number of errors per minute made by 20 trained cockroaches and 20 previously yoked controls when both groups were tested under identical conditions, receiving shocks for errors. The initial learning curve for the trained animals is shown for comparison with the performance of the yoked animals. (After Horridge, 1962.)

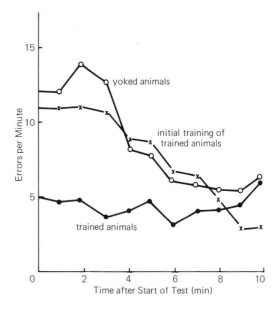

Another process that has sometimes been used in learning models (for example, Eccles, 1953; Fessard & Szabo, 1961) is post-tetanic potentiation, which was described in Chapter 5. There are several reasons for questioning the value of these attempts; the change is only temporary and occurs in the spinal cord, which appears to be incapable of learning. But the most important objection is that the change is not specific enough; there is no way to confine it to the required path. Other short-term changes like fatigue and hypersensitivity of disuse or denervation (Sharpless, 1964) are open to the same objection even as mechanisms for short-term storage.

The problem is that neurons, certainly those likely to be involved in learning, have many axonal branches and transmit to large numbers of other neurons. If all the endings become more effective transmitters of impulses, many paths that have nothing to do with the habit to be learned will be activated. Post-tetanic potentiation, in the course of improving transmission at one synaptic junction, would thus also potentiate many others, producing random and mostly undesirable changes in behavior. In disuse hypersensitivity and fatigue, the receiving cell changes its response to all its afferents, not only that from the source involved in learning, and similar lack of specificity results.

To make this criticism more concrete, let us consider an animal being conditioned to raise a paw at the sound of a bell. We could just as easily arrange the situation so that the animal would make any of a large number of other responses—vocalization, tail wagging, blinking, salivation, or the like—to the same stimulus; the stimulus must thus have potential access to circuits controlling all these responses. If conditioning depended upon some process like post-tetanic potentiation, there would seem to be no way for one of these paths to be selected for potentiation while the others were left unaffected. It may be possible to design special networks in which post-tetanic potentiation could provide more specific new associations, but so many ad hoc assumptions would have to be made about the connections and so many neurons would be necessary to store each bit

of information that the advantage of basing a model on a known physiological phenomenon would be considerably diminished.

Most theorists consider that a change in the relationship between cells should take place only if both the afferent and the efferent cells fire simultaneously (see Hebb, 1949). This postulate results in the most straightforward learning networks, but simplicity does not guarantee the correctness either of the network or of the postulated conditions for change. Some physiological learning theorists (for example, Hydén, 1959; John, 1964) have adopted a quite different model, in which learning cells become more sensitive, not to synaptic input from another neuron, but to the temporal pattern of electrical activity in the neighborhood.

This model has the advantage that, as many neurons are exposed to similar patterns of input, there is no problem of explaining the lack of localization of the engram. As we have seen, however, this problem is not insuperable for "synaptic" theories of learning; many methods of reduplication of stored information are possible. In the absence of data crucial to discriminating among the models, our preference must depend upon whether we think it more likely that a membrane can become "tuned" to a particular pattern of input or that a synapse can be changed to make it more effective. The synapse is the better-documented avenue of input to neurons, and membrane resonance has not yet been shown to have any significance for cell firing; a synaptic theory therefore seems somewhat more likely, but this view could be changed by further evidence.

HUMAN MEMORY DISTURBANCES AND THE PHENOMENON OF CONSOLIDATION

Korsakoff, a Russian physician, was the first to describe a syndrome commonly found in chronic alcoholic patients, one of the symptoms of which is almost complete loss of "memory" (inability to learn anything new; see Korsakoff, 1889; Victor & Yakovlev, 1955). B. Milner calls this disability loss of *recent memory* (B. Milner & Teuber, 1968) an expression used by patients and their friends to denote inability to remember recent events though memory for remote events remains intact. It is important not to confuse recent memory with *immediate memory* (see discussion later in this chapter), which may be quite normal in patients with impaired recent memory. A careful study of the brains of patients with Korsakoff's syndrome (Adams, Collins & Victor, 1962) revealed variable amounts of brain damage, with lesions in the medial thalamus common to those patients who had had the most severe memory loss.

Many patients showed considerable mental deterioration in addition to memory loss, but some remained quite intelligent, and Korsakoff's original patient could play a good game of chess despite being unable to remember what had happened to bring about the current positions on the board. (Of course, he had learned to play the game before the onset of his disease.) M. Williams and Pennybacker (1954) found similar memory disturbances in patients with tumors in the vicinity of the third ventricle.

Bechterev (1900) described a patient with bilateral damage to the hippocampal formation resulting from strokes, who suffered from chronic *anterograde amnesia* (loss of memory of events occurring *after* trauma) similar to that of the Korsakoff syndrome. Glees and Griffith (1952) also reported a case of this kind.

Several patients who have sustained bilateral damage to the hippocampal zone during operations for the relief of epilepsy have been studied by Milner (see B. Milner, 1959; 1966; B. Milner & Teuber, 1968; Scoville & Milner, 1957) and found to have varying degrees of anterograde amnesia. Some patients were operated upon bilaterally; in two patients the operation was unilateral, but the contralateral hippocampus had been injured previously. A post-mortem examination of one of these patients, who died a number of years later, showed that the hippocampus on the surgically intact side was completely atrophied and that all other structures in that temporal lobe were substantially undamaged. This finding adds weight to the theory that the hippocampus and not some neighboring structure is the crucial region for recent memory. De Jong, Itabashi,

and Olson (1968) have presented similar evidence.

One patient with bilateral medial temporal lobectomy and two patients with memory loss after unilateral temporal-lobe ablations were trained on a fairly simple visual stylus maze and on a tactually guided maze of comparable difficulty. On the visual maze the patient with the bilateral operation received 215 trials over a period of three days and failed to make any progress at all (Figure 20.11). The other two patients learned the maze eventually but took more trials than almost any patient with neocortical lesions. The results on the tactual maze were similar.

The patient with the bilateral operation was, however, able to learn a motor skill at a normal rate. He was trained on a mirror-drawing task (tracing a line between the double outline of a star while seeing the star and his pencil only in a mirror). He retained the skill the next day, although he did not remember having performed the task before (Figure 20.12).

Some kinds of perceptual learning are also relatively unimpaired by bilateral hippocampal

Figure 20.11 A learning curve on the bolt-head maze for a patient with bilateral ablations of the medial temporal lobe. (After B. Milner, 1962a.)

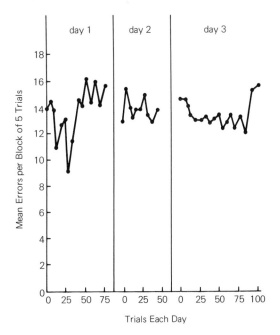

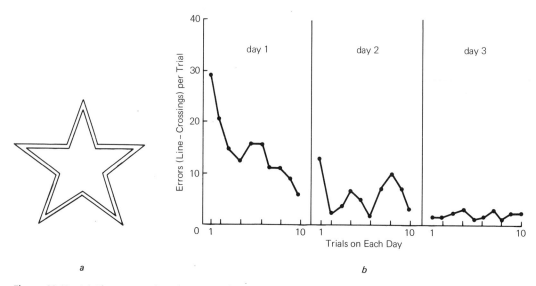

Figure 20.12 (a) The star used in the mirror-drawing test. The subject must trace a complete path between the lines while watching his hand only through a mirror. (b) A learning curve for patient with bilateral ablation of the medial temporal lobe. (After B. Milner, 1962a.)

lesions. If sets of broken drawings (Figure 20.13) are presented, with the least complete set first followed by more and more finished versions of the same drawings until the subject recognizes the objects, normal subjects are found to have improved when retested weeks later with the same set of stimuli (Gollin, 1960). This result is presumably based partly on memory of what the objects were—reducing the range of possible objects to fit the drawings to—and partly on acquisition of memory traces of the complete drawings, which can be reinstated by the partial stimulation provided by the broken drawings.

Warrington and Weiskrantz (1968) found that amnesic patients also showed improvement, though not as much as normal subjects did, even when the second test was given several months later. The amnesic patients did not remember what the drawings were, but they presumably retained some form of perceptual trace. B. Milner has confirmed that long-lasting improvement on this test occurred in the patient with a bilateral medial temporal lobectomy, who had been completely unable to learn a maze (B. Milner & Teuber 1968).

None of the amnesic patients were in the least impaired on immediate memory span, as measured by the Memory Span for Digits test of the Wechsler-Bellevue Scale. They could repeat as many digits forward and backward as normal subjects could. When undisturbed they could also retain short numbers for many minutes by continuous rehearsal, but permanent storage did not result even then. As soon as the patient was distracted he completely forgot the number.

Memory loss is a disability as severe as, or worse than, the epileptic seizures eliminated by the operation, and precautions are now taken to avoid that outcome. If there is any suspicion that a patient about to have a temporal lobectomy has an unhealthy hippocampal region contralateral to the intended ablation, he is subjected to an Amytal test (see "Cerebral Dominance and Handedness," Chapter 13). Each hemisphere is anesthetized on successive days, and the effectiveness of the other hemisphere is determined by giving the patient a few simple memory tests involving remembering a sentence and pictures of common objects (B. Milner & Teuber, 1968). If he fails to remember them when the side to be ablated is anesthetized (as occasionally happens) great care is taken to avoid damage to the medial temporal region during the operation. When the "good" hemisphere is anesthetized, memory disturbances frequently occur, and they provide further information on the relation of the medial temporal region to recent memory.

Patients who become amnesic during a unilateral Amytal test are unable to recall events that took place during testing even after they recover from the anesthetic, though they can remember things they were told just before the test. The hippocampal deficit is thus more easily explained as an impairment of storage than as interference with the recall mechanism, a conclusion also suggested by amnesic patients' ability to recall many events of their lives up to the time of their lesion.

The asymmetry of the human brain with respect to language and nonlinguistic functions (Chapter 13) also allows investigation of the structures responsible for recent memory. It has been found that impairment of verbal memory is correlated with the amount of hippocampal tissue removed from the dominant hemisphere at operation (Corsi, 1969). Similarly, memory for faces after nondominant temporal lobectomy is impaired in proportion to the amount of hippocampus ablated (B. Milner & Teuber, 1968).

Another observation that implicates the temporal lobe in some types of human learning is that of Bickford, Mulder, Dodge, Svien, and Rome (1958), who stimulated the area with a depth electrode in two candidates for temporal lobectomy. They found that for some time after the stimulation the patients were unable to remember events that had taken place just before the stimulation and that sometimes patients had a brief period of amnesia for events that had occurred just after the stimulation. The retrograde amnesia was not permanent and cannot therefore be attributed to failure of memory consolidation. It is interesting that the longer the period of stimulation, the further back the period of retrograde amnesia extended.

Very similar results were obtained by Chapman, Walter, Markham, Rand, and Crandall (1967), who stimulated 2 epileptic patients bilaterally in the hippocampus and another 13 patients unilaterally in the same region. The bilateral stimulations produced retrograde amnesia extending back two weeks. Immediate (digit-span) memory and remote memories were intact. The amnesia disappeared after a few hours. The unilateral stimulations had less effect upon memory, but in four patients stimulation of the amygdala elicited hallucinatory reenactments of past experiences similar to those reported by Penfield (1954). Repeated stimulation through the same electrode on successive days produced the same experience, but

Figure 20.13 A sample figure from a perceptual-learning test. The figures of set 1 are shown first, then those of set 2, and so on until the subject recognizes the object. (After Gollin, 1960.)

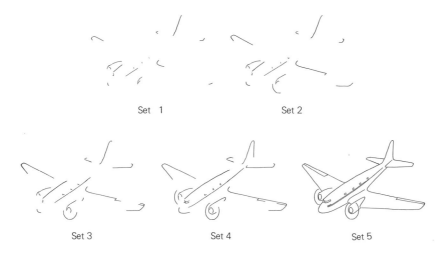

Set 1   Set 2

Set 3   Set 4   Set 5

the patient could voluntarily direct his attention to different aspects of it and report additional details. Six patients with hippocampal electrodes also experienced visual images, sounds, feelings, concepts, and the like, usually very fragmentary and not recognizably related to past experience.

One of Penfield's patients repeatedly heard an orchestra playing the "War March of the Priests" whenever she was stimulated at a particular point on the temporal cortex and could hum the tune along with her hallucination (1954). She had a recording of the piece at home. In another case,

During stimulation of the superior surface of the left temporal lobe within the fissure of Sylvius, R. M. [the patient] said "A guy coming through the fence at the baseball game, I see the whole thing." Afterward he said, "I just happened to watch those two teams play when the fellow came through the fence. . . . That would be like the beginning of an attack, anything might come up." He went on to explain that such scenes from his past came to him suddenly at the beginning of a seizure, when he was thinking of something else, things he had forgotten all about. (Penfield, 1954).

The data from observations by Korsakoff and from patients with temporal-lobe epilepsy can be interpreted in various ways, but they seem to imply that firmly established associations are not localized in the medial temporal or thalamic structures, as they survive lesions there. Similarly, the associations of immediate memory do not occur there, as patients have no difficulty in remembering the various parts of a sentence or repeating the stimulus words of the digit-span test. The impairment seems to be in the transfer of material from short-term storage to long-term storage, that is, in consolidation.

It is possible that the hippocampus, or some other limbic structure of the temporal lobe, plays a direct role in consolidation in human beings. An alternative possibility is that the structure has an amplifying effect upon weak associations in the cortex or elsewhere, an effect that may be essential for retrieval of weak long-term traces. Long-term traces that have been used for a period of months or years are as-

sumed to have become strong enough to be accessible without amplification; only recent memories are impaired by lesions or interfering stimulation of the hippocampal area. This theory assumes that long-term traces do not automatically become stronger with time but that frequent recall and rehearsal are necessary. As the latter are prevented, no recent memories can be consolidated.

On the other hand, there is strong evidence, as we saw in Part Five, that the limbic system is important for arousal and motivated behavior in animals. We also know that we remember events connected in some way with arousing or motivating situations more reliably than we remember events that have little significance for us; another hypothesis for the role of the hippocampal region in consolidation is therefore that it is involved in the mechanism of reinforcement. Activity of the hippocampal system may provide the cortex or other storage area with a neural signal or chemical agent required for the formation of permanent associations.

HIPPOCAMPAL INVOLVEMENT IN ANIMAL LEARNING

Unfortunately for the experimental study of the hippocampal amnesic effect, efforts to reproduce it in animals have so far proved unsuccessful. Orbach, Milner, and Rasmussen (1960) tested monkeys with bilateral lesions of the medial temporal lobe that were as nearly as possible identical with those most effective in producing recent-memory loss in man, but the deficits were much less marked and of a quite different character. For example, the monkeys learned a visual object discrimination with almost no impairment, even when distracting tasks were interpolated between trials. They could also learn a delayed-response task with distraction (being offered a free peanut during the delay), though delayed-alternation learning was impaired. Monkeys with medial temporal lesions also showed deficits in learning and retaining more difficult visual discriminations, but the deficits did not in any way approach the severity of the global learning difficulties in human patients. These negative results have been confirmed by other investigators similarly attempting to reproduce the human memory-loss syndrome in monkeys (Correll & Scoville, 1965; Drachman & Ommaya, 1964).

Rats with hippocampal lesions also show mixed deficits. Some types of active-avoidance learning even seemed to be improved by hippocampal lesions (Isaacson, Douglas & Moore, 1961), though passive avoidance was usually impaired (Douglas Kimura, 1958; Kimble, 1963). Simultaneous brightness discriminations were not impaired by hippocampal lesions, but successive brightness discriminations were (Kimble, 1963). Maze learning was usually impaired by such lesions (Kaada, Rasmussen & Kveim, 1961; Kimble, 1963).

The difference between hippocampal function in man and in animals has thus been firmly established, but it is nevertheless puzzling. We might speculate that man's use of language has changed his technique of learning, but this theory is difficult to uphold in the face of deficits in tasks especially chosen for their nonverbal character. Prisko (see B. Milner & Teuber, 1968) has shown that patients with bilateral damage to the hippocampal region cannot match different shades of pink or the frequencies of clicks or flashes when the stimuli are separated by a minute or more, whether or not the patients must perform a distracting task in the interval. Control patients are capable of accurate matching over much longer intervals.

At present we can assume only that the difference is caused by an evolutionary discontinuity between monkey and man in the function of the hippocampus and nearby structures. Such a discontinuity would not be unprecedented; the hippocampus at one time had a primarily olfactory function, which it no longer has in mammals.

TESTS OF THE CONSOLIDATION HYPOTHESIS

The results of other animal experiments on retrograde amnesia and consolidation have proved even more variable and controversial than those on hippocampal lesions. Much of the early work has been reviewed by Glickman (1961) and Hudspeth and Gerbrands (1965).

Duncan (1949) subjected rats to electro-convulsive shock (ECS) at various intervals ranging from 20 seconds to 14 hours after each trial in an avoidance problem and found that learning was retarded in those rats that had received ECS shortly after the trials. This finding supports the idea that traces need a period of undisturbed gestation in order to become permanent, the so-called "consolidation hypothesis." But Coons and Miller (1960) have pointed out that ECS might have aversive effects, resulting in a conflict situation for the animal. The subject has the choice of not responding and receiving a shock to the feet or of responding and receiving a shock to the head; choice of the former alternative does not necessarily imply that the response has been forgotten.

To test this theory Coons and Miller trained rats to run promptly to food and then started to shock them as they reached it. ECS was administered at varying times after the foot shocks. They found that rats with ECS 20 seconds after each trial learned to stay away from the food more quickly than did rats receiving ECS after a longer delay. They also replicated Duncan's experiment but added a further stage, in which rats that had learned an avoidance response then had to learn to withhold it, again with ECS at various intervals after each trial. In this passive-avoidance situation the experimenters found once more that ECS shortly after each trial speeded up the learning. These results support the theory that ECS has aversive effects, but subsequent experiments, especially those in which ECS has been presented only once, suggest that this component is relatively unimportant.

If rats are placed in an apparatus consisting of two communicating compartments, one large and one small, they will tend to spend most of their time in the small compartment. If they are then shocked in that compartment and placed back in the apparatus the next day, they will avoid that compartment. Bureš and Burešová (1963) found that rats given ECS up to six hours after the shock in the small compartment would return to it on the next day more often than unconvulsed control rats.

Chorover and Schiller (1965) used a slightly different passive-avoidance situation, originally developed by Pearlman, Sharpless, and Jarvik (1961). Rats stepped down from a small elevated platform onto the floor, a natural response that is normally performed with short latency. Some of the rats received foot shock as they reached the floor, and some of these rats were given ECS at different times (0.5, 2.0, 5.0, and 30 seconds) after the foot shock. Another group received no foot shock, but some of them were also given ECS at the same intervals after stepping down as were the first group. The results showed that when ECS followed the foot shock by less than 10 seconds there was amnesia for the foot shock, as indicated by an unchanged latency of stepping down on subsequent tests, but that when the ECS was delayed longer it had little effect upon retention.

ECS without foot shock produced an inverted-U type of avoidance curve. It had little effect upon behavior when given either immediately after stepping down or 30 seconds after stepping down, but at 10 seconds it produced avoidance. These results were interpreted as indicating that consolidation is a brief process, complete in a little more than 10 seconds and that ECS interferes with it. ECS is also shown to have aversive effects, but when it is presented less than 10 seconds after the response the amnesia it engenders prevents learning; when presented much more than 10 seconds after the response the delay of reinforcement reduces its effectiveness. A delay of 10 seconds between the response and the ECS thus gives optimal avoidance learning.

This explanation seems reasonable at first, but it is difficult to understand how ECS can become associated with any response or stimulus if it is an anticonsolidation agent, for its aversive effect is presumably contiguous with its anticonsolidation effect. It should therefore always erase the memory of itself, whatever its temporal relationship to other events.

The most surprising aspect of Chorover and Schiller's experiment, in view of the previous results, is the very short time required for consolidation. The discrepancy between their experiment and that of Bureš and Burešová

already mentioned induced Chorover and Schiller to repeat the latter (Chorover & Schiller, 1966). They obtained the same results as had Bureš and Burešová: Rats subjected to ECS one hour after shock in the small compartment did not avoid the compartment the next day. They also showed, however, that the rats receiving ECS were more active than the others and suggested that the cause of the apparent amnesia was the adverse effect of ECS upon inhibitory mechanisms, a suggestion previously made by Vanderwolf (1963b).

This suggestion seems the most reasonable explanation for the failure of the rats to avoid the dangerous compartment on the second day, but it leaves some questions unanswered. It does not explain, for example, why ECS six hours after the training trial produces less effect than ECS two hours after training. If the effect were entirely on the second day's performance we would expect the ECS to be more effective when administered after a longer interval. Nor is it clear why inhibition of entry into the small compartment is interfered with by ECS but inhibition of the step-down response is not.

Another explanation for the discrepancy has been suggested by the work of Lee-Teng (1969), who used chicks, and A. J. Miller (1968), who used rats; they have shown that the extent of retrograde amnesia produced by ECS is a function of the intensity of the convulsing current. In rats 35 ma ECS produced significant amnesia 24 hours later only if presented less than 30 seconds after the event to be remembered. A current of 100 ma, however, produced significant amnesia covering events occurring 50 minutes before the ECS.

Miller also found that over a period of two days there was some recovery of memory of foot shock given 30 seconds or more before the ECS, even when the more intense ECS current was used. This finding has been complemented by that of Pagano, Bush, Martin, and Hunt (1969), who found some recovery of memory over time when the ECS current was low, even when it was administered immediately after the foot shock. These results are in keeping with the usual course of amnesia in people who have suffered concussion. The retrograde amnesia immediately upon return to consciousness may stretch back for many years, but the blank period shrinks over the next few days until it includes only the last few minutes before the accident.

Another theory about how ECS affects behavior has been put forward by D. J. Lewis and Adams (1963). They argue that certain aspects of the convulsion become conditioned to the surrounding stimuli and that, when the animal is next introduced to the situation after it has received ECS there, it performs badly because components of the seizure are reestablished.

There is substantial evidence that ECS produces effects other than retrograde amnesia, for example those suggested by Coons and Miller (1960) and Lewis and Adams (1963), but demonstration of these effects does not prove that they are the only phenomena to be taken into account. The evidence in favor of an anticonsolidation effect is now very strong.

Another confounding effect of one-trial avoidance-learning situations in tests of consolidation theory is the delayed appearance of avoidance after shock pointed out by Hudson (1950). Avoidance of the dangerous situation appears to incubate over time. Pinel and Cooper (1966) and Pinel (1968) have suggested that ECS may arrest the incubation of fear and thus cause poor avoidance on later trials. Of course, the incubation process may be related to consolidation in some way, but the important point is that in normal learning memory is apparently available immediately, even before it has been consolidated, whereas the incubation hypothesis implies that memory is not available until consolidation has taken place.

To what extent the assumption of a steadily decaying trace is justified in connection with material that exceeds the span of immediate memory is an interesting question. The phenomenon of reminiscence indicates that under certain conditions the immediate trace may be weaker than the later one. B. Milner has shown that recognition of faces by normal subjects is poorer after a delay of 2-3 seconds than after 120 seconds. Damage to the right hippocampal region prevents this reminiscence effect (B. Milner & Teuber, 1968).

The reason for the popularity of the one-trial avoidance situation for tests of consolidation is the relative ease with which the interval between the event to be learned and the ECS or other treatment can be controlled, but it does lead to misgivings about the generality of the consolidation process. Tenen (1965) has devised an ingenious method of obtaining one-trial reward learning with rats. He measured the number of times that very thirsty rats explored a hole in the side of a testing box during several short individual testing sessions. At the last session water was presented to some of the rats at the hole for 10 seconds. Rats that were given ECS immediately after the presentation of the water subsequently explored the hole only slightly longer than did the control rats that received no water. Other control rats received water but were given shock to the feet instead of ECS; they showed almost as great an increase in exploration of the hole as rats receiving neither ECS nor shock (Figure 20.14). In a group of rats that received ECS three hours after presentation of water the animals explored

Figure 20.14 The mean number of hole explorations for five groups of rats in a water-reinforcement situation. The curves for the groups overlap closely during the adaptation period and are not shown individually. (After Tenen, 1965.)

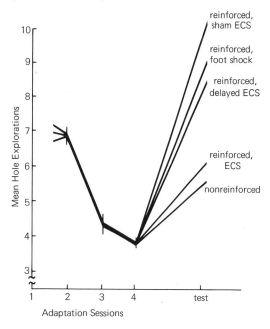

the hole to an extent intermediate between the "immediate ECS" and "no ECS" groups. There is thus no reason to suppose that the disturbance of consolidation produced by ECS is confined to avoidance-training situations.

Other methods of disturbing brain function can also produce retrograde amnesia in animals. Goddard (1964b) has demonstrated an anticonsolidation effect of low-intensity electrical stimulation of the amygdala in rats. The stimulation was maintained for five minutes after each pairing of a buzzer with foot shock. Under these conditions the rats receiving stimulation learned the association more slowly than did rats receiving the same stimulation during a three-minute presentation of the buzzer just before the foot shock.

Rapid anesthetization with ether was used by Pearlman, Sharpless, and Jarvik (1961) on mice in the stepping-down situation described previously, and it disturbed consolidation. Bureš and Burešová (1963) were not able to influence consolidation in rats with ether anesthesia in their two-compartment passive-avoidance test, but they did find that bilateral spreading depression (see Chapter 4, Lesions) induced by potassium chloride applied to the dura immediately after the foot shocks, interfered with consolidation. Albert (1966a) observed a similar influence. As with ECS in this apparatus, spreading depression induced six hours after the learning trial produced a decrement in passive avoidance the next day, though not as great as that produced by spreading depression induced immediately after the shock.

Bureš and Burešová (1960) have also demonstrated that cortical spreading depression can be used to produce temporary functional decortication or, when confined to one hemisphere, functional hemidecortication, and they have used this technique in the study of interhemispheric transfer of memory traces. I. S. Russell and Ochs (1963) later used the same technique and were able to show that, although a bar-pressing response for food was not transferred from one hemisphere to the other spontaneously if one hemisphere was always depressed during training sessions and the

"trained" hemisphere depressed during test sessions, it required only one reinforced bar-press with both hemispheres functioning to ensure complete interhemispheric transfer of the traces necessary for the behavior.

This one-trial transfer situation seems ideal for studying the process of consolidation, and it was used for this purpose by Ray and Emley (1964). Water-deprived rats were trained during unilateral spreading depression to make *successive* brightness discriminations in a T-maze (that is, to turn one way when the light was on and the other way when it was off). When they had learned the discrimination under this condition they were given one trial with neither hemisphere depressed; then either 15 seconds or 10 minutes later potassium-chloride solution was applied to the "trained" hemisphere to produce spreading depression there. Thirty minutes after the single trial, and with the previously trained hemisphere still depressed, the rats were tested again; those in which spreading depression had begun 15 seconds after the transfer trial not only did not know which way to turn in the maze, they seemed to turn more often than chance to the wrong side. Those rats that were allowed 10 minutes with both hemispheres functional performed correctly.

The tendency to turn to the wrong side was also observed in rats that had had no transfer trial, and it may thus indicate learning in subcortical circuits that have connections to both hemispheres. Any subcortical learning occurring when one hemisphere was depressed might produce the reverse motor effect when the other hemisphere was depressed. Carlson (1967) has demonstrated that subcortical learning takes place under certain conditions during cortical spreading depression.

The consolidation results suggest that during the transfer of training from one hemisphere to another there is a period of persistent activity during which the trace on the trained side helps to consolidate the new trace on the previously depressed side. If the trained side is prevented by spreading depression from participating in this consolidation, the transfer is disrupted. If this evidence is reliable, it suggests that consolidation does depend upon an active process, as Müller and Pilzecker, Hebb, and others have postulated.

Bilateral injections of the anticholinesterase *diisopropylfluorophosphate* (DFP) into the hippocampus of rats immediately after they have learned an avoidance response impairs performance 24 hours later, but performance returns to normal after a few days (Deutsch, Hamburg & Dahl, 1966). More interestingly, DFP injected three days after training has practically no effect, but if it is injected two or three weeks after training it again impairs performance (Figure 20.15). Deutsch has explained this U-shaped curve by assuming a two-stage memory process. The initial trace fades as the second trace is consolidated and grows in strength. The effect of DFP is to inactivate acetylcholinesterase, the enzyme that breaks down free acetylcholine released at synapses during neural transmission. Neurons can then be fired by smaller quantities of released acetylcholine, but when the amount of acetylcholine released is normal, enough of it may accumulate at the synapses to produce long-lasting depolarization and either to block or to reduce the firing rates of affected neurons.

According to Deutsch, when the memory trace is recent and strong, the DFP tends to block performance. Later, when the initial trace has weakened and the permanent trace has not yet been fully consolidated, the DFP may help the weak traces, but later still, when consolidation is complete, DFP blocks transmission again.

In another experiment (cited by Deutsch & Deutsch, 1966), scopolamine, which antagonizes acetylcholine and therefore produces most effective synaptic blocking when small amounts of acetylcholine are released, was found to have an effect opposite to that of DFP. Impairment of avoidance was greatest when the injection was given three days after training. Whether or not the hypothesis about the changing strengths of the trace is correct, it seems clear from the data that the hippocampus in the rat plays different roles in performance at different times after learning has taken place.

Some of the experiments with puromycin, a

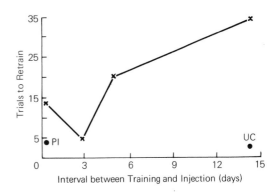

Figure 20.15 Effects upon habit retention of injections of diisopropylfluorophosphate (DFP) into the brains of rats at various times after training, measured 24 hours after injection. UC is the score for an uninjected control group 14 days after training. PI is the score for a placebo injection group injected 30 minutes after training. (After Deutsch, Hamburg & Dahl, 1966.)

protein-synthesis inhibitor, also seem relevant to the problem of consolidation, but as most of them were done with a different problem in mind we shall postpone discussion of them until the next chapter.

The original theory of consolidation, put forward by Müller and Pilzecker and still retaining many supporters, was that the information is initially stored as some form of persistent reverberatory activity, and is gradually converted into structural changes at synapses. This is a common-sense view, because we know that in order to fix a memory we "rehearse" it, that is, repeat it to ourselves a number of times, and it seems logical that if a certain amount of synaptic change takes place when a pair of neurons fire together, the change will be greater if they fire together a number of times.

When we rehearse consciously the pattern to be learned is reactivated intermittently—or so it seems from introspection. Accordingly, in the intervals between rehearsals the information would have to be stored in some other way, which is not quite what most psychologists understand by "reverberatory trace." Hebb (1949), for example, assumed that the information was carried entirely by the neural activity pursuing its tail round closed circuits for a time.

The pure activity trace is an attractive concept at first sight, but there are several difficulties. How, for example, are the impulses that constitute the information kept from straying into other pathways and producing unwanted neural changes there? How is the beginning of the message to be located again once the activity has started to circulate around loops? The further difficulties seem formidable, if not insurmountable, when the actual mechanics of setting up a chain of activity that can link two complex activities (representing two words, for example) are seriously contemplated. Many neurons must inevitably be tied up in the storage of quite small amounts of information, and, as the type of circuit suitable for holding information by circulating activity is not suited to permanent storage, smooth transfer from one mode of storage to the other becomes a problem.

These objections are not so serious if we can assume that stored information does not circulate in loops made up of completely unmodified neurons. The initial firing might produce a temporary increase in synaptic efficiency, a temporary reduction in threshold, or a withdrawal of inhibition from the neurons of the loop, as suggested by P. M. Milner (1957) and Walker (1958). As a result of some such change it would be possible for all activity to cease in a loop and later to start up again in the same pattern, provided the pause were not long enough to allow the temporary change to fade.

The presentation of additional information during reverberation might establish mutual inhibition between the old and new traces and might block the firing of some neurons, resulting in inferior consolidation. A generalized convulsion or other severe disturbance of neural firing would also interfere with the patterned activity, and if it interfered long enough the reverberation would not reestablish itself properly, and consolidation would again be prevented.

It seems very likely that some internal control over the degree of consolidation is exerted through the motivation system (in man, possibly through the hippocampus) and that it serves the purpose of separating the information to be saved for future use from that to be discarded as useless clutter. The agent that serves this selective function is usually called "reinforcement," and, although the question of whether or not reinforcement enhances learning has never been definitely settled, the fact that latent learning is relatively weak (MacCorquodale & Meehl, 1954) suggests that it does. In most learning situations reinforcement is not presented until some time after the events to be learned have occurred, and it is presumably useful therefore to be able to store the greater part of the incoming information for a short time in order to determine whether or not it will turn out to be interesting and important. If not, the chances are that the information will not be consolidated to any appreciable extent. If the information is made interesting by the presentation of some reinforcing event shortly afterward, it will be stored more effectively.

In man the process of deciding what is important enough to be worth remembering is often conscious, and learning may involve acquired tricks like rehearsing. The evidence from human patients with memory loss suggests that other consolidation mechanisms of which we are not conscious are also set in motion by reinforcement.

If reinforcement did enhance consolidation, it could do so in various ways. One, suggested by P. M. Milner (1957), is that reinforcing stimuli may fire the arousal system and thus lead to a higher level of firing in all active cells. It was assumed that the more often a cell fired, the greater would be the synaptic change. Another possibility is that some firing must take place in a "reinforcing" system of neurons or some substance must be released into the cerebral circulation, in order to fix any synaptic changes, which would otherwise fade rapidly away. No evidence has so far been found for or against either of these mechanisms.

Albert (1966b) has postulated that consolidation may be furthered by small potential gradients across cortical cells. He based this suggestion primarily upon the work of Rusinov (1953). In Rusinov's experiments a small anodal (surface-positive) polarizing current of 2–10 μa was applied to the rabbit motor cortex at a point from which limb movements could be elicited by electrical stimulation. He found that the direct current (DC) sensitized the cortex so that any stimulus (a flash, a touch, click, or the like) would trigger a motor response. The aspect of the experiment that aroused most interest was that, if a movement had been elicited many times by a flash, for example, while the cortex was polarized, flashes would continue to elicit the movement after the polarizing current had been turned off for as long as 20 minutes. Only stimuli that had been presented frequently during the polarization had this effect; other stimuli, which also elicited movements when presented during the polarization but which were presented infrequently, did not trigger movements when the current was turned off, showing that the effect was not simply sensitization of the cortex near the electrode.

This work was replicated by Morrell (1961a), who extended it by recording from the polarized region with microelectrodes instead of using a motor response as the detector of firing. He also used electrical stimulation of the cortex, instead of peripheral stimuli, to trigger the activity.

These results could be interpreted as meaning that surface-positive polarization of the cortex facilitates learning or consolidation. Bureš, Burešová, and Záhorová (1958) pointed out that the cortex became surface-negative during cortical spreading depression, which, of course, interferes with consolidation.

Following up the implications of these findings, Morrell and Naitoh (1962) implanted electrodes so that the visual cortex of the rabbit could be polarized as the animal learned an avoidance. Cathodal polarization of the visual cortex impaired performance, but the effect upon learning was equivocal. Kupfermann (1965) obtained decrements of visual-discrimination learning in rats by a similar cathodal-polarization technique, but they were not statistically significant. Albert (1966b) claimed that a very small cathodal current, waxing and waning in a way that mimicked the waves of surface-negative polarization accompanying spreading depression, interfered with consolidation of an avoidance response. He regarded this finding as further evidence that the effect of spreading depression on consolidation results

from absence of the required surface-positive potential.

Neither Morrell nor Kupfermann found any evidence that the Rusinov effect extends to behavioral learning. Anodal polarization was not found to enhance avoidance learning or visual discrimination, but it is possible that the natural reinforcing effect was optimal in these experiments, leaving no margin for improvement by artificial manipulation of the cortical polarization. Albert, reported, however, that anodal polarization, although it did not enhance learning, could restore information that had been lost by spreading depression if applied at the right time.

There have been many attempts to determine what steady-potential (SP) changes occur at the cortex during learning and other behavior, but so far they have not thrown much light on the questions raised by the theory just described. Caspers (1961, 1965) found that arousal from sleep was accompanied by a surface-negative shift in cortical potential and that a positive shift occurred at the onset of sleep. Some psychologists believe that sleep promotes consolidation, which would be the effect predicted by the theory, but few would argue that arousal is bad for learning, which should also follow.

Rowland & Goldstone (1963) found that changes in cortical SP (usually surface-positive ones) occurred when food was presented to hungry cats (Figure 20.16). The response could be conditioned to flash or click stimuli, and the conditioned SP change could be extinguished and differentiated like any other conditioned response. Rowland, Bradley, School, and Deutschman (1967) reported shifts in cortical potential of up to 0.5 mv during feeding and sexual stimulation in cats (Figure 20.17) and during noxious and hypothalamic reward stimulation in rats, but changes in both positive and negative directions were observed, depending upon the placement of the electrodes and upon the animal.

It is possible that only certain areas of the cortex undergo SP shift. Depending on the arrangement of the recording electrodes, other areas might then appear to have SP shifts of the opposite polarity. Like much of the research

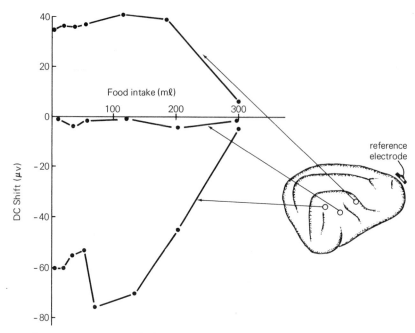

Figure 20.16 A DC shift during consumption of a liquid diet by a cat. The curves are for the three different electrode sites shown in the lateral view of the brain. The reference electrode in each case was on the frontal bone. (After Rowland & Goldstone, 1963.)

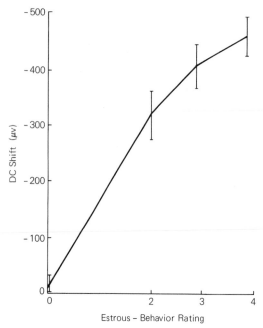

Figure 20.17 The shift in potential of the cat cortex in response to genital stimulation at different stages of estrus. The rating scale ranged from 0, when the cat warded off the male, to 4, when the afterreaction included more than 10 rolls onto the back. (After Rowland, Bradley, School & Deutschman, 1967.)

in this field, these results are still uncertain and can be cited either in support of the notion that cortical polarization is a factor in reinforcement and consolidation or against it.

Several investigators have claimed that neural excitants such as strychnine, Metrazol, or magnesium Pemoline, can improve learning. Lashley (1917b) was, as usual, early in the field. He gave strychnine to rats a few minutes before running them through a maze and found that they learned faster than controls did. McGaugh and Petrinovich (1959) thought this effect might be upon consolidation, so they injected strychnine once a day immediately after a single maze run. They found, as had Lashley, faster learning in the strychnine group, but the interpretation of this result as showing an effect upon consolidation has been criticized by Cooper and Krass (1963), who found that strychnine improved maze learning when injected as long as three days before training. It is thus unclear whether McGaugh and Petrinovich's results reflected the effect of the drug upon consolidation of the immediately previous run or upon the next day's learning.

It should be noted that facilitation of learning by strychnine or other convulsant drugs is, in any case, a capricious phenomenon. Apparently the optimum dose is critical and varies from one strain of rat to another. There have been many failures to replicate this type of experiment, and we cannot consider the effect as incontrovertibly established.

Magnesium Pemoline is an excitant drug that has recently received attention because of reports that it enhances learning (Plotnikoff, 1966), but again it is disappointing to have to state that more extensive work has cast doubt on the result. Claims of improved learning should never be made on the basis of improved performance of a single type of response in a single species. There seems to be evidence that Pemoline increases the tendency of some rats to jump; if jumping is the response to be learned the drug may appear to produce some improvement. In many other types of performance it either has no effect or, as has been reported for maze running, may cause a deficit.

On the somewhat doubtful grounds that sodium glutamate is an important constituent of nerve cells, it was at one time proposed that intelligence might be improved by addition of glutamic acid to the diet, but, although Zimmerman and Ross (1944) obtained positive results, subsequent investigations have repeatedly failed to confirm their finding.

Of course, it would be wonderful if we could find some drug or other treatment that would turn us all into geniuses or even overcome some types of mental deficiency, and the search for learning enhancers will continue. Apart from any applied value, however, if some substance could be found to modify learning, it would have the additional value of telling us something about the mechanism of learning. On the other hand, it is more likely that improved understanding of the processes of learning will come first and may then lead to practical methods of increasing learning ability.

Summary

Learning is a phenomenon that we can describe and, up to a point, measure but that has so far defeated all efforts at explanation. Our best hope of reaching an understanding of the physiological basis of learning is from the converging effects of improved knowledge about neural transmission and increased behavioral knowledge about learning, especially learning under conditions of physiological intervention.

Classical learning experiments tell us that there are at least two stages of memory in man, immediate memory and long-term memory. Man's immediate memory capacity is limited to about seven concepts, but each concept can be quite complex, depending upon previous long-term learning. The transfer of information to long-term memory in man and probably in animals seems to require repetition, either external or internal through rehearsal, and the resulting memory trace (engram) is susceptible to interference from subsequent stimuli for some hours or days after learning. The process of stabilizing long-term traces is called "consolidation."

Reinforcement may effect consolidation by facilitating the transfer of items from immediate memory to long-term memory. It may also aid learning by increasing the distinctiveness of reinforced items and by providing the motivation required for learning to be demonstrated during subsequent tests.

An important first step in the physiological investigation of learning is to discover where it takes place and where memory traces are stored. Despite half a century of research, all we can say at present is that in the mammal most, but not all, learning depends upon the cortex and that each memory is dispersed widely through the brain. No lesion will selectively destroy a particular habit, and no one has pinpointed with certainty a neural change corresponding to a long-term memory.

Changes in electrographic activity during learning have been studied exhaustively, but so far these methods have proved no more informative than others, and the results have raised more questions than they have answered.

Learning has been studied in simple organisms like *paramecia* and *planaria* and in parts of more complex animals—the abdominal ganglion of *Aplysia* and the ventral-cord ganglia of arthropods, for example. Various changes have been observed in such preparations, but it is not certain that these changes bear any relation to learning in higher animals. One of the most promising preparations from the point of view of generating learning changes in observable tissue is the secondary (or mirror) epileptogenic focus produced by intermittent concentrated stimulation of a cortical region. The resulting change in cortical activity can hardly be called "learning," but it may involve a similar basic process.

Human learning seems to be severely disturbed by damage to the hippocampus. This region is apparently not where information is permanently stored because old memories survive the damage; presumably, however, it contributes to the establishment of long-term memories. Immediate memory is not affected by hippocampal lesions, and patients are still capable of motor learning and some types of perceptual learning.

Hippocampal lesions in animals do not produce a widespread learning deficit, but maze learning and some forms of delayed response are impaired. Whether this finding means that animal learning is very different from most human learning or that the role of the hippocampus has changed in man is not yet clear.

Consolidation studies on animals have not provided such clear-cut demonstrations of the phenomenon as are observed in man after brain trauma. Some investigators have found that memory of a task can be impaired by electroconvulsive shock or some other strong disturbance of brain activity applied up to several hours after learning; others have found that consolidation is complete in a few seconds. Although there is little doubt that various procedures will interfere with consolidation in animals, there are many confounding factors that make interpretation of the experiments difficult. In some cases the anticonsolidation procedure has been shown to have aversive effects and it usually also has other effects upon behavior—increasing general activity or making the animal fatigued or sick, for example.

One theory about the consolidation mechanism is that it involves maintenance of a potential gradient (surface-positive) across the cortex. Most anticonsolidation treatments produce surface-negative gradients. If the cortex is cathodally polarized by having a small current passed through it between implanted electrodes, some hint that learning is impaired results, but the effect is weak. The surface of the cortex often goes positive during reinforcing situations, but this effect is not sufficiently universal to justify postulating a causal relationship.

Several attempts to improve consolidation and learning with drugs have been made but with doubtful success at best and in most cases no success at all.

CHAPTER 21

BIOCHEMISTRY AND LEARNING

In recent years much research effort has concentrated on the mechanisms of protein synthesis in nerve and glial cells as they relate to learning. Most of the structural features and metabolic processes of cells depend upon the nature and quantities of proteins that the cells manufacture, and there is, therefore, a good *a priori* reason to suppose that this mechanism may play a part in the neural changes that underlie learning and memory. Before we discuss the behavioral evidence for these ideas, however, let us briefly review what is known at present about the synthesis of proteins in cells.

DNA AND THE CONTROL OF PROTEIN SYNTHESIS

Proteins consist of polymerized amino acids. There are only 20 amino acids, but an unlimited number of different proteins can be made from them by changing the order in which they are joined together along the chain, the length of the chain, and the ways in which the chain tangles itself in knots after it has been formed. In order to synthesize a particular protein, therefore, it is necessary to specify in some way the sequence in which the amino acids are linked.

This information is believed to be derived initially from the genetic material in the nucleus of the cell, which has been identified as deoxy-ribonucleic acid (DNA). As every biology student knows, DNA consists of a double helix of the sugar deoxyribose and phosphate, with cross links between the helical chains consisting of pairs of nitrogenous bases, either thymine and adenine or cytosine and guanine. When a cell divides in mitosis, the two helices separate, and new *nucleotides* (sugar-phosphate-base units) join the free ends of the bases attached to the original helices to form two new double helices (Figure 21.1).

Information is coded according to the sequence of bases along each helix of the DNA, and it has been shown that this sequence is directly related to the sequence of amino acids along a *polypeptide* (that is, polyamino acid) chain. As there are 20 amino acids and only 4 nucleotide bases, a sequence of several bases must be necessary to specify each amino acid. In order to obtain 20 code "words" from the 4-letter base alphabet, each word must have at least 3 letters, and in fact each sequence of 3 bases along the DNA molecule does specify an amino acid to be fitted onto the polypeptide chain.

The mechanics of the translation from DNA to protein are not as straightforward as might be inferred from this account; the information is first transferred from the DNA to single-strand ribonucleic acid (RNA) molecules (called "messenger RNA"), which attach themselves to *ribosomes*. The amino-acid molecules are brought to the ribosomes by short molecules of transfer RNA, of which there is one type for each amino acid. The transfer RNA is coded to bind itself to an amino acid and to fit the appropriate base code of the messenger RNA. If the next three bases of the messenger RNA specify a particular amino acid, say glutamic acid, the transfer RNA bound to glutamic acid will have the complementary set of three bases and will attach itself to the messenger RNA, towing its amino acid into a position where it will be combined with the growing peptide chain. As each amino acid is assembled the messenger RNA passes through the ribosome like a tape through a tape-recorder head and exposes the next code word (Figure 21.2).

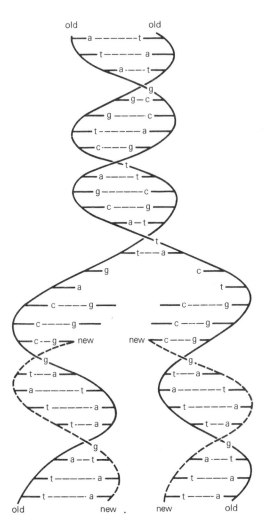

Figure 21.1 The replication process in a DNA molecule. The solid helical chains consist of deoxyribose and phosphate. The cross links consist of *a*, adenine; *c*, cytosine; *g*, guanine; *t*, thymine. (Redrawn from H. E. Sutton, 1961.)

DIFFERENTIATION OF CELLS

The preceding account of the production of different proteins by the genetic information coded in the DNA of the cell is very much simplified. We know that in multicellular organisms all the cells are not alike; they do not all produce the same proteins, despite having been derived from the same parent cell. Either the DNA is changed during cell division, or not all its information is used all the time. The latter explanation is the more widely accepted one for most organisms. One theory is that parts of the DNA molecule are masked by operator genes. Environmental substances called "derepressors" can react with particular operators, unmasking part of the DNA so that it can act as a template for the production of RNA.

Different derepressors can thus cause some cells to become liver cells, others neurons, others bone, and so on. Once a cell has begun to differentiate in a particular way it apparently produces its own derepressors for the substances it will need for its growth and functioning. For example, a liver cell may require a slight nudge in the form of a hormone-like substance released by its neighbors, but once the appropriate sections of DNA have been exposed not only the proteins required by the cell but also the derepressor substances necessary to keep those bits of DNA active are synthesized, and the cell is prevented from regressing to a more primitive form if and when the external influence is removed.

Nowhere in the body does the effect of neighboring cells seem so important as in the nervous system. Not only do neurons and glial cells coexist in symbiotic relationship, each providing substances necessary for the proper development of the other, but each nerve also grows under the influence of others, especially those with which it will eventually synapse. When an axonal branch finally reaches its target and establishes a synaptic connection, its growth ceases, and changes in the membranes of both cells take place at the point of contact. Sperry (1944, 1948, 1963), in a very elegant series of experiments, showed that the course of axonal growth was very accurately determined in amphibians and that the process was recapitulated with precision after nerve tracts had been cut and frayed (Figure 21.3).

It is difficult to believe that all these interactions among brain cells depend only upon the action of derepressor substances on the genetic material of the cells. A more plausible hypothesis is that the "organizers" released by one set of neurons act directly on the membrane growth of other cells they influence.

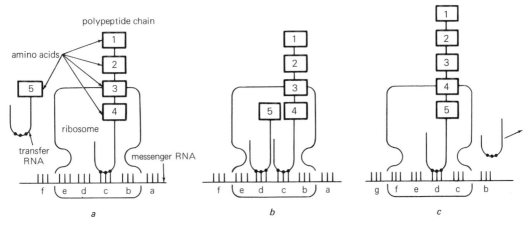

Figure 21.2   Growth of the polypeptide chain on the ribosome. (a) Site *d* on messenger RNA is exposed by the ribosome, as transfer RNA coded to match the site approaches carrying its amino acid. (b) The transfer RNA attaches itself to site *d* and places its amino acid so that it can become attached to the growing polypeptide chain. (c) Messenger RNA moves one "triplet step" through the ribosome, releasing the previous molecule of transfer RNA and bringing the second into line with the polypeptide chain. Site *e* is now exposed and will capture a suitably coded molecule of transfer RNA. (After J. D. Watson, 1965.)

Very little is known about how a cell membrane grows. It is usually assumed that the protein and lipoid molecules that constitute it fit together spontaneously as do atoms building a crystal, but the behavior of the growing axon, for example, suggests a more directed process in which external substances play an important role. If some sort of a growth hormone is required to facilitate the assembly of the membrane from the molecules in the cell, two factors must be involved: First, each growing neuron must be coded in some way, and, second, specific growth hormones must be present along the path of axonal growth to encourage the neuron to grow in that direction. The coding of the cell almost certainly involves the production of specific proteins, possibly proteins destined to form part of the membrane. As already pointed out, specificity will depend upon local derepressor substances that determine which parts of the total information coded on the DNA will be used in that particular cell.

We may now speculate that the individual mix of proteins and lipoids available within our neuron can be assembled in a membrane most efficiently in the presence of traces of a substance released by neurons in the target zone. The membrane thus grows most rapidly in the direction of the target, forming a projection in that direction, which becomes the axon. The specific growth substance has no effect upon the membrane components of other neurons not destined to grow toward that target. The membranes of those cells are influenced by other growth hormones, and they grow toward their own targets, so that axons can grow in opposite directions in the same path at the same time or tracts can grow through one another at angles without confusion. The growth substances released by the target neurons are almost certainly also polypeptides, manufactured

Figure 21.3   Regeneration of the optic nerve in the newt. Functional connections are reestablished despite the fact that the eye and distal stump of the nerve were inverted before the two ends of the nerve were rejoined. (After Sperry, 1951.)

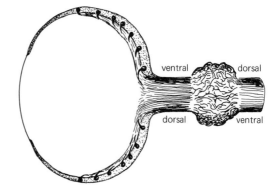

under genetic control, and they too presumably depend upon local derepressors for their specificity.

When the tip of the advancing axon reaches the dendritic membrane of a neuron in the target area, changes in the type of membrane produced at both sides of the synapse occur. Probably substances emitted by the advancing tip cause reorganization of the membrane of the target cell to form the subsynaptic membrane. At the same time substances emitted by the target cell modify the growth of the axon tip and induce it to form a synaptic knob. At some synapses there is microscopic evidence of filaments from one membrane to the other (Figure 21.4), which supports the idea that the synaptic structures are formed under joint control of substances from both cells and that there is an exchange of material between the neurons at this point.

A picture thus emerges of membrane growth under dual control of the local environment (which determines in the first place, through the action of derepressor substances, which types of membrane protein a cell will produce) and specific growth hormones (which determine how these proteins along with lipoids will be assembled to form different types and shapes

of membrane). These environmental effects can, of course, work only because there is a substrate of DNA that both produces and is acted upon by the environmental substances. The interplay of heredity and environment, which Hebb (1949) has stressed in relation to behavior, thus extends in a sense to the individual cell. It is easy to see how an abnormal chemical environment in the growing organism could thoroughly disrupt the "innate" pattern.

Of course, in this chapter, we are not primarily interested in how innate connections are formed, but the possibility that learned connections are produced by some modification of the same mechanism must be entertained. If we understood how innate connections were formed, it would almost certainly help us to find out how they could be modified by experience.

The basic requirement of a learning process is that impulses be enabled to fire certain neurons that they could not fire before learning. The particular connection made in this way is usually between two circuits that are active at the same time or nearly so. In view of the infinite number of possible conjunctions of events that we would be able to remember if we ever observed them or even imagined them, it seems likely that there is an almost infinite number of *potential* connections between neurons, few of which are functional when the organism is naïve. We can think of many reasons why the potential connections may not function without help: The synaptic knobs may be too big and insensitive to be fired by an impulse along the very thin terminal section of the axon (P. M. Milner, 1961b); the knob may fire but fail to release enough transmitter substance to affect the next neuron; the subsynaptic membrane may not be sensitive to the transmitter substance released; and so on. It is even possible that the transsynaptic filaments are essential for synaptic transmission and that only in a minority of synapses are these filaments formed innately. This nonconductivity must remain unaltered during the firing of either the presynaptic or the postsynaptic membrane alone; otherwise countless false associations would take place that would not represent con-

Figure 21.4 A cortical synapse with filaments extending between the membranes, as seen under the electron microscope. The continuation of the filaments within the dendrite suggests that they are involved in the transfer of substances from one cell to the other. (After De Robertis, 1964.)

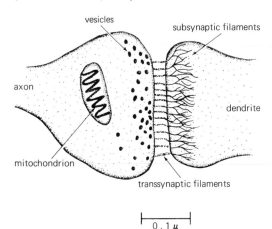

vesicles

subsynaptic filaments

axon

dendrite

mitochondrion

transsynaptic filaments

$0.1\ \mu$

junctions of actual events. Only when both membranes are fired almost simultaneously must we assume that something happens to make the synapse functional. Again, this result could arise from a vast number of changes, but one strong possibility is that substances released by the firing are exchanged between the membranes, resulting in completion of the process that was not completed by innate mechanisms in these learning synapses.

These speculations run rather far ahead of the experimental evidence. So far most investigations into the neurochemical concomitants of learning have dealt more with the possibility that learning involves changes in RNA, or even DNA, thus influencing the metabolism of the whole cell. The results have not been very encouraging, however, and the changed-RNA hypothesis may well have to be abandoned.

INVESTIGATIONS OF NEUROCHEMICAL CONCOMITANTS OF LEARNING

During the last decade several experiments have been performed to determine what relationship there might be between learning and the metabolism of neurons and glial cells, but there are still not enough data to justify confident interpretation.

One of the first major efforts to relate protein synthesis to behavior was that of Krech and his associates at Berkeley. Their early work has been reviewed by Rosenzweig, Krech, and Bennett (1958) and their more recent work by Bennett, Diamond, Krech, and Rosenzweig (1964). In most of the experiments the protein under investigation was the enzyme cholinesterase (ChE), which was chosen because of its relation to the process of neural transmission and because it is relatively easy to measure reliably.

The early experiments indicated that the most adaptive rats had higher concentrations of ChE in their brains, at least when they were older than about 120 days. Later experiments have been aimed at the effect of experience upon brain metabolism, and it has been found that rats reared in a complex "free" environment had heavier and thicker cortices than did rats reared in isolation. The total enzyme content of the rats raised in a free environment was higher than that of the restricted rats, but, because of the greater cortical weight, there was actually a lower proportion of the enzyme in the cortices of experienced rats. Analysis of the enzyme change suggests that the free rats had more nonneural tissue (glia, blood vessels, and the like) relative to neural tissue than the isolated rats did. The cortical weight changes were not permanent and disappeared after a few weeks in a standard environment; they were not therefore directly associated with memory. Nor can the changes be attributed to any general change in body metabolism with activity, for example, because the "free" animals were about 7 per cent lighter than the isolated animals; the subcortical parts of the brain were also lighter.

About the only conclusion that can be drawn from these data is that neural activity does affect the structure and chemical composition of the brain. The effects are most likely related to processes regulating the production of proteins to keep pace with their consumption.

Krech and his colleagues have not devoted much effort to relating their findings to possible changes in the genetic material of brain cells, but this topic has been the main preoccupation of many other investigators in recent years. A major difficulty with such research is that all neural transmission obviously depends upon the synthesis of transmitter substances, and it is highly likely that such synthesis depends upon RNA (and therefore indirectly upon DNA and derepressor substances). It has been known for some time that increased activity of neurons usually results in an increase in the amount of RNA in the cytoplasm (Brattgård, 1952; Morrell, 1961b); interference with RNA or protein synthesis would then be expected to impair all neural activity, performance as well as learning. Similarly, any change in RNA observed during learning experiments might result from the increased neural activity evoked by the stimuli or responses and thus only indirectly from the learning itself.

The historical background of these investigations, with an evolving hypothetical framework, further complicates the task of trying to interpret the results. At first, scientists were influenced by the enormous amount of information that could be stored in the DNA molecule, and, recognizing the need for concentration of information in memory, they saw the nucleic-acid molecule as the ideal store for this information also. Either DNA or RNA was assumed to be modified by the patterns of electrical activity impinging upon the neuron, and it was rather vaguely specified that such modified material would produce proteins that would make the cell more sensitive to the same patterns of electrical activity.

What these theorists did not take into account was the complexity of the neural networks in the brain, which relieves the individual neuron of the job of storing all incoming information. All each neuron has to store is the information that input at synapse x helped to fire it—much simpler than the total event to be remembered—and certainly far less than the capacity of a molecular coding mechanism. The rather misleadingly named "genetic memory" does not produce innate behavior directly; it acts as a blueprint from which the networks that determine innate behavior are constructed. The blueprint must be reduced to molecular form simply because it must fit into the single egg cell during reproduction. Memory based on individual experience almost certainly is the result of a direct modification of the resulting network; the information is not inherited and need not therefore be compressed into a single molecule. If any molecular mechanisms are important for learning they are presumably those responsible for effecting and maintaining the synaptic change, and there has been a steady drift in theoretical orientation toward this point of view.

Like most theories, good and bad, the idea that RNA is changed by experience led to some provocative experiments. One of the originators of the theory (Hydén, 1959) had developed a very delicate technique for measuring the composition of minute quantities of RNA, and he applied the technique to material from the nuclei of sensory cells in the vestibular nucleus of rats that had learned to climb a sloping wire ("tightrope") to obtain food (Hydén & Egyházi,

1962). Rats that had been swung round for an equivalent time to stimulate their vestibular cells but had not learned to balance were used as controls. The investigators found that both treatments caused an increase in the total amount of RNA in the nuclei of the neurons, but in the rats that had learned to balance on the wire they also found changes in the proportions of the various nucleotide bases. There was a higher proportion of adenine and less uracil (which in RNA replaces the thymine of DNA) than in the RNA of control rats. The other two bases, guanine and cytosine were present in approximately the usual proportions.

This result points to the emergence of new types of RNA (or to differences in the proportions of RNA previously present) as a result of tightrope walking, and it could thus be construed as supporting Hydén's hypothesis. Other explanations are possible, however, and it has been pointed out that a sensory nucleus is an improbable site for learning changes. The questionable validity of the chosen control group, whose vestibular stimulation was certainly not identical to that of the experimental group, also makes us hesitate to accept the findings as conclusive.

Hydén and Egyházi (1963) later found similar changes in the base ratios of RNA in the glial cells surrounding the neurons of the vestibular nucleus in rats after tightrope walking. Hydén's suggestion that the glial RNA changes were related to short-term memory and the neural changes to long-term memory is sheer speculation and does not follow from the experiments. The finding does, however, seem to support the hypothesis that exchange of genetic material can take place between neurons and their satellite glial cells.

Hydén and Lange (1965) repeated their RNA measurements on neurons from the motor cortex of rats that had been forced to reach with their nonpreferred paw for food at the end of a tube, the change in "handedness" having been regarded as learning. Control neurons were collected from the contralateral motor cortex in the same rats. The total amount of RNA was found to increase on the active side, and the new RNA turned out to be somewhat higher in adenine and much lower in cytosine than was that on the control side. Later in the training the main change was an increase in the proportion of guanine. These changes differed from those in vestibular cells during "learning."

It should be mentioned that by 1965 Hydén had abandoned his earlier theory in favor of the idea that the new RNA is produced from the DNA template in the usual way, presumably under the influence of a new derepressor substance, but he still seemed to believe that the RNA contained information about outside events and not just about local synaptic changes.

John (1967) has criticized the controls in Hydén's experiments. In an attempt to remedy certain flaws, he trained some flatworms, using classical conditioning, with controls for sensitization, pseudoconditioning and the like. Four groups of flatworms were presented with light and shock, but in only one group were the timing of stimuli and polarity of shock conducive to the appearance of a conditioned response. At the end of the light-shock treatments all the worms were killed and sent to Hydén, who dissected neurons from the head ganglia and analyzed the RNA in them. He was not able to distinguish between conditioned and pseudoconditioned worms. It is not clear whether this failure should be interpreted as evidence that Hydén's techniques do not work when proper controls are used (and when the neurochemist is ignorant of the history of each animal) or that flatworms do not learn by the same mechanism as rats.

The changes of RNA that can be detected by Hydén's method of analysis are quite gross. It would be possible to rearrange the same quantities of adenine, uracil, guanine and cytosine along the RNA molecule, leaving the base ratios quite unchanged, and yet to produce completely different polypeptides. The limitations and great difficulty of the technique have discouraged its widespread use, and other investigators have preferred to adopt a sort of biological assay for changes in neural metabolism (that is, they determine the effect of cell extracts from one group of animals upon the behavior of another group).

Early work on the problem of the relationship between genetic materials and learning used flatworms. R. Thompson and McConnell (1955) claimed to have developed a technique for conditioning these primitive invertebrates by exposing them to light paired with shock. The response to shock was a contraction, or curling movement, which unfortunately is also the way that the worms respond to bright light; great precautions must therefore be (and not always are) taken to ensure that the "conditioned" response is not simply sensitization of an innate response.

McConnell, Jacobson, and Kimble (1959) next showed that, when a conditioned planarian was cut into two or more pieces and the pieces allowed to regenerate into whole worms, each worm retained the conditioned response. This finding suggested that the genetic mechanism, which ensured that the worms would grow back into the normal shape, was also responsible for the regeneration of connections that permitted retention of conditioning. This interpretation was partly reinforced by the discovery that when worms were regenerated in a medium containing small quantities of *ribonuclease*, an enzyme that destroys RNA, only the worms regenerated from the head ends retained the conditioned response (Corning & John, 1961).

Another experiment leading to a similar conclusion was that of McConnell (1962), in which untrained worms, fed on minced trained worms, were found to have acquired the conditioned response. Again it was assumed that the RNA of the trained worms had found its way to the nerve cells of the naïve worms and had brought about changes either in the connections or in the sensitivity of the neurons. Attempts by McConnell to transfer learning to naïve worms by injecting them with purified RNA from trained worms have not been very successful, however.

In a controversial experiment (even for this field) Babich, Jacobson, Bubash, and Jacobson (1965) claimed to have transferred a learned response (approach to a food cup at the sound of a food-delivery mechanism) from trained rats to naïve rats by injecting RNA, extracted from the brains of the trained rats, intraperitoneally into the naïve rats. Injections of RNA from the brains of untrained rats were ineffective in facilitating the approach response.

RNA is rapidly broken down in the body by the enzyme ribonuclease, and none of it passes the blood-brain barrier (Luttges, Johnson, Buck, Holland & McGaugh, 1966). The investigators' interpretation, that RNA generated during training finds its way to neurons in the brain of the naïve recipient and there establishes the same neural relationships as were formed in the brains of the donor rats during training, must thus be viewed with some skepticism. Most attempts to replicate the experiment have failed (Byrne, Samuel, Bennett, Rosenzweig, Wasserman, Wagner, Gardner, Galambos, Berger, Margules, Fenichel, Stein, Corson, Enesco, Chorover, Holt, Schiller, Chiappetta, Jarvik, Leaf, Dutcher, Horovitz & Carlson, 1966), though Rosenblatt, Farrow, and Herblin (1966) claimed to have transferred learning in a brain extract from which RNA had been removed, implying that the transfer agent was a protein.

Albert (1966c) claimed to have transferred the engram of an avoidance response from one hemisphere to the other of the same rat through a brain extract. Rats with one hemisphere incapacitated by spreading depression were trained to avoid one side of a two-compartment box. The cortex of the trained hemisphere of each rat was then ablated, ground up, and injected into the peritoneum of the same rat. Rats treated in this way relearned the avoidance with greater savings than did other rats treated in exactly the same way except that they did not receive injections of their own cortex.

The arguments that these differences do not result from incorporation of "trained" RNA are the same as those raised against the interpretation of the experiment by Babich and his colleagues, except that the brain lesion may have caused a partial breakdown of the blood-brain barrier. It is conceivable that a protein involved in some aspect of avoidance (activity, fear, or the like) might have been transferred and might thus have influenced behavior, but this possibility is remote because, contrary to the findings of Babich and his colleagues, in-

jections from the brains of other trained rats did not facilitate learning; the extract had to be from the brain of the recipient.

Even more difficult to interpret are those experiments in which purified RNA from a low form of life like yeast is supposed to influence vertebrate learning. Cameron and Solyom (1961) gave large quantities of such RNA to senile human patients and claimed that it improved their memories and learning abilities. The coding of yeast RNA could hardly have been supposed to contain the personal memories of the patients, even if the substance had been able to reach the brain in its original form, which of course it could not. It may be that the neurons of these old people were short of RNA nucleotides with which to synthesize their own forms of RNA and obtained them from the digested yeast RNA, but this possibility seems unlikely. From personal discussion with one of those involved in collecting data for this experiment, it seems that the controls and precautions against artifacts were not as careful as the published accounts of the work indicate, and the results must be regarded as still in need of confirmation.

A rat experiment by Cook, Davidson, Davis, Green, and Fellows (1963) seemed at one time to offer support for the study by Cameron and Solyom. Rats injected with yeast RNA learned a pole-climbing avoidance response more rapidly than did controls not so injected. Corson and Enesco (1966) confirmed that RNA injections produced faster learning of the response but were unable to find any other learning task that was facilitated by the injection. The specificity of the effect is intriguing (there is no evidence of an innate pole-climbing tendency in yeast cells!), but the overall evidence renders it unlikely that large doses of RNA are helpful in general learning ability.

MANIPULATION OF CELL METABOLISM

Instead of trying to detect changes in RNA produced by learning, some experimenters have used cell metabolism as the independent variable and learning as the dependent variable. An early study of this sort was that by Dingman and Sporn (1961). Rats were trained on a maze, and then some of them were injected with *8-azaguanine*, which blocks the uptake of guanine and inhibits or distorts RNA synthesis. Fifteen minutes later the rats were tested for retention of the maze. Under these conditions there was no statistical difference between the injected rats and the control groups, but when the drug was injected before training it produced a significant impairment of learning.

This difference may mean that RNA is important for learning and not for retention, as Dingman and Sporn at first claimed, or it may mean that impairment of RNA synthesis has a generally debilitating effect upon the animals. It is known that less effort is required to perform a previously well-learned task than to learn a new one; thus almost any treatment that makes an animal sick will have a more severe effect upon learning than upon performance or retention. In a later paper Dingman and Sporn (1964) pointed out the difficulties of interpreting the effects upon learning of interfering with neural metabolism. They suggested that a study of lipids and synaptic membranes might be more fruitful. Using another, more potent RNA synthesis inhibitor, *actinomycin-D*, Barondes and Jarvik (1964) and H. D. Cohen and Barondes (1966) were unable to demonstrate any deficits in the retention of maze learning by mice when the drug had been injected into the brain shortly after learning was completed.

J. B. Flexner, Flexner, and Stellar (1963), and Flexner (1967) studied the effect of blocking protein synthesis in the brain. As a blocking agent they used the antibiotic *puromycin*, which is incorporated into the growing polypeptide chain and causes its premature release from the ribosome. Small quantities of the chemical were injected into the brains of mice that had previously learned a Y-maze under shock motivation. Control mice injected with saline retained the discrimination for at least five weeks, but mice injected one day after training with puromycin in both temporal lobes showed no retention of the discrimination three days later.

If the puromycin was injected more than about six days after training, the response was not impaired by temporal injections, but it

could still be disturbed if the drug was more widely distributed throughout the brain. These results were interpreted to mean that memories are stored for a few days in the temporal region, perhaps in the hippocampus, and that over a period of time they are transferred into less localized long-term storage. The investigators suggested that these results were consistent with the deficits of recent memory produced by bilateral ablations of the temporal lobe in man, a finding mentioned in Chapter 20, but, as we have seen, other experiments offer little encouragement for the idea that these human data can be extrapolated to mice.

Nevertheless, hippocampal lesions in the rodent did produce selective and severe impairment of maze learning (Kimble, 1963; Kaada, Rasmussen & Kveim, 1961); if the drug had caused a hippocampal dysfunction it might well have been reflected in poor maze performance. Other learning situations must be used before it can be assumed that injections of puromycin produce a general learning and memory deficit, however.

In another experiment with puromycin, Agranoff and Klinger (1964) found that intracranial injections impaired retention of shock avoidance in the goldfish. The injections were made immediately after the fish had experienced 20 trials in a shuttle tank. Three days later the fish that had been injected with puromycin made more errors than did trained fish injected with saline; they made fewer errors than naïve fish, however. Injections of puromycin before training had no effect upon the acquisition rate.

Another group of goldfish was trained to the point of 80 per cent correct avoidances, then half were injected with puromycin. Three days later no difference between the injected and normal fish was found. This result was rather different from that in mice reported by Flexner and his colleagues, though many experimental conditions, most conspicuously the species of subject, were different in the two experiments.

In a later paper Agranoff, Davis, and Brink (1966) reported that a more potent protein-synthesis inhibitor, *acetoxycycloheximide*, (cycloheximide) had less effect upon retention than did puromycin. Barondes and Cohen (1966, 1967) also found differences in the effectiveness of different protein-synthesis inhibitors. They were interested in the time course of the change from short- to long-term storage and set out to test the theory that short-term storage results from temporary redistribution of proteins at synapses, whereas long-term changes depend upon the triggering of a self-replicating protein-synthesis mechanism.

They used the same Y-maze that Flexner and his colleagues had used but injected the puromycin into the hippocampal region several hours before the mice were trained, so that protein synthesis was maximally inhibited during the training period. Learning was only slightly impaired by the injection; the injected mice did not learn significantly more slowly than controls. (L. B. Flexner and Flexner, 1968, seem to have had more difficulty under the same conditions, however.) Fifteen minutes after the training the injected mice showed only 80 per cent savings, 60 minutes after training only 35 per cent and after a total of three hours the mice had essentially lost the habit. Saline controls showed 100 per cent savings several hours after training, and so did other control mice injected with puromycin in the frontal cortex.

This result seemed to support the hypothesis that protein synthesis was needed only for long-term retention. When the experiment was repeated with cycloheximide as the protein inhibitor, however, the injected mice had 80–90 per cent savings one hour after training, although protein synthesis was more effectively inhibited. The cycloheximide had even less effect upon later retention when injected one hour after training. A similar result was reported by L. B. Flexner, Flexner, and Roberts (1967).

Cycloheximide inhibits protein synthesis by preventing amino acids from leaving the transfer RNA to join the polypeptide chain. Flexner and his colleagues thus proposed that puromycin produces its effect by using the experientially coded messenger RNA to produce abnormal polypeptides, whereas cycloheximide

prevents the RNA from being used at all, leaving it available to produce its proper protein when the antibiotic wears off. That cycloheximide protects the engram from puromycin if both are injected at the same time might be regarded as support for this theory.

On the other hand, the theory is considerably weakened by two other recent discoveries. It had been assumed that puromycin produced an irreversible loss of memory of recent events. The memory for the correct turn in the Y-maze did not return even when mice were tested three months after the puromycin injections, though protein synthesis in the brain as a whole returned to normal in a few days. Recently, however, L. B. Flexner and Flexner (1968) have found that injections of saline at the sites into which the puromycin had previously been injected, brought about recovery of a conditioned avoidance habit as long as 60 days after the habit had been eliminated by puromycin. This is an extraordinary finding, very difficult to explain by any current theory.

The other damaging finding was that injections of puromycin into the hippocampus of mice produced very abnormal electrographic activity. H. D. Cohen, Ervin, and Barondes (1966) injected either puromycin, cycloheximide, or saline into the hippocampus of groups of mice and recorded the hippocampal EEG when the mice awoke from the anesthetic. Except in those injected with puromycin, the activity took the form of the usual four-to-six per second theta waves, with an amplitude of about 50 μv, but there was less than 10 μv of activity in the puromycin group, and that was at a high frequency (Figure 21.5). Macrides and Chorover (1968) found that puromycin not only inhibited the hippocampal theta rhythm in rats but also evoked paroxysmal activity there for several days.

The effect of puromycin on the retention of maze learning probably results not from a general effect upon learning at the molecular level but from a functional lesion of the hippocampus. Nevertheless, it is obvious that puromycin does have an interesting effect upon neural function, either directly or, more likely,

0 . 04 M Na Cl

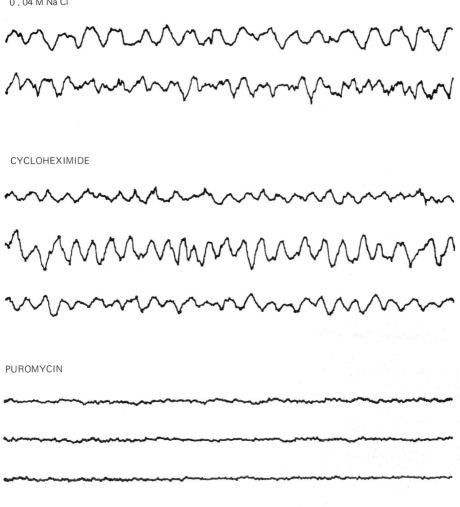

CYCLOHEXIMIDE

PUROMYCIN

50 μV

1 SEC.

Figure 21.5 Hippocampal activity recorded from mice injected with saline, cycloheximide, or puromycin. The records were taken from different mice. (From H. D. Cohen, Ervin & Barondes, 1966.)

because of the abnormal peptides to which it gives rise. The action of these peptides at synapses is something that might repay study. Such study might lead to better understanding of the molecular basis of neural transmission, a step on the way to discovering what happens at the synapse during learning.

At present, therefore, the evidence of RNA changes in learning is still not conclusive. There is an urgent need to use a greater variety of learning situations in studies of this sort. The alternative hypothesis that learning involves an interchange of polypeptides essential for determining membrane structure at the synapse has not been sufficiently tested to allow its evaluation at this time.

Summary

The discovery that an enormous amount of genetic information is compressed into nucleic-acid molecules aroused speculation that learned information might be similarly coded. Such speculation has led to various experiments in which the RNA of neurons and glia has been analyzed to discover whether or not changes resulting from learning can be detected. Unfortunately, the best analysis that can be performed in the laboratory is very crude and tells us essentially nothing about the information stored in the molecules. The only way to read out this information is to use the RNA to produce proteins, and attempts have been made to do so. "Educated" RNA from trained animals is injected into naïve animals, and the behavior of the latter in the training situation is observed. Although some successful transfers of learning have been reported, the technique rarely works; when it does it seems unlikely that RNA is the vehicle by which the information is carried.

RNA is potentially capable of storing all our memories, so that each neuron could contain a record of everything learned by an organism. Very few scientists now believe that memory works this way, however. Probably the only information that has to be stored in a particular neuron is which of its synapses have contributed to its firing in the past. The complexity of the learned event is managed by the complexity of the neuronal network.

The storage of information of even this rela-tively simple order may still involve the mechanism of protein synthesis involving DNA and RNA. This mechanism can act as an on-off switch for the production of proteins necessary for the transmission of impulses at synapses. According to this theory, a derepressor substance uncovers part of the DNA not previously in use, and one of the new proteins coded by that section of DNA can act as a further source of derepressor substance to keep itself uncovered; production, once started, thus continues as long as necessary.

If this mechanism is important in learning, we should be able to interfere with learning by suppressing synthesis of RNA or of protein, but the evidence is to the contrary. One protein-synthesis inhibitor, puromycin, has been found to interfere with retention, but it has also been found to produce abnormal electrographic activity in parts of the brain. It thus seems likely that its main effect is to produce fragmented polypeptides that interfere with neural transmission.

Unless some methodological flaw is discovered that will explain away the negative findings of recent experiments on the neurochemistry of learning, it seems that the search for molecular changes in learning should be directed to the proteins and lipoids of the membrane and to those hormone-like substances that determine the structure of such polymacromolecular aggregations as cell membranes.

REFERENCES

Ables, M. F. & Benjamin, R. M. 1960. Thalamic relay nucleus for taste in albino rat. *Journal of Neurophysiology*, **23**, 376-382.

Adams, R. D., Collins, G. H. & Victor, M. 1962. Troubles de la mémoire et de l'apprentissage chez l'homme; leurs relations avec des lésions des lobes temporaux et du diencéphale. In P. Passouant (Ed.), *Physiologie de l'hippocampe*. Paris: Centre Nationale de Recherche Scientifique. Pp. 273-291.

Adey, W. R. 1959. The sense of smell. In J. Field (Ed.), *Handbook of physiology. Neurophysiology*. vol. 1. Washington, D.C.: American Physiological Society. Pp. 535-548.

Adey, W. R. 1961. Studies of hippocampal electrical activity during approach learning. In J. F. Delafresnaye (Ed.), *Brain mechanisms and learning*. Springfield, Ill.: Thomas, Pp. 577-588.

Adey, W. R. 1962. EEG studies of hippocampal system in the learning process. In P. Passouant (Ed.), *Physiologie de l'hippocampe*. Paris: Centre Nationale de Recherche Scientifique. Pp. 203-222.

Adey, W. R., Merrillees, C. R. & Sunderland, S. 1956. The entorhinal area: Behavioural, evoked potential, and histological studies of its interrelationships with brainstem regions. *Brain*, **79**, 414-439.

Adey, W. R., Walter, D. O. & Lindsley, D. F. 1962. Subthalamic lesions. Effects on learned behavior and correlated hippocampal and subcortical slow-wave activity. *Archives of Neurology*, **6**, 194-207.

Adolph, E. F. 1964. Regulation of body water content through water ingestion. In M. J. Wayner (Ed.), *Thirst*. New York: Macmillan. Pp. 5-17.

Adrian, E. D. 1928. *The basis of sensation*. London: Christophers.

Adrian, E. D. 1942. Olfactory reactions in the brain of the hedgehog. *Journal of Physiology*, **100**, 459-473.

Adrian, E. D. 1943. Discharges from vestibular receptors in the cat. *Journal of Physiology*, **101**, 389-407.

Adrian, E. D. 1951. Olfactory discrimination. *Année Psychologique*, **50**, 107-113.

Adrian, E. D. 1953. Sensory messages and sensation. The response of the olfactory organ to different smells. *Acta Physiologica Scandinavica*, **29**, 5-14.

Adrian, E. D., Cattell, M. & Hoagland, H. 1931. Sensory discharges in single cutaneous nerve fibers. *Journal of Physiology*, **72**, 392-404.

Agranoff, B. W., Davis, R. E. & Brink, J. J. 1966. Chemical studies on memory fixation in goldfish. *Brain Research*, **1**, 303-309.

Agranoff, B. W. & Klinger, P. D. 1964. Puromycin effect on memory fixation in the goldfish. *Science*, **146**, 952-953.

Åkerman, B. 1966. Behavioural effects of electrical stimulation in the forebrain of the pigeon I. Reproductive behaviour. *Behaviour*, **26**, 323-338.

Albert, D. J. 1966a. The effect of spreading depression on the consolidation of learning. *Neuropsychologia*, **4**, 49-64.

Albert, D. J. 1966b. The effect of polarizing currents on the consolidation of learning. *Neuropsychologia*, **4**, 65-78.

Albert, D. J. 1966c. Memory in mammals: Evidence for a system involving nuclear ribonucleic acid. *Neuropsychologia*, **4**, 79-92.

Albino, R. C. & Lucas, J. W. 1962. Mutual facilitation of self-rewarding regions within the limbic system. *Journal of Comparative and Physiological Psychology*, **55**, 182-185.

Allen, W. F. 1941. Effect of ablating the pyriform-amygdaloid areas and hippocampi on positive and negative olfactory conditioned reflexes and on conditioned olfactory differentiation. *American Journal of Physiology*, **132**, 81-92.

Allen, W. F. 1949. Effect of prefrontal brain lesions on correct conditioned differential responses in dogs. *American Journal of Physiology*, **159**, 525-532.

Allison, A. C. & Warwick, R. T. T. 1949. Quantitative observations on the olfactory system of the rabbit. *Brain*, **72**, 186-197.

Amoore, J. E. 1952. The stereochemical specificities of human olfactory receptors. *The Perfumery and Essential Oil Record*, **43**, 321-323, 330.

Amoore, J. E. 1964. Current status of the steric theory of odor. *Annals of the New York Academy of Sciences*, **116**, 457-476.

Anand, B. K. & Brobeck, J. R. 1951. Hypothalamic control of food intake in rats and cats. *Yale Journal of Biology and Medicine*, **24**, 123-140.

Anand, B. K. & Brobeck, J. R. 1952. Food intake and spontaneous activity of rats with lesions in the amygdaloid nuclei. *Journal of Neurophysiology*, **15**, 421-430.

Anand, B. K., Chhina, G. S., Sharma, K. N., Dua, S. & Singh, B. 1964. Activity of single neurons in the hypothalamic feeding centers: Effect of glucose. *American Journal of Physiology*, **207**, 1146-1154.

Anand, B. K., Chhina, G. S. & Singh, B. 1962. Effect of glucose on the activity of hypothalamic "feeding centers." *Science*, **138**, 597-598.

Anand, B. K., Dua, S. & Singh, B. 1961. Electrical activity of the hypothalamic "feeding centres" under the effect of changes in blood chemistry.*Electroencephalography and Clinical Neurophysiology*, **13**, 54-59.

Andersen, P., Eccles, J. C. & Sears, T. A. 1964. Cortically evoked depolarization of primary afferent fibers in the spinal cord. *Journal of Neurophysiology*, **27**, 63-77.

Andersson, B. 1953. The effect of injections of hypertonic NaCl-solutions into different parts of the hypothalamus of goats. *Acta Physiologica Scandinavica*, **28**, 188-201.

Andersson, B., Ekman, L., Gale, C. C. & Sundsten, J. W. 1963. Control of thyrotrophic hormone (TSH) secretion by the "heat loss center." *Acta Physiologica Scandinavica*, **59**, 12-33.

Andersson, B., Gale, C. C. & Sundsten, J. W. 1964. Preoptic influences on water intake. In M. J. Wayner (Ed.), *Thirst*. New York: Macmillan. Pp. 361-379.

Andersson, B., Grant, R. & Larsson, S. 1956. Central control of heat loss mechanisms in the goat. *Acta Physiologica Scandinavica*, **37**, 261-280.

Andersson, B. & Larsson, B. 1961. Influence of local temperature changes in the preoptic area and rostral hypothalamus on the regulation of food and water intake. *Acta Physiologica Scandinavica*, **52**, 75-89.

Andersson, B. & Larsson, S. 1956. An attempt to condition hypothalamic polydipsia. *Acta Physiologica Scandinavica*, **36**, 377-382.

Andersson, B. & McCann, S. M. 1955. Drinking, antidiuresis and milk ejection from electrical stimulation within the hypothalamus of the goat. *Acta Physiologica Scandinavica*, **35**, 191-201.

Andersson, B. & Wyrwicka, W. 1957. The elicitation of a drinking motor conditioned reaction by electrical stimulation of the hypothalamic "drinking area" in the goat. *Acta Physiologica Scandinavica*, **41**, 194-198.

Andersson, S. & Gernandt, B. E. 1954. Cortical projection of vestibular nerve in cats. *Acta Oto-laryngologica*, (Suppl. 116), 10-18.

Andy, O. J., Peeler, D. F. & Foshee, D. P. 1967. Avoidance and discrimination learning following hippocampal ablation in the cat. *Journal of Comparative and Physiological Psychology*, **64**, 516-519.

Angel, A., Magni, F. & Strata, P. 1965. Evidence for pre-synaptic inhibition in the lateral geniculate body. *Nature*, **208**, 495-496.

Anokhin, P. K. 1947. The theory of functional systems as the basis of understanding of compensatory processes in the body. *Transactions of a conference on the restoration of function after war injuries*. Moscow State University. (Uchenyye zapiski Kafedry psikhologii MGU). Cited by A. R. Luria, *Restoration of function after brain injury*. New York: Macmillan, 1963. Pp. 35-39.

Arduini, A. & Pinneo, L. R. 1962. Properties of the retina in response to steady illumination. *Archives Italiennes de Biologie*, **100**, 425-448.

Asdourian, D., Stutz, R. M. & Rocklin, K. W. 1966. Effects of thalamic and limbic system lesions on self-stimulation. *Journal of Comparative and Physiological Psychology*, **61**, 468-472.

Aserinsky, E. & Kleitman, N. 1955. A motility cycle in sleeping infants as manifested by ocular and gross bodily activity. *Journal of Applied Physiology*, **8**, 11-18.

Axelrod, S. & Diamond, I. T. 1965. Effects of auditory cortex ablation on ability to discriminate between stimuli presented to the two ears. *Journal of Comparative and Physiological Psychology*, **59**, 79-89.

Babich, F. R., Jacobson, A. L., Bubash, S. & Jacobson, A. 1965. Transfer of a response to naive rats by injection of ribonucleic acid extracted from trained rats. *Science*, **149**, 656-657.

Bacq, Z. M. 1931. Impotence of the male rodent after sympathetic denervation of the genital organs. *American Journal of Physiology*, **96**, 321-330.

Bagshaw, M. H., Kimble, D. P. & Pribram, K. H. 1965. The GSR of monkeys during orienting and habituation and after ablation of the amygdala, hippocampus and inferotemporal cortex. *Neuropsychologia*, **3**, 111-119.

Bagshaw, M. H. & Pribram, K. H. 1953. Cortical organization in gustation (*Macaca mulatta*). *Journal of Neurophysiology*, **16**, 499-508.

Bailey, P., Bonin, G. von, Garol, H. W. & McCulloch, W. S. 1943. Functional organization of temporal lobe of monkey (*Macaca mulatta*) and chimpanzee (*Pan satyrus*). *Journal of Neurophysiology*, **6**, 121-128.

Bárány, R. 1907. *Physiologie und Pathologie des Bogengangsapparates beim Menschen*. Vienna: Deuticke.

Bard, P. 1928. A diencephalic mechanism for the expression of rage with special reference to the sympathetic nervous system. *American Journal of Physiology*, **84**, 490-515.

Bard, P. 1940. The hypothalamus and sexual behavior. *Research Publications of the Association for Research in Nervous and Mental Disease*, **20**, 551-579.

Bard, P. & Macht, M. B. 1958. The behavior of chronically decerebrate cats. In G. E. W. Wolstenholme & C. M. O'Connor (Eds.), *Neurological basis of behavior*. London: Churchill. Pp. 55-75.

Bard, P. & Mountcastle, V. B. 1948. Some forebrain mechanisms involved in expression of rage with special reference to suppression of angry behavior. *Research Publications of the Association for Research in Nervous and Mental Disease*, **27**, 362-404.

Bard, P., Woolsey, R. S., Snider, R. S., Mountcastle, V. B. & Bromiley, R. B. 1947. Delimitation of central mechanisms in motion sickness. *Federation Proceedings*, **6**, 72.

Barfield, R. J. 1965. Induction of aggressive and courtship behavior by intracerebral implants of androgen in capons. *American Zoologist*, **5**, 203.

Bargmann, W. & Scharrer, E. 1951. The site of origin of the hormones of the posterior pituitary. *American Scientist*, **39**, 255-259.

Barker, D. 1948. The innervation of the muscle spindle. *Quarterly Journal of Microscopical Science*, **89**, 143-186.

Barlow, H. B. & Hill, R. M. 1963. Selective sensitivity to direction of movement in ganglion cells of rabbit retina. *Science*, **139**, 412-414.

Barnett, S. A. 1963. *The rat. A study in behaviour*. London: Methuen.

Barondes, S. H. & Cohen, H. D. 1966. Puromycin effect on successive phases of memory storage. *Science*, **151**, 594-595.

Barondes, S. H. & Cohen, H. D. 1967. Comparative effects of cycloheximide and puromycin on cerebral protein synthesis and consolidation of memory in mice. *Brain Research*, **4**, 44-51.

Barondes, S. H. & Jarvik, M. E. 1964. The influence of actinomycin-D on brain RNA synthesis and on memory. *Journal of Neurochemistry*, **11**, 187-195.

Barraclough, C. A. & Cross, B. A. 1963. Unit activity in the hypothalamus of the cyclic female rat: Effect of genital stimuli and progesterone. *Journal of Endocrinology*, **26**, 339-359.

Barrera, S. E., Kopeloff, L. M. & Kopeloff, N. 1944. Brain lesions associated with experimental "epileptiform" seizures in the monkey. *American Journal of Psychiatry*, **100**, 727-737.

Bartoshuk, A. K. 1955a. Electromyographic gradients in goal-directed activity. *Canadian Journal of Psychology*, **9**, 21-28.

Bartoshuk, A. K. 1955b. Electromyographic gradients as indicants of motivation. *Canadian Journal of Psychology*, **9**, 215-230.

Bartoshuk, L. M., McBurney, D. H. & Pfaffmann, C. 1964. Taste of sodium chloride solutions after adaptation to sodium chloride: Implication for the "water taste." *Science*, **143**, 967-968.

Basmajian, J. V. 1963. Control and training of individual motor units. *Science*, **141**, 440-441.

Bastian, H. C. 1882. *The brain as an organ of mind.* London: Kegan Paul & Trench.

Batini, C., Moruzzi, G., Palestini, M., Rossi, G. F. & Zanchetti, A. 1958. Persistent patterns of wakefulness in the pretrigeminal midpontine preparation. *Science,* **128,** 30-32.

Battig, K., Rosvold, H. E. & Mishkin, M. 1960. Comparison of the effects of frontal and caudate lesions on delayed response and alternation in monkeys. *Journal of Comparative and Physiological Psychology,* **53,** 400-404.

Bauer, J. H. & Cooper, R. M. 1964. Effects of posterior cortical lesions on performance of a brightness-discrimination task. *Journal of Comparative and Physiological Psychology,* **58,** 84-92.

Baumgartner, G., Brown, J. L. & Schulz, A. 1964. Visual motion detection in the cat. *Science,* **146,** 1070-1071.

Bazett, H. C., McGlone, B., Williams, R. G. & Lufkin, H. M. 1932. Studies in sensation. I. Depth, distribution, and probable identification in the prepuce of sensory end-organs in sensation of temperature and touch; thermometric conductivity. *Archives of Neurology and Psychiatry,* **27,** 489-517.

Bazett, H. C. & Penfield, W. G. 1922. A study of the Sherrington decerebrate animal in the chronic as well as the acute condition. *Brain,* **45,** 185-265.

Beach, F. A. 1940. Effects of cortical lesions upon the copulatory behavior of male rats. *Journal of Comparative Psychology,* **29,** 193-244.

Beach, F. A. 1944. Effects of injury to the cerebral cortex upon sexually-receptive behavior in the female rat. *Psychosomatic Medicine,* **6,** 40-55.

Beach, F. A. 1947. A review of physiological and psychological studies of sexual behavior in mammals. *Physiological Review,* **27,** 240-307.

Beach, F. A. 1949. A cross-species survey of mammalian sexual behavior. In P. H. Hoch & J. Zubin (Eds.), *Psychosexual development in health and disease.* New York: Grune & Stratton. Pp. 52-78.

Beach, F. A. & Gilmore, R. W. 1949. Response of male dogs to urine from females in heat. *Journal of Mammalogy,* **30,** 391-392.

Beach, F. A. & Rasquin, P. 1942. Masculine copulatory behavior in intact and castrated female rats. *Endocrinology,* **31,** 393-409.

Beach, F. A., Zitrin, A. & Jaynes, J. 1956. Neural mediation of mating in male cats: I. Effects of unilateral and bilateral removal of the neocortex. *Journal of Comparative and Physiological Psychology,* **49,** 321-327.

Bechterev, W. von. 1900. Demonstration eines Gehirns mit Zerstörung der vorderer und innerer Theile der Hirnrinde beider Schläfenlappen. *Neurologisches Zentralblatt,* **19,** 990-991.

Beck, K. 1912. Untersuchungen über den statischen Apparat von Gesunden und Taubstummen. *Zeitschrift für Psychologie, Abteilung 2, Sinnesphysiologie,* **46,** 362-378.

Beidler, L. M. 1961. Mechanisms of gustatory and olfactory receptor stimulation. In W. A. Rosenblith (Ed.), *Sensory communication.* New York: Wiley. Pp. 143-157.

Beidler, L. M. 1963. Dynamics of taste cells. In Y. Zotterman (Ed.), *Olfaction and taste.* Oxford: Pergamon. Pp. 133-145.

Békésy, G. von. 1949. The vibration of the cochlear partition in anatomical preparations and in models of the inner ear. *Journal of the Acoustical Society of America,* **21,** 233-244.

Békésy, G. von. 1962. The gap between the hearing of external and internal sounds. *Symposia of the Society for Experimental Biology,* **16,** 267-288.

Békésy, G. von. & Rosenblith, W. A. 1951. The mechanical properties of the ear. In S. S. Stevens (Ed.), *Handbook of experimental psychology.* New York: Wiley. Pp. 1075-1115.

Bellows, R. T. 1939. Time factors in water drinking in dogs. *American Journal of Physiology,* **125,** 87-97.

Bender, M. B. & Teuber, H. L. 1946. Nystagmoid movements and visual perception. *Archives of Neurology and Psychiatry,* **55,** 511-529.

Benjamin, R. M. 1959. Absence of deficits in taste discrimination following cortical lesions as a function of the amount of preoperative practice. *Journal of Comparative and Physiological Psychology,* **52,** 255-258.

Benjamin, R. M. 1963. Some thalamic and cortical mechanisms of taste. In Y. Zotterman (Ed.), *Olfaction and taste.* Oxford: Pergamon. Pp. 309-329.

Benjamin, R. M. & Akert, K. 1959. Cortical and thalamic areas involved in taste discrimination in the albino rat. *Journal of Comparative Neurology,* **111,** 231-259.

Benjamin, R. M. & Pfaffmann, C. 1955. Cortical localization of taste in albino rat. *Journal of Neurophysiology,* **18,** 56-64.

Bennett, E. L., Diamond, M. C., Krech, D. & Rosenzweig, M. R. 1964. Chemical and anatomical plasticity of the brain. *Science,* **146,** 610-619.

Benzinger, T. H. 1962. The thermostatic regulation of human heat production and heat loss. *Proceedings of the 22nd International Congress of Physiological Sciences,* **1,** 415-438.

Berger, H. 1929. Über das Elektrenkephalogramm des Menschen. *Archiv für Psychiatrie und Nervenkrankheiten,* **87,** 527-570.

Berman, A. L. 1961. Interaction of cortical responses to somatic and auditory stimuli in anterior ectosylvian gyrus of cat. *Journal of Neurophysiology,* **24,** 608-620.

Berry, C. M. Hagamen, W. D. & Hinsey, J. C. 1952. Distribution of potentials following stimulation of olfactory bulb in cat. *Journal of Neurophysiology,* **15,** 139-148.

Bianchi, L. 1895. The functions of the frontal lobes. *Brain,* **18,** 497-522.

Bickford, R. G., Mulder, D. W., Dodge, H. W., Svien, H. J. & Rome, H. P. 1958. Changes in memory function produced by electrical stimulation of the temporal lobe in man. *Research Publications of the Association for Research in Nervous and Mental Disease,* **36,** 227-243.

Bindra, D. 1968. Neuropsychological interpretation of the effects of drive and incentive-motivation on general activity and instrumental behavior. *Psychological Review,* **75,** 1-22.

Bishop, M. P., Elder, S. T. & Heath, R. G. 1963. Intracranial self-stimulation in man. *Science,* **140,** 394-396.

Bizzi, E. 1966a. Changes in the orthodromic and antidromic response of optic tract during the eye movements of sleep. *Journal of Neurophysiology,* **29,** 861-870.

Bizzi, E. 1966b. Discharge patterns of single geniculate neurons during the rapid eye movements of sleep. *Journal of Neurophysiology,* **29,** 1087-1095.

Blake, L. 1959. The effect of lesions of the superior colliculus on brightness and pattern discriminations in the cat. *Journal of Comparative and Physiological Psychology*, **52**, 272–278.

Blix, M. 1884. Experimentelle Beiträge zur Lösung der Frage über die specifische Energie der Hautnerven. *Zeitschrift für Biologie*, **20**, 141–156.

Block, R. A. & McConnell, J. V. 1967. Classically conditioned discrimination in the planarian, *Dugesia dorotocephala*. *Nature*, **215**, 1465–1466.

Blomquist, A. J., Benjamin, R. M. & Emmers, R. 1962. Thalamic localization of afferents from the tongue in squirrel monkey (*Saimiri sciureus*). *Journal of Comparative Neurology*, **118**, 77–87.

Blum, J. S. 1951. Cortical organization in somesthesis. *Comparative Psychology Monographs*, **20**, 219–249.

Blumer, D. & Walker, E. 1967. Sexual behavior in temporal lobe epilepsy. *Archives of Neurology*, **16**, 37–43.

Bodian, D. 1962. The generalized vertebrate neuron. *Science*, **137**, 323–326.

Bogacz, J., St. Laurent, J. & Olds, J. 1965. Dissociation of self-stimulation and epileptiform activity. *Electroencephalography and Clinical Neurophysiology*, **19**, 75–87.

Bolles, R. C., Rapp, H. M. & White, G. C. 1968. Failure of sexual activity to reinforce female rats. *Journal of Comparative and Physiological Psychology*, **65**, 311–313.

Booth, D. A. 1967. Localization of the adrenergic feeding system in the rat diencephalon. *Science*, **158**, 515–517.

Boring, E. G. 1929. *A history of experimental psychology*. New York: Appleton.

Bower, G. H. & Miller, N. E. 1958. Rewarding and punishing effects from stimulating the same place in the rat's brain. *Journal of Comparative and Physiological Psychology*, **51**, 669–674.

Bowlker, T. J. 1908. On the factors serving to determine the direction of sound. *Philosophical Magazine*, **15**, 318–332.

Bowsher, D., with Albe-Fessard, D. 1965. The anatomophysiological basis of somatosensory discrimination. *International Review of Neurobiology*, **8**, 35–75.

Boyd, E. S. & Gardner, L. C. 1962. Positive and negative reinforcement from intracranial stimulation of a teleost. *Science*, **136**, 648–649.

Boyd, I. A. & Roberts, T. D. M. 1953. Proprioceptive discharges from stretch receptors in the knee-joint of the cat. *Journal of Physiology*, **122**, 38–58.

Boynton, R. M., Schafer, W. & Neun, M. E. 1964. Hue-wavelength relation measured by color-naming method for three retinal locations. *Science*, **146**, 666–668.

Brady, J. V. 1958a. The paleocortex and behavioral motivation. In H. F. Harlow & C. N. Woolsey (Eds.), *Biological and biochemical bases of behavior*. Madison: University of Wisconsin Press. Pp. 193–235.

Brady, J. V. 1958b. Temporal and emotional factors related to electrical self-stimulation of the limbic system. In H. H. Jasper, L. D. Proctor, R. S. Knighton, W. C. Noshay & R. T. Costello (Eds.), *Reticular formation of the brain*. Boston: Little, Brown. Pp. 689–703.

Brady, J. V. 1960. Temporal and emotional effects related to intracranial electrical self-stimulation. In E. R. Ramey & D. S. O'Doherty (Eds.), *Electrical studies on the unanesthetized brain*. New York: Hoeber. Pp. 52–77.

Brady, J. V., Boren, J. J., Conrad, D. & Sidman, M. 1957. The effect of food and water deprivation upon intra-

cranial self-stimulation. *Journal of Comparative and Physiological Psychology*, **50**, 134–137.

Brady, J. V. & Nauta, W. J. H. 1953. Subcortical mechanisms in emotional behavior: Affective changes following septal forebrain lesions in the albino rat. *Journal of Comparative and Physiological Psychology*, **46**, 339–346.

Brady, J. V. & Nauta, W. J. H. 1955. Subcortical mechanisms in emotional behavior: The duration of affective changes following septal and habenular lesions in the albino rat. *Journal of Comparative and Physiological Psychology*, **48**, 412–420.

Brady, J. V., Schreiner, L., Geller, I. & Kling, A. 1954. Subcortical mechanisms in emotional behavior: The effect of rhinencephalic injury upon the acquisition and retention of a conditioned avoidance response in cats. *Journal of Comparative and Physiological Psychology*, **47**, 179–186.

Brain, R. 1961. *Speech disorders*. London: Butterworth.

Brambell, F. W. R. 1944. The reproduction of the wild rabbit *Oryctolagus cuniculus* (*L.*). *Proceedings of the Zoological Society of London*, **114**, 1–45.

Brattgård, S. O. 1952. The importance of adequate stimulation for the chemical composition of retinal ganglion cells during early postnatal development. *Acta Radiologica* (Suppl. 96), 1–80.

Bremer, F. 1935. Cerveau isolé et physiologie du sommeil. *Comptes Rendus de la Société de Biologie*, **118**, 1235–1242.

Bremer, F. 1936. Nouvelles recherches sur le mécanisme du sommeil. *Comptes Rendus de la Société de Biologie*, **122**, 460–464.

Briggs, M. H. & Kitto, G. B. 1962. The molecular basis of memory and learning. *Psychological Review*, **69**, 537–541.

Broadbent, D. E. 1954. The role of auditory localization in attention and memory span. *Journal of experimental Psychology*, **47**, 191–196.

Broadbent, D. E. 1956. Successive responses to simultaneous stimuli. *Quarterly Journal of Experimental Psychology*, **8**, 145–162.

Brobeck, J. R. 1948. Food intake as a mechanism of temperature regulation. *Yale Journal of Biology and Medicine*, **20**, 545–552.

Brobeck, J. R., Tepperman, J. & Long, C. N. H. 1943. Experimental hypothalamic hyperphagia in the albino rat. *Yale Journal of Biology and Medicine*, **15**, 831–853.

Broca, P. 1861. Remarques sur le siège de la faculté du langage articulé, suivies d'une observation d'aphémie (perte de la parole). *Bulletin de la Société Anatomique de Paris* (2nd series), **6**, 330–357.

Brodal, A. 1960. Fiber connections of the vestibular nuclei. In G. L. Rasmussen & W. F. Windle (Eds.), *Neural mechanisms of the auditory and vestibular systems*. Springfield, Ill.: Thomas. Pp. 224–246.

Brodal, A., Pompeiano, O. & Walberg, F. 1962. *The vestibular nuclei and their connections: Anatomy and functional correlations*. Edinburgh: Oliver & Boyd.

Brodmann, K. 1909. *Vergleichende Lokalisationslehre der Grosshirnrinde in ihren Prinzipien dargestellt auf Grund des Zellenbaues*. Leipzig: Barth.

Bromiley, R. B. 1948. Conditioned responses in dog after removal of neocortex. *Journal of Comparative and Physiological Psychology*, **41**, 102–110.

Brookhart, J. M. & Dey, F. L. 1941. Reduction of sexual

behavior in male guinea pigs by hypothalamic lesions. *American Journal of Physiology*, **133**, 551-554.

Brooks, C. M. 1937. The role of the cerebral cortex and of various sense organs in the excitation and execution of mating activity in the rabbit. *American Journal of Physiology*, **120**, 544-553.

Brooks, C. M., Lambert, E. F. & Bard, P. 1942. Experimental production of obesity in the monkey (*Macaca mulatta*). *Federation Proceedings*, **1**, 11. (Abstract)

Brown, A. G. & Iggo, A. 1963. The structure and function of cutaneous "touch corpuscles" after nerve crush. *Journal of Physiology*, **165**, 28P-29P.

Brown, B. M. & Noble, E. P. 1967. Cycloheximide and learning in the isolated cockroach ganglion. *Brain Research*, **6**, 363-366.

Brown, P. K. & Wald, G. 1964. Visual pigments in single rods and cones of the human retina. *Science*, **144**, 45-52.

Brown, S. & Schäfer, E. A. 1888. An investigation into the functions of the occipital and temporal lobes of the monkey's brain. *Philosophical Transactions of the Royal Society of London*, **179B**, 303-327.

Brown, T. S., Rosvold, H. E. & Mishkin, M. 1963. Olfactory discrimination after temporal lobe lesions in monkeys. *Journal of Comparative and Physiological Psychology*, **56**, 190-195.

Brown-Séquard, C. -E. 1889. Le sommeil normal, comme le sommeil hypnotique, est le résultat d'une inhibition de l'activité intellectuelle. *Archives de Physiologie Normale et Pathologique* (5th series), **1**, 333-335.

Bruce, H. M. & Parrott, D. M. V. 1960. Role of olfactory sense in pregnancy block by strange males. *Science*, **131**, 1526.

Brügger, M. 1943. Fresstrieb als hypothalamisches Symptom. *Helvetica Physiologica et Pharmacologica Acta*, **1**, 183-198.

Brush, E. S., Mishkin, M. & Rosvold, H. E. 1961. Effects of object preferences and aversions on discrimination learning in monkeys with frontal lesions. *Journal of Comparative and Physiological Psychology*, **54**, 319-325.

Brush, F. R. & Levine, S. 1966. Adrenocortical activity and avoidance learning as a function of time after fear conditioning. *Physiology and Behavior*, **1**, 309-311.

Brutkowski, S., Fonberg, E. & Mempel, E. 1961. Angry behavior in dogs following bilateral lesions in the genual portion of the rostral cingulate gyrus. *Acta Biologiae Experimentalis*, **21**, 199-205.

Buffery, A. W. H. 1965. Attention and retention following frontal and temporal lesions in the baboon. *Proceedings of the 73rd Annual Convention of the American Psychological Association*, **1**, 103-104.

Buffery, A. W. H. 1967. Learning and memory in baboons with bilateral lesions of frontal or inferotemporal cortex. *Nature*, **214**, 1054-1056.

Bureš, J. & Burešová, O. 1960. The use of Leão's spreading depression in the study of interhemispheric transfer of memory traces. *Journal of Comparative and Physiological Psychology*, **53**, 558-565.

Bureš, J. & Burešová, O. 1963. Cortical spreading depression as a memory disturbing factor. *Journal of Comparative and Physiological Psychology*, **56**, 268-272.

Bureš, J., Burešová, O. & Záhorová, A. 1958. Conditioned reflexes and Leão's spreading cortical depression. *Journal of Comparative and Physiological Psychology*, **51**, 263-268.

Burns, B. D. 1950. Some properties of the cat's isolated cerebral cortex. *Journal of Physiology*, **111**, 50-68.

Burns, B. D. 1954. The production of after-bursts in isolated unanesthetized cerebral cortex. *Journal of Physiology*, **125**, 427-446.

Burns, B. D. 1958. *The mammalian cerebral cortex*. London: Arnold.

Burns, B. D., Heron, W. & Grafstein, B. 1960. Responses of cerebral cortex to diffuse monocular and binocular stimulation. *American Journal of Physiology*, **198**, 200-204.

Burns, B. D. & Salmoiraghi, G. C. 1960. Repetitive firing of respiratory neurones during their burst activity. *Journal of Neurophysiology*, **23**, 27-46.

Buser, P., Bornstein, P. & Bruner, J. 1959. Étude des systèmes "associatifs" visuels et auditifs chez le chat anesthésié au chloralose. *Electroencephalography and Clinical Neurophysiology*, **11**, 305-324.

Butler, R. A. 1953. Discrimination learning by rhesus monkeys to visual-exploration motivation. *Journal of Comparative and Physiological Psychology*, **46**, 95-98.

Butler, R. A. 1954. Incentive conditions which influence visual exploration. *Journal of Experimental Psychology*, **48**, 19-23.

Butler, R. A. 1957. Discrimination learning by rhesus monkeys to auditory incentives. *Journal of Comparative and Physiological Psychology*, **50**, 239-241.

Butler, R. A., Diamond, I. T. & Neff, W. D. 1957. Role of auditory cortex in discrimination of changes in frequency. *Journal of Neurophysiology*, **20**, 108-120.

Byrne, W. L., Samuel, D., Bennett, E. L., Rosenzweig, M. R., Wasserman, E., Wagner, A. R., Gardner, F., Galambos, R., Berger, B. D., Margules, D. L., Fenichel, R. L., Stein, L., Corson, J. A., Enesco, H. E., Chorover, S. L., Holt, C. E., III, Schiller, P. H., Chiappetta, L., Jarvik, M. E., Leaf, R. C., Dutcher, J. D., Horovitz, Z. P. & Carlson, P. L. 1966. Memory transfer. *Science*, **153**, 658-659.

Caggiula, A. R. & Hoebel, B. G. 1966. "Copulation-reward site" in the posterior hypothalamus. *Science*. **153**, 1284-1285.

Cameron, D. E. & Solyom, L. 1961. Effects of ribonucleic acid on memory. *Geriatrics*, **16**, 74-81.

Campbell, A. W. 1905. *Histological studies on the localisation of cerebral function*. Cambridge: Cambridge University Press.

Campbell, B. A. & Sheffield, F. D. 1953. Relation of random activity to food deprivation. *Journal of Comparative and Physiological Psychology*, **46**, 320-322.

Cannon, W. B. 1929. Hunger and thirst. In C. Murchison (Ed.), *The foundations of experimental psychology*. Worcester, Mass.: Clark University Press. Pp. 434-448.

Cannon, W. B. & Washburn, A. L. 1912. An explanation of hunger. *American Journal of Physiology*, **29**, 441-454.

Carlson, K. R. 1967. Cortical spreading depression and subcortical memory storage. *Journal of Comparative and Physiological Psychology*, **64**, 422-430.

Carpenter, M. B. 1960. Experimental anatomical-physiological studies of the vestibular nerve and cerebellar connections. In G. L. Rasmussen & W. F. Windle (Eds.), *Neural mechanisms of the auditory and vestibular systems*. Springfield, Ill.: Thomas. Pp. 297-323.

Carr, W. J., Loeb, L. S. & Wylie, N. R. 1966. Responses to feminine odors in normal and castrated male rats. *Journal of Comparative and Physiological Psychology*, **62**, 336-338.

Carreras, M. & Andersson, S. A. 1963. Functional properties of neurons of the anterior ectosylvian gyrus of the cat. *Journal of Neurophysiology*, **26**, 100-126.

Casey, K. L. 1966. Unit analysis of nociceptive mechanisms in the thalamus of the awake squirrel monkey. *Journal of Neurophysiology*, **29**, 727-750.

Caspers, H. 1961. Changes of cortical D.C. potentials in the sleep-wakefulness cycle. In G. E. W. Wolstenholme & M. O'Connor (Eds.), *The nature of sleep*. London: Churchill. Pp. 237-253.

Caspers, H. 1965. Shifts of the cortical steady potential during various stages of sleep. In M. Jouvet (Ed.), *Aspects anatomo-fonctionnels de la physiologie du sommil*. Paris: Centre Nationale de Recherche Scientifique. Pp. 213-224.

Caton, R. 1877. Interim report of investigations on the electric currents of the brain. *British Medical Journal*. (May 5 Suppl.)

Chang, H. -T., Ruch, T. C. & Ward, A. A., Jr. 1947. Topographical representation of muscles in motor cortex of monkeys. *Journal of Neurophysiology*, **10**, 39-56.

Chapman, L. F., Walter, R. D., Markham, C. H., Rand, R. W. & Crandall, P. H. 1967. Memory changes induced by stimulation of hippocampus or amygdala in epilepsy patients with implanted electrodes. *Transactions of the American Neurological Association*, **92**, 50-56.

Chiles, W. D. 1954. Performance during stimulation of the diencephalic activating system. *Journal of Comparative and Physiological Psychology*, **47**, 412-415.

Chomsky, N. 1967. The formal nature of language. In E. H. Lenneberg, *Biological foundations of language*. New York: Wiley. Pp. 397-442.

Chorazyna, H. & Konorski, J. 1962. Absolute versus relative cues in differentiation of tones in dogs. *Acta Biologiae Experimentalis*, **22**, 90-100.

Chorover, S. L. & Schiller, P. H. 1965. Short-term retrograde amnesia in rats. *Journal of Comparative and Physiological Psychology*, **59**, 73-78.

Chorover, S. L. & Schiller, P. H. 1966. Reexamination of prolonged retrograde amnesia in one-trial learning. *Journal of Comparative and Physiological Psychology*, **61**, 34-41.

Chow, K. L. 1952. Further studies on selective ablation of associative cortex in relation to visually mediated behavior. *Journal of Comparative and Physiological Psychology*, **45**, 109-118.

Chow, K. L. 1954a. Lack of behavioral effects following destruction of some thalamic association nuclei in monkey. *A.M.A. Archives of Neurology and Psychiatry*, **71**, 762-771.

Chow, K. L. 1954b. Effects of temporal neocortical ablation on visual discrimination learning sets in monkeys. *Journal of Comparative and Physiological Psychology*, **47**, 194-198.

Christopher, M. & Butter, C. M. 1968. Consummatory behaviors and locomotor exploration evoked from self-stimulation sites in rats. *Journal of Comparative and Physiological Psychology*, **66**, 335-339.

Cizek, L. J., Semple, R. E., Huang, K. C. & Gregerson, M. I. 1951. Effect of extracellular electrolyte depletion on water intake in dogs. *American Journal of Physiology*, **164**, 415-422.

Clark, C. V. H. & Isaacson, R. L. 1965. Effect of bilateral hippocampal ablation on DRL performance. *Journal of Comparative and Physiological Psychology*, **59**, 137-140.

Clark, G. 1942. Sexual behavior in rats with lesions in the anterior hypothalamus. *American Journal of Physiology*, **137**, 746-749.

Clark, S. L. 1939. Responses following electrical stimulation of the cerebellar cortex in the normal cat. *Journal of Neurophysiology*, **2**, 19-35.

Clark, W. E. Le Gros & Russell, W. R. 1938. Cortical deafness without aphasia. *Brain*, **61**, 375-383.

Cohen, B., Suzuki, J. I. & Bender, M. B. 1965. Nystagmus induced by electrical stimulation of ampullary nerves. *Acta Oto-laryngologica*, **60**, 422-436.

Cohen, B. D., Brown, G. W. & Brown, M. L. 1957. Avoidance learning motivated by hypothalamic stimulation. *Journal of Experimental Psychology*, **53**, 228-233.

Cohen, H. D. & Barondes, S. H. 1966. Further studies of learning and memory after intracerebral actinomycin-D. *Journal of Neurochemistry*, **13**, 207-211.

Cohen, H. D., Ervin, F. & Barondes, S. H. 1966. Puromycin and cycloheximide: Different effects on hippocampal electrical activity. *Science*, **154**, 1557-1558.

Cohen, M. J., Landgren, S., Ström, L. & Zotterman, Y. 1957. Cortical reception of touch and taste in the cat: A study of single cortical cells. *Acta Physiologica Scandinavica*, **40** (Suppl. 135), 1-50.

Cohen, R. L. & Johansson, B. S. 1967. Some relevant factors in the transfer of material from short-term to long-term memory. *Quarterly Journal of Experimental Psychology*, **19**, 300-308.

Cole, J. & Glees, P. 1954. Effects of small lesions in sensory cortex in trained monkeys. *Journal of Neurophysiology*, **17**, 1-21.

Collins, W. E. 1964. Task-control of arousal and the effects of repeated unidirectional angular acceleration on human vestibular responses. *Acta Oto-laryngologica* (Suppl. 190), 1-34.

Cook, L., Davidson, A. B., Davis, D. J., Green, H. & Fellows, E. J. 1963. Ribonucleic acid: Effect on conditioned behavior in rats. *Science*, **141**, 268-269.

Coons, E. E. 1964. Motivational correlates of eating elicited by electrical stimulation in the hypothalamic feeding area. Doctoral dissertation, Yale University. (Microfilm obtainable from University Microfilms Inc., Ann Arbor, Mich., No. 64-13, 166).

Coons, E. E. & Cruce, J. A. F. 1968. Lateral hypothalamus: Food and current intensity in maintaining self-stimulation of hunger. *Science*, **159**, 1117-1119.

Coons, E. E., Levak, M. & Miller, N. E. 1965. Lateral hypothalamus: Learning of food-seeking response motivated by electrical stimulation. *Science*, **150**, 1320-1321.

Coons, E. E. & Miller, N. E. 1960. Conflict versus consolidation of memory traces to explain "retrograde amnesia" produced by ECS. *Journal of Comparative and Physiological Psychology*, **53**, 524-531.

Cooper, R. M. & Krass, M. 1963. Strychnine: Duration of the effects on maze-learning. *Psychopharmacologia*, **4**, 472-475.

Cooper, R. M. & Taylor, L. H. 1967. Thalamic reticular system and central grey: Self-stimulation. *Science*, **156**, 102-103.

Corcoran, M. E. 1968. Recovery of hypothalamic self-stimulation following ventral tegmental lesions in the rat. Unpublished Masters thesis, McGill University.

Corkin, S. H. 1964. Somesthetic function after focal cerebral damage in man. Unpublished doctoral thesis, McGill University.

Corkin, S. H. 1965. Tactually-guided maze learning in man: Effects of unilateral cortical excisions and bilateral hippocampal lesions. *Neuropsychologia*, 3, 339-351.

Corkin, S., Milner, B. & Rasmussen, T. 1964. Effects of different cortical excisions on sensory thresholds in man. *Transactions of the American Neurological Association*, 89, 112-116.

Cornil, L., Gastaut, H. & Corriol, J. 1951. Appréciation du degré de conscience au cours des paroxysmes épileptiques "petit mal." *Revue Neurologique*, 84, 149-151.

Corning, W. C. & John, E. R. 1961. Effect of ribonuclease on retention of response in regenerated planarians. *Science*, 134, 1363-1365.

Correll, R. E. & Scoville, W. B. 1965. Performance on delayed match following lesions of medial temporal lobe structures. *Journal of Comparative and Physiological Psychology*, 60, 360-367.

Corsi, P. 1969. Verbal memory impairment after unilateral hippocampal excisions. Paper read at 40th annual meeting of the Eastern Psychological Association, Philadelphia.

Corson, J. A. & Enesco, H. E. 1966. Some effects of injections of ribonucleic acid. *Psychonomic Science*, 5, 217-218.

Courtois, G. 1954. Discussion of R. Jung. Correlation of bioelectrical and autonomic phenomena with alterations of consciousness and arousal in man. In J. F. Delafresnaye (Ed.), *Brain mechanisms and consciousness*. Springfield, Ill.: Thomas. P. 340.

Coury, J. N. 1967. Neural correlates of food and water intake in the rat. *Science*, 156, 1763-1765.

Covian, M. R. 1967. Studies on the neurovegetative and behavioral functions of the brain septal area. *Progress in Brain Research*, 27, 189-217.

Cowey, A. 1967. Perimetric study of field defect in monkeys after cortical and retinal ablations. *Quarterly Journal of Experimental Psychology*, 19, 232-245.

Cowey, A. & Weiskrantz, L. 1963. A perimetric study of visual field defects in monkeys. *Quarterly Journal of Experimental Psychology*, 15, 91-115.

Cowie, A. T. 1944. Fracture of the pelvic bones in bovines implanted with tablets of synthetic oestrogens. *Journal of Endocrinology*, 4, 19-22.

Cox, V. C. & Valenstein, E. S. 1965. Attenuation of aversive properties of peripheral shock by hypothalamic stimulation. *Science*, 149, 323-325.

Cragg, B. G. & Temperley, H. N. V. 1955. Memory: The analogy with ferromagnetic hysteresis. *Brain*, 78, 304-316.

Craig, W. 1911. Oviposition induced by the male in pigeons. *Journal of Morphology*, 22, 299-305.

Creed, R. S., Denny-Brown, D., Eccles, J. C., Liddell, E. G. T. & Sherrington, C. S. 1932. *Reflex activity of the spinal cord*. Oxford: Clarendon.

Critchley, M. 1953. *The parietal lobes*. Baltimore: Williams & Wilkins.

Crow, L. T. 1964. Subcommissural organ, lateral hypothalamus and dorsal longitudinal fasciculus in water and salt metabolism. In M. J. Wayner (Ed.), *Thirst*. New York: Macmillan. Pp. 473-481.

Cuénod, M., Casey, K. L. & MacLean, P. D. 1965. Unit analysis of visual input to posterior limbic cortex. I. Photic stimulation. *Journal of Neurophysiology*, 28, 1101-1117.

Dahlström, A. & Fuxe, K. 1964. Evidence for the existence of monoamine-containing neurons in the central nervous system. *Acta Physiologica Scandinavica*, 62 (Suppl. 232), 1-55.

Dallenbach, K. M. 1955. Phrenology versus psychoanalysis. *American Journal of Psychology*, 68, 511-525.

Danilewski, V. J. 1891. Electrical phenomena in the brain. *Fiziologicheskom Sbornik*, 2, 77-88.

Darrow, D. C. & Yannet, H. 1935. The changes in the distribution of body water accompanying increase and decrease in extracellular electrolyte. *Journal of Clinical Investigation*, 14, 266-275.

Davis, C. D. 1939. The effect of ablations of neocortex on mating, maternal behavior and the production of pseudopregnancy in the female rat and on copulatory activity in the male. *American Journal of Physiology*, 127, 374-380.

Davis, C. M. 1928. Self selection of diet by newly weaned infants. *American Journal of Diseases of Children*. 36, 651-679.

Davis, C. M. 1939. Results of self selection of diets by young children. *Canadian Medical Association Journal*, 41, 257-261.

Davis, H. 1947. *Hearing and deafness. A guide for laymen*. New York: Murray Hill.

Davis, H. 1961. Peripheral coding of auditory information. In W. A. Rosenblith (Ed.), *Sensory communication*. New York: Wiley. Pp. 119-141.

Davis, H. 1964. Enhancement of evoked cortical potentials in humans related to a task requiring a decision. *Science*, 145, 182-183.

Davis, H. 1966. A model for transducer action in the cochlea. *Cold Spring Harbor Symposia of Quantitative Biology*, 30, 181-189.

Davis, H. & associates. 1953. Acoustic trauma in the guinea pig. *Journal of the Acoustical Society of America*, 25, 1180-1189.

Davis, H., Deatherage, H. B., Eldredge, D. H. & Smith, C. A. 1958. Summating potentials of the cochlea. *American Journal of Physiology*, 195, 251-261.

Davis, J. D., Gallagher, R. L. & Ladove, R. 1967. Food intake controlled by a blood factor. *Science*, 156, 1247-1248.

Day, L. & Bentley, M. 1911. A note on learning in *Paramecium*. *Journal of Animal Behavior*, 1, 67-73.

De Groot, J. 1959. The rat forebrain in stereotaxic coordinates. *Verhandelingen der Koninklijke Nederlandse Akademie van Wetenschappen Afd. Natuurkunde*, 52, 1-40.

Dejerine, J. 1914. *Sémiologie des affections du système nerveux*. Paris: Masson.

De Jong, R. N., Itabashi, H. H. & Olson, J. R. 1968. "Pure" memory loss with hippocampal lesions. A case report. *Transactions of the American Neurological Association*, 93, 31-34.

Delattre, P. C., Liberman, A. M. & Cooper, F. S. 1955. Acoustic loci and transitional cues for consonants. *Journal of the Acoustical Society of America*, 27, 769-773.

Delgado, J. M. R. 1955. Cerebral structures involved in

transmission and elaboration of noxious stimulation. *Journal of Neurophysiology*, **18**, 261-275.

Delgado, J. M. R. 1963. Electrodes for extra-cellular recording and stimulation. In W. L. Nastuk, *Physical techniques in biological research*. Vol. 5. New York: Academic Press. Pp. 88-143.

Delgado, J. M. R. 1965. Sequential behavior induced repeatedly by stimulation of the red nucleus in free monkeys. *Science*, **148**, 1361-1363.

Delgado, J. M. R., Roberts, W. W. & Miller, N. E. 1954. Learning motivated by electric stimulation of the brain. *American Journal of Physiology*, **179**, 587-593.

Delgado, J. M. R., Rosvold, H. E. & Looney, E. 1956. Evoking conditioned fear by electrical stimulation of subcortical structures in the monkey brain. *Journal of Comparative and Physiological Psychology*, **49**, 373-380.

De Lorenzo, A. J. D. 1963. Studies on the ultrastructure and histophysiology of cell membranes, nerve fibers and synaptic junctions in chemoreceptors. In Y. Zotterman (Ed.), *Olfaction and taste*. Oxford: Pergamon. Pp. 5-17.

Dement, W. 1960. The effect of dream deprivation. *Science*, **131**, 1705-1707.

Dement, W., Henry, P., Cohen, H. & Ferguson, J. 1967. Studies on the effect of REM deprivation in humans and animals. *Research Publications of the Association for Research in Nervous and Mental Disease*, **45**, 456-468.

Dement, W. & Kleitman, N. 1955. Incidence of eye motility during sleep in relation to varying EEG pattern. *Federation Proceedings*, **14**, 216.

Dement, W. & Kleitman, N. 1957. Cyclic variations in EEG during sleep and their relation to eye movements, body motility, and dreaming. *Electroencephalography and Clinical Neurophysiology*, **9**, 673-690.

De Robertis, E. 1964. *Histophysiology of synapses and neurosecretion*. Oxford: Pergamon Press.

Desmedt, J. E. 1962. Auditory-evoked potentials from cochlea to cortex as influenced by activation of the efferent olivo-cochlear bundle. *Journal of the Acoustical Society of America*, **34**, 1478-1496.

Desmedt, J. E. & LaGrutta, V. 1963. Function of the uncrossed efferent olivo-cochlear fibres in the cat. *Nature*, **200**, 472-474.

Dethier, V. G. & Bodenstein, D. 1958. Hunger in the blowfly. *Zeitschrift für Tierpsychologie*, **15**, 129-140.

Deutsch, J. A. 1960. *The structural basis of behavior*. Chicago: University of Chicago Press.

Deutsch, J. A. 1964. Behavioral measurement of the neural refractory period and its application to intracranial self-stimulation. *Journal of Comparative and Physiological Psychology*, **58**, 1-9.

Deutsch, J. A. & Deutsch, D. 1966. *Physiological psychology*. Homewood, Ill.: Dorsey.

Deutsch, J. A. & DiCara, L. 1967. Hunger and extinction in intracranial self-stimulation. *Journal of Comparative and Physiological Psychology*, **63**, 344-347.

Deutsch, J. A., Hamburg, M. D. & Dahl, M. 1966. Anticholinesterase-induced amnesia and its temporal aspects. *Science*, **151**, 221-223.

Deutsch, J. A. & Howarth, C. I. 1963. Some tests of a theory of intracranial self-stimulation. *Psychological Review*, **70**, 444-460.

De Valois, R. L., Jacobs, G. H. & Abramov, I. 1964. Responses of single cells in visual system to shifts in the wavelength of light. *Science*, **146**, 1184-1186.

De Valois, R. L., Smith, C. J., Karoly, A. J. & Kitai, S. T. 1958. Electrical responses of primate visual system: I. Different layers of macaque lateral geniculate nucleus. *Journal of Comparative and Physiological Psychology*, **51**, 662-668.

DeVito, J. L. & Smith, O. A., Jr. 1959. Effects of temperature and food deprivation on the random activity of *Macaca mulatta*. *Journal of Comparative and Physiological Psychology*, **52**, 29-32.

De Vries, H. & Stuiver, M. 1961. The absolute sensitivity of the human sense of smell. In W. A. Rosenblith, (Ed.), *Sensory communication*. New York: Wiley. Pp. 159-167.

Dewson, J. H. III. 1964. Speech sound discrimination by cats. *Science*, **144**, 555-556.

Dey, F. L., Fisher, C., Berry, C. M. & Ranson, S. W. 1940. Disturbances in reproductive functions caused by hypothalamic lesions in female guinea pigs. *American Journal of Physiology*, **129**, 39-46.

Diamond, I. T., Chow, K. L. & Neff, W. D. 1958. Degeneration of caudal medial geniculate body following cortical lesion ventral to auditory area II in cat. *Journal of Comparative Neurology*, **109**, 349-362.

Dingman, W. & Sporn, M. B. 1961. The incorporation of 8-azaguanine into rat brain RNA and its effect on maze learning by the rat: an inquiry into the biochemical bases of memory. *Journal of Psychiatric Research*, **1**, 1-11.

Dingman, W. & Sporn, M. B. 1964. Molecular theories of memory. *Science*, **144**, 26-29.

Ditchburn, R. W. & Fender, D. H. 1955. The stabilised retinal image. *Optica Acta*, **2**, 128-133.

Ditchburn, R. W., Fender, D. H. & Mayne, S. 1959. Vision with controlled movements of the retinal image. *Journal of Physiology*, **145**, 98-107.

Ditchburn, R. W., & Ginsborg, B. L. 1952. Vision with a stabilised retinal image. *Nature*, **170**, 36-37.

Ditchburn, R. W. & Ginsborg, B. L. 1953. Involuntary eye movements during fixation. *Journal of Physiology*, **119**, 1-17.

Dodt, E. & Zotterman, Y. 1952. The discharge of specific cold fibres at high temperatures. *Acta Physiologica Scandinavica*, **26**, 358-365.

Donald, M. W. 1968. Electrocortical correlates of fixed foreperiod decision tasks. Unpublished doctoral dissertation, McGill University.

Dondey, M., Albe-Fessard, D. & Le Beau, J. 1962. Premières applications neurophysiologiques d'une méthode permettant le blocage électif et réversible de structures centrales par réfrigération localisée. *Electroencephalography and Clinical Neurophysiology*, **14**, 758-763.

Doty, R. W. 1951. Influence of stimulus pattern on reflex deglutition. *American Journal of Physiology*, **166**, 142-158.

Doty, R. W. 1958. Potentials evoked in cat cerebral cortex by diffuse and by punctiform photic stimuli. *Journal of Neurophysiology*, **21**, 437-464.

Doty, R. W. & Bosma, J. F. 1956. An electromyographic analysis of reflex deglutition. *Journal of Neurophysiology*, **19**, 44-60.

Doty, R. W. & Rutledge, L. T. 1959. "Generalization" between cortically and peripherally applied stimuli eliciting conditioned reflexes. *Journal of Neurophysiology*, **22**, 428-435.

Doty, R. W. Rutledge, L. T. & Larsen, R. M. 1956. Conditioned reflexes established to electrical stimulation of cat cerebral cortex. *Journal of Neurophysiology*, **19**, 401-415.

Douglas, R. J. 1967. The hippocampus and behavior. *Psychological Bulletin*, **67**, 416-442.

Douglas, W. W. & Ritchie, J. M. 1957. Non-medullated fibres in the saphenous nerve which signal touch. *Journal of Physiology*, **139**, 385-399.

Dowling, J. E. 1965. Foveal receptors of the monkey retina: Fine structure. *Science*, **147**, 57-59.

Downer, J. & Zubek, J. P. 1954. Role of the cerebral cortex in temperature discrimination in the rat. *Journal of Comparative and Physiological Psychology*, **47**, 199-203.

Drachman, D. A. & Ommaya, A. K. 1964. Memory and the hippocampal complex. *Archives of Neurology*, **10**, 411-425.

Dua, S. & MacLean, P. D. 1964. Localization for penile erection in medial frontal lobe. *American Journal of Physiology*, **207**, 1425-1434.

Duncan, C. P. 1949. The retroactive effect of electroshock on learning. *Journal of Comparative and Physiological Psychology*, **42**, 32-44.

Durup, G. & Fessard, A. 1935. L'électroencéphalogramme de l'homme. *Année Psychologique*, **36**, 1-32.

Ebbinghaus, H. 1885. *Über das Gedächtnis*. Leipzig: Duncker & Humblot. (Translated by H. A. Ruger & C. E. Bussenius: *Memory*. New York; Dover, 1964.)

Ebner, F. F. & Myers, R. E. 1962. Corpus callosum and the interhemispheric transmission of tactual learning. *Journal of Neurophysiology*, **25**, 380-391.

Eccles, J. C. 1953. *The neurophysiological basis of mind*. Oxford: Clarendon.

Eccles, J. C. 1957. *The physiology of nerve cells*. Baltimore: Johns Hopkins Press.

Eccles, J. C. 1964. Ionic mechanism of postsynaptic inhibition. *Science*, **145**, 1140-1147.

Eccles, J. C., Eccles, R. M. & Magni, F. 1960. Presynaptic inhibition in the spinal cord. *Journal of Physiology*, **154**, 28P.

Eccles, J. C., Eccles, R. M. & Magni, F. 1961. Central inhibitory action attributable to presynaptic depolarization produced by muscle afferent volleys. *Journal of Physiology*, **159**, 147-166.

Economo, C. von. 1918. *Die Encephalitis lethargica*. Vienna: Deuticke.

Economo, C. von & Koskinas, G. N. 1925. *Die Cytoarchitectonik der Hirnrinde des erwachsenen Menschen*. Vienna: Springer.

Egger, M. D. & Flynn, J. P. 1963. Effects of electrical stimulation of the amygdala on hypothalamically elicited attack behavior in cats. *Journal of Neurophysiology*, **26**, 705-720.

· Ehrlich, A. 1963. Effects of tegmental lesions on motivated behavior in rats. *Journal of Comparative and Physiological Psychology*, **56**, 390-396.

Ehrlich, A. 1964. Neural control of feeding behavior. *Psychological Bulletin*, **61**, 100-114.

Eldred, E., Granit, R. & Merton, P. A. 1953. Supraspinal control of the muscle spindles and its significance. *Journal of Physiology*, **122**, 498-523.

Emmers, R., Benjamin, R. M. & Blomquist, A. J. 1962. Thalamic localization of afferents from the tongue in albino rat. *Journal of Comparative Neurology*, **118**, 43-48.

Endröczi, E., Lissák, K. & Telegdy, G. 1958. Influence of sexual and adrenocortical hormones on the maternal aggressivity. *Acta Physiologica Academiae Scientiarum Hungaricae*, **14**, 353-357.

Engström, H. 1960. Electron micrographic studies of the receptor cells of the organ of Corti. In G. L. Rasmussen & W. F. Windle (Eds.), *Neural mechanisms of the auditory and vestibular systems*. Springfield, Ill.: Thomas. Pp. 48-64.

Enström, H. & Wersäll, J. 1958. The ultrastructural organization of the organ of Corti and of the vestibular sensory epithelia. *Experimental Cell Research* (Suppl. 5), 460-492.

Epstein, A. N. 1959. Suppression of eating and drinking by amphetamine and other drugs in normal and hyperphagic rats. *Journal of Comparative and Physiological Psychology*, **52**, 37-45.

Epstein, A. N. 1960. Reciprocal changes in feeding behavior produced by intra-hypothalamic chemical injections. *American Journal of Physiology*, **199**, 969-974.

Epstein, A. N. & Milestone, R. 1968. Showering as a coolant for rats exposed to heat. *Science*, **160**, 895-896.

Epstein, A. N. & Teitelbaum, P. 1962. Regulation of food intake in the absence of taste, smell, and other oropharyngeal sensations. *Journal of Comparative and Physiological Psychology*, **55**, 753-759.

Epstein, A. N. & Teitelbaum, P. 1964. Severe and persistent deficits in thirst produced by lateral hypothalamic damage. In M. J. Wayner (Ed.), *Thirst*. New York: Macmillan. Pp. 395-410.

Estable, C. 1961. Considerations on the histological bases of neurophysiology. In J. F. Delafresnaye (Ed.), *Brain mechanisms and learning*. Springfield, Ill.: Thomas. Pp. 309-334.

Ettlinger, G. & Kalsbeck, J. E. 1962. Changes in tactile discrimination and in visual reaching after successive and simultaneous bilateral posterior parietal ablations in the monkey. *Journal of Neurology, Neurosurgery, and Psychiatry*, **25**, 256-268.

Evans, D. R. 1963. Chemical structure and stimulation by carbohydrates. In Y. Zotterman (Ed.), *Olfaction and taste*. Oxford: Pergamon. Pp. 165-176.

Evarts, E. V. 1964. Temporal patterns of discharge of pyramidal tract neurons during sleep and waking in the monkey. *Journal of Neurophysiology*, **27**, 152-172.

Evarts, E. V. 1966. Pyramidal tract activity associated with a conditioned hand movement in the monkey. *Journal of Neurophysiology*, **29**, 1011-1027.

Evarts, E. V. 1967. Discussion of O. Pompeiano. The neurophysiological mechanisms of the postural and motor events during desynchronized sleep. *Research Publications of the Association for Research in Nervous and Mental Disease*, **45**, 450.

Evarts, E. V. 1968. Relation of pyramidal tract activity to force exerted during voluntary movement. *Journal of Neurophysiology*, **31**, 14-27.

Everett, N. B. 1965. *Functional neuroanatomy* (5th ed.) Philadelphia: Lea & Febiger.

Evvard, J. M. 1916. Is the appetite of swine a reliable indication of physiological needs? *Proceedings of the Iowa Academy of Sciences*, **22**, 375-414.

Falk, J. L. 1961. The behavioral regulation of water-electrolyte balance. In M. R. Jones (Ed.), *Nebraska Symposium on Motivation*. Vol. 9. Lincoln: University of Nebraska Press. Pp. 1-33.

Falk, J. L. 1964. Studies on schedule-induced polydipsia. In M. J. Wayner (Ed.), *Thirst*. New York: Macmillan. Pp. 95-116.

Feder, H. H. & Whalen, R. E. 1965. Feminine behavior

in neonatally castrated and estrogen-treated male rats. *Science*, **147**, 306-307.

Fehrer, E. 1956. The effects of hunger and familiarity of locale on exploration. *Journal of Comparative and Physiological Psychology*, **49**, 549-552.

Feindel, W. 1961. Response patterns elicited from the amygdala and deep temporoinsular cortex. In D. E. Sheer (Ed.), *Electrical stimulation of the brain*. Austin: University of Texas Press. Pp. 519-532.

Feldberg, W. & Myers, R. D. 1963. A new concept of temperature regulation by amines in the hypothalamus. *Nature*, **200**, 1325.

Feldman, S. M. & Waller, H. J. 1962. Dissociation of electrocortical activation and behavioural arousal. *Nature*, **196**, 1320-1322.

Fernandez de Molina, A. & Hunsperger, R. W. 1959. Central representation of affective reactions in forebrain and brain stem: Electrical stimulation of amygdala, stria terminalis, and adjacent structures. *Journal of Physiology*, **145**, 251-265.

Fernandez de Molina, A. & Hunsperger, R. W. 1962. Organization of the subcortical system governing defence and flight reactions in the cat. *Journal of Physiology*, **160**, 200-213.

Fernández-Guardiola, A., Roldán, E. R., Fanjul, M. L. & Castells, C. 1961. Role of the pupillary mechanism in the process of habituation of the visual pathways. *Electroencephalography and Clinical Neurophysiology*, **13**, 564-576.

Ferrier, D. 1876. *The functions of the brain*. London: Smith Elder.

Fessard, A. & Szabo, T. 1961. La facilitation de post-activation comme facteur de plasticité dans l'établissement des liaisons temporaires. In J. F. Delafresnaye (Ed.), *Brain mechanisms and learning*. Springfield, Ill.: Thomas, Pp. 353-373.

Fessard, A. & Tauc, L. 1960. Variations prolongées du rhythme de neurones autoactifs provoquées par la stimulation synaptique. *Journal de Physiologie*, **52**, 101. (Abstract)

Finan, J. L. 1942. Delayed response with pre-delay reinforcement in monkeys after removal of the frontal lobes. *American Journal of Psychology*, **55**, 204-214.

Fisher, A. E. 1956. Maternal and sexual behavior induced by intracranial chemical stimulation. *Science*, **124**, 228-229.

Fisher, A. E. & Coury, J. N. 1962. Cholinergic tracing of a central neural circuit underlying the thirst drive. *Science*, **138**, 691-692.

Fitzsimons, J. T. 1961. Drinking by rats depleted of body fluid without increase in osmotic pressure. *Journal of Physiology*, **159**, 297-309.

Fitzsimons, J. T. 1966. Hypovolaemic drinking and renin. *Journal of Physiology*, **186**, 130P-131P.

Fitzsimons, J. T. 1967. The kidney as a thirst receptor. *Journal of Physiology*, **191**, 128P-129P.

Fitzsimons, J. T. & Simons, B. J. 1968. The effect of angiotensin on drinking in the rat. *Journal of Physiology*, **198**, 39P-41P.

Fletcher, H. 1929. *Speech and hearing*. New York: Van Nostrand.

Flexner, J. B., Flexner, L. B. & Stellar, E. 1963. Memory in mice as affected by intracerebral puromycin. *Science*, **141**, 57-59.

Flexner, L. B. 1967. Dissection of memory in mice with antibiotics. *Proceedings of the American Philosophical Society*, **111**, 343-346.

Flexner, L. B. & Flexner, J. B. 1968. Intracerebral saline: Effect on memory of trained mice treated with puromycin. *Science*, **159**, 330-331.

Flexner, L. B., Flexner, J. B. & Roberts, R. B. 1967. Memory in mice analysed with antibiotics. *Science*, **155**, 1377-1383.

Flourens, P. 1823. Recherches physiques sur les propriétés et fonctions du système nerveux dans les animaux vertébrés. *Archives Générales de Médecine*, **2**, 321-374.

Flynn, J. P. & Wasman, M. 1960. Learning and cortically evoked movement during propagated hippocampal afterdischarges. *Science*, **131**, 1607-1608.

Foerster, O. 1936. Symptomatologie der Erkrankungen des Grosshirns. Motorische Felder und Bahnen. In O. Bumke & O. Foerster (Eds.), *Handbuch der Neurologie*, Vol. 6. Berlin: Springer. Pp. 358-448.

Folley, S. J. & Malpress, F. H. 1944. The artificial induction of lactation in the bovine by the subcutaneous implantation of synthetic oestrogen tablets. *Journal of Endrocrinology*, **4**, 1-18.

Fonberg, E. & Delgado, J. M. R. 1961. Avoidance and alimentary reactions during amygdala stimulation. *Journal of Neurophysiology*, **24**, 651-664.

Forster, R. E., II & Ferguson, T. B. 1952. Relationship between hypothalamic temperature and thermoregulatory effectors in unanesthetized cat. *American Journal of Physiology*, **169**, 255-269.

Fraenkel, G. S. & Gunn, D. L. 1961. *The orientation of animals*. New York: Dover.

Frank, K. & Fuortes, M. G. F. 1957. Presynaptic and postsynaptic inhibition of monosynaptic reflexes. *Federation Proceedings*, **16**, 39-40.

Franz, S. I. & Lashley, K. S. 1917. The retention of habits by the rat after destruction of the frontal portion of the cerebrum. *Psychobiology*, **1**, 3-18.

Freeman, W. J. & Davis, D. D. 1959. Effects on cats of conductive hypothalamic cooling. *American Journal of Physiology*, **197**, 145-148.

French, G. M. & Harlow, H. F. 1955. Locomotor reaction decrement in normal and brain-damaged monkeys. *Journal of Comparative and Physiological Psychology*, **48**, 496-501.

Frey, M. von. 1895. Beiträge zur Sinnesphysiologie der Haut. *Sitzungsberichte sächs Gesamte (Akademische) Wissenschaft Leipzig*, **47**, 166.

Frisch, K. von. 1950. *Bees. Their vision, chemical senses, and language*. Ithaca, N. Y.: Cornell University Press.

Fritsch, G. & Hitzig, E. 1870. Über die elektrische Erregbarkeit des Grosshirns. *Archiv für Anatomie Physiologie und Wissenschaftliche Medicin*, **37**, 300-332.

Fröhlich, A. 1901. Ein Fall von Tumor der *hypophysis cerebri* ohne Akromegalie. *Wiener Klinische Rundschau*, **15**, 883-886, 906-908. (Reprinted: *Research Publications of the Association for Research in Nervous and Mental Disease*, 1940, **20**, xvi-xxviii.)

Frommer, G. P. 1961. Gustatory afferent responses in the thalamus. In M. R. Kare & B. P. Halpern (Eds.), *The physiological and behavioral aspects of taste*. Chicago: University of Chicago Press. Pp. 50-59.

Fulton, J. F. & Ingraham, F. D. 1929. Emotional disturbances following experimental lesions of the base of the brain (pre-chiasmal). *Journal of Physiology*, **67**, xxvii-xxviii.

Fulton, J. F. & Sherrington, C. S. 1932. State of the flexor reflex in paraplegic dog and monkey respectively. *Journal of Physiology*, **75**, 17-22.

Fuster, J. M. 1958. Effects of stimulation of brain stem on tachistoscopic perception. *Science*, **127**, 150.

Fuster, J. M. 1961. Excitation and inhibition of neuronal firing in visual cortex by reticular stimulation. *Science*, **133**, 2011-2012.

Gabor, D. 1968. Improved holographic model of temporal recall. *Nature*, **217**, 1288-1289.

Galambos, R. 1952. Microelectrode studies on medial geniculate body of cat. III. Response to pure tones. *Journal of Neurophysiology*, **15**, 381-400.

Galambos, R. 1956. Suppression of auditory nerve activity by stimulation of efferent fibers to the cochlea. *Journal of Neurophysiology*, **19**, 424-437.

Galambos, R., Schwartzkopf, J. & Rupert, A. 1959. Microelectrode study of superior olivary nuclei. *American Journal of Physiology*, **197**, 527-536.

Galambos, R., Sheatz, G. & Vernier, V. G. 1956. Electrophysiological correlates of a conditioned response in cats. *Science*, **123**, 376-377.

Gall, F. J. 1810-1819. *Anatomie et physiologie du système nerveux en générale et du cerveau en particulier, avec des observations sur la possibilité de reconnâitre plusieurs dispositions intellectuelles et morales de l'homme et des animaux par la configuration de leurs têtes.* Paris: Schoell.

Garcia, J., Ervin, F. R., Yorke, C. H. & Koelling, R. A. 1967. Conditioning with delayed vitamin injections. *Science*, **155**, 716-718.

Garcia, J., Kimeldorf, D. J. & Hunt, E. L. 1961. The use of ionizing radiation as a motivating stimulus. *Psychological Review*, **68**, 383-395.

Gardner, E. 1968. *Fundamentals of neurology.* (5th ed.) Philadelphia: Saunders.

Gassel, M. M. & Williams D. 1963. Visual function in patients with homonymous hemianopia: Part II. Oculomotor mechanisms. *Brain*, **86**, 1-36.

Gasser, H. S. 1935. Conduction in nerves in relation to fiber types. *Research Publications of the Association for Research in Nervous and Mental Disease*, **15**, 35-59.

Gastaut, H. & Collomb, H. 1954. Étude du comportement sexuel chez les épileptiques psychomoteurs. *Annales Médico-psychologique*, **112**, 657-696.

Gastaut, H., Vigouroux, R., Corriol, J. & Badier, M. 1951. Effets de la stimulation électrique (par électrodes à demeure) du complexe amygdalien chez le chat non narcosé. *Journal de Physiologie*, **43**, 740-746.

Gelber, B. 1952. Investigations of the behavior of *Paramecium aurelia*. Modification of behavior after training with reinforcement. *Journal of Comparative and Physiological Psychology*, **45**, 58-65.

Gelber, B. 1957. Food or training in *Paramecium*. *Science*, **126**, 1340-1341.

Geldard, F. A. 1953. *The human senses.* New York: Wiley.

Gerall, A. A. 1966. Hormonal factors influencing masculine behavior of female guinea pigs. *Journal of Comparative and Physiological Psychology*, **62**, 365-369.

Gerall, A. A. & Ward, I. L. 1966. Effects of prenatal exogenous androgen on the sexual behavior of the female albino rat. *Journal of Comparative and Physiological Psychology*, **62**, 370-375.

Gerall, H. D., Ward, I. L. & Gerall, A. A. 1967. Disruption of the male rat's sexual behavior induced by social isolation. *Animal Behaviour*, **15**, 54-58.

Gergely, J. 1959. The relaxing factor of muscle. *Annals of the New York Academy of Sciences*, **81**, 490-504.

Gergely, J. 1964. The relaxing factor in muscle. Introductory remarks. *Federation Proceedings*, **23**, 885-886.

Gernandt, B. 1949. Response of mammalian vestibular neurons to horizontal rotation and caloric stimulation. *Journal of Neurophysiology*, **12**, 173-184.

Gernandt, B. E. 1959. Vestibular mechanisms. In J. Field (Ed.), *Handbook of physiology. Neurophysiology.* Vol. 1. Washington, D.C.: American Physiological Society. Pp. 549-564.

Gesteland, R. C., Lettvin, J. Y., Pitts, W. H. & Rojas, A. (1963). Odor specificities of the frog's olfactory receptors. In Y. Zotterman (Ed.), *Olfaction and taste.* Oxford: Pergamon. Pp. 19-34.

Ghent, L., Mishkin, M. & Teuber, H. L. 1962. Short-term memory after frontal-lobe injury in man. *Journal of Comparative and Physiological Psychology*, **55**, 705-709.

Gibson, E. J. & Walk, R. D. 1960. The "visual cliff." *Scientific American*, **202**, (4), 46-71.

Gibson, W. E., Reid, L. D., Sakai, M. & Porter, P. B. 1965. Intracranial reinforcement compared with sugar-water reinforcement. *Science*, **148**, 1357-1359.

Gilbert, G. J. 1958. Subcommissural organ secretion in the dehydrated rat. *The Anatomical Record*, **132**, 563-567.

Gilbert, G. J. 1964. The subcommissural organ and water-electrolyte metabolism. In M. J. Wayner (Ed.), *Thirst.* New York: Macmillan. Pp. 457-471.

Girden, E. & Culler, E. 1937. Conditioned responses in curarized striate muscle in dogs. *Journal of Comparative Psychology*, **23**, 261-274.

Glees, P. & Cole, J. 1950. Recovery of skilled motor functions after small repeated lesions of motor cortex in macaque. *Journal of Neurophysiology*, **13**, 137-148.

Glees, P. & Griffith, H. B. 1952. Bilateral destruction of the hippocampus (*Cornu Ammonis*) in a case of dementia. *Monatsschrift für Psychiatrie und Neurologie*, **123**, 193-204.

Glickman, S. E. 1961. Perseverative neural processes and consolidation of the memory trace. *Psychological Bulletin*, **58**, 218-233.

Glickman, S. E. & Jensen, G. D. 1961. The effects of hunger and thirst on Y-maze exploration. *Journal of Comparative and Physiological Psychology*, **54**, 83-85.

Glickman, S. E. & Schiff, B. B. 1967. A biological theory of reinforcement. *Psychological Review*, **74**, 81-109.

Glickman, S. E. & Sroges, R. W. 1966. Curiosity in zoo animals. *Behaviour*, **26**, 151-188.

Gloor, P. 1954. Autonomic functions of the diencephalon. *A.M.A. Archives of Neurology and Psychiatry*, **71**, 773-790.

Gloor, P. 1960. Amygdala. In J. Field (Ed.), *Handbook of physiology. Neurophysiology.* Vol. 2. Washington, D.C.: American Physiological Society. Pp. 1395-1420.

Glusman, M. & Roizin, L. 1960. Role of the hypothalamus in the organization of agonistic behavior in the cat. *Transactions of the American Neurological Association*, **85**, 177-181.

Goddard, G. V. 1964a. Functions of the amygdala. *Psychological Bulletin*, **62**, 89–109.

Goddard, G. V. 1964b. Amygdaloid stimulation and learning in the rat. *Journal of Comparative and Physiological Psychology*, **58**, 23–30.

Goddard, G. V. 1967. Development of epileptic seizures through brain stimulation at low intensity. *Nature*, **214**, 1020–1021.

Gol, A., Kellaway, P., Shapiro, M. & Hurst, C. M. 1963. Studies of hippocampectomy in the monkey, baboon, and cat. *Neurology*, **13**, 1031–1041.

Goldberg, J. M., Diamond, I. T. & Neff, W. D. 1957. Frequency discrimination after ablation of temporal and insular cortex in cat. *Federation Proceedings*, **16**, 47.

Gollin, E. S. 1960. Developmental studies of visual recognition of incomplete objects. *Perceptual and Motor Skills*, **11**, 289–298.

Goltz, F. 1892. Der Hund ohne Grosshirn. *Archiv für die gesamte Physiologie des Menschen und der Tiere*. **51**, 570–614.

Goodman, I. J. & Brown, J. L. 1966. Stimulation of positively and negatively reinforcing sites in the avian brain. *Life Sciences*, **5**, 693–704.

Goolker, P. & Schein, J. 1953. Psychic effects of ACTH and cortisone. *Psychosomatic Medicine*, **15**, 589–612.

Gorzalka, B. 1970. Reinforcing effects of pre-copulatory activity on the behavior of female rats. Honors thesis, McGill University.

Gouras, P. 1965. Primate retina: Duplex function of dark-adapted ganglion cells. *Science*, **147**, 1593–1594.

Goy, R. W., Bridson, W. E. & Young, W. C. 1964. Period of maximal susceptibility of the prenatal female guinea pig to masculinizing actions of testosterone propionate. *Journal of Comparative and Physiological Psychology*, **57**, 166–174.

Grady, K. L., Phoenix, C. H. & Young, W. C. 1965. Role of the developing rat testis in differentiation of the neural tissues mediating mating behavior. *Journal of Comparative and Physiological Psychology*, **59**, 176–182.

Graff, H. & Stellar, E. 1962. Hyperphagia, obesity, and finickiness. *Journal of Comparative and Physiological Psychology*, **55**, 418–424.

Grafstein, B. 1956. Mechanism of spreading cortical depression. *Journal of Neurophysiology*, **19**, 154–171.

Granit, R. 1943. The spectral properties of the visual receptors of the cat. *Acta Physiologica Scandinavica*, **5**, 219–229.

Granit, R. 1947. *Sensory mechanisms of the retina*. London: Oxford University Press.

Granit, R. 1955a. *Receptors and sensory perception*. New Haven, Conn.: Yale University Press.

Granit, R. 1955b. Centrifugal and antidromic effects on ganglion cells of the retina. *Journal of Neurophysiology*, **18**, 388–411.

Grant, D. A. & Berg, E. A. 1948. A behavioral analysis of degree of reinforcement and ease of shifting to new responses in a Weigl-type card-sorting problem. *Journal of Experimental Psychology*, **38**, 404–411.

Grastyán, E. 1968. Commentary. In E. Gellhorn (Ed.), *Biological foundations of emotion*. Glenview, Ill.: Scott, Foresman. Pp. 114–127.

Grastyán, E. & Ángyán, L. 1967. The organization of motivation at the thalamic level of the cat. *Physiology and Behavior*. **2**, 5–13.

Grastyán, E., Czopf, J., Ángyán, L. & Szabó, I. 1964.

Neural mechanisms of motivation. *Nova Acta Leopoldina*, **169**, 153–170.

Grastyán, E., Czopf, J., Ángyán, L. & Szabó, I. 1965. The significance of subcortical motivational mechanisms in the organization of conditional connections. *Acta Physiologica Academiae Scientiarum Hungaricae*, **26**, 9–46.

Grastyán, E., Karmos, G., Vereczkey, L. & Kellényi, E. E. 1966. The hippocampal electrical correlates of the homeostatic regulation of motivation. *Electroencephalography and Clinical Neurophysiology*, **21**, 34–53.

Grastyán, E., Karmos, G., Vereczkey, L., Martin, J. & Kellényi, L. 1965. Hypothalamic motivational processes as reflected by their hippocampal electrical correlates. *Science*, **149**, 91–93.

Grastyán, E. Lissák, K., Madarász, I. & Donhoffer, H. 1959. Hippocampal electrical activity during the development of conditioned reflexes. *Electroencephalography and Clinical Neurophysiology*, **11**, 409–430.

Grastyán, E., Szabó, I., Molnar, P. & Kolta, P. 1968. Rebound, reinforcement and self-stimulation. *Communications in Behavioral Biology*, **A2**, 235–266.

Gray, E. G. 1962. A morphological basis for pre-synaptic inhibition? *Nature*, **193**, 82–83.

Gray, J. A. B. 1959. Initiation of impulses at receptors. In J. Field, (Ed.), *Handbook of Physiology. Neurophysiology*. Vol. 1. Washington D.C.: American Physiological Society. Pp. 123–145.

Gray, J. A. B. & Sato, M. 1953. Properties of the receptor potential in Pacinian corpuscles. *Journal of Physiology*, **122**, 610–636.

Green, J. D. 1958. The rhinencephalon: Aspects of its relation to behavior and the reticular activating system. In H. H. Jasper, L. D. Proctor, R. S. Knighton, W. C. Noshay & R. T. Costello (Eds.), *Reticular formation of the brain*. Boston: Little, Brown. Pp. 607–619.

Green, J. D. & Arduini, A. 1954. Hippocampal electrical activity in arousal. *Journal of Neurophysiology*, **17**, 533–557.

Green, J. D., Clemente, C. D. & De Groot, J. 1957. Rhinencephalic lesions and behavior in cats. An analysis of the Klüver-Bucy syndrome with particular reference to normal and abnormal sexual behavior. *Journal of Comparative Neurology*, **108**, 505–545.

Green, H. H. 1925. Perverted appetites. *Physiological Review*, **5**, 336–348.

Green, R. H., Beatty, W. W. & Schwartzbaum, J. S. 1967. Comparative effects of septo-hippocampal and caudate lesions on avoidance behavior in rats. *Journal of Comparative and Physiological Psychology*, **64**, 444–452.

Greer, M. A. 1955. Suggestive evidence of a primary "drinking center" in the hypothalamus of the rat. *Proceedings of the Society for Experimental Biology and Medicine of New York*, **89**, 59–62.

Griffin, D. R. 1953. Sensory physiology and the orientation of animals. *American Scientist*, **41**, 209–244.

Griffin, D. R. 1958. *Listening in the dark*. New Haven, Conn.: Yale University Press.

Grinker, R. R. 1939. Hypothalamic functions in psychosomatic interrelations. *Psychosomatic Medicine*, **1**, 19–47.

Gross, C. G. 1963. Comparison of the effects of partial and total lateral frontal lesions on test performance by monkeys. *Journal of Comparative and Physiological Psychology*, **56**, 41–47.

Gross, C. G. & Weiskrantz, L. 1962. Evidence for dissociation between impairment on auditory discrimination and delayed response in frontal monkeys. *Experimental Neurology*, 5, 453-476.

Gross, C. G. & Weiskrantz, L. 1964. Some changes in behavior produced by lateral frontal lesions in the macaque. In J. M. Warren & K. Akert (Eds.), *The frontal granular cortex and . behavior*. New York: McGraw-Hill. Pp. 74-101.

Grossman, R. G. 1958. Effects of stimulation of nonspecific thalamic system on locomotor movements in cat. *Journal of Neurophysiology*, 21, 85-93.

Grossman, S. P. 1960. Eating or drinking elicited by direct adrenergic or cholinergic stimulation of hypothalamus. *Science*, 132, 301-302.

Grossman, S. P. 1962. Direct adrenergic and cholinergic stimulation of hypothalamic mechanisms. *American Journal of Physiology*, 202, 872-882.

Grossman, S. P. & Grossman, L. 1963. Food and water intake following lesions or electrical stimulation of the amygdala. *American Journal of Physiology*, 205, 761-765.

Grossman, S. P. & Rechtschaffen, A. 1967. Variations in brain temperature in relation to food intake. *Physiology and Behavior*, 2, 379-383.

Grüsser-Cornehls, U., Grüsser, O. J. & Bullock, T. H. 1963. Unit responses in the frog's tectum to moving and nonmoving visual stimuli. *Science*, 141, 820-822.

Guiot, G., Hertzog, E., Rondot, P. & Molina, P. 1961. Arrest or acceleration of speech evoked by thalamic stimulation in the course of stereotaxic procedures for Parkinsonism. *Brain*, 84, 363-379.

Hagamen, W. D., Zitzmann, E. K. & Reeves, A. G. 1963. Sexual mounting of diverse objects in a group of randomly selected, unoperated male cats. *Journal of Comparative and Physiological Psychology*, 56, 298-301.

Hagbarth, K. E. & Fex, J. 1959. Centrifugal influences on single unit activity in spinal sensory paths. *Journal of Neurophysiology*, 22, 321-338.

Hagbarth, K. E. & Kerr, D. I. B. 1954. Central influences on spinal afferent conduction. *Journal of Neurophysiology*, 17, 295-307.

Hagen, E., Knoche, H., Sinclair, D. C. & Weddell, G. 1953. The role of specialized nerve terminals in cutaneous sensibility. *Proceedings of the Royal Society*, B141, 279-287.

Hainsworth, F. R. & Epstein, A. N. 1966. Severe impairment of heat-induced saliva-spreading in rats recovered from lateral hypothalamic lesions. *Science*, 153, 1255-1257.

Hammel, H. T., Hardy, J. D. & Fusco, M. M. 1960. Thermoregulatory responses to hypothalamic cooling in unanesthetized dogs. *American Journal of Physiology*, 198, 481-486.

Han, P. W. 1967. Obesity in force-fed, hypophysectomized rats bearing hypothalamic lesions. Paper presented at the meeting of the New York Academy of Sciences, New York, November.

Hanson, M. E. & Grossman, M. I. 1948. The failure of intravenous glucose to inhibit food intake in dogs. *Federation Proceedings*, 7, 50. (Abstract)

Hardy, J. D., Hellon, R. F. & Sutherland, K. 1964. Temperature-sensitive neurones in the dog's hypothalamus. *Journal of Physiology*, 175, 242-253.

Harlow, H. F. 1949. The formation of learning sets. *Psychological Review*, 56, 51-65.

Harlow, H. F. 1958. Behavioral contributions to interdisciplinary research. In H. F. Harlow and C. N. Woolsey (Eds.), *Biological and biochemical bases of behavior*. Madison: University of Wisconsin Press. Pp. 3-23.

Harlow, H. F. 1962. The heterosexual affectional system in monkeys. *American Psychologist*, 17, 1-9.

Harper, E. H. 1904. The fertilization and early development of the pigeon's egg. *American Journal of Anatomy*, 3, 349-386.

Harris, G. W. 1964. Sex hormones, brain development and brain function. *Endocrinology*, 75, 627-648.

Harris, G. W. & Levine, S. 1965. Sexual differentiation of the brain and its experimental control. *Journal of Physiology*, 181, 379-400.

Harris, G. W. & Michael, R. P. 1964. The activation of sexual behaviour by hypothalamic implants of oestrogen. *Journal of Physiology*, 171, 275-301.

Harris, L. J., Clay, J., Hargreaves, F. J. & Ward, A. 1933. Appetite and choice of diet. The ability of the vitamin B deficient rat to discriminate between diets containing and lacking the vitamin. *Proceedings of the Royal Society*, B113, 161-190.

Hart, B. L. 1967. Sexual reflexes and mating behavior in the male dog. *Journal of Comparative and Physiological Psychology*, 64, 388-399.

Hartline, H. K. 1938. The response of single optic nerve fibers of the vertebrate eye to illumination of the retina. *American Journal of Physiology*, 121, 400-415.

Hartline, H. K. & Graham, C. H., 1932. Nerve impulses from single receptors in the eye. *Journal of Cellular and Comparative Physiology*, 1, 277-295.

Hartline, H. K. & Ratliff, F. 1957. Inhibitory interaction of receptor units in the eye of *Limulus*. *Journal of General Physiology*, 40, 357-376.

Hartline, H. K., Wagner, H. G. & Ratliff, F. 1956. Inhibition in the eye of *Limulus*. *Journal of General Physiology*, 39, 651-673.

Haugen, F. P. & Melzack, R. 1957. The effects of nitrous oxide on responses evoked in the brain stem by tooth stimulation. *Anesthesiology*, 18, 183-195.

Head, H. 1920. *Studies in neurology*. London: Oxford University Press.

Head, H. 1926. *Aphasia and kindred disorders of speech*. London: Cambridge University Press.

Hearst, E. & Pribram, K. H. 1964. Facilitation of avoidance behavior by unavoidable shocks in normal and amygdalectomized monkeys. *Psychological Reports*, 14, 39-42.

Hebb, D. O. 1939. Intelligence in man after large removals of cerebral tissue: Defects following right temporal lobectomy. *Journal of General Psychology*, 21, 437-446.

Hebb, D. O. 1949. *The organization of behavior*. New York: Wiley.

Hebb, D. O. 1951. The role of neurological ideas in psychology. *Journal of Personality*, 20, 39-55.

Hebb, D. O. 1955. Drives and the C.N.S. (conceptual nervous system). *Psychological Review*, 62, 243-254.

Hebb, D. O. 1961. Distinctive features of learning in the higher animal. In J. F. Delafresnaye (Ed.), *Brain mechanisms and learning*. Springfield, Ill.: Thomas. Pp. 37-51.

Hebb, D. O. 1966. *A textbook of psychology*. (2nd ed.) Philadelphia: Saunders.

Hebb, D. O. & Penfield, W. 1940. Human behavior after extensive bilateral removals from the frontal lobes. *Archives of Neurology and Psychiatry*, 44, 421-438.

Hécaen, H. & Angelergues, R. 1964. Localization of symptoms in aphasia. In A. V. S. de Reuck & M. O'Connor (Eds.), *Ciba foundation symposium on disorders of language*. London: Churchill. Pp. 222-256.

Hécaen, H., Penfield, W., Bertrand, C. & Malmo, R. 1956. The syndrome of apractognosia due to lesions of the minor cerebral hemisphere. *Archives of Neurology and Psychiatry*, 75, 400-434.

Hécaen, H., Talairach, J., David, M. & Dell, M. B. 1949. Coagulations limitées du thalamus dans les algies du syndrome thalamique. *Revue neurologique*, 81, 917-931.

Hecht, S. 1929. Vision: II. The nature of the photoreceptor process. In C. Murchison (Ed.), *The foundations of experimental psychology*. Worcester, Mass.: Clark University Press. Pp. 216-272.

Heinroth, O. 1910. Beiträge zur Biologie, namentlich Ethologie und Physiologie der Anatiden. *Verhandlungen des 5th Internatzional Ornithologie Kongress*, 1, 589-702.

Helmholtz, H. von. 1862. *Die Lehre von den Tonempfindungen als physiologische Grundlage für die Theorie der Musik*. Brunswick: Vieweg. (Translated: *Sensations of tone*. New York; Longmans, 1930.)

Hemphill, R. E. & Stengel, E. 1940. A study of pure word-deafness. *Journal of Neurology and Psychiatry*, 3, 251-262.

Hendry, D. P. & Rasche, R. H. 1961. Analysis of a new nonnutritive positive reinforcer based on thirst. *Journal of Comparative and Physiological Psychology*, 54, 477-483.

Henry, J. P. & Pearce, J. W. 1956. The possible role of cardiac atrial stretch receptors in the induction of changes in urine flow. *Journal of Physiology*, 131, 572-585.

Hensel, H., Iggo, A. & Witt, I. 1960. A quantitative study of sensitive cutaneous thermoreceptors with C afferent fibres. *Journal of Physiology*, 153, 113-126.

Hensel, H. & Zotterman, Y. 1951. Quantitative Beziehungen zwischen der Entladung einzelner Kältefasern und der Temperatur. *Acta Physiologica Scandinavica*, 23, 291-319.

Herberg, L. J. 1960. Hunger reduction produced by injecting glucose into the lateral ventricle of the rat. *Nature*, 187, 245-246.

Herberg, L. J. 1962. Physiological drives investigated by means of injections into the cerebral ventricles of the rat. *Quarterly Journal of Experimental Psychology*, 14, 8-14.

Herberg, L. J. 1963a. Seminal ejaculation following positively reinforcing electrical stimulation of the rat hypothalamus. *Journal of Comparative and Physiological Psychology*, 56, 679-685.

Herberg, L. J. 1963b. Determinants of extinction in electrical self-stimulation. *Journal of Comparative and Physiological Psychology*, 56, 686-690.

Hering, E. 1878. *Zur Lehre vom Lichtsinne*. Vienna: Gerhold's Sohn.

Herman, M. 1950. Role of somesthetic stimuli in the development of sexual excitation in man. *Archives of Neurology and Psychiatry*, 64, 47-56.

Hernández-Peón, R. 1961. Reticular mechanisms of sensory control. In W. A. Rosenblith (Ed.), *Sensory communication*. New York: Wiley. Pp. 497-520.

Hernández-Peón, R., Chávez-Ibarra, G., Morgane, P. J. & Timo-Iaria, C. 1963. Limbic cholinergic pathways involved in sleep and emotional behavior. *Experimental Neurology*, 8, 93-111.

Hernández-Peón, R., Scherrer, H. & Jouvet, M. 1956. Modification of electric activity in cochlear nucleus during "attention" in unanesthetized cats. *Science*, 123, 331-332.

Herrick, C. J. 1948. *The brain of the tiger salamander*. Chicago: University of Chicago Press.

Heschl, R. L. 1878. Über die vorderequere Schläfenwindung des menschlichen Grosshirns. Vienna: Braumüller.

Hess, R., Jr., Koella, W. P. & Akert, K. 1953. Cortical and subcortical recordings in natural and artifically induced sleep in cats. *Electroencephalography and Clinical Neurophysiology*, 5, 75-90.

Hess, W. R. 1931. Le sommeil. *Comptes Rendus de la Société de Biologie*, 107, 1333-1360.

Hess, W. R. 1932. *Beiträge zur Physiologie des Hirnstammes*. Vol. 1. *Die Methodik der lokalisierten Reizung und Ausschaltung subkortikaler Hirnabschnitte*. Leipzig: Thième.

Hess, W. R. 1957. *The functional organization of the diencephalon*. New York: Grune & Stratton.

Hess, W. R. & Brügger, M. 1943. Das subkortikale Zentrum der affektiven Abwehrreaktion. *Helvetica Physiologica et Pharmacologica Acta*, 1, 33-52.

Hetherington, A. W. & Ranson, S. W. 1940. Hypothalamic lesions and adiposity in the rat. *Anatomical Record*, 78, 149-172.

Hetherington, A. W. & Ranson, S. W. 1942. Effect of early hypophysectomy on hypothalamic obesity. *Endocrinology*, 31, 30-34.

Higginbotham, A. C. & Koon, W. E., 1955. Temperature regulation in the Virginia opossum. *American Journal of Physiology*, 181, 69-71.

Hild, W. & Tasaki, I. 1962. Morphological and physiological properties of neurons and glial cells in tissue culture. *Journal of Neurophysiology*, 25, 277-304.

Hill, R. M. & Horn, G. 1964. Responsiveness to sensory stimulation of cells in the rabbit mid-brain. *Journal of Physiology*, 175, 40P-41P.

Hilton, S. M. & Zbrożyna, A. W. 1963. Amygdaloid region for defense reactions and its afferent pathway in the brain stem. *Journal of Physiology*, 165, 160-173.

Hind, J. E. 1953. An electrophysiological determination of tonotopic organization in auditory cortex of cat. *Journal of Neurophysiology*, 16, 473-489.

Hobhouse, L. T. 1901. *Mind in evolution*. New York: Macmillan.

Hodgkin, A. L. 1951. The ionic basis of electrical activity in nerve and muscle. *Biological Review*, 6, 339-409.

Hodgkin, A. L. & Huxley, A. F. 1939. Action potentials recorded from inside nerve fibre. *Nature*, 144, 710-711.

Hodos, W. & Valenstein, E. S. 1960. Motivational variables affecting the rate of behavior maintained by intracranial stimulation. *Journal of Comparative and Physiological Psychology*, 53, 502-508.

Hodos, W. & Valenstein, E. S. 1962. An evaluation of response rate as a measure of rewarding intracranial stimulation. *Journal of Comparative and Physiological Psychology*, 55, 80-84.

Hoebel, B. G. 1965. Hypothalamic lesions by electrocauterization: Disinhibition of feeding and self-stimulation. *Science*, 149, 452-453.

Hoebel, B. G. & Teitelbaum, P. 1962. Hypothalamic control of feeding and self-stimulation. *Science*, 135, 375-377.

Holmes, J. H. & Montgomery, A. V. 1951. Observations

on relation of hemorrhage to thirst. *American Journal of Physiology*, 167, 796. (Abstract)

Holmes, J. H. & Montgomery, A. V. 1953. Thirst as a symptom. *American Journal of Medical Science*, 225, 281-286.

Holst, E. von & Saint Paul, U. von. 1963. On the functional organization of drives. *Animal Behaviour*, 11, 1-20.

Hongo, T., Kubota, K. & Shimazu, H. 1963. EEG spindle and depression of gamma motor activity. *Journal of Neurophysiology*, 26, 568-580.

Horn, G. 1960. Electrical activity of the cerebral cortex of unanaesthetised cats during attentive behaviour. *Brain*, 83, 57-76.

Horn, G. 1963. The response of single units in the striate cortex of unrestrained cats to photic and somaesthetic stimuli. *Journal of Physiology*, 165, 80P-81P.

Horn, G. 1965. Physiological and psychological aspects of selective perception. In D. S. Lehrman, R. A. Hinde & E. Shaw (Eds.), *Advances in the study of behavior*. Vol. 1. New York: Academic Press. Pp. 155-215.

Horn, G. & Hill, R. M. 1964. Habituation of the response to sensory stimuli of neurons in the brain stem of rabbits. *Nature*, 202, 296-298.

Horridge, G. A. 1962. Learning of leg position by the ventral nerve cord in headless insects. *Proceedings of the Royal Society*, B157, 33-52.

Horridge, G. A. 1965. The electrophysiological approach to learning in isolatable ganglia. *Animal Behaviour* (Suppl. 1.), 163-182.

Horsley, V. & Clarke, R. H. 1908. The structure and function of the cerebellum examined by a new method. *Brain*, 31, 45-124.

Horvath, F. E. 1963. Effects of basolateral amygdalectomy on three types of avoidance behavior in cats. *Journal of Comparative and Physiological Psychology*, 56, 380-389.

Howarth, C. I. & Deutsch, J. A. 1962. Drive decay: The cause of fast "extinction" of habits learned for brain stimulation. *Science*, 137, 35-36.

Hubel, D. H. & Wiesel, T. N. 1962. Receptive fields, binocular interaction and functional architecture in the cat's visual cortex. *Journal of Physiology*, 160, 106-154.

Hubel, D. H. & Wiesel, T. N. 1963. Receptive fields of cells in striate cortex of very young, visually inexperienced kittens. *Journal of Neurophysiology*, 26, 994-1002.

Hubel, D. H. & Wiesel, T. N. 1965. Binocular interaction in striate cortex of kittens reared with artificial squint. *Journal of Neurophysiology*, 28, 1041-1059.

Hudson, B. B. 1950. One-trial learning in the domestic rat. *Genetic Psychology Monographs*, 41, 99-145.

Hudspeth, W. J. & Gerbrandt, L. K. 1965. Electroconvulsive shock: Conflict, competition, consolidation and neuroanatomical functions. *Psychological Bulletin*, 63, 377-383.

Hull, C. L. 1943. *Principals of behavior*. New York: Appleton.

Hull, C. L., Livingston, J. R., Rouse, R. O. & Barker, A. N. 1951. True, sham, and esophageal feeding as reinforcements. *Journal of Comparative and Physiological Psychology*, 44, 236-245.

Humphrey, M. E. & Zangwill, O. L. 1952. Dysphasia in left-handed patients with unilateral brain lesions. *Journal of Neurology, Neurosurgery, and Psychiatry*, 15, 184-193.

Hunt, C. C. 1961. On the nature of vibration receptors in the hind limb of the cat. *Journal of Physiology*, 155, 175-186.

Hunt, C. C. & Kuno, M. 1959. Background discharge and evoked responses of spinal interneurones. *Journal of Physiology*, 147, 364-384.

Hunt, C. C. & McIntyre, A. K. 1960a. Properties of cutaneous touch receptors in cat. *Journal of Physiology*, 153, 88-98.

Hunt, C. C., & McIntyre, A. K. 1960b. An analysis of fibre diameter and receptor characteristics of myelinated cutaneous afferent fibres in cat. *Journal of Physiology*, 153, 99-112.

Hunt, H. F. & Diamond, I. T. 1957. Some effects of hippocampal lesions on conditioned avoidance behavior in the cat. *Proceedings of the 15th International Congress of Psychology*, 203-204.

Hunter, J. & Jasper, H. H. 1949. Effects of thalamic stimulation in unanaesthetised animals. *Electroencephalography and Clinical Neurophysiology*, 1, 305-324.

Hurvich, L. M. & Jameson, D. 1957. An opponent-process theory of color vision. *Psychological Review*, 64, 384-404.

Huxley, A. F. & Niedergerke, R. 1954. Structural changes in muscle during contraction. *Nature*, 173, 971-973.

Huxley, H. E. 1965. The mechanism of muscular contraction. *Scientific American*, 213, (6), 18-27.

Huxley, H. & Hanson, J. 1954. Changes in the cross-striations of muscle during contraction and stretch and their structural interpretation. *Nature*, 173, 973-976.

Hydén, H. 1959. Biochemical changes in glial cells and nerve cells at varying activity. *Proceedings of the 4th International Congress of Biochemistry*, 3, 64-89.

Hydén, H. & Egyházi, E. 1962. Nuclear RNA changes of nerve cells during a learning experiment in rats. *Proceedings of the National Academy of Sciences of the United States of America*, 48, 1366-1373.

Hydén, H. & Egyházi, E. 1963. Glial RNA changes during a learning experiment in rats. *Proceedings of the National Academy of Sciences of the United States of America*, 49, 618-624.

Hydén, H. & Lange, P. W. 1965. A differentiation in RNA response in neurons early and late during learning. *Proceedings of the National Academy of Sciences of the United States of America*, 53, 946-952.

Hydén, H. & Pigeón, A. 1960. A cytophysiological study of the functional relationship between oligodendroglial cells and nerve cells of Deiters' nucleus. *Journal of Neurochemistry*, 6, 57-72.

Iggo, A. 1959. Cutaneous heat and cold receptors with C afferent fibres. *Quarterly Journal of Experimental Physiology*, 44, 362-370.

Iggo, A. 1960. Cutaneous mechanoreceptors with afferent C-fibres. *Journal of Physiology*, 152, 337-353.

Irwin, D. A., Knott, J. R., McAdam, D. W. and Rebert, C. S. 1966. Motivational determinants of the "contingent negative variation." *Electroencephalography and Clinical Neurophysiology*, 21, 538-543.

Isaac, W. & DeVito, J. L. 1958. Effect of sensory stimulation on the activity of normal and prefrontal-lobectomized monkeys. *Journal of Comparative and Physiological Psychology*, 51, 172-174.

Isaacson, R. L., Douglas, R. J. & Moore, R. Y. 1961. The effect of radical hippocampal ablation on acquisition of avoidance response. *Journal of Comparative and Physiological Psychology*, 54, 625-628.

Isaacson, R. L., Olton, D. S., Bauer, B. & Swart, P. 1966.

The effect of training trials on passive avoidance deficits in the hippocampectomized rat. *Psychonomic Science*, 5, 419-420.

Isaacson, R. L. & Wickelgren, W. O. 1962. Hippocampal ablation and passive avoidance. *Science*, 138, 1104-1106.

Jabbur, S. J. & Towe, A. L. 1961. Cortical excitation of neurons in dorsal column nuclei of cat, including an analysis of pathways. *Journal of Neurophysiology*, 24, 499-509.

Jackson, J. H. 1870. A study of convulsions. *Transactions St. Andrews Medical Graduates' Association*, 3, 162-207. (Reprinted: J. Taylor (Ed.), *Selected writings of John Hughlings Jackson*, Vol. 1. London, Hodder and Stoughton, 1931. Pp. 8-36.)

Jacobsen, C. F. 1936. Studies of cerebral function in primates: I. The functions of the frontal association areas in monkeys. *Comparative Psychology Monographs*, 13, 3-60.

James, W. 1890. *The principles of psychology*, Vol. 2, New York: Holt.

Jane, J. A., Smirnov, G. D. & Jasper, H. H. 1962. Effects of distraction upon simultaneous auditory and visual evoked potentials. *Electroencephalography and Clinical Neurophysiology*, 14, 344-358.

Janowitz, H. D. & Grossman, M. I. 1949. Some factors affecting the food intake of normal dogs and dogs with esophagostomy and gastric fistulae. *American Journal of Physiology*, 159, 143-148.

Janowitz, H. D., Hanson, M. E. & Grossman, M. I. 1949. Effect of intravenously administered glucose on food intake in the dog. *American Journal of Physiology*, 156, 87-91.

Janowitz, H. D. & Hollander, F. 1953. Effect of prolonged intragastric feeding on oral ingestion. *Federation Proceedings*, 12, 72. (Abstract)

Jasper, H., Hunter, J. & Knighton, R. 1948. Experimental studies of thalamocortical systems. *Transactions of the American Neurological Association*, 73, 210-212.

Jasper, H. H., Khan, R. T. & Elliott, K. A. C. 1965. Amino acids released from the cerebral cortex in relation to its state of activation. *Science*, 147, 1448-1449.

Jasper, H., Ricci, G. F. & Doane, B. 1958. Patterns of cortical neuronal discharge during conditioned responses in the monkey. In G. E. W. Wolstenholme & C. M. O'Connor (Eds.), *Neurological basis of behavior*. London: Churchill. Pp. 277-290.

Jasper, H., Ricci, G. F. & Doane, B. 1960. Microelectrode analysis of cortical cell discharge during avoidance conditioning in the monkey. *Electroencephalography and Clinical Neurophysiology*, (Supplement 13), 137-155.

Jasper, H. H. & Shagass, C. 1941a. Conditioning the occipital alpha rhythm in man. *Journal of Experimental Psychology*, 28, 373-388.

Jasper, H. & Shagass, C. 1941b. Conscious time judgements related to conditioned time intervals and voluntary control of the alpha rhythm. *Journal of Experimental Psychology*, 28, 503-508.

Jeffress, L. A. 1948. A place theory of sound localization. *Journal of Comparative and Physiological Psychology*, 41, 35-39.

Jensen, D. D. 1957. Experiments on "learning" in paramecia. *Science*, 125, 191-192.

John, E. R. 1964. Information storage in behavior. (Discussion). In R. W. Gerard & J. W. Duyff (Eds.), *Information processing in the nervous system*. Amsterdam: Excerpta Medica Foundation. Pp. 288-298.

John, E. R. 1967. *Mechanisms of memory*. New York: Academic Press.

John, E. R. & Killam, K. F. 1959. Electrophysiological correlates of avoidance conditioning in the cat. *Journal of Pharmacology and Experimental Therapeutics*, 125, 252-274.

John, E. R., Ruchkin, D. S. & Villegas, J. 1964. Signal analysis and behavioral correlates of evoked potential configurations in cats. *Annals of the New York Academy of Sciences*, 112, 362-420.

Johnson, L. C., Davidoff, R. A. & Mann, S. H. 1962. Brain activity, seizure discharges and behavior. *Proceedings of the San Diego Symposium on Biomedical Engineering*. Pp. 233-244.

Johnston, J. W. 1963. An application of the steric odor theory. *Georgetown Medical Bulletin*, 17, 40-42.

Jones, G. M. 1966. Vestibular inaptitude in the environments of flight and space. *Journal of Laryngology and Otology*, 80, 207-221.

Jouvet, D., Vimont, P., Delorme, F. & Jouvet, M. 1964. Étude de la privation de phase paradoxale du sommeil chez le chat. *Comptes Rendus de la Société de Biologie*, 158, 756-759.

Jouvet, M. 1962. Recherches sur les structures nerveuses et les méchanismes responsables des différentes phases du sommeil physiologique. *Archives Italiennes de Biologie*, 100, 125-206.

Jouvet, M. 1967. Mechanisms of the states of sleep. A neuropharmacological approach. *Research Publications of the Association for Research in Nervous and Mental Disease*, 45, 86-126.

Jouvet, M. & Delorme, J. 1965. Locus coeruleus et sommeil paradoxal. *Comptes Rendus de la Société de Biologie*, 159, 895-899.

Jouvet, M. & Michel, F. 1958. Recherches sur l'activité électrique cérébrale au cours du sommeil. *Comptes Rendus de la Société de Biologie*, 152, 1167-1170.

Judd, D. B. 1951. Basic correlates of the visual stimulus. In S. S. Stevens (Ed.), *Handbook of experimental psychology*. New York: Wiley. Pp. 811-867.

Jung, R. 1954. Correlation of bioelectrical and autonomic phenomena with alterations of consciousness and arousal in man. In J. F. Delafresnaye (Ed.), *Brain mechanisms and consciousness*. Springfield, Ill.: Thomas. Pp. 310-344.

Justesen, D. R., Sharp, J. C. & Porter, P. B. 1963. Self-stimulation of the caudate nucleus by instrumentally naive cats. *Journal of Comparative and Physiological Psychology*, 56, 371-374.

Kaada, B. R. 1951. Somato-motor, autonomic and electrocorticographic responses to electrical stimulation of "rhinencephalic" and other structures in primates, cat and dog. *Acta Physiologica Scandinavica*, 24 (Suppl. 83), 1-285.

Kaada, B. R., Rasmussen, E. W. & Kveim, O. 1961. Effects of hippocampal lesions on maze learning and retention in rats. *Experimental Neurology*, 3, 333-355.

Kaada, B. R., Rasmussen, E. W. & Kveim, O. 1962. Impaired acquisition of passive avoidance behavior by subcallosal, septal, hypothalamic, and insular lesions in rats. *Journal of Comparative and Physiological Psychology*, 55, 661-670.

Kandel, E. R. & Spencer, W. A. 1968. Cellular neurophysiological approaches in the study of learning. *Physiological Reviews*, 48, 65-134.

Kandel, E. R. & Tauc, L. 1965. Heterosynaptic facilitation in neurones of the abdominal ganglion of *Aplysia depilans*. *Journal of Physiology*, **181**, 1-27.

Kaplan, J. 1968. Approach and inhibitory reactions in rats after bilateral hippocampal damage. *Journal of Comparative and Physiological Psychology*, **65**, 274-281.

Kaplan, R. 1963. Rat basal resistance level under stress and nonstress conditions. *Journal of Comparative and Physiological Psychology*, **56**, 775-777.

Kare, M. R. & Ficken, M. S. 1963. Comparative studies on the sense of taste. In Y. Zotterman (Ed.), *Olfaction and taste*. Oxford: Pergamon. Pp. 285-297.

Karmos, G. & Grastyán, E. 1962. Influence of hippocampal lesions on simple and delayed conditional reflexes. *Acta Physiologica Academiae Scientiarum Hungaricae*, **21**, 215-224.

Kasper, P. 1964. Attenuation of passive avoidance by continuous septal stimulation. *Psychonomic Science*, **1**, 219-220.

Kasper, P. 1965. Disruption of position habit reversal by septal stimulation. *Psychonomic Science*, **3**, 111-112.

Katsuki, Y. 1961. Neural mechanisms of auditory sensation in cats. In W. A. Rosenblith (Ed.), *Sensory communication*. New York: Wiley. Pp. 561-583.

Katsuki, Y., Watanabe, T. & Suga, N. 1959. Interaction of auditory neurons in response to two sound stimuli in cat. *Journal of Neurophysiology*, **22**, 603-623.

Katz, B. 1950. Depolarization of sensory terminals and the initiation of impulses in the muscle spindle. *Journal of Physiology*, **111**, 261-282.

Keller, A. D. 1932. Autonomic discharges elicited by physiological stimuli in mid-brain preparations. *American Journal of Physiology*. **100**, 576-586.

Kellogg, W. N. 1959. Size discrimination by reflected sound in a bottle-nose porpoise. *Journal of Comparative and Physiological Psychology*, **52**, 509-514.

Kellogg, W. N. 1961. *Porpoises and sonar*. Chicago: University of Chicago press.

Kellogg, W. N., Deese, J., Pronko, N. H. & Feinberg, M. 1947. An attempt to condition the chronic spinal dog. *Journal of Experimental Psychology*, **37**, 99-117.

Kennard, M. A. 1939. Alterations in response to visual stimuli following lesions of frontal lobe in monkeys. *Archives of Neurology and Psychiatry*, **41**, 1153-1165.

Kennedy, G. C. 1950. The hypothalamic control of food intake in rats. *Proceedings of the Royal Society*, **B137**, 535-549.

Kennedy, G. C. 1953. The role of depot fat in the hypothalamic control of food intake in the rat. *Proceedings of the Royal Society*, **B140**, 578-592.

Kenyon, J. 1962. The effect of septal lesions upon motivated behavior in the rat. Unpublished doctoral dissertation, McGill University.

Kenyon, J. & Krieckhaus, E. E. 1965a. Enhanced avoidance behavior following septal lesions in the rat as a function of lesion size and spontaneous activity. *Journal of Comparative and Physiological Psychology*, **59**, 466-468.

Kenyon, J. & Krieckhaus, E. E. 1965b. Decrements in one-way avoidance learning following septal lesions in rats. *Psychonomic Science*, **3**, 113-114.

Kerr, D. I. B., Haugen, F. P. & Melzack, R. 1955. Responses evoked in the brain stem by tooth stimulation. *American Journal of Physiology*, **183**, 253-258.

Kety, S. S. 1967. Relationship between energy metabolism of the brain and functional activity. *Research Publications of the Association for Research in Nervous and Mental Disease*, **45**, 39-45.

Kim, C. 1960. Sexual activity of male rats following ablation of hippocampus. *Journal of Comparative and Physiological Psychology*, **53**, 553-557.

Kimble, D. P. 1963. The effects of bilateral hippocampal lesions in rats. *Journal of Comparative and Physiological Psychology*, **56**, 273-283.

Kimble, D. P., Kirby, R. J. & Stein, D. G. 1966. Response perseveration interpretation of passive avoidance deficits in hippocampectomized rats. *Journal of Comparative and Physiological Psychology*, **61**, 141-143.

Kimble, D. P., Rogers, L. & Hendrickson, C. W. 1967. Hippocampal lesions disrupt maternal, not sexual, behavior in the albino rat. *Journal of Comparative and Physiological Psychology*, **63**, 401-407.

Kimura, Doreen. 1961. Some effects of temporal-lobe damage on auditory perception. *Canadian Journal of Psychology*, **15**, 156-165.

Kimura, Doreen. 1963. Right temporal-lobe damage. *Archives of Neurology*, **8**, 264-271.

Kimura, Doreen. 1964a. Cognitive deficit related to seizure pattern in centrencephalic epilepsy. *Journal of Neurology, Neurosurgery, and Psychiatry*, **27**, 291-295.

Kimura, Doreen. 1964b. Left-right differences in the perception of melodies. *Quarterly Journal of Experimental Psychology*, **16**, 355-358.

Kimura, Douglas. 1958. Effects of selective hippocampal damage on avoidance behaviour in the rat. *Canadian Journal of Psychology*, **12**, 213-218.

Kimura, K. & Beidler, L. M. 1961. Microelectrode study of taste receptors of rat and hamster. *Journal of Cellular and Comparative Physiology*, **58**, 131-139.

King, F. A. 1958. Effects of septal and amygdaloid lesions on emotional behavior and conditioned avoidance responses in the rat. *Journal of Nervous and Mental Disease*, **126**, 57-63.

King, H. E. 1961. Psychological effects of excitation in the limbic system. In D. E. Sheer (Ed.), *Electrical stimulation of the brain*. Austin: University of Texas Press. Pp. 477-486.

Kish, G. B. 1955. Learning when the onset of illumination is used as reinforcing stimulus. *Journal of Comparative and Physiological Psychology*, **48**, 261-264.

Kitchell, R. L. 1963. Comparative anatomical and physiological studies of gustatory mechanisms. In Y. Zotterman (Ed.), *Olfaction and taste*. Oxford: Pergamon. Pp. 235-255.

Kleinsmith, L. J. & Kaplan, S. 1964. Paired associate learning as a function of arousal and interpolated interval. *Journal of Experimental Psychology*, **65**, 190-193.

Kleitman, N. 1939. *Sleep and wakefulness*. Chicago: University of Chicago Press.

Kling, A. 1968. Effects of amygdalectomy and testosterone on sexual behavior of male juvenile macaques. *Journal of Comparative and Physiological Psychology*, **65**, 466-471.

Klüver, H. 1936. An analysis of the effects of the removal of the occipital lobes in monkeys. *Journal of Psychology*, **2**, 49-61.

Klüver, H. & Barrera, E. 1953. A method for the combined staining of cells and fibers in the nervous system. *Journal of Neuropathology and Experimental Neurology*, **12**, 400-403.

Klüver, H. & Bucy, P. C. 1938. An analysis of certain effects of bilateral temporal lobectomy in the rhesus monkey with special reference to "psychic blindness." *Journal of Psychology*, 5, 33-54.

Klüver, H. & Bucy, P. C. 1939. Preliminary analysis of functions of the temporal lobes in monkeys. *Archives of Neurology and Psychiatry*, 42, 979-1000.

Koh, S. D. & Teitelbaum, P. 1961. Absolute behavioral taste thresholds in the rat. *Journal of Comparative and Physiological Psychology*, 54, 223-229.

Komisaruk, B. R. 1967. Effects of local brain implants of progesterone on reproductive behavior in ring doves. *Journal of Comparative and Physiological Psychology*, 64, 219-224.

Kopa, J. Szabó, I. & Grastyán, E. 1962. A dual behavioral effect from stimulating the same thalamic point with identical stimulus parameters in different conditional reflex situations. *Acta Physiologica Academiae Scientiarum Hungaricae*, 21, 207-214.

Korsakoff, S. S. 1889. Étude médico-psychologique sur une forme des maladies de la mémoire. *Revue de Philosophie*, 28, 501-530.

Krieckhaus, E. E. 1964. Ultrasound and psychology. In D. Gordon (Ed.), *Ultrasound as a diagnostic and surgical tool*. Edinburgh: Livingstone. Pp. 272-287.

Krieckhaus, E. E., Simmons, H. J., Thomas, G. J. & Kenyon, J. 1964. Septal lesions enhance shock avoidance behavior in the rat. *Experimental Neurology*, 9, 107-113.

Kruger, L. & Porter, P. 1958. A behavioral study of the functions of the rolandic cortex in the monkey. *Journal of Comparative Neurology*, 109, 439-469.

Kryter, K. D. & Ades, H. W. 1943. Studies on the function of the higher acoustic nervous centers in the cat. *American Journal of Psychology*, 56, 501-536.

Kuffler, S. W. 1953. Discharge patterns and functional organization of mammalian retina. *Journal of Neurophysiology*, 16, 37-68.

Kupfermann, I. 1965. Effects of cortical polarization on visual discriminations. *Experimental Neurology*, 12, 179-189.

Land, E. H. 1959. Color vision and the natural image. *Proceedings of the National Academy of Sciences of the United States of America*, 45, 115-129.

Landau, W. M., Goldstein, R. & Kleffner, F. R. 1960. Congenital aphasia: A clinicopathologic study. *Neurology*, 10, 915-921.

Landgren, S. 1957a. Cortical reception of cold impulses from the tongue of the cat. *Acta Physiologica Scandinavica*, 40, 202-209.

Landgren, S. 1957b. Convergence of tactile, thermal and gustatory impulses on single cortical cells. *Acta Physiologica Scandinavica*, 40, 210-221.

Landgren, S. 1960. Thalamic neurones responding to cooling of the cat's tongue. *Acta Physiologica Scandinavica*, 48, 255-267.

Lansdell, H. & Mirsky, A. F. 1964. Attention in focal and centrencephalic epilepsy. *Experimental Neurology*, 9, 463-469.

Larsson, S. 1954. On the hypothalamic organization of the nervous mechanism regulating food intake. *Acta Physiologica Scandinavica*, 32 (Suppl. 115), 1-40.

Lashley, K. S. 1917a. The accuracy of movement in the absence of excitation from the moving organ. *American Journal of Physiology*, 43, 169-194.

Lashley, K. S. 1917b. The effect of strychnine and caffeine upon rate of learning. *Psychobiology*, 1, 141-170.

Lashley, K. S. 1920. Studies of cerebral function in learning. *Psychobiology*, 2, 55-135.

Lashley, K. S. 1921. Studies of cerebral function in learning: III. The motor areas. *Brain*, 44, 255-286.

Lashley, K. S. 1924. Studies of cerebral function in learning: V. The retention of motor habits after destruction of the so-called motor areas in primates. *Archives of Neurology and Psychiatry*, 12, 249-276.

Lashley, K. S. 1929. *Brain mechanisms and intelligence*. Chicago: University of Chicago Press.

Lashley, K. S. 1930a. Basic neural mechanisms in behavior. *Psychological Review*, 37, 1-24.

Lashley, K. S. 1930b. The mechanism of vision: II. The influence of cerebral lesions upon the threshold of discrimination for brightness. *Journal of Genetic Psychology*, 37, 461-480.

Lashley, K. S. 1935. The mechanism of vision: XII. Nervous structures concerned in habits based on reactions to light. *Comparative Psychology Monographs*, 11, 43-79.

Lashley, K. S. 1941. Patterns of cerebral integration indicated by the scotomas of migraine. *Archives of Neurology and Psychiatry*, 46, 331-339.

Lashley, K. S. 1942. The problem of cerebral organization in vision. *Biological Symposia*, 7, 301-322.

Lashley, K. S. 1950. In search of the engram. In *Symposia of the Society for Experimental Biology*, 4, 454-482.

Lashley, K. S. 1951. The problem of serial order in behavior. In L. A. Jeffress (Ed.), *Cerebral mechanisms in behavior*. New York: Wiley. Pp. 112-136. (Reprinted: In F. A. Beach, D. O. Hebb, C. T. Morgan & H. W. Nissen [Eds.], *The neuropsychology of Lashley*. New York; McGraw-Hill, 1960. Pp. 506-528.)

Lashley, K. S. & Clark, G. 1946. The cytoarchitecture of the cerebral cortex of Ateles: A critical examination of architectonic studies. *Journal of Comparative Neurology*, 85, 223-306.

Lashley, K. S. & Franz, S. I. 1917. The effects of cerebral destruction upon habit-formation and retention in the albino rat. *Psychobiology*, 1, 71-139.

Lashley, K. S. & McCarthy, D. A. 1926. The survival of the maze habit after cerebellar injuries. *Journal of Comparative Psychology*, 6, 423-433.

Law, T. & Meagher, W. 1958. Hypothalamic lesions and sexual behavior in the female rat. *Science*, 128, 1626-1627.

Lawicka, W. M. 1957. The effect of the prefrontal lobectomy on the vocal conditioned reflexes in dogs. *Acta Biologiae Experimentalis*, 17, 317-325.

Lawrence, D. G. & Kuypers, H. G. J. M. 1965. Pyramidal and non-pyramidal pathways in monkeys: Anatomical and functional correlation. *Science*, 148, 973-975.

Leão, A. A. P. 1944. Spreading depression of activity in the cerebral cortex. *Journal of Neurophysiology*, 7, 359-390.

Leaton, R. N. 1965. Exploration behavior in rats with hippocampal lesions. *Journal of Comparative and Physiological Psychology*, 59, 325-330.

Ledsome, J. R., Linden, R. J. & O'Connor, W. J. 1961. The mechanisms by which distension of the left atrium produces diuresis in anesthetized dogs. *Journal of Physiology*, 159, 87-100.

Lee-Teng, E. 1969. Retrograde amnesia in relation to subconvulsive and convulsive currents in chicks. *Journal of Comparative and Physiological Psychology*, 67, 135-139.

Legendre, R. & Piéron, H. 1912. Recherches sur le besoin de sommeil consécutif à une veille prolongée. *Zeitschrift für Allgemeine Physiologie*, 14, 235-262.

Lehrman, D. S. 1958a. Induction of broodiness by participation in courtship and nest-building in the ring dove. (*Streptopelia risoria*). *Journal of Comparative and Physiological Psychology*, 51, 32-36.

Lehrman, D. S. 1958b. Effect of female sex hormones on incubation behavior in the ring dove (*Streptopelia risoria*). *Journal of Comparative and Physiological Psychology*, 51, 142-145.

Lehrman, D. S. 1961. Gonadal hormones and parental behavior in birds and infrahuman mammals. In W. C. Young (Ed.), *Sex and internal secretions*. Baltimore: Williams & Wilkins. Pp. 1268-1382.

Leksell, L. 1945. The action potential and excitatory effects of the small ventral root fibres to skeletal muscle. *Acta Physiologica Scandinavica*, 10 (Suppl. 31), 1-84.

Lele, P. P. & Weddell, G. 1956. The relationship between neurohistology and corneal sensibility. *Brain*, 79, 119-154.

Lende, R. A. 1963. Cerebral cortex: A sensorimotor amalgam in the marsupialia. *Science*, 141, 730-732.

Lenneberg, E. H. 1967. *Biological foundations of language*. New York: Wiley.

Levine, S. & Jones, L. E. 1965. Adrenocorticotropic hormone (ACTH) and passive avoidance learning. *Journal of Comparative and Physiological Psychology*, 59, 357-360.

Levine, S. & Mullins, R. 1964. Estrogen administered neonatally affects adult sexual behavior in male and female rats. *Science*, 144, 183-185.

Levine, S. & Soliday, S. 1960. The effects of hypothalamic lesions on conditioned avoidance learning. *Journal of Comparative and Physiological Psychology*, 53, 497-501.

Lewis, D. J. & Adams, H. E. 1963. Retrograde amnesia from conditioned competing responses. *Science*, 141, 516-517.

Lewis, M. 1964. Behavior resulting from calcium deprivation in parathyroidectomized rats. *Journal of Comparative and Physiological Psychology*, 57, 348-352.

Lewis, M. 1968. Discrimination between drives for sodium chloride and calcium. *Journal of Comparative and Physiological Psychology*, 65, 208-212.

Lhermitte, F., Gautier, J. C., Marteau, R. & Chain, F. 1963. Troubles de la conscience et mutisme akinétique. *Revue Neurologique*, 109, 115-131.

Liberman, A. M. 1957. Some results of research on speech perception. *Journal of the Acoustical Society of America*, 29, 117-123.

Liberman, A. M., Cooper, F. S., Shankweiler, D. P. & Studdert-Kennedy, M. 1967. Perception of the speech code. *Psychological Review*, 74, 431-461.

Liberman, A. M., Delattre, P. C. & Cooper, F. S. 1958. Some cues for the distinction between voiced and voiceless stops in initial position. *Language and Speech*, 1, 153-167.

Liberman, A. M., Harris, K. S., Hoffman, H. S. & Griffith, B. C. 1957. The discrimination of speech sounds within

and across phoneme boundaries. *Journal of Experimental Psychology*, 54, 358-368.

Liberman, A. M., Ingeman, F., Lisker, L., Delattre, P. & Cooper, F. S. 1959. Minimal rules for synthesizing speech. *Journal of the Acoustical Society of America*, 31, 1490-1499.

Licklider, J. C. R. 1959. Three auditory theories. In S. Koch (Ed.), *Psychology: A study of a science*. Vol. 1. New York: McGraw-Hill. Pp. 41-144.

Licklider, J. C. R. & Kryter, K. D. 1942. Frequency localization in the auditory cortex of the monkey. *Federation Proceedings*, 1, 51.

Lilly, J. C. 1963. Distress call of the bottlenose dolphin: Stimuli and evoked behavioral responses. *Science*, 139, 116-118.

Lilly, J. C. 1965. Vocal mimicry in Tursiops: Ability to match numbers and durations of human vocal bursts. *Science*, 147, 300-301.

Lilly, J. C. & Miller, A. M. 1962. Operant conditioning of the bottlenose dolphin with electrical stimulation of the brain. *Journal of Comparative and Physiological Psychology*, 55, 73-79.

Lindauer, M. 1961. *Communication among social bees*. Cambridge, Mass.: Harvard University Press.

Lindsley, D. B., Schreiner, L. H., Knowles, W. B. & Magoun, H. W. 1950. Behavioral and EEG changes following chronic brain stem lesions in the cat. *Electroencephalography and Clinical Neurophysiology*, 2, 483-498.

Lissák, K. & Endröczi, E. 1961. Neurohumoral factors in the control of animal behaviour. In J. F. Delafresnaye (Ed.), *Brain mechanisms and learning*. Springfield, Ill.: Thomas. Pp. 293-308.

Livanov, M. N. & Poliakov, K. L. 1945. The electrical reactions of the cerebral cortex of a rabbit during the formation of a conditioned defense reflex by means of rhythmic stimulation. *Bulletin of the Academy of Science of the U.S.S.R.*, 3, 286-298.

Lloyd Morgan, C. 1894. *Introduction to comparative psychology*. London: Scott.

Loeb, J. 1884. Die Sehstörungen nach Verletzung der Grosshirnrinde. Nach Versuchen am Hunde. *Archiv für die gesamte Physiologie des Menschen und der Tiere*, 34, 67-172.

Loewenstein, W. R. 1959. The generation of electrical activity in a nerve ending. *Annals of the New York Academy of Sciences*, 81, 367-387.

Longuet-Higgins, H. C. 1968. Holographic model of temporal recall. *Nature*, 217, 104.

Lorens, S. A. 1966. Effect of lesions in the central nervous system on lateral hypothalamic self-stimulation in the rat. *Journal of Comparative and Physiological Psychology*, 62, 256-262.

Lorente de Nó, R. 1933a. Anatomy of the eighth nerve. The central projections of the nerve endings of the internal ear. *Laryngoscope*, 43, 1-33.

Lorente de Nó, R. 1933b. Vestibulo-ocular reflex arc. *Archives of Neurology and Psychiatry*, 30, 245-291.

Lorente de Nó, R. 1935a. Facilitation of motoneurones. *American Journal of Physiology*, 113, 505-523.

Lorente de Nó, R. 1935b. The summation of impulses transmitted to the motoneurones through different synapses. *American Journal of Physiology*, 113, 524-528.

Lorente de Nó, R. 1949. Cerebral cortex: Architecture,

intracortical connections, motor projections. In J. F. Fulton, *Physiology of the nervous system.* New York: Oxford University Press. Pp. 288-312.

Loucks, R. B. 1961. Methods of isolating stimulation effects with implanted barriers. In D. E. Sheer (Ed.), *Electrical stimulation of the brain.* Austin: University of Texas Press.

Low, M. D., Borda, R. P., Frost, J. D. & Kellaway, P. 1966. Surface-negative, slow-potential shift associated with conditioning in man. *Neurology,* **16,** 771-782.

Low, M. D., Borda, R. P. & Kellaway, P. 1966. "Contingent negative variation" in rhesus monkeys: An EEG sign of a specific mental process. *Perceptual and Motor Skills,* **22,** 443-446.

Löwenstein, O. & Sand, A. 1940a. The individual and integrated activity of the semicircular canals of the elasmobranch labyrinth. *Journal of Physiology,* **99,** 89-101.

Löwenstein, O. & Sand, A. 1940b. The mechanism of the semicircular canal. A study of the responses of single-fibre preparations to angular accelerations and to rotation at constant speed. *Proceedings of the Royal Society,* **B129,** 256-275.

Lubar, J. F. & Perachio, A. A. 1965. One-way and two-way learning and transfer of an active avoidance response in normal and cingulectomized cats. *Journal of Comparative and Physiological Psychology,* **60,** 46-52.

Lubar, J. F., Perachio, A. A. & Kavanagh, A. J. 1966. Deficits in active avoidance behavior following lesions of the lateral and posterolateral gyrus of the cat. *Journal of Comparative and Physiological Psychology,* **62,** 263-269.

Lubar, J. F., Schostal, C. J. & Perachio, A. A. 1967. Non-visual functions of visual cortex in the cat. *Physiology and Behavior,* **2,** 179-184.

Lundberg, A., Norrsell, U. & Voorhoeve, P. 1963. Effects from the sensorimotor cortex on ascending spinal pathways. *Acta Physiologica Scandinavica,* **59,** 462-473.

Luria, A. R. 1964. Factors and forms of aphasia. In A. V. S. de Reuck & M. O'Connor (Eds.), *Ciba foundation symposium on disorders of language.* London: Churchill. Pp. 143-167.

Luria, A. R. & Homskaya, E. D. 1964. Disturbance in the regulative role of speech with frontal lobe lesions. In J. M. Warren & K. Akert (Eds.), *The frontal granular cortex and behavior.* New York: McGraw-Hill. Pp. 353-371.

Luttges, M., Johnson, T., Buck, C., Holland, J. & McGaugh, J. 1966. An examination of "transfer of learning" by nucleic acid. *Science,* **151,** 834-837.

MacCorquodale, K. & Meehl, P. E. 1954. Edward C. Tolman. In A. T. Poffenberger (Ed.), *Modern learning theory.* New York: Appleton. Pp. 177-266.

MacDonnell, M. F. & Flynn, J. P. 1964. Attack elicited by stimulation of the thalamus of cats. *Science,* **144,** 1249-1250.

Mach, E. 1865. Über die Wirkung der räumlichen Vertheilung des Lichtreizes auf die Netzhaut. I. *Sitzungsberichte der Wiener Akadamie Wissenschafts,* **52** (II), 303-322.

Macht, M. B. & Bard, P. 1942. Studies on decerebrate cats in the chronic state. *Federation Proceedings,* **1,** 55-56.

MacLean, P. D. 1957. Chemical and electrical stimulation of hippocampus in unrestrained animals. *A.M.A. Archives of Neurology and Psychiatry,* **78,** 113-142.

MacLean, P. D. & Ploog, D. W. 1962. Cerebral representation of penile erection. *Journal of Neurophysiology,* **25,** 29-55.

MacNichol, E. F. Jr., 1958. Subthreshold excitatory processes in the eye of *Limulus. Experimental Cell Research,* (*Suppl. 5*), 411-425.

MacNichol, E. F., Jr. 1966. Retinal processing of visual data. *Proceedings of the National Academy of Sciences of the United States of America,* **55,** 1331-1344.

MacNichol, E. F., Jr. & Svaetichin, G. 1958. Electric responses from isolated retinas of fishes. *American Journal of Opthalmology,* **46,** 26-40.

MacPhail, E. M. 1966. Self-stimulation in pigeons: The problem of "priming." *Psychonomic Science,* **5,** 7-8.

MacPhail, E. M. & Miller, N. E. 1968. Cholinergic brain stimulation in cats: Failure to obtain sleep. *Journal of Comparative and Physiological Psychology,* **65,** 499-503.

Macrides, F. & Chorover, S. L. 1968. Neuro-electrical disturbances produced by intracerebral injection of puromycin dihydrochloride in rats. Paper presented at the meeting of the Eastern Psychological Association, Washington, D.C., April.

Magnes, J., Moruzzi, G. & Pompeiano, O. 1961. Synchronization of the EEG produced by low-frequency electrical stimulation of the region of the solitary tract. *Archives Italiennes de Biologie,* **99,** 33-67.

Magni, F., Melzack, R., Moruzzi, G. & Smith, C. J. 1959. Direct pyramidal influences on the dorsal-column nuclei. *Archives Italiennes de Biologie,* **97,** 357-377.

Magni, F., Moruzzi, G., Rossi, G. F. & Zanchetti, A. 1959. EEG arousal following inactivation of the lower brain stem by selective injection of barbiturate into the vertebral circulation. *Archives Italiennes de Biologie,* **97,** 33-46.

Magnus, O. & Lammers, H. J. 1956. The amygdaloid-nuclear complex. *Folia Psychiatrica Neurologica et Neurochirurgica Neerlandica,* **59,** 555-582.

Magoun, H. W. 1952. The ascending reticular activating system. *Research Publications of the Association for Research in Nervous and Mental Disease,* **30,** 480-492.

Magoun, H. W., Harrison, F., Brobeck, J. R. & Ranson, S. W. 1938. Activation of heat loss mechanisms by local heating of the brain. *Journal of Neurophysiology,* **1,** 101-114.

Makous, W., Nord, S., Oakley, B. & Pfaffmann, C. 1963. The gustatory relay in the medulla. In Y. Zotterman (Ed.), *Olfaction and taste.* Oxford: Pergamon. Pp. 381-393.

Malmo, R. B. 1942. Interference factors in delayed response in monkeys after removal of frontal lobes. *Journal of Neurophysiology,* **5,** 295-308.

Malmo, R. B. 1961. Slowing of heart rate after septal self-stimulation in rats. *Science,* **133,** 1128-1130.

Malmo, R. B. 1964. Heart rate reactions and locus of stimulation within the septal area of the rat. *Science,* **144,** 1029-1030.

Malmo, R. B. 1965. Psychological gradients and behavior. *Psychological Bulletin,* **64,** 225-234.

Malmo, R. B. & Shagass, C. 1949. Physiologic study of symptom mechanisms in psychiatric patients under stress. *Psychosomatic Medicine,* **11,** 25-29.

Mangold, R., Sokoloff, L., Conner, E., Kleinerman, J.,

Therman, P. O. G. & Kety, S. S. 1955. The effects of sleep and lack of sleep on the cerebral circulation and metabolism of normal young men. *Journal of Clinical Investigation*, **34**, 1092-1100.

Margules, D. L. & Olds, J. 1962. Identical "feeding" and "rewarding" systems in the lateral hypothalamus of rats. *Science*, **135**, 374-375.

Marks, W. B., Dobelle, W. H. & MacNichol, E. F., Jr. 1964. Visual pigments of single primate cones. *Science*, **143**, 1181-1183.

Marshall, J. 1951. Sensory disturbances in cortical wounds with special reference to pain. *Journal of Neurology, Neurosurgery and Psychiatry*, **14**, 187-204.

Marshall, N. B., Barrnett, R. J. & Mayer, J. 1955. Hypothalamic lesions in goldthioglucose injected mice. *Proceedings of the Society for Experimental Biology and Medicine of New York*, **90**, 240-244.

Marshall, W. H. & Talbot, S. A. 1942. Recent evidence for neural mechanisms in vision leading to a general theory of sensory acuity. In H. Klüver (Ed.), *Biological symposia*. Vol. 7. *Visual mechanisms*. Lancaster, Pa.: Cattell. Pp. 117-164.

Maruhashi, J., Mizuguchi, K. & Tasaki, I. 1952. Action currents in single afferent nerve fibres elicited by stimulation of the skin of the toad and the cat. *Journal of Physiology*, **117**, 129-151.

Marx, M. H., Henderson, R. L. & Roberts, C. L. 1955. Positive reinforcement of the bar-pressing response by a light stimulus following dark operant pretests with no aftereffect. *Journal of Comparative and Physiological Psychology*, **48**, 73-76.

Mason, W. A. 1960. The effects of social restriction on the behavior of rhesus monkeys: I. Free social behavior. *Journal of Comparative and Physiological Psychology*, **53**, 582-589.

Masserman, J. H. 1941. Is the hypothalamus a center of emotion? *Psychosomatic Medicine*, **3**, 3-25.

Masserman, J. H. 1943. *Behavior and neurosis*. Chicago: University of Chicago Press.

Masters, W. & Johnson, V. 1966. *Human sexual response*. Boston: Little, Brown.

Masterton, R. B. & Diamond, I. T. 1964. Effects of auditory cortex ablation on discrimination of small binaural time differences. *Journal of Neurophysiology*, **27**, 15-36.

Masterton, R. B., Jane, J. A. & Diamond, I. T. 1967. Role of brainstem auditory structures in sound localization. I. Trapezoid body, superior olive, and lateral lemniscus. *Journal of Neurophysiology*, **30**, 341-359.

Matsuzaki, M., Takagi, H. & Tokizane, T. 1964. Paradoxical phase of sleep: Its artificial induction in the cat by sodium butyrate. *Science*, **146**, 1328-1329.

Matthews, B. H. C. 1931. The response of a single end organ. *Journal of Physiology*, **71**, 64-110.

Matthews, B. H. C. 1933. Nerve endings in mammalian muscle. *Journal of Physiology*, **78**, 1-33.

Matthews, B. H. C. 1934. A special purpose amplifier. *Journal of Physiology*, **57**, 28P-29P.

Matthews, L. H. 1939. Visual stimulation and ovulation in pigeons. *Proceedings of the Royal Society*, **B126**, 557-560.

Maturana, H. R. & Frenk, S. 1963. Directional movement and horizontal edge detectors in the pigeon retina. *Science*, **142**, 977-978.

Maturana, H. R., Lettvin, J. Y., McCulloch, W. S. & Pitts, W. H. 1960. Anatomy and physiology of vision in the frog (*Rana pipiens*). *Journal of General Physiology*, **43** (Suppl. 2), 129-175.

Mayer, J. 1953. Glucostatic mechanisms of regulation of food intake. *New England Journal of Medicine*, **249**, 13-16.

Mayer, J. & Bates, M. W. 1952. Blood glucose and food intake in normal and hypophysectomized alloxan-treated rats. *American Journal of Physiology*, **168**, 812-819.

Mayer, J., French, R. G., Zighera, C. F. & Barrnett, R. J. 1955. Hypothalamic obesity in the mouse: Production, description and metabolic characteristics. *American Journal of Physiology*, **182**, 75-82.

Mayer, J. & Sudsaneh, S. 1959. Mechanism of hypothalamic control of gastric contractions in the rat. *American Journal of Physiology*, **197**, 274-280.

Mayne, R. 1950. The dynamic characteristics of the semicircular canals. *Journal of Comparative and Physiological Psychology*. **43**, 309-319.

McAdam, D. W. 1962. Electroencephalographic changes and classical aversive conditioning in the cat. *Experimental Neurology*, **6**, 357-371.

McCabe, B. F. 1960. Vestibular suppression in figure skaters. *Transactions of the American Academy of Opthalmology and Otolaryngology*, **64**, 264-268.

McCance, R. A. 1936. Experimental sodium chloride deficiency in man. *Proceedings of the Royal Society*, **B119**, 245-268.

McCleary, R. A. 1953. Taste and post-ingestion factors in specific-hunger behavior. *Journal of Comparative and Physiological Psychology*, **46**, 411-421.

McCleary, R. A. 1961. Response specificity in the behavioral effects of limbic system lesions in the cat. *Journal of Comparative and Physiological Psychology*, **54**, 605-613.

McConnell, J. V. 1962. Memory transfer through cannibalism in planarians. *Journal of Neuropsychiatry*, **3** (Suppl. 1), 542-548.

McConnell, J. V., Jacobson, A. L. & Kimble, D. P. 1959. The effects of regeneration upon retention of a conditioned response in the planarian. *Journal of Comparative and Physiological Psychology*, **52**, 1-5.

McDougall, W. 1901. Experimentelle Beiträge zur Lehre vom Gedächtniss. Von G. E. Müller and A. Pilzecker. *Mind*, **10**, 388-394. (Review).

McGaugh, J. L. & Petrinovich, L. 1959. The effect of strychnine sulphate on maze-learning. *American Journal of Psychology*, **72**, 99-102.

Mehler, W. H., Feferman, M. E. & Nauta, W. J. H. 1960. Ascending axon degeneration following anterolateral cordotomy. An experimental study in the monkey. *Brain*, **83**, 718-750.

Melton, A. W. 1963. Implications of short-term memory for a general theory of memory. *Journal of Verbal Learning and Verbal Behavior*, **2**, 1-21.

Melzack, R. 1952. Irrational fears in the dog. *Canadian Journal of Psychology*, **6**, 141-147.

Melzack, R. & Casey, K. L. 1968. Sensory, motivational, and central control determinants of pain: A new conceptual model. In D. R. Kenshalo (Ed.), *The skin senses*. Springfield, Ill.: Thomas. Pp. 423-443.

Melzack, R., Rose, G. & McGinty, D. 1962. Skin sensitivity to thermal stimuli. *Experimental Neurology*, **6**, 300-314.

Melzack, R., Stotler, W. A. & Livingstone, W. K. 1958. Effects of discrete brainstem lesions in cats on perception of noxious stimulation. *Journal of Neurophysiology*, **21**, 353-367.

Melzack, R. & Wall, P. D. 1962. On the nature of cutaneous sensory mechanisms. *Brain*, **85**, 331-356.

Melzack, R. & Wall, P. D. 1965. Pain mechanisms: A new theory. *Science*, **150**, 971-979.

Mendelson, J. 1965. Electrical stimulation in the hypothalamic feeding area of the rat: Motivational, reinforcing and cue properties. Doctoral dissertation, Massachusetts Institute of Technology.

Mendelson, J. 1966. Role of hunger in T-maze learning for food by rats. *Journal of Comparative and Physiological Psychology*, **62**, 341-349.

Mendelson, J. 1967. Lateral hypothalamic stimulation in satiated rats: The rewarding effects of self-induced drinking. *Science*, **157**, 1077-1079.

Mendelson, M. & Loewenstein, W. R. 1964. Mechanisms of receptor adaptation. *Science*, **144**, 554-555.

Mendelssohn, M. 1902. Recherches sur la thermotaxie des organismes unicellulaires. *Journal de Physiologie et de Pathologie Générale*, **4**, 393-409.

Mettler, F. A. & Mettler, C. 1942. The effects of striatal injury. *Brain*, **65**, 242-255.

Meyer, D. R. & Woolsey, C. N. 1952. Effects of localized cortical destruction on auditory discriminative conditioning in cat. *Journal of Neurophysiology*, **15**, 149-162.

Meyer, P. M. 1963. Analysis of visual behavior in cats with extensive neocortical ablations. *Journal of Comparative and Physiological Psychology*, **56**, 397-401.

Meyer, P. M., Horel, J. A. & Meyer, D. R. 1963. Effects of dl-amphetamine upon placing responses in neodecorticate cats. *Journal of Comparative and Physiological Psychology*, **56**, 402-404.

Meyer, V. & Yates, A. J. 1955. Intellectual changes following temporal lobectomy for psychomotor epilepsy. *Journal of Neurology, Neurosurgery, and Psychiatry*, **18**, 44-52.

Meyers, W. J., Valenstein, E. S. & Lacey, J. I. 1963. Heart rate changes after reinforcing brain stimulation in rats. *Science*, **140**, 1233-1235.

Michael, C. R. 1966a. Receptive fields of directionally selective units in the optic nerve of the ground squirrel. *Science*, **152**, 1092-1095.

Michael, C. R. 1966b. Receptive fields of opponent color units in the optic nerve of the ground squirrel. *Science*, **152**, 1095-1097.

Michael, R. P. 1962. Estrogen-sensitive neurons and sexual behavior in female cats. *Science*, **136**, 322-323.

Mickle, W. A. & Ades, H. W. 1952. A composite sensory projection area in the cerebral cortex of the cat. *American Journal of Physiology*, **170**, 682-689.

Mihailović, L. & Delgado, J. M. R. 1956. Electrical stimulation of the monkey brain with various frequencies and pulse durations. *Journal of Neurophysiology*, **19**, 21-36.

Milgram, W. N. 1969. Effect of hippocampal stimulation on feeding in the rat. *Physiology and Behavior*, **4**, 665-670.

Miller, A. J. 1968. Variations in retrograde amnesia with parameters of electroconvulsive shock and time of testing. *Journal of Comparative and Physiological Psychology*, **66**, 40-47.

Miller, G. A. 1956. The magical number seven, plus or minus two: Some limits on our capacity for processing information. *Psychological Review*, **63**, 81-97.

Miller, N. E. 1969. Learning of visceral and glandular responses. *Science*, **163**, 434-445.

Miller, N. E., Bailey, C. J. & Stevenson, J. A. F. 1950. Decreased "hunger" but increased food intake resulting from hypothalamic lesions. *Science*, **112**, 256-259.

Miller, R. E. & Ogawa, N. 1962. The effect of adrenocorticotrophic hormone (ACTH) on avoidance conditioning in the adrenalectomized rat. *Journal of Comparative and Physiological Psychology*, **55**, 211-213.

Milner, B. 1954. Intellectual function of the temporal lobes. *Psychological Bulletin*, **51**, 42-62.

Milner, B. 1958. Psychological defects produced by temporal lobe excision. *Research Publications of the Association for Research on Nervous and Mental Disease*, **36**, 244-257.

Milner, B. 1959. The memory defect in bilateral hippocampal lesions. *Psychiatric Research Reports*, **11**, 43-52.

Milner, B. 1962a. Les troubles de la mémoire accompagnant des lésions hippocampiques bilatérales. In P. Passouant (Ed.), *Physiologie de l'hippocampe*. Paris: Centre Nationale de Recherche Scientifique. Pp. 257-272. (Translated by the author: In P. M. Milner & S. E. Glickman [Eds.], *Cognitive processes and the brain*. Princeton; N.J.; Van Nostrand, Pp. 97-111.)

Milner, B. 1962b. Laterality effects in audition. In V. B. Mountcastle (Ed.), *Interhemispheric relations and cerebral dominance*. Baltimore: Johns Hopkins Press. Pp. 177-195.

Milner, B. 1963. Effects of different brain lesions on card sorting. *Archives of Neurology*, **9**, 90-100.

Milner, B. 1964. Some effects of frontal lobectomy in man. In J. M. Warren & K. Akert (Eds.), *The frontal granular cortex and behavior*. New York: McGraw-Hill. Pp. 313-334.

Milner, B. 1965. Visually-guided maze learning in man: Effects of bilateral hippocampal, bilateral frontal, and unilateral cerebral lesions. *Neuropsychologia*, **3**, 317-338.

Milner, B. 1966. Amnesia following operation on the temporal lobes. In C. W. M. Whitty & O. L. Zangwill (Eds.), *Amnesia*. London: Butterworth. Pp. 109-133.

Milner, B. 1967. Brain mechanisms suggested by studies of temporal lobes. In F. L. Darley (Ed.), *Brain mechanisms underlying speech and language*. New York: Grune & Stratton. Pp. 122-145.

Milner, B., Branch, C. & Rasmussen, T. 1964. Observations on cerebral dominance. In A. V. S. de Reuck & M. O'Connor (Eds.), *Ciba foundation symposium on disorders of language*. London: Churchill. Pp. 200-214.

Milner, B., Branch, C. & Rasmussen, T. 1966. Evidence for bilateral speech representation in some non-right-handers. *Transactions of the American Neurological Association*, **91**, 306-308.

Milner, B. & Teuber, H. L. 1968. Alteration of perception and memory in man: Reflections on methods. In L. Weiskrantz (Ed.), *Analysis of behavioral change*. New York: Harper. Pp. 268-375.

Milner, P. M. 1950. A study of the mode of development of food preferences in rats. Masters thesis, McGill University.

Milner, P. M. 1957. The cell assembly: Mark II. *Psychological Review*, **64**, 242–252.

Milner, P. M. 1958. Sensory transmission mechanisms. *Canadian Journal of Psychology*, **12**, 149–158.

Milner, P. M. 1960. Learning in neural systems. In M. C. Yovits & S. Cameron (Eds.), *Self-organizing systems*. New York: Pergamon. Pp. 190–202.

Milner, P. M. 1961a. The application of physiology to learning theory. In R. A. Patton (Ed.), *Current trends in psychological theory*. Pittsburgh: University of Pittsburgh Press. Pp. 111–133.

Milner, P. M. 1961b. A neural mechanism for the immediate recall of sequences. *Kybernetik*, **1**, 76–81.

Milner, P. M. & Zucker, I. 1965. Specific hunger for potassium in the rat. *Psychonomic Science*, **2**, 17–18.

Mirsky, A. F., Primac, D. W., Ajmone Marsan, C., Rosvold, H. E. & Stevens, J. R. 1960. A comparison of the psychological test performance of patients with focal and nonfocal epilepsy. *Experimental Neurology*, **2**, 75–89.

Mirsky, A. F. & Van Buren, J. M. 1965. On the nature of the "absence" in centrencephalic epilepsy: A study of some behavioral, electroencephalographic and autonomic factors. *Electroencephography and Clinical Neurophysiology*, **18**, 334–348.

Mishkin, M. 1954. Visual discrimination performance following partial ablations of the temporal lobe: II. Ventral surface vs. hippocampus. *Journal of Comparative and Physiological Psychology*, **47**, 187–193.

Mishkin, M. 1964. Perseveration of central sets after frontal lesions in monkeys. In J. M. Warren & K. Akert (Eds.), *The frontal granular cortex and behavior*. New York: McGraw-Hill. Pp. 219–241.

Mishkin, M. 1966. Visual mechanisms beyond the striate cortex. In R. W. Russell (Ed.), *Frontiers in physiological psychology*. New York: Academic Press. Pp. 93–119.

Mishkin, M. & Pribram, K. H. 1954. Visual discrimination performance following partial ablations of the temporal lobe: I. Ventral vs. lateral. *Journal of Comparative and Physiological Psychology*, **47**, 14–20.

Mishkin, M. & Pribram, K. H. 1955. Analysis of the effects of frontal lesions in monkeys: I. Variations of delayed alternations. *Journal of Comparative and Physiological Psychology*, **48**, 492–495.

Mishkin, M. & Pribram, K. H. 1956. Analysis of the effects of frontal lesions in the monkey: II. Variations of delayed response. *Journal of Comparative and Physiological Psychology*, **49**, 36–40.

Mishkin, M., Prockop, E. S. & Rosvold, H. E. 1962. One-trial object-discrimination learning in monkeys with frontal lesions. *Journal of Comparative and Physiological Psychology*, **55**, 178–181.

Mogenson, G. J. 1962. Electrical stimulation of the visual cortex as the conditioned stimulus in peripherally blind rats. *Journal of Comparative and Physiological Psychology*, **55**, 492–494.

Mogenson, G. J. 1964. Effects of sodium pentobarbital on brain self-stimulation. *Journal of Comparative and Physiological Psychology*, **58**, 461–462.

Mogenson, G. J. 1965. An attempt to establish secondary reinforcement with rewarding brain stimulation. *Psychological Reports*, **16**, 163–167.

Mogenson, G. J. 1969. Test of a possible influence of the drinking system of the lateral hypothalamus on the mechanisms controlling antidiuretic hormone. *Canadian Journal of Physiology and Pharmacology*, **47**, 109–111.

Mogenson, G. J., Cinnamon, A. D. & Stevenson, J. A. F. 1967. The anorexigenic effects of amphetamine in mice treated with aurothioglucose. *Canadian Journal of Physiology and Pharmacology*, **45**, 564–567.

Mogenson, G. J. & Morgan, C. W. 1967. Effects of induced drinking on self-stimulation of the lateral hypothalamus. *Experimental Brain Research*, **3**, 111–116.

Mogenson, G. J. & Stevenson, J. A. F. 1966. Drinking and self-stimulation with electrical stimulation of the lateral hypothalamus. *Physiology and Behavior*, **1**, 251–254.

Mogenson, G. J. & Stevenson, J. A. F. 1967. Drinking induced by electrical stimulation of the lateral hypothalamus. *Experimental Neurology*, **17**, 119–127.

Molnár, P. & Grastyán, E. 1966. Effect of hippocampal lesion on self-stimulatory reactions. *Acta Physiologica Academiae Scientiarum Hungaricae*, **30**, 304–305. (Abstract)

Moltz, H., Geller, D. & Levin, R. 1967. Maternal behavior in the totally mammectomized rat. *Journal of Comparative and Physiological Psychology*, **64**, 225–229.

Moltz, H. & Wiener, E. 1966. Effects of ovariectomy on maternal behavior of primiparous and multiparous rats. *Journal of Comparative and Physiological Psychology*, **62**, 382–387.

Moncrieff, R. W. 1954. The characterization of odours. *Journal of Physiology*, **125**, 453–465.

Moncrieff, R. W. 1955. The sorptive properties of the olfactory membrane. *Journal of Physiology*, **130**, 543–558.

Money, J. 1961. Sex hormones and other variables in human eroticism. In W. C. Young, (Ed.), *Sex and internal secretions*. Baltimore: Williams & Wilkins. Pp. 1383–1400.

Monnier, M. & Hösli, L. 1964. Dialysis of sleep and waking factors in blood of the rabbit. *Science*, **146**, 796–798.

Montgomery, K. C. 1953. The effect of the hunger and thirst drives upon exploratory behavior. *Journal of Comparative and Physiological Psychology*, **46**, 315–319.

Montgomery, M. F. 1931. The rôle of the salivary glands in the thirst mechanism. *American Journal of Physiology*, **96**, 221–227.

Mook, D. G. 1963. Oral and postingestional determinants of the intake of various solutions in rats with esophageal fistulas. *Journal of Comparative and Physiological Psychology*, **56**, 645–659.

Mook, D. G. & Blass, E. M. 1968. Quinine-aversion thresholds and "finickiness" in hyperphagic rats. *Journal of Comparative and Physiological Psychology*, **65**, 202–207.

Morgan, C. T. 1957. Physiological mechanisms of motivation. *Nebraska symposium on motivation*. **5**, 1–35.

Morgane, P. J. 1961a. Medial forebrain bundle and "feeding centers" of the hypothalamus. *Journal of Comparative Neurology*, **117**, 1–25.

Morgane, P. J. 1961b. Alterations in feeding and drinking behavior of rats with lesions in globi pallidi. *American Journal of Physiology*, **201**, 420–428.

Morgane, P. J. 1961c. Electrophysiological studies of feeding and satiety centers in the rat. *American Journal of Physiology*, **201**, 838–844.

Morgane, P. J. 1964. Limbic-hypothalamic-midbrain

interaction in thirst and thirst motivated behavior. In M. J. Wayner (Ed.), *Thirst*. Oxford: Pergamon Press. Pp. 429–453.

Morgane, P. J. & Kosman, A. J. 1957. Alterations in feline behavior following bilateral amygdalectomy. *Nature*, **180**, 598–600.

Morgane, P. J. & Kosman, A. J. 1959. A rhinencephalic feeding center in the cat. *American Journal of Physiology*, **197**, 158–162.

Morgane, P. J. & Kosman, A. J. 1960. Relationship of the middle hypothalamus to amygdalar hyperphagia. *American Journal of Physiology*, **198**, 1315–1318.

Morin, F. 1955. A new spinal pathway for cutaneous impulses. *American Journal of Physiology*, **183**, 245–252.

Morin, F., Kitai, S. T., Portnoy, H. & Demirjian, C. 1963. Afferent projections to the lateral cervical nucleus: A microelectrode study. *American Journal of Physiology*, **204**, 667–672.

Morrell, F. 1961a. Effect of anodal polarization on the firing pattern of single cortical cells. *Annals of the New York Academy of Sciences*, **92**, 860–876.

Morrell, F. 1961b. Lasting changes in synaptic organization produced by continuous neuronal bombardment. In J. F. Delafresnaye (Ed.), *Brain mechanisms and learning*. Springfield, Ill.: Thomas. Pp. 375–392.

Morrell, F. & Jasper, H. H. 1956. Electrographic studies of the formation of temporary connections in the brain. *Electroencephalography and Clinical Neurophysiology*, **8**, 201–215.

Morrell, F. & Naitoh, P. 1962. Effect of cortical polarization on a conditioned avoidance response. *Experimental Neurology*, **6**, 507–523.

Morrison, G. R. 1955. The relation of rewarding intracranial stimulation to biological drive. Unpublished master's thesis, McGill University.

Moruzzi, G. 1954. The physiological properties of the brain stem reticular system. In J. F. Delafresnaye (Ed.), *Brain mechanisms and consciousness*. Springfield, Ill.: Thomas. Pp. 21–53.

Moruzzi, G. & Magoun, H. W. 1949. Brain stem reticular formation and activation of the EEG. *Electroencephalography and Clinical Neurophysiology*, **1**, 455–473.

Motokawa, K., Oikawa, T. & Tasaki, K. 1957. Receptor potential of vertebrate retina. *Journal Neurophysiology*, **20**, 186–199.

Moulten, D. G. & Tucker, D. 1964. Electrophysiology of the olfactory system. *Annals of the New York Academy of Sciences*, **116**, 380–428.

Mountcastle, V. B. 1961a. Some functional properties of the somatic afferent system. In W. A. Rosenblith (Ed.), *Sensory communication*. New York: Wiley, Pp. 403–436.

Mountcastle, V. B. 1961b. Duality of function in the somatic afferent system. In M. A. B. Brazier (Ed.), *Brain and behavior*. Vol. 1. Washington, D. C.: American Institute of Biological Sciences. Pp. 67–93.

Mountcastle, V. B., Poggio, G. F. & Werner, G. 1963. The relation of thalamic cell response to peripheral stimuli varied over an intensive continuum. *Journal of Neurophysiology*, **26**, 807–834.

Mountcastle, V. B. & Powell, T. P. S. 1959a. Central nervous mechanisms subserving position sense and kinesthesis. *Bulletin of the Johns Hopkins Hospital*, **105**, 173–200.

Mountcastle, V. B. & Powell, T. P. S. 1959b. Neural mechanisms subserving cutaneous sensibility, with spe-

cial reference to the role of afferent inhibition in sensory perception and discrimination. *Bulletin of the Johns Hopkins Hospital*, **105**, 201–232.

Moyer, K. E. 1958. The effect of adrenalectomy on anxiety motivated behavior. *Journal of Genetic Psychology*, **92**, 11–16.

Mozell, M. M. 1958. Electrophysiology of olfactory bulb. *Journal of Neurophysiology*, **21**, 183–196.

Mullan, S. & Penfield, W. 1959. Illusions of comparative interpretation and emotion. *Archives of Neurology and Psychiatry*, **81**, 269–284.

Müller, G. E. & Pilzecker, A. 1900. Experimentelle Beiträge zur Lehre vom Gedächtniss. *Zeitschrift für Psychologie und Physiologie der Sinnesorgane*, Erganzungsband, **1**, 1–288.

Munk, H. 1880. Über die Sehsphären der Grosshirnrinde. *Monatsberich der Preussischen Akadamie der Wissenschaften*, 484–507.

Munro, D., Horne, H. W. & Paull, D. P. 1948. The effect of injury to the spinal cord and cauda equina on the sexual potency of men. *New England Journal of Medicine*, **239**, 903–911.

Murphy, J. V. & Miller, R. E. 1955. The effect of adrenocorticotrophic hormone (ACTH) on avoidance conditioning in the rat. *Journal of Comparative and Physiological Psychology*, **48**, 47–49.

Myers, R. D. 1964a. Emotional and autonomic responses following hypothalamic chemical stimulation. *Canadian Journal of Psychology*, **18**, 6–14.

Myers, R. D. 1964b. Modification of drinking patterns by chronic intracranial infusion. In M. Wayner (Ed.), *Thirst*. New York: Macmillan. Pp. 533–549.

Nachman, M. 1959. The inheritance of saccharin preference. *Journal of Comparative and Physiological Psychology*. **52**, 451–457.

Nachman, M. 1962. Taste preferences for sodium salts by adrenalectomized rats. *Journal Comparative Physiological Psychology*, **55**, 1124–1129.

Nachman, M. 1963. Learned aversion to the taste of lithium chloride and generalization to other salts. *Journal of Comparative and Physiological Psychology*, **56**, 343–349.

Nachman, M. & Pfaffmann, C. 1963. Gustatory nerve discharge in normal and sodium deficient rats. *Journal of Comparative and Physiological Psychology*, **56**, 1007–1011.

Nadel, L. 1968. Dorsal and ventral hippocampal lesions and behavior. *Physiology and Behavior*, **3**, 891–900.

Nafe, J. P. 1934. The pressure, pain, and temperature senses. In C. Murchison (Ed.), *A handbook of general experimental psychology*. Worcester, Mass.: Clark University Press. Pp. 1037–1085.

Nakajima, Shigehiro. 1964. Adaptation in stretch receptor neurons of crayfish. *Science*, **146**, 1168–1170.

Nakajima, Shinshu. 1964. Effects of chemical injection into the reticular formation of rats. *Journal of Comparative and Physiological Psychology*, **58**, 10–15.

Nakayama, T., Eisenman, J. S. & Hardy, J. D. 1961. Single unit activity of anterior hypothalamus during local heating. *Science*, **134**, 560–561.

Nakayama, T., Hammel, H. T., Hardy, J. D. & Eisenman, J. S. 1963. Thermal stimulation of electrical activity of single units of the preoptic region. *American Journal of Physiology*, **204**, 1122–1126.

Nalbandov, A. V. & Card, L. E. 1945. Endocrine identification of the broody genotype of cocks. *Journal of Heredity*, **36**, 34-39.

Naquet, R., Denavit, M. & Albe-Fessard, D. 1962. Mise en évidence du rôle d'une zone subthalamique dans le mecanisme de l'éveil. *Comptes Rendus de l'Académie de Science*, **255**, 1473-1475.

Naquet, R., Denavit, M., Lanoir, J. & Albe-Fessard, D. 1965. Altérations transitoires ou définitives de zones diencéphaliques chez le chat. Leurs effets sur l'activité électrique corticale et le sommeil. In M. Jouvet (Ed.), *Aspects anatomo-fonctionnels de la physiologie du sommeil.* Paris: Centre Nationale de Recherche Scientifique. Pp. 107-130.

Natanson, 1844. *Archiv für Physiologische Heilkunde*, **3**, 515-535. Cited by E. G. Boring, *A history of experimental pyschology.* New York: Appleton, 1929. P. 88.

Nathanson, M., Bergman, P. S. & Gordon, G. G. 1952. Denial of illness. *A.M.A Archives of Neurology and Psychiatry*, **68**, 380-387.

Nauta, W. J. H. 1946. Hypothalamic regulation of sleep in rats; an experimental study. *Journal of Neurophysiology*, **9**, 285-316.

Nauta, W. J. H. 1957. Silver impregnation of degenerating axons. In W. F. Windle (Ed.), *New research techniques of neuroanatomy.* Springfield Ill.: Thomas. Pp. 17-26.

Nauta, W. J. H. 1964. Some efferent connections of the prefrontal cortex in the monkey. In J. M. Warren & K. Akert (Eds.), *The frontal granular cortex and behavior.* New York: McGraw-Hill. Pp. 397-409.

Nauta, W. J. H. & Mehler, W. R. 1966. Projections of the lentiform nucleus in the monkey. *Brain Research*, **1**, 3-42.

Neff, W. D. 1961a. Discriminatory capacity of different divisions of the auditory system. In M. A. B. Brazier (Ed.), *Brain and behavior.* Vol. 1. Washington, D.C.: American Institute of Biological Sciences. Pp. 205-262.

Neff, W. D. 1961b. Neural mechanisms of auditory discrimination. In W. A. Rosenblith (Ed.), *Sensory communication.* New York: Wiley. Pp. 259-278.

Neff, W. D. & Diamond, I. T. 1958. The neural basis of auditory discrimination. In H. F. Harlow & C. N. Woolsey (Eds.), *Biological and biochemical bases of behavior.* Madison: University of Wisconsin Press. Pp. 101-126.

Netter, F. H. 1957. *The Ciba collection of medical illustrations.* Vol. 1. *The nervous system.* Summit, N.J.: Ciba.

Nevins, W. B. 1927. Experiments in the self-feeding of dairy cows. *University of Illinois Agriculture Experimental Station Bulletin*, No. 289.

Nichols, I. C. & Hunt, J. McV. 1940. A case of partial bilateral frontal lobectomy. *American Journal of Psychiatry*, **96**, 1063-1087.

Noordenbos, W. 1959. *Pain.* Amsterdam: Elsevier.

Novin, D. 1962. The relation between electrical conductivity of brain tissue and thirst in the rat. *Journal of Comparative and Physiological Psychology*, **55**, 145-154.

Oakley, B. & Pfaffmann, C. 1962. Electrophysiologically monitored lesions in the gustatory thalamic relay of the albino rat. *Journal of Comparative and Physiological Psychology*, **55**, 155-160.

Oatley, K. 1964. Changes of blood volume and osmotic pressure in the production of thirst. *Nature*, **202**, 1341-1342.

Ogle, W. 1867. Aphasia and agraphia. *St. George's Hospital Reports*, **2**, 83-122.

Olds, J. 1956a. A preliminary mapping of electrical reinforcing effects in the rat brain. *Journal of Comparative and Physiological Psychology*, **49**, 281-285.

Olds, J. 1956b. Runway and maze behavior controlled by basomedial forebrain stimulation in the rat. *Journal of Comparative and Physiological Psychology*, **49**, 507-512.

Olds, J. 1958a. Effects of hunger and male sex hormone on self-stimulation of the brain. *Journal of Comparative and Physiological Psychology*, **51**, 320-324.

Olds, J. 1958b. Satiation effects in self-stimulation of the brain. *Journal of Comparative and Physiological Psychology*, **51**, 675-678.

Olds, J. 1958c. Self-stimulation experiments and differentiated reward systems. In H. H. Jasper, L. D. Proctor, R. S. Knighton, W. C. Noshay & R. T. Costello (Eds.), *Reticular formation of the brain.* Boston: Little, Brown. Pp. 671-687.

Olds, J. 1960. Differentiation of reward systems in the brain by self-stimulation technics. In E. R. Ramey & D. S. O'Doherty (Eds.), *Electrical studies on the unanesthetized brain.* New York: Hoeber. Pp. 17-51.

Olds, J. 1962. Hypothalamic substrates of reward. *Physiological Review*, **42**, 554-604.

Olds, J. & Milner, P. 1954. Positive reinforcement produced by electrical stimulation of septal area and other regions of rat brain. *Journal of Comparative and Physiological Psychology*, **47**, 419-427.

Olds, J. & Olds, M. E. 1961. Interference and learning in paleocortical systems. In J. F. Delafresnaye (Ed.), *Brain mechanisms and learning.* Springfield, Ill.: Thomas. Pp. 153-183.

Olds, J. & Olds, M. E. 1965. Drives, rewards, and the brain. In *New directions in psychology.* Vol. 2. New York: Holt. Pp. 327-410.

Olds, J. & Peretz, B. 1960. A motivational analysis of the reticular activating system. *Electroencephalography and Clinical Neurophysiology*, **12**, 445-454.

Olds, J. & Travis, R. P. 1960. Effects of chlorpromazine, meprobamate, pentobarbital, and morphine on self-stimulation. *Journal of Pharmacology and Experimental Therapeutics*, **128**, 397-404.

Olds, M. E. & Olds, J. 1963. Approach-avoidance analysis of rat diencephalon. *Journal of Comparative Neurology*, **120**, 259-295.

Olton, D. S. & Isaacson, R. L. 1967. Effects of lateral and dorsomedial thalamic lesions on retention of active avoidance tasks. *Journal of Comparative and Physiological Psychology*, **64**, 256-261.

Oomura, Y., Kimura, K., Ooyama, H., Maeno, T., Iki, M. & Kunioshi, M. 1964. Reciprocal activities of the ventromedial and lateral hypothalamic areas in cats. *Science*, **143**, 484-485.

Oppenheimer, D. R., Palmer, E. & Weddell, G. 1958. Nerve endings in the conjunctiva. *Journal of Anatomy*, **92**, 321-352.

Orbach, J. 1959. "Functions" of striate cortex and the problem of mass action. *Psychological Bulletin*, **56**, 217-292.

Orbach, J. & Fantz, R. L. 1958. Differential effects of temporal neo-cortical resections on overtrained and non-overtrained visual habits in monkeys. *Journal of Comparative and Physiological Psychology*, **51**, 126-129.

Orbach, J., Milner, B. & Rasmussen, T. 1960. Learning

and retention in monkeys after amygdala-hippocampus resection. *Archives of Neurology*, 3, 230-251.

Oswaldo-Cruz, E. & Kidd, C. 1964. Functional properties of neurons in the lateral cervical nucleus of the cat. *Journal of Neurophysiology*, 27, 1-14.

Ottoson, D. 1958. Studies on the relationship between olfactory stimulating effectiveness and physico-chemical properties of odorous compounds. *Acta Physiologica Scandinavica*, 43, 167-181.

Ottoson, D. 1959. Studies on slow potentials in the rabbit's olfactory bulb and nasal mucosa. *Acta Physiologica Scandinavica*, 47, 136-148.

Ottoson, D. 1963. Generation and transmission of signals in the olfactory system. In Y. Zotterman (Ed.), *Olfaction and taste*. Oxford: Pergamon. Pp. 35-44.

Overton, D. A. 1964. State-dependent or "dissociated" learning produced with pentobarbital. *Journal of Comparative and Physiological Psychology*, 57, 3-12.

Pagano, R. R., Bush, D. F., Martin, G. & Hunt, E. B. 1969. Duration of retrograde amnesia as a function of electroconvulsive shock intensity. *Physiology and Behavior*, 4, 19-21.

Paintal, A. S. 1954. A study of gastric stretch receptors. Their role in peripheral mechanisms of satiation of hunger and thirst. *Journal of Physiology*, 126, 255-270.

Palay, S. L. 1958. The morphology of synapses in the central nervous system. *Experimental Cell Research* (Suppl. 5), 275-293.

Parry, D. A. 1947. The function of the insect ocellus. *Journal of Experimental Biology*, 24, 211-219.

Patel, M. D. 1936. The physiology of the formation of "pigeon's milk." *Physiological Zoology*, 9, 129-152.

Patton, H. D. 1960. Taste, olfaction and visceral sensation. In T. C. Ruch & J. F. Fulton (Eds.), *Medical physiology and biophysics*. Philadelphia: Saunders. Pp. 369-385.

Pavlov, I. P. 1927. *Conditioned reflexes*. Oxford: Oxford University Press. (reprinted: New York; Dover, 1960.)

Pearl, R. & Fairchild, T. E. 1921. Studies in the physiology of reproduction in the domestic fowl. XIX. On the influence of free choice of food materials on winter egg production and body weight. *American Journal of Hygiene*, 1, 253-277.

Pearlman, C. A., Sharpless, S. K. & Jarvik, M. E. 1961. Retrograde amnesia produced by anesthetic and convulsant agents. *Journal of Comparative and Physiological Psychology*, 54, 109-112.

Penfield, W. 1938. The cerebral cortex in man. I. The cerebral cortex and consciousness. *Archives of Neurology and Psychiatry*, 40, 417-442.

Penfield, W. 1952. Memory mechanisms. *Archives of Neurology and Psychiatry*, 67, 178-198.

Penfield, W. 1954. The permanent record of the stream of consciousness. *Proceedings of the 14th International Congress of Psychology*, 47-69.

Penfield, W. & Boldrey, E. 1937. Somatic motor and sensory representation in the cerebral cortex of man as studied by electrical stimulation. *Brain*, 60, 389-443.

Penfield, W. & Jasper, H. H. 1954. *Epilepsy and the functional anatomy of the human brain*. Boston: Little, Brown.

Penfield, W. & Perot, P. 1963. The brain's record of auditory and visual experience. *Brain*, 86, 595-696.

Penfield, W. & Rasmussen, T. 1950. *The cerebral cortex of man*. New York: Macmillan.

Penfield, W. & Roberts, L. 1959. *Speech and brain mechanisms*. Princeton, N.J.: Princeton University Press.

Perez-Cruet, J., Black, W. C. & Brady, J. V. 1963. Heart rate: Differential effects of hypothalamic and septal self-stimulation. *Science*, 140, 1235-1236.

Perl, E. R., Whitlock, D. C. & Gentry, J. R. 1962. Cutaneous projection to second-order neurons of the dorsal column system. *Journal of Neurophysiology*, 25, 337-358.

Persson, N. 1962. Self-stimulation in the goat. *Acta Physiologica Scandinavica*, 55, 276-285.

Peters, R. H., Rosvold, H. E. & Mirsky, A. F. 1956. The effect of thalamic lesions upon delayed response-type tests in the rhesus monkey. *Journal of Comparative and Physiological Psychology*, 49, 111-116.

Pfaffmann, C. 1955. Gustatory nerve impulses in rat, cat and rabbit. *Journal of Neurophysiology*, 18, 429-440.

Pfaffmann, C. 1960. The pleasures of sensation. *Psychological Review*, 67, 253-268.

Pfaffmann, C. & Bare, J. K. 1950. Gustatory nerve discharges in normal and adrenalectomized rats. *Journal of Comparative and Physiological Psychology*, 43, 320-324.

Pfaffmann, C., Erickson, R. P., Frommer, G. P. & Halpern, B. P. 1961. Gustatory discharges in the rat medulla and thalamus. In W. A. Rosenblith (Ed.), *Sensory communication*. New York: Wiley. Pp. 455-473.

Phoenix, C. H., Goy, R. W., Gerall, A. A. & Young, W. C. 1959. Organizing action of prenatally administered testosterone propionate on the tissues mediating mating behavior in the female guinea pig. *Endocrinology*, 65, 369-382.

Piercy, M., Hécaen, H. & Ajuriaguerra, J. de. 1960. Constructional apraxia associated with unilateral cerebral lesions—left and right sided cases compared. *Brain*, 83, 225-242.

Pilgrim, P. J. & Patton, R. A. 1947. Pattern of self-selection of purified dietary components by the rat. *Journal of Comparative and Physiological Psychology*, 40, 343-348.

Pinel, J. P. J. 1968. Evaluation of the one-trial passive avoidance task as a tool for studying ECS-produced amnesia. *Psychonomic Science*, 13, 131-132.

Pinel, J. P. J. & Cooper, R. M. 1966. Demonstration of the Kamin effect after one-trial avoidance learning. *Psychonomic Science*, 4, 17-18.

Pliskoff, S. S. & Hawkins, T. D. 1963. Test of Deutsch's drive-decay theory of rewarding self-stimulation of the brain. *Science*, 141, 823-824.

Pliskoff, S. S., Wright, J. E. & Hawkins, T. D. 1965. Brain stimulation as a reinforcer: Intermittent schedules. *Journal of the Experimental Analysis of Behavior*, 8, 75-88.

Ploog, D. W. & MacLean, P. D. 1963. Display of penile erection in squirrel monkey (*Saimiri sciureus*). *Animal Behavior*, 11, 32-39.

Plotnikoff, N. 1966. Magnesium pemoline: Enhancement of learning and memory of a conditioned avoidance response. *Science*, 151, 703-704.

Plutchik, R., McFarland, W. L. & Robinson, B. W. 1966. Relationships between current intensity, self-stimulation rates, escape latencies, and evoked behavior in rhesus monkeys. *Journal of Comparative and Physiological Psychology*, 61, 181-188.

Podolsky, R. J. & Costantin, L. L. 1964. Regulation by

calcium of the contraction and relaxation of muscle fibers. *Federation Proceedings*, **23**, 933-939.

Poggio, G. F. & Mountcastle, V. B. 1960. A study of the functional contributions of the lemniscal and spinothalamic systems to somatic sensibility. *Bulletin of the Johns Hopkins Hospital*, **106**, 266-316.

Poggio, G. F. & Mountcastle, V. B. 1963. The functional properties of ventrobasal thalamic neurons studied in unanesthetized monkeys. *Journal of Neurophysiology*, **26**, 775-806.

Pollack, M., Battersby, W. S. & Bender, M. B. 1957. Tachistoscopic identification of contour in patients with brain damage. *Journal of Comparative and Physiological Psychology*, **50**, 220-227.

Poltyrew, S. S. & Zeliony, G. P. 1930. Grosshirnrinde und Assoziationsfunktion. *Zeitschift für Biologie*, **90**, 157-160.

Polyak, S. 1932. *The main afferent fiber systems of the cerebral cortex in primates*. Berkeley: University of California Press.

Polyak, S. L. 1941. *The retina*. Chicago: University of Chicago Press.

Pomerat, C. M., Hendelman, W. J., Raiborn, C. W., Jr. & Massey, J. F. 1967. Dynamic activities of nervous tissue *in vitro*. In H. Hydén (Ed.), *The neuron*. Amsterdam: Elsevier. Pp. 119-178.

Pompeiano, O. 1967. The neurophysiological mechanisms of the postural and motor events during desynchronized sleep. *Research Publications of the Association for Research in Nervous and Mental Disease*, **45**, 351-423.

Pompeiano, O. & Swett, J. E. 1962. EEG and behavioral manifestations of sleep induced by cutaneous nerve stimulation in normal cats. *Archives Italiennes de Biologie*, **100**, 311-342.

Poppelreuter, W. 1917. *Die psychischen Schädigungen durch Kopfschuss im Kriege 1914-1917*. Vol. 1. Leipzig: Voss.

Porter, R. W., Cavanaugh, E. B., Critchlow, B. V. & Sawyer, C. H. 1957. Localized changes in electrical activity of the hypothalamus in estrous cats following vaginal stimulation. *American Journal of Physiology*, **189**, 145-151.

Porter, R. W., Conrad, D. G. & Brady, J. V. 1959. Some neural and behavioral correlates of electrical self-stimulation of the limbic system. *Journal of the Experimental Analysis of Behavior*. **2**, 43-55.

Poschel, B. P. H. 1966. Comparison of reinforcing effects yielded by lateral versus medial hypothalamic stimulation. *Journal of Comparative and Physiological Psychology*, **61**, 346-352.

Powell, T. P. S. & Mountcastle, V. B. 1959. Some aspects of the functional organization of the cortex of the monkey: A correlation of findings obtained in single unit analysis with cytoarchitecture. *Bulletin of the Johns Hopkins Hospital*, **105**, 133-162.

Prescott, R. G. W. 1966. Estrous cycle in the rat: Effects on self-stimulation behavior. *Science*, **152**, 796-797.

Pribram, H. B. & Barry, J. 1956. Further behavioral analysis of parieto-temporo-preoccipital cortex. *Journal of Neurophysiology*, **19**, 99-106.

Pribram, K. H. 1950. Some physical and pharmacological factors affecting delayed response performance of baboons following frontal lobotomy. *Journal of Neurophysiology*, **13**, 373-382.

Pribram, K. H. 1958. Neocortical function in behavior.

In H. F. Harlow & C. N. Woolsey (Eds.), *Biological and biochemical bases of behavior*. Madison: University of Wisconsin Press. Pp. 151-172.

Pribram, K. H. 1960. The intrinsic systems of the forebrain. In J. Field (Ed.), *Handbook of physiology: Neurophysiology*. Vol. 2. Washington, D.C.: American Physiological Society. Pp. 1323-1344.

Pribram, K. H. & Kruger, L. 1954. Functions of the "olfactory brain." *Annals of the New York Academy of Sciences*, **58**, 109-138.

Pribram, K. H., Rosner, B. S. & Rosenblith, W. A. 1954. Electrical responses to acoustic clicks in monkey: Extent of neocortex activated. *Journal of Neurophysiology*, **17**, 336-344.

Pribram, K. H. & Weiskrantz, L. 1957. A comparison of the effects of medial and lateral cerebral resections on conditioned avoidance behavior of monkeys. *Journal of Comparative and Physiological Psychology*, **50**, 74-80.

Pribram, K. H., Wilson, W. A. & Connors, J. 1962. Effects of lesions of the medial forebrain on alternation behavior of rhesus monkeys. *Experimental Neurology*, **6**, 36-47.

Pritchard, R. M., Heron, W. & Hebb, D. O. 1960. Visual perception approached by the method of stabilized images. *Canadian Journal of Psychology*, **14**, 67-77.

Raab, D. H. & Ades, H. W. 1946. Cortical and midbrain mediation of a conditioned discrimination of acoustic intensities. *American Journal of Psychology*, **59**, 59-83.

Racine, R. J. 1969. The modification of afterdischarge and convulsive behaviour in the rat by electrical stimulation. Ph.D. thesis, McGill University.

Ramón y Cajal, S. 1952. *Histologie du système nerveux de l'homme et des vertébrés*. Madrid: Instituto Ramón y Cajal.

Rampone, A. J. & Shirasu, M. E. 1964. Temperature changes in the rat in response to feeding. *Science*, **144**, 317-319.

Ranson, S. W. 1937. Some functions of the hypothalamus. *Harvey Lectures*, **32**, 92-121.

Ranson, S. W. 1939. Somnolence caused by hypothalamic lesions in the monkey. *Archives of Neurology and Psychiatry*, **41**, 1-23.

Ranson, S. W. 1940. Regulation of body temperature. *Research Publications of the Association for Research in Nervous and Mental Disease*. **20**, 342-399.

Rasmussen, G. L. 1946. The olivary peduncle and other fiber projections of the superior olivary complex. *Journal of Comparative Neurology*, **84**, 141-219.

Rasmussen, G. L. 1960. Efferent fibers of the cochlear nerve and cochlear nucleus. In G. L. Rasmussen & W. F. Windle (Eds.), *Neural mechanisms of the auditory and vestibular systems*. Springfield, Ill.: Thomas. Pp. 105-115.

Ratliffe, F. & Hartline, H. K. 1959. The responses of *Limulus* optic nerve fibers to patterns of illumination on the receptor mosaic. *Journal of General Physiology*, **42**, 1241-1255.

Ray, O. S. & Emley, G. 1964. Time factors in intrahemisphere transfer of learning. *Science*, **144**, 76-78.

Rebert, C. S., McAdam, D. W., Knott, J. R. & Irwin, D. A. 1967. Slow potential change in human brain related to level of motivation. *Journal of Comparative and Physiological Psychology*, **63**, 20-23.

Reid, L. D., Gibson, W. E., Gledhill, S. M. & Porter, P. B. 1964. Anticonvulsant drugs and self-stimulating behavior. *Journal of Comparative and Physiological Psychology*, 57, 353-356.

Replogle, A. 1960. Motivational effects of lesions in the thalamus. Unpublished master's thesis, McGill University.

Restorff, H. von. 1933. Über die Wirkung von Bereichsbildung im Spurenfeld. *Psychologische Forschung*, 18, 299-342.

Revusky, S. H. & Bedarf, E. W. 1967. Association of illness with prior ingestion of novel foods. *Science*, 155, 219-220.

Reynolds, R. W. 1963. Ventromedial hypothalamic lesions without hyperphagia. *American Journal of Physiology*, 204, 60-62.

Reynolds, R. W. 1965a. An irritative hypothesis concerning the hypothalamic regulation of food intake. *Psychological Review*, 72, 105-116.

Reynolds, R. W. 1965b. Hypothalamic lesions and disinhibition of feeding. *Science*, 150, 1322.

Rheingold, H. L. & Hess, E. H. 1957. The chick's "preference" for some visual properties of water. *Journal of Comparative and Physiological Psychology*, 50, 417-421.

Richter, C. P. 1947. Biology of drives. *Journal of Comparative and Physiological Psychology*, 40, 129-134.

Richter, C. P. 1967. Sleep and activity: Their relation to the 24-hour clock. *Research Publications of the Association for Research in Nervous and Mental Disease*, 45, 8-27.

Richter, C. P. & Eckert, J. F. 1937. Increased calcium appetite of parathyroidectomized rats. *Endocrinology*, 21, 50-54.

Richter, C. P. & Eckert, J. F. 1938. Mineral metabolism of adrenalectomized rats studied by the appetite method. *Endocrinology*, 22, 214-224.

Richter, C. P. & Hines, M. 1938. Increased spontaneous activity produced in monkeys by brain lesions. *Brain*, 61, 1-16.

Richter, C. P., Holt, L. E., Jr. & Barelare, B., Jr. 1938. Nutritional requirements for normal growth and reproduction in rats studied by the self-selection method. *American Journal of Physiology*, 122, 734-744.

Riddle, O. & Lahr, E. L. 1944. On broodiness of ring doves following implants of certain steroid hormones. *Endocrinology*, 35, 255-260.

Riddoch, G. 1917. The reflex functions of the completely divided spinal cord in man, compared with those associated with less severe lesions. *Brain*, 40, 264-402.

Riggs, L. A., Ratliffe, F., Cornsweet, J. C. & Cornsweet, T. N. 1953. The disappearance of steadily fixated testobjects. *Journal of the Optical Society of America*, 43, 495-501.

Riley, C. V. 1895. The senses of insects. *Nature*, 52, 209-212.

Riley, D. A. & Rosenzweig, M. R. 1957. Echolocation in rats. *Journal of Comparative and Physiological Psychology*, 50, 323-328.

Riopelle, A. J., Alper, R. G., Strong, P. N. and Ades, H. W. 1953. Multiple discrimination and patterned string performance of normal and temporal-lobectomized monkeys. *Journal of Comparative and Physiological Psychology*, 46, 145-149.

Roberts, W. W. 1958a. Rapid escape learning without avoidance learning motivated by hypothalamic stimulation in cats. *Journal of Comparative and Physiological Psychology*, 51, 391-399.

Roberts, W. W. 1958b. Both rewarding and punishing effects from stimulation of posterior hypothalamus of cat with same electrode at same intensity. *Journal of Comparative and Physiological Psychology*, 51, 400-407.

Roberts, W. W. 1962. Fear-like behavior elicited from dorsomedial thalamus of cat. *Journal of Comparative and Physiological Psychology*, 55, 191-197.

Roberts, W. W. & Kiess, H. O. 1963. Effect of dorsomedial thalamic lesions on fear in cats. *Journal of Comparative and Physiological Psychology*, 56, 950-958.

Roberts, W. W. & Carey, R. J. 1965. Rewarding effect of performance of gnawing aroused by hypothalamic stimulation in the rat. *Journal of Comparative and Physiological Psychology*, 59, 317-324.

Roberts, W. W. & Kiess, H. O. 1964. Motivational properties of hypothalamic aggression in cats. *Journal of Comparative and Physiological Psychology*, 58, 187-193.

Roberts, W. W., Steinberg, M. L. & Means, L. W. 1967. Hypothalamic mechanisms for sexual, aggressive, and other motivational behaviors in the opossum, *Didelphis virginiana*. *Journal of Comparative and Physiological Psychology*, 64, 1-15.

Robinson, B. W. 1964. Forebrain alimentary responses: Some organizational principles. In M. J. Wayner (Ed.), *Thirst*, New York: Macmillan. Pp. 411-427.

Robinson, B. W. & Mishkin, M. 1962. Alimentary responses evoked from forebrain structures in *Macaca mulatta*. *Science*, 136, 260-262.

Robinson, B. W. & Mishkin, M. 1968. Alimentary responses to forebrain stimulation in monkeys. *Experimental Brain Research*, 4, 330-366.

Robinson, B. W., Warner, H. & Rosvold, H. E. 1965. Brain telestimulator with solar cell power supply. *Science*, 148, 1111-1113.

Robinson, J. S. 1953. Stimulus substitution and response learning in the earthworm. *Journal of Comparative and Physiological Psychology*, 46, 262-266.

Rodgers, W. L. 1967. Specificity of specific hungers. *Journal of Comparative and Physiological Psychology*, 64, 49-58.

Rodgers, W. L., Epstein, A. N. & Teitelbaum, P. 1965. Lateral hypothalamic aphagia: Motor failure or motivational deficit. *American Journal of Physiology*, 208, 334-342.

Rodgers, W. L. & Rozin, P. 1966. Novel food preferences in thiamine-deficient rats. *Journal of Comparative and Physiological Psychology*, 61, 1-4.

Rogers, F. T. 1922. Studies of the brain stem. VI. An experimental study of the corpus striatum in the pigeon as related to various instinctive types of behavior. *Journal of Comparative Neurology*, 35, 21-59.

Rolando, L. 1809. *Saggio sopra la vera struttura del cervello dell'uomo e degl'animali e sopra le funzioni del sistema nervoso*. Sassari, It.: Stamperia Privilegiata.

Root, W. S. & Bard, P. 1937. Erection in the cat following removal of lumbo-sacral segments. *American Journal of Physiology*, 119, 392-393.

Rose, J. E., Galambos, R. & Hughes, J. R. 1959. Microelectrode studies of the cochlear nuclei of the cat. *Bulletin of the Johns Hopkins Hospital*, 104, 211-251.

Rose, J. E., Greenwood, D. D., Goldberg, J. M. & Hind, J. E. 1963. Some discharge characteristics of single neurons in the inferior colliculus of the cat. I. Tonotopical organization, relation of spike-counts to tone intensity, and firing patterns of single elements. *Journal of Neurophysiology*, **26**, 294-320.

Rose, J. E., Gross, N. B., Geisler, C. D. & Hind, J. E. 1966. Some neural mechanisms in the inferior colliculus of the cat which may be relevant to localization of a sound source. *Journal of Neurophysiology*, **29**, 288-314.

Rose, J. E. & Mountcastle, V. B. 1959. Touch and kinesthesis. In J. Field, (Ed.), *Handbook of physiology. Neurophysiology*. Vol. 1. Washington, D.C.: American Physiological Society. Pp. 387-429.

Rose, J. E. & Woolsey, C. N. 1958. Cortical connections and functional organization of the thalamic auditory system of the cat. In H. F. Harlow & C. N. Woolsey (Eds.), *Biological and biochemical bases of behavior*. Madison: University of Wisconsin Press.

Rosenblatt, F., Farrow, J. T. & Herblin, W. F. 1966. Transfer of conditioned responses from trained rats to untrained rats by means of a brain extract. *Nature*, **209**, 46-48.

Rosenblatt, J. S. 1967. Nonhormonal basis of maternal behavior in the rat. *Science*, **156**, 1512-1514.

Rosenzweig, M. R. 1961. Development of research on the physiological mechanisms of auditory localization. *Psychological Bulletin*, **58**, 376-389.

Rosenzweig, M. R., Krech, D. & Bennett, E. L. 1958. Brain chemistry and adaptive behavior. In H. F. Harlow and C. N. Woolsey (Eds.), *Biological and biochemical bases of behavior*. Madison: University of Wisconsin Press, Pp. 367-400.

Rosenzweig, M. R. & Sutton, D. 1958. Binaural interaction in lateral lemniscus of cat. *Journal of Neurophysiology*, **21**, 17-23.

Rosvold, H. E. & Delgado, J. M. R. 1956. The effect on delayed alternation test performance of stimulating or destroying electrically structures within the frontal lobes of the monkey's brain. *Journal of Comparative and Physiological Psychology*, **49**, 365-372.

Rosvold, H. E., Mirsky, A. F. & Pribram, K. H. 1954. Influence of amygdalectomy on social behavior in monkeys. *Journal of Comparative and Physiological Psychology*, **47**, 173-178.

Rosvold, H. E., Mishkin, M. & Szwarcbart, M. K. 1958. Effects of subcortical lesions in monkeys on visual-discrimination and single alternation performance. *Journal of Comparative and Physiological Psychology*, **51**, 437-444.

Rosvold, H. E. & Szwarcbart, M. K. 1964. Neural structures involved in delayed-response performance. In J. M. Warren & K. Akert (Eds.), *The frontal granular cortex and behavior*. New York: McGraw-Hill. Pp. 1-15.

Routtenberg, A. 1968. The two-arousal hypothesis: Reticular formation and limbic system. *Psychological Review*, **75**, 51-80.

Routtenberg, A. & Huang, Y. H. 1968. Reticular formation and brainstem unitary activity: Effects of posterior hypothalamic and septal-limbic stimulation at reward loci. *Physiology and Behavior*, **3**, 611-617.

Routtenberg, A. & Kramis, R. C. 1967. "Foot-stomping" in the gerbil: Rewarding brain stimulation, sexual behavior, and foot shock. *Nature*, **214**, 173-174.

Routtenberg, A. & Lindy, J. 1965. Effects of the availability of rewarding septal and hypothalamic stimulation on bar pressing for food under conditions of deprivation. *Journal of Comparative and Physiological Psychology*, **60**, 158-161.

Routtenberg, A. & Malsbury, C. 1969. Brainstem pathways of reward. *Journal of Comparative and Physiological Psychology*, **68**, 22-30.

Routtenberg, A. & Olds, J. 1966. Stimulation of dorsal midbrain during septal and hypothalamic self-stimulation. *Journal of Comparative and Physiological Psychology*, **62**, 250-255.

Rowan, W. 1938. Light and seasonal reproduction in animals. *Biological Review*, **13**, 374-402.

Rowland, V. 1961. Simple non-polarizable electrode for chronic implantation. *Electroencephalography and Clinical Neurophysiology*, **13**, 290-291.

Rowland, V., Bradley, H., School, P. & Deutschman, D. 1967. Cortical steady-potential shifts in conditioning. *Conditional Reflex*, **2**, 3-22.

Rowland, V. & Goldstone, M. 1963. Appetitively conditioned and drive-related bioelectric baseline shift in cat cortex. *Electroencephalography and Clinical Neurophysiology*, **15**, 474-485.

Rozin, P. 1965. Specific hunger for thiamine: Recovery from deficiency and thiamine preference. *Journal of Comparative and Physiological Psychology*, **59**, 98-101.

Rozin, P. 1967. Specific aversions as a component of specific hungers. *Journal of Comparative and Physiological Psychology*, **64**, 237-242.

Rozin, P. 1968. Are carbohydrate and protein intakes separately regulated? *Journal of Comparative and Physiological Psychology*, **65**, 23-29.

Ruch, T. C. 1960. Somatic sensation. In T. C. Ruch & J. F. Fulton (Eds.), *Medical physiology and biophysics*. Philadelphia: Saunders.

Ruch, T. C., Fulton, J. F. & German, W. J. 1938. Sensory discrimination in monkey, chimpanzee and man after lesions of the parietal lobe. *Archives of Neurology and Psychiatry*, **39**, 919-937.

Ruch, T. C. & Shenkin, H. A. 1943. The relation of area 13 on orbital surface of frontal lobes to hyperactivity and hyperphagia in monkeys. *Journal of Neurophysiology*, **6**, 349-360.

Rusinov, V. S. 1953. An electrophysiological analysis of the connecting function in the cerebral cortex in the presence of a dominant region area. *Abstracts of Communications of the 19th International Physiology Congress*, 719-720.

Russek, M. & Morgane, P. J. 1963. Anorexic effect of intraperitoneal glucose in the hypothalamic hyperphagic cat. *Nature*, **199**, 1004-1005.

Russell, I. S. & Ochs, S. 1963. Localization of a memory trace in one cortical hemisphere and transfer to the other hemisphere. *Brain*, **86**, 37-54.

Russell, W. R. & Nathan, P. W. 1946. Traumatic amnesia. *Brain*, **69**, 280-300.

Rutherford, W. 1886. A new theory of hearing. *Journal of Anatomy and Physiology*, **21**, 166-168.

Salmoiraghi, G. C. & Burns, B. D. 1960. Notes on mechanism of rhythmic respiration. *Journal of Neurophysiology*, **23**, 14-26.

Santibañez, G. & Pinto Hamuy, T. 1957. Olfactory discrimination deficits in monkeys with temporal lobe ablations. *Journal of Comparative and Physiological Psychology*, **50**, 472-474.

Satinoff, E. 1964. Behavioral thermoregulation in response to local cooling of the rat brain. *American Journal of Physiology*, **206**, 1389-1394.

Satterfield, J. H. 1965. Evoked cortical response enhancement and attention in man. A study of responses to auditory and shock stimuli. *Electroencephalography and Clinical Neurophysiology*, 19, 470-475.

Satterfield, J. H. & Cheatum, D. 1964. Evoked cortical potential correlates of attention in human subjects. *Electroencephalography and Clinical Neurophysiology*, 17, 456-457.

Scharlock, D. P., Tucker, T. J. & Strominger, N. L. 1963. Auditory discrimination by the cat after neonatal ablation of temporal cortex. *Science*, 141, 1197-1198.

Scharrer, E. & Scharrer, B. 1963. *Neuroendocrinology*. New York: Columbia University Press.

Schiff, B. B. 1964. The effects of tegmental lesions on the reward properties of septal stimulation. *Psychonomic Science*, 1, 397-398.

Schmaltz, L. W. & Isaacson, R. L. 1966. The effects of preliminary training conditions upon DRL performance in the hippocampectomized rat. *Physiology and Behavior*, 1, 175-182.

Schnieden, H. 1962. Solution drinking in rats after dehydration and after hemorrhage. *American Journal of Physiology*, 203, 560-562.

Schreiner, L. & Kling, A. 1953. Behavioral changes following rhinencephalic injury in cat. *Journal of Neurophysiology*, 16, 643-659.

Schulman, J. L., Carleton, J. L., Whitney, G. & Whitehorn, J. C. 1957. Effect of glucagon on food intake and body weight in man. *Journal of Applied Physiology*, 11, 419-421.

Schulman, S. 1964. Impaired delayed response from thalamic lesions. *Archives of Neurology*, 11, 477-499.

Scott, E. M. 1946. Self selection of diet. I. Selection of purified components. *Journal of Nutrition*, 31, 397-406.

Scott, E. M. & Quint, E. 1946a. Self selection of diet. III. Appetite for B vitamins. *Journal of Nutrition*, 32, 285-291.

Scott, E. M. & Quint, E. 1946b. Self selection of diet. IV. Appetite for protein. *Journal of Nutrition*, 32, 293-301.

Scott, E. M. & Verney, E. L. 1947. Self selection of diet. VI. The nature of appetite for B vitamins. *Journal of Nutrition*, 34, 471-480.

Scott, E. M., Verney, E. L. & Morissey, P. 1950. Self selection of diet: XI. Appetites for calcium, magnesium, and potassium. *Journal of Nutrition*, 41, 187-202.

Scoville, W. B., 1954. The limbic lobe in man. *Journal of Neurosurgery*, 11, 64-66.

Scoville, W. B., & Milner, B. 1957. Loss of recent memory after bilateral hippocampal lesions. *Journal of Neurology, Neurosurgery, and Psychiatry*, 20, 11-21.

Semans, J. H. & Langworthy, O. R. 1938. Observations on the neurophysiology of sexual function in the male cat. *Journal of Urology*, 40, 836-846.

Sem-Jacobsen, C. W. & Torkildsen, A. 1960. Depth recording and electrical stimulation in the human brain. In E. R. Ramey & D. S. O'Doherty (Eds.), *Electrical studies on the unanesthetized brain*. New York: Hoeber. Pp. 275-290.

Semmes, J. 1965. A non-tactual factor in astereognosis. *Neuropsychologia*, 3, 295-315.

Semmes, J. & Mishkin, M. 1965. Somatosensory loss in monkeys after ipsilateral cortical ablation. *Journal of Neurophysiology*, 28, 473-486.

Semmes, J., Weinstein, S., Ghent, L. & Teuber, H. L. 1955. Spatial orientation in man after cerebral injury—

I: Analysis by locus of lesion. *Journal of Psychology*, 39, 227-244.

Semmes, J., Weinstein, S., Ghent, L. & Teuber, H. L. 1960. *Somatosensory changes after penetrating brain wounds in man*. Cambridge, Mass.: Harvard University Press.

Sengstake, C. B. 1968. Habituation and activity patterns of rats with large hippocampal lesions under various drive conditions. *Journal of Comparative and Physiological Psychology*, 65, 504-506.

Settlage, P. H. & Bogumill, G. P. 1955. Use of radioactive cobalt for the production of brain lesions in animals. *Journal of Comparative and Physiological Psychology*, 48, 208-210.

Seward, J. P., Uyeda, A. A. & Olds, J. 1959. Resistance to extinction following cranial self-stimulation. *Journal of Comparative and Physiological Psychology*, 52, 294-299.

Seward, J. P., Uyeda, A. A., & Olds, J. 1960. Reinforcing effect of brain stimulation on runway performance as a function of interval between trials. *Journal of Comparative and Physiological Psychology*, 53, 224-228.

Shankweiler, D. & Studdert-Kennedy, M. 1967. Identification of consonants and vowels presented to left and right ears. *Quarterly Journal of Experimental Psychology*, 19, 59-63.

Share, I., Martyniuk, E. & Grossman, M. I. 1952. Effect of prolonged intragastric feeding on oral food intake in dogs. *American Journal of Physiology*, 169, 229-235.

Sharma, K. N., Anand, B. K., Dua, S. & Singh, B. 1961. Role of stomach in regulation of activities of hypothalamic feeding centers. *American Journal of Physiology*, 201, 593-598.

Sharpless, S. 1964. Reorganization of function in the nervous system—use and disuse. *Annual Review of Physiology*, 26, 357-388.

Sharpless, S. & Jasper, H. 1956. Habituation of the arousal reaction. *Brain*, 79, 655-680.

Shealy, C. N. & Peele, T. L. 1957. Studies on amygdaloid nucleus of cat. *Journal of Neurophysiology*, 20, 125-139.

Sherrington, C. S. 1906. Observations on the scratch-reflex in the spinal dog. *Journal of Physiology*, 34, 1-50.

Sholl, D. A. 1956. *The organization of the cerebral cortex*. London: Methuen.

Shower, E. G. & Biddulph, R. 1931. Differential pitch sensitivity of the ear. *Journal of the Acoustical Society of America*. 3, 275-287.

Shurrager, P. S. & Culler, E. 1940. Conditioning the spinal dog. *Journal of Experimental Psychology*, 26, 133-159.

Sidman, M. 1953. Avoidance conditioning with brief shock and no exteroceptive warning signal. *Science*, 118, 157-158.

Sidman, M., Brady, J. V., Boren, J. J., Conrad, D. G. & Schulman, A. 1955. Reward schedules and behavior maintained by intracranial self-stimulation. *Science*, 122, 830-831.

Simmons, F. B., Epley, J. M., Lummis, R. C., Guttman, N., Frishkopf, L. S., Harmon, L. D. & Zwicker, E. 1965. Auditory nerve: Electrical stimulation in man. *Science*, 148, 104-106.

Sinclair, D. C. 1955. Cutaneous sensation and the doctrine of specific energy. *Brain*, 78, 584-614.

Singh, D. & Meyer, D. R. 1968. Eating and drinking by rats with lesions of the septum and the ventromedial hypothalamus. *Journal of Comparative and Physiological Psychology*, 65, 163–166.

Sivian, L. J. & White, S. D. 1933. On minimum audible sound fields. *Journal of the Acoustical Society of America*, 4, 288–321.

Skoglund, S. 1956. Anatomical and physiological studies of knee joint innervation in the cat. *Acta Physiologica Scandinavica*, 36 (Suppl. 124), 1–101.

Smith, C. J. 1959. Mass action and early environment in the rat. *Journal of Comparative and Physiological Psychology*, 52, 154–156.

Smith, M. H., Jr. 1966. Effects of intravenous injections on eating. *Journal of Comparative and Physiological Psychology*, 61, 11–14.

Smith, R. W. & McCann, S. M. 1964. Increased and decreased water intake in the rat with hypothalamic lesions. In M. J. Wayner (Ed.), *Thirst*. New York: Macmillan. Pp. 381–394.

Smith, S. 1908. The limits of educability in *Paramecium*. *Journal of Comparative Neurology*, 18, 499–510.

Snider, R. S. 1950. Recent contributions to the anatomy and physiology of the cerebellum. *Archives of Neurology and Psychiatry*, 64, 196–219.

Snyder, F. 1967. Autonomic nervous system manifestations during sleep and dreaming. *Research Publications of the Association for Research in Nervous and Mental Disease*, 45, 469–487.

Sokolov, E. N. 1960. Neuronal models and the orienting reflex. In M. A. B. Brazier (Ed.), *The central nervous system and behavior: Transactions of third conference.* New York: Macy Foundation. Pp. 187–276.

Solomon, R. L. & Wynne, L. C. 1954. Traumatic avoidance learning: The principles of anxiety conservation and partial irreversibility. *Psychological Review*, 61, 353–385.

Sommer, S. R., Novin, D. & LeVine, M. 1967. Food and water intake after intrahypothalamic injections of carbachol in the rabbit. *Science*, 156, 983–984.

Sommers, P. van. 1963. Carbon dioxide escape and avoidance behavior in the brown rat. *Journal of Comparative and Physiological Psychology*, 56, 584–589.

Sperry, R. W. 1944. Optic nerve regeneration with return of vision in anurans. *Journal of Neurophysiology*, 7, 57–70.

Sperry, R. W. 1948. Orderly patterning of synaptic association in regeneration of intracentral fiber tracts mediating visuomotor coordination. *Anatomical Record*, 102, 63–76.

Sperry, R. W. 1951. Mechanisms of neural maturation. In S. S. Stevens (Ed.), *Handbook of experimental psychology*. New York: Wiley. Pp. 236–280.

Sperry, R. W. 1952. Neurology and the mind-brain problem. *American Scientist*, 40, 291–312. (Reprinted: R. L. Isaacson [Ed.], *Basic readings in neuropsychology*. New York: Harper, 1964. Pp. 403–429.)

Sperry, R. W. 1962. Some general aspects of interhemispheric integration. In V. B. Mountcastle (Ed.), *Interhemispheric relations and cerebral dominance*. Baltimore: Johns Hopkins Press. Pp. 43–49.

Sperry, R. W. 1963. Chemoaffinity in the orderly growth of nerve fiber patterns and connections. *Proceedings of the National Academy of Sciences of the United States of America*, 50, 703–710.

Sperry, R. W. & Gazzaniga, M. S. 1967. Language following surgical disconnection of the hemispheres. In F. L. Darley (Ed.), *Brain mechanisms underlying speech and language*, New York: Grune & Stratton. Pp. 108–121.

Sperry, R. W. & Miner, N. 1955. Pattern perception following insertion of mica plates into visual cortex. *Journal of Comparative and Physiological Psychology*, 48, 463–469.

Spiegel, E. A., Miller, H. R. & Oppenheimer, M. J. 1940. Forebrain and rage reaction. *Transactions of the American Neurological Association*, 66, 127–131.

Spiegel, E. A. & Price, J. B. 1939. Origin of the quick component of labyrinthine nystagmus. *Archives of Otolaryngology*, 30, 576–588.

Spiegel, E. A. & Wycis, H. T. 1961. Stimulation of the brain stem and basal ganglia in man. In D. E. Sheer (Ed.), *Electrical stimulation of the brain*. Austin: University of Texas Press.

Spinelli, D. N. 1966. Visual receptive fields in the cat's retina: Complications. *Science*, 152, 1768–1769.

Spinelli, D. N. & Pribram, K. H. 1966. Changes in visual recovery functions produced by temporal lobe stimulation in monkeys. *Electroencephalography and Clinical Neurophysiology*, 20, 44–49.

Spinelli, D. N., Pribram, K. H. & Weingarten, M. 1965. Centrifugal optic nerve responses evoked by auditory and somatic stimulation. *Experimental Neurology*, 12, 303–319.

Spinelli, D. N. & Weingarten, M. 1966. Afferent and efferent activity in single units of the cat's optic nerve. *Experimental Neurology*, 15, 347–362.

Spong, P., Haider, M. & Lindsley, D. B. 1965. Selective attentiveness and cortical evoked responses to visual and auditory stimuli. *Science*, 148, 395–397.

Sprague, J. M. 1966. Interaction of cortex and superior colliculus in mediation of visually guided behavior in the cat. *Science*, 153, 1544–1547.

Sprague, J. M. & Chambers, W. W. 1954. Control of posture by reticular formation and cerebellum in the intact, anesthetized and unanesthetized and in the decerebrated cat. *American Journal of Physiology*, 176, 52–64.

Sprague, J. M., Chambers, W. W. & Stellar, E. 1961. Attentive, affective, and adaptive behavior in the cat. *Science*, 133, 165–173.

Stamm, J. S. 1955. The function of the median cerebral cortex in maternal behavior of rats. *Journal of Comparative and Physiological Psychology*, 48, 347–356.

Stark, P. & Boyd, E. S. 1963. Effects of cholinergic drugs on hypothalamic self-stimulation response rates of dogs. *American Journal of Physiology*, 205, 745–748.

Stein, D. G. & Kirkby, R. J. 1967. The effects of training on passive avoidance deficits in rats with hippocampal lesions: A reply to Isaacson, Olton, Bauer, and Swart. *Psychonomic Science*, 7, 7–8.

Stein, L. 1958. Secondary reinforcement established with subcortical stimulation. *Science*, 127, 466–467.

Stein, L. 1962a. Effects and interactions of imipramine, chlorpromazine, reserpine and amphetamine on self-stimulation: Possible neurophysiological basis of depression. *Recent Advances in Biological Psychiatry*, 4, 288–308.

Stein, L. 1962b. An analysis of stimulus-duration preference in self-stimulation of the brain. *Journal of Comparative and Physiological Psychology*, 55, 405–414.

Stein, L. 1965. Facilitation of avoidance behavior by positive brain stimulation. *Journal of Comparative and Physiological Psychology*, **60**, 9–16.

Stein, L. 1966. Noradrenergic substrates of positive reinforcement: Site of motivational action of amphetamine and chlorpromazine. *Proceedings of the 5th International Congress of the Collegium Internationale Neuropsychopharmacologicum*, P. 765.

Stellar, E. 1954. The physiology of motivation. *Psychological Review*, **61**, 5–22.

Stevens, S. S. 1957. On the psychophysical law. *Psychological Review*, **64**, 153–181.

Stevens, S. S. 1961. The psychophysics of sensory function. In W. A. Rosenblith (Ed.), *Sensory communication*. New York: Wiley.

Stone, C. P. 1925. The effects of cerebral destruction on the sexual behavior of rabbits. II. The frontal and parietal regions. *American Journal of Physiology*, **72**, 372–385.

Stotler, W. A. 1953. An experimental study of the cells and connections of the superior olivary complex of the cat. *Journal of Comparative Neurology*, **98**, 401–431.

Stowe, F. R. & Miller, A. T. 1957. The effect of amphetamine on food intake in rats with hypothalamic hyperphagia. *Experientia*, **13**, 114–115.

Stricker, E. M. 1966. Extracellular fluid volume and thirst. *American Journal of Physiology*, **211**, 232–238.

Strümpell, A. 1877. Ein Beitrag zur Theorie des Schlafs. *Archiv für die Gesamte Physiologie des Menschen und der Tiere*, **15**, 573–574.

Stunkard, A. J., Van Itallie, T. B. & Reis, B. B. 1955. The mechanism of satiety: Effect of glucagon on gastric hunger contractions in man. *Proceedings of the Society for Experimental Biology and Medicine of New York*, **89**, 258–261.

Stunkard, A. J. & Wolff, H. G. 1954. Correlation of arteriovenous glucose differences, gastric hunger contractions and the experience of hunger in man. *Federation Proceedings*, **13**, 147. (Abstract)

Subirana, A. 1958. The prognosis in aphasia in relation to cerebral dominance and handedness. *Brain*, **81**, 415–425.

Supa, M., Cotzin, M. & Dallenbach, K. M. 1944. "Facial vision:" The perception of obstacles by the blind. *American Journal of Psychology*, **57**, 133–183.

Sutton, H. E. 1961. *Genes, enzymes and inherited diseases*. New York: Holt.

Swann, H. G. 1934. The function of the brain in olfaction. II. The results of destruction of olfactory and other nervous structures upon the discrimination of odors. *Journal of Comparative Neurology*, **59**, 175–201.

Swisher, L. P. 1967. Auditory intensity discrimination in patients with temporal-lobe damage. *Cortex*, **3**, 179–193.

Szentágothai, J. 1948. Anatomical considerations of monosynaptic reflex arcs. *Journal of Neurophysiology*, **11**, 445–454.

Szentágothai, J. 1950. The elementary vestibulo-ocular reflex arc. *Journal of Neurophysiology*, **13**, 395–407.

Szentágothai, J. 1964a. Anatomical aspects of junctional transformation. In R. W. Gerard & J. W. Duyff (Eds.), *Information processing in the nervous system*. Amsterdam: Excerpta Medica Foundation. Pp. 119–136.

Szentágothai, J. 1964b. Neuronal and synaptic arrangement in the substantia gelatinosa Rolandi. *Journal of Comparative Neurology*, **122**, 219–239.

Talairach, J., Hécaen, H., David, M., Monnier, M. & Ajuriaguerra, J. de. 1949. Recherches sur la coagulation thérapeutique des structures souscorticales chez l'homme. *Revue Neurologique*, **81**, 4–24.

Talland, G. A. 1965. A test of the consolidation theory with ECT patients. *Psychonomic Science*, **2**, 339–340.

Tapper, D. N. 1964. Cutaneous slowly adapting mechanoreceptors in the cat. *Science*, **143**, 53–54.

Tasaki, I. 1954. Nerve impulses in individual auditory nerve fibers of guinea pig. *Journal of Neurophysiology*, **17**, 97–122.

Taylor, A. N. & Farrell, G. 1962. Effects of brain stem lesions on aldosterone and cortisol secretion. *Endocrinology*, **70**, 556–566.

Teitelbaum, H. 1964. A comparison of effects of orbitofrontal and hippocampal lesions upon discrimination learning and reversal in the cat. *Experimental Neurology*, **9**, 452–462.

Teitelbaum, H. & Milner, P. M. 1963. Activity changes following partial hippocampal lesions in rats. *Journal of Comparative and Physiological Psychology*, **56**, 284–289.

Teitelbaum, H., Sharpless, S. K. & Byck, R. 1968. Role of somatosensory cortex in interhemispheric transfer of tactile habits. *Journal of Comparative and Physiological Psychology*, **66**, 623–632.

Teitelbaum, P. 1955. Sensory control of hypothalamic hyperphagia. *Journal of Comparative and Physiological Psychology*, **48**, 156–163.

Teitelbaum, P. 1957. Random and food-directed activity in hyperphagic and normal rats. *Journal of Comparative and Physiological Psychology*, **50**, 486–490.

Teitelbaum, P. & Cytawa, J. 1965. Spreading depression and recovery from lateral hypothalamic damage. *Science*, **147**, 61–63.

Teitelbaum, P. & Epstein, A. N. 1962. The lateral hypothalamic syndrome: Recovery of feeding and drinking after lateral hypothalamic lesions. *Psychological Review*, **69**, 74–90.

Teitelbaum, P. & Stellar, E. 1954. Recovery from failure to eat produced by hypothalamic lesions. *Science*, **120**, 894–895.

Tenen, S. S. 1965. Retrograde amnesia from electroconvulsive shock in a one-trial appetitive learning task. *Science*, **148**, 1248–1250.

Terzian, H. & Dalle Ore, G. 1955. Syndrome of Klüver and Bucy reproduced in man by bilateral removal of the temporal lobes. *Neurology*, **5**, 373–380.

Teuber, H. L. 1955. Physiological psychology. *Annual Review of Psychology*, **6**, 267–296.

Teuber, H. L. 1960. Perception. In J. Field (Ed.), *Handbook of physiology. Neurophysiology*, Vol. 3. Washington, D.C.: American Physiological Society, Pp. 1595–1668.

Teuber, H. L., Battersby, W. S. & Bender, M. B. 1960. *Visual field defects after penetrating missile wounds of the brain*. Cambridge, Mass.: Harvard University Press.

Teuber, H. L. & Mishkin, M. 1954. Judgment of visual and postural vertical after brain injury. *Journal of Psychology*, **38**, 161–175.

Thomas, G. J. & Otis, L. S. 1958. Effects of rhinencephalic lesions on conditioning of avoidance responses in the rat. *Journal of Comparative and Physiological Psychology*, **51**, 130–134.

Thompson, E. L. 1917. An analysis of the learning process

in the snail. *Physa gyrina* Say. *Behavioral Monographs,* 3, (14), 1-97.

Thompson, R. 1963. Thalamic structures critical for retention of an avoidance conditioned response in rats. *Journal of Comparative and Physiological Psychology,* 56, 261-267.

Thompson, R. & McConnell, J. V. 1955. Classical conditioning in the planarian, *Dugesia dorotocephala. Journal of Comparative and Physiological Psychology,* 48, 65-68.

Thompson, R. F. 1960. Function of auditory cortex of cat in frequency discrimination. *Journal of Neurophysiology,* 23, 321-334.

Thompson, R. F. & Sindberg, R. M. 1960. Auditory response fields in association and motor cortex of cat. *Journal of Neurophysiology,* 23, 87-105.

Thompson, R. F. & Spencer, W. A. 1966. Habituation: A model phenomenon for the study of neuronal substrates of behavior. *Psychological Review,* 73, 16-43.

Thompson, W. R. 1953. Exploratory behavior as a function of hunger in "bright" and "dull" rats. *Journal of Comparative and Physiological Psychology,* 46, 323-326.

Thorndike, E. L. 1898. Animal intelligence: An experimental study of the associative processes in animals. *Psychological Review Monograph Supplements,* 2, (4 Whole No. 8), 1-109.

Thorndike, E. L. 1931. *Human learning.* New York: Century.

Thorpe, W. H. 1956. *Learning and instinct in animals.* London: Metheun.

Tinbergen, N. 1951. *The study of instinct.* Oxford: Clarendon.

Tolman, E. C. 1932. *Purposive behavior in animals and man.* New York: Appleton.

Tonndorf, J. 1960. Discussion of anatomy and physiology of peripheral auditory mechanisms. In G. L. Rasmussen & W. F. Windle (Eds.), *Neural mechanisms of the auditory and vestibular systems.* Springfield, Ill.: Thomas. Pp. 100-103.

Towbin, E. J. 1955. Thirst and hunger behavior in normal dogs and the effects of vagotomy and sympathectomy. *American Journal of Physiology,* 182, 377-382.

Towe, A. L. & Jabbur, S. J. 1961. Cortical inhibition of neurons in dorsal column nuclei of cat. *Journal of Neurophysiology,* 24, 488-498.

Tsuchitani, C. & Boudreau, J. C. 1966. Single unit analysis of cat superior olive S segment with tonal stimuli. *Journal of Neurophysiology,* 29, 684-697.

Tucker, D. 1963. Olfactory, vomeronasal and trigeminal receptor responses to odorants. In J. Zotterman (Ed.), *Olfaction and taste.* Oxford: Pergamon. Pp. 45-69.

Tucker, D. & Beidler, L. M. 1956. Autonomic nervous system influence on olfactory receptors. *American Journal of Physiology,* 187, 637. (Abstract)

Tunturi, A. R. 1944. Audio frequency localization in the acoustic cortex of the dog. *American Journal of Physiology,* 141, 397-403.

Tunturi, A. R. 1945. Further afferent connections of the acoustic cortex of the dog. *American Journal of Physiology,* 144, 389-394.

Tunturi, A. R. 1952. A difference in the representation of auditory signals for the left and right ears in the isofrequency contours of right middle ectosylvian auditory cortex of the dog. *American Journal of Physiology,* 168, 712-727.

Ursin, R., Ursin, H. & Olds, J. 1966. Self-stimulation of

hippocampus in rats. *Journal of Comparative and Physiological Psychology,* 61, 353-359.

Valenstein, E. S. 1965. Independence of approach and escape reactions to electrical stimulation of the brain. *Journal of Comparative and Physiological Psychology,* 60, 20-30.

Valenstein, E. S. & Campbell, J. F. 1966. Medial forebrain bundle—lateral hypothalamic area and reinforcing brain stimulation. *American Journal of Physiology,* 210, 270-274.

Valenstein, E. S., Cox, V. C. & Kakolewski, J. W. 1968. Modification of motivated behavior elicited by electrical stimulation of the hypothalamus. *Science,* 159, 1119-1121.

Valenstein, E. S. & Meyers, W. J. 1964. Rate-independent test of reinforcing consequences of brain stimulation. *Journal of Comparative and Physiological Psychology,* 57, 52-60.

Valenstein, E. S., Riss, W. & Young, W. C. 1955. Experiential and genetic factors in the organization of sexual behavior in male guinea pigs. *Journal of Comparative and Physiological Psychology,* 48, 397-403.

Valenstein, E. S. & Valenstein, T. 1964. Interaction of positive and negative reinforcing neural systems. *Science,* 145, 1456-1458.

Valenstein, E. S. & Young, W. C. 1955. An experiential factor influencing the effectiveness of testosterone propionate in eliciting sexual behavior in male guinea pigs. *Endocrinology,* 56, 173-177.

Vanderwolf, C. H. 1962. Medial thalamic functions in voluntary behavior. *Canadian Journal of Psychology,* 16, 318-330.

Vanderwolf, C. H. 1963a. The effect of medial thalamic lesions on previously established fear-motivated behavior. *Canadian Journal of Psychology,* 17, 183-187.

Vanderwolf, C. H. 1968. Hippocampal electrical activity and voluntary movement in the rat. Technical Report No. 17, May, MacMaster University.

Vaughan, E. & Fisher, A. E. 1962. Male sexual behavior induced by intracranial electrical stimulation. *Science,* 137, 758-760.

Verney, E. B. 1947. The antidiuretic hormone and the factors which determine its release. *Proceedings of the Royal Society,* B135, 25-106.

Victor, M. & Yakovlev, P. I. 1955. S. S. Korsakoff's psychic disorder. *Neurology,* 5, 394-407.

Villablanca, J. 1965. The electrocorticogram in the chronic *cerveau isolé* cat. *Electroencephalography and Clinical Neurophysiology,* 19, 576-586.

Vogt, O. & Vogt, C. 1919. Ergebnisse unserer Hirnforschung. *Journal für Psychologie und Neurologie,* 25, 277-462.

Volkmann, A. W. 1844. In R. Wagner (Ed.), *Handwörterbuch der Physiologie.* Vol. 2. Pp. 521-526. Cited by E. G. Boring, *A history of experimental psychology.* New York: Appleton, 1929. P. 89.

Wada, J. 1949. [A new method for the determination of the side of cerebral speech dominance. A preliminary report on the intracarotid injection of Sodium Amytal in man.] *Igaku to Seibutsugaku* [*Medicine and Biology*], 14, 221-222. (In Japanese).

Wade, M. 1947. The effect of sedatives upon delayed response in monkeys following removal of the prefrontal lobes. *Journal of Neurophysiology,* 10, 57-61.

Wagner, J. W. & De Groot, J. 1963. Changes in feeding

behavior after intracerebral injections in the rat. *American Journal of Physiology,* **204,** 483-487.

Wald, G. 1959. The photoreceptor process in vision. In J. Field (Ed.), *Handbook of physiology. Neurophysiology.* Vol. 1. Washington, D.C.: American Physiological Society. Pp. 671-692.

Waldeyer, W. 1891. Über einige neuere Forschungen im Gebiete der Anatomie des Centralnervensystems. *Deutsche medizinische Wochenschrift,* **17,** 1352-1356.

Walk, R. D. & Gibson, E. J. 1961. A comparative and analytical study of visual depth perception. *Psychological Monographs,* **75,** 1-44.

Walker, A. E. 1940. A cytoarchitectural study of the prefrontal area of the macaque monkey. *Journal of Comparative Neurology.* **73,** 59-86.

Walker, E. L. 1958. Action decrement and its relation to learning. *Psychological Review,* **65,** 129-142.

Wall, P. D. 1960. Cord cells responding to touch, damage, and temperature of skin. *Journal of Neurophysiology,* **23,** 197-210.

Wall, P. D. 1961. Two transmission systems for skin sensations. In W. A. Rosenblith, (Ed.), *Sensory communication.* New York: Wiley. Pp. 475-496.

Waller, W. H. 1940. Progression movements elicited by subthalamic stimulation. *Journal of Neurophysiology,* **3,** 300-307.

Walsh, E. G. 1957. *Physiology of the nervous system.* London: Longmans, Green.

Walsh, R. R. 1956. Single cell spike activity in the olfactory bulb. *American Journal of Physiology,* **186,** 255-257.

Walter, W. G., Cooper, R., Aldridge, V. J., McCallum, W. C. & Winter, A. L. 1964. Contingent negative variation: An electric sign of sensorimotor association and expectancy in the human brain. *Nature,* **203,** 380-384.

Wang, G. H. 1923. Relation between "spontaneous" activity and oestrus cycle in the white rat. *Comparative Psychology Monographs,* **2,** No. 6.

Wangensteen, O. H. & Carlson, A. J. 1931. Hunger sensations in a patient after total gastrectomy. *Proceedings of the Society for Experimental Biology and Medicine of New York,* **28,** 545-547.

Ward, J. W. 1938. The influence of posture on responses elicitable from the cortex cerebri of cats. *Journal of Neurophysiology,* **1,** 463-475.

Warren, J. M. 1964. The behavior of carnivores and primates with lesions in the prefrontal cortex. In J. M. Warren & K. Akert (Eds.), *The frontal granular cortex and behavior.* New York: McGraw-Hill. Pp. 168-191.

Warren, R. M. & Pfaffmann, C. 1959. Suppression of the sweet taste by potassium gymnemate. *Journal of Applied Physiology,* **14,** 40-42.

Warrington, E. K. & Weiskrantz, L. 1968. New method of testing long-term retention with special reference to amnesic patients. *Nature,* **217,** 972-974.

Wasman, M. & Flynn, J. P. 1962. Directed attack elicited from hypothalamus. *Archives of Neurology,* **6,** 220-227.

Watson, J. B. 1926. Behaviorism: A psychology based on reflexes. *Archives of Neurology and Psychiatry,* **15,** 185-204.

Watson, J. D. 1965. *Molecular biology of the gene.* New York: Benjamin.

Weddell, G. 1941. The pattern of cutaneous innervation in relation to cutaneous sensibility. *Journal of Anatomy,* **75,** 346-367.

Weddell, G. 1961. Receptors for somatic sensation. In M. A. B. Brazier (Ed.), *Brain and behavior.* Vol. 1. Washington, D.C.: American Institute of Biological Sciences. Pp. 13-48.

Weddell, G., Sinclair, D. C. & Feindel, W. H. 1948. An anatomical basis for alterations in quality of pain sensibility. *Journal of Neurophysiology,* **11,** 99-109.

Weinberger, N. M. & Lindsley, D. B. 1964. Behavioral and electroencephalographic arousal to contrasting novel stimuli. *Science,* **144,** 1355-1356.

Weingarten, M. & Spinelli, D. N. 1966. Retinal receptive field changes produced by auditory and somatic stimulation. *Experimental Neurology,* **15,** 363-376.

Weinstein, S. 1962. Differences in effects of brain wounds implicating right or left hemispheres: Differential effects on certain intellectual and complex perceptual functions. In V. B. Mountcastle (Ed.), *Interhemispheric relations and cerebral dominance.* Baltimore: Johns Hopkins Press. Pp. 159-176.

Weisenberg, T. & McBride, K. E. 1935. *Aphasia, a clinical and psychological study,* New York: Commonwealth Fund.

Weiskrantz, L. 1956. Behavioral changes associated with ablation of the amygdaloid complex in monkeys. *Journal of Comparative and Physiological Psychology,* **49,** 381-391.

Weiskrantz, L. 1963. Contour discrimination in a young monkey with striate cortex ablation. *Neuropsychologia,* **1,** 145-164.

Weiskrantz, L., Mihailović, C. & Gross, C. G. 1960. Effects of stimulation of frontal cortex and hippocampus on behavior in the monkey. *Science,* **131,** 1443-1444.

Weiskrantz, L. & Mishkin, M. 1958. Effects of temporal and frontal cortical lesions on auditory discrimination in monkeys. *Brain,* **81,** 406-414.

Weiss, B. & Laties, V. G. 1961. Behavioral thermoregulation. *Science,* **133,** 1338-1344.

Weiss, J. M., McEwen, B. S., Silva, M. T. A. & Kalkut, M. F. 1969. Pituitary-adrenal influences on fear responding. *Science,* **163,** 197-199.

Weiss, P. 1926. The relations between central and peripheral coordination. *Journal of Comparative Neurology,* **40,** 241-251.

Weiss, P. 1952. Central versus peripheral factors in the development of coordination. *Research Publications of the Association for Research in Nervous and Mental Disease.* **30,** 3-23.

Welch, K. & Stuteville, P. 1958. Experimental production of unilateral neglect in monkeys. *Brain,* **81,** 341-347.

Wernicke, C. 1874. *Der aphasische Symptomencomplex.* Breslau: Cohn & Weigert.

Wersäll, J. 1960. Electron micrographic studies of vestibular hair cell innervation. In G. L. Rasmussen & W. F. Windle (Eds.), *Neural mechanisms of the auditory and vestibular systems.* Springfield, Ill.: Thomas. Pp. 247-257.

Wetzel, M. C. 1963. Self-stimulation aftereffects and runway performance in the rat. *Journal of Comparative and Physiological Psychology,* **56,** 673-678.

Wever, E. G. & Bray, C. W. 1930. Present possibilities for auditory theory. *Psychological Review,* **37,** 365-380.

Wheatley, M. D. 1944. The hypothalamus and affective behavior in cats: A study of the effects of experimental lesions with anatomical correlations. *Archives of Neurology and Psychiatry,* **52,** 296-316.

Wichterman, R. 1953. *The biology of Paramecium.* New York: Blakiston.

Wiesel, T. N. & Hubel, D. H. 1963a. Effects of visual deprivation on morphology and physiology of cells in the cat's lateral geniculate body. *Journal of Neurophysiology*, 26, 978-993.

Wiesel, T. N. & Hubel, D. H. 1963b. Single-cell responses in striate cortex of kittens deprived of vision in one eye. *Journal of Neurophysiology*, 26, 1003-1017.

Wiesel, T. N. & Hubel, D. H. 1965. Comparison of the effects of unilateral and bilateral eye closure on cortical unit responses in kittens. *Journal of Neurophysiology*, 28, 1029-1040.

Wiesel, T. N. & Hubel, D. H. 1966. Spatial and chromatic interactions in the lateral geniculate body of the rhesus monkey. *Journal of Neurophysiology*, 29, 1115-1156.

Wilkins, L., Jones, H. W. Holman, G. H. & Stempfel, R. S. 1958. Masculinization of the female fetus associated with administration of oral and intramuscular progestins during gestation. Nonadrenal female pseudohermaphrodism. *Journal of Clinical Endocrinology*, 18, 559-585.

Wilkinson, H. A. & Peele, T. L. 1963. Intracranial self-stimulation in cats. *Journal of Comparative Neurology*, 121, 425-440.

Williams, D. & Gassel, M. M. 1962. Visual function in patients with homonymous hemianopia: Part I. The visual fields. *Brain*, 85, 175-250.

Williams, D. R. & Teitelbaum, P. 1959. Some observations on the starvation resulting from lateral hypothalamic lesions. *Journal of Comparative and Physiological Psychology*, 52, 458-465.

Williams, M. & Pennybacker, J. 1954. Memory disturbance in third ventricle tumours. *Journal of Neurology, Neurosurgery, and Psychiatry*, 17, 115-123.

Wilson, M. 1957. Effects of circumscribed cortical lesions upon somesthetic and visual discrimination in the monkey. *Journal of Comparative and Physiological Psychology*, 50, 630-635.

Wilson, M., Wilson, W. A. & Chiang, H.-M. 1963. Formation of tactual learning sets. *Journal of Comparative and Physiological Psychology*, 56, 732-734.

Wilson, W. A. & Mishkin, M. 1959. Comparison of the effects of inferotemporal and lateral occipital lesions on visually guided behavior in monkeys. *Journal of Comparative and Physiological Psychology*, 52, 10-17.

Witt, D. M., Keller, A. D., Batsel, H. L. & Lynch, J. R. 1952. Absence of thirst and resultant syndrome associated with anterior hypothalamectomy in the dog. *American Journal of Physiology*, 171, 780. (Abstract)

Wolf, G. 1968a. Thalamic and tegmental mechanisms for sodium intake: Anatomical and functional relations to lateral hypothalamus. *Physiology and Behavior*, 3, 997-1002.

Wolf, G. 1968b. Lateral hypothalamic function: Relations between data and theory. Discussion at Eastern Psychological Association meeting. Washington, D.C., April.

Wolf, G. & Sutin, J. 1966. Fiber degeneration after lateral hypothalamic lesions in the rat. *Journal of Comparative Neurology*, 127, 137-156.

Woodbury, D. M. 1952. Effect of adrenocortical steriods and adrenocorticotrophic hormone on electroshock seizure threshold. *Journal of Pharmacology and Experimental Therapeutics*, 105, 27-36.

Woodbury, D. M. 1954. Effect of hormones on brain excitability and electrolytes. *Recent Progress in Hormone Research*, 10, 65-104.

Woods, J. W. 1964. Behavior of chronic decerebrate rats. *Journal of Neurophysiology*, 27, 635-644.

Woodworth, R. S. & Sherrington, C. S. 1904. A pseud-affective reflex and its spinal path. *Journal of Physiology*, 31, 234-243.

Woolsey, C. N. 1958. Organization of somatic sensory and motor areas of the cerebral cortex. In H. F. Harlow & C. N. Woolsey (Eds.), *Biological and biochemical bases of behavior.* Madison: University of Wisconsin Press. Pp. 63-81.

Woolsey, C. N. 1960. Organization of cortical auditory system: A review and a synthesis. In G. L. Rasmussen & W. F. Windle (Eds.), *Neural mechanisms of the auditory and vestibular systems.* Springfield, Ill.: Thomas. Pp. 165-180.

Woolsey, C. N. 1961. Organization of cortical auditory system. In W. A. Rosenblith Ed., *Sensory communication.* New York: Wiley. Pp. 235-257.

Woolsey, C. N. & Walzl, E. M. 1942. Topical projection of nerve fibers from local regions of the cochlea to the cerebral cortex of the cat. *Bulletin of the Johns Hopkins Hospital*, 71, 315-344.

Worden, F. G. & Marsh, J. T. 1963. Amplitude changes of auditory potentials evoked at cochlear nucleus during acoustic habituation. *Electroencephalography and Clinical Neurophysiology*, 15, 866-881.

Wortis, H., Stein, M. H. & Joliffe, N. 1942. Fibre dissociation in peripheral neuropathy. *Archives of Internal Medicine*, 69, 222-237.

Wurtz, R. H. & Olds, J. 1963. Amygdaloid stimulation and operant reinforcement in the rat. *Journal of Comparative and Physiological Psychology*, 56, 941-949.

Wyrwicka, W., Dobrzecka, C. & Tarnecki, R. 1959. On the instrumental conditioned reaction evoked by electrical stimulation of the hypothalamus. *Science*, 130, 336-337.

Wyrwicka, W. & Doty, R. W. 1966. Feeding induced in cats by electrical stimulation of the brain stem. *Experimental Brain Research*, 1, 152-160.

Yerkes, R. M. 1912. The intelligence of earthworms. *Journal of Animal Behavior*, 2, 332-352.

Yoshii, N. & Hockaday, W. J. 1958. Conditioning of frequency-characteristic repetitive electroencephalographic response with intermittent photic stimulation. *Electroencephalography and Clinical Neurophysiology*, 10, 487-502.

Yoshii, N. & Ogura, H. 1960. Studies on the unit discharge of brainstem reticular formation in the cat. I. Changes of reticular unit discharge following conditioning procedure. *Medical Journal of Osaka University*, 11, 1-17.

Young, W. C., Goy, R. W. & Phoenix, C. H. 1964. Hormones and sexual behavior. *Science*, 143, 212-218.

Zbrożyna, A. W. 1960. Defense reactions from the amygdala and the stria terminalis. *Journal of Physiology*, 153, 27P-28P.

Zimmerman, F. T. & Ross, S. 1944. Effect of glutamic acid and other amino acids on maze learning in the white rat. *Archives of Neurology and Psychiatry*, 51, 446-451.

Zingg, R. M. 1940. Feral man and extreme cases of isolation. *American Journal of Psychology*, 53, 487-517.

Zotterman, Y. 1939. Touch, pain and tickling: An electro-physiological investigation on cutaneous sensory nerves. *Journal of Physiology*, **95**, 1–28.

Zotterman, Y. 1959. Thermal sensations. In J. Field, *Handbook of physiology. Neurophysiology.* Vol. 1. Washington, D. C.: American Physiological Society. Pp. 431–458.

Zubek, J. P. 1951. Studies in somesthesis: I. Role of the somesthetic cortex in roughness discrimination in the rat. *Journal of Comparative and Physiological Psychology*, **44**, 339–353.

Zubek, J. P. 1952a. Studies in somesthesis: II. Role of somatic sensory areas I and II in roughness discrimination. *Journal of Neurophysiology*, **15**, 401–408.

Zubek, J. P. 1952b. Studies in somesthesis: III. Role of somatic areas I and II in the acquisition of roughness discrimination in the rat. *Canadian Journal of Psychology*, **6**, 183–193.

Zubek, J. P. 1952c. Studies in somesthesis: IV. Role of somatic areas I and II in tactual "form" discrimination in the rat. *Journal of Comparative and Physiological Psychology*, **45**, 438–442.

Zubek, J. P. & De Lorenzo, A. J. 1952. The cerebral cortex and locomotor activity in rats. *Canadian Journal of Psychology*, **6**, 55–70.

Zucker, I. 1965. Short-term salt preference of potassium-deprived rats. *American Journal of Physiology*, **208**, 1071–1074.

Zucker, I. & McCleary, R. A. 1964. Perseveration in septal cats. *Psychonomic Science*, **1**, 387–388.

ADDITIONAL REFERENCES:

Rutledge, L. T. & Doty, R. W. Surgical interference with pathways mediating responses conditioned to cortical stimulation. *Experimental Neurology*, **6**, 478–491.

Vanderwolf, C. H. 1963b. Improved shuttle-box performance following electroconvulsive shock. *Journal of Comparative and Physiological Psychology*, **56**, 983–986.

AUTHOR INDEX

SUBJECT INDEX

This index can also be used as a glossary. The page numbers in bold type refer to definitions in the text.